SIXTH EDITION

Strategic Management

A CASEBOOK

MARY M. CROSSAN
Richard Ivey School of Business, University of Western Ontario

JOSEPH N. FRY
Richard Ivey School of Business, University of Western Ontario

J. PETER KILLING
International Institute for Management Development

RODERICK E. WHITE
Richard Ivey School of Business, University of Western Ontario

Prentice
Hall

Toronto

National Library of Canada Cataloguing in Publication Data

Crossan, Mary M.
      Strategic management: a casebook

6th ed.
Includes index.
ISBN 0-13-066163-5

1. Business planning–Canada–Case studies. 2. Business planning–Case studies. 3. Industrial management–Canada–Case studies. 4. Industrial management–Case studies. I. Fry, Joseph N., 1936-II. White, Roderick E. III. Title

HF5351.C76 2002   658.4'01'0971   C2001-901247-0

ISBN 0-13-066163-5

Vice President, Editorial Director: Michael Young
Marketing Manager: Cas Shields
Associate Editor: Veronica Tomaiuolo
Production Editor: Julia Hubble
Production Coordinator: Janette Lush
Page Layout: Jodie Guthrie and Nicki Smith
Art Director: Mary Opper
Cover Design: Amy Harnden
Cover Image: Gettyone

   3 4 5   06 05 04 03 02

Printed and bound in the USA.

All cases in the book were prepared as a basis for class discussion rather than to illustrate either effective or ineffective handling of an administrative situation.

CONTENTS

PART ONE: Introduction to Strategic Management

1   London Telecom Network   1
Joseph N. Fry and John Bogert

London Telecom Network (LTN) is a fast-growing reseller of long distance telephone services. The company has survived where many have failed and is starting to generate significant profits. Now management is beginning to look at a range of initiatives to further build the business. The situation raises some interesting questions for Rob Freeman, the founder and owner of the business. Are the circumstances right for LTN to be pursuing new ideas? If so, which of several proposals deserves priority attention?

2   Asiasports: Hockey Night in Hong Kong   16
Andrew Delios

Tom Barnes, executive director of Asiasports Ltd., is evaluating several options for growth for the sports management company. Asiasports principal sports properties are the South China Ice Hockey League and the World Ice Hockey 5's tournament, both based in Hong Kong. Among the alternatives available: Barnes could develop hockey in other countries in Southeast Asia; he could acquire new sports properties; or he could expand into in-line hockey promotion in Hong Kong.

PART TWO: Strategy—Environment

3   Aikenhead's   31
Mary M. Crossan and Katy Paul-Chowdhury

Stephen Bebis, the CEO of Aikenhead's, is opening the first warehouse home improvement centre in Toronto, which will radically alter the competitive landscape. He must assess how he should roll out the business given competitive pressures.

4   Cola Wars Continue: Coke vs. Pepsi in the 1990s   44
David B. Yoffie and Sharon Foley

The competition between Coke and Pepsi is a classic corporate battle that began in America at the turn of the century and has expanded into worldwide competitive warfare in the 1990s. This case examines the economics of the soft drink and bottling industries, and describes the history and internationalization of the cola wars.

After years of success with its vaunted "Direct Model" for computer manufacturing, marketing, and distribution, Dell Computer Corp. faces efforts by competitors to match its strategy. This case describes the evolution of the personal computer industry, Dell's strategy, and efforts by Compaq, IBM, Hewlett-Packard, and Gateway 2000 to capture the benefits of Dell's approach.

One of Dow Jones & Company's most respected brands, The Wall Street Journal, is threatened by Internet news providers, including their own Interactive Edition. The company is unsure whether the Interactive Edition will be a substitute or a complement to the Print Edition. The case focuses on changing industry boundaries, new technology, potential cannibalization, and a threat to the company's traditional business model.

Pete Vanexan, President of Grand & Toy, is reviewing his company's 2001 budget forecast in preparation for a meeting with the other senior managers. He wanted to focus on this opportunity to rethink Grand & Toy's strategy and assess whether there was something they had missed in the previous strategy review.

The music industry has changed dramatically as a result of technological and business innovations that have transformed how music is acquired, and how value is created and distributed. Napster Inc. operates one of several Web sites that allow Internet users free access to MP3 music files. The case requires examination of the forces at play in the transformation of the music industry, the strategic alternatives for players in the industry and the legal context of the strategic alternatives.

iCraveTV intends to retransmit network broadcast television signals to Internet-connected PCs, reaching a worldwide extension market. There are several obstacles to overcome while entering the fiercely competitive broadcasting industry and building competitive advantage. Several issues remain unresolved as they move towards the launch of iCraveTV.

The management team at WestJet is reviewing its growth plans in light of an anticipated merger of Air Canada and Canadian Airlines. The merger would result in a near monopoly of domestic air travel in Canada and a new set of opportunities and challenges for the handful of smaller airlines in the country. Under the circumstances, WestJet is considering whether it should shift from its focus of building on its success in Western Canada and expand into the East.

PART THREE: Strategy—Resources

Harlequin, the world's largest and most successful publisher of romantic fiction, is ending a decade of solid growth and profitability. What should be the firm's strategy to sustain this performance?

Starbucks must decide how it should leverage its core competencies against various opportunities for growth. Some options include introducing its coffee in McDonalds, pursuing further expansion of its retail operations, and leveraging the brand into other product areas.

The Saws and Tools division of Sandvik has invested heavily in development for a world-class competency in ergonomic hand tool design and manufacture. The Ergo strategy appears to be working in Europe, but North American results are disappointing. Göran Gezelius, the division president, must decide how to proceed with the Ergo strategy.

Service Corporation International, the world's largest funeral consolidator, has just made a formal takeover bid for the Loewen Group, its key competitor. The offer is approximately 50 per cent above the price at which Loewen Group stock traded 30 days ago. Should Loewen Group fight the takeover, or accept the offer?

In less than 20 years, Canadel, based in Louiseville, Quebec, had become Canada's leading manufacturer of casual dining room furniture. Canadel's top management team, the three Deveault brothers, Guy, Michel, and Jean, were discussing recent results and future prospects for the firm. Some questions that surfaced included growth in existing and new markets, and competition from established industry giants and new upstarts.

Despite the substantial investments Harley Davidson had made in growth and development—including expanding sales and distribution outside the US, the new assembly plant in Kansas City, the acquisition of Buell Motorcycle Company and Eaglemark Financial Services, gross margins had widened, and net income had increased. Jeffrey Bleustein, president and CEO is considering to what extent changing market forces and competition will affect Harley Davidson in the future.

PART FOUR: Strategy—Organization

Workbrain Corporation is a young firm that offers Web-based time and attendance management systems solutions to companies with a "blue-collar" workforce. The newly hired vice-president of corporate development is responsible for the strategic growth of the firm both internally and externally. He is faced with the task of organizing and re-orienting the company, and needs to develop a plan for growth.

Phil McLeod had been appointed as the editor of The London Free Press (LFP) with a mandate to make changes. Despite its ability to remain profitable, McLeod thought that the paper was not living up to its potential. He wondered if it would be possible to stop the slow decline of the newspaper, or if its shrinkage was an inevitable consequence of broader trends in the information industry and Canadian society. In pursuing a new strategy McLeod must consider whether they need to rethink how they are organized.

Top management at the Bank of Montreal is considering a proposal for a pilot launch of a direct banking venture (Direct banking bypasses the traditional branch network and deals directly with the customers by phone, fax personal computer and ABM). At issue are such matters as the nature, scope and independence of the venture and the pace of introduction.

PART FIVE: Strategy—Management Preferences

Diane McGarry, Chairman, CEO and President of Xerox Canada has been meeting with her leadership team since eight o'clock in the morning to craft the organization's new vision statement. Three and a half hours into the meeting the team hits a roadblock. With 30 minutes left in the session, McGarry must decide whether and how to proceed.

Roy Vagelos, head of Merck research labs was considering a request by Merck researchers to pursue a cure for river blindness, a disease plaguing millions in developing countries. Vagelos had to decide whether to invest in research for a drug that, even if successful, might never pay for itself.

The case describes the start-up and rapid growth of a company whose founder holds strong, non-traditional beliefs about the role of the corporation and its responsibility to society. Are the strong values and beliefs imposed by Anita Roddick transferable to the United States and what will happen as Roddick steps back from the business?

PART SIX: Scope of the Firm

After acquiring Greyhound U.S., Laidlaw, Inc. became the principal provider of intercity transit in North America. Nine months later, the board of Laidlaw asked its CEO to resign, citing performance problems and the need to divest certain operations to strengthen its balance sheet. Laidlaw's attempts to enter and to consolidate selected transportation service industries are examined. Something has gone terribly wrong and the search for the reasons pushes back to fundamental issues associated with growth by acquisition and corporate management.

The Newell Company, a multi-billion dollar company dealing in hardware and home furnishings, office products and housewares, is contemplating a merger with Rubbermaid, a renowned manufacturer of plastic products. Newell has a remarkable record of success in growth by acquisition. Rubbermaid would mark a quantum step in this program, but equally, would pose a formidable challenge to Newell's capacity to integrate and strengthen acquisitions.

This case explores a proposal by Labatt management to purchase a 22 per cent interest in a Mexican brewing business and to strike associated agreements for cooperative activities throughout North America. An evaluation of the deal requires an assessment of the venture prospects in the Mexican and U.S. beer markets, the potential for synergies in cooperative activities and ultimately the pricing and financing of an investment in a developing economy.

Trojan Technologies sells water disinfecting equipment, and the senior market associate's job is to find new areas for growth. China is particularly intriguing because it has as much water as Canada, but 40 times the population, and its economic boom will further stress current water resources. Trojan has set growth hurdles of 30 per cent per year, and needs new markets to reach that objective. The task in new market development is to determine if Trojan should enter China, and if so, when, where and how.

PART SEVEN: Implementing Strategy

Guru.com intends to transform the global labour market by creating the world's largest online marketplace for independent professionals (IPs)—freelancers, consultants, "knowledge workers" and "hired guns"—known as gurus. One month into the launch of its preview site, and preparing for its first major release scheduled in three months, management needs to define its priorities for implementation.

This Calgary-based carpet manufacturer has been suffering serious losses. Its president, hired only one year earlier to correct the situation, has resigned. The major shareholder must consider anew the possibilities and means of recovery.

Provincial Papers is a very troubled manufacturer of coated paper located in Thunder Bay, Ontario. The director and chairman of the board of Provincial Papers is being informally pressed to take on the CEO role. He is assessing the possibility of rescue in the face of depressed market prices, an over-supplied industry, departing personnel and money-losing operations.

Murray Wallace has just taken over as CEO and President of Wellington Insurance, a "company without hope" according to a recent consultant's report. Wallace is faced with the challenge of effecting a complete revitalization at Wellington when the prospects for the industry and the company look bleak.

Silent Witness Enterprises Ltd. is one of Canada's fastest growing technology-based firms. The 14-year-old publicly traded company created a new market niche in the security surveillance industry by introducing novel applications of VCR-based technology. The company's founder forecasted growth that would take the company from annual revenues of $34 million in 1999 to $250 million by 2005. In achieving these goals, he must decide how to balance the need to sustain innovation and new product development, while at the same time, develop the capabilities needed to manage the firm's increasingly complex operations.

PART EIGHT: Strategic Analysis and Personal Action

32   Sabena Belgian World Airlines (A)   508
Mary M. Crossan and Barbara Pierce

When Pierre Godfroid took over as Sabena's CEO, Sabena was in crisis and facing imminent bankruptcy. On the strength of a restructuring plan developed by Godfroid and his staff, the Belgian government had agreed to bail out the airline in return for assurances that this would be the last time government assistance would be requested. Godfroid's task was to transform the company into a viable private enterprise. The case provides the opportunity to evaluate the viability of Godfroid's strategy. More importantly, it sets the stage for a sequence of follow-on cases dealing with the implementation of the strategy.

33   The GE Energy Management Initiative (A)   522
Joseph N. Fry and Julian Birkinshaw

Raj Bhatt, Business Development Manager for GE Canada, met with executives from GE Supply, a U.S.-based distribution arm of GE. The purpose of the meeting was to discuss new business opportunities in Energy Efficiency. Bhatt had identified some opportunities for business development in Canada, while GE Supply had just put together an energy-efficiency joint venture in the U.S. Bhatt was keen to work with GE Supply and retain a high level of operating autonomy. The challenge was to put together an appropriate organizational structure.

34   Procter & Gamble Canada (A): The Febreze Decision   529
Roderick E. White and Ken Mark

Lynn Mepham, marketing director for Procter & Gamble Canada, is evaluating the potential success of launching a new product, Febreze. Procter & Gamble had reorganized operations with the intent to promote reasonable risk-taking. While trying to adjust to the new culture, Mepham had to evaluate the risks associated with launching the product not knowing if the new marketing tools would generate the additional volumes needed, and the risk of losing the competitive edge if she postponed the launch.

PART NINE: Comprehensive

35   Nestlé-Rowntree (A)   534
James C. Ellert, J. Peter Killing and Dana G. Hyde

Nestlé is the world's largest food company. For some time it has been attempting, without success, to develop a link with Rowntree PLC, one of the world's top chocolate companies. As a matter of policy, Nestlé does not make hostile takeovers, but now its hand seems to be forced by the sudden purchase of 14.9 per cent of Rowntree by Jacobs Suchard, one of Nestlé's keenest rivals in the European chocolate business. Rowntree is preparing to fight all comers; the stakes are enormous.

PREFACE

Appropriate for Strategic Management and Business Policy courses, this sixth edition continues to effectively present the concept of strategy and the high quality, class-tested cases that have made it the premier strategic management casebook in Canada. The underlying theme of the cases remains that of a general manager facing issues of strategy formulation and implementation, strategic change and personal action.

New to this edition

Twenty new cases have been introduced, all of which have been tested at Ivey. We have focused on companies that are inherently interesting to study, yet provide a rich learning experience. One of our primary efforts in writing new cases has been in the area of e-commerce. We recently tested these cases in Ivey's newly launched eLeadership course, with the intent of drawing the cases back into the Strategy course. The selection of new cases include companies such as Dell, Coke and Pepsi, Napster, iCraveTV, Harley Davidson, Merck, The Body Shop, Newell Rubbermaid, Guru.com, and Procter and Gamble.

Improved structure

We have made one modification to the structure. Since many of the cases, particularly in the area of e-commerce, have a global orientation, we have not included a separate section on "Competing in Foreign Markets" as we have done in the past. Instead, we have included cases that would have traditionally fallen into this area under the new section, "Scope of the Firm", as they deal with questions of expanding geographic scope. Note that many of the other sections also contain cases with an international orientation. However, where the geographic scope issue is salient, we have incorporated the case in the new section. Overall, we have attempted to achieve a balance of cases in each section, recognizing that a number of the cases could be used in different areas.

Mirroring the structure of *Strategic Analysis and Action* by Crossan, Fry and Killing, the first five parts cover each of the elements in the Diamond-E Framework. These elements are then extended to deal with issues of firm scope. The cases in Part Seven can be used to examine strategy formulation, but they offer the added benefit of a detailed assessment of strategy implementation and the management of strategic change. It has become increasingly important to us over time to anchor concepts of strategy formulation and implementation in the personal action of the manager and, where possible, recent graduates of business schools. The cases in the Strategic Analysis and Personal Action section are designed to make the concept of strategy more meaningful to the business school graduate. Several of the cases in this section also reinforce the real-time nature of strategy by requiring students to respond in the moment to a variety of situations. The cases in this section also provide a strong closing to the book by integrating all strategic management aspects learned in the course.

Supplements

The following supplements have been carefully prepared to accompany this new edition:
- videos featuring managers reflecting on the case situations, helping to bridge the gap between theory and practice.

- an Instructor's Resource Manual containing detailed teaching notes for all of the cases, including suggestions for case sequencing, assignments, teaching approach and supplementary readings and references.
- a Transparency Resource package containing electronic slides prepared in PowerPoint 7.0.

Acknowledgments

The cases in this book were prepared with the generous cooperation and assistance of a large number of executives. One of the continuing delights of the case writing process is the opportunity for us to meet and to learn from these individuals. We owe them a great, collective vote of thanks.

Case writing is an expensive process. It would not be possible without continued support from the Richard Ivey School of Business. Some of the businesses that we were studying also helped us indirectly by picking up expenses ranging from airline tickets to the proverbial free lunch. Thank you all. We would also like to thank the Harvard Business School, the International Institute for Management Development (IMD) in Lausanne, Switzerland, The Lear Family Foundation, and Robert M. Grant for permission to use their cases.

The encouragement that is essential in sustaining a case development program comes from a supportive administrative context and from the help of our immediate colleagues. Paul Beamish, the Associate Dean of Research, has been a consistent supporter, as have our Deans past and present: Bud Johnston, Al Mikalachki, Adrian Ryans and Larry Tapp. We have been greatly assisted by our teaching colleagues and former colleagues who have contributed cases and who have been an essential part of the work of testing, refining and, indeed, figuring out how to teach the cases. We have also had the opportunity of working with a cooperative and skilled group of Ph.D. candidates and research assistants, whose names and individual contributions are acknowledged in the cases on which they worked. We are also extremely grateful to the following reviewers for their comments and suggestions: Gordon Holmes, Mohawk College; Sam Boutilier, University College of Cape Breton; Allan Ryan, University of Alberta; Ian Lee, Carleton University; John C. Banks, Wilfrid Laurier University; B.J. Austin, Brock University.

We are indebted to our publisher, Pearson Education Canada, and in particular Michael Young, Steven Iacovelli, Veronica Tomaiuolo, Deborah Starks, Janette Lush, and Deanne Walle for their help in producing and promoting this book. At our school we are, in particular, obliged to Jodi Guthrie, Penni Pring, Nicki Smith, Shirley Koenig, Pegg Saunders, and Bill McGrath and for their diligent and industrious effort in bringing everything together. Ruzena Andrysek, Laurie Craik, Carole Kinahan, Diana Lee and Jeannett Weston from Ivey were also extremely helpful in helping to prepare the final document.

Mary M. Crossan
Joseph N. Fry
J. Peter Killing
Roderick E. White

London, Ontario

INTRODUCTION

All of the cases in this book deal with problems facing general managers. Although some are disguised, all are based on real situations and raise issues that are in some way related to a firm's strategy. We have presented the cases in a logical and orderly progression—from analysis (what are the key elements in this firm's situation?) through desired action (what should be done?) to detailed implementation (how should it be done?). However, we do not recommend that the casebook be used alone. It should be employed in conjunction with either a strategy textbook or an organized set of readings that present the basic concepts of strategy formulation and implementation and the management of strategic change.

Our preferred text is *Strategic Analysis and Action*, Fifth Edition, and the Diamond-E model on which it is based. This model links the firm's strategy with its environment, its resources, the preferences of its managers and its organization. We have used it for a number of years, and have found that it permits useful insights not only into the cases presented in this book but also into a wide variety of other general management situations.

The key to using the Diamond-E model is to begin by identifying the firm's existing or proposed strategy. In *Strategic Analysis and Action*, Fifth Edition, we suggest that a description of a firm's strategy should include its goals, product-market focus, value proposition, and core activities. The Diamond-E model can then be used to assess methodically the new or existing strategy by means of the following questions:
1.   Is the strategy internally consistent?
2.   Is the strategy consistent with the environment?
3.   Is the strategy consistent with present or obtainable resources?
4.   Is the strategy consistent with the firm's organizational attributes?
5.   Is the strategy consistent with the personal preferences and beliefs of top management?

The Diamond-E Framework

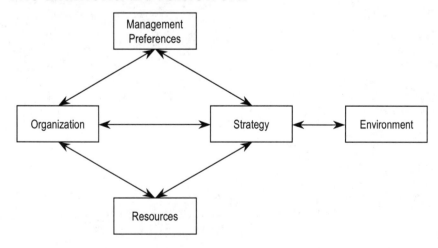

Source: M.M. Crossan, J.N. Fry and J.P. Killing, *Strategic Analysis and Action*, Fifth Edition. Scarborough, Ontario: Pearson Education Canada Inc., 2001.

We have grouped the cases according to the strategy relationships in the Diamond-E model that they emphasize. This is a rough cut as strategic issues do not come in neat packages, but it does provide for a flow of emphasis over the progression of a course. The first five sections of the casebook correspond to the Diamond-E framework. Part Six provides the opportunity to examine all elements of the Diamond-E in dealing with questions of Business Scope. The five cases that comprise Part Seven, Implementing Strategy, are the most difficult in the book. In these, the questions of what must be done and how it should be done need to be addressed simultaneously. The section in *Strategic Analysis and Action* dealing with this topic considers three variables: the pace at which the general manager should attempt to effect change, the targets to focus efforts on, and the tactics that should be employed. Each issue deserves close examination in these cases.

Part Eight, Strategic Analysis and Personal Action, presents three cases that accomplish three objectives: 1) to present strategic analysis from the perspective of a new manager rather than a CEO or senior manager; 2) to demonstrate the incremental and emergent nature of strategy as a "pattern" of decisions; and 3) to challenge students to understand and internalize the personal attributes required to think and act strategically.

The Nestlé-Rowntree Series in Part Nine is a comprehensive case series. The (A) case provides a vehicle to do a thorough assessment of a global industry. The follow-on cases require the students to decide and act.

We hope that you find these cases enjoyable as well as instructive. The new cases as well as our favourites give us a great deal of satisfaction, provoke dialogue among us and give us new insights.

LONDON TELECOM NETWORK

John Bogert and
Joseph N. Fry

On a snowy Thursday in December 1995, Rob Freeman, chairman and sole owner of London Telecom Network Inc. (LTN), was driving to Hamilton for his bi-weekly meeting with senior management. LTN was one of Canada's more prominent long distance resellers, servicing over 22000 customers and generating annualized revenues of $23 million. Profits had improved in the past year from a break even in the first five months to a cumulative $1 million forecast by the end of December. (See Exhibit 1 for further financial information.)

Rob and his management team were encouraged by the developing profitability of the business. They were now turning their attention to longer term issues, and particularly to opportunities for further growth. The problem here was not one of generating new ideas, rather of deciding which ideas made sense. Rob's aims were high — to pursue the prospect of offering "flat rate long distance to everyone" and becoming a billion dollar, debt-free telecommunications corporation.

IVEY

John Bogert prepared this case under the supervision of Professor Joseph N. Fry solely to provide material for class discussion. The author does not intend to illustrate either effective or ineffective handling of a managerial situation. The author may have disguised certain names and other identifying information to protect confidentiality.

THE CANADIAN LONG DISTANCE TELECOMMUNICATIONS INDUSTRY

Overview

The 1995 Canadian market for telephone telecommunications services was estimated at $16 billion per year. Of this amount, $8 billion was for local service and $8 billion was for long distance. The local service market included local phone service and phone equipment. The long distance market — including phone calls, data transmission, and fax — encompassed all calls that originated and terminated in Canada and the Canadian portion of calls that originated or terminated outside Canada. Overall, the long distance market was growing at a rate of five to 10 per cent per year.

Background

Until the mid 1980s, Canadian telecommunications services had been controlled by a series of regulated provincial monopolies. A notable exception to this situation was Bell Canada, which was a public company that operated as a regulated monopoly in southern Ontario and southern Quebec (60 per cent of the total market). Bell and the provincial monopolies were organized into a consortium called the Stentor Alliance, which provided a unified front for them to lobby on regulatory matters and other industry-wide issues. The Stentor Alliance was comprised of: BCTel (British Columbia), SaskTel (Saskatchewan), AGT(Alberta), MTS (Manitoba), Bell Canada (Ontario and Quebec), Quebec-Tel (northern Quebec), IslandTel (Prince Edward Island), MT&T (New Brunswick and Nova Scotia), NewfoundlandTel (Newfoundland), and NorthwestTel (Northwest Territories and Yukon).

The CRTC

Radio, television and telecommunications in Canada were controlled by the Canadian Radio-television and Telecommunications Commission (CRTC). In the late 1980s the CRTC had come under immense pressure from industry to deregulate the long distance market. Canadian industry, which had watched long distance rates in the U.S. drop some 40 per cent in the five years since U.S. deregulation, wanted the same opportunities in Canada. In addition, some companies were using technical and legal loopholes to enter the long distance market. This practice undermined the CRTC's control. As a result, the CRTC passed Ruling 90-3 in the spring of 1990, deregulating 90 per cent of all long distance services, and Ruling 92-12 in late 1992, deregulating the remaining 10 per cent. These revisions forced the Stentor Alliance to rent long distance lines and time to registered resellers.

The CRTC's mandate had thence become one of ensuring the smooth deregulation of the telecommunications market. In this passage, rate re-balancing became a major issue. Under regulation, the Stentor Alliance companies' had been charged with providing all Canadians with "affordable" local phone service. As a result residential users paid $11-$15 per month for a service that cost $38 to deliver. Long distance charges subsidized local service costs. As lower prices and competition cut into the Stentor Alliance's long distance income, it became difficult to continue to cross-subsidize local residential service. Therefore, the CRTC decided to allow the Stentor Alliance to phase in rate re-balancing. Over a five-year period, long distance charges would drop 35 to 50 per cent, while local residential line charges would go up 30 to 40 per cent.

It was thought that the CRTC's increase in local access charges would pave the way for deregulation of the local loop (lines that run from individual houses to the main switch). Local charges needed to reflect actual costs if competition was to be successful. Most recently, the CRTC had ruled to allow the Stentor Alliance to deliver cable television and the cable companies to deliver local telephone service. Experts were curious as to what would happen to phone charges as local loops were privatized. If the cable companies could deliver an individualized movie to a house for $5, how would they justify charging $0.20/minute for a phone call that used 1/10,000 of the bandwidth?

The Canadian Long Distance Market

There were three basic ways in which a company could provide long distance service:

Buy time on a per minute basis: Renting the use of another carrier's network, one call at a time.

Rent lines and switch space: Stentor Alliance companies and alternative carriers had excess capacity on their switches and fibre optic lines. Alternative carriers rented a dedicated amount of capacity for a flat monthly fee, to supplement their dedicated networks.

Build a dedicated network: Buying lines and switches was very capital intensive, but resulted in the lowest cost per minute, once capacity was filled.

There were three types of companies that provided long distance service to end-users: the Stentor Alliance, the alternative carriers, and the resellers. The Stentor Alliance controlled 82 per cent of the $8 billion long distance market, with the remaining 18 per cent divided among 270 resellers and the alternative carriers.

Stentor Alliance

The Stentor Alliance companies had traditionally controlled 100 per cent of the long distance market. With the advent of deregulation, however, they had lost 18 per cent of the market to resellers and alternative carriers. The Alliance continued to control 100 per cent of the market for local phone service, however, and were the only providers of long distance that reached into all the small towns and cities across Canada. Therefore, many resellers and alternative carriers bought long distance services from the Stentor Alliance.

Resellers

There were 265 resellers of long distance in Canada which had collectively captured about nine per cent of the end-user market. They were called resellers because they rented time from Bell or the alternative carriers. Take, for example, a reseller which buys time from Bell. When a customer places a long distance phone call, Bell carries the call, tracks the fact that this was customer of the reseller, and invoices the reseller instead of the customer. Bell forwards individualized call data to the reseller when invoicing, so that the reseller could repackage it to the customer's needs. Typically, the reseller bought time at a 50 per cent discount and then resold it at a 35 per cent discount. These businesses, with low overheads and low advertising, focused on capturing mid-size businesses which were looking for additional services such as calling cards, data lines, and customized billing.

Resellers lived in a constant cash crunch. They often had to pay their provider in advance for service (at least until they built up a credit history), and had to wait 30 to 60 days to collect from their customers. It was easy to enter the industry, and easy to fail as well.

Alternative Carriers

There were four major alternative long distance carriers in Canada, Sprint, fonorola, ACC and Unitel (see Table 1). These companies had all started as resellers, but over the past five years they had invested in their own dedicated networks, which were typically installed between major hubs, and connected to their U.S. parent. The alternative carriers all supplemented their networks by leasing lines and space on switches from the Stentor Alliance companies. Each firm had its own discount plan, often complicated by different discounts for specific areas, and customers. Although competition was stiff, customers could generally expect to receive up to 25 per cent off Bell rates. (See Exhibit 2 for an example of discounts.)

Table 1   Canadian Alternative Carriers — Revenue and Performance

1995 Data	Sprint	Fonorola	ACC	Unitel
Revenue ($ MM)	457	209	109	1118E
Profits ($ MM)	-65	-7.2	0.6	-181E

Source: Company financial statements, Unitel figures are estimates

Alternative carriers had financed their network expansion with equity and debt issues (see Exhibits 3 and 4 for financial data on ACC and Sprint Canada). These funds were spent to install fibre optic cable between major hubs and switches. The expectation was that lower costs per unit would result once the network was filled. All of these companies (with the exception of Unitel) were expected to start turning a profit in 1996.

LONDON TELECOM NETWORK

History

In 1988, Rob Freeman, a real estate broker living in Strathroy, Ontario was bothered by the $0.35/minute charge for calling London, only 12 miles away. Rob knew something about telecommunications (telecom) switches, having studied two years of electrical engineering at the University of Waterloo, and having toyed with telecom as a hobby for years.

Through a friend who worked at Bell Canada, he inquired about the legality of setting up a phone in Mount Bridges, halfway between Strathroy and London, to forward phone calls. He could then make a local call to Mount Bridges from Strathroy. The phone in Mount Bridges would forward a second local call from Mount Bridges to London. The net effect was that a long distance call would be converted into two local calls, and no long distance charges would apply.

Bell, of course, claimed that such a system was illegal. Rob disagreed; his research had not revealed any preventative regulations. He decided to proceed without Bell's permission. Selling long distance was illegal in 1988, so he started a sharing group, and convinced 100 Strathroy residents to join. Because he had no money, he asked the members to prepay two months. He then set up a switch in Mount Bridges with 10 lines in and 10 lines out. Later, he added Exeter and St. Thomas.

Bell filed a complaint with the CRTC. The ruling came out in Rob's favour: as long as the call was forwarded only once, he could continue. However, call forwarding more than once was ruled to be illegal.

In 1990, when the CRTC deregulated the Canadian long distance market, Rob acquired the interests of the other members of the sharing group, and formed London Telecom. Rob knew that, to survive, LTN had to grow. Therefore, he established a line through Oakville to link Burlington to Toronto, and rented his first trunk line to carry long distance calls. In the first week LTN signed up 400 customers. By the end of 1991, the company had 1,000 customers. From this starting point LTN grew rapidly, and by December 1995, the company provided services to over 22,000 customers.

The Organization

LTN was a flat organization. A group of six managers — Jim Weisz, president, Rob Belliveau, vice-president, sales and marketing; Gary Campbell, vice president, finance and information services; Greg Cope, manager, regulatory issues and special projects; Maureen Merkler, manager, human resources; and Randy Patrick, vice president, network services — handled virtually all the business operating decisions and the supervisory activities for a roster of about 100 employees. Rob Freeman, as chairman, confined his involvement primarily to policy issues and to developing the management group. Jim Weisz explained the management approach:

> We try to keep ourselves lean. We need to keep costs down in this market and at the same time we need to be able to make decisions quickly. The CRTC keeps us on our toes. That's why I have Greg Cope keeping an eye on the CRTC for us.
>
> The organization is growing and Rob Freeman would like LTN to hire from within whenever possible. Maureen Merkler was hired a year ago to help in this area. We are working to get job descriptions down for all positions, and have sent a few employees who were not performing out for training.

LTN's Product Offering

As of late 1995 LTN operated a network connecting 41 Canadian cities (see Exhibit 5). LTN rented all of its equipment and lines at flat monthly rates from the Stentor Alliance companies. Between different cities, depending on call traffic, LTN could vary the amount of bandwidth rented on lines and switches. There were significant economies of scale in renting long distance bandwidth. For example, a DS-0 line could carry 12 calls at a time at a cost of $4,100 per month, while a DS-3 line could carry 504 calls and at a cost $37,800 per month. To ensure customer service levels, LTN had an agreement with Fonorola to carry overflow calls.

LTN had been rapidly increasing the scope and capacity of its network. Randy Patrick commented:

We had a problem last January with growth. The network was growing faster than marketing could keep up. Bell requires that we give them two months' notice on changes to the network, so we have to order the lines before we know for sure if the sales are going to materialize. Up until then, we had been growing at a rate of one city a week. We have cut back to one city every three weeks. Of course, our network still has a lot of empty space on it, but unfortunately our technology doesn't allow us to pin down exactly where very easily.

We are Bell's second largest customer. None of the long distance resellers get the kind of discounts we do. While Bell's sales guys might not like us because we are stealing business from them, they realize that losing a sale to us is better than losing a sale to Unitel.

Unlike its competitors LTN charged a flat rate for its long distance service: $74.95 per month to residential customers and $94.95 per month to business customers. For this customers received 40 hours of long distance covering calls placed anytime of the day. If they exceeded the 40 hours, customers were automatically sold time in additional five hour blocks. LTN's service included a reverse calling feature; for example, relatives could call the customer using the customer's LTN account.

There were regulatory and economic reasons why few companies charged a flat rate like LTN. Until recently, The Stentor Alliance, Sprint and Unitel had not been allowed to do so; as inter-exchange carriers they had been limited by the CRTC in the way in which they could bill for services. In September 1995, the CRTC decided to allow Sprint and Unitel to charge in whatever way they pleased, leaving only the Stentor companies strictly controlled by pricing tariffs. Resellers, which could legally sell flat rate services, usually sold on a per-minute basis because they bought their services on a per-minute basis and avoided the risk associated with fixed cost line rentals.

LTN also departed from industry norms in not offering direct access service. To use LTN, customers first had to call the LTN network using a local access number, and then dial the number of the party they wanted to reach (see brochure — Exhibit 5). LTN had configured its network this way to take advantage of the lower rates set by the CRTC for non-direct access service.

The net result of buying services on a flat rate and operating a non-direct access network meant that LTN's costs were lower than a reseller buying time on a per-minute basis, providing LTN could achieve a minimum utilization of 40 per cent.

Rob Belliveau summed up how the customers felt about the flat rate, and the extra dialing:

Our product is simple to understand. The flat rate concept sets us apart from the other resellers. We offer the security of a constant long distance phone bill and we don't try to force our customers to make their calls in the middle of the night if they want to save money. In fact, our nights are full. We wish more customers would call during the day.

Customers don't mind dialing the extra numbers. With speed dialing it's just not a big deal. As far as I'm concerned, it's actually a bonus. A customer can sign up with Unitel for overseas calls and still keep us for Canadian calls.

Billing

Since the inception of the call-sharing group, Rob had always required that customers pay first and last month when joining. As the business grew, he saw no reason to change this system, although recently LTN had been hearing complaints about the high up-front cost to join. For example, a residential customer joining LTN would have pay to $150 in advance ($75 — first month, and $75 — last month).

LTN billed every day of the month, based on the day the customer signed up. This helped the accounting staff to smooth the workload. Billing was further simplified by the fact that all customers received a one-line invoice for either $74.95 or $94.95. The occasional customer who used more than 40 hours in a month received a second invoice. This procedure was quite different from the industry standard of multi-line invoices detailing the length and cost of every call.

Marketing

LTN relied heavily on advertising through direct mail. As each new city was added to the network, LTN would blanket the area with brochures. More recently, Rob Belliveau had begun experimenting with focused mailing efforts directed at certain demographic pockets and had run a 30-second TV spot in the World Series. LTN used sales representatives to follow up on leads:

Sales Agents: 10 sales agents across the country went door-to-door, cold calling residential and small business customers.

Inside Sales: LTN had 15 people in its call centre who answered inquiries and received a commission for customers that they closed.

Direct Sales: Two full time sales representatives handled inquiries from business prospects and made site visits to close sales.

Most of LTN's customers fell into three categories (see Table 2):
- residential customers, calling primarily within Canada;
- small and medium sized businesses, especially home-based businesses and outbound telemarketers; and
- large businesses, willing to use more than one company to minimize costs.

Table 2 LTN's Current Canadian Market Segmentation and Share

	High Use Residential	Med. Use Residential	Low Use Residential	Small /Med. Business	Large Business	Total
Total Market:						
% Accounts (residential only)	5%	35%	60%			
Spending per month	>$100	$10-100	<$10			
Total $ (mil.)	$750	$1,680	$432	$2,000	$3,138	$8,000
% Market	9.4%	21.0%	5.4%	25%	39.1%	100%
LTN:						
# Customers	14,000	0	0	9,300	1	23,300
Revenue ($ mil.)	$12.6	0	0	$10.2	$0.2	$23.0
Current Market Share	1.7%	0.0%	0.0%	0.5%	0.01%	0.3%

Source: Consultant estimates

The Call Centre

The 15 employees in LTN's call centre handled all inbound calls, with customers often waiting 10 to 15 minutes for service. Monday mornings were especially busy because potential customers would be calling after seeing advertisements on the weekend. Simultaneously, customers with billing problems would be calling, wondering why they had received two, and sometimes three, invoices. When call loads were especially heavy, the call centre would forward calls related to invoices to the accounting department.

Gary Campbell, vice-president finance and information systems, commented:

> We are still using the ACCPAC accounting package. It was designed for a few thousand customers at most, and we have 22,000. We figure that 50 per cent of the calls received by the call center are related to billing problems. We are hoping to have a new accounting system in place in the next few months. Once that is done, call center traffic should drop substantially.
>
> Confounding the problem was that we are adding 1,000 customers a month. The computer system can't handle it. Call centre staff trying to add a new customer over the phone typically wait five minutes to pull up a file on the computer.

Wintel

Wintel was a separate company controlled by LTN management that was established in the summer of 1995 to deal with start-up competitors in the Toronto area. These companies were using the call forwarding technique that Rob Freeman had originally developed. LTN had been looking for a way to compete effectively with these new competitors without cannibalizing its own product line. The Wintel start-up provided the solution by offering a package of $29.95 flat rate for 40 hours, covering a limited area around Toronto. By December 1995, Wintel had 600 customers of its own.

LOOKING AHEAD

The LTN senior management team had several ideas for continued expansion. The options included:

1. Going public;
2. Expanding into the U.S.;
3. Expanding the Canadian product offering;
4. Introducing new products; and
5. Building a permanent network.

Going Public

LTN senior management had approached Rob Freeman with the idea of going public. They felt that this option would provide funding for some of the ideas they were considering. One plan, which had been discussed in a preliminary way with an investment banker involved issuing $10 million worth of shares: $5 million would be new issue, with funds to be used by the company, while $5 million would be sold by Rob Freeman. After the issue, Rob Freeman would retain 46 per cent of the shares, the public would hold 46 per cent, and the remaining eight per cent would be divided equally among the senior managers.

Expanding into the U.S.

The management team had been working on and off on this expansion possibility for months. Originally, they had been interested in the possibility of providing Canadian customers with access to the U.S.; however, they had been looking more recently at full entry into the U.S. market.

The $80 billion U.S. long distance market had been deregulated five years longer than the Canadian market. Twenty-eight per cent of all long distance traffic was carried by 150 alternative carriers, seven per cent by the 3,800 resellers, and the remainder by AT&T. The regulatory aspects of the long distance market were controlled by the Federal Communications Commission (FCC). This body was similar to the CRTC in mandate; but unlike the CRTC, its rulings had to be passed by Congress before they became law.

LTN had two potential plans for entry. The first was to ease into the market, growing slowly as it had in Canada, by starting in upstate New York, or around Chicago, and expanding outward. Advertising would be primarily by direct mail, and word of mouth. The second possibility was to go after traffic between the major centres by connecting the six biggest cities in the U.S. The advantage of this option was that LTN would immediately cover 30 per cent of the population of the U.S. The network would gradually expand out to the smaller centres.

In either case, LTN expected to offer a flat rate service. Although some competitors were already offering flat rates per minute, none was offering a flat monthly rate. LTN hoped to manage the network from Canada, but realized it would need a U.S. call centre to give customers service with a local feel. Randy Patrick (network) and Greg Cope (regulatory) had been working hard to determine whether FCC regulations would allow LTN to set up a low cost network similar to the one in Canada. Even without favourable FCC regulations, LTN was optimistic. With over 100 alternative carriers in the U.S., the competition to sell to resellers was intense. LTN had been quoted a cost of five cents a minute for nationwide coverage, and anticipated that it would be able to sell time for eight cents a minute.

Expanding the Canadian Product Offering

The average customer used only 20 of the 40 hours available. Management was concerned that they might lose some customers who decided that they were not getting their money's worth. Therefore, they were considering two new products:

- five hours for $29.95
- ten hours for $49.95

Rob Freeman, who was concerned about cannibalization, was also excited about the prospect of expanding the customer base by offering packages with more universal appeal. Rob Belliveau (marketing) had inquired with marketing research companies, but data on new customer potential were not available. Management was also considering automatic billing for the new products. Customers who submitted their credit card numbers would be billed automatically once a month.

Introducing New Products

Jim Weisz had recently been in contact with Calldex Inc., the manufacturer of a new technology: a calling card with a digital display that showed a new PIN number every minute. The advantage of this system was that the calling card number could not be stolen by someone looking over the shoulder of a caller entering the code.

LTN intended to use this new technology to target the cellular market. LTN could not offer cellular long distance service with their current network setup. Regular phone calls carried with them the number from which they had originated, which was used for services like call-display. LTN used this number to verify that calls into their network came from registered customers.

Unfortunately for LTN, cellular calls did not carry this number. LTN planned to reconfigure the network so that customers could input a calling card number, in this way solving the cellular problem.

LTN wanted to charge flat rate for long distance calls placed with the calling card. The Calldex card was perfect for this, because the user could not pass the number around to friends or coworkers; the customer had to have the card in hand to place a call. LTN's proposal was that customers would use the Calldex cards to circumvent per minute long distance charges by using the local access numbers to call the LTN network. Once connected, they would input their calling card number, the PIN number currently being displayed, and the number they want to reach. Customers would pay a flat amount in advance, as well as an additional $160 to buy the card.

An alternative idea was to sell disposable calling cards with a fixed amount of long distance time pre-loaded with amounts of $10, $25 or $50. Disposable cards were popular in Europe, where people paid a per-minute charge for local calls. LTN hoped to sell the cards directly to current customers, as well as to packaged-goods companies which might want to put $2 worth of long distance credit into every cereal box as a promotion.

Building a Permanent Network

With projectability building and the possibility of going public, management felt LTN should plan on building a permanent network. To transmit calls, the company was considering using microwave towers which, although susceptible to weather, were much cheaper than fibre optic cable. Rob Freeman thought that LTN could easily arrange a contract with one of the alternative carriers to carry calls when the weather was bad.

DECISION

Rob Freeman had almost reached the Hamilton office, where he would be meeting with his management team to discuss the options at 10 a.m. Although each option had potential, he was uncertain about how to make a choice and unwilling to take any big risks.

Exhibit 1: **LONDON TELECOM NETWORKS: FINANCIAL STATEMENTS 1992-1995**

Income Statement					11 month ending
	Jan 31,1992	Jan 31,1993	Jan 31,1994	Jan 31,1995	Dec 31 , 1995
Revenue	253 387	1 625 012	5 899 065	12 368 252	20 036 062
Line costs	127 987	860 832	3 919 194	8 836 132	13 273 814
Gross Margin	125 400	764 180	1 979 871	3 532 120	6 762 248
Sales. General & Admin	117 678	906 566	1 820 178	4 007 550	5 305 266
Amortization	9 514	49 785	100 428	704 110	456 725
Operating Profit	(1 792)	(192 170)	59 265	(1 179 540)	1 000 257
Other Income	2 240	0	0	92 465	0
Unusual Item (1)	0	0	0	(1 000 000)	0
Taxes	0	0	0	0	0
Net Profit	448	(192 170)	59 265	(2 087 075)	1 000 257

Balance Sheet					
Assets					
Cash	17 948	0	354 037	299 450	1 675 700
Accounts Receivable	32 716	471 915	1 330 838	1 983 534	3 138 090
Prepaids	0.00	3 273	13 348	51 660	560 004
Due from Shareholders	0	0	31 233	96 630	201 980
Total Current Assets	50 664	475 188	1 729 456	2 431 274	5 575 774
Capital Assets (net)	69 944	296 663	509 452	772 134	1 469 330
Due from Related Companies	0	0	15 487	286 465	908 358
Other Assets	63 058	56 591	50 123	43 657	0
Total Assets	183 666	828 442	2 304 518	3 533 529	7 953 462
Liabilities					
Short term debt	0	48 162	0	0	0
Accounts Payable	139 278	198 184	614 073	1 069 528	2 672 297
Deferred Revenue	45 268	456 014	1 163 008	2 043 873	3 393 849
Customer Deposits	0	313 810	658 343	1 638 109	2 105 040
Shareholders Advance	(2 880)	2 443	0	0	0
Non competition A/P	0	0	0	1 000 000	1 000 000
Total Liabilities	181 666	1 018 613	2 435 424	5 751 510	9 171 186
Equity					
Capital Stock	2 000	2 000	2 000	2 000	2 000
Retained Earnings	0	(192 170)	(132 906)	(2 219 981)	(1 219 724)
Total Liabilities and Equity	183 666	828 442	2 304 518	3 533 529	7 953 462

Note: 1) Unusual item in 1995: non competition agreement paid to past shareholder.

Source: LTN internal documents.

Exhibit 2: COMPARISON OF COMPETITIVE LONG DISTANCE PRICES AND COSTS

	cost/min. (cents)
1. Bell Canada: Prices	
base rate (Quebec-Windsor corridor):	37.0
Residential	
evening discount (6-11pm) - 35%	24.1
late night (after 11pm)/weekend discount - 60%	14.8
Business	
large business (over $300,000/month)	
day rate	14.8
late night rate	10.4
medium business (over $2,500/month)	
day rate	16.7
late night rate	11.7
Bell Canada: Costs	
Cost per MOU (minute of use) - average	8.0
2. Large Alternative Carriers -(ACC, fonorola, Unitel, Sprint): Prices	
Business and Residential	
Best discount -25% off Bell rate	
day rate	27.8
evening	18.0
late night / weekend	11.1
Large Alternative Carriers: Costs	
Cost per MOU (minute of use) - average	12.0-16.7
3. Small Resellers: Prices	
Business and Residential	
best discount - 35% off Bell rate	
day rate	24.1
evening	15.6
late night / weekend	9.6
Small Resellers: Costs	
Cost per MOU (minute of use)	77% of selling price

Source: Discount rates based on literature search. Better discounts may be available to key clients.

Exhibit 3: **ACC TelEnterprises Overview and Financial Statements 1994/1995**

Overview

ACC TelEnterprises was a subsidiary of ACC Corp. of Rochester, New York. ACC rented all of its long distance equipment, but had invested in switching technology and frame relay equipment to ensure that it was able to offer a full range of services to its customers. As a part of this, the Canadian ACC network was interconnected with ACC's networks in the U.S. and in the U.K. In 1995, ACC TelEnterprises spent $4.2 million on switches and equipment.

ACC's motto was to be "all things to some people". ACC ended 1995 with 136,000 residential and 25,000 commercial customers, an increase of 58,000 over December, 1994. ACC had exclusive marketing rights at 30 universities in Canada, provided private label services to The Bay, and had recently introduced internet services.

Income Statement
($000s)

	Dec. 31, 1994	Dec. 31, 1995
Revenue	95,511	120,002
Network costs	65,482	76,130
Operating Expenses	36,729	40,231
EBITDA	(347)	10,005
Net Profit	(11,002)	631
Balance Sheet		
Assets		
Current	17,350	23,147
Fixed	13,604	16,017
Other	10,997	20,317
Total Assets	41,951	59,481
Liabilities & Equity		
Accounts Payable	15,350	20,612
Debt	354	3,437
Due to Affiliates	20,440	28,167
Other	185	1,008
Capital Stock	22,990	22,994
Deficit	(17,368)	(16,737)
Total	41,951	59,481

Source: ACC TelEnterprises Annual Report.

Exhibit 4: CALL-NET (SPRINT CANADA) OVERVIEW AND FINANCIAL STATEMENTS 1994/1995

Overview

Call-Net Enterprises (Sprint Canada) was 25% owned by Sprint U.S., and had signed special distribution agreements with Sprint U.S. that ensured Call-Net exclusive Canadian rights to Sprint U.S.'s switched voice network and trademarks. Sprint Canada had over 700,000 circuit miles of company-owned fibre optic cable, and state-of-the-art switching equipment in Vancouver, Toronto, Calgary, and Montreal. Call-Net had spent $110 million on network expansion over the last two years and had planned an additional $50 million for 1996.

Sprint Canada was involved in all areas of the Canadian long distance market, including residential and business long distance services, toll free services, bill analysis software, global frame relay (for interconnecting LANs), private line, data packet switching, and Internet access services.

Over the past two years, most of Sprint's new revenues had come from residential and small/medium business clients, but in 1996 Sprint had planned to focus more effort on large business clients, and on the cellular market.

Income Statement	($000s) Dec. 31, 1994	Dec. 31, 1995
Revenue 176,287	457,461	
Network costs	125,093	302,016
Operating Expenses	82,382	171,238
EBITDA	(31,188)	(15,793)
Net Profit	(55,359)	(64,751)
Balance Sheet		
Assets		
Cash	157,730	179,626
Other Current	41,507	92,643
Fixed	85,290	132,008
Other	115,446	120,481
Total Assets	399,973	524,758
Liabilities & Equity		
Accounts Payable	53,498	104,367
Debt	139,634	164,853
Due to Affiliates		
Other	2,587	5,900
Capital Stock	262,638	372,593
Deficit	(58,384)	(123,135)
Total Liabilities	399,973	524,578

Source: Call-Net Enterprises Annual Report.

Exhibit 5: LTN NETWORK AND NETWORK ACCESS

Welcome to London Telecom.™

Canada's flat rate long distance company.

Here's the fast and simple way to start using our flat rate service and start saving money. For easy reference, keep this brochure and your London Telecom™ Directory by your phone.

1. If you're at work, select the line designated for London Telecom's™ flat rate service. At home, just pick up your receiver.

2. Dial your local seven digit access number _____, and wait for a continuous dial tone. It's best to set this number up in speed dial.*

3. Enter the area code and the seven digit number you are calling. **(Never dial 1 or 0 before the area code).**

4. Talk without worrying about per minute charges.

The London Telecom Network™ uses only the latest technology. All your calls will be placed with fast, clear connections, quickly and with no lengthy numbers to call and without delays for authorization. All you need is London Telecom's™ service and a touch tone phone. If you do not dial your local London Telecom™ access number, you will be calling long distance through your regular long distance carrier.

* Note: Write your access number in the space provided. If your telephone service does not provide call identity on your line, London Telecom™ flat rate services can not be accessed.

Source: LTN promotional brochure

Your Local London Telecom™ Office

ONTARIO

ALLISTON	(705) 435-3450
BARRIE	(705) 734-1017
BELLEVILLE	(613) 966-7373
BRANTFORD	(519) 751-9410
BROCKVILLE	(613) 342-4885
CAMBRIDGE	(519) 658-6667
CHATHAM	(519) 352-2900
COBOURG	(905) 377-0750
COLLINGWOOD	(705) 446-2575
CORNWALL	(613) 933-3242
GEORGETOWN	(905) 873-6060
GUELPH	(519) 766-4997
HAMILTON	(905) 570-8700
KITCHENER	(519) 741-5990
KINGSTON	(613) 544-7212
LINDSAY	(705) 324-0001
LONDON	(519) 646-3131
MIDLAND	(705) 526-5445
NEWMARKET	(905) 895-3020
NORTH BAY	(705) 474-5095
ORANGEVILLE	(519) 940-4400
ORILLIA	(705) 327-5117
OSHAWA	(905) 404-6666
OTTAWA	(613) 567-4881
OWEN SOUND	(519) 371-4213
PETERBOROUGH	(705) 743-2382
ST. CATHARINES	(905) 685-5155
SARNIA	(519) 337-1060
SLT. STE. MARIE	(705) 256-7718
SIMCOE	(905) 428-2600
STEVENSVILLE	(519) 382-4448
STRATFORD	(519) 273-4910
SUDBURY	(705) 669-1300
TORONTO	(416) 777-2600
WINDSOR	(519) 257-2900
WOODSTOCK	(519) 537-1000

QUÉBEC

MONTREAL	(514) 879-8502
QUÉBEC CITY	(418) 694-2500

WESTERN CANADA

KELOWNA	(604) 470-4999
VANCOUVER	(604) 606-6949
VICTORIA	(604) 953-9449

Our Coverage Area is Constantly Expanding

COMING SOON

Cobourg, Ontario	Nov. 20, 1995
Sault Ste. Marie, Ontario	Nov. 27, 1995
Calgary, Alberta	Dec. 11, 1995

OUR COVERAGE AREA

LOCAL CALLING AREAS OF ALL CITIES SHOWN ARE ALSO INCLUDED IN LONDON TELECOM'S™ FLAT RATE NETWORK.

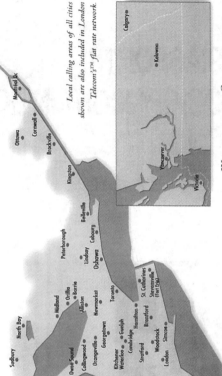

Local calling areas of all cities shown are also included in London Telecom's™ flat rate network.

WESTERN CANADA

ASIASPORTS: HOCKEY NIGHT IN HONG KONG

case 2

Andrew Delios

On March 5, 1999, Tom Barnes, executive director of Asiasports Limited (Asiasports), spent several hours in a meeting with the two main shareholders of the private company, Shane Weir and Bill Gribble. In the meeting, the trio discussed the business strategy for Asiasports for the next five years. Asiasports, a sports management company, was involved in the development of ice hockey in Hong Kong. Barnes, Weir and Gribble had to make decisions about whether the company should promote hockey outside of Hong Kong and its choice of sports properties. An implementation plan also had to be developed for the chosen strategy.

TOM BARNES

Tom Barnes, 32, was born in St. Louis, Missouri, in the United States. He had been active in hockey since his high school days, where he served as captain of his high school team. After

Ivey

Andrew Delios prepared this case solely to provide material for class discussion. The author does not intend to illustrate either effective or ineffective handling of a managerial situation. The author may have disguised certain names and other identifying information to protect confidentiality.

completing an undergraduate degree in organizational behavior at the University of Miami at Ohio, Barnes worked for Enterprise Leasing in St. Louis and Seattle, Washington. In February 1993, following the suggestions of relatives who were living in Hong Kong, Barnes moved there.

Once he arrived in Hong Kong, Barnes began to work for the large cable programmer, Star TV. This job gave Barnes an entry back into the sports world as he worked as a program researcher for the prime sports channel of Star TV. Six months into his term at Star TV, Barnes discovered the existence of a hockey league in Hong Kong while on a hiking trip in rural Lantau Island. In the fall of 1993, he joined the fledgling ice hockey league, which was the predecessor of one of Asiasports' main properties.

HISTORY OF HOCKEY

Ice hockey had been played for several hundred years. Forerunners to the present version of the game were played on frozen lakes and ponds in Great Britain, France and Holland in the 18th century. From these beginnings, hockey began to take more shape in the 19th century in Canada. A primitive variant of today's game emerged near Halifax, Nova Scotia, Canada in the early 1800s. Local schoolboys adopted hurley, a form of field hockey played with a stick and ball, to winter conditions. In the 1870s, students at McGill University in Montreal, Quebec, Canada assigned a set of rules to hockey and played the first exhibition game. The first formal ice hockey league was launched in Kingston, Ontario, Canada in 1885.

Ice hockey was originally played with seven players on the ice. In 1911 the seventh position, the 'rover', was dropped. Later amendments to the rules permitted player substitutions, and the number of players on a team began to exceed ten. Various other initiatives and rule changes shaped the game into its 1990s version. These rule changes facilitated the opening-up of the game, and made hockey into a faster sport.

In the 1990s, hockey was a sport of power, speed, agility and knowledge. Players had to master the ability to skate; they had to learn to control the puck (the sport's ball) with a stick while maneuvering at high speeds; they had to interact well with teammates; and they had to have endurance and strength. Speed was one of the compelling aspects of the game. The fastest players skated at speeds of 50 kilometres per hour, and the hardest shooters propelled the puck at nearly 200 kilometres per hour. Hockey also had an aggressive aspect. Body contact between players was allowed, but not to the extent seen in rugby or American football.

INTERNATIONAL SPREAD OF HOCKEY

From its beginnings in Eastern Canada, hockey gradually spread to Western Canada and the northern states of the U.S. Hockey also spread east across the Atlantic to Scandinavian countries like Sweden, Finland, Norway, and other northern European countries like Russia, Belarus, Lithuania, Latvia and the Czech and Slovak Republics. Later, regions in Europe with warmer climates, Great Britain, Switzerland, Germany and Italy, embraced the sport.

This spread led to hockey's inclusion in the inaugural Olympic Winter Games, held in 1924 in Chamonix, France. Participating countries were drawn from Western European and North American countries. In the 1950s, Eastern Europe countries began to participate in Olympic and

World Championship events. This growth continued, and in 1998, Japan and China also competed in Olympic hockey.

Women's hockey made its debut in the 1998 Winter Olympics. Prior to that, women's hockey had been recognized internationally, through sanctioned World Championships. At a national level, women's hockey leagues were prominent in the U.S., where several college leagues had operated since the mid-1970s. In the 1990s, women's hockey was played in North America, Europe and Asia. China, Japan and South Korea were the principal countries in Asia in which women's hockey was played. In Canada, close to 20,000 women were enrolled in hockey leagues in 1997. In the U.S. this number was greater as participation had grown four-fold since 1990.

When hockey spread internationally, its growth in new countries was supported by two factors. The first factor was that hockey had to be seen as an exciting and attractive sport for both viewing and participation. Hockey faced competition for the participant and viewer from a variety of other sports. In the United States, for example, hockey had to compete with team sports such as baseball, American football, basketball and soccer, as well as individual sports like tennis and golf. The second factor was that hockey had to develop at a grassroots level. Children had to have the opportunity to play hockey when young, to help develop an interest that would carry over into participation as a player, viewer, and volunteer in hockey associations when an adult.

HOCKEY ASSOCIATIONS

International Ice Hockey Federation[1]

Representatives of Bohemia, Switzerland, France, Belgium and Great Britain founded the International Ice Hockey Federation (IIHF, or Ligue Internationale de Hockey sur Glace) in 1908. The aim of the IIHF was to control the sports of ice hockey and in-line hockey and to organize international competitions.

In its first ten years, the IIHF was purely a European institution. However, in the last two decades of the 20th century, and with the growth of in-line hockey, the sport of hockey became increasingly global. The IIHF grew along with hockey. In 1999, it consisted of 55 member federations.

The IIHF was involved directly with a number of tournaments and leagues, such as the European Senior Championships, the World Senior and Junior Tournaments, the Asia/Oceania Junior Championships and the European and World Women Championships. The IIHF had indirect, but substantive involvement in other tournaments. These tournaments included the well-known Olympic Games, as well as lesser-known ones like the Continental Cup and the Super Cup. Aside from ice hockey tournaments, the IIHF helped to organize several in-line competitions and tournaments. These were organized at the grassroots level, for generating new interest in specific cities and countries, and at a national competitive level. Finally, the IIHF ran a development program for hockey. This program focused on development in four areas: coaching, officiating, playing and administration.

---

[1] Information in this section was derived in part from the International Ice Hockey Federation's homepage: http://www.iihf.com., April 1999.

National Hockey Associations

A number of European, North American and Asian countries had national-level ice hockey associations. These bodies oversaw the development and promotion of the sport within the national domain, as well as in national competitions. National associations, such as the Canadian Hockey Association or USA Hockey, ran development programs for coaches, players and officials. The associations organized national championships and put together the junior and senior teams that competed in international championships.

As an example, the Canadian Hockey Association (CHA) was the sole governing body of amateur hockey in Canada. It worked in conjunction with 13 branch associations, the Canadian Hockey League, and the Canadian Inter-University Athletic Union. The CHA maintained offices in several major cities in Canada, and operated on an annual budget of Cdn$15.1 million (US$9 million, see Exhibit 1). With a relatively small budget, it relied on the co-operation of volunteers to fulfil its mandate to the approximately 500,000 registered hockey players in Canada.

National Hockey League[2]

The National Hockey League (NHL) was the premier hockey league in 1999. The league had teams based in Canada and the U.S. The players in the NHL had a variety of nationalities: American, British, Canadian, Czech, Finnish, German, Russian, Slovak and Swedish, to name a few. The largest group of players was Canadian, but in the 1990s the percentage of players from the U.S. and Europe had been increasing.

The NHL, which was not the first professional league formed in North America, commenced operations in 1917. Initially, it had four Canadian teams: the Montreal Canadiens, the Montreal Wanderers, the Ottawa Senators and the Toronto Arenas. After several decades of sporadic growth and a bout of competition from a since-disbanded rival league, the World Hockey Association, in 1999 the NHL had expanded to 27 teams.

In the 1990s, the NHL adopted an aggressive marketing stance in which promotional activities in the U.S. and elsewhere in the world were an important component. The NHL ran several programs designed to grow the game of hockey. NHL Skate was one of these. NHL Skate aided the creation of multi-purpose ice skating facilities. A related program was NHL Hockey Playground. This program had the goal of creating off-ice hockey rinks in urban environments. A third program, NHL A.S.S.I.S.T., helped youth organizations defray costs associated with playing the sport: equipment costs, costs of travel and the cost of renting an ice rink. NHL A.S.S.I.S.T. had a worldwide mandate and had financed teams in Canada, China, Hungary, Ireland, Romania and the United States.

As a further aid to the promotion of the sport, the NHL actively sought greater penetration of U.S. television markets. Despite success as a television product in Canada and several European countries, the popularity of professional hockey on U.S. television had waned in the late 1990s. To increase television viewership, the NHL had continued to increase the number of U.S.-based franchises through the 1990s. In the late 1990s, the NHL planned to add new teams in such places as Atlanta, Georgia in the U.S. The 30-team league would have teams placed throughout North America, including cities in the south and southwest portions of the U.S.

---

[2] Material in this section was drawn from material available on the National Hockey League's official web-site: www.nhl.com., April 1999.

It was in these cities, in which snow and ice were a rarity, that the NHL had faced its greatest growing pains in the 1970s and 1980s. However, in the 1990s, expansion had been successful because the game's premier player was a member of a Los Angeles-based team for the first half of the 1990s. The adoption of hockey in the south was also aided by an innovation: the creation of the in-line skate.

IN-LINE HOCKEY

In the mid-1980s, two brothers in Minnesota developed an in-line skate that could be used to play hockey. Their efforts led to the incorporation of the Rollerblade company. Subsequently, the popularity of in-line skating as a form of recreation and exercise exploded in the U.S. and elsewhere in the world. In the late 1980s and early 1990s, in-line hockey leagues began to mushroom in the U.S. In-line hockey was particularly well liked in the southern states of the U.S., in places where ice hockey had traditionally had difficulty gaining acceptance as a legitimate sport. California, where in-line skating had been adopted enthusiastically, saw the growth of several professional, semi-professional, amateur and development in-line hockey leagues. Children's participation in in-line hockey was also widespread and growing.

To deal with the rapid growth of in-line hockey, national hockey associations worked to organise the sport on a national and sub-national basis. For instance, in December 1994, USA Hockey created USA Hockey InLine to address the growth in demand for playing, coaching and officiating programs within in-line hockey in the U.S. Accordingly, the mission of USA Hockey was "to promote and facilitate the growth of in-line hockey in America and to provide the best possible experience for all participants by encouraging, advancing and administering the sport."[3]

USA Hockey InLine provided many services to its members. It offered resources and educational programs to coaches, referees and league administrators. It organised and sanctioned tournaments for players of all ages and skill levels. It coordinated national teams that competed in IIHF-sanctioned tournaments.

National associations were not the only ones to adopt and help in-line hockey. As part of its efforts to expand the sports fan base, the NHL created the NHL Breakout program. This program sponsored street and in-line hockey in 22 NHL North American cities in 1999. The tournaments concluded with a National Championship, which was held in January 2000. The NHL Breakout tournament was open to players of all ages and skill levels. Games were played on portable, inflatable in-line hockey rinks, which were also developed by the NHL.

Private companies also became involved in the promotion and organisation of in-line hockey. TOHRS was one such company. TOHRS was an in-line hockey tournament organisation that was sanctioned by USA Hockey. It provided 50 tournaments in the U.S. each year, drawing a total of more than 100,000 participants. Players from all ages and all levels competed in these tournaments. The majority of these tournaments were held in southern U.S. states such as Florida, California, Texas and Georgia, places where ice hockey was played infrequently at a grassroots level.

One reason for the popularity of in-line hockey in southern locations was its suitability to warm weather conditions. Unlike ice hockey, which required an outdoor ice surface (and a cold climate) or an indoor ice arena, in-line hockey could be played anywhere there was a hard, paved surface. Parking lots were a popular location for in-line hockey games as were indoor roller skating

---

[3] The mission statement and other material on USA Hockey were sourced from USA Hockey's web-site: http://www.usahockey.com., April 1999.

rinks. In-line hockey was also played on portable rinks. The NHL Breakout tournament was played on this type of rink. Other tournaments and leagues also used these rinks. California's Pro Beach Hockey Series, which was broadcast on ESPN and ESPN2, was played on a portable Pro Beach Hockey rink. This rink (50 metres by 23 metres) was three-quarters the size of an ice hockey rink. It had 1,200 seats for spectators.

ASIASPORTS

Sports Management

Asiasports was a sports management company (sometimes called a sports marketing company). Sports marketing companies generally carried out a variety of activities. Among these were the organization of fund raisers and sport event design and development, event production and consulting, sponsorship sales and management, media advertising, direct marketing, sales promotion and public relations.

Sports marketing companies often became synonymous with a particular form of sport. For example, Ryno Sports, which was based in California, principally promoted beach volleyball and beach softball. It sold sports that typified the California lifestyle. In connection with these sports, Ryno Sports provided a variety of services ranging from complete event management to professional athletic exhibitions, instructional clinics, turnkey events, consulting and the merchandising of gifts and merchandise.

Some sports marketing companies held a variety of sports properties. Lanier Sports Marketing, which operated out of Cary, North Carolina in the U.S., created, marketed and produced several types of sports in North Carolina. The company helped to create a boxing event called "King of the Ring", and it broadcast boxing. The company's other projects included sponsoring of golf tournaments and distributing and selling tickets for the local university basketball team. Finally, aside from these promotional activities, the company had an advertising arm that created and produced commercials and provided media planning and placement services.

Structure of Asiasports

Asiasports was formally incorporated on July 1, 1996. It was a widely held private company. The main shareholders were Shane Weir and Bill Gribble, each with a 30 per cent share. Barnes possessed 10 per cent, a Hong Kong venture capital company owned 10 per cent, and the remaining 20 per cent was held by thirty other people. The company had a board of directors. Seven to eight shareholders sat on the board; however, Weir and Gribble held most of the decision-making power. While it was a widely held company, its financial resources were limited to the pockets of Weir, Gribble and Barnes, which were not exceptionally deep.

Barnes made quarterly reports to the board, and the company had an annual general meeting. The board helped to set the strategic direction of the company, while Barnes had the autonomy to make day-to-day operating decisions. To aid his tasks, Barnes had one assistant, Keith Fong, and he contracted out secretarial support. When needed, Asiasports made use of volunteers comprising hockey league members and their families. However, all of the hands-on work for the company was done by Barnes and his assistant.

Growth of Asiasports

Weir, Gribble and Barnes founded Asiasports in response to opportunities for the promotion of hockey in Hong Kong. Prior to the founding of Asiasports, hockey in Hong Kong had been played on an informal basis for many years. Following the conclusion of a hockey tournament in March 1995, Barnes spoke with Weir and Gribble about their idea to create a sports marketing company for the promotion of hockey in Hong Kong. Barnes, who was looking for a new position at that time, began working for Asiasports on a full-time basis in July 1996.

Asiasports was founded with the mandate to manage hockey and other activities. In 1999, Asiasports was still in the entrepreneurial stage and Barnes was considering adding a variety of new hockey and non-hockey-related sports properties. It was by the addition of new properties and the expansion of existing ones, that sponsorship income had increased by 50 per cent from 1996 to 1999. During the same period, player fees had grown by 20 to 25 per cent on an annual basis. With the exception of the World Ice Hockey 5's event, all sports properties were individually profitable. Even so, the company had experienced a loss on its 1998 operations.

In its first three years of operations, Asiasports had organised and managed several leagues and events. Some of these were hockey-related, while others involved other sports such as slo-pitch softball and golf. Hockey itself did not have as high a profile in Hong Kong as other sports such as horse racing, soccer and tennis. Horse racing was a popular spectator event, with nightly broadcasts of race results on Hong Kong's main TV channels. Soccer and tennis were the main participant sports. A multitude of tennis courts and soccer fields were squeezed into the tight land space in Hong Kong.

Sources of Revenues

As a sports management company, Asiasports derived its revenues from a variety of sources. Its two primary sources of revenues were player fees and sponsorship income. Player fees represented money collected from participants in the leagues and tournaments organised by Asiasports. As an example, for a player in the South China Ice Hockey League (SCIHL), the fee for the 1998-99 season was HK$1,800 (US$230) (also see Exhibit 2).

For most of Asiasports' activities conducted in Hong Kong, player fees represented 50 per cent of its income. The other 50 per cent came from sponsorship income. Asiasports had engaged a number of sponsors for the SCIHL, and for its annual ice hockey tournament, the World Ice Hockey 5's. The main sponsors for the SCIHL were Budweiser, the SUNDAY network, Nortel networks, the Hong Kong Yellow Pages, Caltex and Jack-in-the-Box. The number of sponsors for the World Ice Hockey 5's was the greatest, as shown in Exhibit 3.

In return for sponsorship, Asiasports gave sponsoring companies exposure. The principal sponsor for the ice hockey tournament was identified in the tournament's title — SUNDAY World Ice Hockey 5's. Tournament and league sponsors also had their names placed on the sweaters of competing teams, a practice similar to European hockey and football leagues, and auto-racing circuits in the U.S. and Europe. Sponsors were likewise identified in programs developed for tournaments. Sponsors also received name exposure through print and electronic media coverage of Asiasports-sponsored events. The two primary events, or sports properties, were the South China Ice Hockey League and the World Ice Hockey 5's.

ASIASPORTS PROPERTIES

South China Ice Hockey League

The South China Ice Hockey League (SCIHL) stimulated much interest in hockey in Hong Kong. The league began in the fall of 1995 with four teams and about 60 players. In the 1996-97 season, six teams competed in the league which involved about 100 players. In the fourth and most recent season (1998-99), six teams and more than 100 players competed in the first division, and another six teams competed in the second division. The first division was the competitive league. The second division was a developmental league. Both men and women who were new to hockey, and children, were members of second division teams.

The SCIHL was originally founded in response to Hong Kong expatriates' desire to play hockey while living in Hong Kong. However, the current coverage of SCIHL extended beyond that original objective. The players came from many of the expatriates that lived in Hong Kong: Canada, China, Finland, France, Japan, Sweden, Switzerland and the United States, among other countries (see Exhibit 4). The majority of the players in the second division were from Hong Kong.

The growth of participation of players from Hong Kong echoed the mushrooming popularity of hockey throughout Asia. Barnes believed Asia's fascination with ice skating owed much to the exposure to figure skating in the Winter Olympics and the success of Asian figure skating champions, like Michelle Kwan, Chen Lu and Kristi Yamaguchi. This interest, he said, often leads skaters to turn to ice hockey. Barnes noted, "Once you master skating around in circles, you'll eventually get bored and want to try something else like ice hockey."

In the SCIHL, as in other areas of Southeast Asia, games were played in ice rinks located in shopping malls. There were five ice rinks in Hong Kong in 1999, with the most recent built in 1998. The venue for the SCIHL was the Skyrink, which was located in the Dragon Centre Shopping Mall, Kowloon. The size of a shopping mall rink was two-thirds that of a standard rink. Consequently, five players — two forwards, two defence and one goaltender — played on a team, rather than the six used in a standard ice hockey game (see Appendix). Fewer players meant that the game was faster and higher scoring than the six-player version. It was more entertaining for the casual spectators that watched the game while shopping in the mall.

World Ice Hockey 5's

The World Ice Hockey 5's was an annual event that had been held since the early 1990s. The idea for the tournament had sprung from a group of American and Canadian hockey players who played hockey at the City Plaza Rink, in Tai Koo Shing, Hong Kong. Four teams competed in this tournament, in which five games were played over a weekend. It was named Hockey 5's because five, rather than six players, played for each team (see the Appendix for a summary of rules for this game).

The first World Ice Hockey 5's tournament was held in 1994. The Swedish company Ericsson sponsored this tournament which saw three local teams and three overseas teams (Beijing, Bangkok and Bahrain) compete for the title. The number of teams grew to nine in 1995, with Moosehead as the lead sponsor.

The event continued to grow through the next three years. In 1996, ten teams competed, with overseas teams from Tokyo, South Korea, Dubai, Bangkok, Singapore and Beijing. In 1997, the number of teams grew by 50 per cent and the name, World Ice Hockey 5's — Hong Kong, was coined. This tournament also marked the introduction of women's teams, from Hong Kong, Japan and Harbin, China, to the tournament. With the continued expansion of the tournament, two venues were used to stage the tournament.

The 1998 tournament saw the introduction of a Kids Division and an All-Asia Men's Division. The number of teams in this tournament more than doubled to 34. Sixty-four games were played over four days at the Skyrink and the City Plaza rink. The 1999 tournament was billed as Asia's largest ice hockey tournament and the world's largest ice hockey 5's tournament. It had more than 40 teams competing in four divisions: Kid's Division, Women's Division, Men's Division 1 and Men's Division 2 (see Exhibit 5). Because of the growth in the tournament, it was held over a period of 10 to 11 days, rather than one weekend.

The growth in the number of teams in the tournament sparked wider media coverage of the event. The tournament had 49 clippings and stories written about it in Chinese and English language print media in Hong Kong, and in print media in Japan and Canada. In the electronic media, ATV, a Hong Kong broadcaster, covered the tournament's final two days. A special five-minute feature was also carried on TVB Pearl. Other coverage was received from CNN and the Asia Sports show.

Asiasports' special guest for the 1999 tournament, Gordie Howe, enhanced media coverage because Howe was widely regarded as one of the greatest players in the sport of hockey. Both local and international media mentioned Howe's attendance at the tournament in their coverage of the 7th annual World Ice Hockey 5's.

In observing the tournament, Howe noticed parallels between the present situation for hockey in Hong Kong, and that in the southern United States in the 1970s. Howe said, "When I heard they played hockey in Hong Kong, I had the same reaction as when they started playing hockey in Florida." (reported in Hong Kong Standard, 12/03/1999.) In 1999, Florida had two professional teams competing in the NHL.

Other Properties / Events

Asiasports organised a number of other hockey tournaments in different parts of Asia and Southeast Asia. In 1997, Asiasports ran tournaments in Macao, Bangkok, Thailand and Jakarta, Indonesia. In 1998 and 1999, the company continued to be active in Asian tournament hockey. Manila in the Philippines, Dubai, and Bangkok were each the site of an Asiasports hockey tournament. Asiasports also assisted with signing up teams for a tournament in 1998 in Ulaan Baatar, Mongolia.

Aside from running hockey tournaments, Asiasports supported the development of hockey. It ran programs for coaches and training programs for children who wanted to play ice hockey or in-line hockey. Occasionally, Asiasports promoted non-hockey sporting events, such as softball or golf, but when it did this, it competed directly with other sports management companies in Hong Kong. When Asiasports concentrated on hockey it had no direct competition in Hong Kong, and little across the rest of Southeast Asia. Even rink operators were not competitors because ice skating rinks were concerned with attracting a figure skating audience.

FUTURE GROWTH

Setting for Expansion

By the spring of 1999, Asiasports had been successful in developing the SCIHL and the World Ice

Hockey 5's tournament. However, these properties alone were not enough to meet the company's mandate, and Barnes' goal of bringing hockey to prominence in Southeast Asia. In 1999, hockey still existed as a fringe sport in Hong Kong and other Southeast Asian countries like the Philippines, Taiwan, Thailand, Malaysia and Singapore. No national bodies organised the sport in these countries.

The growth of hockey in these countries had been sporadic and slow, especially compared to the more northerly Asian countries, China, Japan and South Korea. In Japan, for example, hockey was played at many levels. Developmental leagues existed for children, many universities had their own teams, a variety of people played in informal leagues, and a semi-professional (semi-pro) league, similar to what could be seen in Europe, China and South Korea, also existed. Women's hockey in all three countries was strong. China's women's national team was the third best in the world in the latter half of the 1990s.

The growth in the popularity of hockey in China, Japan and South Korea had attracted the attention of the IIHF. It was involved in linking ice hockey in these countries to the hockey world at large. However, ice hockey in Hong Kong and other Southeast Asian countries had yet to draw any serious attention from the IIHF. Even so, the IIHF was aware of Asiasport's activities in Hong Kong. Unlike the IIHF, the NHL had expressed some interest in hockey in Southeast Asia. It had offices in Japan and Australia. It played two league games in Japan each year. Further, the NHL had provided Asiasports with merchandise and logos for Asiasports' events.

Options

Several options existed for Asiasports. These options included both geographic and product diversification, as well as an increased focus on existing products. Barnes wanted to bring hockey to Asia, but in considering these options, he thought "he would take Asiasports where the money was, to keep the company alive."

1. **Set up Hockey Leagues in Southeast Asia.** In 1999, the only established hockey league in Southeast Asia was SCIHL in Hong Kong. The opportunity existed to set up similar leagues in Bangkok, Manila, Taipei, Singapore and Ho Chi Minh City. The state of hockey in these cities was similar to that in Hong Kong in the early 1990s, and each city possessed a viable rink on which hockey could be played. Further, Bill Gribble was located in Taiwan, and he had done some groundwork on establishing hockey in Taipei.

2. **Develop and Expand Existing Tournaments.** Asiasports organized four to five tournaments each year across several cities in Southeast Asia. One option was to deepen its involvement in these tournaments. It could do this by committing more time to developing sponsors for the various events, by seeking a wider coverage of cities for the tournaments, and by giving tournament partners in various cities access to players that competed in the SCIHL.

3. **Develop in-line hockey**. In 1999, in-line hockey did not enjoy as good a penetration in Hong Kong as ice hockey because it was still new. Furthermore, in-line skating was difficult to do as a recreation in Hong Kong because of the danger caused by the crowded roads, and steep inclines found on many roads. Even so, in-line hockey had begun to sprout in Hong Kong and was played at two locations: Discovery Bay on Hong Kong Island, and Diamond Hill in Kowloon. An advantage to developing in-line hockey was that the NHL had expressed an interest in promoting in-line hockey in Hong Kong. If this option was pursued, there was the chance for Asiasports to develop a tie-in with the NHL for the promotion of the sport and the sale of NHL-branded merchandise.

4. **Develop other properties**. This option included the development of a series of golf and softball tournaments. While this activity would bring Asiasports into more direct competition with other sports management companies in Hong Kong, it would broaden the base of Asiasports' properties and increase the number of potential participants and sponsors.

5. **Develop a Semi-Pro League in Hong Kong.** This option represented a shift in the way Asiasports did business. Developing a semi-pro league meant that players would receive a salary for playing, rather than paying a fee. The loss of user revenues and the higher cost structure would have to be offset by increases in sponsorship revenues. A semi-pro league would have a higher profile, as did the World Hockey 5's tournament, than the SCIHL. As well, the league could be an avenue by which hockey in Hong Kong could be linked to that in China, Japan, South Korea and perhaps elsewhere in the world.

As Barnes considered these options, he could not divorce himself from the context of Asiasports. It was a young, entrepreneurial company that had the financial and human resource constraints typically faced by such companies. It could not pursue all options, and its biggest challenge might be to solidify its current activities in Hong Kong before expanding. Even so, whichever option was selected, it had to be selected soon because the 1999-2000 season was approaching rapidly.

Exhibit 1: SOURCES OF FUNDING FOR CANADIAN HOCKEY ASSOCIATION (1997 to 1998)

Source	Funding (Canadian dollars)
Sponsors	4,055,000
Program/Event Revenue	4,690,000
Membership/Service Fees	1,809,000
Merchandise	1,743,000
Sport Funding Agencies	1,465,000
Government	1,110,000
Other	268,000
Total	**$ 15,140,000**

Note: Major sponsors included Nike Inc., Royal Bank of Canada, Esso (Imperial Oil) and Air Canada.

Source: Canadian Hockey Association web-page: www.canadianhockey.ca/e/index.html, April 1999.

Exhibit 2: **REVENUES AND EXPENSES FOR WORLD ICE HOCKEY 5's TOURNAMENT (1999) (HK$)**

CONSOLIDATED FINANCIAL STATUS

Revenue (all sources)	Gordie Howe Event	235.520
	Sponsorship	542,000
	Players' Fees	148,759
	Merchandise	<u>40,110</u>
	Total Revenue	**966,389**
Expenses (all sources)	Gordie Howe Event	389,826
	Tournament Costs	<u>843,970</u>
	Total Expenses	**1,233,796**
Net Profit		**(267,407)**

TOURNAMENT COSTS

Expenses	Asia Sports Management Fees	85,000
	Video Production	30,000
	Working Staff	70,000
	Ice Rental	450,000
	Program Production	43,000
	Merchandise	88,750
	Other Expenses	<u>77,220</u>
	Total Expenses	**843,970**

GORDIE HOWE EVENT

Revenue	Friday Dinner and Gala	65,000
	Gala Dinner	<u>170,520</u>
	Total revenue	**235,520**
Expenses	Appearance Fee	78,000
	Friday Dinner	11,626
	Books	68,000
	Personnel Costs	30,000
	Hotel costs	194,000
	Miscellaneous costs	<u>8,200</u>
	Total Expenses	**389,826**
Net Income — Gordie Howe Event		**(154,306)**

SPONSORSHIP

Revenue	Title Sponsor Sunday	—
	Co-Title Sponsor Nortel	250,000
	Associate Sponsor (Yellow Pages)	80,000
	Associate Sponsor (Budweiser)	80,000
	Dragon Centre/Sky Rink Team sponsorship	30,000
	Distacom — Team sponsorship	30,000

Continued

	French restaurant — Team sponsorship	15,000
	Cap. Z — Team sponsorship	15,000
	Ski at Whistler — Team sponsorship	15,000
	Lan Kwai Fong Holdings	10,000
	Drink Sponsors	—
	HK Land	7,000
	Dresdner Bank	5,000
	Kan and Co.	5,000
	Total Sponsorship Revenue	**542,000**

PLAYER FEES' AND MERCHANDISE SALES

Player Entrance Fees	Foreign	83,359
	Local	65,400
	Total Player Fees	**148,759**
Merchandise Sales	**Total**	**40,110**
	Total Player's Fees and Merchandise Revenues	**730,869**

Source: Company documents.

Exhibit 3: SPONSORS FOR WORLD ICE HOCKEY 5's (1999)

Main Sponsors	Other Sponsors
SUNDAY	Hong Kong Land
Nortel Networks	Distacom
Budweiser	Ski AT Whistler
Yellow Pages	Fred Kan & Co.
Swire Coca Cola	The Hong Kong Tourist Association
Air Canada	Hong Kong St. John's Ambulance
The Festival Walk	Texon Media
The Empire Hotel	Empire Brew
	Hong Kong Club
	Conrad International Hotel
	Dresdner RCM Global Investors
	API Prism
	Comforce Advertising and Promotion
	Asia Business Group
	Can-Am Ice Hockey Association

Source: Company documents

Exhibit 4: **POPULATION AND NATIONALITY OF HONG KONG RESIDENTS (1996)**

Place of Birth / Nationality	Number of People	Per cent of Population
Place of Birth		
Hong Kong	3,749,332	60.30
China and Macau	2,096,511	33.72
Elsewhere	371,713	5.98
Nationality for Elsewhere category		
Filipino	118,449	1.91
Chinese	57,393	0.92
British	44,703	0.72
United States American	18,502	0.30
Japanese	17,999	0.29
Indian, Pakistani, Bangladeshi	17,379	0.28
Thai	15,494	0.25
Canadian	10,816	0.17
Australian	7,777	0.13
Portuguese	323	0.01
Others	62,878	1.01
Total	**6,217,556**	**100.00**

Note: People born in Hong Kong, China and Macau held a variety of nationalities.

Source: 1996 Population By-census. Census and Statistics Department, Hong Kong.

Exhibit 5: **PARTICIPATION IN WORLD ICE HOCKEY 5's TOURNAMENT (1999)**

Kid's Division	Women's Division	Men's Division 1	Men's Division 2
Number of Teams:			
11 Teams	6 Teams	15 Teams	10 Teams
Sources of Teams:			
Hong Kong	Canada	Canada	Hong Kong
Philippines	Hong Kong	Bangkok	Macao
Singapore	Japan	Hong Kong	Philippines
Taiwan	Philippines	Japan	Singapore
	Singapore	Singapore	United Arab Emirates
		Taiwan	
		United States	
		United Arab Emirates	

Source: Company documents.

APPENDIX

Understanding the game of
ICE HOCKEY 5's

The rink 場地

溜冰場的基本形狀為長方形，兩端四角呈弧狀。一個標準的NHL溜冰場是200呎X85呎，但場地大小可應不同需要而變改。西九龍中心的天龍溜冰場和太古城溜冰場只有120呎X60呎，所以較為適合舉行5人賽。

Basically, a hockey rink is a large rectangle with rounded corners. The ice surface of a standard NHL rink is 200 feet by 85 feet, but dimensions can vary. The surface at Skyrink and City Plaza is 120 feet by 60 feet, ideal for a smaller five-a-side team format.

The markings 記號

溜冰場上設有兩條藍線，用作分辨進攻及防守區域以辨別越位犯規。溜冰場兩端的紅線是用作判斷射球是否得分。在兩端及中場的圈圈，中端的用作兩隊開球或爭球時的標誌。

The rink is marked with two blue lines which designate offensive and defensive zones and used in determining offside violations. The goal line is the red line at each end of the rink that is used in determining whether a goal has been scored. The rink also has two faceoff circles at each end and another at center ice. The dots located just outside the blue lines at each end of the rink also are used as faceoff locations.

The nets 籠門

籠門高4呎，闊6呎。通常是用釘子固定在冰上，避免在比賽中因球員碰撞球門而移動。

The goal nets have openings that are four feet high and six feet wide. The nets are anchored to the ice by pins that give way when players crash into the goals.

Players 球員

每隊球隊最多可有12位球員及2位門將。一般出場比賽的有4位球員及1位門將。但當有球員犯規被逐出場時，該隊便要在缺一位球員的情況下比賽。球隊亦可以選擇換入另一位進攻球員取代門將以加強攻擊力。

Teams are allowed to dress 12 skaters and two goalies. Teams generally have four skaters and one goalie on the ice. Exceptions occur when teams are short-handed because of penalties or when the goalies pulled in favor of an extra skater.

Team benches 球員席

球員席設於溜冰場同一邊的兩端。

The team benches are on the same side of the rink but at opposite ends to each other.

Penalty box 懲罰箱

懲罰箱位於兩個球員席的中間，是處罰球員時所用的

The penalty box is located between the two team benches at center ice. This is where players go to serve penalties.

The boards 圍板

溜冰場四週的圍板是4呎高，而圍板之上是加上特製的玻璃或膠懸板。這些板是比圍板高幾呎，用途是阻止冰球在比賽中被擊出場外。

The rink is surrounded by boards that are four feet high. In some portions of the rink, extending from the boards are plexiglass panes, or "the glass." These panes generally extend several feet above the boards which often prevents the puck from going out of play.

Officials (Referees) 裁判

每場球賽均是由兩位裁判執法，負責吹罰越位和犯規。有些時候，裁判也需要分隔及勸阻球員間之衝突或打架。

The game is officiated by two referees. They call offside passes and penalties. They have also been known to break up confrontations and on occassion fights.

The crease 守門員禁區

印於球門前紅色的方形區域是守門員禁區。除了冰球停在禁區，否則攻方不准進入。

The red square area marked in front of each goal is the crease. No Player from the attacking team is allowed inside the crease unless the puck is there.

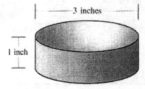

3 inches

1 inch

The puck 冰球

冰球是由硫化橡膠製成，直徑3吋，厚1吋。通常冰球會在比賽前需藏幾小時，減低它的柔軟度，避免冰球在比賽中彈跳。

A four-ounce vulcanized rubber disc that is one inch thick and three inches in diameter. Pucks generally are frozen for a few hours before a game to make them less flexible and more likely to slide instead of bouncing.

Source: Company documents.

AIKENHEAD'S

Mary M. Crossan and
Katy Paul-Chowdhury

When Stephen Bebis placed his business plan in front of Molson Companies Ltd. in 1991, the landscape of Canadian companies in the home improvement industry did not include any warehouse stores. His proposal for the first in a series of home improvement warehouses (HIW) would change the face of Canadian retailing.

Warehouse Concept

Having its origins in U.S. retailing, the warehouse concept was burgeoning, and impacting on almost every area of retailing. In the U.S., Wal-Mart, Kmart, Toys "R" Us, Home Depot, Circuit City Stores, Office Depot, Target Stores, and Costco were among the giant power retailers who were expected to put 50% of retailers out of business by the year 2000.

Every mega-retailer had its own formula. Some focused solely on price, while others attempted to combine the traditional advantages of large volume discount stores, in terms of price and selection, with the customer service of its smaller competitors. Doing so meant gaining the maximum benefit out of every aspect of operations.

The mega-stores sought more than volume discounts and low prices from their suppliers, although this was clearly one of their major strengths. For example, Wal-Mart and Kmart both

IVEY

Mary Crossan and Katy Paul-Chowdhury prepared this case solely to provide material for class discussion. The authors do not intend to illustrate either effective or ineffective handling of a managerial situation. The authors may have disguised certain names and other identifying information to protect confidentiality.

abandoned the brand named "Totes" slippers in favour of a manufacturer who was able to knock-off the concept at a 25% discount. Their strengths, however, extended beyond the clout they wielded to obtain preferential pricing. They worked with their suppliers to develop products that customers wanted, often getting exclusives on some merchandise. One of the areas in which they had made their greatest gains was in inventory management, which enabled them to substantially reduce costs. From electronic hook-ups with suppliers to mandatory bar coding, the mega-retailers had been able to hold operating and selling expenses to as low as 15% of sales versus 28% for their counterparts. As a result they needed only operating margins in the low teens to cover their costs as opposed to traditional retailers who required margins around 30%.

In-store management of merchandise was also critical. Products that didn't move were quickly identified and replaced. While a number of the chains varied on the degree of in-store customer service, some of the more successful warehouses actually provided more in-store service than traditional retailers.

Marketing costs were significantly reduced, since most of the mega-retailers promised "everyday low prices," often with some associated guarantee of having the lowest prices. The focus was, therefore, placed on advertising the store concept, as opposed to a myriad of individual products.

Aikenhead's Concept

The Aikenhead's name had a rich history in the Toronto market. Founded in 1830 as Canada's first hardware chain, it grew into a major wholesaling operation with 19 retail stores when it was purchased by Molson in 1971. The Molson companies, which also owned Beaver Lumber, were very interested in the warehouse concept since they had witnessed the impact of the concept in the U.S. market on mid-level home centres, like Beaver. They believed that in order to protect and strengthen their market share in Canada, they would have to pursue warehouse retailing early in the game. The proposed Aikenhead's concept would be radically different from the original flagship store in downtown Toronto, which had recently undergone a name change to "Armoury Hardware" to reflect the difference in concept.

The proposed Aikenhead's concept was intended to mirror the very successful U.S. Home Depot chain, which was founded in 1978. Home Depot was the largest home improvement retailer with sales of $5.1 billion from 178 outlets in 15 states. Given the higher margins and lower operating expenses of Home Depot, it was estimated that its EBIT of 6.4%, and its return on net assets of 27.5% in 1988 were double that of competitors who followed a traditional retail format. As stated in Aikenhead's business plan:

> The high sales volumes, better buying techniques, focused advertising, intense customer service, everyday low pricing and deep and wide assortments combine to make warehouse home centre retailing one of the fastest growing success stories in terms of sales, profit and investment.

Table 1 provides a comparison of the proposed Aikenhead's home improvement warehouse (HIW) concept and the typical home centre as identified in the Aikenhead's business plan. Table 2 provides a comparison of the sales and profitability of the two concepts. Examples of some of the special customer services to be offered by Aikenhead's, including computerized deck and kitchen designs, and free "how to" videos, can be found in Exhibit 1.

Table 1:   **Comparison between HIW and Typical Home Centre**

	HIW	Typical Home Centre
Size	100 000 sq. ft. 22´–26´ ceilings	40–60 000 sq. ft. 10´–14´ ceilings
SKUs	30–40 000 SKUs	10–20 000 SKUs
Asst/Mix	In-depth assortment of all HI products including professional quality	Limited to the best-sellers of each category
Fixtures	All pallet racking and cantilever racking	Gondola with some pallet and cantilever
Display Format	Bulk oriented Goods are cut cased and massively displayed	Most goods are hung on pegs, hooks or displayed neatly on shelves
Staffing	90% full time	Split to mostly part timers with full-time management
Service	Knowledgeable tradespeople committed to customer service Teach customers to do it themselves Knowledgeable tradespeople on staff in all departments	Most employees are utilized to stock away merchandise Limited service
Supply & Logistics	Worldwide manufacturers Purchase direct from the manufacturers Large quantity, bulk buying, solid trucks, container loads, rail cars 2–4 week lead-time	Worldwide manufacturers Purchase through distributors, wholesalers and brokers Small quantities, common carriers, mixed trucks 7–10 day lead-time
Capital Requirements	$6–7 million/store (excluding real estate)	$3–4 million/store (excluding real estate)
Pricing	Everyday low pricing Always the best price on every item, everyday; pricing driven by the market Negotiate special buys from vendors on key products with savings passed onto the customer The price leader on key commodity items	Higher pricing with sales Selectively sharp on some items, others are based on the store margin budget Run sales on items and absorb profit loss Follows behind the warehouse stores or ignores them
Customer Mix	Do-it-yourselfers Buy-it-yourselfers Professional business customer Customer profile is determined by store placement; insures store will be heavily oriented to the homeowner Over 50% of the customers are female	Not focused on any particular type of customer; some have strong contractor orientation Customer profile varies depending on store location; could be mostly contractors Mostly men with women a smaller minority

Table 2: **Comparative Sales and Profitability**

Performance	HIW	Typical Home Centre
Sales	$24.2 million	$10–12 million
Operating exp.	20.6%	25.9%
EBIT	6.4%	3.4%
RONA (before tax)	27.5%	12.9%

Market Studies

While the HIW concept had been extremely successful in the U.S., there was no Canadian precedent to test the viability of the concept in the new market. However, Price Club and Toys "R" Us had already successfully penetrated the Canadian market. To probe the level of receptivity of Canadians to the HIW concept, $1 million was spent on market studies in the Toronto area, which is where the "roll-out" would begin. Focus groups in the Toronto market indicated that consumers were not particularly loyal as shown by the following types of comments on their shopping habits:

> I drove around until I found the best deal.
> We shop through catalogues in advance.
> I make up a list and look for sales over the next two to three weeks.

While customers perceived that the HIW concept might provide value in terms of convenient shopping, they indicated some skepticism about whether it would provide a high level of service, low prices, convenient location and a wide assortment of branded products. Further research showed that over 80% of shoppers in metropolitan markets were willing to drive 30 minutes to a store with competitive prices. Most consumers would be attracted to the store for its large selection of products and competitive prices.

As well, the research indicated that Canada's 14 largest urban areas, representing one third of its population, could support close to 40 stores with an estimated market size of $3.6 billion.

Competition

Aikenhead's would be stepping into a market with well-established and successful competitors. In 1990, Canadian Tire dominated the industry with sales of $3.1 billion through 418 outlets. Beaver Lumber, which was also owned by Molson's, generated sales of $1.1 billion through 158 outlets. While Canadian Tire and Beaver Lumber characterized the retailing format of the larger retailers, there were chains of independent retailers such as Home Hardware that generated significant sales volumes. Through 985 outlets, Home Hardware generated sales of $850 million. A synopsis of Canadian Tire, Beaver Lumber and Home Hardware is provided in Exhibit 2.

In the Toronto market, with estimated sales for retail home improvement of $482 million, Canadian Tire was the dominant player with a market share of 37% from a base of 33 stores. Beaver Lumber had a 14% market share with 11 stores. Lansing Buildall, Lumber City and Pascal Hardware each had less than 10% of the market. Many smaller retailers such as Home Hardware or other independents made up the remainder of the market. While Bebis viewed every retailer or contractor who sold home improvement products as a competitor, he was confident that Aikenhead's concept would provide it with a superior competitive position in the Canadian context. His primary concern was to establish Aikenhead's before Home Depot entered the market. Molson's believed it would have a few years before Home Depot entered the Canadian market, since in early 1990, when Molson approached Home Depot to form a joint venture, Home Depot indicated they were more interested in pursuing growth opportunities in the U.S.

However, Aikenhead's expected to expand the market, not just to divide the pie a little differently. It viewed itself competing for the consumer's discretionary dollars, and not just for the existing amount spent on home improvement. By making home improvement projects easier and more affordable, it was felt that the entire market had much more room to grow.

In spite of the success U.S. retailers had enjoyed, and the potential that existed in the market according to the research conducted, Bebis was concerned about implementation. The most difficult aspect of the plan was its execution. One of the first things Bebis discovered about the Canadian market was the general lack of pride in the retail sector. He suggested that "in the U.S., individuals do an MBA to get into retail, while in Canada they do an MBA to get out of retail." Executing the Aikenhead's concept would require a revolution in the way retail was conducted; but, more importantly, what was needed was a revolution in the way people thought of retail.

Philosophy/Execution

Execution would go far beyond the words on the page of the business plan that attempted to capture the Aikenhead's corporate philosophy:

> Aikenhead's believes that performing to a standard of excellence in everything we do will optimize the earnings potential of the enterprise.

Fundamental to this standard of excellence are the following philosophical underpinnings:

> Our customers will decide our destiny. We work as a team in which every transaction must convey integrity, value and satisfaction.
> Our employees are our greatest resource. Each is an individual who must be treated with dignity and respect. This will be achieved through providing a work environment which embraces open communications, opportunity, equality and individual fulfillment.

At the outset, the plan tried to identify some of the behaviours that would support the philosophy of a high level of customer service, including getting a carriage for the customer, walking a customer to a product location rather than pointing, and helping the customer carry products to the checkout.

A critical part of the plan was to employ knowledgeable salespeople, and to provide even further training on the culture of the company and the products offered. However, candidates would have to be more than just knowledgeable. Aikenhead's would be looking for individuals who were self-starters, had a high degree of energy, were social, confident, ambitious and could communicate well. Since the organizational structure would be very flat, it was important that all individuals be capable of making decisions. The 200 people to be recruited for the first store opening in March 1992 would swell to 1500, with nine stores, by 1994.

Aikenhead's would have no commissions, or associate (Aikenhead's referred to employees as associates) discounts, as it was felt that they got in the way of customer service and were costly to track. However, associates would be well compensated. Aikenhead's expected to be one of the highest paying retailers in Canada. As well, associates would be provided with the opportunity to earn a financial stake in the business, and bonuses based on store performance. Bebis stated this philosophy:

> In order to get high calibre people, we must: a) pay well; b) offer benefits which are equal to if not better than those offered elsewhere in the industry; c) treat the associates like human beings; d) offer them an environment in which they can grow as individuals; e) encourage them to use their creativity and intelligence; and f) listen to them.

Bebis stated that he would rather hire one associate at $10 per hour than two associates at $6 per hour. With motivated and knowledgeable associates, Bebis saw the benefits of a higher level of sales turnover, arising from the extra care and attention provided to customers and to merchandising products. Training would be used extensively to aid in the development of a new retail mindset. Many of the associates would be coming from traditional retail backgrounds in which the standard was that "there was never enough time to do something right the first time, but enough time to do it over." At Aikenhead's, associates would be encouraged to seek out labour-saving devices to free up the time required to do things right in the first place. Information systems would play a major role in executing the strategy. Systems would be used to reduce costs and to enhance service throughout the organization.

Bebis envisioned that systems would tie Aikenhead's into its supplier network in order to garner efficiencies in ordering, shipping, receiving and billing. If Aikenhead's could reduce a supplier's operating expenses, it was expected that these savings would be passed on to Aikenhead's in the form of lower product costs. Aikenhead's expected to have a partnership relationship with its suppliers that, for many, would require dramatic changes to their business, including selling directly to Aikenhead's. Selling directly meant that manufacturers would have to learn how to service a retailer, while absorbing the additional costs of acting as a warehouse and distribution centre that delivers directly to individual stores. A synopsis of two major suppliers is provided in Exhibit 3.

As well, Aikenhead's would use the same information systems to reduce its own operating expenses and to enhance service. For example, systems designed to track products could be used to manage inventory levels, respond to customer inquiries, establish sales patterns to support decisions about product mix, staffing levels, and to provide information on performance levels.

The company would be organized along functional lines as outlined in Exhibit 4. Each of the vice-presidents had already been recruited. Their profiles are provided in Exhibit 5. Given the flat structure, and the close proximity of the Aikenhead's "home office," which would be adjacent to their first store, executives would be able to stay close to the customer and to remain aware of the cross-functional challenges in running the business.

Leadership

When Molson's decided to pursue the HIW business, they decided that they needed a CEO who was knowledgeable about warehouse retailing, was an entrepreneur, a self-starter and one who could "make it happen." They hired Bebis as their first employee. Bebis described his view of the business as follows:

> I always wanted to open and operate my own business as an entrepreneur but never had the money. The opportunity to come to Canada and to open the first full size warehouse store in the industry and to run the show from scratch using someone else's money was a dream come true. The

reasons I chose Canada were that it was virgin territory for our concept; we would blaze new trails and this was very exciting. I was with Home Depot for six years. I was a small fish in a big pond. By coming to Canada, I was able to become the number one guy and to create a new company from the ground up. This opportunity only comes around once in a lifetime and I wanted to take advantage of it.

When Bebis joined Aikenhead's, Molson's had bought into the concept and had agreed to one store. At that time the name had not even been selected. Bebis described his introduction to the business:

> The one thing I remember fondly is showing up for work the first day and not having a phone or a pencil and certainly not an office. It truly was a greenfield start. I worked out of a hotel room and had to rent office space for myself and buy office furniture. Bob Wittman and I also designed the first store.

Bebis described his leadership role in implementing the concept:

> It was a matter of setting high goals, demanding excellence in the execution of achieving those goals and never wavering from our focus. I have an unwavering commitment to customer service. I am focused and never let up. I believe that constant hammering, constant retraining, constant reinforcement of our mission and why we are here are critical to our success. Being able to go through brick walls to make things happen is definitely one of my strong points.

Bebis knew that to execute the concept, leadership would be required at every level of the organization. Teeth were put into the concept of "empowerment" through the design of the systems and the structure of the organization. The flat organizational structure meant that associates would be required to make key decisions. Training provided them with the knowledge to make the decisions, and the tools were put in place to aid in the process. For example, information systems and in-store terminals enabled them to advise customers on the status of products. Furthermore, each of the 200 store associates would be authorized to contact suppliers as needed, in an industry in which supplier contact had previously only been made at the most senior levels of the organization.

Résumés were already pouring in for the first store. While many people questioned opening the store during a recession, Bebis suggested that it was an ideal time to establish a new business. Deals could be made on real estate, suppliers were hungry for business, and Bebis had his pick of some of the best people in the industry. With construction at a standstill, there were hundreds of professional plumbers, electricians and carpenters who would jump at the chance to supplement their sporadic business with the opportunity for steady work. As Bebis submitted the business plan to Molson's, the question in his mind was not whether the Aikenhead's concept would work, but how big and how fast he should grow the business.

Exhibit 1: **Special Customer Services**

- Computerized Kitchen Design
- Computerized Deck Design
- Product Fairs
- Department Demos
- Multiple Credit Plans
- Lock Keying/Duplicate Keys
- Glass Cutting
- Lumber Cutting—Mini Blinds Cutting
- Delivery
- Special Orders—Kitchen, Bath, Millwork
- Free Project Advice
- Computerized Colour Matching/Mixing
- Short/No Wait Checkouts
- Cash Only Lines
- Scanning
- Free Use of How To Videos
- Use of Car Carrier Racks
- Free Use of Insulation Blower With Purchase
- Sprinkling System Design
- Assistance in Loading Cars
- Equipment Rentals, i.e., Post Hole Digger; Insulation Blower; File Cutter

Exhibit 2: **Competitors**

Beaver Lumber

Beaver Lumber was owned by The Molson Companies Limited, Aikenhead's parent. With 158 locations across Canada, Beaver Lumber was a retailer of building and lumber supplies. As well, it carried a full range of home improvement merchandise. The company served two distinct sets of customers: individuals and, in rural areas, contractors. It was billed as "Canada's largest do-it-yourself retailer." The chain had sales of $1,074 million in 1991, down from $1,129 million in 1990. Operating profit was $29.1 million in 1991, down from $44.8 million in 1990.

Beaver Lumber had a mixture of corporate-owned and franchised stores. Stores were free to purchase products either from a Beaver Lumber distribution centre or from other distributors. The corporation earned its return partly on the sale of goods through the distribution centre, but mainly from the 50–50 split of net income from the franchised stores. The typical Beaver Lumber store was 30,000 square feet in size, with approximately 50 employees. Over 50% of the stores were in secondary urban or rural markets.

Traditionally, the urban stores had performed poorly. They had higher prices and limited product breadth and depth compared to their competitors. Stores in the smaller centres, however, profited from extensive high-margin business with building contractors. Beaver Lumber differentiated itself from its competitors by offering credit to contractors. For this reason, the stores typically had unusually high levels of accounts receivable. Indeed, it was the infrastructure required to support these financing activities which contributed to Beaver Lumber's higher costs and prices.

Beaver Lumber introduced a number of strategic and operating initiatives in 1991. It began to move toward a more centralized organizational structure, in order to exercise greater control over inventories. The company announced plans to increase the number of products carried by its stores by up to 5,000 stocking units. It introduced six different standardized store layouts, and doubled the number of hours of training for store managers. The information system at Beaver Lumber had been in place for approximately 15 years.

Canadian Tire

Canada's largest hardgoods retailer, Canadian Tire had sales of $3.0 billion in 1991, down from approximately $3.1 billion the year before. Net earnings were $127 million, a 12% drop from 1990 levels. Sales of hardware represented 25% of Canadian Tire's revenues, while sales of automotive and sporting goods comprised the remaining 75%.

Canadian Tire had two operating divisions: the Merchandise Business Group, representing 80% of revenues, which supplied goods and services to the company's Associate stores, and the Diversified Business Group comprised mainly of the Petroleum Division and Canadian Tire Acceptance, the financial services division.

The company employed approximately 3,800 full-time and 1,500 part-time workers across the country, in addition to those hired by the firm's Associate Dealers. The Associate Dealer stores were not franchises. Instead, they functioned much like auto dealerships, with five-year contracts to purchase their products from Canadian Tire's Merchandise Business Group. The corporation wielded significant power in its relationship with the Associated Dealers. Margins had traditionally been evenly split between the Corporation and the Dealer, but in the mid-1980s Canadian Tire forced up its share by several percentage points. Canadian Tire earned its return from selling goods and services to its Associated Dealers, and required that Dealers purchase all but the most specialized products from the Corporation.

Canadian Tire had identified the trend toward an increasingly competitive marketplace. It saw its challenge as balancing short-term seasonality and business cycle fluctuations with longer-term changes in buying behaviour, demographics and technology. The company described their customers as demanding low-cost distribution of commodity products, as well as better quality, service and selection.

Canadian Tire considered its competitive advantages to be its entrepreneurial Associate Dealers, convenience of location (77% of the Canadian population lives within a 15-minute drive of a Canadian Tire store), and consumer awareness. Its interrelated business units allowed synergies in cross-merchandising, marketing and information management. Traditionally, information systems played a crucial role in the company's development and competitive positioning. It invested heavily in information technology, resulting in inventory control and management systems at both corporate and store levels which were far superior to those of competitors. Investment in IS was ongoing, with individual stores upgrading their systems every couple of years.

Canadian Tire stores varied widely in size, from 2,500 to 40,000 square feet. Approximately 25,000 products or product sizes were sold.

In summary, the distribution channels at both Beaver Lumber and Canadian Tire were as follows:

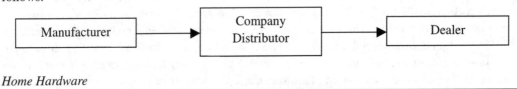

Home Hardware

Home Hardware, with 985 outlets, was Canada's largest dealer-owned chain. Approximately 80 of these stores were located in the Metro Toronto area. The dealers were independents who had organized themselves into a buying group. In 1990, Home Hardware generated $850 million in sales.

Home Hardware considered its competitive advantage to be convenient location. It believed that, while customers might be willing to drive across town for a lower price on big-ticket items, they would choose the closest store for smaller purchases.

Because Home Hardware dealers did not have the backing of a large corporation, they sometimes had difficulty securing bank financing. As a result, the stores tended to be understocked compared to their competitors. The outlets varied greatly in size, but tended to be smaller overall than their competitors.

Exhibit 3: **Suppliers**

Suppliers of products to the Canadian home improvement industry operated within similar distribution channels. Manufacturers sold to distributors, who in turn serviced retail outlets. Distributors were responsible for meeting the demands of the retailer which included on-time delivery, in-store merchandising and servicing, and "hands on" product knowledge and training. They were also responsible for dealing with special shipping instructions, EDI requirements, UPC packaging requirements and the handling of any problems with product quality.

Suppliers did, however, differ from each other along at least three dimensions. The first dimension was the degree of perceived elasticity of demand for their products. For example, Manco, a major manufacturer of a fairly standard product for the home improvement industry, believed that the overall demand for their products was relatively inelastic; a lower price would not result in an increase in demand. In general, it was felt that demand was reasonably fixed and a change in distribution would not impact purchase decisions to a great extent. On the other hand, Hardco, a major manufacturer of tools for the home improvement industry, believed that the overall demand for its product was affected by the efforts on the part of retailers to market their product in ways that expanded the home improvement industry's share of customer's discretionary dollars.

The second way that suppliers differed was the degree to which they dominated distribution channels and shelf space. For example, given Manco's market dominance, it was extremely difficult for new competitors to enter the business. Customers did not demand a wide selection in the product category and therefore retailers were not willing to give a lot of shelf space to the product. Similarly, distributors carried only a few products, and therefore Manco dominated the channel.

Finally, suppliers differed in terms of their geographic market focus and the degree of integration of their operations. For example, Manco Canada was part of Manco Worldwide, which was amongst the largest manufacturers of the product line in the world. However, there was little integration between the Canadian company and its parent. This meant that the Canadian operation had not closely observed other parts of the organization, which were responding to dramatic industry change. At Hardco, however, international operations were well integrated. The Canadian operation had watched its U.S. counterpart deal with radical changes in the U.S. industry, and had been waiting for the same pressures to be exerted on the Canadian market.

Exhibit 4: **A. Organizational Chart 1991**

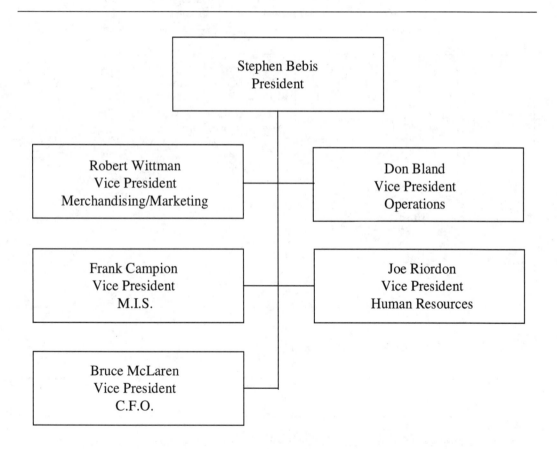

Exhibit 4: **B. Store Operations Model**

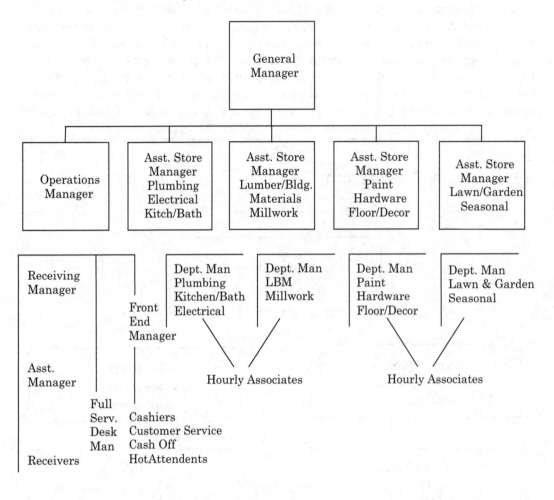

Exhibit 5: **The Management Team**

Stephen Bebis (President)

Steve is a superbly qualified retailing executive. His 20 years of experience have given him a clear understanding of the synergies required to keep all components of an enterprise functioning optimally for the achievement of superior results. His increasingly significant marketing and merchandising responsibilities with Sears Roebuck & Co., Grossman's and, most recently, Home Depot have provided him with the cross-category knowledge necessary to guarantee merchandising success and customer acceptance.

Robert J. Wittman (Vice-President, Merchandising and Marketing)

Bob has a wide range of business experience acquired through 25 years in retailing. He has served in various merchandising capacities with such organizations as Supermarkets General, Loblaws (Canada), Grossman's, Bradlees Department Stores, Somerville Lumber and Home Quarters Warehouse Inc. Bob is an intuitive marketer with a thorough understanding of the categories, assortments and presentations essential to the success of a warehouse home improvement store.

Donald C. Bland (Vice-President, Operations)

Don is a seasoned specialist with 25 years of experience. His progressively increased responsibilities in both merchandising and operations with such companies as Target Stores, Montgomery Ward, The J.L. Hudson Division of Dayton Hudson Corporation, Lechemere Inc. and Home Quarters Warehouse Inc. have provided him with top-flight retail executive credentials. His strategic as well as operational management competence will contribute a great deal to the success of this enterprise.

Frank D. Campion (Vice-President, Information Systems)

Frank is an Information Systems specialist whose experience in the United States Navy, Haines Furniture, Camellia Food Stores and Home Quarters Warehouse Inc. have given him the superb qualifications needed to provide this organization with state-of-the-art systems support. Frank understands the systems needs and the solutions essential to enhancing warehouse store operations through systems that optimize both customer and management information services.

Joseph P. Riordon (Vice-President, Human Resources)

Joe is the epitome of the consummate retailing Human Resources executive. His experience with the Allstate Insurance Company, Royal Trust, Boots Drugstores (Canada) Ltd. and F.W. Woolworth Company Ltd. have provided him with a broad operational and human resource base. He has a thorough understanding of all the component aspects of people management and will be a highly effective link in the cross-functional optimization of people in our company.

Bruce W. McLaren (Vice-President, Finance)

Bruce McLaren is a highly competent financial executive who has, during his career, designed and implemented virtually every type of financial system and/or process relating to the retail sector. His progressive experience with Thorne Riddell, Sears Canada and Kmart has provided Bruce with a profound understanding of the retail environment, and the role of the finance function in it, which will allow him to be a strong contributor to the organization's success.

Source: Aikenhead's Business Plan.

COLA WARS CONTINUE: COKE VS. PEPSI IN THE 1990s

Sharon Foley and
David Yoffie

For decades, competition between Coke and Pepsi has been described as a "carefully waged competitive struggle." The most intense battles in the cola wars were fought over the $48 billion industry in the United States, where the average American drank over 48 gallons per year. However, industry analysts contended that the U.S. soft drink industry had plateaued, and that total consumption was unlikely to increase significantly in the near future. As a consequence, the cola wars were moving to international markets. "Coca-Cola used to be an American company with a large international business. Now we are a large international company with a sizable American business," explained Coke's CEO Roberto Goizueta.[1] Coke, the world's largest soft drink company

---

[1]John Huey, "The World's Best Brand," *Fortune*, May 31, 1993.

This case was prepared by Research Associate Sharon Foley under the direction of Professor David B. Yoffie as the basis for class discussion rather than to illustrate either effective or ineffective handling of an administrative situation. Reprinted by permission of Harvard Business School.

with a 45% share of the worldwide soft drink market, earned 80% of its profits outside of the United States in 1993. Pepsi, with only 15% of its beverage operating profits coming from overseas, was using "guerilla warfare" to attack Coke in selected international markets, noting that "as big as Coca-Cola is, you certainly don't want a shootout at high noon," said Wayne Calloway, CEO of PepsiCo.[2] Roger Enrico, former CEO of Pepsi-Cola, described it this way:

> The warfare must be perceived as a continuing battle without blood. Without Coke, Pepsi would have a tough time being an original and lively competitor. The more successful they are, the sharper we have to be. If the Coca-Cola company didn't exist, we'd pray for someone to invent them. And on the other side of the fence, I'm sure the folks at Coke would say that nothing contributes as much to the present-day success of the Coca-Cola company than . . . Pepsi.[3]

As the cola wars continued into the 1990s, Coke and Pepsi had to struggle with age-old questions: could they maintain their phenomenal growth at home and abroad? What will happen to their margins with on-going warfare? And would the changing economics of their industry keep the average industry profits at historic levels?

ECONOMICS OF THE U.S. INDUSTRY

Americans consumed 23 gallons of soft drinks a year in 1970 compared to 48 gallons in 1993 (see Exhibit 1). This growth was fueled by the increasing availability and affordability of soft drinks in the marketplace, as well as the introduction and growth of diet soft drinks. There were many alternatives to soft drinks: coffee, beer, milk, tea, bottled water, juices, powdered drinks, wine, distilled spirits, and tap water. Yet Americans drank more soft drinks than any other beverage, with the soft drink and bottled water categories being the only ones to increase each year. Since the early 1980s, however, real prices of soft drinks fell. Using 1978 as a base year, the Consumer Price Index (CPI) grew at an average rate of 5.9%, compared with soft drink price growth of 3.8%. Consumer demand appeared to be sensitive to price increases. The cola segment of the soft drink industry held the dominant (68%) share of the market in 1992, followed by lemon/lime with 12%, pepper flavor 7%, orange 3%, root beer 2%, and other 8%.

Concentrate Producers

Soft drinks consisted of a flavor base, a sweetener, and carbonated water. Three major participants in the value chain produced and distributed soft drinks: 1) concentrate and syrup producers; 2) bottlers; and 3) distributors. Packaging and sweetener firms were the major suppliers to the industry.

The concentrate producer (CP) blended the necessary raw material ingredients (excluding sugar or high fructose corn syrup), packaged it in plastic canisters, and shipped the blended ingredients to the bottler. The CP added artificial sweetener (aspartame) for making concentrate for diet soft drinks, while bottlers added sugar or high fructose corn syrup themselves.[4] The process

---

[2]The Wall Street Journal, June 13, 1991.

[3]Roger Enrico, The Other Guy Blinked and Other Dispatches From the Cola Wars (New York: Bantam Books, 1988).

[4]Coke was the exception to this general rule. Coke added sugar prior to shipping the syrup to its bottlers.

involved little capital investment in machinery, overhead or labor. A typical concentrate manufacturing plant cost approximately $5–$10 million to build in 1993, and one plant could serve the entire United States. A CP's most significant costs were for advertising, promotion, market research, and bottler relations. Marketing programs were jointly implemented and financed by CPs and bottlers. The CPs usually took the lead in developing the programs, particularly in product planning, market research, and advertising. Bottlers assumed a larger role in developing trade and consumer promotions, and paid an agreed percentage of promotional and advertising costs. CPs employed extensive sales and marketing support staff to work with and help improve the performance of their franchised bottlers. They set standards for their bottlers and suggested operating procedures. CPs also negotiated directly with the bottlers' major suppliers—particularly sweetener and packaging suppliers—to encourage reliable supply, faster delivery, and lower prices. Coca-Cola and Pepsi-Cola were CPs and bottlers, while Dr Pepper/Seven-Up, Cadbury Schweppes, and RC Cola were involved only in concentrate production in the U.S. (see Exhibit 2 for financial data on the leading soft drink competitors). Throughout most of the 1980s and 1990s, the price of concentrate sold to bottlers increased annually.

Bottlers

Bottlers purchased concentrate, added carbonated water and high fructose corn syrup, bottled or canned the soft drink, and delivered it to customer accounts. Coke and Pepsi bottlers offered "direct store door" delivery (DSD) which involved route delivery sales people physically placing and managing the soft drink brand in the store. Smaller national brands, such as Shasta and Faygo, distributed through food store warehouses. DSD included managing the shelf space by stacking the product, positioning the trademarked label, cleaning the packages and shelves, setting up point-of-purchase displays and end-of-aisle displays. The importance of the bottler's relationship with the retail trade was crucial to continual brand availability and maintenance. Cooperative merchandising agreements (CMAs) between retailers and bottlers were used to promote soft drink sales. Promotional activity and discount levels were agreed in the CMA with the retailer in exchange for a payment from the bottler.

The bottling process was capital-intensive and involved specialized, high-speed lines. Lines were interchangeable only for packages of similar size and construction. Bottling and canning lines cost from $4-$10 million for one line, depending on volume and package type. The minimum cost to build a small bottling plant, with warehouse and office space, was $20-$30 million. The cost of an efficient large plant, with about five lines and a 15 million case volume, was $30-$50 million. Roughly 80-85 plants were required for full national distribution within the United States. Packaging accounted for approximately 48% of bottlers' cost of goods sold, concentrate for 35%, and nutritive sweeteners for 12%. Labor accounted for most of the remaining variable costs. Bottlers also invested capital in trucks and distribution networks. Bottlers' gross profits often exceeded 40%, but operating margins were razor thin. See Exhibit 3 for the cost structures of a typical CP and bottler as of 1993.

Historically, CPs used franchised bottling networks. The typical bottler owned a manufacturing and sales operation in a small exclusive territory, with rights granted in perpetuity by the franchiser. In the case of Coca-Cola, the territorial rights did not extend to fountain accounts—Coke delivered to its fountain accounts directly, not through its bottlers. The rights granted to the bottlers were subject to termination by the CP only in the event of default by the bottler. The contracts did not contain provisions specifying the required performance of the bottlers or the CP.

In the original Coca-Cola bottling contracts, the price of concentrate was fixed in perpetuity, subject to quarterly adjustments to reflect changes in the quoted price of sugar. There was no requirement for renegotiation due to changes in the cost of concentrate ingredients. Coke eventually amended the contract in 1978, which allowed it to raise the price of concentrate according to the CPI, and in the case of syrup, to adjust the price quarterly based upon changes in the average price per pound of sugar in the United States. In return, Coke was required to adjust pricing to reflect any cost savings realized as a result of a modification of ingredients, and allow bottlers to purchase unsweetened concentrate in order to buy sweetener on the open market. In late 1986, Coca-Cola proposed that its 1978 franchise agreement be replaced with the Master Bottler Contract, which provided additional pricing flexibility. By 1993, over 70% of Coke's U.S. volume was covered by the Master Bottler Contract. Pepsi negotiated concentrate prices with its bottling association, and normally based price increases on the CPI.

Coke and Pepsi's franchise agreements allowed bottlers to handle the non-cola brands of other CPs. Franchise agreements also allowed bottlers to choose whether or not to market new beverages introduced by the CP. Some restrictions applied, however, as bottlers were not allowed to carry directly competitive brands. For example, a Coca-Cola bottler could not sell RC Cola, but it could distribute Seven-Up, if it did not carry Sprite. Bottlers had the freedom to participate in or reject new package introductions, local advertising campaigns and promotions, and test marketing. The bottler had the final say in decisions concerning pricing, new packaging, selling, advertising and promotions in its territory. Bottlers, however, could only use packages authorized by the franchiser. In 1971, the Federal Trade Commission initiated action against eight major CPs, charging that exclusive territories granted to franchised bottlers prevented intrabrand competition (two or more bottlers competing in the same area with the same beverage). The CPs argued that interbrand competition was sufficiently strong to warrant continuation of the existing territorial agreements. After nine years of litigation, Congress enacted the "Soft Drink Interbrand Competition Act" in 1980, preserving the right of CPs to grant exclusive territories.

Distributors

In the mid-1980s, U.S. distribution of soft drinks was through food stores (42%), fountain (20%), vending (12%), and other outlets (26%). By 1994, distribution of soft drinks shifted slightly: food stores (40%), fountain (17%), vending (8%), convenience stores and gas marts (14%), and other (21%). Mass merchandisers, warehouse clubs and drug stores made up about 12% of the other outlets. Profits for the bottlers varied by retail outlet (see Exhibit 4). Profits were driven by delivery method and frequency, drop size, advertising and marketing. In 1993, the Pepsi-Cola brand and the Coca-Cola Classic brand each had a 16% share of all retail channel volume.

The main distribution channel for soft drinks was supermarkets. Soft drinks were among the five largest selling product lines sold by supermarkets, traditionally yielding a 15%-20% gross margin (about average for food products) and accounting for 4% of food store revenues in 1993. Soft drinks represented a large percentage of a supermarket's business, and was a big traffic draw. Bottlers fought for retail shelf space to ensure visibility and accessibility for its products, and looked for new locations to increase impulse purchases, such as placing coolers at checkout counters. Supermarkets' share of soft drink sales fell slightly due to consolidation in this sector, the rise of new retail formats, shelf space pressures due to increasing numbers of products, the introduction of supermarket private label soft drinks, and widespread discounting.

Discount retailers, warehouse clubs, and drug stores sold about 12% of soft drinks. Discount retailers and warehouse clubs often had their own private label soft drink, or they sold a private label such as President's Choice. Private label soft drinks were usually delivered to a retailer's warehouse, while branded soft drinks were delivered directly to the store. According to soft drink companies, retailers made a higher margin on DSD delivered soft drinks than on either private label, which was delivered to store warehouses, or warehouse-delivered branded soft drinks (see Exhibit 5). Doug Ivester, Coca-Cola COO for North America, had this to say, "Coke delivers and stocks its soda, while Cott drops its pop at retailers' warehouses. The trouble is, most retailers have never had a good understanding of what their costs really are."[5] Soft drink companies made attempts to educate the trade about this difference in margins, although the issue was controversial. With the warehouse delivery method, the retailer was responsible for storage, transportation, merchandising and labor to get the product on the shelves. In effect, the retailer paid for additional labor, occupancy, inventory, and carrying costs. The extra costs reduced the private label net profit margin to the retailer versus the national brands.

Historically, Pepsi focused on sales through retail outlets, while Coke had always been dominant in fountain sales. Coca-Cola had a 59% share of the fountain market in 1993, while Pepsi had 27%. Competition for fountain was intense, and was characterized by "significant everyday discounting to national and local customers."[6] National fountain accounts were essentially "paid sampling," with soft drink companies breaking even at best. For local fountain accounts, soft drink companies earned operating profit margins before tax of around 2%. Soft drink companies used fountain to increase the availability of its brands. For restaurants, fountain was extremely profitable—soft drinks were one of their highest margin products. Coke and Pepsi invested in the development of fountain equipment, such as service dispensers, and provided their fountain customers with cups, point-of-sale material, advertising, and in-store promotions in order to increase trademark presence. After PepsiCo entered the restaurant business with the acquisitions of Pizza Hut, Taco Bell, and Kentucky Fried Chicken, Coca-Cola persuaded food chains such as Wendy's and Burger King to carry Coke, by positioning these chains as competitors to PepsiCo's three restaurants.

Coca-Cola and Pepsi were the largest suppliers of soft drinks to the vending channel. Bottlers purchased and installed vending machines, and CPs offered rebates to encourage them. The owners of the property on which vending equipment was located usually received a sales commission. Vending machine sales of soft drinks competed with the sale of competing beverages in vending machines, such as juice, tea, and lemonade.

Suppliers

CPs and bottlers purchased two major inputs: packaging, which included $3.4 billion in cans (29% of total can consumption), $1.3 billion in plastic bottles, and $0.6 billion in glass; and sweeteners, which included $1.1 billion in sugar and high fructose corn syrup, and $1.0 billion in aspartame. In 1993, the majority of soft drinks were packaged in metal cans (55%), then plastic bottles (40%), and glass (5%). Cans were an attractive packaging material due to a variety of factors: vendibility, multi-packing capability, lightweight, unbreakability, recyclability, and the ability to be heated or cooled quickly. Aluminum cans were the least expensive package per unit for soft drinks, due in

---

[5]Patricia Sellers, "Brands—It's Thrive or Die," *Fortune*, August 23, 1993.
[6]*Beverage World*, 1989.

part to the fact that Russia was dumping aluminum on the world market, cutting aluminum prices in half in 1993. Plastic bottles, introduced in 1978, boosted home consumption of soft drinks due to its larger 1-liter, 2-liter, and 3-liter sizes.

CPs' strategy towards can manufacturers was typical of their supplier relationships. Coke and Pepsi negotiated on behalf of their bottling networks, and were among the metal can industry's largest customers. Since the can constituted about 40% of the total cost of a packaged beverage, bottlers and CPs often maintained relationships with more than one supplier. In the 1960s and 1970s, Coke and Pepsi backward integrated to make some of their own cans, but largely exited the business by 1990. In 1994, Coke and Pepsi sought to establish long-term relationships with their suppliers to secure supply. The major producers of metal cans included American National Can, Crown Cork & Seal, and Reynolds Metals. Metal cans were viewed as commodities, and there was chronic excess supply in the industry. Often two or three can manufacturers competed for a single contract, which resulted in low margins.

With the advent of diet soft drinks, Coke and Pepsi negotiated with artificial sweetener companies, most notably the Nutrasweet Company, and sold its concentrate to bottlers already sweetened. A second source of aspartame was the Holland Sweetener Company which was based in the Netherlands. Nutrasweet's U.S. patent for aspartame expired in December 1992, which subsequently led to a weakening of Nutrasweet's supplier power. As the cost of aspartame dropped, Coca-Cola amended its franchise bottler contract to pass along two-thirds of any savings or increase to its bottlers. In practice, Pepsi did the same thing so as to not disadvantage its bottlers in the marketplace compared to Coke's, although it was not specified in its bottler contract. This was one of many examples in the cola wars where the competitors tracked and imitated each other.

HISTORY OF THE COLA WARS

The structure and character of the U.S. soft drink industry was molded by the 100-year competitive battle between Coke and Pepsi. Once a fragmented business with hundreds of local vendors, the soft drink industry in 1994 was highly concentrated. Coke and Pepsi had a combined 73% of the U.S. soft drink market. The top six companies, Coca-Cola, Pepsi, Dr Pepper/Seven Up, Cadbury Schweppes, Royal Crown, and A&W Brands, had a combined 89% share of the market. The remaining 11% represented regional soft drink companies and private label brand manufacturers (see Exhibit 6).

The cola wars were fought on many fronts, such as advertising, packaging, and new products. Brand recognition was a competitive advantage that differentiated the soft drinks among consumers. Coke and Pepsi invested heavily in their trademark over time, with the marketing campaigns of Coke and Pepsi recognized as among the most innovative, sophisticated and aggressive of all major advertisers (see Exhibit 7 for soft drink advertising expenditure). Coke and Pepsi sold only their flagship brand, until Coke introduced Sprite in 1961 and Tab in 1963. The next move was Pepsi's, with the introduction of Diet Pepsi and Mountain Dew in 1964. There was no looking back, and between the years 1961-1993, Coke introduced 21 new brands, and Pepsi introduced 24 new brands.

EMERGENCE OF THE DUOPOLY

Coca-Cola and Pepsi-Cola were both invented in the late 1800s as a fountain drink. They each expanded through franchised bottlers—Coke with its uniquely contoured 6-ounce "skirt" bottle and Pepsi with a 12-ounce bottle; both sold for a nickel. Robert Woodruff, one of the most dominant figures in Coca-Cola's history, worked with the company's franchised bottlers to make Coke available wherever and whenever a consumer might want it. He pushed the bottlers to place the beverage "in arm's reach of desire," and argued that if Coke were not conveniently available when the consumer was thirsty, the sale would be lost forever. Woodruff developed Coke's international business, principally through export. One of his most memorable decisions, made at the request of General Eisenhower at the beginning of World War II, was to see "that every man in uniform gets a bottle of Coca-Cola for 5 cents wherever he is and whatever it costs." The company was exempted from wartime sugar rationing beginning in 1942, when the product was sold to the military or retailers serving soldiers. Coca-Cola bottling plants followed the movements of American troops, with 64 bottling plants established during the war—largely at government expense. This led to Coke's dominant market share in most European and Asian countries, a lead which the company still had in 1994.

In contrast to Coke's success prior to WWII, Pepsi struggled, nearing the brink of bankruptcy several times in the 1920s and 1930s. By 1950, Coke's share of the soft drink market was 47% and Pepsi's was 10%. Over the next 20 years, the Coca-Cola company never referred to its closest competitor by name. Coke's management also referred to its famous brand name as "Mother Coke," which was sacred and never extended to other products. "Merchandise 7X", the formula for Coca-Cola syrup, was closely guarded. "Merchandise 7X has long been one of the best-kept secrets in the world. Coke was so protective of it that, when India demanded that they disclose the formula to its government, Coke closed its business in that hot and thirsty country of 850 million souls."[7]

Beginning in the 1950s, Coca-Cola began using advertising that finally recognized the existence of competitors, as evidenced by slogans such as "American's Preferred Taste" (1955), "Be Really Refreshed" (1958), and "No Wonder Coke Refreshes Best" (1960). In the 1960s, Coke along with Pepsi began to experiment with new cola and non-cola flavors, packaging options, and advertising campaigns. They pursued market segmentation strategies, leading to new product introductions such as Pepsi's Teem and Mountain Dew and Coke's Fanta, Sprite, and Tab. New packages included non-returnable glass bottles and 12-ounce cans. Coke and Pepsi both looked outside the soft drink industry for growth in the 1960s: Coke purchased Minute Maid, Duncan Foods, and Belmont Springs Water; Pepsi merged with Frito-Lay to become PepsiCo, claiming synergies based on shared customer targets, store-door delivery systems, and marketing orientations (see Appendix A on the corporate histories of Coke and Pepsi).

Through most of this period, Coke did not aggressively attack Pepsi head-on. Coke maintained a highly fragmented bottler network, with 800 bottlers, that focused on U.S. cities of 50,000 or less. In fact, much of Coke's efforts during this period was on overseas markets, where it generated almost two-thirds of its volume by the mid-1970s. In the meantime, Pepsi aggressively fought for share in the United States, doubling its share between 1950 and 1970. Pepsi's franchise bottling network was generally larger, more flexible, and often offered lower prices to national chain stores. Slowly but surely, Pepsi crept up on Coke, mainly by focusing its attention on take-home sales through supermarkets. In fact, Pepsi's growth largely tracked the growth of supermarkets and convenience stores. There were about 10,000 supermarkets in the United States in 1945, 15,000 in

---

[7]Roger Enrico, The Other Guy Blinked and Other Dispatches From the Cola Wars, 1987.

1955, and 32,000 at the height of their growth in 1962. There were about 24,000 convenience stores in 1970.

Pepsi's 1963 "Pepsi Generation" campaign communicated to the young, emphasized consumer life style, and gave Pepsi an image that could not be confused with Coke's nostalgic, small-town America image. Pepsi's ad agency created an intense and visual commercial using sports cars, motorcycles, helicopters, non-actors, a catchy jingle, and the phrase, "Come Alive—You're in the Pepsi Generation." The campaign was so successful that Pepsi narrowed Coke's lead to a 2-to-1 margin. But the most aggressive move by Pepsi was about to come.

THE PEPSI CHALLENGE

The "Pepsi Challenge" in 1974 was considered Coke and Pepsi's first head-on collision in public. When the Pepsi Challenge was invented in Dallas, Texas, Coke was the dominant brand in the city. Pepsi ran a distant third behind Dr Pepper, which had its headquarters in Dallas. In blind taste tests, run by Pepsi's small local bottler, the company demonstrated that consumers preferred Pepsi to Coke. After Pepsi sales shot up, the company started to roll out the campaign nationwide. Coke countered with rebates, rival claims, price cuts, and a series of advertisements questioning the tests' validity. Coke's price discounting response was mostly in markets where the Coke bottler was company owned and the Pepsi bottler was an independent franchisee. But the Pepsi Challenge fueled the erosion of Coke's market share; in 1979 Pepsi passed Coke in food store sales for the first time with a 1.4 share point lead. Advertising expenditure increased significantly from 1975-1980, when Coca-Cola's advertising doubled from $34 million to over $70 million, with Pepsi's advertising rising from $25 million to $67 million.

Coke's attention was diverted at this crucial time towards the negotiation of the new bottling franchise contract in 1978. In May of that year, Don Keough took what derisive bottlers called his "dog and pony show" to six meetings around the country to persuade hesitant bottlers to sign.[8] Approval came only after the company agreed to supply Coca-Cola concentrate to bottlers without sweetener. This brought Coke's policies in line with Pepsi, which sold its concentrate unsweetened to its bottlers. Pepsi countered with a price increase to its bottlers of 15%, announced shortly after Coke's increase.

The FTC inquiry over exclusive franchise territories occurred during this period (1971-1980), and Coca-Cola officials admitted that they took their eye off the ball while Pepsi kept its cola business sharply in focus. Don Keough said of this period, "Our system was immobilized. Looking back, I should have hired a room full of lawyers and told them to deal with it, and we could have gotten on with the business."[9] Coke was so rattled that Brian Dyson, president of Coca-Cola, broke precedent and uttered the name Pepsi in front of most of Coke's bottlers at a 1979 bottlers conference, by saying, "Coca-Cola's corporate share has grown a mere three-tenths of one percent in ten years. In the same period, Pepsi's corporate share has grown from 21.4% to 24.2%"[10]

---

[8]Mark Pendergrast, For God, Country and Coca-Cola, 1993.
[9]Thomas Oliver, The Real Coke, The Real Story (New York: Random House, 1986).
[10]Mark Pendergrast, For God, Country and Coca-Cola, (New York: Macmillan Publishing Company, 1993).

COLA WARS HEAT UP

In 1980 Coca-Cola experienced a change in management when Roberto Goizueta became CEO and Don Keough president. Goizueta described the corporate culture when he took over: "Unprofessional would be an understatement. We were there to carry the bottlers' suitcases. We used to be either cheerleaders or critics of bottlers. Now we are players."[11] Under Goizueta, Coke began buying up its bottlers in earnest. Coke was first to drop sugar and adopt the lower-priced high fructose corn syrup, a move which Pepsi eventually imitated in 1983. Pepsi's president Roger Enrico had this to say, "Coke's fructose decision was probably the first that Roberto Goizueta and Don Keough—the management team that was about to take charge of the Coca-Cola company—made using their ready-fire-aim philosophy. Given that new philosophy, they probably didn't do much testing. More likely they just looked at the cost savings, bet that it wouldn't hurt sales, and blasted away."[12] Goizueta sold off most non-soft drink businesses that he inherited, including wine, coffee, tea and industrial water treatment. Coca-Cola intensified its marketing effort, with advertising expenditure rising from $74 million in 1981 to $181 million in 1984. Pepsi also stepped up advertising from $66 million to $125 million over the same period. Coca-Cola continued to pursue its expansion overseas with growing investments.

For the first time ever, the Coca-Cola company used the "Coke" brand as a line extension when it introduced diet Coke in 1982. Opposed by company lawyers as a risk to the copyright, this was a major departure in strategy. But, diet Coke was a phenomenal success—probably the most successful consumer product launch of the Eighties. By the end of 1983, it was the nation's most popular diet cola, and in 1984, it became the third-largest seller among all domestic soft drinks. In addition to diet Coke, new soft drink brands proliferated, with Coke introducing 11 new products including Cherry Coke, Caffeine Free Coke, and Minute-Maid Orange. Pepsi introduced 13 products including Caffeine Free Pepsi-Cola, Lemon Lime Slice, and Cherry Pepsi. The battle for shelf space in supermarkets and other food stores became fierce. One of Pepsi's most visible responses to Coke was an advertising blitz, featuring rock star Michael Jackson.

As new brands exploded, price discounting also emerged which eroded margins for all carbonated soft drink manufacturers. Industrywide, there was a sharp increase in the level of discounting in the struggle for market share. Consumers were constantly exposed to cents-off promotions, and a host of other discounts. Consumers, who formerly bought only one soft drink brand, bought whatever was on sale, switching brands each time they made a purchase.

The most dramatic shot in the cola wars came in 1985 when Coke changed the formula of Coca-Cola. Explaining this break from tradition, Goizueta saw the "value of the Coca-Cola trademark going downhill" as the "product and the brand had a declining share in a shrinking segment of the market."[13] Coca-Cola was not prepared for the intensely negative reaction from its core group of loyal customers, most of whom consumed huge amounts of Coca-Cola each day. As a result of this reaction, the company brought back the original formula three months later under the name Coca-Cola Classic, while keeping the new formula as the flagship brand under the name New Coke. With consumers still unhappy, Coke announced six months later that Coca-Cola Classic (the original formula) would be considered its flagship brand. Reflecting on the introduction of new Coke, some insiders said that the reformulation would have been dropped if Coke had not been

---

[11]John Huey, "The World's Best Brand," *Fortune*, May 31, 1993.

[12]Roger Enrico, *The Other Guy Blinked and Other Dispatches From the Cola Wars*, 1987.

[13]*Wall Street Journal*, April 24, 1986.

intent on finding new ways to attack Pepsi. Similarly, Pepsi's early introduction of a 3-liter bottle in 1984 was continued despite lukewarm reception by consumers. A Pepsi marketer explained, "Even if it wasn't working, we had to stay out front on this . . . basically we wanted to jump off the cliff before Coke."[14]

In the ongoing battle for market share, Coke and Pepsi tried to buy the most prominent niche players in the United States. In January 1986, Pepsi announced its intention to acquire Seven-Up from Philip Morris. In response, Coca-Cola countered with an announcement one month later that it planned to acquire Dr Pepper. In June of that year, the Federal Trade Commission voted to oppose both acquisitions. Pepsi did, however, acquire Seven-Up's international operations.

In the 1980s, the smaller CPs were shuffled from one owner to another. In a period of five years, Dr Pepper would be sold (all and in part) a couple of times, Canada Dry twice, Sunkist once, Shasta once, and A&W Brands once. Some of the deals were made by food companies, but several were leveraged buyouts by investment firms. At the same time, many formerly independent bottlers were being absorbed and merged (see Appendix B).

REORGANIZING THE INDUSTRY

Buying-Up Bottlers

Beginning in the mid-1980s, Coke and Pepsi began a process of altering the structure of the franchise system. At the start of the 1980s, Pepsi and Coke each owned about 20-30% of their bottlers. Pepsi company-owned bottling operations in the United States made up 55.7% of Pepsi's volume in 1993, with Pepsi's equity partner volume at 70.8%; Coca-Cola had equity in four bottlers representing 70.1% of volume. Pepsi's top 10 bottlers had 81% of volume, and Coke's had 86%. Analysts gave several reasons for purchasing bottlers. At the outset, the cola wars weakened many independent bottlers, leading franchises to seek buyers. Some of the bottlers were small, producing under 10 million cases a year, and did not have the capability or the time frame to handle corporate goals in a particular market. Others were bought because they were located near a company-owned bottler, or they were underinvesting in plant and equipment.

In 1986 Pepsi-Cola made the decision to proactively acquire its bottling system. Over the next few years, Pepsi acquired MEI Bottling for $591 million, Grand Metropolitan's bottling operations for $705 million, and General Cinema's domestic bottling operations for $1.8 billion. Because PepsiCo was an asset-intensive company—the concentrate business of Pepsi-Cola was the exception—the company believed it had strong competencies in managing the capital-intensive bottling business. Coca-Cola, on the other hand, wanted a clean balance sheet. In 1985, 11% of Coca-Cola's volume was produced by company-owned bottlers. One year later, Coca-Cola bought two large bottling concerns which together with bottling plants it already owned, brought its share of Coke production to one-third. The acquisitions culminated in the creation and sale of 51% of Coca-Cola Enterprises (CCE) to the public, with Coke retaining a 49% share. By 1992, CCE was the largest Coca-Cola bottler with sales of $5 billion. CCE was moving towards "mega-facilities" or 50-million case production facilities with high levels of automation, and with large warehouse and delivery capabilities.

---

[14]*Forbes*, November 27, 1989.

Pepsi, like Coke, saw several advantages in controlling bottlers. Pepsi went from 435 bottlers down to 120 bottlers, with Pepsi owning 56% of them outright, and equity positions in most of the others. The trend towards buying bottlers was set to continue in the 1990s, though the franchise system was predicted to be around for the foreseeable future. Pepsi had no corporate owners, and tended to keep its bottling network more local, and its bottling plants smaller than Coke's. The most efficient Pepsi plant size produced a 10-15 million case volume.

The consolidation of bottlers meant that the smaller concentrate producers, with the exception of RC Cola, had to sell their products through the Pepsi or Coke bottling system. Not surprisingly, the Federal Trade Commission kept the soft drink industry high on its list of priority industries. Pepsi and Coke nonetheless continued to look at the industry as a total system rather than individual markets, and despite greater vertical integration, they continued to run their bottlers as independent businesses. Both companies raised concentrate prices through the early 1990s, and required bottlers to share marketing expenditures.

Changing Distribution Channels and Private Label

With the rapid growth of discount retailers such as Wal-Mart and K mart, and warehouse clubs such as Sam's Clubs and PriceCostco, this became an increasingly important outlet for soft drink distribution. With sales estimated to reach $87 billion in 1994, Wal-Mart was predicted to use the supercenter format (a combination supermarket and discount store) as its primary growth vehicle for the 1990s. Wal-Mart stocked both Coke and Pepsi in its discount stores, warehouse clubs, and supercenters. Although Coke and Pepsi sold their products to Wal-Mart and to supermarkets at the same price, Wal-Mart had lower operating costs and earned higher margins. As a result, supermarkets were putting pressure on soft drink companies to offer them lower prices.

Wal-Mart, along with other retailers, sold its own private label cola. With soft drink growth slowing, this presented a challenge to national brand growth. Although Americans still drank more soft drinks than any other beverage, sales volume registered only a 1.5% increase in 1992, to just under 8.2 billion cases (a case was equivalent to 24 eight-ounce containers, or 192 ounces). This slow growth was in contrast to the 5%-7% annual growth in the 1980s. According to industry analysts, store brands often sold for up to 35% less than national brands. The major supplier to private label retailers in the United States was the Cott Corporation, which bought its concentrate from RC Cola. Cott bottled or canned the cola, sold it under private labels such as President's Choice, and had arrangements with more than 40 retail chain stores, including American Stores, Safeway, A&P, and Wal-Mart. Cott produced four different formulas for cola and could tailor a product to meet individual customer demands.

Private label colas were not a new phenomenon. Their share of foodstore sales reached a peak of 12.8% in 1971, slowly declined each year in the 1970s, and hovered around 7% throughout the 1980s. In 1993, private label had 9% of volume. In the 1990s, supermarkets were developing private label colas as they questioned the profitability of national brands, and they used private label products to enhance the store identity and build patronage. Coke executives met with security analysts in May 1993 to address the issue of private label, "We, along with our major competitor, have addressed consumer needs with sugar-free, caffeine-free, and other variations. We understand how to deal with this [private label] phenomenon. We have been dealing with it effectively for years."[15] Coke executives noted that private label competed only on price, and consumers paid the

---

[15]Jesse Meyers, *Beverage Digest*, May 14, 1993.

same price for a Coke in 1993 that they paid ten years earlier.

New Age Beverages

Another challenge for carbonated soft drink companies were "new age" beverages such as bottled waters and tea-based drinks. When measured in gallons, sales of new age beverages rose by 17% in 1992, compared to 1.5% for bottled water and 1.5% for all soft drinks. While this gain came from a much smaller base (250 million gallons were sold in 1992, compared with 12 billion gallons of all soft drinks), such growth interested Coke and Pepsi. In the 1990s, Coke introduced PowerAde, Nordic Mist and Tab Clear; Pepsi introduced Crystal Pepsi, Diet Crystal Pepsi, All Sport, Tropical Chill, and Strawberry Burst. In tea drinks, Coke joined up with Nestea and Pepsi with Lipton, with Pepsi planning to invest $50 million to upgrade and expand its hot-fill capacity for its ready to drink iced tea brands. In 1993, the new age beverage segment was worth $900 million. Leading the charge was Clearly Canadian's array of 11-ounce blue-tinted bottles of clear, naturally flavored sodas, followed by Snapple's variety of bottled drinks. Snapple's net revenue increased from $13 million in 1988 to $232 million in 1992. The company had several flavors, and a 33% share of the ready-to-drink tea market, the largest share in this category.

In 1993, flavored soda sales grew more than twice as fast as cola sales in supermarkets. Dr. Pepper and Mountain Dew sales, for example, were up 10% each at grocery stores, for the 40 weeks ending October 3, 1993. Pepsi promoted its nine fruit-flavored Slice brands, and Coke was pushing its Dr Pepper-competitor Mr. Pibb as well as an expanded line of Minute Maid flavors. In contrast to flavored sodas, growth of diet soft drinks slowed dramatically from the double-digit expansion in the late 1980s. In 1992, the diet segment did not increase for the first time in its history. Analysts predicted little or no growth in 1993 due to new age beverages, private label brands, and declining brand loyalty. In part to address these trends, Pepsi pronounced itself a "total beverage company," while Coca-Cola appeared to be moving in the same direction. The philosophy behind the strategy, according to Pepsi's VP for new business, was that whenever an American sipped a beverage, that beverage should be a Pepsi-Cola product. "If Americans want to drink tap water, we want it to be Pepsi tap water."[16] Both companies predicted increased market share from beverages outside of carbonated soft drinks. As part of this repositioning, Coca-Cola embarked on a strategy to change its image by dropping McCann-Erickson, its principal ad agency since 1955, and hiring Creative Artists Agency (CAA), a Hollywood talent firm. Coke wanted to revitalize its advertising and overcome the perception that the hip soft drink for the youth market was Pepsi.[17]

INTERNATIONALIZING THE COLA WARS

In the 1990s, some of the most intense battles of the cola wars were being waged in international markets. The opportunities for international soft drink unit case growth and profits were enormous, because per capita consumption levels worldwide were a fraction of the U.S. market. For example, the average American drank 296 eight-ounce Coca-Cola soft drinks in 1993; the average person in China drank one. If Coke boosted Chinese purchases to the annual per-person consumption of Australia, which was 217, "it would be the equivalent of another Coca-Cola company the size it is

---

[16]Marcy Magiera, "Pepsi Moving Fast To Get Beyond Colas," *Advertising Age*, July 5, 1993.
[17]Kevin Goldman, "Coke Blitz Keeps Successful '93 Strategy," *Wall Street Journal*, February 8, 1994.

today. It would be 10 billion cases a year," Goizueta said.[18] Industry analysts believed that the international market would grow by 7%-10% per year.[19] Some of the more exciting areas included Eastern Europe, China and India, where Coke and Pepsi's business had been limited, or prohibited, in the past. Coca-Cola had a global market share of 45% in 1993, compared to Pepsi's 14%. Coke's profitability was particularly strong in Germany, where it had a 50% share of the market. Coke was also the market leader in Western Europe, Japan and Mexico. Pepsi's greatest strength was in the Middle East, Eastern Europe, and Russia (see Exhibit 8).

Coke and Pepsi took different long-term approaches to the international soft drink market. Pepsi had company-owned bottlers in many international territories, while Coca-Cola made equity investments in franchisees. Unlike the U.S. market, international bottling contracts usually did not contain restrictions on concentrate pricing, which gave CPs much more flexibility to raise the price of concentrate. Overseas bottling contracts were not perpetual, and were usually for a 3-10 year duration. Operating margins were as much as ten percentage points higher in many international markets compared to the U.S. CPs made concentrate pricing decisions on a country-by-country basis taking into account local conditions. Retail pricing was established by the local bottlers with input from the franchiser, and was based on channel development, growth in disposable income, and availability of alternative beverages. There were barriers to growth in many countries including price controls, lack of remittable profits, foreign exchange controls, political instability, restrictions on advertising, raw material sources, and environmental issues.

In 1992, Coke earned 80% of its profits outside of the United States, while Pepsi-Cola earned 15%-20% of its profits outside the U.S. Coke executives predicted that international operations would contribute 85% of operating income by the end of the decade. Beginning in the 1980s, Coke refranchised and restructured its international bottlers, particularly those who were having difficulty managing their territories, by providing capital and management expertise to promote profitable volume growth. Coke employed a strategy of "anchor bottlers"—large, committed, and experienced bottling outfits like Norway's Ringnes and Australia's Amatil—who were pioneering new markets like China, Eastern Europe, and the former Soviet Union. Similar to its U.S. approach, Coke tended to own stakes of less than 50% in its overseas bottlers. Yet, Coke also liked to invest enough to influence local management. Coke built brand presence in markets where soft drink consumption was low but where the long-term profit potential was large, such as Indonesia with a population of 180 million, a median age of 18, and a per-person consumption of only four Coca-Cola soft drinks a year. As one Coke executive noted, "They sit squarely on the equator and everybody's young. It's soft drink heaven."[20] From 1981-1993, Coke invested over $3 billion internationally. Goizueta said, "We have really just begun reaching out to the 95% of the world's population that lives outside the United States. Today our top 16 markets account for 80% of our volume, and those markets only cover 20% of the world's population.[21] Coke's equity or joint venture interest was in more than 38% of its worldwide volume in 1993.

Pepsi was slower off the mark than Coke in focusing its international effort. In the mid-1970s, Pepsi was concerned with domestic operations, and after experiencing problems in Mexico and the Philippines in the early 1980s, began selling off its international bottling investments. The money went towards buying back domestic bottlers and increasing efficiency and profitability. But,

---

[18]Martha T. Moore, "Fountain of Growth Found Abroad," *USA Today*, August 16, 1994.
[19]Value Line, *Soft Drink Industry*, August 20, 1993.
[20]Martha T. Moore, "Fountain of Growth Found Abroad," *USA Today*, August 16, 1993.
[21]John Huey, "The World's Best Brand," *Fortune*, May 31, 1993.

PepsiCo Foods International (PFI) continued to operate in seven countries, and the company found it could perform well overseas. By the late 1980s, Pepsi-Cola began to rethink its international effort, and decided that if it wanted to grow 17%-18% annually, it would have to invest outside the United States. Many of its remaining foreign bottling operations were run inefficiently: they were under-marketing, the product quality was inconsistent, and there was no uniformity in graphics standards. Pepsi-Cola International's president, Chris Sinclair, had this to say,

> We were horrible operators internationally. I can't be more blunt than that. It was not uncommon to find 20%-30% levels of distribution in certain markets. We had bottling operations that didn't know their customers and didn't really think about things like, "How do I optimize selling and delivery?" We had cost structures that were woefully uncompetitive. We had to attack not only the cost issues out there in the system, but, more importantly, the customer service issues.[22]

Pepsi utilized a niche strategy which targeted geographic areas where per capitas were relatively established and the markets presented high volume and profit opportunities. These were often "Coke fortresses," and Pepsi put its guerilla tactics to work. One example of such an assault was in Monterrey, Mexico, where 90% of the market belonged to Coke's local bottler. In the Spring of 1992, with the precision of an infantry battalion, Pepsi tripled its market share to 24% in four months, using a well-trained team, 250 new trucks, and a new state-of-the-art bottling plant. Another Coke fortress was Japan, where a "Pepsi Challenge" was launched before a judge issued an injunction against Pepsi to stop using its competitor's name in its advertising. Coke responded to these attacks by lowering its prices in international markets in order to build volume.

Pepsi established local bottling partners either through joint ventures, equity investments or direct control. Unlike Coke who used anchor bottlers to quickly enter a new market, Pepsi was faced with finding bottling partners who possessed adequate business skills. Its bottlers worked closely with the local retail trade to build brand presence and availability. Pepsi restructured or refranchised about half of its international bottling network since 1990, investing almost $2 billion. Including company-owned bottling operations, Pepsi maintained equity control in over 20% of its bottling system on a volume basis, and about 50% on a revenue basis.

Analysts believed that the international game would ultimately be played in Latin America, India, China, and Eastern Europe. With several of these markets expanding rapidly, the question for all soft drink companies in the late 1990s was: will the battle for the global soft drink market evolve into another dominant duopoly like the United States, or will a different pattern emerge, with different players, different vertical structures, and different margins?

---

[22]Larry Jabbonsky, "Room To Run," *Beverage World*, August 1993.

Exhibit 1: U.S. Industry Statistics

	1965	1970	1975	1981	1985	1986	1987	1988	1989	1990	1991	1992	1993E
Historical Soft Drink Consumption													
Cases (millions)	NA	3,090	3,780	5,180	6,500	6,770	7,155	7,530	7,680	7,914	8,040	8,160	8,395
Gallons/capita	17.8	22.7	26.6	34.5	40.8	42.1	44.1	46.0	46.6	47.4	47.2	48.0	48.9
As a % of total beverage consumption	9.8	12.4	14.4	18.7	22.4	23.1	24.2	25.2	25.5	26.0	26.2	26.3	26.8
U.S. Market Share by Flavor (%)													
Cola		57.6	58.0	64.0	67.5	68.8	69.0	69.0	69.5	69.9	69.7	68.3	67.0
Lemon-lime		12.0	12.7	12.6	12.2	11.3	10.6	10.4	12.0	11.7	11.8	12.0	12.1
Pepper		4.1	6.6	5.7	4.9	4.6	4.7	5.1	5.3	5.6	6.2	6.9	7.3
Root beer		4.4	4.1	3.0	2.7	2.2	2.4	2.4	2.6	2.7	2.8	2.7	2.7
Orange		4.8	3.9	5.7	0.8	1.4	1.0	0.8	2.4	2.3	2.3	2.2	2.3
Others		17.1	14.7	9.0	11.9	11.7	12.3	12.3	8.2	7.8	7.2	7.9	8.6
		100.0	100.0	100.0	100.0	100.0	100.0	100.0	100.0	100.0	100.0	100.0	100.00
Caffeine-Free							4.1	4.6	5.2	6.0	6.1	6.0	5.6
Diet					23.1	24.0	24.8	25.9	27.7	30.0	29.8	29.3	28.2
U.S. Liquid Consumption Trends (gallons/capita)													
Soft drinks		22.7	26.3	34.2	40.8	42.1	44.1	46.1	46.7	47.7	47.8	48.0	48.9
Coffee		35.7	33.0	27.2	26.8	27.1	27.1	26.5	26.4	26.4	26.5	26.1	25.9
Beer		18.5	21.6	24.3	23.8	24.1	23.9	23.7	23.6	24.1	23.3	23.1	22.9

	1965	1970	1975	1981	1985	1986	1987	1988	1989	1990	1991	1992	1993E
Milk		22.8	21.8	20.6	19.8	19.9	19.7	19.4	19.6	19.4	19.4	19.2	18.9
Tea		5.2	7.3	7.3	7.3	7.3	7.3	7.4	7.2	7.0	6.7	6.8	6.9
Bottled water		-	1.2	2.7	5.2	5.7	6.4	7.2	8.1	9.2	9.6	9.9	10.5
Juices		6.5	6.8	6.9	7.4	7.3	7.0	7.1	6.8	6.2	6.4	6.6	7.0
Powdered drinks		-	4.8	6.0	6.3	5.2	4.9	5.3	5.4	5.7	5.9	5.6	6.0
Wine		1.3	1.7	2.1	2.4	2.4	2.4	2.2	2.1	2.0	1.9	1.8	1.7
Distilled spirits		1.8	2.0	2.0	1.8	1.7	1.6	1.5	1.5	1.5	1.4	1.3	1.3
Subtotal		114.5	126.5	133.3	141.6	142.8	144.4	146.4	147.4	149.2	148.9	148.4	149.4
Imputed water consumption		68.0	56.0	49.2	40.9	39.7	38.1	36.1	35.1	33.3	33.6	34.1	32.6
Total[a]		182.5	182.5	182.5	182.5	182.5	182.5	182.5	182.5	182.5	182.5	182.5	182.5

[a]This analysis assumes that each person consumes on average one-half gallon of liquid per day.

Source: John C. Maxwell, Jr., Beverage Industry Annual Manual 1992/1993, and The Maxwell Consumer Report, Feb. 3, 1994.

Exhibit 2: Financial Data for the Leading Soft Drink Competitors ($ millions)

	1975	1980	1985	1986	1987	1988	1989	1990	1991	1992	1993
Coca-Cola Company[a]											
Soft drinks, United States											
Sales	NA	1,486	1,865	2,016	2,120	2,012	2,222	2,461	2,646	2,813	2,966
Operating profits/sales	NA	11.1%	11.6%	14.5%	15.3%	17.5%	17.6%	16.5%	17.7%	18.1%	20.8%
Soft drinks, International											
Sales	NA	2,349	2,677	3,629	4,109	4,504	4,759	6,125	7,245	8,551	9,205
Operating profit/sales		21.0%	22.9%	24.5%	27.0%	29.7%	31.9%	29.4%	29.7%	29.5%	29.9%
Consolidated											
Sales	2,773	5,475	5,879	6,977	7,658	8,065	8,622	10,236	11,572	13,074	13,957
Net profit/sales	9.0%	7.7%	12.3%	13.4%	12.0%	13.0%	14.0%	13.5%	14.0%	12.7%	15.6%
Net profit/equity	21.0%	20.0%	24.0%	27.0%	29.0%	31.0%	49.0%	36.0%	38.0%	43.0%	51.7%
Long-term debt/assets	3.0%	10.0%	23.0%	19.0%	15.0%	14.0%	10.0%	8.0%	10.0%	10.0%	11.9%
Coca-Cola Enterprises (CCE)[b]											
Sales				1,951	3,329	3,821	3,822	3,933	3,915	5,127	5,465
Operating profit/sales				8.6%	10.1%	9.3%	8.1%	8.3%	3.1%	6.0%	7.0%
Net profit/sales				1.4%	2.7%	4.0%	1.9%	2.4%	-2.1%	-3.6%	-0.3%
Net profit/equity				2.0%	6.0%	8.0%	4.0%	6.0%	-5.8%	-14.8%	-1.2%
Long-term debt/assets				47.0%	49.0%	44.0%	37.0%	39.0%	51.0%	43.4%	47.0%
PepsiCo, Inc.[c]											
Soft drinks, United States											
Sales	1,065	2,368	2,725	3,450	3,113	3,667	4,623	5,035	5,172	5,485	5,918
Operating profit/sales	10.4%	10.3%	10.4%	10.1%	11.7%	11.1%	12.5%	13.4%	14.4%	14.6%	15.8%
Soft drinks, International											
Sales	NA	NA	NA	NA	863	971	1,153	1,489	1,744	2,120	2,720
Operating profit/sales					5.4%	5.5%	6.8%	6.3%	6.7%	6.7%	6.3%
Consolidated											
Sales	2,709	5,975	7,585	9,017	11,018	12,381	15,241	17,515	19,292	21,970	25,021
Net profit/sales	4.6%	4.4%	5.6%	5.1%	5.5%	6.2%	6.0%	6.2%	5.6%	5.9%	6.4%
Net profit/equity	18.0%	20.0%	30.0%	22.0%	24.0%	24.0%	23.0%	22.0%	19.5%	23.0%	25.1%
Long-term debt/assets	35.0%	31.0%	36.0%	33.0%	25.0%	21.0%	38.0%	33.0%	42.0%	38.0%	31.4%

	1975	1980	1985	1986	1987	1988	1989	1990	1991	1992	1993
Dr Pepper											
Sales	138	339	174	181	207						
Net profit/sales	8.6%	7.8%	2.3%	2.5%	-0.1%						
Net profit/equity	24.0%	24.0%	30.0%	NA	-1.0%						
Long-term debt/assets	NA	38.0%	47.0%	50.0%	38.0%						
Seven-Up[d]											
Sales	214	353	678	271	297						
Net profit/sales	9.5%	NA	NA	-2.4%	2.5%						
Net profit/equity	24.0%	NA	NA	-2.5%	14.8%						
Long-term debt/assets	2.0%	NA	NA	42.0%	66.0%						
Dr Pepper/Seven-Up Co.s[e]											
Sales						511	514	540	601	659	707
Operating profit/sales						11.7%	22.2%	22.8%	23.0%	24.4%	25.9%
Net loss/profit						(79)	(42)	(33)	(38)	(140)	78
Long-term debt/assets						140.6%	149.0%	152.2%	138.5%	163.4%	116.3%
Royal Crown Corporation[f]											
Sales	258	438	986	1,102	1,109	1,122	1,175	1,231	1,027	1,075	1,058
Net profit/sales	5.2%	2.3%	0.6%	-0.8%	1.6%	3.2%	-0.1%	-0.9%	-1.6%	-0.7	-5.7%
Net profit/equity	17.0%	10.0%	5.0%	-9.0%	15.0%	23.0%	-1.0%	-11.0%	-39.0%	-7.7%	NA
Long-term debt/assets	NA	38.0%	47.0%	50.0%	38.0%	46.0%	46.0%	46.0%	34.0%	35.3%	53.7%

[a]Coca-Cola's soft drink sales were comprised primarily of concentrate sales. Coke's 44% stake in CCE was accounted for by the equity method of accounting. Coke's share of CCE's net earnings was included in its consolidated net income figure.

[b]CCE's net loss in 1991 and 1992 was due to debt transactions which increased net income expense.

[c]PepsiCo's soft drink sales included sales from company-owned bottlers.

[d]Seven-Up was purchased by Philip Morris in 1978; in 1986, Seven-Up's domestic operation was sold to Hicks and Haas, and its international operation was sold to PepsiCo. Seven-Up had negative shareholders equity in 1988, 1989, and 1990.

[b]Dr Pepper/Seven-Up was formed in 1988. The company experienced net losses due to charges relating to new financial accounting rules, and to a company recapitalization plan.

[c]Royal Crown was purchased by DWG Corporation in late 1984. Royal Crown Corporation was made up of RC Cola and Arby's, a franchised restaurant system.

Source: Company annual reports

Exhibit 3: **Comparative Cost Structure and Financial Structure of a Typical U.S. Concentrate Producer and Bottler (per standard 8-oz./24-bottle case), 1993**

	Concentrate Producer		Bottler	
	Dollars per Case	**Percent of Total**	**Dollars per Case**	**Percent of Total**
Profit and Loss Data				
Net sales	.66	100%	2.99	100%
Cost of sales	.11	17	1.69	57
Gross profit	.55	83	1.30	43
Selling and delivery	.01	2	.85	28
Advertising and marketing	.26	39	.05	2
General and administration	.05	13	.13	4
Pretax profit	.23	29	.27	9
Balance Sheet Data				
Cash, investments	.12		.16	
Receivables	.32		.30	
Inventories	.02		.16	
Net property, plant & equipment	.07		.82	
Goodwill	.03		1.37	
Total assets	.56		2.81	
Pretax profit/total assets	.41		.10	

Source: Industry analysts and casewriter estimates.

Exhibit 4: **U.S. Soft Drink Retail Outlets, 1993**

	Food Stores	Convenience and gas	Fountain	Vending	Other	Total
Percent of industry volume	40.0%	14.0%	17.0%	8.0%	21.0%	100.0%
Share of channel:						
Coca-Cola (all brands)	32.8	29.6	58.9	48.6	45.4	40.7%
Pepsi-Cola (all brands)	28.5	37.4	27.0	40.6	32.5	31.3%
Other brands	38.7	33.0	14.1	10.8	22.1	28.0%
Bottling Profitability Per Case (192 ounces per case):						
Net Price	$3.14	$3.09	$1.52	$6.05	$1.90	$3.13
NOPBT[a]	$0.25	$0.40	$0.05	$0.69	$0.31	$0.34

[a]Net Operating Profit Before Tax

Source: Industry analysts and casewriter estimates.

Exhibit 5: **Comparative Profit Margin Analysis for Door-Store Delivery, Private Label, and Warehouse Delivered Soft Drinks in the United States, 1993**

Category	Retail Price	Cost of Goods	Gross Profit	Handling Costs	Net Profit / Unit	Net Profit / Case	Net Margin
DSD	$1.01	$.86	$.15	$.07	$.08	$.48	7.9%
Private Label	.69	.55	.14	.17	(.03)	(.18)	N/A
Warehouse	.82	.65	.17	.17	.00	.00	.00

Source: Jesse Meyers' Beverage Digest, July 1993. Used with permission, John Sicher, President, March 2000. © *Beverage Digest*.

Exhibit 6: **U.S. Soft Drink Market Share by Case Volume (percent)**

	1966	1970	1975	1980	1985	1986	1987	1988	1989	1990	1991	1992	1993E
Coca-Cola Company													
Classic					5.8	19.1	19.8	19.9	19.5	19.4	19.5	19.4	19.6
Coca-Cola	27.7	28.4	26.2	25.3	14.4	2.4	1.7	1.3	0.9	0.7	0.6	0.4	0.2
Cherry Coke					1.6	1.7	1.2	0.9	0.7	0.6	0.5	0.6	0.5
diet Coke					6.3	7.2	7.7	8.1	8.8	9.1	9.2	9.0	8.8
diet Cherry Coke						0.2	0.4	0.3	0.3	0.2	0.2	0.2	0.2
Tab	1.4	1.3	2.6	3.3	1.1	0.6	0.4	0.3	0.2	0.2	0.1	0.1	0.1
Caffeine Free Coke, diet Coke, and Tab					1.8	1.7	1.7	1.9	2.2	3.1	3.3	3.2	3.0
Sprite and diet Sprite	1.5	1.8	2.6	3.0	4.2	4.3	4.3	4.3	4.4	4.4	4.6	4.7	4.9
Others	2.8	3.2	3.9	4.3	1.9	2.6	2.7	2.8	3.0	2.7	2.7	3.1	3.8
Total	**33.4**	**34.7**	**35.3**	**35.9**	**37.1**	**39.8**	**39.9**	**39.8**	**40.0**	**40.4**	**40.7**	**40.7**	**41.1**
PepsiCo, Inc.													
Pepsi-Cola	16.1	17.0	17.4	20.4	18.2	18.6	18.6	18.4	17.8	17.3	16.6	16.3	16.0
Diet Pepsi	1.9	1.1	1.7	3.0	3.7	4.4	4.8	5.2	5.7	6.2	6.2	6.2	6.1
Caffeine-Free Pepsi. & Diet Pepsi					2.3	2.0	1.8	2.0	2.1	2.3	2.3	2.3	2.0
Mountain Dew	1.4	0.9	1.3	3.3	2.9	3.0	3.3	3.4	3.6	3.8	4.1	4.3	4.6
Diet Mountain Dew							0.4	0.4	0.5	0.5	0.5	0.6	0.6
Slice					0.7	1.5	1.3	1.1	1.0	0.9	0.9	0.9	1.0
Diet Slice					0.6	1.0	1.0	0.7	0.6	0.4	0.3	0.3	0.2
Others	1.0	0.8	0.7	1.1	0.2	0.1	0.0	0.1	0.4	0.4	0.6	0.4	0.5
Total	**20.4**	**19.8**	**21.1**	**27.8**	**28.6**	**30.6**	**30.8**	**31.3**	**31.7**	**31.8**	**31.5**	**31.3**	**31.0**
Seven-Up	6.9	7.2	7.6	6.3	5.7	5.0	5.1	4.7	4.3	4.0	3.9	4.0	3.9
Dr Pepper	2.6	3.8	5.5	6.0	4.7	4.8	5.0	5.3	5.6	5.8	6.6	7.1	7.5
Royal Crown Co.	6.9	6.0	5.4	4.7	2.9	3.0	2.9	2.8	2.6	2.6	2.5	2.3	2.2
Cadbury-Schweppes	NA	NA	NA	NA	4.5	4.2	3.7	3.5	3.1	3.2	3.1	3.2	3.1
Other companies	29.8	28.5	25.1	19.3	16.5	12.6	12.6	12.6	12.6	12.2	11.7	11.4	11.2
Total (mil. cases)	**2,927**	**3,670**	**4,155**	**5,180**	**6,500**	**6,770**	**7,155**	**7,530**	**7,680**	**7,914**	**8,040**	**8,160**	**8,395**

E — Estimate

Source: John C. Maxwell, Jr., Beverage Industry Annual Manual 1992/1993, and The Maxwell Consumer Report, February 3, 1994.

Exhibit 7: Advertising Spending by Brand in the U.S. ($ millions)

	1975	1980	1985	1986	1987	1988	1989	1990	1991	1992
Coca-Cola Company										
Coca-Cola	$25.3	$47.8	$71.6	$57.4	$57.8	$85.2	$77.4	$90.4	$89.1	$112.1
Diet Coke			40.6	40.3	40.0	56.8	59.2	69.1	71.2	70.0
Cherry Coke			6.6	10.0	7.2	1.0	0.5	0.1	0.2	0.5
Sprite	2.6	10.7	22.2	24.6	22.2	22.4	22.5	23.4	27.4	28.5
Diet Sprite			6.7	5.0	3.3	7.5	2.2	7.6	5.9	a
Tab	6.5	12.6	15.6	5.1	0.5	a	a	a	0.2	0.4
Total	34.4	71.1	163.3	142.4	131.0	172.9	161.8	190.6	194.0	211.5
Pepsi-Cola Company										
Pepsi-Cola	17.9	40.2	56.9	54.9	60.2	70.9	71.9	79.4	74.8	76.2
Diet Pepsi	3.7	11.6	32.9	33.8	35.5	48.5	57.2	76.5	67.5	43.4
Pepsi Free (regular & sugar-free)			9.1	a	a	a	a	a	1.5	8.1
Mountain Dew	2.8	10.2	9.0	8.3	8.0	5.7	9.1	11.7	15.3	11.6
Diet Mountain Dew				a		4.2	1.6	1.6	a	8.0
Pepsi Light	0.9	5.2	0.4	a		a	a	a	a	a
Total	25.3	67.2	108.3	97.0	103.7	129.3	139.8	169.2	159.1	147.3
Dr Pepper Company										
Dr Pepper	6.2	15.1	9.6	9.6	11.3	14.5	17.8	24.1	23.6	29.4
Pepper Free			0.5	0.3	a	a	a	a	NA	NA
Diet Dr Pepper	1.6	2.9	5.7	6.8	9.2	9.7	9.4	6.6	23.6	18.8
Total	7.8	18.0	15.8	16.7	20.5	24.2	27.2	30.7	47.2	48.2
Seven-Up Company										
7-Up	10.2	25.5	22.3	33.3	27.1	27.6	27.2	31.4	28.1	13.6
Diet 7-Up	3.3	7.9	15.6	8.2	11.0	7.3	5.2	8.5	9.9	12.8
Cherry 7-Up				a	8.7	14.5	4.4	0.2	a	a
Like			1.5		a	a	a	a	a	a
Total	13.5	33.4	39.4	41.5	46.8	49.4	36.8	40.1	38.0	26.4
Royal Crown Cola										
Royal Crown	10.9	6.6	5.1	6.4	6.4	5.9	6.2	1.4	2.7	3.0
Diet Rite Cola	3.5	3.4	3.5	2.9	3.5	2.3	1.9	3.2	0.8	a
Total	14.4	10.0	8.6	9.3	9.9	8.2	8.1	4.6	3.5	3.0

	1975	1980	1985	1986	1987	1988	1989	1990	1991	1992
Canada Dry	5.2	10.1	12.4	11.6	8.0	7.1	4.6	4.5	NA	NA
Shasta	2.8	4.4	4.6	[a]	[a]	1.4	[a]	[a]	[a]	1.2
All Others	10.5	26.3	30.4	70.5	72.1	65.5	49.7	58.3	55.0	60.0
Industry Total	114	241	383	389	392	458	428	498	502	503

[a]Advertising under $250,000.

Source: Advertising Age, Beverage Industry, company annual reports.

Exhibit 8: **Soft Drink Industry—Selected International Market Shares, 1993 (192 ounces per case, in thousands)**

	Gallons Per Capita	Industry	Unit Cases Coca-Cola	PepsiCo	Share Coca-Cola	Share PepsiCo
Asia						
Japan	6	2,020,000	646,400	141,400	32%	7%
Philippines	7	324,000	246,240	64,800	76	20
Australia	25	260,850	153,900	26,100	59	10
Korea	8	215,460	107,710	17,230	50	8
Thailand	5	185,740	107,730	16,700	58	9
China	0.8	666,700	76,950	33,330	12	5
Other		377,350	200,070	57,780	53	15
Total		**4,050,100**	**1,539,000**	**357,340**	**38%**	**9%**
Europe						
Germany	27	1,281,450	627,910	102,520	49%	8%
Great Britain	14	651,510	201,970	78,180	31	12
Spain	19	513,000	277,020	66,690	54	13
Italy	13	436,520	240,080	48,020	55	11
France	8	300,640	129,280	21,040	43	7
Other		746,240	370,540	115,780	50	16
Total		**3,929,360**	**1,846,800**	**432,230**	**47%**	**11%**
Latin America						
Mexico	33	1,925,150	1,058,830	481,290	55%	25%
Brazil	8	902,880	541,730	108,340	60	12
Argentina	16	397,160	246,240	142,980	62	36
Chile	18	158,865	98,500	28,590	62	18
Other		1,175,945	517,100	59,600	54	5
Total		**4,560,000**	**2,462,400**	**820,800**	**54%**	**18%**
Northeast Europe/Africa		2,972,970	1,126,000	501,000	38%	17%
Canada	27	603,530	205,200	193,130	34	32
Total		**16,115,960**	**7,179,400**	**2,304,500**	**45%**	**14%**
United States	48	**8,160,000**	**3,345,600**	**2,529,600**	**41%**	**31%**

Source: Andrew Conway, "Thirsting for Growth, Soft Drinks in the 1990s," *Salomon Brothers,* June 1993; industry analysts; casewriter estimates.

Appendix A: **Corporate History of Coke and Pepsi Major Acquisitions and Divestitures**

Coca-Cola

Coca-Cola was incorporated in 1919. Its main business was the production of carbonated soft drink concentrate and syrups. Over the years, Coca-Cola bought and sold many different businesses (the following list contains the acquisitions and sales of franchised bottlers which were over $200 million).

1960: Acquired Minute Maid, the maker of chilled and frozen concentrated citrus juices.

1964: Acquired Duncan Foods Company. In 1967, consolidated operations of Minute Maid and Duncan Foods into the Coca-Cola Foods Division.

1968: Acquired Belmont Springs Water Co. for 13,250 shares.

1977: Acquired The Taylor Wine Co. and Sterling Vineyards of California. Also acquired Gonzales & Co., which operated The Monterey Vineyard in California.

1978: Acquired Presto Products, maker of plastic film products such as plastic wrap, sandwich bags, garbage bags, and moist towelettes.

1981: Sold Aqua-Chem, maker of water conversion systems, to Lyonnaise American Holdings.

1982: Acquired Columbia Pictures for a purchase price of $333 million in cash and stock valued at $692 million. Acquired Ronco Foods Company, a manufacturer and distributor of pasta products. In June, purchased Associated Coca-Cola Bottling Co. for $419 million; by the end of the year, 70% of Associated's operating assets had been sold.

1983: Sold its wine business for $230 million.

1984: Sold Ronco Foods Company.

1985: Sold Presto Products and Winkler Flexible Products for $112 million. Bought certain assets and properties of Embassy Communications and Tandem Productions for $267 million, comprised of 7.1 million shares of the company's common stock and the payment of existing debt. Tandem was purchased for $178 million in cash. Embassy and Tandem were producers and distributors of television programs. In 1986, sold Embassy Home Entertainment to Nelson Entertainment for $85 million. Acquired Nutri-Foods International, a manufacturer of juice-based frozen desserts, for $30 million.

1986: Acquired January Enterprises (now Merv Griffin Enterprises) for $200 million. Transferred the operating assets of company owned bottling companies in the U.S. to

Coca-Cola Enterprises, a 49% owned subsidiary. Acquired the Coca-Cola Bottling Company of Southern Florida for $325 million, and Coca-Cola bottling companies affiliated with Mr. Crawford Rainwater for $211 million.

1987: Cadbury Schweppes and Coke formed a joint venture company known as Coca-Cola and Schweppes Beverage Ltd., which handled bottling, canning and distributing of the companies' products in Great Britain.

1988: Acquired the citrus food service assets of H.P. Hood for $45 million. Sold Coca-Cola Bottling Cos. of Memphis, Miami and Maryland, and a portion of the Delaware operation, to Coca-Cola Enterprises for $500 million.

1989: Acquired S.P.B.G., a subsidiary of Pernod Ricard. Sold Coca-Cola Foods' coffee business to Maryland Club Foods. Acquired the outstanding stock of Frank Lyon Co, the sole shareholder of Coca-Cola Bottling Company of Arkansas, for $232 million. Acquired all of the Coca-Cola bottling operations of Pernod Ricard for an aggregate purchase price of $285 million, and liabilities assumed were $145 million. Acquired a 59.5% share in Coca-Cola Amatil Ltd. for an aggregate purchase price of $491 million. Sold Belmont Springs Water Co. to Suntory Water Group. Sold Columbia Pictures Entertainment to Sony for $1.55 billion.

1990: Sold Coca-Cola Bottling Company of Arkansas to CCE for $250 million.

1991: Coke and Nestle formed the Coca-Cola Nestle Refreshments Company, which manufactured ready to drink coffee, tea, and chocolate beverages under the Nescafe, Nestea, and Nestle brand names.

PepsiCo

The Pepsi-Cola company was mainly a beverage company until 1965 when Pepsi acquired Frito-Lay and became PepsiCo. PepsiCo later purchased Pizza Hut, Taco Bell, and Kentucky Fried Chicken to become the world's largest restaurant group.

1959: Acquired Dossin's Food Products in exchange for 200,000 common shares.

1964: Acquired The Tip Corporation of America, makers of Mountain Dew, for 60,000 shares.

1965: Acquired Frito-Lay for 3,052,780 shares.

1966: Acquired Lease Plan International Corp., a transportation equipment leasing company, for 705,444 shares.

1968: Acquired North American Van Lines for 638,818 common shares, and Chandler Leasing Corp. for 482,498 shares.

1972: Acquired Wilson Sporting Goods Company. In 1985, sold Wilson for $134 million in cash and 10% Wilson preferred stock. Acquired 82% of Rheingold Corp, and in 1973, acquired remaining shares. In 1974, sold Rheingold's brewing operations and changed Rheingold Corp's name to United Beverages. Sold Lease Plan to Gelco-IVM Leasing Co. of Minneapolis for $6.7 million.

1976: Acquired Lee Way Motor Freight. In 1984, sold Lee Way to Commercial Lovelace Motor Freight.

1977: Acquired Pizza Hut through the exchange of 1.55 Pepsi shares for each Pizza Hut share.

1978: Acquired Taco Bell through the exchange of shares valued at $148 million.

1985: Acquired the bottling subsidiary of Allegheny Beverage Corp. for $160 million in cash. Sold North American Van Lines for $376 million.

1986: Acquired MEI Bottling Corp for $591 million in cash. Acquired Seven Up International for $246 in cash. Acquired Kentucky Fried Chicken for $841 million in cash.

1987: Sold La Petite Boulangerie for $15 million.

1988: Acquired bottling operation of Grand Metropolitan for $705 million.

1989: Acquired the domestic franchised bottling operations of General Cinema for $1.77 billion. Acquired the capital stock of Smiths Crisps Ltd. and Walker Crisps Holding Ltd., two snack food companies in the U.K., for $1.34 billion.

1990: PFI, through its Mexican snack food subsidiary, Sabritas S.A., acquired over 70% of the stock of Empresas Gamesa for $300 million.

1991: PFI purchased the remaining 50% interest in the Hostess Frito-Lay Company from Kraft General Foods Canada Inc. Terms were not disclosed.

1992: PFI acquired Evercrisp Snack Productos de Chile S.A. for $12.6 million, one of the leading snack food producers in Chile.

Appendix B: **Other Concentrate Producers**

Dr Pepper/Seven-Up Companies

Seven-Up, a lemon-lime drink, was introduced in 1929. The majority of its bottlers also bottled Coke, Pepsi, or RC Cola. By the 1950s, Seven-Up achieved national distribution through its franchise network and owned a small number of bottling operations. Dr Pepper, formulated in 1885 in Texas, had a unique taste based on a combination of juices, and called for less sugar than the leading brands. It started out as a small, regional producer in the southwest. In 1962, a court ruled that Dr Pepper was not a cola, therefore Coke and Pepsi bottlers could carry it. Dr Pepper expanded its geographic base by granting franchises to Coke and Pepsi bottlers across the country. Eighty percent of Dr Pepper was distributed through the Coke or Pepsi bottling systems in 1993.

Philip Morris acquired Seven-Up in 1978 for a big premium, and then racked up huge losses in the early 1980s. By 1985, Philip Morris was looking for a buyer. The FTC blocked Pepsi's purchase of Seven-Up, although Pepsi purchased Seven-Up's Canadian and international operations for $246 million. Philip Morris sold Seven-Up's domestic operations to an investment firm led by Hicks & Haas for $240 million. By October 1986, Hicks & Haas completed leveraged buyouts of A&W Brands, a specialty concentrate producer, for $75 million, and Dr Pepper's concentrate business for $416 million. At the end of 1986, Hicks & Haas had a 14% share of the U.S. soft drink market. Dr Pepper/Seven-Up Companies was a holding company formed in 1988 to acquire the Dr Pepper Company and the Seven-Up Company. It was the largest noncola soft drink franchiser in the U.S. in 1993 with a market share of 11%. More than 70% of its volume was distributed by Coke and Pepsi bottlers. Cadbury Schweppes held 26% of the company's stock in 1993.

Royal Crown Cola (RC Cola)

Royal Crown introduced its first cola in 1935, and was the first to introduce regular and decaffeinated diet cola. Its franchise bottlers, mostly located in the midwest, also sold Seven-Up, Dr Pepper, and other small brands. In 1984, Royal Crown was acquired by financier Victor Posner's DWG Corporation. RC Cola was a subsidiary of Royal Crown Corporation, which was a subsidiary of CFC Holdings Corporation, a subsidiary of DWG Corporation. In 1993, Posner sold a controlling interest in DWG to Nelson Peltz and Peter May, who changed the name from DWG to Triarc. RC Cola was the third largest national brand cola in 1993, with sales outside of the U.S. accounting for 7.5% of sales. RC Cola was the exclusive supplier of cola concentrate to Cott, a private label soft drink supplier to major retailers.

Other Brands

In 1984, Canada Dry was sold to R.J. Reynolds, which also purchased Sunkist from General Cinema, combining it with earlier purchases of Del Monte's Hawaiian Punch and Cott Beverages. By 1985, R.J. Reynolds controlled 4.6% of the U.S. soft drink industry. In June 1986, R.J. Reynolds sold Canada Dry and Sunkist to Cadbury Schweppes. In 1989, Cadbury-Schweppes acquired Crush International from Proctor & Gamble, which included the Hires brand. In the same year, the company also relocated its beverage headquarters from London, England, to Stamford, Connecticut. In 1990, Cadbury Schweppes refranchised its Canada Dry, Hires and Crush products, with the goal of making the brands national.

MATCHING DELL

case 5

Jan W. Rivkin and
Michael E. Porter

Between 1994 and 1998, the revenue of Dell Computer Corporation rose from $3.5 billion to $18.2 billion, and profits increased from $149 million to $1.5 billion. The company's stock price rose by 5,600%. During the same period, Dell grew twice as fast as its major rivals in the personal computer market and tripled its market share. In the first half of 1998, Dell reported operating earnings that were greater than the personal computer earnings of Compaq, Gateway, Hewlett-Packard, and IBM combined.[1] On *Forbes* magazine's list of the richest Americans, Michael Dell, the 33-year-old founder of Dell Computer, ranked fourth with an estimated worth of $13 billion. He trailed only Bill Gates, Warren Buffett, and Paul Allen on the list and was worth more than Gates had been at the same age.[2]

Dell Computer had pioneered the widely publicized "Direct Model" in the personal computer (PC) industry. While competitors sold primarily through distributors, resellers, and retail sites, Dell took orders directly from customers, especially corporate customers. Once it received an order, Dell rapidly built computers to customer specifications and shipped machines directly to the customer.

The success of the Direct Model attracted the intense scrutiny of Dell's competitors. By 1997, headlines such as "Now Everyone in PCs Wants to Be Like Mike," "Compaq Reengineers the

---

[1] Evan Ramstad, "Dell Profit Jumps 62%, Beating Expectations," *Wall Street Journal,* August 19, 1998, p. A3.
[2] "The *Forbes* 400: The Richest People in America," *Forbes,* October 12, 1998, pp. 165-361.

This case was prepared by Professors Jan W. Rivkin and Michael E. Porter from public sources with the assistance of Research Associate Faramarz Nabavi as the basis for class discussion rather than to illustrate either effective or ineffective handling of an administrative situation. The case draws on a report prepared by Charlie Bruin, Markus Cappel, Tom Galizia, and Laila Worrell, all MBA 1998. Reprinted by permission of Harvard Business School.

Channel: Will It Be Enough to Slow Dell's Momentum?" and "In Search of Greener Pastures, Gateway Moves on Dell's Turf" peppered the PC trade press.[3] By late 1998, virtually every major PC manufacturer had taken some step to match Dell's approach.

THE PERSONAL COMPUTER INDUSTRY

History. Electronic computers emerged from military research undertaken during World War II. In 1949, the magazine *Popular Mechanics* predicted that "Computers in the future may…perhaps only weigh 1.5 tons." For the following three decades, large mainframe and minicomputers, produced by vertically integrated firms such as IBM and Digital Equipment Corporations (DEC), dominated the market. As late as 1977, Kenneth Olsen, founder of minicomputer maker DEC, opined, "There is no reason for any individual to have a computer in their home."[4]

However, electronic hobbyists were already purchasing mail-order and retail kits which allowed them to assemble primitive computers at home. These kits pieced together components that were either altogether new or newly affordable: microprocessors made by start-ups such as Intel, random-access and read-only memories, power supplies, and so forth. (A **Glossary** at the end of the case defines technical terms.)

Between 1975 and 1981, a series of firms began to offer increasingly integrated, pre-assembled personal computers.[5] Start-ups such as Apple Computer and MITS, and midsize firms such as Tandy / Radio Shack and Commodore, led the early market, gaining popularity among hobbyists and educational institutions with easy-to-use machines for ordinary people. Established firms including Texas Instruments, Hewlett-Packard, Zenith, NEC, Xerox, IBM, Toshiba, Sanyo, Sony, Olivetti, Wang, and DEC soon joined the entrepreneurs and began to produce PCs.

IBM launched its first PC in 1981 and, two years later, held 42% of the market. With a world-renowned corporate sales force and service organization, IBM commanded 61% of the market for mainframe computers and produced many of the components for its mainframes.[6] In launching its PC, however, IBM purchased many components. It commissioned a start-up software firm, Microsoft, to write the operating system for its PC and adopted a microprocessor architecture designed by Intel. Publishing most of the specifications for its PC system, IBM established an "open architecture" to encourage software developers to write programs for the IBM PC and to spur other firms to make compatible peripherals such as printers. Most of the industry rapidly rallied around the IBM standards. By 1983, the major alternative standard, a proprietary system championed by Apple, held only 20% of the market.[7]

IBM used its huge sales force to sell personal computers to large corporate accounts. Volume discounts encouraged large firms to centralize PC purchases through corporate MIS departments,

---

[3] David Kirkpatrick, "Now Everyone in PCs Wants to Be Like Mike," *Fortune,* September 8, 1997, pp. 91-92. Steven Fortuna and Pamela Pappachan, "Compaq Reengineers the Channel: Will It Be Enough to Slow Dell's Momentum?", Deutsche Morgan Grenfell Technology Group, June 11, 1997. Andy Zisper, "In Search of Greener Pastures, Gateway Moves on Dell's Turf," *Barron's,* September 15, 1997, p. 10.

[4] John MacIntyre, "Fact of Life: Computers," *Spirit,* p. 170.

[5] Das Narayandas and V. Kasturi Rangan, "Dell Computer Corporation," HBS Case 596-058.

[6] John Steffens, *Newgames: Strategic Competition in the PC Revolution* (Oxford: Pergamon Press, 1994), p. 181.

[7] Source either old case, Steffans, or other.

with whom IBM sales people had strong relationships. To serve small businesses and individuals, IBM turned to retail stores such as Sears and Computerland.[8] It also encouraged the development of a network of distributors and dealers known as *value-added resellers.* These resellers not only sold PCs to customers, but also guided them through the purchase of what was still an unfamiliar product. Resellers commonly handled installation, configured software, pieced together customer networks, and serviced machines on an on-going basis. In small and midsize businesses, employees rarely had the skills to do what resellers did, and few companies had enough PCs to justify hiring trained personnel.

As demand for IBM's PCs exploded, other firms began to offer "IBM clones." Compaq entered the market with a low-priced portable clone in 1982 and booked $100 million of revenue during its first year, making it the fastest growing firm in American history. A host of other start-ups followed Compaq's lead and entered the market with IBM clones. Among these entrants was Dell Computer Corporation, incorporated in 1984. During the same period, most established competitors such as Hewlett-Packard shifted from proprietary architectures to the IBM standard.

Like IBM, makers of IBM clones relied on resellers and retail stores to reach customers. While IBM initially steered resellers away from the largest corporate accounts, start-ups such as Compaq without internal sales forces encouraged resellers to cater to large customers. In time, even IBM relied heavily on resellers to service large accounts.

By 1986, IBM realized that it had set a standard, but in doing so, had spawned a set of imitators while ceding the rights to the most valuable components of the PC—the microprocessor and the operating system—to Intel and Microsoft. In 1986, IBM declined to adopt Intel's third-generation microprocessor, the 386 chip. In introducing its PS/2 line of computers in 1987, IBM tried to make the PC more proprietary. Compaq both adopted the 386 chip and led a group of nine clone makers in affirming the existing industry standards. Though IBM subsequently accepted the 386, its market share fell from 37.0% in 1985 to 16.9% in 1989.[9]

Throughout the 1980s and 1990s, PC performance improved and prices fell at a rapid clip. Intel's 386DX microprocessor, introduced in 1985, was priced at $299 and could perform 2.5 million instructions per second (MIPS)—a price of $120 per MIPS. Intel's Pentium II microprocessor, launched in 1998, was priced at $699 and could carry out 675 MIPS—$1 per MIPS.[10] In addition, the range of software available for the personal computer expanded dramatically.

Microsoft released its new operating system Windows 3.0 in 1990, and over the next four years, the user-friendly Windows became ubiquitous on PCs configured to the IBM standard. Indeed, the standard soon became known as "Wintel," reflecting the combination of the Windows operating system and Intel's x86 microprocessor architecture. By 1991, between 85% and 90% of computers sold conformed to Microsoft / Intel standards, with the remainder using the proprietary Apple operating system and a Motorola microprocessor.

The initial surge in sales of personal computers crested in 1990, just as a recession gripped the United States. In newspapers around the world, Dell Computer ran advertisements showing that its prices were much, much lower than Compaq's list prices. Compaq usually discounted its PCs well below the list price, but the advertising campaign was highly effective. In response, Compaq

---

[8] James Chposky and Ted Leonsis, *Blue Magic,* New York: Facts on File Books, 1988, pp. 65-66.

[9] Das Narayandas and V. Kasturi Rangan, "Dell Computer Corporation," HBS Case 596-058, p. 16.

[10] Lee Gomes, "Bigger and Smaller: Personal Computers Will Be a Lot More Powerful; But They May Not Be Where the Action Is," *Wall Street Journal,* November 16, 1998, p. R6.

slashed its prices by as much as 32%, introduced 41 new products in 1992, and added new distribution channels.[11] A vigorous price war followed.

Demand growth recovered in the mid-1990s, buoyed by strong economic growth and the emergence of new, popular services involving computer networks. Proliferation of electronic mail and growth of the World Wide Web gave customers, especially individual consumers, new reasons to purchase a personal computer. PC prices continued to decline. Compaq offered a powerful personal computer for less than $1,000 in 1997, and other companies rushed to offer similarly inexpensive PCs. By December 1998, the prices of the least expensive PCs had plunged to $499. In the United States, 45.5% of households owned a computer in 1998, and the figure was expected to rise to 49.5% by 2000.[12] Household ownership levels were lower but also growing in Europe and Asia. See Exhibits 1 and 2 for market size and share data over time.

Products in 1998. PC makers followed well-established standards to piece together modular components of hardware and software. The resulting machines differed widely in their processing speeds, memory capacities, portability, software configurations, modem speeds, and screen sizes, for instance.

Hardware components such as housings, keyboards, memory chips, motherboards, disk drives, monitors, modems, and connectors could be purchased in highly competitive global markets served by numerous companies. In contrast, microprocessors were supplied by only a handful of companies. Intel dominated this market, providing 80-90% of the microprocessors for Wintel PCs.[13] By 1998, roughly 96% of new PCs followed the Wintel standard.[14] Virtually all of the rest employed the Apple standard with PowerPC microprocessors. Other semiconductor makers such as AMD and Cyrix offered low-priced microprocessors which competed with Intel's and used a similar architecture, but historically, these companies had made few inroads into Intel's near-monopoly. In the sub-$1,000 market, AMD and Cyrix appeared finally to have made some headway in unseating Intel. Roughly half of the sub-$1,000 PCs sold during 1998 were equipped with an AMD processor.[15]

Intel ordinarily made its microprocessors available to all major purchasers at a standard price, thereby maintaining a level playing field among the leading PC makers. When Intel released a new generation of microprocessors, demand typically exceeded supply. Intel then rationed its new product, allotting microprocessors to PC makers in proportions that were based roughly on past purchases. The price of a microprocessor of a given generation declined rapidly as a generation aged, as did the price of PCs made with them. PC margins were typically highest during the early days of a microprocessor generation.

The core piece of software on a PC was the operating system. Virtually all PCs with x86 microprocessors employed an operating system made by Microsoft, usually some version of Windows. A number of vendors offered "application software" such as word processors, spreadsheets, database management systems, financial organizers, Web browsers, and electronic messaging software. In this market, also, Microsoft held a preeminent position, accounting for

---

[11] John Steffens, *Newgames: Strategic Competition in the PC Revolution* (Oxford: Pergamon Press, 1994), p. 253.

[12] Data from International Data Corporation.

[13] Andy Reinhardt, "Computers and Chips: Prognosis 1999," *Business Week,* January 11, 1999, pp. 94-95.

[14] Mary Kwak and David B. Yoffie, "Apple Computer 1999," Harvard Business School Case 799-108, p. 16.

[15] "Semiconductors: The Money and the Gorilla," *The Economist,* December 5, 1998, p. 71.

nearly 80% of the market for so-called "office productivity applications" (e.g., word processors, spreadsheets) and 10% of the overall $56 billion market for application software.[16]

The hardware and software that comprised a PC were often sold as an integrated bundle. PC makers such as IBM, Compaq, and Dell would deliver computers with a Microsoft operating system already installed and, in turn, would pay a fee to Microsoft. Increasingly, PCs were delivered with pieces of application software also already installed.

As processing costs declined, the lines between PCs and other devices blurred. At the lower end of the processing and memory spectrum, handheld electronic organizers had begun to compete with the personal computer for applications such as electronic mail and portable computing. At the higher end, PCs had become increasing hard to distinguish from workstations. Historically, workstations had been several times faster and more expensive than PCs and had employed specially designed microprocessors and distinct operating systems. In recent years, however, PCs based on the fastest x86 microprocessors and Windows NT had begun to compete with the low end of the workstation market. PC makers had also extended their product lines to include servers, powerful computers that sat at the hubs of computer networks.

Customers. PC buyers were usually divided into four categories: large and midsize businesses government; small businesses and offices; individual consumers; and educational institutions. Exhibit 3 shows the portion of PC units and sales revenue accounted for by each set of customers.

Large and midsize businesses and government institutions usually had significant MIS departments that purchased, maintained, and supported PCs in a centralized fashion. Staff members were highly knowledgeable about PCs. They were charged with providing a reliable network of high-performance computers while also controlling information system costs. The capital cost of a PC was only a portion of the total cost associated with the machine. Once a PC was purchased, MIS staff had to tag it for identification purposes, configure software, install the machine at the user location, train the users, and help users when they encountered problems. By one estimate, corporations spent between $8,000 and $12,000 annually to support each desktop PC.[17] Most large organizations had a motley collection of PCs of various brands and vintages, making maintenance, support, and reliability of machines problematic.

Small businesses and offices typically lacked MIS staffs. Reliability, performance, support, service, price, brand, and channel recommendations (see below) all played roles in the choice of a PC by such organizations. By 1998, virtually all businesses had extensive experience with personal computers.

Individual consumers purchased PCs for home or home-office use. In choosing among brands, individuals relied heavily on the evaluations of independent organizations such as *Consumer Reports.* Individual buyers were a diverse lot, but tended to be more sensitive to price and more interested in a computer's brand name than were business buyers.[18] Some consumers also paid attention to the brand of the microprocessor. Since 1990, Intel had spent an estimated $3 billion on brand advertising for its microprocessors. Among individual consumers in the U.S., 30% of purchasers were first-time buyers in 1998. This figure was expected to decline to 16% by 2000.[19]

---

[16] Microsoft Corporation, 1998 Annual Report and Brian Goodstadt, "Standard & Poor's Industry Surveys, Computers: Software," March 12, 1999, pp. 9-10.

[17] Jeff Bliss, "Can NCs Live Up to Promise of Lower Cost?" *Computer Reseller News,* April 14, 1997.

[18] Roger Kay, analyst at International Data Corporation, April 22, 1999.

[19] Data from International Data Corporation.

In the eyes of some industry observers, buyers were divided into two true camps: Apple and Wintel. Many long-time owners of Apple computers were highly, almost emotionally, attached to the Apple standard, and they cursed the ascendancy of Wintel. Wintel customers, in contrast, tended to be less attached to a particular brand of computer. Apple was more successful in selling its PCs to individuals and educational institutions than to businesses, though it thrived among desktop publishers.

Channels. Personal computers flowed from manufacturers to customers via four channels: retail stores, distributors (working with small resellers), integrated resellers, and direct distribution.[20] Exhibit 4 shows the portion of PCs passing through each channel in various regions of the world.

Retailers such as Circuit City and CompUSA in the United States and Time Computers in Europe took delivery of PCs directly from manufacturers. Machines then passed through distribution centers owned by the retailers on their way to stores. In stores, retail displays and sales people played a significant role in helping customers select among models and manufacturers. Retail shelf space was limited, and even large superstores typically carried only 3-5 brands of PCs. Computer retailers operated on very thin margins. CompUSA, for example, earned overall gross margins of 14.1% and gross margins of roughly 7-9% on computers. It registered a net margin of 0.6% in 1998.

A handful of large distributors such as Ingram Micro (with 1998 sales of $22.0 billion) and Tech Data ($7.1 billion) supplied a full range of computer hardware and software to nearly 100,000 resellers.[21] These resellers, typically small owner-managed firms, worked with business customers to design, buy, configure, install, and support computer networks. According to one survey, 93% of end users accepted reseller recommendations for computer purchases.[22] Beyond charging for their value-added services, distributors and resellers typically marked up hardware by a total of 5-7%, though this mark-up had fallen in recent years.[23]

A few resellers were large enough to deal directly with manufacturers rather than buy through distributors. Integrated resellers such as MicroAge and Vanstar operated distribution centers, fielded extensive sales and service organizations, and in some cases, managed the PC networks of clients on an on-going basis. Vanstar, for instance, split its operations into three distinct segments. The largest, involved in the procurement and installation of corporate PC networks, earned a gross margin of 9.7% in 1998. A second segment devoted to network design and consulting reported a gross margin of 44.4%, while a third involved in on-going network support and maintenance earned a gross margin of 53.1%. Overall, Vanstar's net margin in 1998 was a thin 1.3%.

A fourth and final channel led directly from the manufacturer to the customer. A handful of PC manufacturers took orders directly from customers, either over the telephone and Internet or by means of internal sales forces. They then delivered PCs via third-party shippers such as UPS.

---

[20] Kasturi Rangan and Marie Bell, "Dell Online," HBS Case 598-116, pp. 7-8.

[21] Hassan Fattah, "1998 Forecast: The Channel Fights Back," *MC Technology Marketing Intelligence,* January 1998.

[22] Hassan Fattah, "1998 Forecast: The Channel Fights Back," *MC Technology Marketing Intelligence,* January 1998.

[23] Steven Fortuna and Pamela Pappachan, "Compaq Reengineers the Channel: Will It Be Enough to Slow Dell's Momentum?", Deutsche Morgan Grenfell Technology Group, June 11, 1997. David Kirkpatrick, "Now Everyone in PCs Wants to Be Like Mike," *Fortune,* September 8, 1997, pp. 91-92. Saul Hansell, "Is This the Factory of the Future?" *New York Times,* July 26, 1998.

Manufacturers usually agreed to buy back channel inventory that did not sell. In addition, they provided price protection to resellers and distributors: if the price of a computer fell while it was in the distribution channel, the manufacturer would reimburse the reseller or distributor accordingly. By one estimate, inventory buy-backs and price protection cost PC manufacturers 2.5 cents on every dollar of revenue. Manufacturers spent another 2.5 cents advertising to resellers and distributors, funding the market development activities of channel players, and managing product returns. PCs typically took four to five weeks to pass from the PC maker through distributors and resellers to customers.[24]

Manufacturing. Computer makers used basic assembly-line techniques to assemble PCs from standard parts. By the early 1990s, a manufacturer could buy and install the capital equipment required for an efficient PC assembly line, capable of assembling 250,000 PCs per year, with an investment of roughly a million dollars.[25] Contract manufacturers, many in Asia, also stood ready to make PCs on behalf of other firms. Exhibit 5 shows the structure of the costs typically incurred to assemble a PC that would retail for roughly $1,000.

The prices of components used to make PCs had typically declined 25-30% per year. In 1998, prices declined even faster, at a rate of roughly 1% per week. The financial crisis in Asia (where many component makers were located), increased competition faced by Intel, and gluts in the markets for several components all contributed to the faster decline in prices.[26]

Marketing and sales. PC manufacturers took a variety of approaches to marketing and sales. Companies such as Apple, Hewlett-Packard, and IBM spent as much as 2-3% of sales on advertising in order to develop recognizable brands. Others produced unbranded "white box" PCs and did not advertise to end users at all. Sales forces varied from the 25,000-strong sales organization of IBM to the virtually nonexistent sales forces of white-box PC makers. White-box manufacturers served 23% of the market in North America, 50% in Europe and Asia, and as much as 90% in China.[27]

DELL COMPUTER CORPORATION

> "It was too late to challenge the technical standard and the dealer network had been done already. Compaq was already very strong in retail. A new marketing and distribution strategy was something new, however."[28]

While a freshman at the University of Texas at Austin, 18-year-old Michael Dell started a part-time business in his dorm room: he formatted hard disks for personal computers and added extra memory, disk drives, and modems to IBM clones, selling them for as much as 40% less than comparable IBM machines. Reluctant to reveal this distraction from his studies, Dell hid PCs in his roommate's bathtub when his parents came to visit.[29]

---

[24] Steven Fortuna and Pamela Pappachan, "Compaq Reengineers the Channel: Will It Be Enough to Slow Dell's Momentum?", Deutsche Morgan Grenfell Technology Group, June 11, 1997.

[25] David B. Yoffie, "Apple Computer 1992," Harvard Business School Case 792-081, p. 4.

[26] Walter J. Winnitzki, "PC Hardware Outlook," Hambrecht and Quist, February 17, 1999.

[27] Mary Kwak and David B. Yoffie, "Apple Computer 1999," Harvard Business School Case 799-108, p. 9.

[28] Michael Dell quoted in John R. Halbrooks, *How to Really Deliver Superior Customer Service.*

[29] http://www.dell.com/

When revenue reached $80,000 per month in 1984, Dell dropped out of college and founded Dell Computer Corporation. Already, companies such as Exxon and Mobil were clamoring for 50 to 100 of Dell's machines at a time.[30] In 1985, Dell shifted from upgrading the machines of other manufacturers to assembling Dell-branded PCs. Revenue rose each subsequent year. (See Exhibit 6 for financial results.)

The basic elements of Dell's Direct Model came together early in the company's history and remained in place in 1998. The company dealt directly with end customers. It served primarily corporate customers and offered them high-performance PCs at relatively low prices. PCs were customized to buyer specifications, and assembly commenced only after Dell received an order.

Sales and marketing. While most competitors supplied machines based on orders from distributors, resellers, and retailers, Dell took orders directly from customers. Businesses and government institutions accounted for 77% of Dell's sales, home and small office users 18%, and educational institutions 5%. Very large customers, who purchased more than $1 million in PCs each year, provided 70% of the firm's revenue.[31] No single customer represented more than 2% of Dell's sales.[32]

Dell used indicators of a company's potential PC purchases, such as the number of employees and the number of PCs per employee, to divide customers into two groups: Relationship buyers and Transaction buyers.[33] Relationship buyers were large companies and institutions that could be counted on to place repeated orders for multiple PCs. Dell assigned a team of outside sales reps and inside sales reps to each Relationship account. Over a thousand outside sales reps spent their time in the field, understanding customer needs, courting customer personnel, helping customers configure their information systems, and promoting Dell's products and services. Inside sales reps, located in call centers, received telephone calls from assigned customers. Because Relationship customers typically specified particular PC configurations that their employees were allowed to order, the inside reps serving such customers simply took orders and provided product and delivery information. Both inside and outside sales reps had access to on-line information about a customer's entire purchase history and worked closely with Dell personnel responsible for after-sale service and technical support. Dell tended to realize its highest gross margins among Relationship buyers.[34]

Transaction buyers included small-to-medium businesses and home computer users. The company reached these customers via advertisements in trade journals and business publications, catalogs, and direct marketing. Customers who wanted to buy a PC or obtain information could reach an inside sales rep by calling 1-800-BUY-DELL (a different number than that used by Relationship buyers). Inside sales reps for Transaction buyers provided product information and actively encouraged customers to purchase more advanced PCs. Traditionally, Dell avoided the inexperienced Transaction buyer. Morton Topfer, Vice Chairman of Dell, explained: "Consumers at

---

[30] Das Narayandas and V. Kasturi Rangan, "Dell Computer Corporation," HBS Case 596-058, p. 5.

[31] Joan Magretta, "The Power of Virtual Integration: An Interview With Dell Computer's Michael Dell," *Harvard Business Review,* March-April 1998, p. 77.

[32] Joan Magretta, "The Power of Virtual Integration: An Interview With Dell Computer's Michael Dell," *Harvard Business Review,* March-April 1998, p. 77.

[33] Dell Computer Corporation, Form 10-K, February 1, 1998, pp. 6-7.

[34] Das Narayandas and V. Kasturi Rangan, "Dell Computer Corporation," HBS Case 596-058, p. 6. Dell Computer Corporation Form 10-K, February 1, 1998, p. 6.

retail don't know what they are looking for, other than price. We, on the other hand, like to sell to the educated consumer."[35]

In late 1990, Dell departed from its Direct Model and entered the retail channel. The move, Michael Dell said, would "[provide] us with the opportunity to generate significant new business and increase Dell's market penetration," especially among "PC customers—particularly at the entry level—who want to physically 'touch and feel' a unit before they buy."[36] Accordingly, Dell produced two lines of standard PCs and reached distribution agreements with computer superstores such as CompUSA and warehouse clubs such as Sam's Club. Sales through the retail channel were brisk, but Dell soon found that it was losing money on retail sales. Exhibit 7 compares the margins which Dell earned in the direct and retail channels. Retail losses contributed to Dell's poor financial results in 1993, as did a major recall of notebook computers. In 1994, Dell withdrew from retail stores.

As Dell had grown, it had subdivided its customer base into finer and finer categories. In 1994, buyers were classified as large customers or small customers. By 1996, the large customer classification had been split into large companies, midsize companies, and government and educational institutions. By 1998, large companies had been split into global enterprise accounts and other large companies; government and educational accounts into federal, state and local, and educational; and small customers into small companies and consumers.[37] In addition, sales efforts were divided by region and, within region, by country. Michael Dell explained that such divisions were accomplished "for a lot of reasons. One is to identify unique opportunities and economics. The other is purely a managerial issue: you can't possibly manage something well if it's too big."[38]

Dell launched its Web site www.dell.com in July of 1996, and increasingly, customers were using the site to contact Dell. Transaction buyers could obtain product information, configure a computer system, check pricing, place an order, and track an order's progress. They could also gain access to the complete catalog of service and support information used by Dell's service representatives.

For thousands of Relationship customers, Dell had designed custom Premier Pages[SM]. On these secure Web pages, an employee of a customer might find pager numbers for their Dell account team or a list of computer configurations that had been approved by the customer's purchasing manager, for instance. By December of 1998, transactions totaling $10 million per day involved www.dell.com.[39]

Occasionally, Dell sold to resellers. In December 1997, for instance, it sent a flyer to a limited number of resellers offering older systems to resellers at prices 15-20% below the prices quoted at

---

[35] Das Narayandas and V. Kasturi Rangan, "Dell Computer Corporation," HBS Case 596-058, p. 5.

[36] Dell press release, "Dell PCs to be Offered Through Soft Warehouse Superstores—Expands Reach to Individuals and Small Businesses," September 10, 1990.

[37] Joan Magretta, "The Power of Virtual Integration: An Interview With Dell Computer's Michael Dell," *Harvard Business Review,* March-April 1998, p. 78.

[38] Joan Magretta, "The Power of Virtual Integration: An Interview With Dell Computer's Michael Dell," *Harvard Business Review,* March-April 1998, p. 78.

[39] Scott Thurm, "Leading the PC Pack: Lots of Computer Companies Offer Services on the Web. Why Does Dell Stand Out?" *Wall Street Journal,* December 7, 1998, p. R27. Dell takes orders totaling $3 million of sales per day via its Web site. Another $7 million per day involve customers who browse online, but order in other ways.

www.dell.com. However, Dell did not allow returns or provide price protection.[40] Roughly 5% of Dell's systems were purchased by resellers.[41]

Production, logistics, and procurement. Dell manufactured machines that were—within the guidelines of a broad menu—tailored to customer needs. The company made customized PCs based on actual orders and held no finished goods inventory of standardized machines. Dell operated manufacturing facilities in Austin, Texas; Limerick, Ireland; Penang, Malaysia; and Xiamen, China. A fifth site was slated for Alvorada, Brazil. Daily meetings matched production schedules with sales flows. Keith Maxwell, Dell's vice president for worldwide operations, commented:[42]

> [The current production system] requires that the whole organization be integrated. You've eliminated buffers. When you have no buffers and you have no inventory, the whole organization has to work together. There is no way to let things pile up, because you have no piles.

Once received, an order was sent electronically to the appropriate manufacturing facility. There, a computer generated a parts list for the order and assigned the order a bar code for tracking purposes. Dell's older facilities were organized in assembly-line fashion: as the chassis of the machine traveled down the line, the hardware specified by the parts list was added. Its newest facility in Austin employed five-person manufacturing cells: parts for a PC were compiled in a bin, the bin sent to a cell, and the computer assembled there. The company found that the cells delivered machines with fewer defects more efficiently.[43]

After assembly, the machine moved to a software loading zone. There, special machines and a very-high-speed computer network installed software specified by the customer: an operating system, commercial application software, and diagnostic software. For some corporate customers, Dell also loaded proprietary software. The fully equipped machine proceeded to a "burn-in" area, where it was tested for several hours. Finally, it was boxed along with accessories and shipped to the customer. Dell maintained shipping contracts with a number of third-party shippers such as UPS and Airborne Express.

The production process, from order entry to shipping, took about a day and a half.[44] In the midst of the Asian economic crisis in October of 1997, for instance, Dell received an emergency order from the Nasdaq stock exchange for eight servers. The exchange's existing servers were being strained by unprecedented trading volumes. Dell shipped the customized, tested servers within 36 hours.[45] At the same time, the production process could handle large orders. Also in late 1997, for example, Dell built 2,000 desktop computers and 4,000 servers for Wal-Mart, loaded the machines with proprietary software, and shipped them to 2,000 Wal-Mart stores.[46]

---

[40] Kimberly Caisse, "Dell Uses Channel to Move System Inventory," *Computer Reseller News,* January 12, 1998.

[41] Data from International Data Corporation.

[42] Kirk Ladendorf, "Dell Computer Works to Improve Custom Assembly Process," *Austin American-Statesman,* September 29, 1998.

[43] Kasturi Rangan and Marie Bell, "Dell Online," HBS Case 598-116, p. 3.

[44] Kasturi Rangan and Marie Bell, "Dell Online," HBS Case 598-116, p. 4.

[45] Dell Computer Corporation, Annual Report, 1998, p. 15.

[46] Dell Computer Corporation, Annual Report, 1998, p. 23.

Dell worked closely with suppliers to arrange just-in-time delivery of parts. Dell had whittled its days of inventory down from 32 in 1995 to 7 in 1998.[47] Since 1992, it had reduced the number of suppliers for its Austin facility from 204 to 47.[48] With remaining suppliers, Dell maintained close electronic links, communicating replenishment needs to some vendors on an hourly basis. The electronic links allowed Dell to direct some suppliers' shipments straight to its customers. Computer monitors supplied by Sony, for instance, never passed through Dell's facilities. Rather, Dell communicated the order for a monitor to Sony and to its shipper. The shipper picked up the computer at Dell's site, picked up the monitor at Sony's, brought the boxes together, and delivered them simultaneously to the customer. A web site customized to Sony gave both Sony and Dell continuous access to ordering and manufacturing information.[49] Michael Dell explained:[50]

> ...what's the point in having a monitor put on a truck to Austin, Texas, and then taken off the truck and sent on a little tour around the warehouse, only to be put back on another truck? That's just a big waste of time and money, unless we get our jollies from touching monitors, which we don't.

Dell encouraged suppliers to locate warehouses and production facilities close to its assembly operations. Co-location was particularly easy to arrange near Dell's major facilities in Austin, where local and state government officials had worked since the 1950s and 1960s to attract high-technology companies. Now known as "Silicon Hills," the Austin region included 72 semiconductor manufacturers and related suppliers, 160 computer and electronics manufacturing firms, more than 600 small and midsized software companies, and 825 technology consulting and services firms.[51]

Products and services. Dell provided two lines of desktop computers, one designed to be reliable, stable, and highly compatible with corporate networks, the other intended to incorporate the latest technology. Desktop computers ranged from $1,250 machines for individual consumers to $4,000 PC for corporate networks. The company also offered two lines of notebook computers, with a similar distinction between the lines. A line of network servers and, since 1998, a line of workstations filled out the company's product range.[52] Dell's workstations and servers used Windows NT and x86 microprocessors.

In addition to selling hardware, Dell offered to install off-the-shelf software and a customer's proprietary software. On a custom basis, it installed and tested computers and networks at customer sites. A new venture, Dell Financial Services, offered leasing, technology planning, and asset management services.

After a sale, Dell supported its products in several ways. Online, Dell offered 50,000 pages of customer support information. A customer with a problem could also reach a technical support staff

---

[47] Dell Computer Corporation, Annual Report, 1998, p. 6.

[48] Kasturi Rangan and Marie Bell, "Dell Online," HBS Case 598-116, p. 4.

[49] David Joachim, "Dell Links Virtual Supply Chain," *InternetWeek,* November 2, 1998.

[50] Joan Magretta, "The Power of Virtual Integration: An Interview With Dell Computer's Michael Dell," *Harvard Business Review,* March-April 1998, p. 76.

[51] Julie Borenstein, Stephan Feldgoise, Mike Harmon, Eric Jeck, and Steve Latham, "Austin, Texas—Silicon Hills," in Michael E. Porter, ed., *Case Studies in Competition and Competitiveness,* Harvard Business School, May 1997.

[52] Dell Computer Corporation, Form 10-K, February 1, 1998, pp. 7-8.

of 1,300 representatives via a hotline that was manned 24 hours a day. Upon receiving a call, support personnel would retrieve a file containing details of the customer's computer, starting with the original order and recording all subsequent service calls. Using the diagnostic software installed in the factory, the customer and the support specialist could resolve the problem over the telephone in approximately 90% of cases. For problems requiring an on-site visit, Dell contracted out service to companies such as Xerox, Wang Global, and Unisys rather than employ service personnel itself. Most problems requiring an on-site visit were resolved with 24 to 48 hours.[53] Dell was working with service providers to create measures of service quality and to improve the flow of data between them and Dell.[54] Dell also conveyed information concerning defective parts from the service providers back to its suppliers.[55]

In most industry surveys, customers rated Dell's sales, products, and services highly relative to the competition. Exhibits 8 and 9 report the results from a survey of corporate PC buyers and from *Consumer Reports*, respectively. Exhibits 10a and 10b show, for the consumer and business portions of the market, the prices of Dell PCs relative to comparably configured machines offered by rivals.

Firm infrastructure. For much of its history, Dell was managed as an entrepreneurial start-up with few formal control systems. Growth pains culminated in a net loss in 1993. Dell's supply of cash fell as low as $20 million in 1993, a thin cushion for a company with annual sales of nearly $3 billion.

Subsequently, Michael Dell hired a number of seasoned managers, including veterans from Motorola, Apple Computer, Sun Microsystems, Intel, and Electronic Data Systems. Morton Topfer, formerly at Motorola, took the position of Vice Chairman and focused especially on operations and manufacturing. Dell himself, at 33 the longest tenured chief executive in the PC industry, concentrated on products and market trends.[56]

In 1998, senior management paid special attention to several performance metrics. The company monitored days of inventory by product component. It managed receivables and payables such that, on average, it received payment for its products five days before it had to pay suppliers. Managers examined margins, selling price, and overhead by customer segment, product, and country.[57] As an overall indicator of company performance, the senior management team focused on return on invested capital.[58] Dell's FY 1998 return on invested capital was 186%.

COMPETITION

Dell's financial returns and rapid growth caused its rivals to take both notice and action. (Exhibit 11 compares Dell's growth rate, profitability, and other characteristics to competitors'.) Dell faced a diverse set of competitors, typified by IBM, Compaq, Hewlett-Packard, and Gateway.

---

[53] Kasturi Rangan and Marie Bell, "Dell Online," HBS Case 598-116, p. 4.

[54] Joan Magretta, "The Power of Virtual Integration: An Interview With Dell Computer's Michael Dell," *Harvard Business Review,* March-April 1998, p. 75.

[55] Kevin Rollins, "Using Information to Speed Execution," *Harvard Business Review,* March-April 1998, p. 81.

[56] Scott McCartney, "Michael Dell Shifts From Whiz to Wisdom," *Houston Chronicle,* February 1, 1995.

[57] Kevin Rollins, "Using Information to Speed Execution," *Harvard Business Review,* March-April 1998, p. 81.

[58] Dell Computer Corporation, Annual Report, 1997, p. 3.

IBM. Since sparking the growth of the PC market in the early 1980s, IBM had fallen to third place among PC makers in terms of dollar market share worldwide. IBM remained the largest information technology corporation in the world, offering an extremely broad range of IT hardware, software, and services. Its personal computing products covered the spectrum from sub-$1,000 PCs to high-end servers and workstations. IBM's vaunted sales and service organization gave it full access to corporate MIS managers. The sales force accounted for 5% of its PC sales, distributors and resellers for 70%, and retailers for 18%.

IBM was among the first PC makers to recognize the challenge posed by direct distribution.[59] Starting in the early 1990s, it launched a series of initiatives to improve coordination with distributors and resellers: a Joint Manufacturing Authorization Program was followed by an Integration and Assembly Program and an Enhanced Integration and Assembly Program. In these programs, IBM shipped "heavily configured" PCs to authorized distributors and resellers, who then completed the configuration of the machine to customer specifications and forwarded it on to the customer.

In 1995, IBM moved to an Authorized Assembly Program (AAP). Here, IBM shipped "lightly configured" PCs, known as Model 0s, to downstream partners. Model 0s were barely functional computers, containing only a motherboard, a floppy drive, and a video card. Partners in the channel completed the assembly to customer specifications, using components purchased from IBM. Until September 1998, components were always shipped from IBM facilities. Hence a microprocessor might travel from Intel's warehouse in Arizona to IBM's facility in North Carolina and back to a partner's assembly plant in Arizona.[60] IBM set component prices such that total costs, including assembly costs, were the same for a channel-assembled and IBM-assembled PC.[61] Under AAP, IBM continued to build Model 0 PCs based on forecasts, not on actual customer orders.

A number of major distributors and resellers, including MicroAge, Ingram Micro, and Tech Data, had invested tens of millions of dollars to build plants that assembled IBM PCs (and by 1998, PCs with other brand names).[62] By 1998, roughly half of IBM's shipments of desktop PCs to MicroAge, for instance, were thought to be Model 0s.[63] Overall, between one-quarter and one-third of IBM's PCs were finished by one of 14 channel partners.[64]

AAP enabled IBM and its partners to deliver customized PCs rapidly without holding large amounts of inventory. One partner reported that the program improved the inventory turnover rate of its IBM stock from 10-12x to 20x. At the same time, the partner's fill rate—the portion of time that it had a desired product in stock—rose from 80% to 95%. The program also reduced the need for resellers to "tear down" new PCs, that is, take them apart and reconfigure them to meet customer needs. Tear downs were costly and appeared to cause quality problems. MicroAge reported that

---

[59] Steven Fortuna and Pamela Pappachan, "Compaq Reengineers the Channel: Will It Be Enough to Slow Dell's Momentum?", Deutsche Morgan Grenfell Technology Group, June 11, 1997.

[60] Daniel Lyons, "Games Dealers Play," *Forbes,* October 19, 1998, pp. 132-134.

[61] Steven Fortuna and Pamela Pappachan, "Compaq Reengineers the Channel: Will It Be Enough to Slow Dell's Momentum?", Deutsche Morgan Grenfell Technology Group, June 11, 1997.

[62] Daniel Lyons, "Games Dealers Play," *Forbes,* October 19, 1998, pp. 132-134.

[63] Steven Fortuna and Pamela Pappachan, "Compaq Reengineers the Channel: Will It Be Enough to Slow Dell's Momentum?", Deutsche Morgan Grenfell Technology Group, June 11, 1997.

[64] Hassan Fattah, "1998 Forecast: The Channel Fights Back," *MC Technology Marketing Intelligence,* January 1998.

2.0% to 2.25% of IBM-built machines had defects after a tear-down while only 0.5% of its AAP-assembled machines had problems.[65]

Even as it increased coordination with channel partners, IBM explored ways to expand its own direct sales. To combat IBM clones, IBM had launched an autonomous division named "Ambra" in 1992. The division produced low-end PCs at low cost by contracting out most operations, and it sold Ambra PCs by mail-order and telephone. The Ambra division was shut down in 1994.[66] In April 1998, IBM opened a web site that allowed customers to buy PCs.[67] The site referred business customers to resellers, who then set prices and fulfilled orders. Individual consumers could use the web site to purchase standardized PCs directly from IBM, without going through a retail outlet. For consumers, the site offered the Aptiva line of PCs, which Taiwan-based Acer built on behalf of IBM. Later in 1998, IBM introduced its first program to enable businesses to buy a small set of products directly: the Netfinity Direct program allowed large enterprises to purchase a particular line of IBM servers without going through resellers.

Exhibit 12 shows financial results for IBM as a whole. Personal computers represented 23% of IBM's corporate revenue. Its PC division lost $39 million before taxes in 1996, $161 million in 1997, and $992 million in 1998. The company reported, however, that PC operations returned to profitability in the fourth quarter of 1998.[68]

Compaq. Founded in 1982, Compaq surpassed IBM in 1994 to become the world's largest manufacturer of personal computers. By 1998, Compaq offered a broad range of computers, from sub-$1,000 PCs to $2 million fail-safe servers.[69] With its $3 billion acquisition of Tandem Computers in 1997, Compaq doubled its sales and support staff to 8,000 people and gained access to the corporate data centers which Tandem's fail-safe computers had served.[70] Its $9 billion acquisition of DEC in 1998 gave Compaq, among other assets, DEC's highly regarded service and consulting staff of 22,000 people. In the words of Eckhard Pfeiffer, Compaq's CEO, "We want to do it all, and we want to do it now."[71]

The company employed the full range of PC channels, selling 67% of its PCs through 44,000 distributors and resellers, 25% at retail, and 4% direct.[72] Compaq served individual consumers and business customers in quite different ways. For consumers, Compaq built standard PCs to stock, either in its own factories or the factories of Asian contractors. It distributed to consumers primarily through retail stores. Compaq launched an online catalog in 1993, but abandoned the initiative in

---

[65] Steven Fortuna and Pamela Pappachan, "Compaq Reengineers the Channel: Will It Be Enough to Slow Dell's Momentum?", Deutsche Morgan Grenfell Technology Group, June 11, 1997, p. 3.

[66] "IBM's Ambra PC: A Lesson Learned," *Marketing,* February 24, 1994. Jaikumar Vijayan, "IBM Cuts PC Force, Kills Ambra Corp.," *Computerworld,* August 1, 1994.

[67] "IBM Announces New Web Site, Enabling Customers to Purchase IBM PC Products Via the Internet," IBM press release, April 17, 1998.

[68] William M. Buckeley, "IBM Had '98 PC Pretax Loss of Nearly $1 Billion," *Wall Street Journal,* March 25, 1999.

[69] Gary McWilliams, Ira Sager, Paul G. Judge, and Peter Burrows, "Power Play," *Business Week,* February 9, 1998, pp. 90-97.

[70] Eric Nee, "Compaq Computer Corp.," *Forbes,* January 12, 1998, pp. 90-94.

[71] Gary McWilliams, Ira Sager, Paul G. Judge, and Peter Burrows, "Power Play," *Business Week,* February 9, 1998, pp. 92.

[72] Gary McWilliams, "Computers: Mimicking Dell, Compaq to Sell its PCs Directly," *Wall Street Journal,* November 11, 1998, p. B1.

the face of channel resistance.[73]   In 1996, Compaq introduced a toll-free telephone number that allowed consumers to order PCs directly from the company. According to one analyst, "the results have been tepid, mainly because Compaq kept its prices high to avoid angering dealers."[74]

Compaq's production and distribution system for business customers had evolved over time. In late 1995, Compaq moved from a production system in which it built business PCs according to its own forecast to one in which it built according to forecasts made by channel members. This permitted Compaq to reduce the inventory it held for PCs from 60 days to 30 days. Because resellers and distributors held 35 more days of inventory, a Compaq computer delivered in mid-1997 was typically 65 days old before it reached a customer through the reseller channel.

In July of 1997, Compaq announced a new effort to coordinate efforts with distributors and resellers, an Optimized Distribution Model (ODM). Under ODM, PCs would be built only after an order was received, and orders and delivery would continue to go through distributors and resellers. Relatively standard machines would be built to order in Compaq's plants and delivered rapidly, ready for installation, to resellers. More complicated, customized machines would be assembled in a two-step process: Compaq would ship stripped-down PCs, similar to IBM's Model 0s, to channel partners. Members of the channel would handle the final assembly and configuration. Compaq expected to finish 80% of its corporate PCs in its own factory, with channel partners completing the other 20%.[75]

Under ODM, Compaq would offer only two weeks of price protection, down from as much as seven weeks. In late 1998, the total inventory in the Compaq / distributor / reseller channel was estimated to have declined to 45-50 days.[76] Analysts thought that ODM might eventually reduce total inventory to 25 days.[77]

Following the DEC acquisition, announced in January of 1998, distributors and resellers were concerned that Compaq would use DEC customer relationships to sell directly to corporate accounts, especially to large corporations. In June, Compaq confirmed that it would do so. Compaq's vice president of marketing and communications assured that "the price of systems bought through the channel will be the same as systems purchased directly from Compaq, and resellers will still make a profit."[78]

In November of 1998, Compaq unveiled its DirectPlus Program, intended to sell customized PCs directly to small and midsize companies. Under the program, Compaq would offer a new line of computers via the telephone and Internet. The line would be available only through DirectPlus, and prices would be lower than those charged by resellers for comparable Compaq machines. Compaq offered to pay resellers a referral fee of 6-7% on orders that they passed along to DirectPlus. To accompany the new computer line, Compaq introduced support services, software modules, and leasing programs that might attract small and midsize business customers. Compaq intended to ship DirectPlus orders as early as the next business day and, on average, within five

---

[73] Gary McWilliams, "Computers: Mimicking Dell, Compaq to Sell its PCs Directly," *Wall Street Journal,* November 11, 1998, p. B1.

[74] Saul Hansell, "Compaq Plans to Sell Directly to Consumers," *New York Times,* November 11, 1998.

[75] David Kirkpatrick, "Now Everyone in PCs Wants to Be Like Mike," *Fortune,* September 8, 1997, pp. 91-92.

[76] Robert P. Anastasi, Neal F. Johnson, J. Drennan Lane, and Stephanie L. Spinner, "The Computer Sales Channel: Third Quarter Demand Survey," Robinson-Humphrey, September 23, 1998.

[77] Steven Fortuna and Pamela Pappachan, "Compaq Reengineers the Channel: Will It Be Enough to Slow Dell's Momentum?", Deutsche Morgan Grenfell Technology Group, June 11, 1997.

[78] Dan Briody and Ed Scannell, "Direct Approach," *InfoWorld,* June 15, 1998.

days.[79] Observers expected Compaq to turn over some manufacturing of the new line to resellers who had invested in assembly operations.[80]

Exhibit 13 provides financial information for Compaq. Prior to recent acquisitions, PCs constituted virtually all of Compaq's revenue. According to analysts, Compaq relied heavily on profits from its PC server business. In February of 1998, IBM cut its server prices sharply, passing along cost savings made possible by its efforts to streamline production and distribution. In March, Compaq announced that it would break even in the first quarter of 1998 rather than post a profit expected to exceed $500 million.[81]

Hewlett-Packard. Hewlett-Packard (HP) was founded in 1939 as a maker of scientific instruments but, by 1998, offered a broad range of scientific equipment, computers, printers, and other computer peripherals. In the PC business, HP maintained a reputation for high quality and performance and sold to more demanding customers. Its product range was comparable to Compaq's, but it earned a smaller portion of its revenue from the low end of the consumer and business markets. The company sold 75% of its PCs through distributors and resellers, 23% through retail channels, and less than 1% directly to customers via its sales force.

In September of 1997, shortly after Compaq announced its ODM program, HP unveiled a similar Extended Solutions Partnership Program (ESPP). Under ESPP, HP would build large corporate orders to customer specifications in its factories. Orders would be delivered to resellers or, at the reseller's request, shipped directly to the customer. Ten channel partners would complete assembly of some HP machines. A Web site would allow customers to order products over the Internet for delivery through resellers. HP hoped that the program would allow it to reduce price protection to two weeks, cut down defects, and shave 5% - 15% off of its prices.[82]

HP courted distributors and resellers and steadfastly refused to attach the word "direct" to any of its efforts related to business customers. Even before Compaq announced its DirectPlus program, 59% of resellers reported that they were more willing to promote HP products as a result of IBM's and Compaq's movement toward direct sales.[83] Following the DirectPlus announcement, HP initiated an advertising campaign aimed at resellers to small and midsize businesses and announced incentives for resellers to switch from Compaq to HP products. Duncan Campbell, HP's worldwide group marketing manager for personal systems, explained, "We are pleased that Compaq is going direct. They have made a bad call, and the channel should make them pay."[84]

Nonetheless, in October 1998, HP launched a modest effort to set up direct sales on the World Wide Web.[85] HP Shopping Village, a web service previously providing refurbished HP computers to individuals, was expanded to allow consumers to buy new PCs directly from HP. Business customers could use a similar web site to purchase HP PCs, but like IBM's web site, HP's required

---

[79] Saul Hansell, "Compaq Plans to Sell Directly to Consumers," *New York Times,* November 11, 1998. Rob Guth, "Compaq Goes After Direct-sales Model," *InfoWorld,* November 16, 1998, p. 10.

[80] "Mimicking Dell, Compaq to Sell Its PCs Directly to Customers," Dow Jones Online News, November 11, 1998.

[81] Evan Ramsted, "Compaq Stumbles as PCs Weather New Blow," *Wall Street Journal,* March 9, 1998, p. B1.

[82] Jeff Bliss, "HP Unveils Assembly Plan," *Computer Reseller News,* September 15, 1997.

[83] John Roberts, "Could Direct Moves Backfire?" *Computer Reseller News,* July 20, 1998.

[84] Kelley Damore and Steven Burke, "HP Responds to Compaq Direct Plan," *Computer Reseller News,* November 23, 1998.

[85] Eric Nee, "Defending the Desktop," *Forbes,* December 28, 1998, pp. 53-54.

business customers to complete purchases through resellers. Lew Platt, CEO of HP, hinted that business customers might not have to go through resellers in the future: "You can't ignore what Dell has done.... I could give you a list of names of really large customers who have said to HP, 'Either do business with us directly or you are not going to do business with us.'"[86]

Exhibit 14 provides financial information for Hewlett-Packard. Personal computers constituted 20-25% of corporate revenue in 1998 and earned an operating margin estimated at 3%.[87]

Gateway 2000. Founded in an Iowa farmhouse in 1985, Gateway 2000 was the world's second largest direct marketer of PCs, trailing only Dell. Like Dell, Gateway took orders from customers, produced PCs to their specifications, loaded software on the PCs, and shipped machines directly to customers. The company maintained a force of inside and some outside sales reps, provided extensive telephone- and Web-based technical support, and contracted with third-parties for on-site technical service. The company prided itself on efficient, high-quality manufacturing facilities in South Dakota, Virginia, Utah, and Malaysia and reported that it was usually among the first PC makers to introduce the latest Intel microprocessors.

Gateway's product line ranged from sub-$1,000 PCs to servers and workstations. Its core customers were sophisticated home and small office users, and accordingly, its sales of both inexpensive and high-end PCs were relatively modest. In 1998, 58% of Gateway's sales were to home and small office computer users, 28% to businesses, and 13% to educational and government institutions.[88] Roughly a third of Gateway's revenue from business customers came from small businesses. The company's advertisements—in newspapers, family-oriented magazines, and computer trade publications as well as on television—featured its mascots, a set of Holstein cows. Black and white Holstein spots were featured on Gateway's distinctive packaging.

Gateway grew at annual clip of 39% from 1991 to 1996 and surpassed Dell's U.S. sales briefly in 1994. In 1997, however, sales growth slowed to 25%, and net income fell by half. Attempts to clear excess inventory, charges related to an acquisition, and an aborted effort to develop a new customer information system were said to have contributed to the decline in profits.

Slowing growth prompted a number of initiatives. The 1997 acquisition of Advanced Logic Research eased Gateway's entry into the PC server business. At the same time, the firm set up Gateway Major Accounts, Inc., a company within the company, to service large corporate, government, and educational accounts. The company also opened 144 Gateway Country Stores, retail showrooms, in the United States in 1997 and 1998. In the stores, customers could view Gateway products and place orders. The stores did not stock products.

In 1998, Gateway scaled back its brief efforts to lure major accounts and refocused its energy on small businesses. Observers reported that "Gateway couldn't afford to pay for the expanded sales team it needed to knock on the doors of big corporate clients."[89] A new division, Gateway Partners, was slated to work with resellers.[90] The firm also removed the Holstein cows from its ads and moved its administrative headquarters—including its IT services, marketing, and finance divisions—from North Sioux City, South Dakota, to San Diego, California. The company had tried

---

[86] Ephraim Schwartz and David Pendery, "HP Expands Direct Sales Offerings," *InfoWorld Daily News,* October 1, 1998.

[87] Eric Nee, "Defending the Desktop," *Forbes,* December 28, 1998, pp. 53-54.

[88] Data from International Data Corporation.

[89] Roger O. Crockett, "Gateway Loses the Folksy Shtick," *Business Week,* July 6, 1998, pp. 80-84.

[90] Evan Ramstad, "Gateway Unit to Bolster Ties to PC Dealers," *Wall Street Journal,* April 20, 1998, p. B2.

but failed to fill roughly 250 job openings in South Dakota. Exhibit 15 provides financial information for Gateway.

RECENT DEVELOPMENTS

In late 1998, Dell claimed that its advantage in inventory turnover remained very large,[91] but the price differential between Dell's products and its competitors' had all but vanished.[92] Manufacturer and channel inventories for PCs from Dell's rivals were declining as planned, but availability was now a problem. Customers reported that they could not obtain certain models of IBM PCs and, to a lesser extent, Compaq PCs.[93] A skeptic of channel assembly argued, "There are so many mechanics involved in this and so many egos to go with it. You have to change cultures before this will work."[94]

An observer of the channel reported that "a number of [distributors, resellers, and retailers are] exploring 'strategic alternatives' as a direct result of moves by these manufacturers."[95] MicroAge, one of the resellers that had set up assembly operations, had established the brand name "Pinacor" for its distribution operation. Its assembly facility was allegedly running at 25% capacity in late 1998.[96] The retailer CompUSA had started to sell inexpensive computers under its own brand name.[97]

In public statements, Dell's senior management appeared unconcerned about the efforts of its rivals. "The things HP, IBM, and company have done have added more credibility to us than anything we could have done," said Vice Chairman Morton Topfer.[98] Concerning Compaq's plan to sell direct, Michael Dell joked, "It's like we're the best baseball player and Compaq is the best basketball player. Now they want to play baseball."[99]

Glossary[1]

Application: a program that helps a user accomplish a specific task, for example, a word processing program or a spreadsheet program. Application programs are distinguished from system programs, which control the computer and run the application programs, and utilities, which are small helper programs.

---

[91] Craig Zarley, "Resellers Fight Dell," *Informationweek,* April 20, 1998.

[92] Hassan Fattah, "1998 Forecast: The Channel Fights Back," *MC Technology Marketing Intelligence,* January 1998. Craig Zarley and Christina Torode, "The Party's Over: Dell Loses Pricing Advantage," *Computer Reseller News,* December 15, 1997.

[93] Robert P. Anastasi, Neal F. Johnson, J. Drennan Lane, and Stephanie L. Spinner, "The Computer Sales Channel: Third Quarter Demand Survey," Robinson-Humphrey, September 23, 1998.

[94] Tony Amico, director of PC Channels at International Data Corporation, quoted in Hassan Fattah, "1998 Forecast: The Channel Fights Back," *MC Technology Marketing Intelligence,* January 1998.

[95] Marty Wolf, "IBM, Compaq Strategies 'Unsettling'," *Computer Reseller News,* July 6, 1998.

[96] Daniel Lyons, "Games Dealers Play," *Forbes,* October 19, 1998, pp. 132-134.

[97] Daniel Lyons, "Games Dealers Play," *Forbes,* October 19, 1998, pp. 132-134.

[98] Christopher Palmeri, "The Perils of Being Number One," *Forbes,* December 1, 1997, p. 44.

[99] Andrew Serwer, "Michael Dell Turns the PC World Inside Out," *Fortune,* September 8, 1997, pp. 76-86.

Microprocessor: the semiconductor in a personal computer that performs mathematical and logical operations based on programmed instructions; the central processing unit in a PC.

Motherboard: the main circuit board inside a computer, which contains the microprocessor, memory, and other basic components. Additional boards, called daughter boards, can be plugged into the motherboard.

Operating system: the main control program of a computer that schedules tasks, manages storage, and handles communication with peripherals. The operating system presents a basic user interface when no applications are open, and all applications must communicate with the operating system.

Random-access memory: the working memory of a computer. RAM is the memory used for storing data temporarily while working on it, running application programs, and so forth. "Random access" refers to the fact that any area of RAM can be accessed directly and immediately, in contrast to other media such as a magnetic tape where the tape must be wound to the point where the data is.

Read-only memory: memory that can be read but not changed. Read-only memory holds its contents even when a PC is turned off. Data is placed in ROM only once and stays there permanently.

Video card: a circuit board that enables a computer to display information on its screen. The resolution, number of colors, and refresh rate of a monitor is determined by the kind of video card used, plus the limitations of the monitor itself.

[1] Based on *Computer Currents* High-Tech Dictionary, http://www.currents.net/resources/ dictionary/dictionary.phtml.

Exhibit 1: **PC Market Size, 1982 – 1998**

	82	84	86	88	90	91	92	93	94	95	96	97	98
United States													
Units (mm)	3.0	6.7	6.9	8.7	9.5	9.5	11.8	15.6	18.7	23.0	26.5	31.5	36.3
Dollars (bn)	4.5	12.8	14.5	20.6	23.3	22.0	24.6	30.1	37.4	53.9	64.8	70.0	74.6
Worldwide													
Units (mm)					23.8	25.8	30.8	39.0	47.0	58.9	69.2	79.9	90.3
Dollars (bn)					60.9	59.8	63.7	73.1	100	131	161	170	170

Source: International Data Corporation

Exhibit 2a: **PC Market Shares in the United States, 1980 – 1998 (unit share, in percent)**

	80	83	87	89	90	91	92	93	94	95	96	97	98
Apple	29.3	20.0	14.0	10.7	10.9	13.7	13.2	13.4	11.5	10.6	6.4	4.1	4.6
AST/Tandy	37.6	5.0	2.0	1.7	1.8	2.7	2.8	4.0	3.5	2.3	2.4	-	-
Compaq	-	-	7.5	4.4	4.5	4.1	5.7	9.4	11.7	10.8	12.9	16.0	16.7
Dell	-	-	-	0.9	1.0	1.6	3.7	4.8	4.2	4.9	6.8	9.3	13.2
Gateway	-	-	-	0.2	1.0	2.5	3.6	4.3	5.1	5.1	6.1	7.1	8.4
HP	5.3	-	-	-	-	-	-	-	2.4	3.8	5.3	6.6	7.8
IBM	-	42.0	28.0	16.9	16.1	14.1	11.7	13.0	8.7	7.9	8.3	8.7	8.2
Packard Bell	-	-	-	3.3	3.9	4.7	5.3	6.4	14.3	14.4	11.4	8.8	6.2
Others	27.8	33.0	48.5	61.9	60.8	56.6	54.0	44.7	38.6	40.2	40.4	39.4	34.9

Source: Data for 1980-91 from Das Narayandas and V. Kasturi Rangan, "Dell Computer Corporation," HBS Case 596-058. Data for 1992-98 from International Data Corporation.

Exhibit 2b: **PC Market Shares Worldwide, 1990 – 1998 (unit share, in percent)**

	90	91	92	93	94	95	96	97	98	Headquarters
Acer	-	-	-	-	2.8	3.6	4.1	3.5	3.1	Taiwan
Apple	7.1	9.6	9.0	9.4	8.5	8.0	5.4	3.2	3.4	California
AST/Tandy	2.7	1.9	1.9	3.0	3.0	-	-	-	-	California
Compaq	3.6	3.4	5.1	7.9	10.3	10.0	10.5	12.7	14.7	Texas
Dell	-	-	2.3	3.0	2.8	3.2	4.3	5.9	8.6	Texas
Gateway	-	-	-	1.8	-	-	-	3.4	4.0	South Dakota / California
HP	-	-	-	1.8	2.8	3.5	4.3	5.6	6.3	California
IBM	12.7	11.1	10.4	10.8	8.7	8.2	8.9	9.0	8.8	New York
Packard Bell	-	2.0	2.3	2.9	7.1	7.3	6.1	5.2	4.2	California
Toshiba	-	2.6	2.0	2.0	2.5	2.5	3.9	4.1	3.5	Japan
Others	73.9	69.4	67	57.4	51.5	53.7	52.5	47.4	43.4	

Source: International Data Corporation

Exhibit 3a: **U.S. PC Sales by Customer Category (market share by dollar value)**

	1994	1995	1996	1997	1998
Large / midsize business & government	45.0%	47.4%	44.6%	43.1%	42.3%
Small business & office	24.3%	22.7%	24.8%	24.1%	23.7%
Consumers (home)	27.4%	34.7%	32.6%	28.0%	28.7%
Education	3.2%	5.2%	5.0%	4.8%	5.4%
Total market size ($ bn)	37.4	53.8	64.7	70.3	74.6

Exhibit 3b: **U.S. PC Sales by Customer Category (market share by units)**

	1994	1995	1996	1997	1998Q2
Large / midsize business & government	39.8%	32.0%	34.7%	38.3%	38.5%
Small business & office	24.0%	22.2%	23.8%	23.3%	22.8%
Consumers (home)	32.7%	39.7%	36.8%	33.7%	32.8%
Education	3.6%	6.0%	4.8%	4.8%	5.8%
Total market size (millions of units)	18.7	23.0	26.5	31.5	36.3

Source: International Data Corporation

Exhibit 4: **Portion of Sales Through Each Channel by Region, 1998 (by dollar value)**

Channel	Americas	Europe / ME /Africa	Asia / Pacific / ROW
Retail	21.7%	17.1%	26.4%
Distributor / Reseller	41.2%	63.3%	49.2%
Direct	29.7%	17.8%	23.5%
Catalog, Phone, Online	17.8%	9.7%	3.1%
Sales Representatives	11.9%	8.1%	20.4%
Other	7.4%	1.8%	0.8%

Source: International Data Corporation

Exhibit 5: **Approximate Manufacturing Cost Structure of a Basic Personal Computer**

Components	Cost
Microprocessor	$50 - 600
Motherboard, hard drive, memory, chassis, power, packaging	$250 - 350
Keyboard, mouse, modem, CD-ROM and floppy disk drives, speakers	$90 - 140
Monitor	$100
Windows 98	$50
Assembly labor	$50
Total	On average, $800-900

Source: Mary Kwak and David B. Yoffie, "Apple Computer 1999," HBS Case 799-108, pp. 7-8.

Exhibit 6: **Summary of Dell Computer Corporation Financial Performance ($ million)**

	1992	1993	1994	1995	1996	1997	1998	1999
Revenue	890	2,014	2,873	3,475	5,296	7,759	12,327	18,243
Gross margin	282	449	433	738	1,067	1,666	2,722	4,106
SG&A	182	268	423	424	595	826	1,202	1,788
R&D	33	42	49	65	95	126	204	272
Operating income	69	139	(39)	249	377	714	1,316	2,046
Net income	51	102	(36)	149	272	518	944	1,460
Current assets	512	853	1,048	1,470	1,957	2,747	3,912	6,339
Inventory	127	303	220	293	429	251	233	273
Total assets	560	927	1,140	1,594	2,148	2,993	4,268	6,877
Stockholders' equity	274	369	471	652	973	1,085	1,293	2,321
Operating cash flow	0	(39)	113	243	175	1,362	1,592	2,346
Capital expenditures	33	47	48	64	101	114	187	296

	1992	1993	1994	1995	1996	1997	1998	1999
Ratios:								
Gross margin / revenue	31.7%	22.3%	15.1%	21.2%	20.1%	21.5%	22.1%	22.5%
SG&A / revenue	20.4%	13.3%	14.7%	12.2%	11.2%	10.6%	9.8%	9.8%
R&D / revenue	3.7%	2.1%	1.7%	1.9%	1.8%	1.6%	1.7%	1.5%
Net income / revenue	5.7%	5.1%	-1.3%	4.3%	5.1%	6.7%	7.7%	8.0%
Revenue / EOY assets	1.59x	2.17x	2.52x	2.18x	2.47x	2.59x	2.89x	2.65x
EOY assets / equity	2.04x	2.51x	2.42x	2.45x	2.21x	3.71x	3.30x	2.96x
Net income / EOY equity	18.6%	27.6%	-7.6%	22.9%	28.0%	64.3%	73.0%	62.9%

Source: Company annual reports; Compustat. Note that fiscal year ends January 31; consequently, "1999" results are predominantly for calendar year 1998.

Exhibit 7: Dell Margins in Direct and Retail Channels in 1994

	Dell Direct	**Dell Retail**
Price	100.0	88.0
Cost of sales	81.0	81.0
Gross margins	19.0	7.0
Operating expense	14.0	10.0
Operating income	5.0%	-3.0%

Source: Das Narayandas and V. Kasturi Rangan, "Dell Computer Corporation," HBS Case 596-058, p. 11.

Exhibit 8: **Ratings of PC Vendors by Corporate Managers with PC-buying Responsibility**

	Dell	Compaq	IBM	Gateway	HP
User satisfaction					
Overall	1st	4th	5th	2nd	3rd
At high price point	2nd	2nd	5th	4th	1st
At midrange price point	2nd	3rd	5th	1st	4th
At low price point	2nd	3rd	5th	1st	4th
Raw technology					
System speed	1st	3rd	5th	2nd	3rd
Reliability	1st	2nd	4th	4th	3rd
Compatibility	1st	5th	3rd	1st	4th
Configurability	1st	5th	3rd	1st	4th
Upgrades	1st	3rd	5th	2nd	4th
Hardware quality	1st	4th	5th	3rd	2nd
System management	1st	4th	5th	2nd	2nd
Pricing					
1998 price cuts	2nd	5th	2nd	1st	4th
Price	2nd	3rd	5th	1st	4th
Value	2nd	4th	5th	1st	4th
Cost of in-house support	2nd	5th	3rd	1st	4th
Ownership costs	1st	4th	5th	1st	3rd
Service and support					
Warranties	2nd	4th	3rd	1st	5th
Support staff	1st	5th	3rd	1st	4th
Repair times	2nd	4th	3rd	1st	5th
Channel-based support	3rd	5th	4th	2nd	1st
Web-based support	1st	3rd	5th	3rd	2nd
Overall service / support	1st	4th	5th	2nd	3rd
Customer relationship					
Vendor reputation	2nd	4th	3rd	5th	1st
Technical direction	2nd	4th	5th	3rd	1st
Overall comfort with	2nd	4th	5th	3rd	1st

Source: James Connolly, Kevin Burden, and Amy Malloy, "Direct Hit," *Computerworld,* November 16, 1998, pp. 81-88. Based on survey of 1,447 corporate managers with PC-buying responsibility for an average of 1,340 users each.

Exhibit 9: **Ratings of High-end Desktop PCs by *Consumer Reports***

Rank	Maker	Model	Price	Speed	Multimedia suitability	Ease of upgrade	Quality of manuals	Software clutter	Energy efficiency	Quality of display
1	Dell	Dimension XPS	$2,400	❶	❸	❶	❸	❷	❸	❹
2	Gateway	G6-266	$2,647	❷	❷	❶	❶	❷	❸	❷
3	HP	Pavilion 8180	$2,800	❷	❸	❷	❸	❸	❶	❸
4	Toshiba	Infinia 7230	$2,200	❷	❸	❷	❷	❶	❹	❸
5	Sony	VAIO PCV-150	$2,200	❷	❸	❶	❸	❸	❺	❷
6	IBM	Aptiva L61	$2,530	❷	❸	❷	❹	❷	❸	❸
7	Compaq	Presario 4850	$2,950	❷	❹	❷	❹	❶	❹	❷
8	HP	Pavilion 8160	$2,200	❷	❸	❷	❸	❸	❶	❸
9	Compaq	Presario 4814	$2,100	❷	❸	❸	❹	❶	❸	❸
10	NEC	Ready 9753	$2,080	❷	❹	❷	❷	❺	❸	❸

❶ = excellent. ❷ = very good. ❸ = good. ❹ = fair. ❺ = poor.

Source: Consumer Reports, "Do You Need All That Speed?" January 1998, pp. 39-42.

Exhibit 10: **Prices of Comparable PCs Configured for the Consumer Market**

	96Q1	96Q2	96Q3	96Q4	97Q1	97Q2	97Q3	97Q4	98Q1	98Q2	98Q3	98Q4
Configuration												
Microprocessor clock speed (MHz)	133	133	166	166	200 MMX	200 MMX	PII-233	PII-233	PII-266	PII-266	PII-350	PII-400
Memory (MB)	16	16	16	32	32	32	32	32	64	64	64	64
Hard drive (GB)	1-2	1-2	1-2	2+	3+	3+	4+	6+	6+	6+	6+	8+
Monitor size (inches)	17	17	17	17	17	17	17	17	17	17	17	17
Bundled software?	Y	Y	Y	Y	Y	Y	Y	Y	Y	Y	Y	Y
LAN card?	N	N	N	N	N	N	N	N	N	N	N	N
CD-ROM	6X	6X	6X	8X	12X+	12X+	12X+	12X+	12X+	12X+	12X+	32X+
Modem speed (kB/sec)	28.8	28.8	28.8	33.6	33.6	33.6+	56K	56K	56K	56K	56K	56K
Speakers?	Y	Y	Y	Y	Y	Y	Y	Y	Y	Y	Y	Y
Price ($)												
Compaq	3,299	3,234	2,949	2,624	2,849	2,560	3,014	2,523	2,448	1,539	1,649	1,575
Dell	2,848	2,264	2,296	2,217	2,290	2,039	2,059	2,005	1,838	1,660	1,606	1,606
Gateway	2,439	2,079	2,399	2,179	2,164	2,139	2,039	1,883	1,825	1,575	1,423	1,546
HP	3,198	2,478	2,948	2,799	3,049	2,660	2,914	2,658	2,459	1,590	1,900	1,808
IBM	3,418	2,848	3,149	2,899	2,974	2,640	N/A	2,579	2,348	1,560	1,722	1,709

Abbreviations: MHz = megahertz, MB = megabyte, GB = gigabyte, LAN = local access network, PII = Pentium II, MMX = multimedia enhanced, Y = yes, N =

Source: James Poyner and James Berlino, CIBC World Markets Quarterly Price Survey

Exhibit 11: **Comparisons of Major PC Manufacturers (All figures 1998 unless noted otherwise)**

	Dell	Compaq	IBM	HP	Gateway
Corporate revenue ($bn)	18.2	31.2	81.7	47.1	7.6
Value of PC sales ($bn)	17.7	27.9	16.9	11.8	7.1
Value of PC sales / corporate revenue	96.8%	89.4%	20.7%	25.0%	92.8%
Worldwide PC market share ($)	10.4%	16.4%	9.9%	6.9%	4.2%
Worldwide PC market share (units)	8.6%	14.7%	8.8%	6.3%	4.0%
Worldwide average selling price ($)	2,271	2,100	2,127	2,054	1,961
U.S. PC market share ($)	15.1%	16.6%	9.1%	7.9%	8.1%
U.S. PC market share (units)	13.2%	16.7%	8.2%	7.8%	8.4%
U.S. average selling price ($)	2,343	2,047	2,278	2,088	1,982
U.S. / worldwide PC sales	63.7%	44.4%	40.2%	50.0%	84.9%
CAGR of worldwide PC business, 1994-1998					
Value	51.9%	24.3%	12.9%	40.1%	27.3%
Units	56.2%	28.7%	18.0%	44.8%	36.5%
Corporate financials					
Return on sales	8.0%	-8.8%	7.7%	6.3%	4.5%
Sales-to-assets ratio	2.65x	1.35x	0.95x	1.40x	2.65x
Assets-to-equity ratio	2.96x	2.03x	4.43x	1.99x	2.15x
Return on equity	62.9%	-24.2%	32.6%	17.4%	25.7%
Return on invested capital (1997)	186%	35%	13%	16%	45%
Days of inventory	7.0	34.2	49.4	70.4	10.0
Cost structure					
Advertising / sales	1.1%	1.1%	2.1%	2.6%	N/A
R&D / sales	1.5%	4.3%	6.2%	7.1%	N/A
SG&A / sales	9.8%	16.0%	20.4%	16.6%	13.8%
PC sales by channel (units; worldwide)					
Direct	86.6%	4.4%	7.5%	0.6%	90.3%
Catalog, Phone, Online	37.4%	3.3%	2.4%	0.0%	88.4%
Sales Representatives	49.2%	1.1%	5.1%	0.6%	1.9%
Distributor / reseller	6.9%	66.6%	69.6%	75.1%	4.7%
Retail	0.0%	24.6%	18.4%	23.2%	1.0%
Other	6.5%	4.4%	4.6%	1.2%	4.0%
PC sales by customer category (units; worldwide)					
Home & small office	18.3%	28.5%	30.6%	33.3%	58.2%
Small & midsize business	37.0%	32.6%	32.7%	30.8%	19.1%
Large business	33.6%	27.5%	26.0%	27.2%	9.3%
Government	6.4%	6.0%	6.2%	5.9%	5.1%
Education	4.6%	5.3%	4.6%	2.8%	8.2%
Stock appreciation, 12/30/94-12/31/98	5,617%	432%	402%	174%	374%

Sources: International Data Corporation; Company Annual Reports. Note: Percentages may not equal 100% due to rounding.

Exhibit 12: **Summary of International Business Machines Financial Performance ($ million)**

	1991	1992	1993	1994	1995	1996	1997	1998
Revenue	64,792	64,523	62,716	64,052	71,940	75,947	78,508	81,667
Gross margin	37,467	38,675	29,926	29,481	24,322	34,215	34,627	43,282
SG&A	22,977	20,965	19,409	15,916	16,766	16,854	16,634	16,662
R&D	5,001	5,083	4,431	4,363	4,170	4,654	4,877	5,046
Operating income	4,340	3,406	308	5,005	9,919	9,031	9,098	9,164
Net income	(2,827)	(4,965)	(8,101)	3,021	4,178	5,429	6,093	6,328
Current assets	40,969	39,693	39,202	41,338	40,691	40,695	40,418	42,360
Inventory	9,844	8,385	7,565	6,334	6,323	5,870	5,139	5,200
Total assets	92,473	86,705	81,113	81,091	80,292	81,132	81,499	86,100
Stockholders' equity	37,006	27,624	19,738	23,413	22,423	21,628	19,816	19,433
Operating cash flow	6,725	6,274	8,327	11,793	10,708	10,275	8,865	9,273
Capital expenditures	6,497	4,751	3,154	3,078	4,744	5,883	6,793	6,520
Ratios:								
Gross margin / revenue	57.8%	59.9%	47.7%	46.0%	33.8%	45.1%	44.1%	53.0%
SG&A / revenue	35.5%	32.5%	30.9%	24.8%	23.3%	22.2%	21.2%	20.4%
R&D / revenue	7.7%	7.9%	7.1%	6.8%	5.8%	6.1%	6.2%	6.2%
Net income / revenue	-4.4%	-7.7%	-12.9%	4.7%	5.8%	7.1%	7.8%	7.7%
Revenue / EOY assets	0.70x	0.74x	0.77x	0.79x	0.90x	0.94x	0.96x	0.95x
EOY assets / equity	2.50x	3.14x	4.11x	3.46x	3.58x	3.75x	4.11x	4.43x
Net income / EOY equity	-7.6%	-18.0%	-41.0%	12.9%	18.6%	25.1%	30.7%	32.6%

Source: Company annual reports; Compustat. Note that fiscal year ends December 31.

Exhibit 13: **Summary of Compaq Computer Corporation Financial Performance ($ million)**

	1991	1992	1993	1994	1995	1996	1997	1998
Revenue	3,271	4,100	7,191	10,866	14,755	18,109	24,584	31,169
Gross margin	1,218	1,195	1,698	2,727	3,388	4,196	7,198	9,786
SG&A	722	699	837	1,235	1,594	1,912	2,947	4,978
R&D	197	173	169	226	270	407	817	1,353
Operating income	305	323	692	1,266	1,524	1,877	2,987	958
Net income	131	213	462	867	789	1,313	1,855	(2,743)
Current assets	1,782	2,318	3,291	5,158	6,527	9,169	12,017	15,167
Inventory	437	834	1,123	2,005	2,156	1,152	1,570	2,005
Total assets	2,826	3,142	4,084	6,166	7,818	10,526	14,631	23,051
Stockholders' equity	1,931	2,007	2,654	3,674	4,614	6,144	9,429	11,351
Operating cash flow	394	(59)	240	(101)	943	3,408	3,688	644
Capital expenditures	189	159	145	357	391	342	729	600
Ratios:								
Gross margin / revenue	37.2%	29.1%	23.6%	25.1%	23.0%	23.2%	29.3%	31.4%
SG&A / revenue	22.1%	17.0%	11.6%	11.4%	10.8%	10.6%	12.0%	16.0%
R&D / revenue	6.0%	4.2%	2.4%	2.1%	1.8%	2.2%	3.3%	4.3%
Net income / revenue	4.0%	5.2%	6.4%	8.0%	5.3%	7.3%	7.5%	-8.8%
Revenue / EOY assets	1.16x	1.31x	1.76x	1.76x	1.89x	1.72x	1.68x	1.35x
EOY assets / equity	1.46x	1.57x	1.54x	1.68x	1.69x	1.71x	1.55x	2.03x
Net income / EOY equity	6.8%	10.6%	17.4%	23.6%	17.1%	21.4%	19.7%	-24.2%

Source: Company annual reports; Compustat. Note that fiscal year ends December 31.

Exhibit 14: **Summary of Hewlett-Packard Financial Performance ($ million)**

	1991	1992	1993	1994	1995	1996	1997	1998
Revenue	14,494	16,410	20,317	24,991	31,519	38,420	42,895	47,061
Gross margin	6,636	7,232	8,194	9,501	11,505	12,291	14,576	14,989
SG&A	3,888	4,165	4,554	4,925	5,635	6,477	7,159	7,793
R&D	1,463	1,620	1,761	2,027	2,302	2,718	3,078	3,355
Operating income	1,335	1,510	1,879	2,549	3,568	3,726	4,339	3,841
Net income	755	549	1,177	1,599	2,433	2,586	3,119	2,945
Current assets	6,716	7,679	10,236	12,509	16,239	17,991	20,947	21,584
Inventory	2,273	2,605	3,691	4,273	6,013	6,401	6,763	6,184
Total assets	11,973	13,700	16,736	19,567	24,427	27,699	31,749	33,673
Stockholders' equity	7,269	7,499	8,511	9,926	11,839	13,438	16,155	16,919
Operating cash flow	1,552	1,288	1,142	2,224	1,613	3,456	4,321	5,442
Capital expenditures	862	1,032	1,405	1,257	1,601	2,201	2,338	1,997
Ratios:								
Gross margin / revenue	45.8%	44.1%	40.3%	38.0%	36.5%	33.6%	34.0%	31.9%
SG&A / revenue	26.8%	25.4%	22.4%	19.7%	17.9%	16.9%	16.7%	16.6%
R&D / revenue	10.1%	9.9%	8.7%	8.1%	7.3%	7.1%	7.2%	7.1%
Net income / revenue	5.2%	3.3%	5.8%	6.4%	7.7%	6.7%	7.3%	6.3%
Revenue / EOY assets	1.21x	1.20x	1.21x	1.28x	1.29x	1.39x	1.35x	1.40x
EOY assets / equity	1.65x	1.83x	1.97x	1.97x	2.06x	2.06x	1.96x	1.99x
Net income / EOY equity	10.4%	7.3%	13.8%	16.1%	20.6%	19.2%	19.3%	17.4%

Source: Company annual reports; Compustat. Note that fiscal year ends October 31.

Exhibit 15:   **Summary of Gateway 2000 Financial Performance ($ million)**

	1991	1992	1993	1994	1995	1996	1997	1998
Revenue	627	1,107	1,732	2,701	3,676	5,035	6,294	7,648
Gross margin	116	193	271	358	616	936	1,076	1,546
SG&A	57	89	122	217	367	608	786	1,052
R&D	N/A	N/A	N/A	N/A	N/A	N/A	N/A	N/A
Operating income	59	103	149	141	249	356	290	494
Net income	39	106	151	96	173	251	110	346
Current assets	117	246	501	654	866	1,318	1,545	2,228
Inventory	N/A	100	178	120	225	278	249	168
Total assets	128	269	564	771	1,124	1,673	2,039	2,890
Stockholders' equity	64	129	280	376	556	816	930	1,344
Operating cash flow	45	39	130	202	71	458	443	908
Capital expenditures	5	16	36	29	77	85	162	222
Ratios:								
Gross margin / revenue	18.5%	19.0%	15.6%	13.3%	16.8%	18.6%	17.1%	20.2%
SG&A / revenue	9.1%	8.8%	7.0%	7.0%	8.0%	10.0%	12.5%	13.8%
R&D / revenue	N/A	N/A	N/A	N/A	N/A	N/A	N/A	N/A
Net income / revenue	6.2%	10.4%	8.7%	8.7%	3.6%	4.7%	1.7%	4.5%
Revenue / EOY assets	4.90x	3.78x	3.07x	3.50x	3.27x	3.01x	3.09x	2.65x
EOY assets / equity	2.00x	2.09x	2.01x	2.05x	2.02x	2.05x	2.19x	2.15x
Net income / EOY equity	60.9%	82.2%	53.9%	25.5%	31.1%	30.8%	11.8%	25.7%

Source: Company annual reports; Compustat. Note that fiscal year ends December 31.

THE WALL STREET JOURNAL: PRINT VERSUS INTERACTIVE

case 6

Amy Hillman

In early January 1999, Peter Kann, chief executive officer of Dow Jones & Company, pondered the future of one of the company's most valuable brands and products, The Wall Street Journal. A meeting with Kann's top management team had been called for the following month to discuss the future of this brand, primarily focusing on the relative positioning and performance of the print and Interactive Journal.

The Wall Street Journal had enjoyed an unrivaled position as the top daily business newspaper in the United States for over 109 years. The Journal was the largest circulation newspaper in the United States with approximately 1.8 million subscribers, reached five million worldwide readers daily, and enjoyed tremendous loyalty among readers. However, the newspaper industry was facing a future of little to no growth and mounting competition from other forms of news delivery, most recently and saliently, the Internet.

Internet news providers threatened the typical newspaper's core product and service of timely, current news reporting and delivery. The threat to The Wall Street Journal was felt not only from competitors on the Web, such as CNN and CBS MarketWatch who operated free sites, but from its own Interactive Journal. The Interactive Journal was introduced in 1996 and within a year became the largest paid subscription site on the Internet. But what would the rising demand for instant, Web-based news do to the company's mainstay business of the print edition? Would the Interactive Journal serve as a complement or a substitute for print? Given this, Peter Kann wondered how the

IVEY

two products should be positioned, priced and promoted in order to maximize revenue for both. The answers to these questions would fundamentally shift the industry as well as Dow Jones & Company.

DOW JONES & COMPANY

Dow Jones & Company was a global provider of business news and information. Its primary operations were in three business segments: print publishing, electronic publishing, and general-interest community newspapers.

The print publishing segment included The Wall Street Journal, Barron's, National Business and Employment Weekly, The Asian Wall Street Journal, The Wall Street Journal Europe, Far Eastern Economic Review and SmartMoney Magazine. The electronic publishing segment included The Wall Street Journal Interactive Edition, Dow Jones Newswires, Dow Jones Interactive and the Dow Jones Indexes.

The Wall Street Journal Print Edition

The Wall Street Journal (WSJ), Dow Jones' flagship publication, was long considered the most respected source of business and financial news in the United States. By 1999, The Wall Street Journal was one of the most recognized brands in the world with a subscription renewal rate of 80 per cent. Its circulation rate of approximately 1.8 million subscribers remained relatively stable in the 1990s.

Over 600 reporters and editors — who also support other Dow Jones products — contributed to an outstanding record of journalistic excellence. In 1997, the company received its 19th Pulitzer Prize, an award also given to its chief executive officer in 1972. Each of the print editions of The Wall Street Journal drew heavily upon The Wall Street Journal's worldwide news staff. The Wall Street Journal Europe, headquartered in Brussels, had an average circulation in 1998 of 71,000 and sold on day of publication in continental Europe, the United Kingdom, the Middle East, and North Africa. The Asian Wall Street Journal, headquartered in Hong Kong, had an average circulation of 62,000 in 1998 and was printed in Hong Kong, Singapore, Japan, Thailand, Malaysia, Korea and Taiwan. In addition, the company distributed special editions of Wall Street Journal news within 30 newspapers in 26 countries, published in 10 languages with a combined circulation of four million.

Despite its long-standing traditional front page format without full paper-width headlines, six columns, dot print photos, and the "What's News" summaries, the Journal innovated many new formats in the 1990s. Starting in 1993, the Journal expanded its business and economic trend regional coverage to select parts of the United States, including Texas, Florida, California, New England, the Northwest and the Southeast. These Journal editions consisted of a four-page weekly section included in papers distributed in those regions. Four-color advertising, introduced in 1995, saw increased revenue of 60 per cent in 1997, contributing to overall advertising linage up 13 per cent, on top of a 14 per cent growth in 1996. 1997 saw the addition of a daily page of international business news and 1998, a two-page technology section. Weekend Journal, introduced in 1998, expanded typical content to include lifestyle issues such as personal finance, food and wine, sports, travel, and residential real estate, as well as other new editorial features appealing to new advertisers and readers.

However, these new innovations in the Journal served as supplements rather than substitutes to the three traditional sections of the five-day-a-week paper. Kann explains, "Visually, the Journal has a unique trademark quality. It's a uniquely recognizable page. But the main reason we haven't changed it is it's a very useful format." Section A included the front page and business and political news. Section B, "Marketplace," focused more on lifestyle and marketing issues, including regional editions, and the technology section. Finally, Section C, "Money & Investing," centered on financial news, daily stock and bond quotes and other financial information. Dow Jones also announced plans to spend US$230 million between 1999 and 2002 to expand the number of color pages and total page capacity. This investment would increase the color page capacity from eight to 24 and the total page capacity from 80 to 96.

Economics of Print Publishing

Within the relevant range (circulation and advertising within 15 per cent), most print WSJ expenses were fixed. Variable components (including newsprint, ink, plates, production and delivery overtime) account for approximately 15 per cent of costs. Print WSJ revenues came from two primary sources: sales/subscriptions and advertising. Advertising rate growth was dependent upon at least roughly preserving the circulation level. Hence, if circulation dropped 10 per cent, ad revenue could fall 10 per cent or more.

The paper was printed in 17 company-owned U.S. and 13 overseas plants, 12 of which were leased. Company employees (through the company's National Delivery Service, Inc. subsidiary) delivered 75 per cent of U.S. subscriber copies by 6:00 a.m. daily. This system provided delivery earlier and more reliably than the postal service. Company plants were unionized, operated one shift daily, six days a week, and were important to maintaining the Journal's traditional size, which was larger than typical print newspapers. This size format was believed to be more appealing to advertisers and to readers alike.

The Print Newspaper Industry

Wall Street had long found newspaper stocks appealing and therefore priced them at a premium to the rest of the market. Exhibit 1 includes stock data for Dow Jones & Company. However, newspapers faced increasing media competition in the 1990s, making advertising sales a harder pitch. Local newspapers in general turned to supplemental advertising flyers and catalogues placed between the pages of daily and Sunday papers in order to provide more dependable cash flow. In addition, growth of classified ads was strong due to the general expansion of the economy resulting in strong real estate, automobile and job markets. Classified volume typically contributed 15 to 25 per cent of total newspaper linage sales and was the industry's most profitable ad category on a per-line basis in the 1990s. However, classified ads also faced increased competition from on-line offerings. Overall, newspapers benefited from the robust economy in 1998 by encouraging more advertisers to buy more linage at increased rates. The total advertising market in the United States for print medium was US$72 billion in 1999, up from US$55 billion in 1995, and projected to exceed US$83 billion by 2001.

Despite relatively stable cash flows in the past, newspaper circulation was in a general downward trend from 1987 through late 1996, although there was some stability starting in 1997. Local distribution of newspapers, both home and newsstands, was increasingly contracted out to third parties.

The Wall Street Journal was the first national daily paper in the United States and enjoyed status as the only national daily until the advent of USA Today in 1985. In the late 1990s, the New York Times and Los Angeles Times also nominally entered into the nationally distributed sector of the industry. However, their entry into the nationally distributed sector did not indicate a shift towards nationally focused news; The New York Times and Los Angeles Times still concentrated on a fairly targeted geographic region in terms of subscribers and content. In addition, the business-versus-general-interest focus of The Wall Street Journal kept it relatively immune from direct competitors until the expansion of UK-based Financial Times in 1998. While the Financial Times's focus was primarily business news, its exposure in the U.S. market was dwarfed by that of The Wall Street Journal, with the circulation level of the Journal around 35 times that of the Financial Times.

The Wall Street Journal Interactive Edition

The Wall Street Journal Interactive Journal (http://wsj.com), introduced in April 1996, was another innovation for Dow Jones as well as for the publishing industry. While initially a free site, subscribers were first asked to pay in August of 1996. Subscribers totaled over 100,000 within the first year of launch, and reached over 266,000 subscribers by the end of 1998. While many competitors were delivering news on the Web for free, The Wall Street Journal Interactive Edition became the largest paid subscription site on the World Wide Web. Around one per cent of the content at the web site was free access, with the remaining 99 per cent accessible only to subscribers. "Our proprietary information has value, and we have the guts to charge," said Peter Kann.

U.S. News & World Report called the Interactive Journal "the best single financial site on the Internet." The Interactive Journal offered continuously updated news and market information, access to the international editions, in-depth background reports on over 20,000 companies and pay-per-view access to the Dow Jones Publication library. In addition, the Interactive Journal included proprietary information and coverage not found in the print editions. Within each story in the Interactive Journal were links to stock quotes and other information about the companies discussed.

Careers.wsj.com was a free site, launched in 1997 and linked to the Interactive Journal, that offered a searchable database of employment listings and content from the National Business and Employment Weekly.

Advertising sales were relatively stable in 1998, coming off two relatively strong years of growth. Subscription renewal rates were approximately 75 to 80 per cent. Further comparison of subscribers, subscriber revenue and acquisition costs for both the print and Interactive editions is given in Exhibits 2 and 3.

Economics of Electronic Publishing

Typically for Web-based publishing, most costs were fixed or step-function fixed, except for subscriber acquisition and advertising selling expenses.

For free sites, primary revenue came from advertising, with the number of people visiting the site largely determining the fees charged to advertisers. For subscription sites, however, revenue came from both advertising and subscriptions, similar to print publishing. A third category of revenue also became possible in electronic publishing: transaction fees. Forrester Research predicted that online revenue from subscriptions, advertising and transaction fees would grow from just over US$520 million in 1997 to US$8.5 billion within five years.

The total advertising market for Internet medium was approximately US$2 billion in 1999 and was projected to exceed US$5 billion in 2001. As a quarterly comparison, the first quarter of 1996 saw total U.S. Internet advertising spending at US$29.9 million. By the first quarter of 1998, this number had grown to US$351.3 million and second quarter of 1998 to US$423.0 million. Unlike television, radio or print advertising, an almost unlimited supply of advertising and a concurrent glut of it accompanied the advent of the Internet. As a result, advertising rates plummeted in 1998 due to the lack of target viewers. However, this trend did not apply to web sites that could offer advertisers access to more targeted demographics.

A 1998 GVU Internet survey indicated the attitudes about pay versus free sites on the Internet. Of those individuals who refused to pay for information on the Internet, 44.5 per cent did so because the information was available elsewhere for free, while 32.7 per cent would not pay for Internet information because they were already paying to gain access to the Internet itself. Other reasons given for the resistance to pay for site access included excessive cost and poor site quality. Similarly, a survey conducted by the BBDO advertising agency found that 60 per cent of respondents replied negatively when asked if they would be willing to pay for an on-line subscription edition of their favorite print publication. Of those that answered "yes," 89 per cent indicated they would not be willing to pay more than the newsstand price for an on-line version.

Unlike print publishing, editorial and news skills for a near-real time environment became necessary skills for electronic publishing. With continual news updates, reliability and quality of journalism reports became subject to increased time pressure. Accuracy, the elimination of bias, clarity and comprehensiveness in the face of a flood of information became critical for electronic publishing. In addition, new skills of technology, ease of Web site navigation, effective layout for a computer screen, etc., became necessary for Web publishing.

The Wall Street Journal Interactive Edition was expected to attain its break-even point in 1999. Forrester Research estimated the average annual operating costs of content Internet sites of US$893,000 and of transactional sites at US$2.8 million in 1998. For Income Statement information for both Print and Electronic products, see Exhibits 4 and 5. Company-wide financial information is provided in Exhibits 6 through 8.

The electronic publishing division, which included Dow Jones Interactive, provided subscribers with a news library of over 5,000 publications, including a full-text archive of The Wall Street Journal and Dow Jones Newswires as well as roughly 1,200 non-U.S. news sources, and the 50 largest U.S. newspapers and business magazines.

The Internet/Web Publishing Market

Growth in the use of the Internet exploded in the 1990s. It was estimated that in 1998, the number of worldwide Internet users was over 147 million with over 57 million in the United States alone. The number of U.S. households joining the Internet was estimated at 760 per hour in 1999 with nearly 38 per cent of households being reached by the Internet. Nearly 90 per cent of Internet users gathered news and information from the Web's news, information and entertainment sites. In 1996, Pew Research Center estimated that only four per cent of Americans got their news online. This number jumped to nearly 20 per cent in 1999.

It was projected that by 2003, over 55 million professionals, managers and executives would be using the Internet at work. In 1999, over 17 per cent of the online population preferred to receive their financial news online.

Internet penetration by age was concentrated in younger generations by the end of 1998. Fifty-nine per cent of 12- to 17-year-olds used the Internet, with the percentage dropping with each higher age group to 27 per cent of the population aged 55 to 64, and only 14 per cent of the population over age 65. In 1996 the male to female ratio of Internet use was 57 to 43 but by 1998, this ratio had changed to 51 to 49.

The Interactive Journal competed with a variety of business news sources on the Internet, including sites maintained by traditional print competitors such as Business Week, Fortune, The New York Times, and The Financial Times. In addition, it faced competition from non-print competitors such as CNNfn, Bloomberg, on-line brokerage firms, CBS MarketWatch, TheStreet.com and Yahoo and others who received their news from Reuters. Many of these competitors provided news and information on their Web site for free (for example, CNNfn, Yahoo, Bloomberg, and The New York Times). Still others provided limited free information for non-print subscribers and free on-line access to print subscribers (e.g., Fortune and Business Week). Due to the ease of entry into Web publishing, as opposed to print publishing, competition was growing and fluid. One important difference between print competitors and purely on-line competitors had to do with branding. Companies with established brand names outside of the Internet had a cost advantage over competitors that were Internet-born (e.g., Yahoo and Amazon) due to the high costs of marketing new brands.

Print versus Interactive Customers

Since its introduction, the Interactive Journal was not aggressively promoted to current print subscribers of the Wall Street Journal. Partially, this was a result of the difference in customer profiles for the two products.

Print WSJ customers had a higher average age than Interactive Journal customers and were more likely to be retired. Print customers tended to use the Internet more at work than at home, to have a higher total value of investments, were more likely to have a home office, and were more likely to live in the eastern United States. Interactive Journal customers, on the other hand, were more likely to have children at home, to use the Internet at home than at work, to have a lower total value of investments, to use online brokers and other online information, and to travel internationally for business.

Simmons Market Research Bureau reported that of WSJ print readers, 9.3 per cent had completed high school, 8.3 per cent had some college education, 33.57 per cent had graduated from a four-year college or university, and 30.68 per cent had attended graduate school. The subscription base of WSJ was characterized by an average age of 52 with an average household income of US$75,000. The majority of print readers were 35 years old or older (75.7 per cent), with only 24.3 per cent within the 18 to 34 age group. Most print subscribers were male with a male to female ratio of 75 to 25. Nearly 74 per cent of WSJ print subscribers read the paper every day, spending on average 50 minutes per issue. As of 1999, 40 per cent of Interactive Journal subscribers read the edition on a daily basis and 36 per cent reported using the edition a few times a week.

Current Pricing, Promotion and Positioning

Currently, the Interactive Journal is positioned as a supplement, not a substitute for the print edition and is priced accordingly. Non-print subscribers pay $59 per year while print subscribers pay $29 per year. The print edition is priced at $175 per year with newsstand copies for seventy-five cents each. The print pricing compares with other print competitors as follows: Business Week—

US$42.95 for 51 issues; Fortune—US$54.55 for 26 issues; Forbes—US$23.97 for 17 issues; USA Today—US$119/year; New York Times—US$208/year for weekly editions only; and Financial Times—US$175/year[1], although most magazine competitors did offer discount subscription rates.

The Challenge

The challenge ahead of Peter Kann was a serious one, but he was no stranger to tensions. His Pulitzer Prize was awarded for coverage of the Indian-Pakistan war. As he looked towards the next month's meeting, which would largely shape the direction of the future for The Wall Street Journal print and interactive, Kann wondered: Would the future mean prosperous co-existence of the two formats or a battle with but one format as the victor?

Exhibit 1: **Stock Performance for Dow Jones & Company**

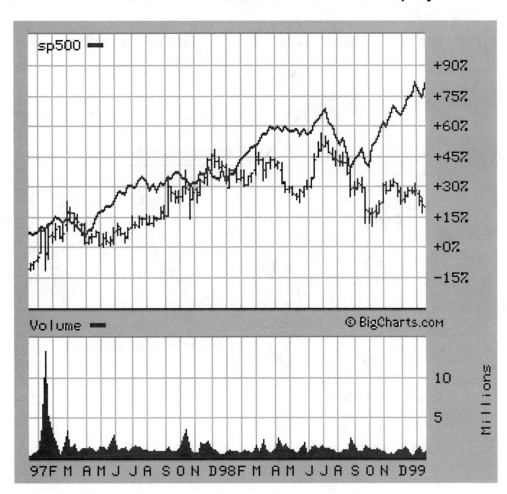

Source: Interactive Chart — dowjones.htm; October 4, 1999.

---

[1] This price is the effective price after taking into consideration widespread discounting.

Exhibit 2: **Per-Subscriber Revenue and Acquisition Costs**

	Print WSJ	Electronic WSJ
1 Year Subscription - Non-Print Subscriber	N/A	$59
1 Year Subscription - Print Subscriber	$175	$29
Advertising Revenue Per Year Per Subscriber	$500	$40
Average Acquisition Cost New Subscriber	$160	$40
Average Renewal Cost	$5	$5
Renewal Rate	80%	75%

Exhibit 3: **The Wall Street Journal — Print Electronic Interaction**

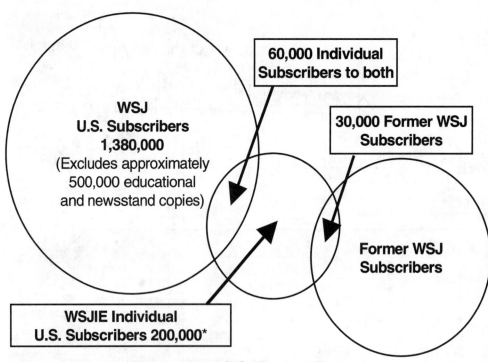

* Excludes corporate and International WSJIE subscribers

Exhibit 4: **Print Publishing Primarily The Wall Street Journal ($ Millions)**

	1997	**1998**
Revenue:		
Advertising	$790	$777
Circ. & Other	$353	$360
TOTAL	$1,143	$1,137
Operating Expenses	$896	$931
Operating Income	$247	$174

Exhibit 5: **ELECTRONIC PRODUCTS**
DOW Jones Interactive
DOW Jones Newswires
The Wall Street Journal Interactive Edition
($ Millions)

	1997	**1998**
Revenue:		
Dow Jones Newswires/Indexes	$204	$220
Interactive Publlishing	$159	$172
TOTAL	$363	$393
Operating Expenses	$302	$315
Operating Income	$ 61	$ 78

Exhibit 6: **Consolidated Statements of Income (Loss)**

For the years ended December 31, 1998, 1997, and 1996

(in thousands except per share amounts)	1998	1997	1996
REVENUES			
Advertising	$1,031,210	$1,011,864	$ 896,981
Information Services	670,441	1,101,696	1,125,625
Circulation and Other	456,455	458,958	458,986
TOTAL Revenues	2,158,106	2,572,518	2,481,592
EXPENSES			
News, Operations and Development	677,381	899,868	820,564
Selling, Administrative and General	762,803	895,707	831,270
Newsprint	163,146	152,478	164,766
Second Class Postage and Carrier Delivery	117,649	114,442	110,256
Depreciation and Amortization	142,439	250,734	217,756
Restructuring	76,115	1,001,263	*
Operating Expenses	1,939,533	3,314,492	2,144,612
Operating Income (Loss)	218,573	(714,974)	336,980
OTHER INCOME (DEDUCTIONS)			
Investment Income	12,266	3,473	4,249
Interest Expense	(7,193)	(19,367)	(18,755)
Equity in Losses of Associated Companies	(21,653)	(49,311)	(5,408)
(Loss) Gain on Disposition of Businesses &			
Investments	(126,085)	52,595	14,315
Other, Net	(4,250)	(9,300)	(121)
Income (Loss) Before Income Taxes &			
Minority Interests	71,658	(763,884)	331,260
Income Taxes	63,083	37,796	147,728
Income (Loss) Before Minority Interests	8,575	(801,680)	183,532
Minority Interests in (Earnings) Losses of			
Subsidiaries	(213)	(452)	6,437
NET INCOME (LOSS)	$ 8,362	$ (802,132)	$ 189,969
PER SHARE			
Net Income (Loss) Per Share:			
Basic	$ .09	$ (8.36)	$ 1.96
Diluted	.09	(8.36)	1.95
Weighted-Average Shares Outstanding:			
Basic	95,180	95,993	96,703
Diluted	96,404	95,993	97,371
Cash Dividends	$ .96	$ .96	$ .96

* This restructuring cost is associated with the divestment of Dow Jones Markets (formerly Telerate).

Exhibit 7: **Financial Highlights**

Income Statement Results (in thousands except per share amounts)	1998	1997	% INCREASE (DECREASE)
CONSOLIDATED			
Revenues	$2,158,106	$2,572,518	(16.1)
Operating Income (Loss)	218,573	(741,974)	-
EBITDA[1]	437,127	510,023	(14.3)
Net Income (Loss)	8,362	(802,132)	-
Net Income (Loss) Per Share – Diluted	.09	(8.36)	-
EXCLUDING SPECIAL ITEMS [2]			
Revenues	1,872,204	1,776,238	5.4
Operating Income	327,915	335,955	(2.4)
EBITDA	416,456	454,071	(8.3)
Net Income	185,039	185,707	(0.4)
Net Income Per Share – Diluted	1.92	1.92	

Financial Position and Cash Flows (in thousands except per share amounts)	1998	1997	% INCREASE (DECREASE)
Long-Term Debt, Including Current Portion	$ 149,889	$ 234,124	(36.0)
Stockholders' Equity	509,340	780,822	(34.8)
Capital Expenditures	225,834	347,797	(35.1)
Cash From Operations	306,226	459,763	(33.4
Purchase of Treasury Stock, Net of Put Premiums	291,215		-

Revenues and Operating Income (Loss) by Segment (in thousands except per share amounts)	1998	1997	% INCREASE (DECREASE)
REVENUES			
Print Publishing	$1,161,939	$1,143,395	1.6
Electronic Publishing [3]	393,178	363,232	8.2
Community Newspapers	317,087	300,611	5.5
Segment Revenues	1,872,204	1,807,238	3.6
Divested/Joint Ventured Operations:			
Print and Television Operations		21,091	-
Telerate	285,902	744,189	(61.6)
Consolidated Revenues	$2,158,106	$2,572,518	(16.1)
OPERATING INCOME (LOSS)[4]			
Print Publishing	$ 173,582	$ 247,191	(29.8)
Electronic Publishing	56,060	61,089	(8.2)
Community Newspapers	44,760	50,584	(11.5)
Corporate	(22,602)	(18,189)	(24.3)
Segment Operating Income	251,800	340,675	(26.1)
Divested/Joint Ventured Operations:			
Print and Televisions Operations		(18,239)	-
Telerate	(33,227)	(1,064,410)	96.9
Consolidated Operating Income (Loss)	$ 218,573	$ (741,974)	-

[1] EBITDA is computed as operating income (loss) excluding depreciation and amortization and restructuring costs.

[2] Consolidated excluding Telerate operations and loss on its sale, and other special charges/gains.

[3] 1997 revenue includes $31 million of one-time index licensing fees.

[4] excluding restructuring charges,, segment operating income was as follows (000's):

	1998	1997
Print Publishing	$223,496	$251,903
Electronic Publishing	65,921	78,138
Community Newspapers	61,100	50,584
Corporate	(22,602)	(18,189)
	$327,915	$362,436

Exhibit 8: **Five-Year Financial Summary**

(in thousands except per share amounts)	1998	1997	1996	1995	1994
REVENUES					
Advertising	$1,031,210	$1,011,864	$ 896,981	$ 771,779	$ 724,990
Information Services	670,441	1,101,696	1,125,625	1,092,002	976,800
Circulation and Other	456,455	458,958	458,986	419,980	389,187
TOTAL Revenues	2,158,106	2,572,518	2,481,592	2,283,761	2,090,977
EXPENSES					
News, Operations and Development	677,381	899,868	820,564	748,945	642,184
Selling, Administrative and General	762,803	895,707	831,270	764,161	681,244
Newsprint	163,146	152,478	164,766	157,047	107,178
Second Class Postage and Carrier Delivery	117,649	114,442	110,256	103,497	96,751
Depreciation and Amortization	142,439	250,734	217,756	206,070	205,303
Restructuring	76,115	1,001,263			
Operating Expenses	1,939,533	3,314,492	2,144,612	1,979,720	1,732,660
Operating Income (Loss)	218,573	(714,974)	336,980	304,041	358,317
OTHER INCOME (DEDUCTIONS)					
Investment Income	12,266	3,473	4,249	5,379	4,884
Interest Expense	(7,193)	(19,367)	(18,755)	(18,345)	(16,858)
Equity in Losses of Associated Companies	(21,653)	(49,311)	(5,408)	14,193	(5,434)
(Loss) Gain on Disposition of Businesses & Investments	(126,085)	52,595	14,315	13,557	3,097
Other, Net	(4,250)	(9,300)	(121)	4,075	(5,981)
Income (Loss) Before Income Taxes & Minority Interests	71,658	(763,884)	331,260	322,900	338,025
Income Taxes	63,083	37,796	147,728	139,878	157,632
Income (Loss) Before Minority Interests	8,575	(801,680)	183,532	183,022	180,393
Minority Interests in (Earnings) Losses of Subsidiaries	(213)	(452)	6,437	6,550	787
Income (Loss) Before Cumulative Effect of Accounting Changes	8,362	(802,132)	189,969	189,572	181,180
Cumulative Effect of Accounting Changes					(3,007)
NET INCOME (LOSS)	$ 8,362	$ (802,132)	$ 189,969	$ 189,572	$ 178,173
PER SHARE Basic					
Income (Loss) Before Cumulative Effect of Accounting Changes	$ .09	$ (8.36)	$ 1.96	$ 1.96	$ 1.83
Net Income (Loss)	.09	(8.36)	1.96	1.96	1.80
PER SHARE Diluted					
Income (Loss) Before Cumulative Effect of Accounting Changes	.09	(8.36)	1.95	1.94	1.82
Net Income (Loss)	.09	(8.36)	1.96	1.94	1.79
Weighted-Average Shares Outstanding ('000's):					
Basic	95,180	95,993	96,703	96,907	99,002
Diluted	96,404	95,993	97,371	97,675	99,662
Dividends	$ .96	$ .96	$ .96	$ .92	$ 84
OTHER DATA					
Long-term debt incl. Current Portion as % of Total Capital	22.7%	23.1%	17.0%	13.9%	16.9%
Newsprint Consumption (Metric Tons)	278,000	270,000	252,000	224,000	221,000
Number of Full Time Employees at Year End	8,253	12,309	11,844	11,232	10,265
Cash From Operations	306,226	459,763	405,157	371,887	403,142
Capital Expenditures	225,834	347,797	232,178	218,765	222,434
Cash Dividends	91,662	92,116	92,969	89,131	83,360
Total Assets	1,491,322	1,919,734	2,759,631	2,598,700	2,445,766
Long-term Debt, Including Current Portion	149,889	234,124	337,618	259,253	300,870
Stockholders' Equity	509,340	780,822	1,643,993	1,601,751	1,481,611

GRAND & TOY: STAPLES' COMPETITIVE THREAT

case 7

Ken Mark and
Mary M. Crossan

INTRODUCTION

Pete Vanexan, president of Grand & Toy (G&T), was reviewing his company's 2001 budget forecast. It was January 13, 2001, in Toronto, Canada, and Vanexan was on his way to a meeting with the other senior managers. Vanexan wanted to focus on this opportunity to rethink G&T's strategy and assess whether there was something they had missed in the previous review.

The History of Grand & Toy[1]

Printer James Grand first began in the stationery business in 1882, working out of a single room in a Toronto house, and selling door-to-door from his wheelbarrow. He soon recognized his customers' greater needs for more than just stationery, and a good idea was born. It wasn't long before his early version of an 'office outfitters' business had grown beyond Grand's solo efforts.

---

[1]Taken from www.grandandtoy.com, January 13, 2001.

IVEY

Grand convinced his brother-in-law, Samuel Toy, to join him as a one-third partner a year later. Together, they opened the first G&T retail store in Toronto. The wheelbarrows were retired.

From such humble beginnings 118 years ago, and through a devastating Toronto fire, the Depression and two World Wars, G&T continued to build their business. They were selling more than office supplies even then. They were selling an unwavering dedication to personal service, uncompromising quality and fair pricing.

In 2001, with over 2,200 employees working in over 90 locations across Canada, G&T (now wholly owned by Boise Cascade Office Products) considered itself an innovator and a market leader in the office products industry. As one of Canada's largest commercial and retail office products distributor, G&T felt that it was equipped to handle every business need, from the home office to the head office.

Grand & Toy's parent company, Boise Cascade Office Products (BCOP), also sold office and computer supplies, office furniture, paper and promotional items (clothing, gifts) directly to business customers, including government offices.[2] BCOP generated 1999 sales of US$3.4 billion, which grew 10.3 per cent compared to 1998. It achieved net income of US$75 million, and employed 12,200 employees worldwide. BCOP operated primarily as a contract stationer to large business accounts (representing 85 per cent of sales). The company also sold its wares through catalogues and the Internet, and made direct sales to small and mid-sized businesses and home offices. BCOP was supported by 65 distribution centres worldwide (ex-U.S. sales made up 25 per cent of sales). Paper producer Boise Cascade owned BCOP.[3]

The Office Products Industry

The size of the global office products marketplace was estimated at US$318 billion annually,[4] with North America representing approximately 35 per cent of the total. The top 10 companies in North America were, in order of sales:

- Office Depot (consumer retail)
- Staples Inc. (consumer retail)
- Buhrmann N.V. (business supplier)
- OfficeMax (consumer retail)
- Avery Dennison Corporation (manufacturer)
- Corporate Express[5] (consumer retail)
- United Stationers (wholesaler)
- Boise Cascade Office Products (business supplier)
- Steelcase (manufacturer)
- U.S. Office Products Company[6] (business supplier)

The Canadian marketplace was estimated at US$8.6 billion (including office computers and software.)

---

[2]Grand & Toy did not sell the promotional items mentioned.
[3]www.hoovers.com accessed January 12, 2001.
[4]1999 figures.
[5]Purchased recently by N.V. Buhrmann.
[6]www.hoovers.com, 1999 figures, January 12, 2001.

Global Office Products Marketplace

	Sales volume (US$ billions)	Percentage of Market	Expected Growth Rate (%)
Office Supplies	32	11.3%	5
Paper and envelopes	33	11.6%	4-5
Other	15	5.3%	4
Furniture	30	10.6%	2-3
Business Machines	33	11.6%	1-2
Computers and software (includes consumables)	140	49.4%	20

It was estimated that by 2003, 50 per cent of the office products sold would be defined as computer supplies (excluding hardware and software). Prospects for economic growth that drove consumption of office products were beginning to sound dim. The Wall Street Journal (WSJ) reported on December 1, 2000, that Canada's third quarter growth was helped by an unexpected inventory buildup. Economists cautioned that the U.S. slowdown, combined with higher energy prices, would have a moderate cooling effect on the Canadian economy in the first half of 2001.

The WSJ followed up with another report on January 5, 2000, indicating that most analysts expected Canadian gross domestic product to grow between 2.75 per cent and three per cent, surpassing the United States's projected 2.25 per cent. Warren Jestin, chief economist at the Bank of Nova Scotia in Toronto, stated:

> The Canadian economy is doing well because our boom wasn't as huge as in the U.S. We've largely been playing catch-up on domestic demand. The last three federal budgets have provided Canada with a lot of fiscal stimuli, particularly with tax cuts.

U.S. competition had been feeling the effects of the slowing U.S. economy. Staples, a well-known U.S. office supplies company, had missed stock analysts' lowered estimates during its third quarter 2000 earning announcement. Analysts such as Salomon Smith Barney attributed the missed targets to increasing competition from discounters, the Internet, Gateway's 300+ stores, Circuit City's home office expansion and CDW.[7] Despite the increased competition, Staples continued to open new stores. Thus, the competition, concurrent with a moderating economic environment, provided the impetus for slower sales and lower margins.[8]

Another U.S. investment bank, Merrill Lynch, speculated that Staples' fundamentals had slowed due to overall industry capacity growing faster than underlying demand. It went on to indicate that the office supplies industry, in the U.S. at least, was on the verge of major store closings on the part of Staples' competitors. If that occurred, the bank's analysts thought that demand would slowly match capacity. Merrill Lynch believed that Staples' two major competitors, OfficeMax and Office Depot, would close five per cent and eight per cent of their stores

---

[7] A high-volume U.S. brand name computer reseller.
[8] Salomon Smith Barney, November 14, 2000.

respectively. The bank expected North American retail operations to have a challenging fourth quarter with slowing PC hardware and software sales overall.[9]

The implications were that increasingly, global competitors would start eyeing G&T's position as Canada's largest business supplier of office products. These competitors would include the traditional consumer retail players, wholesalers, manufacturers, and non-traditional players such as logistics and online companies.

Grand & Toy's Business Operations

Overall sales had grown nearly 35 per cent from 1998 to 2000. In the same period, sales had grown from Cdn$480 million to Cdn$645 million, while profit rose at an even greater rate. There were three business units that delivered G&T's revenue: commercial, retail and the stockroom (SOHO[10] e-commerce). The majority of G&T's revenue came from its commercial operations. Grand & Toy believed the commercial division was broken out into four distinct market segments and three product segments (office supplies, computer supplies and furniture).

Number of Employees	Classification	Of Revenue Derived in %	Of Canadian Market in %*
10-25	Small	3%	1%
25-50	Medium (small)	5%	5%
50-300	Medium (large)	9.5%	8%
300+	Large	92%	15%

*Grand & Toy controlled 7.5 per cent of the total office supply market in Canada

G&T also used wholesalers to augment its product offering. SP Richards was their "first-call" wholesaler for office products; G&T's sales reps had their catalogues, and both companies were linked via computer. SP Richards accounted for one per cent of G&T's sales. Furniture and computer supplies were different. Grand & Toy used wholesalers for stock products in western branches, which allowed them to avoid inventory products. They were trying to expand to move all furniture through wholesalers. This was because furniture required inventory investment and care in delivery.

Grand & Toy was exploring a relationship with United Stationers to stock slower-moving products. For example, if G&T had 8,000 products in total (of which 2,000 were slower moving), the slower products would be outsourced to United Stationers.

United Stationers and SP Richards also sold their services and products to Internet startups, and other G&T competitors. They were available to support any company that did not have a distribution structure on its own.

G&T leveraged the buying power of its parent company to source products at the best price. In 2000, its commercial division accounted for 82 per cent of revenues, and retail operations accounted for 18 per cent. (E-commerce revenues accounted for over 20 per cent of commercial division revenues.) Grand & Toy's logistics and distribution was considered state of the art. Through its relationship with its commercial clients, G&T was able to determine how to personalize its delivery

---

[9]Merrill Lynch Capital Markets, November 14, 2000.
[10]Small office, home office.

of office supplies to meet client specifications. For example, a particular commercial client might want their second-floor supply room stocked on Wednesday between 2:00 pm and 4:00 pm, with product delivered through the west loading doors.

Grand & Toy's Vision and 2001 Objectives

Grand & Toy aimed to achieve sales of Cdn$1 billion. In addition, it aimed to maintain a strong brand, to be the clear leader in the Canadian commercial segment and to operate about 85 commercially focused stores clustered in major markets. Performance objectives against the strategic plan to achieve its vision included:

1. Growing sales;
2. Reducing costs and increasing productivity;
3. Increasing organizational capability and capacity; and
4. Ensuring a strong strategic position.

STAPLES

In pioneering the office supply superstore industry, Staples changed the way people thought about and purchased office supplies. The company's mission was 'to slash the cost and hassle of purchasing office supplies' — a message it thought small businesses identified with. Staples encouraged customers to evaluate what they were spending on office supplies and look for cost savings. To small businesses and consumers, Staples offered access to a wide variety of products at volume purchasing price tags. Exhibit 1 shows some of the retailing milestones that Staples had achieved.

Staples Inc. was a US$9 billion retailer of office supplies, furniture and technology to consumers and businesses. Its clientele ranged from home-based businesses to Fortune 500 companies in the United States, Canada, the United Kingdom, Germany, the Netherlands and Portugal. Headquartered outside Boston, Staples invented the office superstore concept and today was the largest operator of office superstores in the world. The company had over 46,000 employees serving customers through more than 1,100 office superstores, mail order catalogues, e-commerce and contract business.[11] Thomas G. Stemberg, Staples' chairman and chief executive officer commented:

The second quarter (in 2000) marked our 30th consecutive quarter of meeting or beating analysts' earnings expectations. By paying attention to what our customers want and by executing on our business plan, we grew total comparable sales by 10 per cent, the best rate in our industry. These impressive numbers were achieved even though we did not have events such as the Office 2000 and Microsoft Network Internet store promotions that drove sales during the second quarter a year ago.

In order to build on our great momentum, Staples is developing three additional areas to help fuel longer-term growth: Europe, Staples.com and business services.

---

[11]More information about the company is available at http://www.staples.com.

Because of its large number of retail and commercial customers, Staples had very favorable purchasing terms from its suppliers. At Staples, procurement of products was done centrally and thus reaped financial and time resource savings.

Staples Canada had begun to offer additional services to attract the small business market: bizSmart and the Dividend$ program. bizSmart was a resource designed for Canadian small business owners offering no-fee daily business banking, low prices on office products, plus discounts on business products and services from other bizSmart participants. Staples would also provide business associates to service customers who could not find answers online. Its Dividend$ program offered a staggered rebate on products determined by volume purchased.

On November 14, 2000, Staples issued a press release indicating that despite a tough retail climate, its sales were up by 17 per cent for the third quarter of 2000 (see Exhibit 2).

BUHRMANN N.V.[12]

An international business services and distribution group, Buhrmann N.V. was one of the world's leading suppliers of office products, paper and graphic systems for the business market. Headquartered in Amsterdam, Buhrmann generated sales of about 9 billion Euros[13] with approximately 29,000 employees in 28 countries.

The new Corporate Express, a Buhrmann company came about in 1999 when Corporate Express was acquired by Buhrmann N.V. of Amsterdam. BT Office Products (also owned by Buhrmann) and Corporate Express joined forces to become the world's largest business-to-business (B2B) office products supply company, offering office products in 15 of the 28 countries where Buhrmann has businesses. Corporate Express offered its global customers a wide variety of products including office products, computer supplies and consumables, office furniture, and support services.

Corporate Express promised more locations and distribution centres than any business-to-business office supply company in the world, with nearly twice the number of delivery vehicles of its nearest competitor. In addition, the company boasted state-of-the art distribution, Internet and warehouse technologies, and announced that it had the broadest product offering in the industry. Corporate Express would also offer customers their own account manager to assure complete co-ordination.

On October 19, 2000, Corporate Express announced the results of a year-long, integrated international effort to develop a global accounts and merchandising capability. This effort was designed to meet the needs of complex international companies looking for global office products procurement solutions. With significant positions in North America, Europe and Australia/New Zealand, Corporate Express believed that it was the leading B2B office products company servicing large international companies with a true one-company global capability.

Corporate Express's global accounts program was led by an international team who focused on meeting customers' global office products needs. Its global merchandising strategy involved partnering with a core group of international suppliers to provide select products globally, along

---

[12]www.corporateexpress.com, January 14, 2001.
[13]At the beginning of 2001, $1 U.S. dollar = 1.06 Euros.

with developing collateral merchandising and marketing support materials. Mark Hoffman, president of Corporate Express North American Office Products offered:

> Corporate Express's global capabilities differentiate us in the marketplace. Over the past year, we have come to appreciate the challenges associated with multiple languages, currencies, products and cultures across continents. That experience confirms our belief — that the best way to go to market is with one company, one global strategy, one global account team and a single point of accountability supported by local operations in every market we serve. This ensures our global customers receive uniform, consistent high-quality service tailored to their local needs.

Janhein Pieterse, president of Corporate Express European Office Products continued:

> In addition, this strategy provides global accounts with a consistent approach to pricing of products across all countries. It allows pricing efficiencies based on overall global spending and the purchasing power of a multibillion-dollar distribution company.

Ted Nark, president of Corporate Express Australian/New Zealand Office Products added:

> Our global accounts and merchandising teams are made up of top sales and procurement leaders from North America, Europe and Australia/New Zealand. This organization assures local account attention by experienced Corporate Express specialists closely connected to their international colleagues.[14]

Among key global customers, Corporate Express serviced PriceWaterhouse Coopers and Deutsche Bank on three continents. Recently, Deutsche Bank awarded Corporate Express its "Global Supplier of the Year" award for excellence in supporting global operations. The worldwide market account potential for global accounts was estimated to be over US$1 billion.

LYRECO OFFICE PRODUCTS

On a mission to be the number one office products supplier in Canada, Lyreco Office Products was a leading business-to-business distributor of office supplies, office furniture and computer supplies. It offered customers service from coast-to-coast with next-day, free delivery throughout most of Canada. Same-day delivery was offered in Halifax and Calgary for certain orders.

OFFICE DEPOT

The largest seller of office products in North America, Office Depot had more than 950 stores worldwide, most of which were in the United States. Office Depot had 26 retail stores in Canada.[15] It posted 1999 sales of US$10.26 billion, an increase of 14.1 per cent over 1998, and achieved net income of $258 million. In addition to typical office supplies, Office Depot's stores offered computer hardware and software, furniture, printing and copying services, and art and engineering

---

[14]www.corporateexpress.com, January 14, 2001.
[15]Stores: 13 Ontario, 8 Alberta, 3 Manitoba, 2 Saskatchewan. www.officedepot.ca, January 12, 2001.

supplies. The stores (mostly warehouse-styled) mainly sold to small firms, home offices and individual customers. Nearly one-third of Office Depot's sales came from its business services group, which offered contract services and delivery to large firms. Office Depot recently acquired Viking Office Products, which sold office products internationally through catalogues. This move indicated that Office Depot was acquiring capabilities to better serve its business customers. [16]

OFFICEMAX

Number three in North America in terms of office products sales, OfficeMax sold discount-priced office supplies and equipment through about 1,000 stores in the United States and Puerto Rico, as well as through joint ventures in Japan, Brazil and Mexico. Some stores combined office supplies with in-store FurnitureMax (furniture) and CopyMax (printing services) outlets. Gateway was the exclusive computer brand in all OfficeMax stores. OfficeMax also sold products through catalogues and its Web site. Currently, the firm was testing smaller urban OfficeMax PDQ stores. It achieved sales of US$4.84 billion in 2000, an increase of 11.6 per cent over 1999, and net income of US$10 million. OfficeMax employed 41,000 people worldwide.

DELL COMPUTER CORPORATION

G&T considered Dell a valued customer and supplier. However, as in other industries, suppliers like Dell had the opportunity to sell directly to the customer.

In 2000, Dell was number two worldwide in computer market share and was consistently the leader in liquidity, profitability and growth among all major computer systems companies, with approximately 40,000 employees around the globe. The company ranked number one in the United States, where it was a leading supplier of personal computers (PC) to business customers, government agencies, educational institutions and consumers. Company revenue for the last four quarters totalled US$32 billion.

The company was founded in 1984 by Michael Dell, the computer industry's longest-tenured chief executive officer, on a simple concept: that by selling personal computer systems directly to customers, Dell could best understand their needs, and efficiently provide the most effective computing solutions to meet those needs.

Through the direct business model, Dell offered in-person relationships with consumer, corporate and institutional customers; telephone and Internet purchasing; customized computer systems; online and phone technical support; and next-day, on-site product service. Dell was continually enhancing and broadening the fundamental competitive advantages of the direct model by increasingly applying the efficiencies of the Internet to its entire business. About 50 per cent of Dell's sales were Web-enabled, while 50 per cent of Dell's technical support activities and about 76 per cent of Dell's order-status transactions also occurred online.

Dell was a key partner in helping many of its customers deploy the technology they needed to capitalize on the efficiencies of the Internet. Dell arranged for system installation and management, guided customers through technology transitions and provided an extensive range of other services. The company designed and customized products and services to the requirements of organizations

---

[16]www.hoovers.com, January 12, 2001.

and individuals. In addition, it sold an extensive selection of peripheral hardware and computing software. Approximately two-thirds of Dell's revenue was generated through medium and large business and institutional customers. (Dell started in business by serving home and small business PC users.)

Dell's Internet Push

The company was increasingly applying the Internet and realizing associated efficiencies throughout its business, including procurement, customer support and relationship management. At www.dell.com, customers could review, configure and price systems within Dell's entire product line; order systems online; and track orders from manufacturing through shipping. At valuechain.dell.com, Dell shared information on a range of topics, including product quality and inventory, with its suppliers. Dell also used the Internet to deliver customer services such as "E-Support –Direct From Dell" which offered advance online customer support; Dell Talk, an online discussion forum; and Ask Dudley, Dell's natural language technical support tool. More than 58,000 business and institutional customers worldwide used Dell's Premier Dell.com Web pages to do business with the company online.

Expansion of the Direct Model

Dell focused on initiatives such as moving even greater volumes of product sales, service and support to the Internet; using the Internet to improve the efficiency of Dell's procurement, manufacturing, distribution, and other internal processes; and further expanding an already broad range of services that helped customers build an online presence. Dell believed that it still had significant opportunity for expansion in all parts of the world and had expanded the reach of the direct model to new regions and countries such as Latin America and India. Opportunities for expansion also existed in customer segments and in all product categories, from home PCs to enterprise products which played a key role in the build-out of the Internet infrastructure.

UNITED PARCEL SERVICES (UPS)

Founded in 1907 in Seattle, Washington, UPS was the world's largest package distribution company, delivering more than 13 million documents and parcels every day and generating revenues of more than US$27 billion a year (2000). UPS was also the world's largest express package and document delivery company, delivering more packages — in two days or less that were tracked and guaranteed — than any other company in the industry. It served more than 200 countries and territories, operating in five international regions: Europe/Middle East & Africa, Asia Pacific, Latin America/Carribean, Canada and the United States.

UPS had developed what it believed was the world's fastest package tracking system, providing its customers access to tracking and distribution intelligence. Since 1985, UPS had spent more than US$12 billion on information technology. In 2000, UPS spent US$1 billion on information technology, more than it spent for vehicles and nearly as much as it spent on airplanes. A global telecommunications network had been instrumental to UPS's success, linking nearly one million users in 150 international locations. It also operated one of the largest wireless networks in the world.

Specialized Units at UPS

Formed in 1995, UPS Logistics Group (LG) was a wholly owned subsidiary of UPS offering a full spectrum of supply chain services. LG companies provided comprehensive global supply chain solutions aimed at reducing costs, improving customer service, reducing inventory investments and speeding up product delivery. LG integrated the movement of goods with the movement of funds and information, resulting in significant bottom-line improvements. LG operated 420 distribution facilities, ranging from regional logistics and technology centres to small "local" strategic stocking locations. These facilities were located in more than 50 countries. LG's key services included:

- Supply chain management: providing solutions for the re-engineering and managing of global supply chains — from supplier through manufacturing, distributor, dealer and/or the end-consumer.
- Transportation services: designing and managing multimodal shipments and distribution networks around the world.
- Logistics technologies: providing integrated logistics information systems and services that provided visibility for the flow of goods from origin to destination; commercial software for routing, scheduling and dispatching was available under the brand names of MobileCast and Roadnet.
- Service parts logistics: designing and managing urgent parts networks and return-and-repair operations across a wide variety of industries.

For example, its service parts logistics unit specialized in the analysis, design and management of critical parts distribution networks. A worldwide network of transportation carriers, central distribution facilities and strategy stocking locations made it possible to deliver critical parts in one-, two-, four-, and 24-hour time windows. The unit also provided technical repair services for telecommunications and computer equipment, providing warranty turnaround service in 24-to-48 hours.

GRAND & TOY'S E-COMMERCE STRATEGY

E-commerce was an important part of G&T's strategy as the company expected to direct 50 per cent of its orders through its site within three years.[17] Its existing e-commerce offering included www.grandandtoy.com and various customer ordering applications that had general ordering functionality. Grand & Toy believed that the applications were efficiently integrated into its distribution system. Here is a break-out of each ordering application and its intended target market:

	TSR	G&T.com	Order Point	Catalyst
Target Market	SOHO	M-L	Corporation	Multi-Vendor
Functionality	Basic	Basic	Sophisticated	Basic

---

[17]Representing Cdn$500 million in revenues.

Over the next 18 months, G&T intended to correct some of the limitations associated with its multiple applications. These limitations included loss of economies of scale with multiple ordering applications, duplication of effort if new features were added individually to each application, and inconsistent marketing communications and brand dilution.

Thus, G&T's vision of one e-commerce platform would translate into:

- One point of entry for customers (at www.grandandtoy.com);
- Online customer segmentation through user identification;
- Integration with other stakeholders (call centre, retail, commercial etc);
- Customers ordering from multiple channels; and
- New features including credit purchasing, account automation, etc.

By providing a robust ordering tool, coupled with rich product information to customers through electronic presentment, resources from sales and customer service could be focused on more strategic issues such as cost management and strategic sourcing.

Grand & Toy intended to leverage existing online relationships to increase the order size, manage administrative costs and add new value-added services. It also intended to mine existing customer data to target products, promotions and services more effectively.

AN ONLINE COMPETITOR: ONVIA.COM[18]

"Our focus is small b to small b," explained Gary Meehan, President of Onvia Canada. He continued:

> We target entrepreneurs and small businesses, generally with less than 100 employees. There are one million small businesses of between one to 50 people registering and reporting business income in Canada. There are another one and a half million office types who look like consumers. But they're not — we find that only nine per cent of households purchase online.

According to Onvia, the difference between B2B and B2C (business-to-consumer) was complexity of needs and the amount of functionality demanded. Consumers, being purchasing entities of one, were generally less complex than businesses, which themselves contained multiple consumers. Onvia's challenge was to cross the chasm and reach small businesses that were not online, or that were online but not using the Web for commerce.

From an e-business point of view, these businesses were further behind in technological use than consumers. Onvia's closer look at its customer demographics indicated that the newer small businesses (less than a year old) and the ones that had been around for more than seven years were actually going online. The 'laggards' were the businesses in the middle who had been in existence from between one to six years.

Glenn Ballman, founder and CEO elaborated:

---

[18]The Onvia.com section was sourced from the 2000 Ivey case study 'Onvia.com: The Zanova Acquisition', #9B00E019, (Ken Mark and Professor Michael Parent).

We're a closed loop site. As a small business, ideally, you don't have to leave our site to seek out other services because we aim to provide our small business customers with every service they need to both save money and make money. If we keep them in the same loop, we will make money on the seller side.

Onvia's site, or trading hub, included more than 60,000 businesses across 117 services in the RFQ network, which enables buyers to submit requests for quotes for various business services and sellers to respond with pricing and fulfilment information. In Onvia's Purchase Now system, more than 37,000 small business products were available for quick purchase. Their News and Tools section was a collection of breaking news, information, business worksheets and forms designed to help small businesses enhance their operations. The Onvia Community brought entrepreneurs together to exchange ideas, advice and opinions in order to build business-to-business networking relationships. Finally, the most recent addition included a government-to-business exchange that enabled Onvia's small business users access to procurement contracts by matching their specific product and service offering with government agencies and large corporation buyers. "It will take six months for us to build our trading hub to include Purchase Now, RFQ, Auctions, Group Buying, Barter (for points), and Swop (products exchanged)," explained Ballman.

Targeting all vertical markets ranging from industries such as agriculture, automotive, legal and construction, Onvia would build tools to encourage buyers to use the exchange. Services provided would range from seller ratings, Web site hosting, catalogue hosting and payment automation. "We will realize our value when customers can't run their business unless our site is up," offered Ballman.

Offering services such as payroll, financial services, reports, insurance, customer acquisition and other customer services, Onvia intended to manage, for a fee, the non-core, 'business-enabling' functions. Ballman termed this phase 'customer relationship management,' made possible when customers, more and more comfortable with Onvia's services, sought to outsource to Onvia their non-core operations.

REVISITING GRAND & TOY'S STRATEGY

Increasingly, G&T would face global competitors in both its online and offline markets. Furthermore, some of these would be non-traditional competitors. While Vanexan felt that the current strategy was on target, he looked forward to revisiting it with his management team to ensure they had fully considered both the competitive threats and opportunities.

Exhibit 1: **Staples Milestones**

2000	Staples opens 22 retail stores on February 19, setting a company record for the largest number of stores opened on one day.
1999	Staples lays plans to create a tracking stock for Stales.com, its e-commerce business unit. Staples opens the first airport office superstore. Staples acquires 42 European retail stores across Germany, the Netherlands and Portugal. Staples launches Quill catalogue operations in Europe. Staples opens the first 24-hour office superstore. Staples opens its 1,000th store, more than any office supply company.
1998	Based on its ongoing success, Staples is named to the Standard & Poor's 500 Index. Staples launches its e-commerce site, Staples.com. Staples purchases Quill Corporation, a $600 million direct marketer of office supplies for medium-sized companies. Staples acquires Claricom Holdings, Inc., a provider of telecommunications services to medium-sized companies, and later renames it Staples Communications. Staples announces its seventh stock split in eight years.
1996	Staples opens its 500th store and becomes one of six companies U.S. history to achieve annual sales of $3 billion within 10 years.
1993	Staples Contract and Commercial is formed when the company announces plans to purchase contract stationers National Office Supply Company, Inc. and Spectrum Office Products.
1992	Staples enters the European market by acquiring an interest in MAXI-Papier in Germany and forming a joint venture with Kingfisher PLC in the United Kingdom.
1991	Staples crosses the U.S. border into Canada through a joint venture with Business Depot.
1989	Staples raises $36 million through an initial public offering, and launches Staples Direct, its catalogue delivery service.
1986	Staples launches the office products superstore industry with the opening of its first superstore in Brighton, Massachusetts.
1985	Staples Inc. is founded by Tom Stemberg and Leo Kahn, former rivals in Boston's competitive supermarket business.

Source: www.staples.com, March 20, 2001.

Exhibit 2: Staples Press Release

Staples Inc. Revenue Up 17 per cent for the Third Quarter
Nov. 14, 2000--

Economy, Aggressive Investments Impact Results; Staples.com, Staples
Direct and Europe Performances Strong Company Gives Guidance for the Fourth Quarter of 2000
and Fiscal Year 2001

Staples Inc. (NASDAQ:SPLS), the pioneer of the office superstore industry, today announced net income of $84.7 million, or $.19 per common share, on a diluted basis, for the third quarter ending October 28, 2000, compared with $92.5 million, or $.20 per common share, on a diluted basis, in the prior year.

Sales for the quarter rose 17 percent to $2.8 billion, from $2.4 billion reported for the same period last year. Company-wide comparable sales, comprised of the 1,069 stores open for more than one year, as well as Staples Direct and the Staples.com and Business Depot Web sites, increased 7 percent for the third quarter. Pure retail comparable store sales were up 4 percent.

"Given the tough retail climate, our results are respectable, although not up to our usual standards," said Staples Chairman and Chief Executive Officer Thomas G. Stemberg. "The downturn in the economy, combined with our aggressive growth plans, hurt our business. With a strong management team in place, we're managing our way well through a difficult environment."

North American retail store results for the third quarter were negatively impacted by lower consumer spending, competitive pricing, labor and shrink pressures, costs associated with the company's new market entries and a new distribution center that is not yet operating at capacity. In addition, the company's telecommunications subsidiary, Staples Communications, continues to underperform and economic uncertainty caused by the gas crisis in the United Kingdom affected European retail results.

"Although we're dissatisfied with our aggregate results, we continue to lead the industry and are pleased with the performance of a number of our businesses. Staples.com sales continue to exceed our expectations; Staples Direct had its highest operating profit rate ever; and our European retail operations were profitable for the quarter, including corporate expenses. The remedies we're putting in place should have our entire business on track for next year," added Stemberg.

Staples expects earnings per share for the fourth quarter to equal or exceed last year's fourth quarter earnings, but fall short of the current First Call consensus estimates. Staples expects earnings per share in fiscal year 2001 to grow at least 30 percent from fiscal year 2000 levels.

Source: www.staples.com, March 20, 2001.

NAPSTER AND MP3: REDEFINING THE MUSIC INDUSTRY[1]

case 8

Trevor Hunter
Tammy Smith
Mary M. Crossan
Margaret Ann Wilkinson and
Mark Perry

In the summer of 2000, the Recording Industry Association of America (RIAA) was awarded an interim injunction against the Internet's largest facilitator of MP3 file exchanges, Napster Inc. (Napster), forcing it to shut down its system. However, less than a week after the injunction was issued, Napster successfully appealed and the injunction was lifted. The RIAA argued that Napster distributed allegedly "pirated" music (i.e., music that the user uploaded or mounted on their computer for distribution as an MP3 file, thereby allowing people free access to the MP3 files in

[1]This case has been written on the basis of published sources only. Consequently, the interpretation and perspectives presented in this case are not necessarily those of Napster, Inc. or any of its employees.

IVEY

Trevor Hunter and Tammy Smith prepared this case under the supervision of Professors Mary Crossan, Margaret Ann Wilkinson and Mark Perry solely to provide material for class discussion. The authors do not intend to illustrate either effective or ineffective handling of a managerial situation. The authors may have disguised certain names and other identifying information to protect confidentiality.

clear violation of copyright by the user). Although they fought in court, the RIAA and Napster were both members of the Secure Digital Music Initiative (SDMI). The SDMI, established in December 1998, was a forum for the music industry to develop a voluntary open framework for playing, storing and distributing digital music, while at the same time enabling the new market to emerge.[2] The essence of SDMI was to develop a new paradigm in the digital music industry such that alternatives to the current 'in the box' thinking regarding the eradication of music piracy could be explored through mutual agreement and understanding coupled with technological innovation. However, as the Napster/RIAA lawsuit demonstrated, membership did not mean that the fight for a competitive advantage in the industry would end.

The Music Industry

In 1999, the recorded music industry in the United States alone was estimated by the RIAA to be worth close to US$15 billion. The stakes were high, as was the competition. Although there was a seemingly endless source of music from established and new artists, the industry was in a constant search for the newest trend and potential star. The costs of finding the newest superstar were high and the odds of success were low. Record companies could spend between US$150,000 and US$500,000 to sign a new artist, and nearly the same amount to promote them.[3] Exhibit 1 presents a diagram depicting the steps through which recorded music reached the end consumer. The left side of the diagram depicts the value-added stages as artists provide music and lyrics to record companies who record, combine and market music through a variety of distribution channels. The right side depicts the value-added processes involved in the manufacturing and distribution of the technology to play the music. Exhibit 2 presents a breakdown of how the revenues from the sale of a CD are distributed.

As a new channel of distribution, the Internet enabled artists to deal directly with customers, and enabled one customer to access another in order to exchange music. It was the development of MP3 format and player technology that enabled the distribution of music over the Internet.

The MP3 Format

The traditional means of music distribution was for recording artists to use a music publisher that would market compact discs (CDs).

> The typical five-minute track on a CD is a digital file that [contains] around 50 megabytes (MB) of data. … By using file compression technologies such as MP3, it was possible to reduce the file size to around one-twelfth of that of the CD version, whilst achieving good quality for reproduction.[4]

Developed by the Fraunhofer Institute in Germany in 1992, MP3 was a format similar in nature to .jpg. It was used to transfer and store digital music over the Internet.[5] What made it so pervasive was that the file, while significantly compressed, retained near CD-quality sound. This reduced size made the exchange, transfer and storage of digital music far more convenient than ever

[2]http://www.sdmi.org/who_we_are.htm.
[3]Henderson, Richard, "Music & Money: The Billboard Spotlight – How Much Is That Deal In The Window?" Billboard Magazine, April 29, 2000.
[4]Mark Perry, "Audio-files: Good Sounds on Trial," 1 Technology Law Forum, September 2000, p.5.
[5]PC World Magazine, July 2000, p.127.

before. Hundreds of songs, even entire albums could be stored on a computer hard drive and downloaded with relative ease.

MP3 files were routinely exchanged through the Internet. With the advent of digital recording, it became relatively simple and inexpensive to record a CD full of copyrighted material, and further, to upload it onto a computer. Once uploaded, the files could be converted to the MP3 format and made available to anyone in the world having unhindered access to the Internet. Numerous Web sites sprung up, making available MP3 files to download for free. Examples of these sites include the more infamous Napster, MP3.com, Freenet, and Gnutella. Also some users set up file transfer protocol (FTP) sites, allowing other users access to files on their computer. This list is by no means an exhaustive survey of the varied and numerous ways to exchange digitized data.

MP3 Players

Initially a limiting factor to MP3 popularity was the lack of a device to play MP3 files aside from a computer. This changed when Diamond Multimedia introduced its Rio 300 MP3 player.[6] However, the system was relatively expensive at the time and had such limited storage capacity that only a few songs could be stored.

In a relatively short period of time, the number of producers increased dramatically. The door opened to a new industry that quickly filled with competitors who added functions and storage capacity to their models, while at the same time lowering prices to the consumer. By mid-2000, there were numerous models on the market produced by large, established multinationals like Sony and Samsung, as well as new start-ups. (Exhibit 3 presents a list of MP3 players). The machines could store about one hour of music. When consumers wanted to change the music they listened to, they would have to erase what was stored and upload new files onto the player. Depending on the player, this could be a time consuming and confusing process. Although the functionality and ease of use was not at the level of more established competing products (like personal cassette or CD players), the manufacturers continued to innovate. The confluence of the MP3 format, player technology and the Internet greatly simplified the access, transfer, copy and playing of music. In doing so, the issues surrounding copyright became more prevalent. However, challenges to copyright were not new.

Copyright: Historical Perspective

Copyright, itself a legal solution to the challenges of the changes wrought by the industrial and print revolutions, had traditionally been created in works of four kinds: literary, artistic, dramatic and musical. Over time, technology had required the courts and legislatures of various jurisdictions to examine and re-examine the balance created by their copyright legislative regimes.

For example, there was a technological and social challenge to the notion of copyright, particularly in musical works, with the widespread adoption of sound recording technology earlier in the 20th century. Canada early on created a limited right for the producer of the sound recording itself, which existed independent of the copyrights already created for the literary or musical works that might be recorded on the sound recording.

Then, the jukebox, which played the sound recordings of popular copyrighted musical works at the drop of a coin, became a popular addition to restaurants and other gathering places.

---

[6]A&M Records, Inc. et. al. v. Napster Inc., Case Nos. C99-5183 MHP (ADR), C00-0074 MHP (ADR) United States District Court, Northern California District, San Francisco Division, July 26, 2000, p.23.

Technically, the patrons of these establishments could have been considered to be "performing a work in public" when they dropped the coin in and caused the songs to play to the other restaurant patrons and employees. To do this legally, they would have been required to obtain the prior permission of the copyright holders of the musical works and the permission of those who held the rights in the sound recordings. It would then have been within the copyright holders' rights to require payment for these playings.

The Canadian Parliament decided, however, that this situation was unworkable in light of the technical limitations of the new technology and the social demands of Canadians. The *Copyright Act* had therefore been amended to provide that the Copyright Appeal Board, a federal administrative agency, was to provide in advance for the collection of fees from the radio broadcasting stations or the gramophone manufacturers to compensate the rightsholders for the anticipated playing of their works and recordings which would occur through jukeboxes. These moneys would be payable to the Canadian Performing Rights Society and would then be distributed amongst its members (the rightsholders). It was anticipated that these costs would then be passed through to the ultimate consumers of the music by way of pricing mechanisms — the cost to the restaurants of having jukeboxes installed and maintained, or the cost per song for the paying customer.

Although the legislation provided for this administrative mechanism administered by the Copyright Appeal Board, by 1940, it had not yet come into existence. The Canadian Performing Rights Society was not actually getting any recompense for its members from the playing of members' songs on jukeboxes. A case involving this impasse reached the Privy Council (which was then the highest court in Canada) on appeal from the Supreme Court of Canada.[7]

The Court held that the right of 'public performance,' reserved to copyright holders under the copyright regime, did include those performances whereby music is played on a jukebox. However, said the Court, Parliament had expressly removed that right from among those for which the rightsholders were to be compensated in its legislation. This removal operated even though the federal government had failed to implement the alternative administrative scheme they had legislated, which was supposed to have replaced the rightsholders' former statutory rights. The court held that "no charge of any kind is to be collected from the owner or user of the radio receiving set or gramophone."[8] Essentially, the Privy Council exonerated both owners and users of jukeboxes from "all payments in respect of public performances of musical compositions"[9] to the holders of the rights conferred by the *Copyright Act*.

These reactions to earlier music technology illustrated several points about the law relating to copyright. The rights were created through actions of the appropriate legislative bodies. Governments could change the legislation in response to changing social and economic conditions as the political process dictated. They could reallocate rights. They could create new classes of rightsholders. The role of the courts was to apply the law to the individual disputes between users and rightsholders who came before them (or, in criminal proceedings, between the state and the individuals accused), according to the provisions of the legislation as it existed at the time the disputes arose. In periods of technological change, the courts were often faced with disputes in

---

[7]Vigneux et al. v. Canadian Performing Rights Society, [1945] 2 D.L.R. 1, reversing [1943] 3 D.L.R. 369, affirming [1942] 3 D.L.R. 449 [hereinafter Vigneux].
[8]Ibid. at 10.
[9]Ibid.

technological environments that were not clearly covered by the legislation and, in these situations, would still need to resolve the disputes between the litigants before them.

The Recording Industry Association Of America (RIAA)

Working to protect the interests of the industry players on the left side of the chain in Exhibit 1 was the RIAA. The RIAA was the main champion of intellectual property rights in the American recorded music industry. As a lobbying organization, it was influential and proactive both in the United States and around the world in trying to protect the copyrights of its hundreds of members. Its mission was simple:

> The Recording Industry Association of America is the trade group that represents the U.S. recording industry. Our mission is to foster a business and legal climate that supports and promotes our members' creative and financial vitality. Our members are the record companies that comprise the most vibrant national music industry in the world. RIAA members create, manufacture and/or distribute approximately 90 per cent of all legitimate sound recordings produced and sold in the United States.
>
> In support of our mission, we work to protect intellectual property rights worldwide and the First Amendment rights of artists; conduct consumer, industry and technical research; and monitor and review . . . state and federal laws, regulations and policies.[10]

The main thrust of the RIAA activities was in helping members to achieve value from their intellectual property in music in the form of copyright. As an intellectual property right, copyright is that bundle of rights that arises on the creation of original works, including musical works. These rights include the right to control the reproduction and distribution of such works. Copying of musical works without the permission of the copyright holder, either the creator or successor to ownership of the right, was actionable in the courts. However, there was provided in the copyright legislation of most jurisdictions a limited exception to the rights of the copyright holder that permitted copying of musical works for personal use.

As the MP3 technology that enabled the replications and distribution of musical works became increasingly widespread, the RIAA became increasingly proactive in protecting the rights of its members. As part of its strategy, the RIAA became one of the more important groups in championing the creation of SDMI and pushing for focus and standardization of formats in the music industry.

The RIAA was not the only such recording industry association around the world. In Canada, the Canadian Recording Industry Association (CRIA) protected Canadian recording artists, while the British Phonographic Industry (BPI) did the same in the United Kingdom. Interestingly, although both the CRIA and BPI had nearly identical mandates to that of their U.S. counterpart, neither was a member of the SDMI.[11]

---

[10]http://www.riaa.org/About-Who.cfm.

[11]Both CRIA and BPI are members of the International Federation of the Phonographic Industry [IFPI]. Also members of the IFPI are the recording industry associations of: Argentina, Australia, Austria, Belgium, Brazil, Bulgaria, Chile, Colombia, Czech Republic, Denmark, Egypt, Finland, France, Germany, Ghana, Greece, Hong Kong, Hungary, Iceland, India, Ireland, Israel, Italy, Japan, Kenya, Lebanon, Malaysia, Mexico, the Netherlands, New Zealand, Nigeria, Norway, Poland, Portugal, Singapore, Slovak Republic, South Africa, Spain, Sweden, Switzerland, Taiwan, Thailand, Turkey, United States and Venezuela. The IFPI is a member of the SDMI. As such, the IFPI members are represented in the SDMI process. Because of the size of the RIAA

SDMI

Although it was founded in 1998, plans for an initiative such as the SDMI dated back to the mid-1990s. SDMI was an organization of what the administration referred to as "technology" companies. Exhibit 4 presents a list of the SDMI participants. As Cary Sherman, senior vice-president and general counsel of the RIAA put it,

> [SDMI] includes information technology (IT) companies, and consumer electronic (CE) companies, and telecommunications companies, and Internet companies, and vendors of security technologies and everyone else whose technology products and services are critical to the distribution of digital music, in all formats and through all channels.[12]

Together, their aim was to,

> attempt to create an open architecture and specification that [would] make it possible for consumers and content providers to find common ground on the terms on which music can be accessed and used . . . a specification for how music can be marked at the source, identified and labelled with rights-management information that is embedded in the music or carried with it in such a way that it remains with that piece of music no matter what system, network or device it passes through . . . any device in which it is recorded, stored or played on will know how and where to look for and act upon that data.[13]

The mission was at once both reactive and proactive to the MP3 phenomenon, since the members were trying to curb the existing piracy of copyrighted material and develop a strategy by which all members could gain from an innovative technology. As Sherman stated, this technology offered new business models for gaining a competitive advantage in the music industry. The MP3 format provided an easy and efficient format, the Internet provided a pervasive and efficient medium for distribution, and the playing technology provided a new method of listening to music. Under the leadership of Dr. Leonardo Chiariglione, one of the creators of the MPEG format for audio and video exchange through the Internet, SDMI was well connected within the worldwide music industry. What was needed was a way to secure the content to capture the economic gains the SDMI foresaw.

From its inception, the SDMI was intended to be a forum involved in the development of a secure method of transferring and distributing digital music. As a result, it needed to involve content producers, digital music distributors of all sorts (from record labels to Internet sites), and finally, current or potential producers of digital music players and recorders. In February 1999, a meeting with representatives from over 100 different companies was held to announce the plans for the SDMI. Within weeks, more meetings were held and documents were drafted that would establish the ground rules for SDMI. The organization would institute its plan in two phases.

Phase 1 was a solicitation for designs for SDMI-compliant MP3 devices to be available to the market by December 1999. These devices would "accept any content, regardless of format, whether

---

relative to the industry associations of the other member countries, it is feasible that the RIAA maintains an independent membership in the SDMI.

[12]Presentation to the SDMI Organizing Plenary, Feb. 26, 1999. http://www.sdmi.org/present.org.plenary.htm.
[13]Ibid.

secure or insecure, whether legitimate or illegitimate."[14] The purpose for this "open" device was to gain market share for its members before implementing Phase 2. Additionally, and more importantly, within these players there would be a mechanism that would read digitally "watermarked" SDMI-compliant content and eventually filter out content that was illegally obtained. By August 1999, ARIS Technologies had been selected to provide the watermark encryption systems.

Phase 2 was the heart of what SDMI stood for, which was the protection of copyrighted material. Phase 2 was to be implemented by late 2000 or early 2001 and involved the digital "watermark." Phase 2 was described by SDMI as follows:

> The transition from first- to second-generation portable devices would be handled by having Phase 1 and Phase 2 computer applications supporting the devices.
>
> The computer application supporting the device will include a mechanism, or trigger, to prompt the user to upgrade to Phase 2 technology, once such technology is available, in order to play or copy Phase 2 content. The mechanism will be triggered by data incorporated in new, SDMI-compliant music that is released after the Phase 2 technology is available.
>
> The transition mechanism [*Phase 2 technology that is embedded in the device*] will not cut off any function of the Phase 1 application or portable device. However, consumers who want to be able to play or copy new, SDMI-compliant music through an SDMI-compliant computer application will have to upgrade their application to Phase 2 technology. The owner of a Phase 1 device and supporting application may choose not to do so, but that person will not be able to use it for new, SDMI-compliant music. The trigger mechanism will not automatically upgrade the computer application; the individual user will have to choose the upgrade.
>
> The Phase 2 computer application supporting portable devices will enable consumers to "rip" CDs, as they do now, but only for personal use on their own computers or portable devices. That application will not allow the user to make those copies available on pirate sites on the Internet. Moreover, the Phase 2 application will be able to recognize pirated music — i.e., music that has not been authorized to be distributed in insecure, compressed form — and it will refuse to accept a download of that pirated music from the Internet. The application will not reject authorized distributions, such as where an artist or record company chooses to make music available on the Internet for free distribution.
>
> Finally, computer and consumer electronics devices will be able to accommodate both SDMI-compliant and non-SDMI-compliant formats (e.g., MP3) in the same application. The only music files that will be rejected in Phase 2 applications are those that are identified as 'pirated'.[15]

Essentially, Phase 2 of the SDMI would limit the number of times a user could copy a CD or MP3 file to one, for their own personal use. While this limited the extent of the "personal exemption" granted in copyright, such a limitation would be legal since the personal use was an exemption, not a right. As well, Phase 2 applications would not allow a user to copy or download and play an illegally copied CD or file that had been made in the past.

Critics of the SDMI suggested that the organization was designed to limit competition and control the industry. Exhibit 5 presents the position SDMI took against accusations of antitrust violations.

---

[14] SDMI Update: Statement from the Executive Director and Portable Working Group Chair, May 25, 1999, http://www.sdmi.org/statement_May_25_1999.htm.

[15] SDMI Update: Statement from the Executive Director and Portable Working Group Chair, May 25, 1999, http://www.sdmi.org/statement_May_25_1999.htm.

Critics also suggested that the SDMI would not be the secure system it proposed to be. To counteract such criticism, the SDMI looked to a group that they felt would be the best at developing a secure system for help: hackers themselves. In September of 2000, the SDMI launched its "crack SDMI" contest where hackers were given the opportunity to hack into the system and potentially win US$10,000 for their innovativeness. Exhibit 6 presents the open letters on the SDMI Web site explaining the contest, and the following quote presents their rationale.

> The Challenge[16]
>
> Several proposals are currently being considered for the Phase Two screening technology. Some are digital watermarking technologies; others use a different technology to provide the screening functionality. The challenge is to defeat the screening technology. For example, where the proposed technology is a watermark, the challenge is to remove or alter the watermark while not significantly degrading the quality of a digital music sample. Marked samples and files may be downloaded from this site. If you believe you have successfully defeated the security technology you may upload the attacked sample or file to this Web site. We will evaluate your submission. Under certain conditions, challengers may be able to receive compensation for describing and providing to SDMI their successful attack.

Some felt this was an innovative method for the SDMI to deal with a major problem for the protected industry it was trying to create. Others were not as optimistic.

> As things stand, however, SDMI is more likely to be sunk by the forces in the marketplace than by clever hacking. It has been overtaken by events following the rise of Napster. Some of its members of the SDMI consortium are already selling proprietary systems of their own. Most damning of all is the fact that any software-based music-protection system can be attacked by analysing the software player itself — as was shown when the system that protects DVDs was compromised last year. In other words, whatever happens over the next few weeks, SDMI is certain to be cracked sooner or later. So even if nobody defeats the security mechanisms and claims the $10,000, SDMI's triumph will probably be hollow. Worse, if the protection software is cracked straight away, it could deal a fatal blow to what is already an ailing standard.[17]

In some ways the music industry was similar to the computer software industry in that the digital format facilitated easy copying of the original product and mass distribution. As personal computers first became widespread, there were fears that mass pirating of computer software would destroy the legitimate software market. Indeed there was pirating of many programs, but the majority of the software used around the world was purchased legally and the software industry was one of the strongest in the world.

In practice, SDMI appeared to focus solely on the MP3 market.

> Although MP3 files are the most prevalent on the Internet, there are many other audio compression formats in use or under development that achieve better compression and/or quality. A competitor to the portable MP3 player, for example, is the MiniDisc that uses higher quality ATRAC compression though only achieving a reduction of 5:1 in file size.[18]

---

[16]SDMI Website http://www.hacksdmi.org.
[17]The Economist, September 23, 2000, p.96.
[18] Supra note 3 at 2.

It is therefore conceivable that all of SDMI's proverbial eggs were in one basket.

ATTEMPTING TO CONTROL THE INDUSTRY

Prior to the formation of the SMDI, the RIAA had been fighting legal battles to preserve the existing industry order. The introduction of an MP3 player to the market sparked the RIAA to sue the manufacturer for violating the 1992 Audio Home Recording Act because "it does not employ a Serial Copyright Management System ("SCMS") that sends, receives, and acts upon information about the generation and copyright status of the files that it plays."[19] The suit was lost and appealed. The appeal was denied on the ground that while the memory cards that the Rio player used to store music could be viewed as a recording device, the player itself was not a recording device and therefore not subject to the stipulations of the Act. The player was termed a "space-shifting" device that allowed the owner to shift materials from one format to another for their own, non-commercial purposes.

> The Rio's operation is entirely consistent with the Act's main purpose — the facilitation of personal use. As the Senate Report explains, '[t]he purpose of [the Act] is to ensure the right of the consumers to make analog or digital audio recordings of copyrighted music for their private, non-commercial use.' The Act does so through its home taping exemption which 'protects all non-commercial copying by consumers of digital and analogue musical recordings.' The Rio merely makes copies in order to render portable, or 'space-shift,' those files that already reside on a user's hard drive.[20]

The RIAA also attacked the new business models, such as the MP3.com Web site, that did not pay royalties for the music being made available to the public, arguing that they robbed the artists and the record companies of their due revenue. The RIAA sued MP3.com for copyright infringement. Although MP3.com argued that it was merely a "listening post" for subscribers to listen to the songs and then purchase those they liked, the court ruled that the service MP3.com provided was in fact a service that allowed the copying of copyrighted material for commercial use, not for a consumer's personal use, and therefore was done in violation of copyright. As the judge in the case observed,

> The defendant purchased tens of thousands of popular CDs in which the plaintiffs held the copyrights, and, without authorization, copied their recordings onto its computer servers so as to be able to replay the recordings for its subscribers.[21]

Other types of MP3 file sharing sites known as "peer-to-peer" systems allowed members to utilize software that connected their computers to other members on the network, allowing all members to search for and access music files.

---

[19]Recording Industry Association of America v. Diamond Multimedia Systems Inc., No. 98-56727 (9th Cir. 06/15/1999), p.3.

[20]Ibid. p.7.

[21]RIAA v. MP3.com, Inc. United States District Court, Southern District of New York, 00 Civ. 472 (JSR), May 4, 2000, p.2.

The technology, popularized by Napster, [was] that of allowing users to share their MP3 file collection by logging on to a common server. The system allow[ed] users to search and download files from a distributed system that often [had] over 750 GB of files available. There [were] other similar systems online that [used] a centralized server system such as CuteMX and iMesh, which offer[ed] other types of media in addition to MP3 files. A recent potential addition to the menu of online offerings for file sharing called Gnutella, from Nullsoft, [had] for the moment been nipped in the bud by its parent company, America Online.[22]

The service provided by these Web sites operated in a legal grey area. It appeared legal for the owners of a CD to copy it, store it onto their computer hard drives and further upload it onto their MP3 player so long as it was for private use.[23] Private use, by definition, does not indicate that users exchange these copies with others through a computer network. The legality of the above-mentioned file-swapping facilitators was also questionable. It was unclear if it was legal to directly or indirectly make money from the provision of this service. These sites defended their actions as being merely facilitators for Internet users, as opposed to being actual distributors of copied materials in violation of copyright laws. It was this defence that Napster used against the injunction brought against it by the RIAA.

Although the majority of the MP3 files found on the Internet infringed copyright, it was possible to obtain non-infringing MP3 files. In fact, the availability of MP3 files on some Web sites had become a new marketing tool to increase record sales. Often, record companies or established artists would post files containing newly released songs that were free to the public in order to create publicity for an upcoming release, in the hope that such interest would generate additional sales of the album. For example, a 1999 study by Warner music indicated that "following the release of a Tom Petty track in MP3 format on the Internet prior to the album's street release . . . first week sales (of the new album) were considerably higher than the first week for Petty's previous album."[24]

Although this study suggested that the sharing of MP3 files increased CD sales, it was criticized as being focused on the music-buying public in general, not the specific demographic who were most likely to use Napster. Another study presented by the plaintiffs in the case against Napster suggested that among college students (who constituted a large majority of Napster users at the time), "the more songs Napster users have downloaded, the more likely they are to admit or imply that such use has reduced their music purchases," and that, "sales at stores near colleges or universities declined." Ultimately, the judge in the case concluded that "Napster use is likely to reduce CD purchases by college students, whom defendant admits constitute a key demographic."[25]

Occasionally, established artists, themselves, would release entire albums in MP3 format onto the Internet. This occurred under their own label to gain more control over their music and earn more revenue than they would if they were tied to a record company.[26] Additionally, some MP3 sites would pay licensing fees to the record companies and charge consumers for downloading files. For artists who were not established or did not have a recording contract, MP3 files and the Internet

---

[22]Supra note 3 at 4 – 5.

[23]Copyright Act, R.S.C. 1985, c-42 at s.81.

[24]A&M Records, Inc. et. al. v. Napster Inc., Case Nos. C99-5183 MHP (ADR), C00-0074 MHP (ADR) United States District Court, Northern California District, San Francisco Division, July 26, 2000, p.23.

[25]A&M Records, Inc. et. al. v. Napster Inc., Case Nos. C99-5183 MHP (ADR), C00-0074 MHP (ADR) United States District Court, Northern California District, August 10, 2000.

[26]Some artists released newly recorded music online prior to release by their label because they were rebelling against the control extended over their music by their label (i.e., Offspring, Smashing Pumpkins).

were tools to spread their music and hopefully generate sales. There were thousands of MP3 music files available from unknown groups looking to be discovered.

Industry observers thought there was a real opportunity for content providers and MP3 distributors to work together and reap huge revenues. By paying or collecting licensing fees to the record companies and then charging their users a nominal fee, MP3 file distributors or search networks like Napster (who had around 20 million users in July 2000) could make millions. As one analyst noted, "[t]he idea is to sell record companies a minority stake in Napster and split subscription, sponsorship and advertising revenues. If 20 million users pay $100 a year for subscriptions, that's $2 billion."[27] However, many of the MP3 distribution sites on the Internet and their users were staunchly anti-commercial. There was a strong culture of free exchange of ideas and information over the Net, and often the word "free" meant "no-fee" as well as open. The differing philosophies made relations between the two players somewhat adversarial.

Listen.com was launched in August 1999 as a "comprehensive" Web directory for legal downloadable music, garnering unprecedented investments from all five of the major record labels (BMG, EMI, Sony, Universal, Warner). The company hired an editorial staff of about 50 to find, review and categorize hundreds of thousands of music files in genres ranging from "hip-hop" to "cuddlecore."[28]

NAPSTER AND THE SDMI: NEXT STEPS

With the 11th-hour removal of the injunction against them, Napster was free to resume business as usual; however, they were not cleared of any wrongdoing. Although they were allowed to remain in operations until a final decision, they were still being sued for copyright infringement. A final decision would come sometime in September 2000.

The decision would have a number of important ramifications for the industry as well as for the SDMI. The various stakeholders watched with great interest, particularly the SDMI. By early fall 2000, Phase 2 was moving along on schedule, but the infighting between two important members of the initiative posed a major threat to the entire organization.

While Napster was contemplating its next moves, the SDMI was assessing whether its attempts to control the industry would prevail. It needed to assess whether the legal framework within which the industry operated would offer sufficient control, or whether additional efforts to control the technology, as was progressing in Phase 2, were required. Napster realized that while it may be able to succeed with the current players, the global nature of the industry left open the possibility for non-compliant technology and modes of operation.

---

[27]Brull, Steven V., Dennis K. Berman & Mike France, Inside Napster, <u>Business Week</u>, August 14, 2000, p.120.
[28]Lee, H.C., Listen.com chimes in on the layoff trend, <u>The Standard</u>, January 3, 2001.

Exhibit 1: **Distribution Chain for the Consumption of Recorded Music**

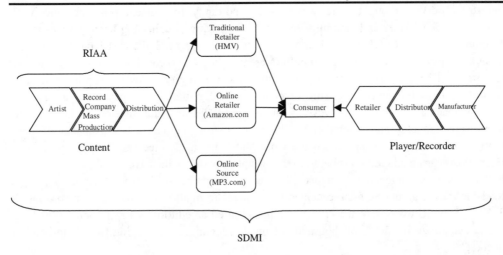

Exhibit 2: **Breakdown of Revenue Distribution from the Sale of One CD[29]**

Assume Retail Selling Price of US$16.98

Where the money goes:	$
Co-op advertising and discounts to retailers:	.85
Pressing album and printing booklet:	.75
Profit to label:	.59
Retail markup:	6.23
Company overhead, distribution and shipping:	3.34
Marketing and promotion:	2.15
Royalties to artist and songwriter:	1.99
Signing act and producing record:	1.08
	16.98

[29]Jeffry, Scott, "Will federal pact slash CD costs?" Atlanta Journal and Constitution, May 12, 2000.

Exhibit 3: **A Sample Comparison of MP3 Players**[30]

Product Name	Price (USD)	Storage Capacity
Audiovox MP-1000	$180	32MB
Casio MP3 Wrist Audio Player	$249	16MB
Creative Labs Nomad II	$330	64MB
HanGo Remote Solution Personal Jukebox	$749	4.86GB
I2Go Ego	$269	64MB
I-Jam	$220	32MB
RCA Lyra Player	$199	32MB
Samsung Yepp	$229	64MB
Sensory Science RaveMP 2100	$269	64MB
Sony Memory Stick Walkman	$400	64MB

---

[30]This information was selected from a list published in PC World, July 2000, pp. 126-127.

Exhibit 4: **SDMI List of Participants as of July 5, 2000**

Adaptec
AegiSoft Corp
AEI Music/Playmedia
Aiwa Limited
Am. Federation of TV and
Radio Artists (AFTRA)
Am. Soc. of Composers,
Authors & Publishers
(ASCAP)
American Federation of
Musicians
AMP3.com/JVWeb
Amplified.com
AOL
ARM Limited
AT&T/a2b
Audible, Inc.
Audio Explosion /Mjuice
Audio Matrix
Audiohighway.com
AudioSoft
AudioTrack
Aureal Semiconductor
Be Inc.
Beatnik, Inc.
Blue Spike, Inc.
BMG Entertainment
BreakerTech
Broadcast Music, Inc. (BMI)
Broadcom HomeNetworking,
Inc
Bureau International des
Sociétés Gérant les Droit
d'Enregistrement et de
Reproduction Méchanique
(BIEM)
Canal Plus
Casio Computer
CDDB, Inc.
Cductive.com
CDWorld
Cinram International
Cirrus Logic
Cognicity, Inc.
Compaq Corp.
Comverse Technology
Confédération Internationale
des Sociétés d'Auteurs et
Compositeurs (CISAC)
Creative Technology Ltd
Dataplay.com, Inc
Dentsu
Deutsche Telekom AG
DigiMarc
Digital Media on Demand
Digital On-Demand /
RedDotNet
Digital Theater Systems
(DTS)

Digitalway Co. Ltd.
DiscoverMusic (formally
Enso Audio Imaging)
DnC Tech, Inc.
Dolby Laboratories
e.Digital Corp.
Earjam, Inc.
EMDES Systems Company
LTD.
EMI Capitol Music
Emusic
Encoding.com / Loudeye
Technology
Entrust
Ericcson
Federation of Music
Producers Japan (FMPJ)
4C Entity, LLC
Fraunhofer Institute
Full Audio Corporation
Funai Corp.
Geidankyo (Japan Council
of Performers Rights
Admin.)
Gemplus
General Instruments
Grundig Digital Systems
Guillemot
Harry Fox Agency
Hewlett-Packard
Hilomusical (Telefonica)
Hitachi
Hithive Inc.
HMV Media Group
I2GO.COM
Infineon (formerly Siemens
Semiconductor)
Intel Corporation
International Federation of
Phonographic Industries
(IFPI)
InterTrust
InterVideo, Inc.
Intervu
Iomega
J.River
JASRAC
JVC Victor
Kenwood Corp.
Lexar Media
LG Electronics
Liquid Audio
Lucent Technologies
M.Ken E
Macrovision
MAGEX (formerly
NatWest)
MarkAny

MARS (Multimedia
Archive and Retrieval
System)
Matsushita
MCY Music
Media Fair, Inc
Media Tag Limited
Mediamatics
Memory Corporation
Midbar Tech Ltd
MHS SA
Micronas Intermetall
Microsoft
MIDI Manufacturers
Association (MMA)
Mitsubishi
Mitsubishi Electric Corp.
MODE (Music-on-
Demand)
Motorola
MPMan.com (formerly
Saehan Information
Systems)
Music Copyright
Operational Services
(MCOS)
Music Producers Guild
(MPG)
Music.co.jp
Musicmaker
MusicMarc, Inc.
MusicMatch
Napster
National Association of
Recording Merchandisers
(NARM)
National Music Publishers
Association (NMPA)
NetActive
News Corp (NDS
Technologies)
Nielsen Media Research
Nokia
NTT
NTT DoCoMo
Oak Technology, Inc.
Oberthur Card
SystemsAnalog Devices
Perception Digital, Ltd.
Philips
Pioneer
PortalPlayer, Inc.
Preview Systems
PricewaterhouseCoopers
QDesign
QPASS
QPICT
Real Networks
Reciprocal

Recording Industry
Association of America
(RIAA)
Recording Industry
Association of Japan
(RIAJ)
Rowe International
RPK SecureMedia, Inc.
S3/Diamond Multimedia
Samsung Electronics
SanDisk
Sanyo
SealTronic Technology
Sharp Electronics
Softlock
Sonic Foundry
Sonic Solutions
Digital World Services
(Sonopress/BMG Storage
Media)
Sony Electronics
Sony Music
Spectra.Net / Throttlebox
Sphere Multimedia
ST Microelectronics
Sun Microsystems
Sunhawk.com Corp.
Supertracks
TDK Electronics
Telecom System
International
Telian
Texas Instruments
Thomson Consumer
Electronics
Tokyo Electron Device
Tornado Group, Inc.
Toshiba
Touchtunes Digital
Jukebox
Unitech Electronics
Universal Music
URocket, Inc. (formerly
Packard Bell NEC)
Vedalabs
Verance Corporation
Voquette, Inc.
Warner Music
Wave Systems
Waveless Radio
Consortium (WLR)
Wavo
World Theater, Inc.
Xerox
Yamaha
ZipLabs

Source: www.sdmi.org, June, 2000.

Exhibit 5: Antitrust Statement on the Secure Digital Music Initiative[31]

Two points of antitrust law govern the SDMI process:

First, many of the companies in this process are competitors of other participants. SDMI is not intended to be, and cannot take the form of, an agreement that limits competition.

Second, the antitrust laws permit, indeed under appropriate circumstances encourage, the creation of neutral standards that benefit the affected industry and consumers.

The SDMI specification is such a standard. Record companies have identified the lack of an open and interoperable standard for security as the single greatest impediment to the growth of legitimate markets for electronic distribution of copyrighted music. Likewise, technology companies developing computer software, hardware and consumer electronics devices that will handle new forms of digital music have realized that an important part of these devices is the presence (or absence) of adequate security for electronic music. The SDMI specification will reflect both the legitimate needs of the record labels for security of digital music and the technical constraints and realistic needs of technology companies. By supporting a wide variety of agreements between rights owners and consumers, such a specification will enable multiple new and flexible business models to emerge in the marketplace.

Technology companies can reasonably conclude that an SDMI-compliant product will meet the security needs of record companies and that consumers purchasing such devices will have broad, legitimate access to music. Moreover, the SDMI process has the potential for facilitating broad interoperability between compliant software and electronic devices. Both results create value for consumers.

The end result of the process however, will be a specification, not an agreement. Each music company, and indeed each participant, will make its own decisions as to the degree of security it finds acceptable in light of marketplace conditions and each technology company will decide whether and the extent to which it incorporates the SDMI specification in its designs.

Exhibit 6: An Open Letter to the Digital Community

Here's an invitation to show off your skills, make some money, and help shape the future of the online digital music economy.

The Secure Digital Music Initiative is a multi-industry initiative working to develop a secure framework for the digital distribution of music. SDMI protected content will be embedded with an inaudible, robust watermark or use other technology that is designed to prevent the unauthorized copying, sharing, and use of digital music.

We are now in the process of testing the technologies that will allow these protections. The proposed technologies must pass several stringent tests: they must be inaudible, robust, and run efficiently on various platforms, including PCs. They should also be tested by *you*.

So here's the invitation: Attack the proposed technologies. Crack them.

---

[31]SDMI Portable Device Specification, Part 1, Version 1.0, Los Angeles, July 8, 1999, Document Number pdwg99070802, p.5.

By successfully breaking the SDMI protected content, you will play a role in determining what technology SDMI will adopt. And there is something more in it for you, too. If you can remove the watermark or defeat the other technology on our proposed copyright protection system, you may earn up to $10,000.

To participate, just go to the website at www.hacksdmi.org after September 15, 2000 and read the public challenge agreement. If you agree to the terms, you will have until at least October 7, 2000 to do your best.

SDMI is a body that includes 200+ companies and organizations from start ups to global enterprises, and from around the world. Participants include leading consumer electronics, information technology, music, and wireless telecom companies. (More information can be found at www.sdmi.org)

Here's your chance to shape the future of digital music.

Sincerely,
Leonardo Chiariglione
Executive Director, SDMI
September 6, 2000

September 28, 2000

SDMI welcomes this opportunity correct a few misconceptions that have surfaced since the public challenge was announced (see www.hacksdmi.org for details about the challenge).

To be clear, with SDMI:

- You will be able to make personal copies of your music. The SDMI specification allows people to make an unlimited number of personal copies of their CDs if in possession of the original CD. Nothing SDMI is doing will conflict with journalists' and educators' use. What will be affected is the ability to make large numbers of perfect digital copies of music, and distribute them instantaneously on the Internet without any compensation to the creator or copyright holder.
- SDMI-compliant players will play music already in your library, as well as new unprotected music, and new SDMI-protected music that has been legitimately acquired.
- You will be able to access more music. SDMI compliant devices will permit consumers to access more music than they currently can over the Internet, because copyright holders will be able to distribute music online without fear that it will be distributed instantaneously worldwide on the Internet.
- You will be able to play the music you already own. The CDs and MP3s you already have will be able to play on any SDMI compliant device.

SDMI will enhance your ability to put music online, whether you are affiliated with a record label or not. Prior to the inception of SDMI, an artist who wanted to distribute his or her music over the Internet could not be assured of retaining control of it. With SDMI, a person will be able to choose SDMI protection if he or she wants. In fact, SDMI is taking pains to be sure its protections are available to all who want them, affiliated or independent, large or small, famous or undiscovered.

SDMI has engaged in dialogue with critics of the SDMI effort. Movements such as open source software and groups such as the Electronic Frontier Foundation play a valuable role in the bringing attention to important policy issues as technology advances and new business models emerge. We have had extensive dialogue with EFF and with representatives of the open source community since the public challenge was announced. While we have agreed to disagree on certain details, SDMI has always welcomed and continues to welcome dialogue on this effort. I hope this answers some misconceptions and unfounded fears that have recently emerged.

Sincerely,

Leonardo Chiariglione
Executive Director, SDMI

Source: SDMI Web site, July, 2000.

iCRAVETV.COM: A NEW MEDIA UPSTART

Ken Mark
Tammy Smith
Mary M. Crossan and
Margaret Ann Wilkinson

Be at the right place, at the right time. Take massive, immediate action.

Attributed to Bill Gates, Founder of Microsoft Corporation

INTRODUCTION

"We've got a plan to create a new extension market for the release of television programming. And in the process, we aim to become the dominant TV aggregator retransmitter on the Internet when we launch iCraveTV in two months," stated Ian McCallum. Located in Montreal, Canada, iCraveTV

IVEY

Ken Mark and Tammy Smith prepared this case under the supervision of Professors Mary Crossan and Margaret Ann Wilkinson solely to provide material for class discussion. The authors do not intend to illustrate either effective or ineffective handling of a managerial situation. The authors may have disguised certain names and other identifying information to protect confidentiality.

was founded by McCallum and William Craig. It was September 30, 1999, and McCallum was looking over his launch options.

iCraveTV was legally permitted to retransmit television signals already carried on Canadian cable channels. But, due to differences in regulation, iCrave might face U.S. broadcast industry objections if U.S. audiences found access to the iCraveTV signal.

[handwritten: Prob b/c plan may not wk in US]

HISTORY OF ICRAVETV

Buying a computer for the first time in May 1999, Craig was not at all tech savvy. But he asked a single question of his group of friends, who had 50 years of broadcast experience behind them: "Why can't you put television on your computer screen?" Reaction from others around Craig led him to think that they thought it an infeasible idea. With the advent of broadband and the realization that its penetration into households would allow the piping of quality streaming video, iCraveTV (Canadian Radio And Video Entertainment) sought to be the first-to-market solution. Taking guidance from watching the growth and penetration of Internet and cable television, McCallum knew that the penetration of fibre optics would rapidly spread, resulting in increased high-speed connections — it was estimated that by the start of 2001, broadband access would comprise 50 per cent of the Internet Service Provider (ISP) market. [1]

[handwritten: Opt more ppl will then have high speed so can watch TV]

AN OVERVIEW OF THE NORTH AMERICAN BROADCAST INDUSTRY[2]

As of January 2000, 98.2 per cent of total U.S. households owned TV sets, and 75.6 per cent owned two or more sets. Average daily U.S. TV household viewing was six hours and 57 minutes, roughly one-third of which was devoted to cable.[3] Neilsen Media Research measured the viewing habits of this audience and ranked audience sizes by "rating points" and "share points." (One rating point equalled one per cent of the total television households in a station's designated market area, while one share point equalled one per cent of the area's total TV households that were using a television at the time. Thus, rating points would be used by media buyers for the purpose of determining advertising rates at the television station level (potential target audience pool), while share points would be used by networks to determine the success of each individual television program.)

The U.S. television market was the largest in the world and was served by three main distribution channels: the national television networks, independent commercial television stations, and cable television services, including pay cable. A commercial broadcast television station might be affiliated with one of the four established national networks (ABC, CBS, NBC, Fox), with one of the two new networks (WB or UPN), or with no network at all. To maintain a network license according to Federal Communications Commission (FCC) rules, commercial TV stations must broadcast at least 28 hours a week and at least two hours every day. Canadian broadcasters

---

[1] Ian McCallum — Speech Notes — Presentation to the Edmonton Business Council, circa May 2000.

[2] Year 2000 Outlook Upbeat for Cable, Radio, and TV. Broadcasting & Cable Industry Survey, January 27, 2000. Broadcasting & Cable Magazine. pp. 1-23.

[3] According to statistics supplied to the National Association of Broadcasters by Nielsen Media Research.

regularly paid to rebroadcast syndicated American programs as established viewing trends showed that Canadians preferred American content — polls continued to indicate that up to 19 of the top 20 television programs in Canada originated from the United States. To encourage the continued production of Canadian-made programs, the government-funded Canadian Broadcasting Corporation (CBC) was given a mandate to purchase and air domestic content.

The radio and broadcast television industries were expected to increase their share of the total U.S. advertising market over the next five years. Broadcast television accounted for 20 per cent of the total U.S. advertising spending, and radio accounted for approximately eight per cent. Combined, advertising spending in broadcast television and radio was expected to rise to US$67.5 billion in 2000, up 13 per cent from the year before.

An Advertising-based Model

The entire North American broadcast industry worked on the assumption that advertisers would pay to promote their wares to consumers. Attracting these consumers required producing consumer-appealing content, acquiring the rights to that content, and finding a means to broadcast it to consumers. AC Neilsen acted as a paid referee, regularly polling consumers to determine the most popular programs. These poll results were termed "Neilsen ratings" and allowed the players in the broadcast industry to price their products appropriately.

A summary of the revenue flows in the broadcast industry would show that almost all stakeholders in the industry depended on advertisers. For example, a content syndicator could be in competition for advertising dollars against the network to which it sold its content programs. (See Table 1.)

Table 1   Revenue Flow in the Broadcast Market

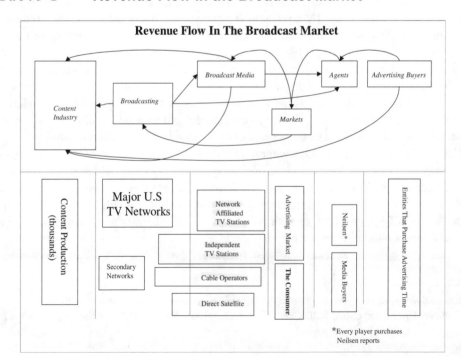

By selling more advertising time, an <u>independent</u> station or new-network affiliate typically garnered a higher share of local advertising revenues than its audience ratings would suggest. But because it broadcast more syndicated programs than a major-network affiliate did, its total programming costs were generally higher than those of a major network affiliate in the same market.

Radio broadcasters, television broadcasters, and cable television operators were similar in that they sought to attract audiences to their programming. To stay in business, they had to satisfy subscribers, viewers or listeners by providing desirable programming. Where they differed was in their means of delivering programming and generating revenues. U.S. radio and TV stations typically got about 90 per cent of their revenues from advertising. Cable system operators also sold advertising, but 65 per cent to 70 per cent of their revenues came from monthly subscriber fees paid by consumers. Content production companies that created basic cable programs received only 15 per cent of their revenues from advertising; most of their earnings came from the carriage fees paid by cable system operators.

Relationships between Content Rights Owners and Broadcast Media

The broadcasting and cable industries comprised tens of thousands of individual companies, most of which were small business operations. Within each segment, however, the biggest players claimed a disproportionately large share of business, and the industry was becoming more top-heavy every year. The Big Three television networks — ABC, CBS, and NBC — generally accounted for more than 40 per cent of the broadcast television industry's annual advertising revenue and as much as 47 per cent or more during Olympic years. Although the Big Three would continue to see their future audience share whittled away by cable and other media outlets, they were still expected to dominate television viewership and advertising for the foreseeable future.

Because the major networks regularly bought and provided first-run programming during prime-time hours (generally 8 p.m. to 11 p.m. in the Eastern and Pacific time zones), network affiliates often achieved higher audience shares than their local rivals did. However, the major networks pre-empted most of their affiliates' prime-time schedule for broadcasting their programs and could sell most of that advertising time themselves. This meant that affiliates of the Big Three networks had substantially fewer prime-time advertisements ("inventory") to sell than did independent stations or affiliates of the newer networks. On the other hand, their large audiences meant higher rates for the slots that they did have, which helped compensate for their limited amount of prime-time advertising.

The newer networks also demanded a high percentage of their affiliates' advertisement inventory during network broadcasts. But because their programming consumed fewer prime-time hours, their affiliates had more slots to sell than did affiliates of the major networks. And despite their generally low advertising rates, new-network affiliates and independent stations enjoyed a large advertisement inventory, which gave them more prime-time slots than their major-network affiliates.

THE ADVERTISERS

Advertisers paid to place their television commercials on programs that would reach their target audience. AC Neilsen regularly polled consumers about their viewing habits and charted the popularity of various television shows. Thus, the future of a television series or program was tied to its Neilsen ratings.

Advertisers usually bought airtime through advertising agencies, for a commission of about 10 per cent to 15 per cent of the cost of placing the advertisement. National advertising time was sold through national sales representatives, who received a commission based on advertising cost. Local advertising time was sold by each station's sales staff; again, the advertiser paid a commission. Networks generally sold about 80 per cent of their available time slots in advance (called "upfront television ad sales"), and the rest was sold on the "scatter" market — the period that began after the start of the fall program season. Upfront market prices usually determined those in the scatter market because they influenced forces of supply and demand. Thus, upfront sales were indicators of the health of television industry revenues in the coming year.

Many contracts came with audience guarantees, so networks could be caught off guard by programs that did not meet expectations of audience appeal or viewership, leading advertisers to cancel their contracts. Some contracts included a "makegood" clause, by which advertisers were to receive "free" advertising time from the network on later programming if audience size for a contracted slot fell below a certain level. Advertisers could also cancel upfront contracts for no other reasons, leaving networks with more advertisement time to fill within the scatter market.

THE TELEVISION NETWORKS[4]

All of the U.S. networks were divisions of larger corporations. ABC was owned by Walt Disney Co., CBS Corp. had agreed to be acquired by Viacom Inc., Fox was a unit of News Corp., and NBC was owned by General Electric Co. WB was 75 per cent-owned by Time Warner Inc. and 25 per cent-owned by Tribune Co. UPN was a 50/50 joint venture of Chris-Craft Industries Inc. and Viacom Inc. ABC, CBS and NBC provided their roughly 650 station affiliates with about 22 hours of primetime programming per week and a substantial amount of programming for other time periods. The terms of most network affiliation contracts ran from two years to 10 years. They paid affiliates for broadcasting their programming and national commercials — each network was thus able to reach virtually every significant U.S. television market.

The Fox network, established in 1996, had 211 affiliates and a primetime audience reach of about 96 per cent of American television homes. (Audience reach meant the percentage of TV-owning households in which a broadcast was available.)

In general, the Big Three networks' share of the prime-time television audience had declined over the past few decades. It had been whittled away by the growing popularity of cable television, the success of the 11-year-old Fox network, and most recently, by the explosion of alternative viewing choices made possible by new cable technologies and regulatory easing. One such technology offered consumers their personalized selection of channels. Instead of paying for a "package" of 200 channels, for example, each consumer could choose a personalized combination of channels and would be billed per selection. According to Neilsen Media Research in 1999, ABC, CBS and NBC collectively commanded a 91 per cent share of the prime-time television audience in the 1978-79 season, and a 75 per cent share in the 1986-87 season. In the most recent television season (September 1998 through May 1999), the Big Three's combined share was down to 45 per cent of the television audience. By network, CBS's share of the prime-time audience was 16 per

---

[4]Broadcasting & Cable Industry Survey, January 27, 2000.

cent, compared with 15 per cent for NBC, 14 per cent for ABC, and 12 per cent for the Fox network. UPN (United Paramount Network) gathered a five per cent share during its six hours of weekly programming, and the WB (Warner Brothers Television Network) network attracted three per cent during its seven hours of weekly prime-time programming. Independent television stations took an 11 per cent share, basic cable attracted 36 per cent, and pay cable garnered six per cent. (These figures added up to more than 100 per cent due to differences in programming schedules and because of the "multiset" phenomenon, in which different sets in one home may be tuned to different channels.)

As competition had eaten into their audience shares while programming costs had escalated, TV networks were increasingly expecting their television station affiliates to help ease the profit squeeze. In the past several years, ABC, CBS, NBC and even Fox had been chipping away at the arrangements whereby they paid their affiliates to carry network programming. More recently, they had asked affiliates to help pay for costly sports rights packages and for renewal rights to certain hit programming.

In April 1999, the Fox network proposed a cut of 22 per cent in its affiliate stations' local commercial slots; it rescinded 20 of the affiliates' 90 prime-time commercial units per week. The 200 affiliates protested strongly at first, but capitulated in late May 1999 on Fox's compromise plan. This plan would give affiliates first refusal rights on purchasing 20 time slots at below-market rates and would grant them 15 new prime-time units to sell locally. As part of the deal, Fox agreed not to take back any more slots, including slots that ran during NFL football games, for three years.

Fox would gain some US$70 million annually from the take-back, as opposed to the US$100 million it originally sought. And while affiliates were collectively losing that US$70 million a year, they would each get 15 more slots per week to sell, along with all the revenue generated.

From the start, some of the newer networks, UPN and WB, established more frugal associate relationships in which case compensation was rare. They charged their affiliates for certain event programming and provided fewer hours of costly primetime programming than the established networks did. To expand their audience reach, the newer networks distributed their programming through cable, as well as across the airwaves.

In Canada, there existed three national television networks: Global, CTV and government-funded Canadian Broadcasting Corporation (CBC). Much of Canadian prime-time television programming originated from the United States.

BROADCAST TELEVISION STATIONS[5]

The top 25 owners of U.S. television stations together controlled 36 per cent of the more than 1,200 U.S. commercial television stations at the end of 1998, up from 33 per cent in 1997 and 25 per cent in 1996. In Canada, the CHUM Group was the majority owner of the largest group of television stations. Of this group, some stations were affiliated with different national networks and some were non-affiliated.

TV station revenues came primarily from three sources: national spot advertising sold to national and regional advertisers; advertising time sold to local advertisers; and network compensation payments (networks' payments to affiliates for broadcasting network commercials and programming). A station's competitive position depended on network affiliation, programming

---

[5]Broadcasting & Cable Industry Survey, January 27, 2000.

quality, management ability and technical factors. Its success relied on the public's response to its programs compared with competing entertainment, as this response affected ratings and, thus, revenues.

Television stations that served a given designated market area (DMA) competed for advertising sales with other broadcast and cable stations, plus other media such as newspapers and radio. Within each DMA, advertising rates depended primarily on the stations' program ratings, the time of day and the program's viewer demographics.

Television stations frequently made substantial financial commitments to guarantee their access to programs that would be syndicated in the future, requiring the station to purchase an entire program series.

As of year-end 1999, there were 1,616 full-power television stations in the United States. Of these, 1,243 were commercial stations and 373 were educational stations. In addition, a total of 2,194 low-power television stations were licensed to operate.

There was a contrast between U.S. and Canadian television stations. Whereas low-powered television stations in the United States served community channels and college markets, Canadian networks used low-powered television stations as "repeaters" to carry programming signals to rural parts of the country.

CABLE TELEVISION SYSTEMS[6]

Cable system operators received signals from their program providers by several means: special antennas, microwave relay systems, Earth stations, and fibre optic cables. The system used amplified the signals, combined them with locally originated programs and ancillary services, and distributed them to subscribers. "Cable providers have retransmitted network broadcasts for years without having a contract or having to pay them any royalties. This is because the networks realized that the cable providers were extending their audience reach for them," stated David Spencer, an associate professor of film and media studies at the University of Western Ontario.

Although there were thousands of cable system operators in the United States, the industry had been dominated by the top 25 players for many years. At the end of May 1999, the top 25 cable operators served about 91 per cent of the U.S. market's subscribers, up from 85 per cent a year earlier. The 10 largest accounted for more than 71 per cent of the 68 million cable subscribers, up from 45 per cent in 1994. In Canada, Rogers Cablesystems was the major player, with roughly similar cable penetration in Canada compared with the United States.

Unlike broadcast television, cable system providers (cable providers) derived most of their revenues from monthly subscriber fees. In addition to recurring subscriber programming revenues, cable providers received revenues from installation charges, sales of pay-per-view movies and events, set-top converter rentals, remote control sales and rentals, advertising, carriage fees from home shopping channels and fees from companies presenting infomercials. In recent years, the industry had upgraded the technological capabilities of its broadband network so that cable providers could offer such new services as digital video, high-speed Internet access, local and long-distance telephone services, and commercial competitive local exchange carrier operations. High-definition television (HDTV), video on demand, and e-commerce were also among the newest offerings. Total revenues for U.S. cable system operators, including subscription fees, advertising,

---

[6]*Broadcasting & Cable Industry Survey*, January 27, 2000.

new services and other fees and charges, was expected to increase 15 per cent in 2000 to US$15.3 billion, with projections for annual 15.4 per cent growth rates through 2004.

Cable providers' advertising revenues continued to grow rapidly as well, expected to increase by 27 per cent in 2000, and expecting to advance 22 per cent on average each year through 2004. By January 2000, cable was available to more than 30,000 U.S. communities, serving nearly 68 per cent of the roughly 102.68 million U.S. households with television.

Cable's growth over the past 15 years had hurt broadcast television by fostering the creation of dozens of new cable networks that battled for advertising dollars. At the same time, it also helped broadcast television networks by providing clear reception for weak stations.

SYNDICATION DEALS

Content producers were free to sell and syndicate their programs to competing and international stations.

Spencer explained,

> This would help the producer recoup the cost of producing the program. Alliance Atlantis (a Canadian syndication content provider) could sell the rights to put "Traders" (their Canadian syndicated show) on air to Global, at which time Global sells advertising and recovers the costs. Alliance then could also sell syndication to CBS, who in turn recoups its costs through advertising. The only caveat is that if Global and CBS aired the same show at the same time, the Canadian television stations carrying Global's signal would be forced to substitute U.S. advertising for Canadian-only advertising.[7]

Regardless of network affiliation, all broadcast stations obtained some programs from independent sources. These programs were mainly syndicated TV shows (some of which had previously aired on a major network) and syndicated feature films that were either made for network TV or previously shown in theatres and on cable television.

Although network audiences were analysed to estimate the future value and potential profitability of program syndication (a program licensed for reruns after it had been aired), there was no assurance that a successful network program would continue to be profitable once syndicated.

Syndicators sometimes sold broadcast stations a license to air a syndicated program, allowing the purchase station to sell the advertising slots and keep the revenues; no barter element was involved. The cash price of such programming varied, depending on its perceived desirability and the number of times it was to be aired. Syndicators also offered programs to stations on a barter basis. Although stations did not pay fees to get such programming, the syndicators often sold most of the associated advertising, keeping the revenues for themselves. This arrangement gave purchasing stations fewer advertisement slots, but reduced their programming slots. A third option was the cash-plus-barter sale, a combination of the first two options. In recent years, barter and cash-plus-barter deals were becoming more prevalent. These exchanges provided programming to stations without requiring as much upfront cash as a direct sale. Of course, they also reduced the amount of advertising time that stations could sell, although the direct impact on broadcasters' operating income was believed to be neutral. Program distributors that acquired airtime by barter

---

[7]David Spencer – Interview September 28, 2000.

must then compete with television stations and broadcasting networks to sell their available slots to advertisers. [8]

SUBSTITUTE ADVERTISING MEDIA TO BROADCAST TELEVISION

Broadcast networks and cable operators alike were seeing significantly greater competition from alternative technologies. Digitalization of the television signal (which was now analogue) allowed for the broadcast and transmission of high-definition television (HDTV), with its incredibly sharp and detailed pictures. Under the current schedule mandated by the FCC, all television signals had to be transmitted digitally by May 1, 2002. By mid-1999, TV stations covering nearly 45 per cent of U.S. homes had been converted to the digital format — the advent of digital television allowed cable providers to tout the crystal-clear picture that had been trumpeted by direct broadcast satellite providers in their marketing campaigns.

Digital television also made it possible for cable providers to transmit more than one signal per channel by means of a technology called broadband compression. This capability, which functioned by condensing numerous signals into one bandwidth, was probably more important to cable providers and broadcasters than picture clarity, allowing a 60-channel cable system to hold 510 channels by giving 50 channels a compression factor of 10 and using the remaining 10 channels for other revenue-producing services involving phones, computers, music and other features. One drawback of this technology, however, was that as more channels were added, the picture quality diminished.

If consumers demanded sharper, clearer picture quality than cable could offer, they would subscribe to Direct Broadcast Satellite service (DBS). DBS systems provided higher picture quality and more programming choice than cable did, but both factors were becoming less advantageous with the cable industry's current rollout of digital broadband capabilities. Thus, DBS's penetration of the cable market had been relatively minor. One shortcoming of DBS was that it was costly — the consumer had to bear the cost of the DBS dish as well as its installation and maintenance. With cable, equipment costs and maintenance were borne by the cable system operator. Another disadvantage was that in most markets, DBS subscribers could not receive locally originated over-the-air broadcast signals; to receive those channels, they had to put up rabbit-ear antennae or subscribe to cable. In addition, DBS reception could be lost or badly disturbed in severe weather — for these reasons, roughly one-fourth of DBS subscribers also subscribed to cable. In 1999, lawmakers eased the rules that currently prevented satellite companies from offering local stations, putting DBS on a more equal footing with cable. According to Neilsen Market Research, the number of DBS subscribers grew from 2.1 million in 1996 to 11.3 million in 1999.

Radio was expected to continue exhibiting stronger growth than broadcast television, enjoying 10.4 per cent annual revenue growth through 2004. As the U.S. business environment changed in response to deregulation in telecommunications and advances in technology, advertisers in various segments were expected to continue to intensify their marketing programs to keep up with the competition.

---

[8]Broadcasting & Cable Industry Survey, January 27, 2000.

ALLIANCES BETWEEN CABLE PROVIDERS AND BROADCASTERS

The Big Three networks had long considered forming formal alliances with cable providers prior to 1999 as a means to reach wider audiences, taking action only in the past year or two, due to the increased pace of audience erosion as digital television replaced analogue television. Fox and the newer networks (UPN, WB, and PAX) had already drawn on cable's reach by forming affiliate relationships with cable channels. In June 1999, NBC reached an agreement with AT&T, the new cable giant, under which AT&T would carry NBC's cable and broadcast programming, including an Olympics package and HDTV signals through 2009. The companies did not disclose financial terms, but NBC stated that the pact would increase distribution of its CNBC and MSNBC cable-news channels from 50 million homes to more than 66 million homes in three years. It would also allow NBC to carry the 2000 Olympics over cable as well as network TV.

REGULATION

Government oversight of broadcasting and cable services fell primarily under the jurisdiction of the Federal Communications Commission (FCC) in the United States, and the Canadian Radio and Television Commission (CRTC) in Canada. The FCC was created through the Communications Act of 1934 and regulated all interstate and international communications by wire and radio. The CRTC had regulated Canadian airwaves since 1968. Canadian ownership regulations prevented foreign nationals from owning more than a 25 per cent controlling stake in networks or television stations. This ruling had largely dissuaded the U.S. broadcasting players from taking a significant equity stake in any Canadian broadcast properties.

The U.S. radio and television industries were transformed during the 1990s by such landmark legislation as the Telecommunications Act of 1996, rule changes by the FCC, and other recent federal legislation. Most of the recent legislation was designed to boost competition and to level the playing field. One major effect of these new laws has been widespread and continuing consolidation in the media arena. Most recently, in August 1999, the FCC revised its local market television ownership rules — the TV duopoly rule and the radio and television cross-ownership (or "one-to-a-market") rule — to permit ownership of two television stations within the same market and to permit cross-ownership of multiple radio stations at the same time.

These rules changes have and would continue to lead consolidation in the marketplace, allowing for the centralization of similar functions and the ability for the growing conglomerates to offer larger audiences and wider advertising reach to clients.

In Canada, the situation had been different stated Spencer,

> We have had extremely restrictive media regulations in Canada since 1932. The CRTC sought to bring all media under the umbrella of Canadian nationalism. This started with the Canadian content rules — 30 per cent of all content on AM Radio, and 55 per cent of prime-time radio and television content has to be Canadian. But there are ways to minimize that restriction because content is counted on a rolling average. Therefore, if a Canadian station picked up Wednesday Night Hockey (three hour broadcast), news and current affairs, plus a Canadian syndicated television series, it would have its quota for the week.

But the CRTC decided in 1996 not to regulate media activities on the Internet, beginning a series of announcements that led industry observers to note that the Canadian media industry was also moving towards deregulation.[9] For example, cable was never treated as a part of the broadcasting system in Canada until amendments were made to the Canadian Broadcasting Act of 1968. Until then, cable was regarded simply as a method by which television signals could be distributed to a wider audience without physical interference. Spencer explained:

> Since most of the television products that appeared between the first cable system and the revised Canadian Broadcasting Act of 1968 were produced and distributed by networks, the networks were only too happy to have expansion of their signals instead of setting up a series of low-power relay transmitters in remote areas. If nothing else, the retransmission enhanced advertising rates for the networks.
>
> The copyright issue first began to become a problem in the United States when Hollywood insisted on royalty payments based on distribution. The U.S. networks refused, claiming that the only audience they should pay for was the audience that they had been licensed to serve — that referred to the audience within the broadcast contour, not those collected on cable.
>
> At least in Canada, the CRTC declared with the 1968 Broadcast Act that cable was in effect a member of the broadcasting community. But here, the definition gets cloudy. In effect, the CRTC stated that there were two ways to approach the definition of "broadcasting." First, providing to consumers cable-specific channels, such as Rogers Cable 13 in London, subjected cable operators to the same conditions that any broadcaster, off air or off cable, had to meet. However, the retransmission of network signals was not considered broadcasting. So in effect, the CRTC stated that cable operators were not stealing product when they retransmitted a signal, and that was that. The U.S. industry disagrees.
>
> Cable operators often retransmitted network signals to audiences already able to receive network broadcasts via affiliated television stations. Therefore, if a U.S. or Canadian broadcaster has already paid for the rights to broadcast the program across the country, why should cable be subject to pay more to retransmit the signal to the same audience?

CONSOLIDATION AND CONVERGENCE

Media giants were emerging. By being the only willing investors in new media and entertainment technologies, software and delivery systems, the industry giants such as the major network broadcasters (ABC, NBC, CBS and Fox) were expected to gain further control of the shape and focus of the media and entertainment industry in the decades to come. In a vicious circle of market power and access to capital, these industry giants, because of their market share and purchasing power, would continue to strengthen their financial and market prospects and further reinforce their powerful gatekeeper positions well into the 21st century. But they offered enormous benefits to consumers, since their fiscal power would allow them to efficiently develop and implement new technologies.[10]

---

[9]David Spencer – Interview September 28, 2000.

[10]Garin, Michael N., and Redmond, Thomas A. The Changing Economic Structures and Relationships among Entertainment Industry Participants in the 21st Century. Firestone, Charles M., Editor: Television for the 21st Century — The Next Wave. 1993. p.34.

BREAKING INTO THE INDUSTRY – A TRADITIONAL APPROACH (PRE-INTERNET)

Starting a traditional television network was theoretically simple. First, one had to have programs, preferably something unique and highly appealing to a mass audience. Next, one would need to get local TV stations to agree to act as affiliates. If enough affiliates were lined up, one could sell advertising time to advertisers. Then, an arrangement with a common carrier company (AT&T, Bell) would be needed to transmit programs to the affiliates. Getting the programs would be fairly easy, although it was the most expensive part. Very few program producers were likely to go to the considerable expense of producing shows without payment in advance, or at least guaranteed. One alternative was to contract with the party that owned the rights to a sports event, for example. Usually the rights could be obtained for a modest advance fee, with the balance to be paid if and when the event actually was used.

Lining up affiliates was the hardest part of forming a new network. Since there were not many independent stations, and the more successful ones were profitable with their usual programming (syndicated old movies and off-network shows), they were not eager to give up their time for an uncertain venture.[11]

For an aspiring new cable system operator entrant, Spencer outlined the Canadian rules of entry:

> A new player must apply to the CRTC, and if the application is accepted, the licensee plays under the same rules as any other cable operator. However, there are virtually no areas of the country not serviced by cable or by satellite through operations such as Bell ExpressVu. The activity then in this area deals largely with companies buying out other companies.

Theoretically, a new cable operator entrant would need to negotiate rights and carriage fees to pay for certain cable programs, but could (at least in Canada) legally retransmit network television signals.

A NEW MEDIA ALTERNATIVE

iCraveTV's founders had two options: work within the existing framework and seek to negotiate Internet rights from syndicators, or pirate network signals and launch the site. Ian McCallum offered:

> Fibre is being installed at about the rate of 2,400 kilometres a minute. About 11 per cent of office workers have high-speed access. We expect there to be 10 million homes passed by mid-2001, and 30 million four years later. In the first quarter, cable modem access jumped 44 per cent and DSL grew by 183 per cent. We expect growth rates in North America to slow to four per cent and in the rest of the world to be about 11 per cent for the next five years. Angus Reid Group has predicted that by the end of 2000, there will be 450 million people on the Internet. China alone jumped from six million to 10 million since February.

---

[11]DeLuca, Stuart M., Television's Transformation for the Next 25 Years. 1980. p.135.

When cable television's copper lines were laid down throughout North American neighborhoods, about 40 per cent of homes in the service areas subscribed. That figure currently stood at about 70 per cent of households; about half of that number subscribe to additional tiers amounting to a total of 220 per cent of pay to basic. (Basic U.S. monthly cable was $29 and per-tier pricing is about $8.) We know that studies have been done to show the online movie viewer profiles, which look very encouraging. Pay-per-view still has a way to go, but the Internet may eventually break through some of the problems experienced in the cable environment.

THE CONCEPT OF "COMPANION TELEVISION"

iCraveTV did not perceive itself to replace television consumption.

McCallum mentioned,

> Companion Television is designed to be part of the online computer experience. It converges continuous live and archival television onto the computer screen. A viewer sitting 18 inches away from their computer, could choose from one of three screen formats: 3"×5" to full screen. The quality is expected to improve as throughput of the online world improves.

McCallum coined the term "extension market" to emphasize that iCraveTV would take television programming to places it had not been before — computer screens in the office, student computers in residences, bedrooms of youths, offices — anywhere, in fact, where one possessed an online computer. He continued:

> We spent a couple of million dollars on equipment (antennae, receivers, servers, digitizers and an operations centre) and around Cdn$13 million in telecom commitments. In addition, we have commissioned two-and-a-half OC3 telecom pipes. To give you an idea of what that means, all of Toronto's traffic to the United States passes along three OC3s.

iCRAVETV'S REVENUE MODEL

The founders intended iCraveTV to realize 60 per cent of revenues from service subscription fees and 40 per cent from online banner advertisement sales. iCraveTV's advertising revenue assumptions were based on management experience and industry information concerning rates and inventories in the cable industry, with the difference being that iCraveTV could insert commercials as well as run ad banners into viewer content. Furthermore, some of the ad banners would be below the picture and therefore would be viewed for an entire 30 seconds.

A DIFFERENT AUDIENCE SERVED VERSUS TRADITIONAL BROADCAST TELEVISION

McCallum felt strongly that he would not be in competition with existing television stations. This was the view that he presented to the public on iCraveTV's relationship with traditional broadcast television:

This service is not, I want to emphasize, to compete with over-the-air broadcasting. Anyone who has seen video on a computer monitor will know that it is not a substitute for television. Typically, the video picture takes up only a small portion of a computer monitor that is itself small compared to current television screens, and if the video is enlarged, it loses resolution. We expect the technology, and so the quality of the picture, to improve, but it will not in the foreseeable future improve to the point where someone who owns a television set — which includes, of course, far more people than own computers — will want to watch a TV show on a computer rather than on TV.

Instead, iCraveTV serves a different audience. It serves those who cannot receive broadcast television, such as those in the shadow of the huge CN broadcast tower in Toronto, and those in universities and offices who cannot receive broadcast television and do not have cable access. And it serves those who are working on a computer and would like to be able to view a television program in a corner of their screen. In these ways we provide a real service to some people, but it is not a service that provides any competition to over-the-air broadcasters or cable or satellite re-transmitters. This is confirmed by the limited capacity of the video server used by iCraveTV: we can serve no more than about 4,000 viewers at a time. This is hardly a threat to television broadcasters with their tens of millions of viewers, and the technology will not permit it to become such a threat, even if we wanted to, which we do not. In the future, we hope to use technological improvements to serve millions of consumers. In fact, within months, we expect to have this capability to serve millions.

THE ISSUE OF ROYALTY PAYMENTS FOR RE-TRANSMITTED SIGNALS

According to Canadian copyright laws, iCraveTV would be permitted to retransmit to Canadians any U.S. programming already carried on Canadian cable channels and to sell advertising on those shows. Spencer commented:

> Rogers Cable Television regularly substitutes commercial messages when re-transmitting A&E, TNN and other signals. So in effect, they are using a foreign product for domestic gain. As well, cable operators are required to black out U.S. television signals and transmit only the Canadian signal when the U.S. networks and the Canadian stations or networks are broadcasting the same program at the same time. However, once a company starts re-broadcasting Canadian signals and selling advertising in those signals, it is acting like a broadcaster. Even though the CRTC has decided that it will not regulate the Internet, programming copyright laws are still in effect.

McCallum commented:

> iCraveTV was launched to provide TV retransmission to Canadian viewers, to pay royalties to copyright holders, including Buffalo, New York broadcasters and international program producers, with payments to be made according to tariffs to be established by the Canadian Copyright Board in negotiation with the broadcasters, iCraveTV and similar companies, and to generate revenues based on banner advertising. Except for the latter point, it will be similar to Canadian cable companies. By this means the Canadian government had established a technologically independent means to cut through the Gordian Knot of conflicting, dispersed or ill-defined rights and thereby to

provide what no contracts could provide — the flow of revenue from the viewers/advertisers, through iCraveTV to broadcasters and program producers.

Initially iCraveTV will be established using best available security techniques to contain the service within Canada. However, U.S. rights holders might be concerned that these techniques are inadequate to stop their programming from entering the U.S. market.[12]

McCallum knew that measures had to be taken to at least attempt to prevent U.S. users from accessing the Canadian site. One option was to require the user to enter a three-digit Canadian telephone area code in order to confirm that they were located in Canada.

CONCLUSION

For McCallum and Craig, several issues remained unresolved as they moved towards the launch of iCraveTV. First, they believed that no broadcasting rights for current television programs existed. They could either negotiate those rights from each of the content syndicators, or attempt to pay Internet royalties for the programming if a suitable tariff were to be retroactively negotiated by broadcasters and the Canadian Copyright Board.

iCraveTV might be able to retransmit to Canadians the same programs already being retransmitted by the cable operators, but what if American audiences gained access to the Internet retransmission? In spite of these issues, McCallum and Craig planned to implement a 'viral marketing' campaign to boost awareness a week before the launch date. It seemed as though they had a great idea and an untapped niche. Now they had to figure out how to capitalize on it.

---

[12]Ian McCallum, Presentation to the Congress Judiciary Committee, June 15, 2000.

WESTJET LOOKS EAST[1]  case 10

Joseph N. Fry and
Roderick E. White

In August 1999, the Canadian airline industry was taken by surprise when the Onex Corporation proposed to acquire and merge Canada's two large system carriers, Canadian Airlines and Air Canada. A long and debilitating rivalry between the two airlines was being pushed to a conclusion. Air Canada countered with a merger proposal of its own, and ultimately prevailed in a high-profile takeover battle. With Onex out of the picture, the way was left clear for Air Canada to achieve a near monopoly of domestic, regularly scheduled air travel. Meanwhile, the federal government, which had helped to ignite the merger initiatives, insisted that it would sustain competition in the industry.

In light of these developments, the management of WestJet Airlines of Calgary were reviewing their growth plans and wondering, in particular, if they should shift from their focus on building and reinforcing their Western Canadian markets to expanding in the East. WestJet was a young, successful, low-fare airline patterned after Southwest Airlines, the most successful U.S. carrier.

[1]This case has been written on the basis of public sources only. Consequently, the interpretation and perspectives presented in this case are not necessarily those of WestJet or any of its employees.

IVEY

Professors Joseph N. Fry and Roderick E. White prepared this case solely to provide material for class discussion. The authors do not intend to illustrate either effective or ineffective handling of a managerial situation. The authors may have disguised certain names and other identifying information to protect confidentiality.

WestJet had been profitable from its start-up in early 1996, and by 1999 was flying 13 Boeing 737s approximately 517 flights per week between 11 destinations in Western Canada. WestJet had just recently completed a $25 million initial public offering and planned to purchase three additional aircraft with the proceeds. At the time of the offering, WestJet's plan was to use the increased flight capacity for further penetration of the western market. A summary of WestJet's financial performance is given in Exhibit 1.

INDUSTRY BACKGROUND: DOMESTIC WARFARE

The epic battle between Air Canada and Canadian had started with the deregulation of Canada's domestic airline industry in the mid-1980s.[2] At that time, Pacific Western Airlines, a successful regional carrier, spurned a potential marriage with Air Canada and set out to become a full-fledged national and international carrier. To achieve this, the company, renamed Canadian Airlines, acquired Canadian Pacific Airlines (which itself had just swallowed Eastern Provincial Airways, Nordair and Quebecair) and a few years later, Wardair. As it emerged from this process, Canadian Airlines had assembled the essentials of an international air carrier; in particular, it held a strong position in Western Canada and important flag carrier routes across the Pacific and to Mexico and South America. On the other hand, Canadian was working from a relatively weak position in Eastern Canada and across the Atlantic. It was experiencing integration difficulties with the acquisitions, and it was saddled with significant debt. Canadian chose, nevertheless, to persist and to engage Air Canada in a winner-takes-all contest to become Canada's dominant, regularly scheduled domestic and international carrier.

In the meantime, Air Canada was in transition from government ownership to publicly traded company. When full privatization was achieved in 1989, Air Canada was seen on the one hand as a carrier that was quite well-off in routes, equipment and finance, but, on the other hand, limited in its potential by overstaffing, low productivity and a pervasive attitude of entitlement.

A 10 Year Dog Fight

While cumbersome, Air Canada was the stronger airline. In a continuing war of attrition — marked by over-capacity in overlapping routes and frequencies, and corresponding price pressures — Canadian, with its burdensome debt, was soon in financial trouble. In 1992, with the economy in recession, Canadian posted a loss of over $500 million, reducing its accumulated equity to zero. Air Canada took note and pursued the possibility of a merger. The reaction from Canadian and its employees ranged from uncooperative to hostile, and Air Canada withdrew, reportedly to wait and pick up the pieces when Canadian fell into bankruptcy. Canadian soon got back into the thick of it, however, largely by way of a strategic alliance with AMR Corp., parent of American Airlines. The alliance provided for a critical $246 million equity investment in return for a service agreement that secured Canadian as a customer for AMR's Sabre information systems business and significant concessions by Canadian's employees, shareholders and creditors.

---

[2]After deregulation, the government would license airlines to fly any domestic route, any time, at any price, subject only to safety requirements. The government also retained provisions requiring that at least 75 per cent of the voting interests of air carrier license holders be owned and controlled by Canadians and that control of the airline be held, in fact, by Canadians.

But, by 1995, Canadian was in serious trouble again. For that matter, Air Canada was suffering too — but it was somewhat better-off in scale, market position and financing. (Collectively, in their six fiscal years from 1990 through 1995, the two airlines posted cumulative losses of $2.15 billion, of which Canadian accounted for $1.26 billion). Given the circumstances, Canadian management took a serious look at downsizing its domestic operations and retrenching to its more profitable international routes. As attractive as this idea looked in concept, there were serious obstacles to successful implementation, ranging from the maintenance of effective domestic feed and distribution for the international routes, to absorbing the tangible and intangible costs of major layoffs and facility closings. Management chose instead to seek further payroll concessions and productivity improvements to sustain their now-quixotic all-fronts contest with Air Canada.

Air Canada was not prepared to disengage, of course, and pressed on with the battle. The inevitable outcome was painfully slow to emerge. But over the next three years, Canadian lost a cumulative $319 million, and by late 1998, the airline was clearly having trouble assembling the cash needed to stay in the air. In March 1999, Canadian approached Federal Transport Department officials to explain its situation and to request that the government use Section 47 of the Transport Act to allow Canada's main airlines to enter into discussions that would normally be forbidden under competition regulations. Meanwhile, with the encouragement of Canadian, Onex Corporation and American Airlines, executives were engaged in on- and off-talks about a venture to merge Canadian and Air Canada. When Section 47 was formally invoked for 90 days in early August, Air Canada was the first mover, with an offer to buy Canadian's international routes. Canadian rejected this out of hand. Then, in short order, Onex announced a plan to buy and merge both airlines in a deal that was heavily backed by American Airlines. Air Canada management was dismayed, to say the least, at the prospect of falling short so close to victory and outraged at the seeming complicity of the government in the process.

The Last Weeks of Canadian Airlines

A fierce takeover battle was joined, full of rancor, legal manoeuvring, bids and counter-bids. The stakes were unprecedented. The competing proposals put forward by Onex and Air Canada were both structured such that the winner would emerge with control of a single airline serving over 80 per cent of Canada's regularly scheduled domestic air travel. Public relations programs were cranked up to a fever pitch. Both sides claimed that they would generate the greatest shareholder benefits, without, of course, abusing their monopoly position. One of Air Canada's promises — which seemed aimed at the not necessarily consistent goals of tying up yet another domestic market segment, while reassuring the public that price competition would continue — was that it would set up a separate low-fare carrier at Hamilton airport.[3] Just to make sure of its position, Air Canada took a pre-emptive step in locking up all of Hamilton's available gates.

After 10 weeks of a very public contest, both sides were claiming that they would emerge the winner. Then, in early November, one of Air Canada's legal defences came through: a judge in the Quebec Superior Court ruled that Onex's bid contravened the terms of the legislation under which Air Canada was privatized. Under the Air Canada Public Participation Act, no single party could control more than 10 per cent of Air Canada. Onex decided to withdraw, leaving Canadian hanging

---

[3]Hamilton airport was located 60 kilometers southwest of Toronto's international airport. It was used by airfreight carriers, local air traffic and the occasional charter flight and had no regularly scheduled passenger traffic.

by a thread and looking for further backing from American Airlines and its Oneworld alliance partners. These last-ditch efforts were unsuccessful, and in early December, the Canadian board announced its approval of a $98 million take-over offer from Air Canada. All that remained for this acquisition to proceed was approval from the federal government. This was expected, although it was not clear what conditions the government might try to, or be able to, impose.

INDUSTRY BACKGROUND: CONCURRENT DEVELOPMENTS

Passenger Traffic

From a historic high point reached in 1990, the number of passengers carried by Canada's domestic airlines dipped about 15 per cent in the recession of the early '90s and did not recover to pre-recession levels until 1995. Thereafter, growth was strong; overall, from 1990 through 1998, passenger counts grew 23 per cent, from 36.8 million to 45.4 million, and the number of revenue passenger kilometres flown increased 41.5 per cent, from 66.8 billion to 94.5 billion. The distribution of demand by major airline and service is given in Table 1.

Table 1: **Passenger Kilometres Flown by Canadian Carriers — 1990 and 1998 (millions)**

	Air Canada	%	Canadian	%	Other Sch.*	%	Charter	%	Total	%
1990	25,504	*37.6*	21,624	*31.9*	3,975	*5.9*	16,675	*24.6*	67,778	*100*
1998	37,296	*39.5*	26,544	*28.1*	10,784	*11.4*	19,843	*21.0*	94,467	*100*

*The growth in "other scheduled" reflected the practice of most charter carriers in the 1990s to add some form of seasonal or peak-time scheduled carriage.

Source: Drawn from Transport Canada, Air Information in Canada, T-Facts. Includes domestic and international carriage.

By Sector. The components of passenger traffic growth over the 1990 to 1998 period reflected the increasing importance of trans-border (United States) and other international traffic. Passenger traffic carried by domestic airlines grew 14 per cent over the period, trans-border traffic grew 39 per cent and other international traffic grew 53 per cent. A particularly important event during the period was the signing of an "Open Skies" agreement with the United States in 1995. This treaty essentially removed pre-existing restrictions on air traffic between the two countries over a three-year period. It sustained the competitive status quo within each country, however, by not providing for cabotage — the right of an airline to carry local traffic within a foreign country. The revenue mix of the two major airlines in 1998, as shown in Table 2, reflected the results of these trends.

Table 2: **Passenger Revenue Mix for Major Airlines—1998 ($ millions)**

	Domestic	Transborder	International	Total
Air Canada	2,294	1,426	1,257	4,977
Canadian	1,403	355	993	2,751

Source: Company Annual Reports.

By Region. The distribution of passenger traffic carried by domestic carriers by region was six per cent for Atlantic Canada, 13 per cent for Quebec, 37 per cent for Ontario, 21 per cent for the Prairies and North, and 23 per cent for the Pacific.

By Airport. Passenger traffic in Canada was concentrated in relatively few airports. Toronto alone accounted for 31 per cent of the passenger traffic flown by Canadian carriers in 1998. Put together, the country's seven largest airports — Toronto, Vancouver, Montreal-Dorval, Calgary, Edmonton, Ottawa, Halifax and Winnipeg — accounted for 83 per cent of all traffic flown by Canadian carriers. By sector, these same airports accounted for 75 per cent of the domestic, 97 per cent of the transborder and 90 per cent of the international passenger traffic flown by Canadian carriers.

By City Pair. Passenger traffic data for origin/destination traffic, or point-to-point traffic, further emphasizes the importance of the Toronto market in domestic air travel. The 10 highest-traffic city pairs is presented in Table 3.

Table 3: **Point-To-Point Traffic for Selected City Pairs—1997 (000s)**

Carriers	Scheduled	Charter	Total
Toronto to Montreal	1,182	NA	1,182
Toronto to Vancouver	830	233	1,063
Toronto to Ottawa	684	NA	684
Toronto to Calgary	495	95	590
Calgary to Vancouver	520	50	570
Toronto to Winnipeg	347	56	403
Toronto to Halifax	289	77	366
Edmonton to Vancouver	312	48	360
Calgary to Edmonton	308	NA	308
Toronto to Edmonton	282	44	326

* Excludes passengers flying the city pair as part of a connecting flight itinerary.

Source: Drawn from Transport Canada, Air Information in Canada, T-Facts Air Folder.

Competition

The competitive context of the air travel market in Canada in the 1990s was a reflection of the seemingly irrational duel between Air Canada and Canadian. It was a hostile environment, marked by over-capacity, price-cutting and heavy losses for the two big airlines. It was remarkable that, under these circumstances, a number of relatively small carriers — namely, Royal Airlines, Canada 3000, AirTransat, Skyservice and WestJet — found viable market niches and were able to stay aloft and to grow. There were also two notable failures — Greyhound and Vistajet.

In the spring of 1996, Greyhound attempted to set up a low-fare, transcontinental service with hubs in Hamilton and Winnipeg. Greyhound's low fares generated high load factors and, interestingly, passenger profiles that were much further upscale than expected by industry observers. However, Greyhound was also saddled by costly delays in securing regulatory approvals, by inefficient second-hand 727 aircraft, by expensive aircraft lease arrangements, and by some questionable operating decisions, such as selling airline tickets in bus stations to avoid travel agent commissions. When the parent bus company was sold to Laidlaw Inc. in the summer of 1997, the airline was cut loose and quickly shut down.

Vistajet hardly got off the ground. It was to be a London, Ontario-based discount airline, but after four months of operation with one 30-year-old 737 and a bird strike that disabled the plane at a critical juncture, the new venture called it quits.

Competition and Government Policy

The federal government may have hoped that deregulation and the privatization of Air Canada would free it from some messy obligations. How wrong. By the early 1990s, Canadian's financial problems had become high-profile political issues. And, for the government, there were no easy solutions. Any significant effort to help Canadian — by, for example, providing financial assistance, moderating competition through re-regulation, or dropping domestic ownership provisions — would fly in the face of the government's political and economic objectives to be, and to be seen to be, even-handed, to avoid interference with market mechanisms and to maintain a domestically controlled industry. Not helping Canadian could result in an Air Canada monopoly, jeopardizing the government's goal of maintaining a healthy and competitive market, and, in the process, generating no small amount of criticism. Caught on the horns of a dilemma, the government tried to provide some aid to Canadian,[4] but it was sufficient only to buy some time for Canadian to pursue its own fate.

Faced with Canadian's failure, the government suspended competition rules, leading to the Air Canada – Onex takeover battle. In the furore that ensued, which included heated attacks on the government's actions and on the motives and intelligence of the transport minister, critics were nevertheless short on constructive alternatives. What the government did do was advise both Air Canada and Onex that it would be taking steps to protect the public interest, including provisions to:

- Prevent price gouging by any emerging monopoly carrier;
- Enhance competition in the domestic market, particularly by ensuring ease of entry and policing predatory practices;
- Maintain Canadian ownership and control of the industry;

---

[4]For example, the government purchased some Canadian aircraft in what some thought was a sweetheart deal.

- Maintain service to small communities;
- Ensure fair treatment of employees.

The precise legislation to accomplish these aims was some weeks off, and some critics questioned whether these objectives could ever be achieved. In response, the government promised that if a competitive industry did not evolve in a reasonable time, it would have no hesitation about initiating further steps, such as the discussion of cabotage with the United States.

The Competitive Situation in Late 1999

As the new Air Canada took shape, the industry was rife with speculation about its strategic intentions and the consequences for travellers and industry players alike. Given the government's position on sustaining competition, it looked as if there would be opportunities for Canada's existing airlines and possibly for new entrants; the issues for the airlines were how and when to take advantage of these possibilities. Following is a brief review of the positions and apparent intentions of the incumbent and announced players.

The New Air Canada. Despite the turmoil of the moment, complete with pending but uncertain government approvals and conditions, union clashes, and unresolved financial and operating issues at Canadian, there were some broad, if not settled, themes in Air Canada's positions. It was expected that as the air cleared the company would:

- Negotiate freedom from Canadian's financial and contractual obligations to American Airlines, the Sabre operating systems contract and the Oneworld alliance (in favor of consolidation with its present Star Alliance partners);
- Rationalize Air Canada's and Canadian's regional feeder carriers to eliminate gross duplication of capacity;
- Rationalize the domestic trunk routes of the two airlines to cut capacity by 15 per cent or more;
- Rationalize and expand its transborder operations (where it already held over 50 per cent of the market) and its other international operations, and use these dominant positions as forcefully as possible to influence domestic patronage and pricing;
- Increase prices and cut promotional spending as much as legally, politically and commercially feasible;
- Pursue, as it had already announced, the creation of a stand-alone low fare airline based in Hamilton, and perhaps parallel stand-alone businesses for the leisure (charter) market and for cargo. This theme was already becoming a sore point in Air Canada's union negotiations since the company had made no secret of its desire for concessions in wages and work rules for the new entities.

Most observers doubted that Air Canada would be able, or would be allowed, to sustain all of the market share accrued through the merger. Air Canada clearly thought otherwise and was setting out to further develop all segments of the industry.

Royal Airlines. Royal was founded in 1979, and for many years operated as a Quebec-based charter carrier with additional cargo, water bombing and aircraft maintenance services. In the early 1990s, the company went public and expanded into charter operations in Canada and abroad. By 1999, Royal's fleet encompassed 11 large passenger aircraft. In anticipation of the opportunities that might be created by an Air Canada-Canadian merger, Royal added domestic scheduled services in October, 1999, with flights at peak times from Toronto, Montreal, Ottawa, Winnipeg, Halifax and Vancouver.

Canada 3000. Canada 3000 was a privately owned carrier that started business in 1988 as a dedicated charter carrier for international pleasure travel, and gradually added scheduled carrier operations in Canada and abroad. By 1999, the company's fleet of 15 large aircraft was focused on long-haul domestic and international routes that varied with seasonal traffic patterns. It was anticipated that Canada 3000 would expand its operations in response to industry restructuring, possibly with an IPO to finance fleet additions.

AirTransat. The parent of AirTransat, Transat A.T. Inc., operated an integrated vacation travel business encompassing every aspect of holiday travel organization and distribution. The airline's fleet of 20 large charter aircraft was dedicated to the vacation travel market in Canada and Europe. There were no indications that Transat intended to change its focus in response to the domestic market turmoil.

Skyservice. Skyservice Airlines flew a charter fleet of four large aircraft mainly for two big tour operators, but also for incidental hire. The airline was a division of privately owned Skyservice Investments. This was an aggressive company and it was expected that it would attempt to expand its operations, possibly by way of long-haul scheduled domestic service.

CanJet. The CanJet Corp. of Toronto had been working since the summer of 1999 on plans for a low-fare airline that would fly out of Hamilton to Montreal, Ottawa, Halifax and Winnipeg. Although the prospective venture was backed by a well-known industry figure, Kenneth Rowe, chairman of the IMP Group Ltd. of Halifax, as of early December it was still regarded as very much a paper airline.

Canadian Regional Airlines. There was an expectation that the government would insist that Air Canada try to sell Canadian's regional feeder subsidiary as a condition of the acquisition. The airline consisted of 54 aircraft, most notably a fleet of 30, 20-to-30-year-old, 60-to-85 passenger Fokker F 28 jets. These aircraft had been described uncharitably, but with some accuracy, by Robert Milton, Air Canada's CEO, as planes that "are rarely flown in the Third World anymore."

Although the strategic role of the regional airlines in Canada was to feed the hub-based trunk flights of their parents, up to 80 per cent of the passengers on regional airlines flew between cities without connecting to the larger jets.[5] It was not clear in December 1999 whether there would be a buyer at an acceptable price, although one industry entrepreneur, Jim Deluce of Regional Airlines Holdings, had proposed purchasing both the Canadian and Air Canada regional subsidiaries.

---

[5]Joe Randall, president of Air Canada's regional airline business, in The Globe and Mail, January 21, 2000.

WESTJET AND THE "SOUTHWEST" BUSINESS MODEL

WestJet commenced operations out of Calgary in 1996. The airline was the brainchild of several local businessmen who were unhappy with the price and service being provided in the West by the major carriers (and this at the height of a price and frequency battle!). The founders hired experienced senior management from the United States and went into business with a strategy that copied the Southwest model, "rivet-for-rivet, stitch-for-stitch."

Other airlines that had successfully adopted this formula included Morris Air (now part of Southwest), Frontier Airlines and Spirit Airlines in the United States, and easyJet, Ryanair and Virgin Express in Europe. Interestingly, major system carriers on both continents had, by and large, experienced serious difficulties in their attempts to establish similar low-fare operating units.

The Southwest Low-Fare Airline Model

In the United States, Southwest Airlines had pioneered, developed and exploited a low-fare airline model to the point of becoming the most consistently profitable airline in the world. Founded in 1971, with three planes serving three Texas cities, Southwest had overcome early problems and had steadily grown its fleet, route structure and financial record. Over the years, Southwest had become well known for its employee-oriented, irreverent, work-hard-play-hard culture which was epitomized in the iconoclastic management style of Herb Kelleher, chairman and CEO.

The Southwest business model departed from the conventional system-airline, hub-and-spoke model in three principal ways, by: (1) focusing on price-sensitive passengers; (2) employing a short-haul, point-to-point route system, and; (3) running a low-cost, no-frills operation. An outline of further differences in the conventional hub-and-spoke and Southwest models is presented in Table 4. There were, of course, other business models being pursued in the industry such as charter, scheduled charter, and full- or luxury-service medium- to long-haul point-to-point carriage, but these were less central to the WestJet situation.

Table 4: Comparison of the Hub-and-Spoke and Southwest Models

	Hub-and-Spoke	Southwest
Market Focus	Business travel	Personal travel
Value Proposition	Frequency, system, amenities	Low fare
Route System	Integrated hub-and-spoke	Point-to-point
Stage Length	Medium- and long-haul	Short-haul
Seating	Reserved	Open
Airport Requirements	Major metropolitan hubs	Secondary airports
Ticketing	Travel Agents	Direct
Fleet	Multi-role/type	Single role/type
Product	Multi-class, frills	Single class, no-frills
Promotional Focus	Service, loyalty programs, restricted price deals	Low price, few restrictions
Culture	Formal	Casual
Structure	Hierarchical, defined roles	Flat, multi-task, relationships
Personnel Systems	Union work rule driven	Task, enterprise success driven

The Competitive Features of the Southwest Model

The Southwest-style airlines took some pains to emphasize that their low-fare/short-haul operations were a complement to the traditional airlines in that they aimed primarily at budget-conscious travelers who might otherwise drive, use a bus or train, or not travel at all. While this was undoubtedly accurate as a point of focus, it was also true that as their systems expanded, low-fare airline routes overlapped city pairs served by the large system carriers, or by their subsidiary regional feeder operations. As a result, the two airline system types invariably ended up in competition for at least part of the potential market. This was not a happy circumstance for the major carriers who were already locked in a tough competitive battle with each other.

The response of the major carriers to the advent of low-fare competitors followed two avenues. First, they counter-attacked through their regular operations — by measures that included selective fare cuts, enhanced promotional incentives, and shifts in frequencies and equipment. Second, if low fare operators continued to grow, some of the majors tried the more direct counter of creating captive low-fare subsidiary operations. All these responses, however, were ultimately limited by the higher cost structures of the conventional airlines and by the difficulty of disentangling a subsidiary from traditional industry practices, including most notably, union restrictions and cultural habits.

The Southwest formula was designed to achieve low cost. The key elements highlighted in Table 1 and other operational practices were designed to contribute to this end. The focus on one aircraft type, for example, contributed to lower employee-to-aircraft ratios, greater flexibility in crew assignments, and simplified maintenance, training programs and administrative procedures relative to the multi-aircraft system carriers. The result of this dedication to low cost meant the low-fare carriers had substantially lower operating costs per unit of capacity than those of the conventional airlines. WestJet estimated, for example, that its operating costs, after equalization for stage length, were 40 per cent to 50 per cent lower than those of Canadian and Air Canada. This put conventional carriers at a terrific disadvantage if they chose to compete on price on any given city pair. Some comparative financial and operating statistics for selected airlines are presented in Exhibit 2.

Setting up a competitive, profitable, low-fare subsidiary had also proven to be a problematic endeavor for the traditional airlines. In the early 1990s, Continental Airlines launched Continental Lite and closed it after a few years of substantial losses. Other entrants included, in the United States, United Airlines' United Shuttle, Delta Airlines' Delta Express and U.S. Airways' MetroJet, and in Europe, British Airways' GO. Although specific financial results were not available for these ventures, industry observers were generally sceptical about their profitability on any kind of fully allocated cost basis. United, for example, had started United Shuttle to compete with Southwest in the Western United States, but had backed off from direct competition after reported losses of $200 million and repositioned the Shuttle as a feeder to its West Coast hubs. British Airways, which had launched GO in 1998 to compete with the challenge of Ryannair and easyJet, had reported operating losses of $32 million in GO's first year of operation — much to the delight of easyJet, which sponsored a contest offering prizes for the most accurate forecast of the losses.

Whatever their willingness to subsidize losses, whether it be on particular routes or with new entries, the conventional airlines faced the limitations of their own fiscal abilities and beyond this, the prospect of legal challenge for engaging in predatory competition. In the United Kingdom, for example, easyJet made a big thing of their underdog status by suing British Airways under Article 26 of the Treaty of Rome, which says that dominant players in a market should not operate below the cost of production.

WESTJET'S PROGRESS

By late 1999, WestJet was on a roll. The company had overcome some early problems with safety regulations; acquired a fleet; established a route structure; built a reputation as an efficient and reliable, if unconventional operator; grown passenger volumes; fought off competitive challenges; completed a successful IPO; and was increasingly profitable.

Route Network. WestJet's route network focused on short-haul point-to-point service in Western Canada. This structure allowed WestJet to provide frequent service and dispense with many of the amenities usually provided on longer flights. The company's service coverage and departure frequencies as of late 1999 are summarized in Table 5. Whenever possible, WestJet picked niche routes where it could compete with non-stop jet service against the turbo-prop service of the majors' regional subsidiaries. On all its routes, WestJet sought to offer low everyday fares while maintaining a friendly service environment. Consistent with the Southwest model, WestJet offered a single class of service, did not interline baggage with other airlines, nor offer meal service, city ticket offices, frequent-flier programs, airport lounges or business class amenities.

Table 5: **WestJet Service Coverage and Weekly Departures, Summer 1999**

Airport	Service Commenced	Weekly Departures
Calgary	February, 1996	156
Vancouver	February, 1996	94
Kelowna	February, 1996	61
Edmonton	February, 1996	88
Victoria	March, 1996	27
Regina	June, 1996	21
Saskatoon	August, 1996	28
Abbotsford, B.C.	June, 1997	20
Winnipeg	March, 1998	27
Prince George	March, 1999	26
Thunder Bay	March, 1999	7

Source: WestJet Prospectus, April 1999.

Passenger Traffic. The impact of WestJet's entry, coupled with the competitive response of the majors, contributed to large increases in traffic on the targeted city pairs, as illustrated in Table 6. It appeared, indeed, that WestJet was correct in claiming that it was opening new demand segments for the industry.

Table 6: **Growth in Passenger Traffic for Largest City Pairs***
(000 passengers)

	Cal-Van	Edm-Van	Cal-Edm	Kel-Van	Cal-Vic	Edm-Vic
1995	422	243	271	87	63	43
1997	674	438	375	192	162	123
% Inc.		60	`80	38	119	155

*For cities served by WestJet; all domestic carriers; traffic does not include domestic portion
of international flights.*

Source: WestJet Prospectus, April 1999.

Competitive Reaction. Air Canada and Canadian counter-attacked in predictable ways. They sought to match WestJet's everyday low prices — which were up to 60 per cent less than the nominal economy prices of the majors — but in doing so they raised "fences" to limit their overall revenue erosion — such as by limiting the number of seats available in varying discount ranges, by restricting the times when the low fares were available and by requiring minimum stay-overs. On the promotional front, both airlines used occasional bonus point offers in their frequent-flyer programs to help stem the loss of high yield customers. Similarly, on occasion, the majors would price under on selected routes. Finally, the majors shuffled equipment and frequencies to try to improve their offer. At one point, for example, Air Canada attempted to compete in some city pairs by introducing its new 70-seat CRJ 700 regional jet, but had backed off after 10 months and little progress. Throughout these various forays, WestJet claimed that it made money on all routes.

In WestJet's assessment, Air Canada and Canadian were engaging in harassment and containment, rather than in trying to "blow 'em out of the sky" — although the two majors would no doubt have been happy to see this happen. The company was confident that, under these circumstances, it had room for continuing profitable growth.

WESTJET'S OPTIONS

In early September 1999, WestJet's CEO, Stephen Smith, reiterated the company's original plan: "We have a business plan we've been following and that plan contemplates the addition of three or four aircraft per year focused primarily on Western Canada...the company doesn't plan to fly further east than Thunder Bay for the foreseeable future...at least three to five years."[6] WestJet was, quite logically, concerned about not overextending itself. The airline had prospered in a tough market by following conservative policies with respect to growth and financing. It took pride, for example, in the fact that it had minimized the use of debt and owned 11 of its 13 aircraft.

As the events of the fall of 1999 unfolded, however, WestJet management was more or less compelled to take the possibility of eastern expansion into consideration. First, there was a matter of growth potential. If the company remained in Western Canada there was growth potential to perhaps 30 to 40 aircraft. A successful move to the East would more than double the potential.

---

[6]The Globe and Mail, September 7, 1999.

Second, there was a matter of timing, and particularly concerns about first-mover advantages. It was quite apparent that it would be just a matter of time before someone entered the East with a low-fare strategy — be it CanJet, or Air Canada, or another start-up. In this respect, there was an expectation that Ottawa would delay Air Canada's promised low-fare entry for a year or two, and facilitate gate access for newcomers at airports such as Hamilton. Finally, there was a chance that by remaining solely in the West, they might create some vulnerability to competition reaching out from their Eastern bases.

Management was clearly dealing with a strong temptation to push east, probably with an operation based at Hamilton airport. Beyond this, they had to consider immediate and fundamental questions of pace — how fast and how significant an entry was necessary from a competitive standpoint, and how fast and how significant an entry could the company digest? And, finally, in the longer haul, what were WestJet's prospects against Air Canada and others?

Exhibit 1: **Selected Financial Information for WestJet, 1998 and Projected 1999 ($000)**

	31 Dec. 1999	31 Dec. 1998
	$	$
Operating Revenues	**204,000**	**125,000**
Operating expenses	173,000	112,000
Operating income	30,000	13,000
Income before taxes	29,000	12,000
Net Income	16,000	7,000
Current assets	61,000	23,000
Capital and other assets	126,000	85,000
Total Assets	**187,000**	**108,000**
Current liabilities	50,000	29,000
Long-term debt	30,000	22,000
Deferred income tax	13,000	8,000
Shareholders equity	94,000	49,000
Total Liabilities and Shareholder Equity	**187,000**	**108,000**

Source: Company Financial Reports.

Exhibit 2: Comparative Financial and Operating Performance for Selected Airlines*

	South-west	WestJet	easyJet	Air Canada	Canadian	United
Financial Results						
Operating Revenues	6,226	126	184	5,932	3,171	26,257
Operating Expenses	5,203	112	181	5,788	3,173	24,016
Operating Income	1,02	14	3	144	(22)	2,209
Net Income	647	7	6	(16)	(138)	1,227
Operating Statistics**						
Avg. Stage Length (miles)***	597	378	NA	955	1,325	NA
Rev. Pass. Miles (RPM, millions)	31,419	639	1,302	23,212	16,695	124,609
Avail. Seat Miles (ASM, millions)	47,544	893	1,737	32,719	23,217	174,008
Load Factor	66	72	75	71	72	72
Pass. Revenue/RPM (cents) ****	19	19	NA	19	14	19
Pass. Revenue/ASM (cents)	13	13	NA	13	10	13
Oper. Revenue/ASM (cents)	13	14	11	16	11	15
Oper. Costs/ASM (cents)	11	13	10	16	11	14
Employees	25,844	629	394	23,000	14,123	91,000
ASM/Employee (millions)	1,840	1,420	4,410	1,430	1,640	1,910
Aircraft	280	11	8	157	81	577

* For fiscal year end, 1998.

** Air Canada, Canadian statistics exclude regional subsidiaries.

*** Typically, airline operating costs per mile decrease with longer flights. WestJet estimated, for example, that its operating costs per available seat mile if it operated with an average stage length of 1,113 miles (Calgary-Thunder Bay) would be about 8.2 cents per mile.

**** Simple passenger revenue comparisons are also confounded by stage length. As costs per mile fall with longer stage lengths, the tendency, under competition, is for prices per mile to fall as well.

Source: Company financial reports. All currencies converted to $ Canadian.

HARLEQUIN ENTERPRISES LIMITED

case 11

Peter Killing

In 1979, Harlequin Enterprises was the largest publisher of romance novels in the world and was judged by many to be North America's most profitable publishing company. Harlequin's sales and profits had increased every year since 1970 and in 1979 were forecasted at $180 million and $20 million, respectively. Harlequin romances were produced in nine languages and sold in more than 90 countries.

As the 1970s drew to a close, the pace of change at Harlequin seemed to be quickening. In 1978, for example, Harlequin had produced its first feature film, based on one of its romance novels, and opened its first retail store, designed to sell educational material produced by the company's "Scholar's Choice" division. In 1979, the company was launching its romance novels in Japan, Scandinavia, Mexico, Venezuela, and Greece, as well as adding new romance series in North America, Germany and Holland. As Larry Heisey, Harlequin's president, looked ahead, he stated:

> Strategies that served us well in the 1970s will be continued into the 1980s. We will work to develop our present resources, to make use of those growth channels that have been established, and to pursue the flexibility that will enable us to react to market opportunities … We look to the 1980s as a time of great promise for this company.

Ivey

Associate Professor Peter Killing prepared this case solely to provide material for class discussion. The author does not intend to illustrate either effective or ineffective handling of a managerial situation. The author may have disguised certain names and other identifying information to protect confidentiality.

THE PUBLISHING INDUSTRY

Apart from educational material, publishing a book is typically a high-risk venture. Each book is a new product with all the risks attendant on any new product introduction. The risks vary with the author's reputation, the subject matter and the predictability of the market's response. Among the numerous decisions facing the publisher are selecting manuscripts out of the thousands submitted each year, deciding how many copies to print and deciding how to promote the book.

Insiders judged that the key to success in hardcover publishing was the creative genius needed to identify good young authors among the hundreds of would-be writers, and then publish and develop them throughout their careers. Sol Stein of Stein and Day Publishers commented:

> Most successful publishers are creative editors at heart, and contribute more than risk capital and marketing expertise to the books they publish. If a publisher does not add value to what he publishes, he's a printer, not a publisher.

Successful hardcover authors and their publishers could profit greatly from the sale of paperback publishing rights and film rights. In the 1970s, prices paid for paperback rights had skyrocketed, as softcover publishers bid astronomical amounts, frequently more than $1 million, for books they judged would sell in the numbers necessary for paperback success.

These high prices raised the already high break-even volumes for paperback publishers. Publishers generally received about 50 per cent of the retail price, of which about 13 per cent (15¢ per book) would pay for printing costs, 10 per cent for distribution, 10 per cent for selling expenses, five to 7.5 per cent for advertising and promotion, and the remainder would, hopefully, cover rights and overheads. If the publisher failed to sell enough books, the loss could be substantial. One result was that the mass paperback publishers in the United States earned only about two per cent on sales of new releases, whereas Harlequin, using a distinctly different approach to the business, earned in the 15 per cent range. (Harlequin's financial results are summarized in Exhibit 1.)

HARLEQUIN'S FORMULA: STANDARDIZATION

Harlequin's formula was fundamentally different from that of traditional publishers: content, length, artwork, size, basic formats and print were all standardized. Each book was not a new product, but rather an addition to a clearly defined product line. The consequences of this uniformity were significant. The reader was buying a **Harlequin novel**, and advertising promoted the Harlequin line rather than a particular book or author. The standardized size made warehousing and distribution more efficient. A comparison of Harlequin's formula and the operations of traditional "one-off" publishers is presented in Table 1.

Table 1:   **The Harlequin Formula**

	Harlequin	**One-Off Publisher**
Editorial	Emphasizes Consistency with established guidelines.	Requires separate judgement on potential consumer demand for each manuscript.
Rights	Uses standardized process, usually for established amounts.	Can be a complex process, involving subrights, hard/soft deals and tying up authors for future books.
Author Management	Is less dependent on specific authors.	Is vulnerable to key authors changing publisher.
Marketing	Builds the imprint/series.	Builds each title/author.
Selling	Emphasizes servicing, rack placement, and maintaining distribution.	Sells on strength of author, cover, critical reviews, special promotional tactics.
Production	Uses consistent format with focus on efficiency.	Emphasizes cover design, cost control secondary.
Distribution/Order Regulation/ Information Systems	Utilizes very sophisticated shipping and returns handling procedures.	Traditionally has not received much attention, and hence, is not as sophisticates.

Source: Adapted from a Canada Consulting Group Report

Because all its novels were aimed at the same target market — "any and all female readers over the age of 15" — Harlequin could afford to do a significant amount of market research, identifying its customers and their likes and dislikes. The average Harlequin reader was 35½ years old, was married, had 2½ children, was equally likely to be working or a housewife, and had probably finished high school. Harlequin described the relationship between its books and its readers as follows:

> The world of romantic fiction offers the reader delights of a kind which are absent from her everyday life. Identifying herself with the heroine, the romance reader can meet the strong, masterful hero of her dreams and be courted by him. Without stirring from her fireside, she can travel to other countries, learn about other ways of life, and meet new people. After the vicarious enjoyment provided by such literature, the reader can return to safe reality, where domineering males seldom have to be confronted and trips to exotic parts of the world never happen, so that illusion is always preserved. The romance provides compulsive reading and leaves a feeling of satisfaction and pleasure.

Harlequin's view that its novels could be sold "like other branded consumer products" perhaps explained why employees hired from mass-marketing companies such as Procter and Gamble had skills and aptitudes that led them to do well at Harlequin. The company's 1974 Annual Report documented its mass market focus, its use of sampling techniques, and its entry into television advertising, which in many cities increased sales by as much as 80 per cent.

We are selling branded literature which can be promoted like other branded consumer products. Sampling techniques, the costs of which are prohibitive to the general publisher because of the variety of books published, are being used by Harlequin to expand its market. For example, several million books were distributed free to the trade in 1973 and 1974 for use in introducing our products to new consumers. Since September 1974, a television advertising campaign has been tested in ten cities in Canada and the United States. Expansion of this advertising will begin in 1975.

Responsibility for the development of Harlequin novels lay with the company's British editorial staff and stable of more than 100 writers, most of whom were also British. Harlequin had acquired this editorial expertise in 1971 when it purchased Mills and Boon, a long-established British publisher of romance novels. The genius of the Mills and Boon editors, according to one observer, was that they were able to produce a consistency in the final product, even though many authors were contributing. Readers always knew what they were getting and were satisfied again and again. In addition to the work of its regular writers, Mills and Boon received approximately 5,000 unsolicited manuscripts per year. Typically, about 50 of these were accepted.

Harlequin's editorial process did not generate or even encourage best-sellers. "Best-sellers would ruin our system," stated Bill Willson, Harlequin's vice president of finance. "Our objective is steady growth in volume. We have no winners and no losers." All Harlequin books published in any month sold about the same number of copies. Unsold paperback books could be returned to the publisher for credit; a consequence of Harlequin's even and predictable sales was that its rate of return of unsold books was much lower than that of its competitors, 25 to 30 per cent of sales versus 40 to 50 per cent.

One industry analyst commented on Harlequin's approach to the industry as follows:

> You've got to realize that these guys at Harlequin revolutionized the North American book industry. They brought professional marketing and business techniques to an industry that seems to publish "for love rather than money." At retail, for instance, they ignored the bookstores. This was a good move because most people never enter bookstores. Instead they built Harlequin book racks and placed them in supermarkets, mass merchandisers and drug stores where women are. They made each of the books 192 pages by changing the type size. This allowed for standard packaging and six books would fit into each pocket on the rack. Once the books were accepted by the trade they went on a monthly standing order system like magazines. This allowed for uniform print runs, shipping containers, and so on. Everything was done for efficiency, prices were kept low and volumes skyrocketed.

Distribution

In late 1977, Harlequin established a national retail sales organization in Canada, ending a joint venture agreement with another publisher in which a single sales force had represented both companies. By early 1979, Harlequin executives declared themselves well satisfied with the new arrangement, which allowed the sales force to focus solely on Harlequin products.

In the United States, Harlequin was represented by the Pocket Books Distribution Corporation, a wholly owned subsidiary of Simon and Schuster. Pocket Books' 120-person sales force was responsible for dealing with the 400 or so independent regional distributors who distributed Harlequin's books and the major chains who bought direct, and for ensuring that Harlequin books were properly displayed and managed at the retail level. In addition to handling the Harlequin romance series, the sales force carried Simon and Schuster's own pocket books which were "one-offs" issued monthly.

Harlequin did not print any of its own books. Harlequin novels that were sold in the United States were printed by a major American printer of mass market books and distributed through a distribution centre in Buffalo, New York. Harlequins sold in Canada were printed in Canada and distributed through the company's Stratford, Ontario warehouse.

HARLEQUIN'S PRODUCTS AND MARKETS

The Romance Novel

The backbone of Harlequin's business was its two major series, Harlequin Presents and Harlequin Romances, which consistently produced over 90 per cent of the company's sales and earnings. Originally, Harlequin had published only the Romances line, consisting of very chaste conservative stories selected from the Mills and Boon line by the wife of one of Harlequin's founders. After a period of time, however, Mills and Boon executives suggested to Harlequin that they were not publishing Mills and Boon's most popular books. Arguing that the British and North American markets were not the same, Harlequin nevertheless tried a blind test — two of its choices and two of the slightly more "racy" Mills and Boon choices — on 500 of its North American customers. To the company's amazement the Mills and Boon selections were very popular and, bowing to its customers' wishes, Harlequin created the Presents line to offer Mills and Boon's less chaste romance stories. In early 1979, the still growing Presents line was increased from four titles per month to six in North America, and sales rose by 50 per cent. At the same time, the Romances line was cut back from eight titles per month to six, with the net result that in North America the two lines were selling very similar quantities of books.

Both the Presents and Romances lines were sold at retail and, since 1970, through Harlequin's "Reader Service" book club. This direct mail operation offered heavy Harlequin readers the possibility of purchasing every book the company published, delivered right to the front door. The book club was an important source of profit; in the United States, six books were sold through the book club for every ten sold at retail. Furthermore, a book sold through the book club yielded Harlequin the full cover price, whereas a book sold at retail netted the company approximately half the retail price, and required advertising, distribution costs, the acceptance of returns from retailers and so on. As one observer put it: "No wonder the company is willing to pay the mailing costs for its book club members!"

Competition

No other publisher concentrated as heavily as Harlequin on the romance novel, although, attracted by Harlequin's profit margins, most of the majors had made attempts to penetrate the market. Bantam Books, the largest and generally considered the best-run conventional paperback publisher in North America, had tried to enter Harlequin's market in the early 1970s with a series titled Red Rose Romances. The line was a failure and had been phased out of existence by 1977. Four or five other major publishers had also attempted to penetrate the romantic novel market in the late 1960s and early 1970s. Consumers were offered Valentine Romances from Curtis Publishing, Rainbow Romances from New American Library, Hamilton House from Fawcett, and Candlelight Romances from Dell. The only one of these series selling in 1979 was Dell's, offering one or two new titles per month. Willson explained that the problem faced by all of these firms was their editorial content. The stories simply were not good enough. Heisey agreed, adding:

> We are good managers and good marketers, I admit, and those things make us more profitable than we otherwise would be, but the essence of this firm is the editorial department and our group of more than 100 authors. It is these resources which make us unique, and it is precisely these resources which our competition cannot duplicate.

International Markets

Commencing in 1975, Harlequin began to establish foreign language ventures for its romance novels in countries around the world. Typically, a new venture would start with two or four titles per month, translated from the <u>Romances</u> or <u>Presents</u> lines, and then expand as the market allowed. In spite of predictions from many (male) publishers that the Harlequin line would not appeal to the women of their country, virtually all of the new ventures prospered. Entry costs were not high in most countries, and profits came quickly. Harlequin's major international moves are listed in Table 2.

Table 2: INTERNATIONAL EXPANSION

1975	Harlequin Holland established. Four titles per month. Extremely successful. Second line introduced in 1976. Further expansion in 1977 and 1978. Holland, together with Canada, has Harlequin's highest per capita (women over 15) penetration rate.
1976	Harlequin paid $2.1 million for a 50 per cent interest in the West German company that had been publishing Mills and Boon novels for several years. The company published five romance titles per month, plus a French detective series. In spite of new competition in the romance area in 1978, the company was performing well.
1977	Harlequin France established. In 1978, a four-title per month series was launched, aimed at French, Belgian and Swiss markets. Line expanded in 1979. Company became profitable in 1979.
1978	Mills and Boon's Australian operation (established in 1973) took a major step forward with the introduction of TV advertising and a new line. A successful operation.
1979	New launches in Japan, Scandinavia, Greece, Mexico, and Venezuela.

Harlequin's major new romance novel venture in 1979, representing an investment of $2 million, was its entry into the Japanese market. Despite scepticism from outsiders, initial market research had indicated that the appeal of Harlequin's product would be even stronger in Japan than North America. In early 1979, the company also entered its smallest foreign-language markets to date (i.e., those of the Scandinavian countries). A Harlequin executive explained the company's rationale:

Harlequin's operation in Stockholm is the headquarters for publishing and marketing activities in the Swedish, Finnish and Norwegian languages. We will begin publishing romance fiction in Sweden and Finland in March, at the rate of four titles per month, and in Norway in April, at two titles per month. Denmark is currently being examined as a potential new market.

The four Scandinavian countries, with populations varying from 4.1 million to 8.3 million, will provide Harlequin with experience in the management of smaller markets. We also believe that, despite their size, they are potentially productive and represent a well-founded investment.

Literary Diversification

Harlequin's heavy dependence on the romance novel had been a source of concern to company executives for a number of years. In 1975, the company had attempted diversification with a line of science fiction (SF) novels for the North American market. They were known as the Laser series. In spite of an intense marketing effort, the series was discontinued after 18 months and 58 titles. Heisey indicated that no one factor was responsible, suggesting that the problem was likely part editorial, part distribution, and part pricing, (see Appendix A).

Subsequent literary diversification attempts were more modest. In 1977, Mills and Boon created a series of romance stories focussing on doctors and nurses. These were introduced at the rate of two titles per month. In 1978, the Masquerade line of historical romances was also introduced at the level of two titles per month. In Willson's view, these were "the same romance stories, but with long dresses." While both lines showed some initial promise, neither was expected to match the success of Harlequin Presents or Harlequin Romances.

In 1979, Harlequin took the somewhat bolder step of creating a new brand, Worldwide Library, which would act as an umbrella imprint for new products. The first of these was Mystique Books, introduced in March 1979. This romantic suspense series, adapted from a successful line of French novels, was introduced at the rate of four titles per month, with heavy television advertising. It did not carry the Harlequin name.

The importance that Harlequin placed on new series such as these was illustrated in the five-year plan of the North American book division, the company's most important business unit. This division's objective was a 30 per cent annual increase in sales and profits throughout the early 1980s, to be achieved by increasing the U.S. penetration rate of the Presents and Romances lines closer to Canadian levels, and at the same time, through the introduction of new "spin-off" products, to reduce the overall dependence on those two lines to 65 per cent of sales and profits by 1985. Harlequin's penetration rate in the United States (sales per women over the age of 15) was approximately half that of the Canadian rate.

Scholar's Choice

Scholar's Choice was created in the early 1970s when Harlequin acquired and merged two small Canadian companies involved in the production of educational material for school boards and teachers. Dissatisfied with what it described as "mixed results" from "less than buoyant Canadian institutional markets for educator supplies" during the mid 1970s, the company opened a retail store in Toronto in 1977. The success of this store led to a second Toronto store in 1978 and plans for seven more stores across Canada in 1979. All of these stores would sell educational material and would be wholly owned by the company.

Harlequin Films

Harlequin entered the movie-making business in 1977 with the $1.1 million film, Leopard in the Snow. The movie featured no well-known actors, but it was based on a successful novel by one of Harlequin's established authors. The venture was a first step toward Harlequin's objective of "becoming to women what Walt Disney is to children." Willson elaborated on Harlequin's rationale:

> In the traditional film-making business, there are a number of quite separate participants. The screenplay and actual creation of the movie are done by one group, financing by another group, distribution and marketing of the finished product by a variety of people. The people who actually create the product virtually lose control of it by the time it is marketed. Because so many conflicting groups are involved with different objectives and skills, the entire process is extremely inefficient.
>
> Harlequin could manage this process quite differently. We have the books for screenplays — over 2,000 on our back list — and we have the finances to make the films. We know how to market and we have far more knowledge about our target market than most movie makers ever do. We could, once we gain confidence, use the distributors only to get the films into the theatres for a flat fee. We would do the promotion ourselves and take the financial risk.
>
> The other advantage to Harlequin is the same one that we have in the publishing business — consistency. For other producers, each film is a new product and new risk and the public has to be educated separately. We could advertise Harlequin films on a pretty intensive scale, and they could reinforce and be reinforced by the book sales. The potential may be tremendous.

The box office results of "Leopard in the Snow" were described by the company as "somewhat inconsistent" and further testing was to be done in 1979 to determine the feasibility of the concept.

Forward Integration

Harlequin's current three-year contract with Pocket Books was going to expire on December 31, 1979 and the company was considering ending the arrangement and establishing its own U.S. sales force. The following factors indicated that such a move might make sense:

Cost

Harlequin paid Pocket Books a set fee per book sold for the use of its U.S. sales force. As volumes continued to rise, so would Harlequin's total selling cost, even though Pocket Book's sales force costs were unlikely to increase. Harlequin executives estimated that they were already paying "well over half" the total cost of the Pocket Book sales force, even though the volumes of books it handled for Simon and Schuster and Harlequin were approximately equal. In fact, since the Simon and Schuster line consisted of "one-offs" which had to be "sold" to the distributors each month and the Harlequin line was all on automatic reorders, there was little doubt that Harlequin received less than half of the sales force's attention. The net result was that Harlequin felt it would get better service at lower cost from its own sales force.

New Products

As new products like the <u>Mystique</u> line were introduced to the U.S. market with increasing frequency, the attention given to each product line by the sales force would become extremely important. If such new lines were to be a success, Harlequin felt that it would need to be able to control the activities of its U.S. sales force directly.

Returns

One of the tasks of a Harlequin sales force was known as "order regulation." This job, which was to check with individual retailers to determine their return rate, was necessary because the independent distributors, set up to handle magazines, could not accurately monitor pocket book returns by customer. If the return rate was too high, books were being printed and distributed for no gain. If it was too low, retailers were stocking out and sales were being lost.

Larry Heisey commented:

> I ran a cheek to see what kind of a job Pocket Books was doing for us on order regulation. We had about 400 distributors, each carrying <u>Romances</u> and <u>Presents</u>. That meant we could have had up to 800 changes in order positions per month as wholesalers fine-tuned their demands to optimize our return rates. As I recall, there were only about 23 changes per month in the time period we checked. The Pocket Book's sales force simply wasn't managing the situation the way they should have been.

The only concern expressed at Harlequin about dropping Pocket Books was the possible reaction of Dick Snyder, the tough and aggressive president of Simon and Schuster. Snyder had become president of Simon and Schuster in 1975, the same year that the New York-based publisher was acquired by Gulf and Western, a large U.S. conglomerate. Snyder was interested in growth and profits, and was achieving results in both areas. Newsweek commented as follows:

> S&S has always been a best-seller house, but Snyder has turned it into the bastion of books-as-product — and the target of derision by other publishers who pride themselves on a commitment to good literature. He expects his editors to bring in twice as many titles per year than are required at other houses ...
> The marketing staff is renowned for its aggressiveness — and high turnover rate. "Simon and Schuster runs a sales contest every year," former sales representative Jack O'Leary says only half jokingly. "The winners get to keep their jobs."

The Acquisition Program

In 1977, Heisey and Willson had estimated Harlequin's potential world market for romance novels (all non-Communist countries) at $250 million, but as Harlequin's prices and volumes continued to rise, it became apparent that this estimate might have been too low. No matter how big the ultimate market, however, neither man felt that the company could penetrate this market any faster than it already was. They also emphasized that Harlequin's romantic fiction business could not profitably absorb all the cash it generated. As a result, Willson, with the approval of the Torstar Corporation (the publisher of the Toronto Star newspaper which had acquired 59 per cent of Harlequin's shares in the late 1970s), hired several staff analysts and began a search for acquisitions. Early investigation revealed that the major U.S. paperback companies were not for sale, and the minor ones were not attractive.

Willson prepared a list to guide the search process (see Exhibit 2), deciding that he was not interested in any company which would add less than 10 per cent to Harlequin's profits. With more than $20 million in cash in 1977 and no debt to speak of, Willson had thought that $40 million would be a reasonable amount to spend on acquisitions; he visualized two major acquisitions, both in the United States. One would be in the publishing business and the other in a related business.

By 1979, Willson and his group had made several acquisitions, but were still searching for one or two really sizeable takeover candidates. In mid-1977, they had purchased the Ideals Corporation of Milwaukee, a publisher of inspirational magazines and books, as well as greeting cards and a line of cookbooks, for $1.5 million. In 1978, Harlequin acquired a 78 per cent interest in the Laufer Company of Hollywood, California for $10.5 million, approximately $8 million of which represented goodwill. In the nine months ended December 31, 1977, Laufer earned US$814,000 on sales of $10 million. Laufer published eight monthly entertainment magazines including Tiger Beat, Right On! and Rona Barrett's Hollywood, for teenage and adult markets. The Laufer and Ideals businesses were subsequently combined to form the Harlequin Magazine Group. (An organization chart is presented in Exhibit 3.) During the first half of 1979, the magazine group acquired a 50 per cent interest in ARTnews ("the most distinguished fine arts magazine in the United States"), a 60 per cent interest in Antiques World, which was launched in 1979 as a sister publication to ARTnews, and a 57.5 per cent interest in a new Toronto publication titled Photo Life.

THE FUTURE

As the financial results for the first six months of 1979 arrived, showing a 45 per cent increase in sales (no doubt in part a result of the 20 and 30 per cent price increases on the Presents and Romances lines in North America — bringing retail prices to $1.50 and $1.25, respectively) and a 23 per cent gain in net income, Larry Heisey looked forward to the 1980s with keen anticipation.

> We believe the 1980s will be very important to Harlequin, even more so than the '70s. Our market research indicates substantial growth potential in the English-language markets. The rapid development of markets in Holland and French Canada to per capita levels nearly equivalent to those of English-speaking Canada, our most mature market, suggests the great potential of Mills & Boon romance fiction in other languages.

> The goals that we established for ourselves at the beginning of the seventies are being realized, generating an outstanding growth pattern. We have every reason to believe that this pattern will continue in the 1980s, for the company's financial resources are more than adequate to support an active expansion and diversification program.

Exhibit 1: **Summary of Financial Performance**

	1978	1977	1976	1975	1974	1973	1972	1971	1970
OPERATING RESULTS									
(millions)									
Net Revenues									
Publishing	-	-	44.1	35.1	24.8	16.4	11.0	4.0	3.0
Learning Materials *	-	-	8.3	8.2	6.2	4.0	4.3	4.0	5.1
Total Net Revenues	125.9	80.5	52.4	43.2	31.0	20.4	15.3	8.0	8.0
Net Earnings	16.8	12.5	5.3	4.4	3.5	3.0	1.6	0.5	0.1
FINANCIAL POSITION									
(millions)									
Cash and Securities	22.5	24.0	9.3	4.2	3.5	3.2	1.1	1.2	
Total Current Assets	58.4	45.8	23.6	19.2	14.3	10.0	6.1	6.2	4.0
Current Liabilities	25.2	21.2	10.5	8.4	7.0	5.0	3.4	4.0	2.1
Working Capital	33.2	24.6	13.1	40.8	7.2	5.0	3.0	2.5	2.0
Net Fixed Assets	2.3	1.7	1.0	0.9	0.7	0.5	0.2	0.2	0.2
Other Assets	14.1	6.4	5.8	3.7	3.7	3.7	4.0	4.0	2.2
Shareholders' Equity	45.2	30.5	19.4	15.4	11.7	9.1	6.8	4.3	3.9
FINANCIAL RATIOS									
Net Earnings on Net Revenues	13.3%	15.6%	10.2%	10.2%	11.4%	13.4%	10.3%	5.7%	1.4%
Net Earnings on Equity	37.1%	41.0%	27.5%	28.8%	30.2%	30.0%	23.2%	10.5%	2.8%
Working Capital Ratio	2.3:1	2.2:1	2.2:1	2.3:1	2.0:1	2.0:1	1.8:1	1.7:1	1.7:1
Fully Diluted Earnings per Share	1.06	0.79	0.34	0.29	0.24	0.18	0.12	0.04	0.01
Dividends Declared (millions)	2.3	1.4	1.3	1.2	1.0	0.4	0.1	-	-
OTHER DATA									
Share Price ** - Low	7.75	3.83	2.75	1.33	0.94	1.30	0.44	0.23	-
- High	16.00	9.00	3.79	3.25	1.72	1.83	4.67	0.46	-
Number of Employees	980	881	584	332	313	240	201	157	188
Number of Books Sold (millions)	125	109	90	72	63	42	29	25	19

* Although exact figures were not available, learning materials were still a relatively low proportion of Harlequin sales in 1978.

** Adjusted for splits. Stock price in mid-1979 was $18 to $20.

Exhibit 2: Harlequin's Guide for Acquisitions

Potential areas to look for acquisition in publishing business:	Areas to consider for acquisition in related industry:
1. Trade Books • Paperback fiction and non-fiction • Hardcover fiction and non-fiction • Continuity series and partworks	1. Entertainment • Movies and television films • Records • Video tapes • Music
2. Reference Books • Text books and learned journals • Professional publishing: legal, medical, accounting • Reference guides and handbooks	2. Mass-marketed, low-technology consumer products • Adult games • Children's games • Children's toys
3. Magazines • Consumer magazines • Trade and business publications	3. Handicraft and hobby products
4. Other Publishing • Greeting cards, stationary • Sewing patterns • Diaries and albums • Music publishing	

Exhibit 3: **Organization**

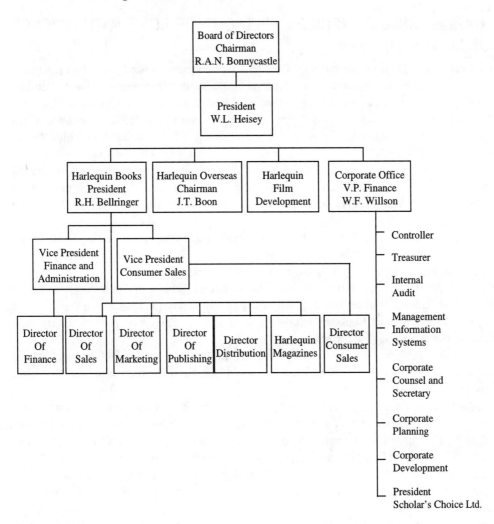

Appendix A

WHY HARLEQUIN ENTERPRISES FELL OUT OF LOVE WITH SCIENCE FICTION by Brian M. Fraser

"It didn't work," says Harlequin Enterprises President W. Lawrence Heisey. "We didn't perceive that it would be profitable in the reasonably short-term future, so we decided to abandon it. Period."

Although noncommittal on the failure, Heisey said no one factor was responsible: "I think it was a lot of problems," he said. "It wasn't any one thing. I don't think the distribution was that bad; it probably begins with editorial and ends with pricing, so it was a whole collection of problems. But it didn't work."

Hard-core SF enthusiasts were against the venture from the start, fearing science fiction would be watered down into pap for the masses. And, indeed, this was essentially true: the plots of the Laser books generally took standard ideas in the genre and sketched new adventure stories, but without much depth.

Like its romances, which are mainly sold in supermarkets and drug stores, Harlequin attempted to produce a uniform product in the science fiction category. It also hoped it would prove as addictive to young male readers as the light romances are for some housewives.

Harlequin put all its marketing expertise and resources behind the new SF paperbacks, beginning with six titles plus a free novel (Seeds of Change by Thomas F. Monteleone) as incentive to anyone who bought a Laser Book and returned a questionnaire. Like good marketers, they used these names to build a mailing list for promotional material.

An extensive publicity and advertising program was tied to the announcement. Major Canadian media carried articles, focussing on the worldwide financial success of the Harlequin Romances line.

To attract potential readers directly, full-page ads were placed in major science fiction digest magazines, such as Analog, and in amateur fan magazines, such as Locus. And, with sage marketing skill, Harlequin also attempted to create a favorable selling environment through ads in Publisher's Weekly and the Coast Review of Books, which are read by bookstore managers.

Harlequin even placed trial direct response ads in a girlie magazine, ran radio commercials in Toronto and U.S. test markets, and its ad agency, Compton Advertising of New York, tried out a television commercial.

These innovative merchandising techniques, not part of the repertoire of most Canadian publishers, have been used with some success on the romances.

"The failure can be attributed to a complete misunderstanding of the special appeal of science fiction and the nature of its addictive readers. Nobody "in the know" ever believed this venture would succeed," says veteran U.S. SF editor Donald Woolheim.

The inside-SF consensus is that Harlequin underestimated the intelligence of the science fiction reader who, unlike the devotees of Harlequin Romances, looks for non-formula fiction, cerebral material with new and well-developed ideas.

It's conceivable that lack of adequate distribution may have been one of the prime reasons Harlequin pulled out. With the Romances line, Harlequin has been phenomenally successful in penetrating the grocery and drugstore markets, placing racks specifically for their interchangeable 12 titles a month. But no such breakthrough was evident with the Laser line.

STARBUCKS

case 12

Ariff Kachra and
Mary M. Crossan

Mr. Howard Schultz, the Chairman and CEO of Starbucks Corporation, had just given a speech on the future of the coffee industry at a well-known business school. As he left the lecture hall, he stopped at the University's most popular coffee shop, the Brewery. The shop's sign indicated that it was "Now Serving Starbucks Coffee". As Mr. Schultz ordered the House Blend, he noticed that the Brewery was a far cry from any Starbucks coffeehouse. The shop was messy, the service was poor, and the coffee was average. As Mr. Schultz was leaving the Brewery, Orin Smith, Starbucks President and COO, called him on his cellular phone. McDonald's, whom Starbucks had turned down a number of times, was once again petitioning for a contract to serve Starbucks coffee. On the plane back to Seattle, Washington, Mr. Schultz's thoughts drifted back to his experience at the Brewery and the call from McDonald's. He asked himself two questions: Was Starbucks growing in the best way possible? Was Starbucks overextending in its quest for growth?

IVEY

Ariff Kachra prepared this case under the supervision of Professor Mary Crossan solely to provide material for class discussion. The author does not intend to illustrate either effective or ineffective handling of a managerial situation. The author may have disguised certain names and other identifying information to protect confidentiality.

SPECIALTY COFFEE INDUSTRY

Coffee was the second most traded commodity next to oil. It was divided into two categories: specialty coffee and basic coffee. Specialty coffee was the highest echelon of quality coffee available in the world. Many people described it as gourmet coffee. There was no one accepted definition in the industry; however, everyone agreed that specialty coffee was of higher quality than basic supermarket brand coffee.

It was estimated in 1994 that the specialty coffee industry was growing at a rate of 15 per cent per year and that the basic coffee industry was suffering. Although most consumers only saw this division at the retail level, specialty vs. basic coffee was a concept that originated with the coffee grower.

SUPPLIERS

Specialty coffee companies did not typically deal with suppliers, i.e., coffee farmers, directly. They dealt with exporters instead. About a third of the coffee farms in the world were less than three acres. These farmers did not have the desire, the volume, the money, the expertise, or the connections to export coffee themselves because most countries regulated coffee sales. Coffee processors or exporters regularly visited smaller farmers and bought their coffee[1] either in cherry or parchment[2]. The coffee would then be moved to a mill where there would be other farmers' production from the same or different regions. After husking the parchment, the millers sold it to the exporter(s). It was common place for coffee to change hands as many as five times before it reached a specialty coffee seller. Typically, coffee was moved from the farmer, to the collector, to the miller, to the exporter, to the importer, and finally, to the specialty coffee seller.

The bean suppliers that managed this process well, typically concentrated on high quality Arabica beans for which they could command premium prices. Lower quality bean suppliers concentrated on Robusta beans. This quality division was somewhat congruent to the way the industry was divided, i.e., lower quality beans were harvested for the commercial industry and higher quality beans for the specialty coffee industry. (Industry experts estimated that specialty coffee made up 31 per cent of the total coffee consumption, See Exhibit 1).

The price of certain coffee was a direct reflection of the quality and quantity of coffee available at a particular time. It was very difficult to get price confirmations because a successful coffee harvest was dependent on so many different factors. These included weather conditions, health of the coffee trees, harvesting practices, disease and infection caused by insects, and the social, political, regulatory and economic environments of the coffee-producing countries. For example, the 1975 Brazilian frost drove the price of coffee up, and U.S. coffee consumption never recovered from the 18.5 per cent decline.

---

[1] This process varied by country.

[2] Once the coffee cherry had been washed and dried, what remained was the coffee bean in some sort of husk.

CONSUMERS

Coffee consumption patterns had changed in the U.S. In 1996, the per capita consumption of coffee was 1.7 cups per day per person, a significant decrease from the two to three cups daily consumption in the '60s and '70s. The National Coffee Association attributed this decrease to poor product development, packaging, and position (price focused) by the industry's leading coffee producers. However, now it seemed that coffee consumption was on the rise. The following compares U.S. consumption rates to global consumption rates:

> In terms of kilograms of coffee per person consumed in 1985, the United States at 4.7 ranked tenth, behind Sweden (11.6), Denmark (11.0), Finland (10.0), Holland (9.5), Germany (6.8), France (5.5), and Italy (4.9) among the coffee-consuming nations and behind Costa Rica (6.5) and Brazil (5.5) among the coffee-producing nations. Overall, in the decade between 1975 and 1985, Europe's levels of imported coffee rose significantly, those of Japan doubled, while those of the United States remained steady despite increased population.[3]

The recent popularity of specialty coffee was the result of four consumer trends: (1) the adoption of a healthier lifestyle had led North Americans to replace alcohol with coffee; (2) coffee bars offered a place where people could meet; (3) people liked affordable luxuries and specialty coffee fit the bill; and (4) consumers were becoming more knowledgeable about coffee.

Profile

According to <u>Avenues for Growth   A 20-Year Review of the U.S. Specialty Coffee Industry</u>,[4] 22 per cent of the U.S. consumers purchased specialty coffee. This 22 per cent of the population typically lived and worked in urban areas, and had an annual income over $35,000. Research had shown that two parent families with a stay-at-home mother, purchased 41 per cent more specialty coffee than the average. Single people, purchased 39 per cent more than the average and consumers with college degrees purchased 49 per cent more than the average. Females purchased slightly more specialty coffee than men and coffee consumption was higher among individuals aged 30 to 59 than those aged 20 to 29.[5] Research by many coffee companies had found that once a consumer learned to appreciate a high-quality specialty coffee, he or she did not go back to his or her favorite average quality brew.

Community Gathering Place

Consumers' patterns of socializing had changed since the eighties. While the mid-eighties were characterized by the pursuit of entertainment outside the home, in the early nineties, people wanted to stay home. There was a move away from restaurants and dance clubs. Now, in the second part of the decade, there seemed to be a resurgence of outside-the-home entertainment. Coffeehouses were able to fill this need and were more accessible than bars. Coffee's image had changed from being purely a breakfast drink to a beverage that could be enjoyed any time and as a social catalyst. Coffee purchasers wanted more than just a place where they could get a higher quality cup of coffee.

---

[3] Encyclopaedia of American Industries, Volume 1, Manufacturing Industries, SIC 2095, Roasted Coffee.
[4] Montgomery Securities, April 30, 1996, Vol. 27.
[5] 1995 Winter Coffee Drinking Study, National Coffee Association of the U.S.A & Montgomery Securities Volume 27.

They wanted a place that answered a life-style need. Increasingly, coffee shops were turning into living rooms, where people sat back and enjoyed a cup of coffee or something else and relaxed with their friends or business associates. Coffeehouses had become community gathering places.

COMPETITION

Product-Based Competition

In retail coffee-house sales, Specialty coffee not only competed with basic coffee, it also competed with tea, juice, soft drinks, alcohol and other coffee and non-coffee-related drinks. However the consumption of all of these beverages relative to specialty coffee was declining.

Specialty Coffee could be divided into flavored coffee which represented 25 per cent of all specialty coffee sold and non-flavored coffee. Flavored coffee referred to coffee that was flavored with a variety of essences during the roasting process. Popular flavors included hazelnut, ammaretto, raspberry etc. Flavored coffee was not offered by specialty coffee companies like Starbucks, Peet's, Caribou Coffee and The Coffee Station, but the opposite was true for Timothy's, and The Second Cup. Flavored coffee was popular among traditionally non-coffee drinkers, younger coffee drinkers, and those interested in a low calorie substitute for desserts or snacks. For a comparison of retail sales of different types of coffee, see Exhibit 2.

Another important product substitute was specialty coffee originating from basic coffee companies in the grocery chain. To respond to the phenomenal growth in speciality coffee in the grocery chain, many large, basic coffee manufacturers were moving into more speciality brands by introducing upscale versions of already popular supermarket brands. However, industry analysts forecasted that there would be a shift in consumer purchasing of specialty coffee. Currently, grocery stores were responsible for 81 per cent of specialty coffee sales; this figure was expected to fall to 46 per cent in 1999. This shift would result in greater amounts of coffee being purchased from specialty stores: 19 per cent currently to 54 per cent in 1999.

Retail-Based Competition

The Specialty Coffee Association of America estimated there would be room for about 10,000 coffee retail outlets in the United States and Canada by 1999. But only 5,500 of those would be coffee bars and cafes; the rest would be carts.[6] The following table depicts the amount of room for growth in the retail coffee industry:

---

[6] Chicago Tribune, Sunday, March 10, 1996

Location	Population (millions)	Number of Starbucks Stores	Current Population /Store	Population necessary to support a coffee house	Maximum number of coffee stores supportable by market	Total Starbucks Stores as a percentage of total possible stores
Top 50 U.S. Markets	144.9	914	158,581	54,470	2,661	34%
Vancouver, Toronto, Ottawa, Montreal, Calgary	11.3	113	99,611	56,000	201	56%
Top 100 U.S. & Major Canadian Markets	180.2	1,074	167,784	55,000	3,276	33%
Total U.S. & Canadian Markets	276.2	1,074	257,128	56,000	4,931	22%

Source: William Blair & Company, Starbucks Corporation, June 20, 1997

Given the low barriers to entry in the retail specialty coffee market, there were more than 3,485[7] competitors in the market. However, most of these were one-store establishments with no real plans for growth. A description of those companies that had developed a strong regional and/or national presence follows.

DIEDRICH'S COFFEE	GREEN MOUNTAIN COFFEE INC.	COFFEE PEOPLE
▪ made with its own freshly roasted beans ▪ sold light food items and whole bean coffee ▪ a few wholesale customers ▪ operated a total of 32 coffeehouses in Texas, Colorado, and California ▪ 1996 sales: $10.2 million	▪ primarily a wholesaler of specialty coffee (3000 customers) ▪ small number of retail operations with in-store roasting facilities ▪ roasted over 25 high quality Arabica coffees to produce over 70 varieties ▪ 1996 sales: $38.3 million.	▪ located in suburban neighborhoods and business districts, averaging about 1,500 to 2,000 square feet in size ▪ used specialty kiosks located in high traffic locations such as airports and shopping malls ▪ hoped to have 100 locations by 1998

---

[7] "Caffeine Rush: Customers are High on Gourmet Coffee and so are Operators" Restaurant Business, January 1, 1996

A.L. VAN HOUTTE	BARNIE'S COFFEE & TEA COMPANY	CARIBOU
<ul><li>offered 36 types of ground coffee, nine types of flavored coffee and 54 types of whole beans</li><li>sold its coffee through restaurants, including its own network of 107 cafe-bistros (only 4 corporate stores)</li><li>good reputation as a vendor of coffee to offices, hotels, etc.</li><li>1996 sales: $164.1 million</li></ul>	<ul><li>focussed on the merchandising aspect of coffee retailing; it offered 400 different branded products</li><li>typically seated about 50 people and was located in malls</li><li>its newest innovation was a restaurant, La Venezia Cafe; seated 200 people and offered 47 different coffees</li></ul>	<ul><li>wanted to be the 3rd place between work and home where people could socialize</li><li>implemented a very American feel to its coffeehouses rather than a European feel</li><li>offered very fast service, magazines, newspapers, free refills, and seating</li><li>had 50 stores; analysts predicted that it would be a growth leader</li></ul>
COFFEE BEANERY	**CHOCK FULL O'NUTS**	**CAFE APPASIONATO**
<ul><li>franchiser who operated 175 units across the U.S.</li><li>coffee beverages and food accounted for 80% of the sales and 20% came from merchandise</li><li>focus had always been on malls but it was now shifting its focus to free-standing locations;</li><li>began franchising coffee carts.</li></ul>	<ul><li>operated as a coffee supplier to the restaurant industry</li><li>enough contracts with restaurants to warrant its own fleet of 150 trucks</li><li>recently, company had begun diversifying into different coffeehouse formats like double drive-throughs and sit-down retail outlets, about 3000 square feet in size</li></ul>	<ul><li>small but aggressive player in the industry</li><li>primarily a coffee roaster</li><li>sold its coffee in its own retail outlets, franchised stores, wholesale coffee to specialty stores and restaurants, grocery division, direct mail, exports to the Pacific Rim, private label coffee production and co-label ventures with fast food chains, such as Taco Bell.</li></ul>

SECOND CUP

Second Cup was primarily a franchiser (90 per cent of all locations), and as a result, the company was consistently cash flow positive and had the benefit of taking little operating risk at the store level. Traditionally, the Second Cup was mall-based, but in the past few years it had moved into more stand-alone locations. These locations were established rather quickly and were not always on prime real estate. In its retail concept, the Second Cup offered specialty coffee drinks, varietals, flavored coffee and snack items.

The Second Cup was very growth-oriented and believed strongly in growth via acquisitions. One of its major acquisitions included Gloria Jean's (247 locations), in the U.S.. Including its own 243 stores, the Second Cup was the second largest player in the specialty coffee industry. Where the Second Cup's revenues came from liquid coffee and snack food items, Gloria Jean's obtained a high percentage of sales from coffee mugs, related items and coffee beans.

In recent times, the Second Cup had become quite active in developing alliances with other food service companies. Through its alliance with Cara Operations Ltd., the Second Cup hoped to gain access to a number of its partners institutional and retail sites such as Harvey's and Swiss

Chalet. The Second Cup also held a 30 per cent interest in the Great Canadian Bagel that operated 120 stores in 1996 and was planning to own 175 by the end of 1997. Finally, the company had also struck a deal to serve its coffee on Air Canada flights. Revenues for 1996 amounted to $63.3 million.

See Exhibit 3 for a comparison of the industry competitors using different financial and growth measures.

STARBUCKS' STRATEGY

Starbucks' strategy for the future was presented in the following extracts of a letter to Starbucks' shareholders. This letter, from Howard Schultz, Chairman and CEO, and Orin Smith, President and Chief Operating Officer, appeared in the company's 1996 Annual Report:

> We have firmly established our leadership position, ending fiscal 1996 with more than 1000 retail locations in 32 markets throughout North America and two new stores in Tokyo, Japan. With more than 20,000 dedicated partners (employees), we are creating opportunities every day for millions of customers around the world to enjoy the Starbucks Experience. From selecting the finest Arabica beans to hiring the most talented people, we are committed to applying the highest standards of quality in everything we do. . . . When you walk into a Starbucks store, when you open a mail order package, when you drink our coffee on United Airlines, it is our goal to offer more than just a great cup of coffee   we want to offer a memorable experience . . . We are excited about the global possibilities as more new customers embrace our business, and we know that we have many brand-building opportunities ahead of us. In 1994, when we entered into a joint venture agreement with Pepsi-Cola to develop ready-to-drink coffee products, we knew that we wanted to redefine the category . . . . we look forward to the positive reception of bottled Frappuccino . . . but most importantly, we know that we have developed a platform for bigger product innovations. During fiscal 1996, we installed proprietary, state-of-the-art roasting and manufacturing equipment to create a world-class logistics and manufacturing organization . . . . Our specialty sales and marketing team has continued to develop new channels of distribution . . . our direct response group launched a new America Online Café Starbucks store...we continue to work towards our long-term goal of becoming the most recognized and respected brand of coffee in the world . . . . We believe more strongly than ever that at the heart of our continuing success lie the company's two cornerstones, coffee and our people . . . .Twenty-five years from now, when we look back again, if we can say that we grew our company with the same values and guiding principles that we embrace today, then we will know we have succeeded.

STARBUCKS' BUSINESS SYSTEM

Sourcing

Starbucks sourced approximately 50 per cent of its beans from Latin America, 35 per cent from the Pacific Rim, and 15 per cent from East Africa. Having a diversified portfolio allowed Starbucks to offer a greater palette of coffees to its customers while being able to maintain a hedged position.

Starbucks maintained close relationships with its exporters by working directly with them and providing them with training. Mary Williams, Senior Vice-President of Coffee at Starbucks, described what it took to be considered an official Starbucks' exporter:

> If I am working with a dealer who has sold me 5000 bags of Guatemalan for January's shipment and he knows that he is not going to be able to deliver, I don't want to hear about it in January. I want him to call me in September and say, "Mary, we are going to have trouble with this January. What can we do? How can we work this problem out? What can I do to help you? Shall we switch it to another coffee?" If I have a quality problem, I expect to be able to call up the person I bought the coffee from and say: "Sorry, I have to reject this; it doesn't meet our standards." I expect them to say: "OK, we will take it back, no problem and we will replace it." Both the customer service and consistency are the things we look for over time.

Exporters of high quality coffee were very anxious to become Starbucks suppliers because Starbucks purchased more high quality coffee than anyone else in the world. Starbucks' relationship with its suppliers was so good that if Supplier "A" sold to a number of different buyers and it had only one container of a certain coffee, Starbucks would be the first to get it.

To ensure quality, Starbucks extracted three different samples of coffee from every shipment of 250 bags. Sample one was an offer sample sent by an exporter trying to make a sale to Starbucks. Sample two was taken just before the shipment was due to be sent. Sample three was extracted from the shipment, which arrived at the coffee roasting plant. At every stage of sampling, Starbucks reserved the right to reject the coffee if it was not in line with its quality standards.

Starbucks hoped to double volumes over the next three years. This could make the ability to find coffees that would meet its quantity/quality requirements difficult. Starbucks needed to offer an increasing number of blends to deal with its increasing volumes, since blends provided more flexibility around components. Mary Williams explained:

> When you blend coffee, it's like baking a cake; you need to put lots of different kinds of spices in a spice cake; you don't necessarily have to have cinnamon, nutmeg and allspice. You can have other kinds of spices, and the consumers of that cake will not know the difference, because it tastes like a spice cake. So a House blend with a particular flavor profile can have different types of the same quality components to reach the same flavor profile. Moving towards offering more blends and revolving varietals is one of the most important things Starbucks can do to ensure the quality/quantity mix of the coffee we buy.

Despite Starbucks' large supply needs, growing its own, high-quality coffee was an option that was never seriously considered.

ROASTING AND BLENDING

Roasting was a combination of time and temperature. Recipes were put together by the coffee department once all the components had been tested and were up to standard. Despite computerized roasters which guaranteed consistency, roasting was not a complete science; it was more of a technological art. This was because the people roasting the coffee had to understand the properties of the roasting process, i.e., managing temperature and being able to roast coffees along different roast curves. Roasting was essential to Starbucks, because how a coffee was roasted could change its entire taste.

Starbucks undertook a great deal of research by roasting its coffees in many different ways, under many different temperature and time conditions to ensure that it was getting as much as possible from the bean. These trial and error sessions allowed Starbucks to build signature roasting curves. These roasting curves were then built into proprietary computer software. The method by which they were developed was as much a result of the technology as the art. This ensured that even if a roaster were to defect to another competitor, he/she would not be able to duplicate Starbucks' signature roasts.

After roasting and air cooling, the coffee was immediately vacuum-sealed in one-way valve bags. This packaging was unique in its ability to ensure freshness, since it allowed gases naturally produced by fresh roasted beans out without letting oxygen in. This one-way valve technology extended the shelf life of Starbucks coffee to 26 weeks. However, Starbucks did not keep any coffee on its shelves for more than three months and for the coffee it used to prepare beverages in the store, the shelf life was limited to seven days, after the bag was opened.

SUPPLY CHAIN OPERATIONS

Starbucks Supply Chain Operations (SCO) claimed it had the best transportation rates in the industry, a complex bakery distribution model, a forecasting process for "who will need coffee when" that was generally very accurate, strong inventory turns for the specialty coffee industry, and a fully integrated manufacturing and distribution process that protected the coffee beans from oxygen from the time beans were roasted to the time they were packaged (closed loop system). Starbucks had developed these skills and benefits because it benchmarked against its competitors, hired experts, and believed strongly in the concept of integrated supply.

Starbucks tried to build its supply chain operations in order to eliminate redundancy and maximize efficiency. Supply chain operations served four business units: the retail store units, the specialty sales and wholesale channels, the mail order business and the grocery channel. According to Ted Garcia, Starbucks' Executive Vice President, Supply Chain Operations, the phenomenal growth in these business units was posing challenges to supply chain operations:

> Supporting four business units in an integrated, effective, efficient, cost-effective method, is a challenge. We are trying new and innovative things. We are not afraid to enter into agreements or challenge our suppliers such as United Parcel Service (UPS) to do things in new and innovative ways.

RETAIL SALES

The retail outlet had been Starbucks' fundamental growth vehicle. For many customers Starbucks was not only a place to drink coffee but also an experience. Howard Schultz's vision for Starbucks was a place that offered interesting coffee-related drinks in a theatrical kind of atmosphere, which pivoted around an espresso machine:

You get more than the finest coffee when you visit Starbucks. You get great people, first-rate music, a comfortable and upbeat meeting place, and sound advice on brewing excellent coffee at home. At home you're part of a family. At work you're part of a company. And somewhere in between there's a place where you can sit back and be yourself. That's what a Starbucks store is to many of its customers   a kind of "third place" where they can escape, reflect, read, chat or listen.[8]

Starbucks' formula was firmly based in its coffee, its employees, its merchandising, its ownership philosophy, its real-estate approach, its image, and its innovativeness.

Employees

Starbucks' store employees (baristas) tended to be either in college or university. They received a great deal of training and were able to talk about a variety of different coffees and processes. Having baristas that had a strong coffee education was essential because Starbucks' consumers were becoming more and more knowledgeable about coffee. Mary Williams, SVP Coffee for Starbucks, outlined the nature of the questions asked of the baristas at Starbucks:

We have very educated consumers. They ask very interesting questions of the people who work in our stores; such as, "I am having chocolate mousse for dessert, what kind of coffee should I serve?"; or "I am having shrimp scampi for dinner and a fruit salad for dessert, what kind of coffee should I serve?" So we have to give the baristas some kind of a basis and background so that they can answer these difficult questions.[9]

Developing coffee knowledge and service expertise demanded a great deal of effort from employees and as Starbucks grew, finding enough good people that could replicate the values, culture and service experiences was an ongoing challenge.

Merchandising

Starbucks only carried the highest quality merchandise. In terms of coffee-making equipment, it purchased its machines from manufacturers like Krups, Gaggia and Bodum. It also offered accessory items bearing the Starbucks Logo such as coffee mugs, grinders, coffee filters, storage containers and other items. In terms of merchandising, Starbucks faced challenges related to the design of a nationally consistent merchandising program, since many of its stores dealt with individual suppliers.

Real-Estate Approach

Starbucks considered itself to be real estate opportunistic. It did not always wait for the perfectly designed location, i.e., a box. It had a design team that could fit a location in many retail spaces, be it a corner, a trapezoid, or triangle. This flexibility, in addition to Starbucks' concept of store clustering, which often placed retail outlets across from one another or on the same block, allowed Starbucks to maximize its market share in given areas of a city and to begin building a regional reputation.

To meet its growth needs Starbucks had approximately 20 real estate managers across the country. These managers worked with "street sniffers", i.e., professionals who specialized in

---

[8]1995 Annual Report, Starbucks Corporation
[9] Mary Williams, SVP Coffee, Starbucks Corporation

identifying the best retail locations. Their commissions were paid either by the landlord or by Starbucks. These real estate brokers were guaranteed a minimum commission per location. If the landlord's brokerage commission did not cover the minimum, Starbucks paid the difference. This engendered a very loyal relationship between Starbucks and the real estate network.

Starbucks was very disciplined about its entire approach to real estate:

> Discipline is the difference between locating a store in a targeted demographic area this year, in order to get in there and gain market share versus being disciplined enough to wait for the corner or the mid-block with a parking lot. Discipline is rooted in the ability to understand the differences and business issues involved with taking a store today that may do $750,000 vs. waiting for a store that may do $1 million. Understanding and acting upon location issues such as corners, parking lots and co-tenants; that's the discipline of it. [10]

As Starbucks grew and the number of "A" sites in "A" markets decreased, one of the key challenges faced by Starbucks was to constantly motivate its real estate staff to continue to generate 20 to 40 solid stores per month. Starbucks had to meet this challenge if it was going to meet its goal of 2000 stores by the year 2000. Traditionally, Starbucks had been focused on the retail store on Main and Main of every major North American city. Now it was expanding to the Main and Main of different regions within a city. See Exhibit 4 for the actual and forecasted income statement of a typical store.

Another way in which Starbucks hoped to reach a new customer base was through the introduction of its new espresso carts or kiosks. By introducing Starbucks Espresso Carts, the company had succeeded in branding the coffee cart, which had always been a brandless, grassroots type of specialty coffee retailer. Starbucks called its version of the espresso cart Doppio. The Doppio was an 8x8-foot cube that unfolded into a larger stand with sides, counters, and Starbucks' trademark finishes. It would allow the company to take advantage of sales areas such as train stations, street corners, malls, etc. Starbucks was in the initial stages of its Doppio strategy.

Domestic vs. International Retail Image

> The retail system is the base or anchor of the brand-building strategy, the essence of the company's passion for quality coffee, and the showcase for the lifestyle that Starbucks is defining. It is this lifestyle attribute of the brand that could catapult the company beyond its roots as a speciality retailer/restaurant with a few closely associated brand extensions. [11]

Starbucks decided to enter the international market place to prevent competitors from getting a head start, to build upon the growing desire for Western brands, and to take advantage of higher coffee consumption rates in different countries. It focused on Asia Pacific simply because it did not have the resources to go into different areas of the globe at once and because one half of the world's population lived a five and a half-hour flight from the area. It was expected that in the next five to ten years, international retail's contribution would be sizeable. See Exhibit 6 for a forecast of International Retail's potential contribution to Starbucks' earnings. Also see Exhibit 5 for a forecast of Starbucks' growth in the Pacific Rim.

---

[10] Arthur Rubinfeld, Senior Vice-President Real Estate, Starbucks Corporation

[11] Merrill Lynch Capital Markets, Starbucks Company Report, September 16, 1996

SPECIALTY SALES

Specialty sales were agreements with retailers, wholesalers, restaurants, service providers, etc. to carry Starbucks coffee. Specialty sales not only provided Starbucks with revenue growth potential but also with increased name recognition. Starbucks partnered with companies that were leaders in their field, companies that had stellar reputations for success and quality. Partnerships existed with many different companies, some of which included:

- **United Airlines** – Starbucks was served on all domestic and international flights
- **Nordstrom** – Starbucks had developed a special blend for Nordstrom.
- **Barnes & Noble Bookstores** – Starbucks operated individual but attached locations. Many of these locations had separate entrances that allowed them to stay open even after Barnes & Noble closed.
- **PepsiCo** – Starbucks and PepsiCo had jointly developed the Frappuccino product, a milk-based cold coffee beverage in a bottle.
- **PriceCostco** – Starbucks had developed a special brand name, Meridian, for PriceCostco.
- **Red Hook Breweries** – Starbucks provided coffee concentrate as an ingredient for one of the brewery's beers, Double Black Stout.
- **Dreyers' Ice Cream** – In this joint venture, Starbucks had its own brand of ice cream that Dreyers' promoted via its grocery channels.
- **ARAMARK** – This was the world's leading provider of a broad range of services to businesses, reaching 10 million people a day at more than 400,000 locations. Through ARAMARK, Starbucks coffee was now being served at over one hundred of those locations, including such college campuses as the University of Florida and Boston University, corporations such as Boeing and Citicorp, and hospitals such as St. Vincent's in New York. ARAMARK also had a few licensed locations.

Some of these partnerships involved serving Starbucks coffee, some were for product development and others were for store development. Starbucks was actively increasing its participation in specialty sales contracts.

NEW VENTURES

Three of Starbucks' newest business ventures included its contract with Dreyers' Ice Cream, its bottled Frappuccino product with Pepsi and its penetration into the grocery channel.

It was estimated that Starbucks' ice cream would perhaps reach $40 million at retail and contribute at least $500,000 to earnings during fiscal 1997. Although the return was somewhat limited (See Exhibit 6), it opened Starbucks to an entirely new customer base, reinforced its premium quality image, and built its reputation with supermarket chains.

Bottled Frappuccino was Starbucks' attempt to introduce a quality ready-to-drink coffee beverage into the North American market place. Starbucks viewed this bottled beverage as a $1 billion opportunity. These estimates were from Pepsi, who said that it had never seen a product test quite as well as bottled Frappuccino, where 70 per cent of testers became repeat purchasers. Other products that had hit the billion dollar mark with less favorable test results were Ocean Spray Juices and Lipton Iced Teas. The product might even do better in countries where there was already a market for cold coffee beverages, like the Pacific Rim. Bottled Frappuccino was currently being offered in all Starbucks retail stores and had begun to be distributed via PepsiCo's national distribution channels. See Exhibit 6 for a forecast of bottled Frappuccino's contribution to Starbucks' future earnings.

In penetrating the grocery market, Starbucks met with a great deal of success when it began test marketing in the Portland area. Now it was test marketing the Chicago market. If it was successful in Chicago, then it would consider initiating a national roll out with the expectation that in five years it would be nationally available. See Exhibit 6 for an estimate of the impact of a national roll out on Starbucks' earnings. Mr. Orin Smith, Starbucks President and COO, explained how he viewed the importance of Starbucks' penetration into the grocery chain:

> Presence in supermarkets is not essential to Starbucks' survival or prosperity. However, in the interest of being a major player in coffee for the home, we have to be available in supermarkets. This is because convenience plays a key role in the decision to purchase coffee for the home. Therefore, no matter how many stores we open, we will never overcome the "convenience" advantage of supermarkets. For us, the choice is clear: Are we going to allow supermarkets to continue to capture 70 to 80 per cent of the home coffee business or are we going to join up and take our piece of that? Supermarkets are very interested in carrying Starbucks Coffee because we can offer them greater margins; we can grow their business and we will help pull consumers out of the lower priced categories into our category.[12]

Other areas of opportunity included the introduction of Starbucks coffee to the higher echelon restaurants and day-part chains. Day-part chains are retail outlets catering to the daytime trade. Examples are bagel shops, juice bars, lunch counters etc.

MAIL ORDER

For a long time, mail order had allowed Starbucks to meet the needs of its customers not located near a Starbucks retail store and its regular home users. The company had a direct mail program entitled Encore. Encore customers received a monthly shipment of a different type of either ground or whole bean coffee. This program helped boost sales by increasing transaction size, and introducing customers to a wider range of company products.

HOWARD SCHULTZ

Howard Schultz began his coffee career with Starbucks Coffee Company in 1982, when it used to be a retailer solely of whole bean coffees. On a buying trip to Italy, in 1983, the vast number of coffee bars in Milan inspired Mr. Schultz. He returned to Starbucks and presented his idea to expand the whole bean retailer into a coffee bar. The Board of Directors rejected his idea and two years later, Mr. Schultz left Starbucks to start his own coffee bar company which he named Il Giornale. After two years of great success, Il Giornale purchased the Starbucks name and assets and changed the names of all of its retail outlets to Starbucks.

---

[12] Orin Smith, Chief Operating Officer, Starbucks Corporation

Howard Schultz came from rather humble beginnings. He remembered how his father used to work hard for little money and no respect. He said his upbringing instilled in him "not a fear of failure but a fear of mediocrity". He was the first in his family to get a college degree and had always been an over-achiever. He was young and energetic at 45 and very hands-on in the company. "Howard is very creative, he is very inspiring, he is exceptionally demanding, he is tremendously competitive, exceptionally ambitious, and has very high standards in everything we can do and he is always ratcheting the bar up. He really cares about people; anything anyone would do to damage the culture   he would be right on it."[13]

Howard Schultz played a very important and unique role at Starbucks. "The barista's interpretation of the vision is the engine of the company, Howard is the on-board computer, and to some extent he is also the fuel that drives through it. People around here feel very much that they are following Howard up some mountain with a flag clenched under their teeth and they give 110 per cent."[14]

HUMAN RESOURCES

Starbucks had a very flat organizational structure. Everyone from the CEO to a barista was a partner and not an employee. Starbucks placed a great deal of effort into seeking the thoughts and opinions of its baristas, because they were in direct contact with Starbucks' customers. Starbucks' retail management, at headquarters, kept in regular contact with field people. Many people in the stores knew Deidra Wager, the Executive Vice-President of Retail, and would not hesitate to call her directly to talk about the retail group's decisions. The head office managers had sessions with people in the field, standard mission reviews where they collected questions from anyone about any topic and then responded, and open forums where they heard from and listened to the partner base.

The coffee service system was built on three principles: hospitality, production and education. Starbucks expected baristas to be customer-service oriented by being hospitable, effective in making exactly the type of drink the customer requested and able to answer the customers' coffee-related questions. This demanded a great deal of effort on behalf of the baristas. To prepare them for the challenge, they all underwent 24 hours of training before they were allowed to serve a cup of coffee to a Starbucks customer. Every employee, even those that were hired for executive positions, went through the same training program, which included a two-week term in a store.

In addition to training, Starbucks paid its partners a slightly higher wage than most food service companies. Also, all employees received health insurance (vision, dental, medical), disability and life insurance, and a free pound of coffee each week. All company employees also received "Bean Stock", an employee stock option plan. This was quite profitable for some employees.

From its baristas to its senior managers, Starbucks took great care in recruitment. For baristas, turnover rates were about 60 per cent; this was less than half of the industry average (150 to 300 per cent). Many of the senior managers came from companies like Taco Bell, Nike, McDonalds, Hallmark, Wendy's, and Blockbuster. These managers knew how to manage a high growth retailer.

---

[13] Orin Smith, Chief Operating Officer, Starbucks Corporation
[14] Scott Bedbury, Senior Vice-President, Marketing, Starbucks Corporation

ORGANIZATIONAL CULTURE

The following six guiding principles, from the company's 1995 Annual Report, helped Starbucks measure the appropriateness of its decisions:

1. Provide a great work environment and treat each other with respect and dignity.
2. Embrace diversity as an essential component of the way we do business.
3. Apply the highest standards of excellence to the purchasing, roasting, and fresh delivery of our coffee.
4. Develop enthusiastically satisfied customers all of the time.
5. Contribute positively to our community and our environment.
6. Recognise that profitability is essential to our future success.

The following statements captured employee sentiments about Starbucks' culture.

When people ask me what I do for a living, I say: I drink coffee and talk about it. That's my job   not too shabby. I have a lot to learn, and a lot of places I can go if I wanted to leave Starbucks, but it's so interesting and I've met the neatest people that work here. I have a lot of passion for it. You know you go through bumps and grinds because we've changed a lot but it's like being in any kind of relationship. You fall in love, its all great, everything is beautiful and then you find out that there are some things like wrinkles or bad habits. You work on those and then you're in puppy love again. I love working at Starbucks; my husband thinks it's pretty twisted. I mean I was a store manager and I lived at my store . . . people would say that you do such a great job and I would say that I couldn't do it without these people   I can't do it alone   none of us can. I totally rely on the wealth and depth of knowledge that other people have, the background they bring to Starbucks, their support and work ethic. And I just embrace that hugely; I can bring my weird ideas and be as goofy as I want one day or as serious as I need to be another day and its OK. When I started at Starbucks someone told me: you tell me what you want to do and I will help you.[15]

In a day offsite, with Jim Collins (author of <u>Built to Last</u>), the senior management team of 40 people or so was divided into 10 groups of four. First, we identified our own set of values and then when we broke into groups of four people and combined our lists of values. It was absolutely mind-boggling that we all came back and had exactly the same list of values. Collins had never seen anything like that. Everyone is passionate about what they do, about life, about everything. Everybody has a sense of integrity, that we want to succeed but we want to do it in a fair, equitable, ethical way. We care about winning; you know we aren't ashamed to admit that we want to be successful, that we do care about people and do respect our partners. The fifth value was our entrepreneurial spirit. We don't want this to become a big company; we want to continually strive to be innovative and continually rejuvenate the company.[16]

FINANCIAL

Starbucks' stock price and EPS had been rapidly increasing over the last five years (See Exhibit 7). In the span of six months, from January to June 1997, four prominent investment companies had

---

[15] Aileen Carrell, Coffee Taster, Starbucks Corporation
[16] Liz Sickler, Director, Special Projects, Starbucks Corporation

rated the company as a "BUY" in their report to investors. See Exhibit 8 for a forecast from each of these companies regarding EPS, P/E ratios and share price. One investment company that rated Starbucks as a long-term buy stated:

> Since its 1992 IPO, Starbucks has executed its strategy to near perfection, achieving its initial goal of building the country's leading branded retailer of specialty coffees. As growth in its North American retail business decelerates from unsustainable rapid rates, the company is now in the early stages of pursuing a more ambitious goal – to build the most recognized and respected coffee brand in the world. Current initiatives include the development of Starbucks stores with local partners in the Pacific Rim, domestic brand extensions into packaged ice cream and bottled beverages, and test-marketing Starbucks whole bean coffees in the supermarket channel. While greatly enhancing the company's long-term growth potential, we believe these new pursuits also raise the risk profile of the stock. With SBUX shares trading at 33 times our estimate of calendar 1998 EPS, we believe extraordinary intermediate-term appreciation relies upon the successful execution of these ventures. Given the strength of the brand, our confidence in management, and impressive joint-venture partners, we are optimistic that these activities, in the aggregate, will contribute significantly to Starbucks' profitability over the next three to five years. We conclude that Starbucks remains a core holding for long-term growth stock investors, albeit with higher risk, as it transitions from a category-dominant domestic branded retailer into a global consumer brand.[17]

In North America, Starbucks owned all of its retail outlets other than host licensing arrangements. However, owning all of its stores, Starbucks was faced with the prospect of depending heavily on equity and debt financing to grow. Its competitors like Seattle's Best Coffee and the Second Cup were all franchised, and consequently, needed less internal financing to roll out stores. For Starbucks' balance sheet, see Exhibit 9. For the income statement, see Exhibit 7.

MARKETING

Of key concern in Starbucks' marketing department was its brand equity. The retail business had historically been Starbucks' source of brand equity. This had meant that Starbucks was never just about the coffee; it was about a place, an experience.

Starbucks now wanted to develop its brand beyond being the preferred outlet from which to purchase coffee to becoming the preferred consumer brand. Scott Bedbury, Starbucks' Senior Vice-President of Marketing, explained its brand:

> We are transitioning from a very retail centric view about the brand to a view that will allow us to say that Starbucks' role is to provide uplifting moments to people every day. I didn't say coffee! If you go beyond coffee, you can get to music, you can get to literature, you can get to a number of different areas. It can also become a license to dilute the brand. Therefore our goal is to remain true to our core, coffee. After all we are the protectors of something that is 900 million years old. Just like when you drop a rock in a pond there will be ripples that come outside that core, Starbucks is not just a pound of coffee, but a total coffee experience.

One of the key challenges faced by Starbucks was trying concretely to define its brand image. Company executives felt that this was essential before Starbucks started mounting grand-scale

---

[17] William Blair and Company on June 20, 1997

national-advertising campaigns and other brand leveraging activities. Liz Sickler, Starbucks Director of Special Projects, commented:

> I don't think that we leverage our size well enough. Very often we have strong competition in local markets from Caribou, to Seattle's Best Coffee to the Second Cup in Canada. And it's always mind-boggling how they can be so competitive in their local markets despite the fact that our national brand image is so much stronger. We need to take advantage of our national presence. We need to compete on our brand recognition. I think that's why we started to do some national advertising this year to see if that's how we can leverage our size. I think going into different distribution channels and leveraging the brand is the answer.

OPTIONS

Howard Schultz and the senior management at Starbucks were committed to the company's strategy. It was felt that Starbucks' current strategic direction would allow it to sustain growth by continuing the development of the Starbucks brand image and by increasing its presence in different markets. Starbucks was growing very rapidly and was consistently evaluating new opportunities in its domestic and international retail markets, new specialty sales partners, penetration in the grocery channel and the future potential of its mail order business. How the company should react to all of these opportunities was one of Mr. Schultz's key concerns.

Exhibit 1: **Specialty Coffee Sales as a % of Total Coffee Sales**

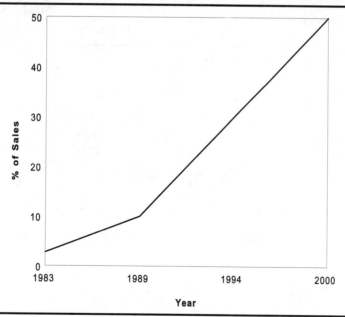

Source: Specialty Coffee Association of America, Montgomery Securities Volume 27

Exhibit 2: **Comparing the Retail Sales Of Coffee (US$ millions)**

	1990	1994	1998E	1990-1994 growth	1994-1998E growth
Ground Regular	2,050	1,240	800	-11.8%	-10.4%
Ground Decaffeinated	650	575	450	-3.0%	-5.9%
Ground Specialty	810	1,315	1,635	12.9%	5.6%
Instant Regular	1,175	1,010	780	-3.7%	-6.3%
Instant Decaffeinated	385	295	170	-6.4%	-12.9%
Whole Bean	255	380	500	10.5%	7.1%
Ready-To-Drink	5	250	1,255	165.9%	49.7%
Total	**5,330**	**5,065**	**5,590**	**-1.3%**	**2.5%**

Source: Yorkton Securities Inc., March 25, 1997

Exhibit 3: **Coffee Chains' Stock Prices and Market Capitalizations**

Company	Year		Market Cap. ($mm)
	High ($)	Low ($)	
U.S. Companies			
Brothers	4.63	2.13	30.8
Coffee People	9.38	6.00	21.4
Diedrich	12.00	3.00	23.6
Green Mountain	7.50	6.88	24.8
Starbucks	40.25	21.50	2,438.5
Canadian Companies			
Cara	4.80	3.30	440.2
Van Houtte	28.35	18.50	225.6
Second Cup	13.35	9.15	137.2

Comparing the Coffee Chains

Company	TEV(1)/ EBITDA (2)	Net Margin
U.S. Companies		
Brothers	6.0	-14.0%
Coffee People	8.4	1.7%
Diedrich	15.6	1.2%
Green Mountain	7.3	3.3%
Starbucks	25.1	6.0%
Average	14.5	
Canadian Companies		
Cara	7.7	5.8%
Van Houtte	7.8	4.7%
Second Cup	13.2	-3.7%
Average	17.9	

(1) TEV is total enterprise value defined as current market cap plus debt less cash. Debt and cash are as latest available balance sheet date.

(2) EBITDA for Brothers and Diedrich is trailing twelve months.

Source: Yorkton Securities Inc., March 25, 1997

Exhibit 4: Analysis of Unit Economic Trends (US$ thousands)

	1994	1995	1996	1997E	1998E	1999E
Cash Investment:						
Store Build Out (1)	330	357	315	310	305	300
Pre-opening	16	23	21	20	20	20
Beginning Inventory	17	20	24	20	20	20
Total Cash Investment	363	400	360	350	345	340
Average Sales/Store (2)	820	820	850	825	790	765
Average Sales/Investment	2.3x	2.1x	2.4x	2.4x	2.3x	2.3x
EBIT Margin (3)	18.9%	17.5%	16.5%	18.0%	17.8%	17.6%
EBIT	155	144	140	150	141	135
ROI (EBIT/Cash Invested)	43.0%	36.0%	39.0%	43.0%	41.0%	40.0%

(1) Estimated Investment per store opened during the fiscal year, (2) Estimated average sales and EBIT for units open at least one year. (3) EBIT includes marketing and field level overhead expenses.

Source: William Blair & Company, 1997

Exhibit 5: **Starbucks Corporation Projected Pacific Rim Development (A) (US$ Millions)**

	1997E	1998E	1999E	2000E
New units	13	30	55	100
Ending units	15	45	100	200
Average unit volume	$1.0	$1.0	$1.0	$1.0
Total sales (a)	$9	$30	$73	$150

(a) Note that total sales reflect sales of joint ventures, partnerships, and licensees. We expect additional partnership agreements in the Pacific Rim to be disclosed before year-end. In fact, an executive of President Foods (the largest food company in Taiwan and a 7-Eleven franchisee) was recently quoted saying that the company expected to develop Starbucks stores in Taiwan, and perhaps China. Given the magnitude of the opportunity in the Pacific Rim, we do not anticipate development in Europe until at least 1999. Whereas the long-term potential of international development is tremendous, we expect expenses of building infrastructure and growing rapidly will be a drag on Starbucks profits at least through 1999. Depending on the structure of future international ventures, this business could become a significant consumer of Starbucks investment capital.

Source: William Blair & Company, 1997

Exhibit 6: **Projected Avenues of Growth - Estimated Contribution from Joint Ventures (US$ millions)**

	1995	1996	1997E	1998E	1999E
Annual Investment					
Ice Cream	0.0	0.9	2.0	1.0	0.5
Bottled Beverages	1.2	2.7	18.0	15.0	10.0
Whole Bean	0.0	0.0	3.0	5.0	9.5
Total	**1.2**	**6.0**	**30.0**	**33.0**	**35.0**
Retail Revenues					
Ice Cream	0.0	15.0	40.0	45.0	50.0
Bottled Beverages	0.0	0.0	65.0	250.0	300.0
Whole Bean	0.0	0.0	1.3	43.8	78.8
Total	**0.0**	**15.0**	**114.8**	**368.8**	**501.3**
Contribution to Starbucks Earnings:					
Ice Cream	0.0	-0.7	0.5	2.4	3.0
Bottled Beverages	-1.2	-0.4	-0.5	4.4	7.9
Whole Bean	0.0	0.0	-0.5	1.6	4.5
Total	**-1.2**	**-1.1**	**-1.5**	**8.4**	**15.4**
Joint Venture Contributions	-1.2	-1.1	-1.5	8.4	15.4

Source: William Blair & Company, 1997

Exhibit 7: Income Statement (US$ thousands)

	1994	1995	1996	1997E	1998E	1999E
Net Revenues						
Retail	248453	402874	600367	827003	1053796	1276840
Specialty Sales	26498	47917	78702	110331	148612	193552
Direct Response	9972	14422	17412	22066	25792	30008
Total Net Revenues	284923	465213	696481	959400	1228200	1500400
Store Operating Expenses	90087	148757	210693	296200	368700	441800
Other Operating Expenses	8698	13932	19787	24200	31800	40200
Cost of Sales and Related Occupancy Costs	162840	262408	409008	548800	687000	827700
Operating Income	23298	40116	56993	90200	140700	190700
Other Expenses	-5544	3027	11508	3600	-2600	-7000
Earnings before income taxes	17754	43143	68501	93800	138100	183700
Income Taxes	7548	17041	26373	36100	53200	70700
Net Earnings	10206	26102	42128	57700	84900	113000
Preferred Stock Dividends Accrued	-270	0	0			
Net Earnings Available to Common Shareholders	9936	26102	42128	57700	84900	113000
Net Earnings Per Share	0.17	0.36	0.47	0.70	1.00	1.30
Weighted Average Shares Outstanding	57575	71909	80831	88600	89500	90400
Average Share Price	25	15	24			
Price Earnings Ratios	148	42	51	51	36	28

Note 1: The $0.47 EPS in 1996 excludes the gains from the sale of Noah's Bagels
Note 2: The $0.17 EPS in 1994 would be $0.22 without the one-time charges associated with the acquisition of Coffee Connection
Note 3: On December 1, 1995, the company recorded a 2 for 1 stock split to holders of record on November 1, 1995. Net earnings per share for all years have been restated to reflect the stock split.

Sources: Starbucks Annual Reports & William Blair & Company

Exhibit 8: Forecast of EPS, P/E Ratio and Share Price

Robinson-Humphrey Company Inc.	1996	1997E	1998E
Earnings Per Share	$0.54*	$0.70	$1.00
Price / Earnings Ratio	55.6 times	42.9 times	30.0 times
Forecasted Share Price			$49.00

Alex Brown & Sons	1996	1997E	1998E
Earnings Per Share	$0.48	$0.70	$0.98
Price / Earnings Ratio		39.0 times	27.8 times
Forecasted Share Price			$45.00

Painwebber Inc..	1996	1997E	1998E
Earnings Per Share	$0.47	$0.70	$0.95
Price / Earnings Ratio		40.5 times	30.0 times
Forecasted Share Price			$42.00

William Blair and Company	1996	1997E	1998E	1999E
Earnings Per Share	$0.47	$0.70	$1.00	$1.30
Price / Earnings Ratio	76.1 times	51.1 times	35.8 times	27.5 times

*   Includes a one-time gain on the Sale of Noah's Bagels

Exhibit 9: **Balance Sheet (US$ thousands)**

	1994	1995	1996	1997E	1998E	1999E
Assets						
Current Assets:						
Cash and Cash Equivalents	8,394	20,944	126,215	128,900	53,200	21,000
Accounts Receivable	5,394	9,852	17,621	24,300	31,100	38,000
Inventories	56,064	123,657	83,370	122,500	149,600	178,100
Other Current Assets	14,728	50,897	112,335	12,500	16,100	19,600
Total Current Assets	84,580	205,350	339,541	288,200	250,000	256,700
Property and Equipment, Net	140,754	244,728	369,477	496,700	617,600	733,600
Other Assets	6,087	18,100	17,595	43,100	78,100	121,100
Total Assets	231,421	468,178	726,613	828,000	945,700	1,111,400
Liabilities and Shareholders' Equity						
Current Liabilities						
Accounts Payable	9,128	28,668	38,034			
Other Current Liabilities	31,290	42,378	63,057			
Total Current Liabilities	40,418	71,046	101,091	134,100	165,800	198,100
Other Liabilities	81,105	84,901	173,862			
Shareholders' Equity:						
Common Stock	89,861	265,679	361,309	519,400	604,300	717,200
Retained Earnings	20,037	46,552	90,351			
Total Shareholders' Equity	109,898	312,231	451,660			
Total Liabilities	231,421	468,178	726,613	828,000	945,700	1,111,400

Sources: Starbucks Corporation Annual Reports & William Blair & Company

AB SANDVIK SAWS & TOOLS: THE ERGO STRATEGY

case 13

Roderick E. White and
Julian Birkinshaw

Fifteen years ago we competed with price. Today we compete with quality. Tomorrow it will be design.

—Robert Hayes, 1991

Göran Gezelius, the president of the Sandvik Saws & Tools Business Area, looked out his office window at the serene waters of Lake Storsjön. It was early spring and the trees had not yet taken on their summer foliage. He had just returned from a two-week trip to North

America a day early and had some free time in his normally hectic schedule. He thought that, overall, Saws and Tools business results for 1995 had been adequate. Early operating results suggested that 1996 would be a challenging year. But from a strategic perspective he was not entirely satisfied with what was being accomplished with the recently introduced Ergo hand tools, especially in North America. There was a meeting of the Ergo Steering Committee later in the week

IVEY

Roderick White and Julian Birkinshaw prepared this case solely to provide material for class discussion. The authors do not intend to illustrate either effective or ineffective handling of a managerial situation. The authors may have disguised certain names and other identifying information to protect confidentiality.

and he needed to review the performance of ergonomic hand tools strategy. He reached for his Ergo file.

OVERVIEW

Over the last three years, beginning in 1993, ergonomically designed hand tools had become an increasingly important part of the strategy for the hand tools component of the Saws and Tools Business Unit. Ergonomics, the science of optimizing the interaction of the person and their work environment, had always been considered in the design process. But in 1991 Sandvik acquired Bahco Verktyg AB, a maker of spanners[1] and wrenches. Bahco had been working with an industrial design firm and they had developed an intensive methodology that set new standards for ergonomic design. In mid-1993 the Ergo Project Group was formed within Saws and Tools and created a common design philosophy and marketing statement across the range of hand tools: from handsaws to screwdrivers. A sequence was established for the conversion of existing tools to the new ergonomic standard and the changeover began. By early 1996 the process was about half completed. A considerable investment had already been made in redesign, retooling production processes and repositioning products in the marketplace. More would be required to complete the conversion.

Even though the complete line of Ergo tools would not be available for another two to three years, Göran was concerned that the initial sales of Ergo tools already introduced were not as strong as hoped. Personally he still felt very committed to the Ergo concept. However, he wondered whether the Ergo Committee should re-examine the strategy and consider alternative courses of action.

COMPANY BACKGROUND

AB Sandvik Saws & Tools was one of six global business areas within Sandvik AB. The others were: cutting tools, rock tools, hard materials, steel and process systems. Exhibit 1 provides a brief description and overview of each business area. Each operated as an autonomous business. Group management provided a few support activities (finance, legal, international sales/trading companies for less developed markets) that were drawn on by the business areas as needed.

With headquarters in Sandviken, Sweden, about 150 kilometers north of Stockholm, Sandvik began in 1862 as a manufacturer of high quality steel. Never a volume producer of steel, Sandvik specialized in applications where quality, uniformity, hardness and sharpness were important. Initially they provided steel for things like saws, fish hooks, drills for rock mining and razors. In 1886 the company started making saws. As expertise accumulated it led into other related businesses like steel tubing and cutting tools.

Although the company had evolved into different businesses there were several themes common to all of Sandvik's businesses. Sandvik products were functional. They provided the customer maximum value in terms of performance, quality, speed, productivity and flexibility. Sandvik's products usually sold at a premium price (on a per unit basis) but had higher performance and overall lower costs to the customer. The performance advantages incorporated into Sandvik products originated with its engineering and R&D efforts. Partly as a consequence of its attention to

---

[1] Called adjustable wrench in North America. The spanner had been invented by Bahco's founder.

customer functionality Sandvik tended to focus on niche markets. For example, Sandvik supplied the steel used by a leading compass manufacturer to make their magnetic compass needles (1,000 kilograms per year); or, the balls for ball-point pens (2 billion annually). In order to maintain direct contact with the customers and ensure that they understood the value of its products, Sandvik forward integrated, as far as feasible, into sales and distribution. Sandvik also manufactured most of what it sold.

The Sandvik Group's activities were global in scope. The group was active in over 60 countries. Over 90 per cent of sales were to customers outside Sweden (see Chart 1) and two-thirds of Sandvik's almost 30,000 employees were located outside Sweden. At the same time, Sandvik was the quintessential Swedish company: conservative, understated and traditional in style with a strong work ethic and a homogeneous corporate culture. As stated by chairman of the board, Percy Barnevik, "Sandvik cannot be described as a company given to excesses...put simply, the company does a darn fine job without a lot of fuss and without any particular recognition for it."

Chart 1:   Sandvik AB: Sales by Region

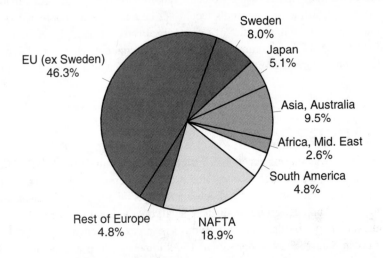

Most of the Group's businesses were industrial. Thus sales, and profits even more so, tended to follow the business cycle. (See Chart 2.) Partly as a consequence of this exposure Sandvik had a very conservative financial structure. Long-term liabilities were just 14 per cent of total capital and the company had 6.9 billion[2] SEK in cash and short-term investments (22.5 per cent of total assets) at the end of 1995. This liquidity allowed Sandvik to make selective acquisitions to develop and strengthen selected business areas. And, the company had been active in this way.

---

[2] As of early 1996 one SEK was equal to approximately US$0.15.

Chart 2: **Sandvik AB: Financial Performance**

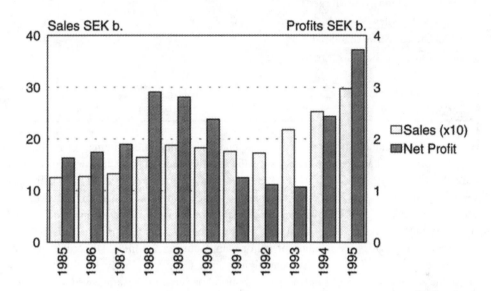

SAWS AND TOOLS GROUP:
PERFORMANCE TOOLS—ALWAYS AVAILABLE

Sandvik Saws and Tools with invoiced sales of 2,674 MSEK accounted for nine per cent of Sandvik AB's turnover. Historical information on sales and profit for this business area are presented below.

millions of SEK	1991	1992	1993	1994	1995
Sales	1437	2049	2363	2583	2674
Profit before financial items	(16)	(82)	(3)	185	184
# of Employees	3676	3275	3060	3050	2998

Saws and Tools had 40 sales units around the world and 16 production units in 8 countries. Saws and Tools made and marketed a wide range of hand tools including: pliers, wrenches, ratchets, screwdrivers, hammers, chisels, scrapers; files; hand saws, bow saws, hacksaws and blades; as well as gardening/agricultural hand tools (pruners, loppers and secateurs). It also manufactured and sold forestry products (chain saw bar and chain) and industrial band saw blades. Sales for 1995 by major product centre were:

Product Centre	% of 1995 sales
Gardening	10%
Hand Tools (carpentry)	16%
Mechanics Hand Tools (forged)	27%
Files and Handles	6%
Metal Cutting Saws (excl: bandsaws)	<u>19%</u>
Hand Tools and associated products	<u>78%</u>
Bandsaws	13%
Forestry Products	9%
Total	2674 MSEK

Saws and Tools' hand tool product range included more than 8,000 items.[3] Over the last five years product offerings had been globally rationalized. All products were the same in all markets and available on a global basis. With its wide range of products customers could meet their needs in hand tools and machine-saw accessories from a single source, almost anywhere in the world.

Manufacturing was globally rationalized. Most products were made at one facility, and for those products made in more than one place the assortment was usually rationalized between the facilities. Exhibit 2 provides the location of major manufacturing facilities. Direct labour costs per hour differed by country. Germany had the highest cost followed closely by Sweden. Costs at facilities in the southern U.S. and England were about 60 per cent of those in Sweden. Portugal and Argentina were even lower labour cost areas. Overall labour costs, including production staff and administration, accounted for 30 to 60 per cent of total manufacturing costs, with the average being 50 per cent.

The business unit's products were designed to appeal to professional users in many different markets. The following statement made this focus clear.

> More than 80 per cent of everything we sell is bought by professionals. Professionals will be our most important customers for a long time, even though nonprofessional use is expanding. If our products are accepted by the professionals and discerning users who often buy their tools privately, then we don't have to worry about the non-professionals. Our reputation will induce them to buy our tools.[4]

Of course quality and performance were very important to professional users. Saws and Tools management felt their "do it ourselves" approach was important to delivering value to their customers.

> A main reason why we manage to maintain a high standard of quality is that we control the entire cycle from basic research, through product development and manufacturing to distribution. The Sandvik Group is a world leader in materials technology. We regularly introduce innovations that put us ahead of competitors: Ergonomic design, hard pointing of hand saws, bimetal hacksaws and roll-top guide bars are just a few examples.[5]

---

[3] This included all SKUs. It was estimated that only about 400 SKUs were amenable to Ergo design.

[4] We're determined..., May 1994, page 16. (Internal publication by company.)

[5] We're determined..., May 1994, page 24.

Distribution

Sandvik was organized with sales units in each major country responsible for local sales and distribution. Global product centres (PCs) were responsible for manufacturing of the product, and with input from the sales units, for marketing and pricing. Product profit responsibility was with the product centres. The management for most hand tool PCs were located in Sweden.

Whenever possible Saws and Tools sold through resellers into each local market. However, its own distribution was increasingly centralized. There were only two distribution points for all of Europe. A new state-of-the-art distribution centre in the Netherlands serviced the EU. Nordic countries were served from Sandviken. This approach was a dramatic change from a few years earlier when each country's Sales Unit held its own inventory and ran its own distribution system. With the new system, delivery was promised anywhere within Europe in 72 hours, and to major cities within 48 hours. Many resellers were linked by EDI to Sandvik's computers. North American distribution was not yet as rationalized. But it had never been as fragmented. Currently it was done from facilities in Scranton, PA and Mississauga, Ontario. Other regions of the world tended to have local, country-based distribution.

Distribution of hand tools was through a number of channels. Consumers, non-professional users, generally bought their tools through hardware stores or mass merchandisers. Most hardware stores were members of large buying groups. Professional users either bought their tools personally, or had them supplied by their employers. In either case they tended to buy from industrial or agricultural supply companies. Distributors tended to work on a regional basis and often carried competing products from different manufacturers.

In most of Europe Saws and Tools had strong distribution for its hand tools. In North America the distribution system had been built around bandsaw blades. The general mill supply distributors carried an assortment of products including bandsaw blades and hand tools. But in almost all instances these distributors already carried the product assortment of one of the major U.S.-based competitors, such as Cooper and Stanley products.

A sales force of 22 Sandvik people (16 in the U.S. and 6 in Canada) and 9 manufacturers representatives[6] serviced industrial distributors. Other channels, like electrical and plumbing supply houses, retail "big box" stores and hardware chains, were served by agencies and manufacturers' representatives. All together they had about 40 field sales people. Saws and Tools had one manager coordinating this channel.

Saws and Tools did not sell hand tools directly to the end user. They had a policy of not bypassing resellers. Sales people would, however, often do joint sales calls on industrial customers with the reseller's representative. Saws and Tools participated in all the major trade shows.

Sandvik Brand: The Fish-and-Hook

The Sandvik brand, represented by the fish-and-hook symbol, was well recognized by many professional users within Europe. It did not have the same degree of recognition in North America, or the Asia-Pacific. As one manager explained:

> In Europe we have strong brand recognition among industrial distributors (the trade) and professional end users. However, our brand recognition does vary between countries and product

---

[6] Manufacturers representatives were not employees of the company. They worked on commission and usually represented several non-competing manufacturers.

lines. The trade knows us everywhere (in Europe); the end users primarily in Scandinavia, UK, Switzerland and Holland; less in Germany and very little in France and southern Europe. Overall we have strong brand recognition for hand saws, adjustable wrenches and electronic pliers. In the USA, our brand recognition with the end user is weak, or even non-existent except for bandsaw blades and electronic pliers. In Latin America Sandvik has very strong brand recognition in Argentina; in the remaining parts we are mainly known for Sandflex™ hand hacksaw blades. In Asia we are recognized for hacksaw blades and to some extent for adjustable wrenches.

Amongst casual users Sandvik was widely known in Scandinavia and the Netherlands for handsaws and adjustable wrenches, in the U.K. for handsaws, in Switzerland for chisels and handsaws and in France for pruning tools and handsaws. In the Americas and Asia Sandvik was not known to casual users.

These differences in brand recognition were reflected in different market shares by region. As shown below Saws and Tools had larger shares in Europe.

	USA			Europe	
Category	Market MUSD 1994	Sandvik Share	Category	Market MUSD 1994	Sandvik Share
Screwdrivers	218	~0	Screwdrivers	~200	3
Adjustable & pipe wrenches	116	~0	Adjustable wrenches	~50	~15
Pliers	140	~0	Pliers	250	4
Handsaws	150	10	Handsaws (carpenter)	100	25
Hacksaw blades	17	5	Hacksaws & Blades	100	20
Mechanics' Tools	~1200	~0	Mechanics' Tools	2000	6
Other	1000	3	Other	2000	6

In the U.S., Saws and Tools did have a more substantial presence in forestry (chain saws bars and chain) and industrial band saw blades. But these products were not amenable to ergonomic design.

Sandvik endeavoured to have the customer associate Sandvik with "performance tools, always available". High performance had always been a Sandvik hallmark. With the new distribution strategy availability was improving.

Sandvik's pricing policy was related to its business strategy. Its prices were based upon the market leader for that (professional) product line in that region. The policy stated, "Our price should stay within a range of 90 to 105 per cent of the market leader. We never undercut the leader by more than 10 per cent."[7] Saws and Tools also tried to keep prices consistent between countries in a region (although not necessarily between regions).

---

[7] We're determined..., May 1994, page 49.

STRUCTURE OF THE HAND TOOL MARKETS

In general, the hand tool industry had been fragmented, with many small, local companies making one or two types of tools. (For example, fifty companies make screwdrivers.) Sandvik was the only European-based manufacturer with a wide range of products for professional users. In Europe the 50 largest companies accounted for 50 per cent of the market. However, the industry was less fragmented in the U.S., where five firms accounted for 50 per cent of the industry.[8] Larger players like Cooper Industries and Stanley produced and sold a range of branded tools. But retailers, like Sears with their Craftsman™ tool line, also had a strong position particularly in the consumer market.

Both Craftsman and Stanley brands were more oriented to the home market, less towards the professional user. Stanley claimed to be the "largest manufacturer of consumer hand tools in the world."[9] Stanley also had a line of products oriented to the professional user. Stanley's tool business included consumer, industrial and engineered segments. The first two segments were most directly competitive with Sandvik. Consumer tools included hand tools such as measuring instruments, planes, hammers, knives and blades, wrenches, sockets, screwdrivers, saws, chisels, boring tools, masonry, tile and drywall tools, paint preparation and paint application tools. Industrial tools included industrial and mechanics' hand tools, and high-density industrial storage and retrieval systems. The consumer segment had 1995 sales of $739 million (US); industrial sales of $552 million. Seventy-two per cent of Stanley total sales were in the U.S.; 16 per cent in Europe. The U.S. accounted for 79 per cent of operating profits.

Professionally oriented products were generally produced by specialized, single product line firms of limited geographic scope: single product, single market companies. Of course Sandvik with a broad product line and wide geographic scope was an exception to this rule, as was Cooper Industries in the U.S. Cooper had 1995 tools and hardware sales of $962 million (US). It competed directly with Sandvik in pliers, conventional and adjustable wrenches, files, saws, hammers and screwdrivers. Cooper also had other products within its tools and hardware segment including: drapery hardware, power tools, chain, soldering equipment torches and cutting products. Cooper had many identifiable brands, e.g., Crescent™ in adjustable wrenches and Kirsch™ in drapery hardware. However, Cooper itself was a holding company with no strong brand identity. Sales outside the U.S. were 37 per cent of total sales, up from 31 per cent two years earlier.

Cooper and Stanley, like Sandvik, produced a range of tools supplying a variety of markets. Snap-on Tools had a very different strategy. It focused exclusively on automotive service technicians and serviced them through 5,400 franchised dealers. These dealers drove large vans stocked with the popular products and visited the customers at their repair shops at least once per week. Snap-on had sales of $1.3 billion (US), 40 per cent in hand tools; 80 per cent in North America, 15 per cent in Europe.

Distribution of hand tools was changing. An interesting North American phenomenon was the emergence of big-box specialty retailers, companies like Home Depot and Builder's Square. With their large stores and wide product assortment these outlets targeted both the professional and the do-it-yourself market.

---

[8] We're determined..., May 1994, page 6.
[9] Stanley Works, 10-K, 1995.

Acquisitions

Many of Saws and Tools' markets were highly fragmented, but restructuring was occurring. This was a situation the company recognized:

> The hand-tool industry in Europe is ripe for restructuring. Sandvik Saws and Tools has taken the initiative in this process... We've acquired competent tool manufacturers and added strong brands. We've gained economies of scale in production, marketing and distribution. We've improved customer service and will continue to do so.[10]

During the last few years Saws and Tools had acquired Bahco (spanners and pliers), Belzer (screwdrivers and ratchets), Lindstrom (electronic pliers) and Milford (industrial band saw blades).

THE ERGO STRATEGY

> The awareness of ergonomics is growing and it is going to continue to grow. The cost of NOT addressing ergonomics is also going to continue to grow.

> Professor Thomas Armstrong
> Center for Ergonomics, The University of Michigan

Saws and Tools had an ongoing interest in ergonomic design. This interest was enhanced when in early 1992 Sandvik acquired the Bahco Tool Group, headquartered in Enköping, Sweden. Bahco, working with an industrial design firm, Ergonomi Design Gruppen, had developed a methodology for designing ergonomic tools. (See Exhibit 3.) Prior to the Sandvik acquisition Bahco had used this process to develop ergonomic screwdrivers (1983), adjustable wrenches (1984), wood chisels (1985), slipjoint pliers (1986), side cutters (1989), combination pliers (1991) and a combination adjustable wrench (1991).

The ergonomic approach to hand tool design fit well with Sandvik's basic strategy and appealed to Saws and Tools management. The 11-point Ergo process became the standard for the Saws and Tools group and the formal Ergo strategy came into being in mid-1993 when the Ergo Project Committee was formed.

The Ergo Project Committee was asked to build, direct and co-ordinate the Ergo Concept across the group, specifically to:

- Ensure that all products designated as Ergo had followed the 11-point process.
- Identify products to add to the Ergo range.
- Establish guidelines for pricing Ergo products.
- Produce documentation and promotional materials.

The committee had eight members; six from different Saws and Tools units and two from EDG. It was chaired by Connie Jansson, R&D manager for Sandvik Bahco.

One of the first tasks of the committee was to identify those products most amenable to the Ergo concept and establish priorities for conversion to the Ergo standard. Major considerations were

---

[10] We're determined..., May 1994, page 6.

volume, existing and potential, and the prospects for global sales, as well as recognizable benefits and the potential to enhance Sandvik's market position. Exhibit 4 provides a list of Ergo products done to date or immediately pending. Each Ergo product had undergone the 11-point process and was done in collaboration with Ergonomi Design Gruppen.

Ergonomi Design Gruppen (EDG)

EDG was an industrial design firm located in an old converted church on the outskirts of Stockholm. Sweden was asserted to have a comparative advantage in design, and EDG was one of the best mid-sized independent industrial design firms in Sweden. EDG assumed a major role in the initial Ergo design process. Olle Bobjer was the senior ergonomist at EDG and Hans Himberg was the principal of the firm. Both played an active role with the Sandvik account. The firm employed 16 professionals, mostly industrial designers.

Sandvik's relationship with EDG was very close. EDG did work on a wide range of products for many different companies but had agreed to do hand tool design only for Sandvik. And, as a portion of their fees was tied to the sales volume of the finished product Sandvik felt the relationship gave them the benefits of an in-house design group, but with a much higher level of expertise.

EDG managed the 11-point development and certification process. Ergonomics was an applied science. The process was based upon feedback from sophisticated professional users of the tool under development. The process began with studies of how end-users worked. Work sites were visited, people interviewed and videos of the tools in use were made. Multiple prototypes were built, tested and assessed by end users. (See Exhibit 5.)

If sufficiently unique, aspects of an Ergo product could be patented by Sandvik. But this type of protection was unusual. Most often design patents were applicable when Ergo tools differed from traditional tools in appearance. Saws and Tools used both types of protection whenever possible. Several competitors had been stopped from copying Sandvik products.

The combined capabilities of EDG and Sandvik provided Saws and Tools with an area of distinctive competence. They felt no competitor could match their ability to design, develop and manufacture ergonomic hand tools. But from the beginning the Ergo Committee had recognized that, "a product can successfully combine all the right things but stumble in the marketplace because of failure to communicate effectively about the product to potential purchasers."[11]

Ergo Benefits

Designing and manufacturing ergonomic hand tools was one thing; selling them was another. Hand tools had been used for centuries. Many of these tools had incorporated local norms and evolved into effective instruments; others remained largely unchanged since the industrial revolution. A better understanding of how the human body functioned in relation to work, the science of ergonomy, and the ongoing development of new materials presented opportunities for significant improvements in most hand tools.

The specific benefits of ergonomic design varied by tool (see Exhibit 6). But generally there were two principal benefits of ergonomic hand tools that were in fact both related to reduced physical stress on the worker:

- reduction in work-related physical disorders, and

---

[11] A Research Approach to Ergonomic Hand Tools, April 1994, page 3.

- increases in productivity.

Work related disorders, more properly called Cumulative Trauma Disorders (CTD) or Repetitive Motion Injuries (RMI) were recognized as the number one occupational hazard of the 1990s by experts. Carpal Tunnel Syndrome was one such work-related injury. Nerves and tendons to the hand pass through the carpal tunnel, inside the wrist. Repetitive, stressful hand motions can cause the tendons to become inflamed, putting pressure on the nerves in this area, resulting in pain and numbness.

The highest risks for CTD was encountered when a job or tool required a combination of force and precision used repeatedly, without sufficient rest time for the body to recover. For example, a vineyard worker pruning grape vines and making up to 10,000 cuts per day would be at high risk.

Properly designed ergonomic tools reduced musculo-skeletal stresses and strains and provided sensory feedback to the user for accuracy and optimum control. They were proportioned to the dimensions of the user and were efficient in the use of human energy. While good styling and ergonomic design often went hand-in-hand there was a difference. Styling looks at the superficial aesthetics of the object. Ergonomics goes deeper. Shapes, materials and textures are selected for their functionality.

Ergonomics had also caught the attention of governmental health and safety agencies. Legislation had been proposed in the U.S. that would make employers liable for damages if they were not using ergonomic best practice. This proposed legislation had been shelved and was not under active consideration.

There were sound economic reasons for a company to use ergonomic tools. These included: fewer on-the-job accidents and worker sick days; reduction in injuries that sometimes result in disability claims, law suits and higher insurance costs. They could also improve worker morale and job satisfaction.

Naturally workers using well-designed tools could be more productive. While this benefit was recognized within Saws and Tools, it was not explicitly mentioned in any of the marketing materials. Groups related to worker health and safety, like unions, were seen as key opinion leaders in getting the Ergo concept accepted. Generally, they were more concerned with the health benefits than the possible productivity improvements.

It was recognized from the outset that, "there is a latent demand within the professional hand tool users for ergonomic products. Many people need them, but few ask or know anything about them."[12] The original report went on to say, "it is our job to educate the users/dealers about real ergonomic tools. This will be difficult as many competitors claim to have ergonomic tools."

Indeed, although the user may prefer one type of tool, it was difficult to conclusively demonstrate the ergonomic benefits of one tool over another. Because most CTD were caused by repetitive motions it took weeks, if not months to emerge. Comparative testing, a technique used to demonstrate the value of many other Sandvik products, was difficult under these circumstances. Thus while Sandvik believed its Ergo tools were better than competitors', they could not easily prove this claim. Instead the initial marketing program relied on Sandvik's reputation for quality and explained the 11-point development program for Ergo tools.

---

[12] A Research Approach to Ergonomic Hand Tools, April 20, 1994, page 23.

Introduction of Ergo Tools

When Sandvik acquired Bahco their product line included a number of Ergo tools. With Sandvik's resources distribution of these tools was broadened and the application of the Ergo concept to other products accelerated.

When first introduced, Ergo products were additions to the top-end of Sandvik's product range. They did not immediately replace an existing product. As a consequence a product range, like screwdrivers, included both Ergo and non-Ergo product. However, the adjustable wrench category had evolved to the point that it included only Ergo product (1st and 2nd generation). Ergo products were positioned as the premium product within the Sandvik assortment and priced to reflect this positioning.

After Sandvik launched the Ergo strategy, the initial marketing/communication program targeted opinion leaders who could influence the tool purchase decision: ergonomists, health and safety engineers, safety (union) representatives, human resource managers, etc. Sales unit staff were trained in the benefits of ergonomic hand tools and provided with aids: brochures, videos, etc. to help them communicate the concept.

Sandvik had not had significant hand tools sales in the U.S. prior to Ergo. Using the Ergo products it was hoped Saws and Tools could expand its position in the U.S. hand tools market. Because of the investment required and the lack of warehouse space only about 2,000 handtool SKUs were currently available in the U.S. (compared to 8,000 in Europe). Because of this limited assortment Sandvik could not offer to replace a distributor's other hand tool suppliers. They positioned themselves as an innovative product specialist targeted on niche markets. Ergo was introduced into the U.S. during the spring of 1995. As part of the introduction Dr. Thomas Armstrong, a well-known U.S. ergonomist, along with Sandvik personnel explained the Ergo concept to interested health and safety professionals, mostly from large automotive and aerospace manufacturers.

Cost of Ergo Tools

The incremental costs of the Ergo strategy were difficult to ascertain precisely. Sandvik periodically redesigned its hand tools and the added cost of employing the Ergo methodology was hard to calculate. Upfront design costs paid to EDG for an Ergo tool and associated with the 11-point program ranged from 200,000 to 1,500,000 SEK depending on the complexity of the project. A typical project would be about 600,000 SEK. In addition to this amount EDG also received a royalty. For a successful product EDG design costs would account for one to two per cent of sales[13] during its first 10 years.

Any design change, ergonomic or otherwise, required the retooling of the manufacturing process. The Ergo strategy had accelerated the number of design changes but it was not necessarily much more expensive. These costs differed. The new Ergo screwdrivers had cost about a million dollars (US), the Ergo ratchet about $200,000. The Ergo loper saw had required a new injection mold for the handle at $100,000 and a new grinding technique for the blade that required an investment of $400,000 in equipment. Generally retooling costs ranged from $500,000 to $1,000,000 (US), assuming the equipment for producing the same type of non-ergo tool was available.

---

[13] Internal transfer price from the product centre to the sales unit.

Ergo products were sometimes more difficult and costly to manufacture. Most often this was the result of a more complex shape and/or a special gripping surface being incorporated into the product. As one manager observed:

> Any increase in costs has to be seen in light of the previous state of the tool. Ergo tools incorporate a higher level of end user input and preference... The cost change, from our experience, and as a rule of thumb is 5 to 10 per cent.

While some of the manufacturing processes were more challenging, none were proprietary. Smaller companies might have difficulty replicating some Ergo products, but larger manufacturers willing to expend the effort would be able to do so.

Price Premium

Sandvik tried to adhere to its normal pricing policy with Ergo products. Because of the unique Ergo design it was often difficult to find a comparable product. But in most instances there was a somewhat similar competitive offering to serve as a benchmark. This product was most likely a niche product and not the market leader, at least in terms of volume. Ergo products were priced at a zero to 20 per cent premium over competitive products. The amount of the premium took into account the cost of the product, the additional value it offered the user and the pricing of competitor products. The price premium over low-end, non-professional products could be much greater. The latest generation of Ergo adjustable wrench was five times the (retail) price of the cheapest product available in the Scandinavian marketplace. In North America the premiums tended to be even greater.

GOING GLOBAL

The Ergo strategy also reinforced Sandvik's global approach to the hand-tool business.

> In the past the hand-tool business was local. Customer preferences varied widely even within one country. Patterns of tool choice and use were passed on from one generation of craftsmen to the next. Local manufacturers and small-town businesses, which were often family-owned, served local customers.
>
> Now...the hand-tool business has gone from local to regional to global. The industry still leans toward tradition. There are still local preferences and idiosyncrasies that we will have to deal with for some time to come... The market as a whole is moving toward universal acceptance of tool types and ranges. It's increasingly feasible to sell the same product design in many countries.[14]

Of course Ergo tools were designed for optimal function with the human hand. Something that did not differ between countries, or cultures. (When required Ergo products came in a range of sizes to accommodate different sized hands.)

Tariffs were not judged to be a significant factor. On hand tools shipped between the EU to the U.S. tariffs ranged from five to nine per cent; from the U.S. to the EU tariffs tended to be slightly lower, from three to four per cent. Adjustable wrenches were an extreme case with tariffs from the EU to the U.S. of nine per cent and from the U.S. to the EU of three per cent.

---

[14] We're determined..., May 1994, page 8.

SITUATION IN EARLY 1996

By 1995, there were seven categories of Ergo products with variations within each category. (See Exhibit 7.) As shown in Chart 3 sales were 224 million SEK, or 8.4 per cent of the groups overall sales and about 10.7 per cent of hand tool sales.

Chart 3: **ERGO Branded Products**

1995 External Invoicing

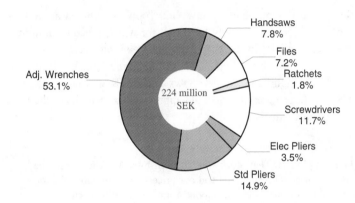

But these sales were not evenly distributed. As shown below Europe accounted for most of the Ergo sales.

Unit Sales (000) of Ergo Product 1995	Europe	North America	Rest Of World
Adjustable Wrenches	1300	8	200
Standard Pliers	300	4	60
Screwdrivers	996	25	16
Handsaws f/c 1996	177	9	28
Files, handles	587	15	38
Electronic Pliers	-	20	-
f/c 1996	10	30	-
Ratchet Wrenches	16	1.1	0.1
f/c 1996	22	0.1	0.4

Of course the Ergo hand tools had just been introduced in a limited range to North America during 1995.

It was difficult to assess the precise impact of the Ergo strategy. As Per Tornell, the Nordic Sale Unit manager, explained:

> We dominate certain product categories in the Nordic countries. In adjustable wrenches we have 50 to 60 per cent share of the unit volume and 90 per cent of the value for professional users. And, we've (Bahco) had this position for a long time. Ergo has helped us to maintain our strong position. But in ratchets we are one of ten competitors with about a 20 per cent share. I feel that the new Ergo ratchet will help us to improve our position but it is too early to tell. It takes years for this type of thing to have a noticeable impact.
>
> Screwdrivers are a good example. Over ten years ago Bahco introduced the Ergo screwdriver. At that time it was a radical redesign; very different from the traditional product. The difference in the product was obvious to the user. We are now the market leader in Sweden and Finland. But it took ten years.

In North America the situation was different. Sandvik Saws and Tools was known in the U.S. for its forestry products, and industrial band saws. The only hand tool for which it had even limited recognition were hand saws and electronic pliers. In the U.S. Ergo had been launched in February 1995. The concept had been well-received by health and safety professionals. But their endorsements had not yet materialized as significant orders. Saws and Tools was targeting large industrial users like Ford and GM. It was hoped these users could appreciate the benefits of the Ergo product and pull it through the distribution channels.

As one U.S. manager observed:

> Distributors will not really push a product. They stock what their customers ask for. Since we have a limited assortment and not much brand recognition and our prices are at, or above the top end it's a difficult sell. The availability of our hand tool products through distributors is not as extensive as we would like. We would like to use Ergo to develop, expand and strengthen our channels.

Another manager went further:

> The health and safety people have not been able to convince the purchasing people to specify our product. They'll look at our product but it usually comes back to an issue of price. Most hand tools are only used occasionally and repetitive motion injuries are not considered to be a major factor. Naturally we try to sell the advantage—the prevention of one lost-time accident will more than pay for the tool. And, where RMI is a factor, like in trimming electronic circuit boards with snippers, we have done well. For the same reason we expect our Ergo metal shears, when they are developed, will be well accepted. But again this is a niche where the benefit is clear.

Meanwhile the ergonomic idea seemed to be gaining popularity with other competitors. Stanley had recently distributed marketing literature stating that their products were ergonomically tested by an independent testing firm. However, there was no evidence that Stanley employed a rigorous process for incorporating ergonomics into the design of their hand tools. It was also known that Cooper had formed an ergonomic working group, including customers and ergonomists, as well as company personnel. Nothing had yet emerged from this group.

CONCLUSION

Göran Gezelius observed:

> Interest and recognition in Ergo from our own sales people, as well as distributors has been excellent. We have not succeeded yet in turning this recognition into big sales figures in markets where we were not previously known with our hand tools. In markets where we are known—Scandinavia, UK, Netherlands—it appears as if Ergo helps us to increase our market share. However, if we are to become a truly global, professional hand tool company, we need to improve our position where we are less well-known, especially North America. It is not clear whether Ergo will help us in a significant way to accomplish this objective; or what more needs to be done.

Exhibit 1: AB SANDVIK Results by Business Area 1995

Business Area	Sales		Operating Profits[14]		Return on
	SEK m.	%	SEK m.	%	Sales (%)
Tooling	9576	32	2436	47	25.4%
Rock Tools	2015	7	219	4	10.9%
Hard Materials	1224	4	185	4	15.1%
Steel	9807	33	1623	31	16.5%
Saws and Tools	2674	9	184	4	6.9%
Process Systems	1810	6	101	2	5.6%
Seco Tools[15]	2555	9	542	10	21.2%
Intra Group	39	/	(96)	/	
Group total	29700	100	5194	100	17.5%

Description of Business Areas

Business Area (# of employees)	Description
Tooling (11010)	Sandvik Coromat was the global leader in cemented carbide inserts used for the machining of metal. Inserts were the cutting edge in machine tools, like lathes. CTT Tools produced principally high-speed steel tools like drills, threading tools and reamers.
Rock Tools (1877)	This business was a leading supplier of cemented-carbide-tipped rockdrilling tools (and tool systems) used in mining, civil engineering and water-well drilling.
Hard Materials	This business manufactures and markets unmachined carbide blanks, as well

[14]After depreciation, before financial charges.

[15]A separately listed public company. Sandvik owned 61 per cent.

(1447)	as customized wear parts (e.g., seal rings). Sandvik was the largest competitor in this business, and the only one with global scope.
Steel (7257)	Steel manufactures tube, strip, wire and bar for demanding applications. Products are produced in stainless and high alloy steels and in titanium, nickel and zirconium alloys.
Saws and Tools (2998)	Used mainly by professionals, S&T products included: hand saws and saw blades; wrenches, spanners, pliers, files, pruning tools, as well as guide bars and saw chains.
Process Systems (888)	Manufactures the steel belts and engineers the complete systems used in automated sorting and chemical and food-processing.

Exhibit 2: Location of Saws and Tools Manufacturing Facilities

Location	Product Center	# of employees
Edsbyn, Sweden	Forestry Tools	147
Bollnäs, Sweden	Hand Tools (handsaws)	160
Sveg, Sweden	Hand Tools (bowsaws)	40
Enköping, Sweden	Pliers (pliers & adjustables)	336
Lidköping, Sweden	Metal Saws (hack)	242
	Bandsaws	23
Hasborn, Germany	Wrenches	90
Wuppertal, Germany	Wrenches	80
Maltby, England	Metal Saws	37
	Bandsaws	23
Vila do Conde, Portugal	Files	243
Branford, CT, USA	Bandsaws	140
Milan, TN, USA	Forestry (chain saw bars)	51
Dyer, TN, USA	Forestry (saw chain)	97
Santo Tome, Argentina	Wrenches	312

Exhibit 3: Development of Ergonomically Designed Hand Tools

11 Points, in Chronological Order

1. Specification of demands
2. Analysis of competitors—tools and markets
3. Background material
4. Production of functioning model
5. User tests I
6. Evaluation and modification of models
7. User tests II
8. Design proposal
9. Product specification
10. User test III and preparation before launching
11. Follow up on statistics

Approved by: The Scientific Committee on Musculoskeletal Disorders of the International Commission on Occupational Health (ICOH).

Exhibit 4: ERGO Tools Since 1992

Type of Tool (by Product Center)	Launch Date
Sandvik Bahco	
Combination Adjustable	Cologne[16] -93 (2nd generation)
Gripping Pliers	1994
Electronic Pliers	1995
Pipe Wrenches	pending
Sandvik Belzer	
Screwdrivers	pending (2nd generation)
Ratchet wrench	1994
Sandvik Gardening	
Secateurs	pending
Plate shears	pending
Sandvik Hand Tools	
Paint scrapers	pending
Hand saw (2600)	1995
Sandvik Files	
File handles	1995
Metal Saws	
Hack Saw frame	pending

[16]A major trade fair held in Cologne, Germany each year in May.

Exhibit 5: **Prototypes of Electronic Nippers**

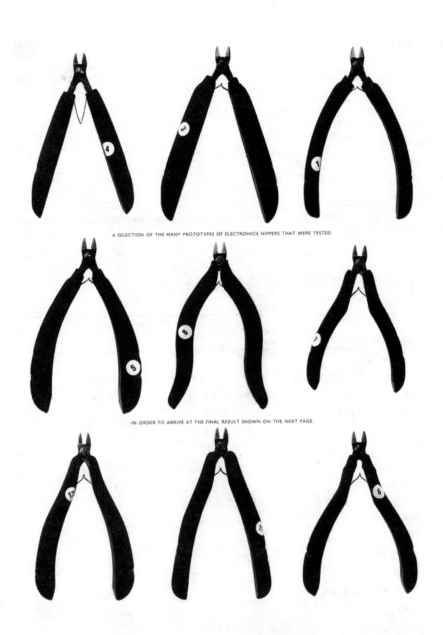

A SELECTION OF THE MANY PROTOTYPES OF ELECTRONICS NIPPERS THAT WERE TESTED

IN ORDER TO ARRIVE AT THE FINAL RESULT SHOWN ON THE NEXT PAGE.

Exhibit 6: **Typical Benefits of Ergo Hand Tool**

1. Hexagonal nut, so you can use a wrench if you need to pull hard.

2. Small diameter lets you tighten or loosen the screw quickly.

3. Plenty of room for precision control with thumb and index finger.

4. Completely rounded handle, so you avoid pressure points on your hand.

5. Fits your hand well – the right diameter provides maximum power. Ridged surface increases friction even when the handle is oily.

6. The handle is designed for both power and precision.

7. Large, rounded end minimizes pressure in your hand.

1. Long, narrow jaws make it easy to reach the places you need to.

2. Jaws grip tightly in three places, so you don't have to squeeze the handles so hard.

3. Larger jaw opening than other slip joint pliers. Can be adjusted with parallel jaws in 11 different positions.

4. Unique thumb grip lets you adjust jaw opening without letting go or losing control of the pliers.

5. Long, softly rounded grip that doesn't end in the middle of your hand.

6. The handles can't close, so your hand won't get caught between them.

Exhibit 7: **ERGO Product Categories—1996**

Sandvik ERGO Products

Accompanying this brochure you will find literature on many of the products that Sandvik is proud to include in their Ergo range. The tools are one important part of the work process which can be improved by the application of ergonomics. Other important factors are the work-stations, posture and rest.

The durability, strength, availability and diversity of the Sandvik tool range is an established fact, as are the fast delivery and service we offer. Ergonomic design adds a whole new dimension of cost-saving through health awareness to our tools. Since the potential benefits to our customers are clear, Sandvik is looking positively and "ergonomically" at the future.

How about you?

An expanding range
A selection from the increasing range of Sandvik "Ergo" hand tools. All of these tools meet the exacting criteria of the Sandvik 11 Point Ergo Program.

10

THE LOEWEN GROUP

case 14

Ariff Kachra and
Mary Crossan

On September 17, 1996, Ray Loewen, Chairman and CEO of the Loewen Group, North America's second largest funeral home consolidator, was seeking approval from his Board for the purchase of the largest cemetery in the U.S., Rose Hills Memorial Park in California. As he was speaking about the $240 million[1] acquisition, one of the investment bankers at the meeting responded to a "911" on his beeper display. He returned with a news wire bulletin announcing the launch of a hostile take-over bid by SCI (Service Corporation International), the world's largest funeral consolidator. What began as a meeting seeking approvals for acquisitions, had turned into a war council. The entire Board turned to Mr. Loewen for his reaction. Should Loewen Group fight the takeover, or should it accept SCI's offer? (See Exhibit 1 for a copy of the letter sent by William Heiligbrodt to Ray Loewen, outlining the parameters of the proposed bid.)

THE FUNERAL SERVICE INDUSTRY

Typically, when a person passed away and had not made provisions for a pre-planned funeral, the process began with a phone call to book a meeting with the funeral director at a home. The funeral

---

[1]All dollar values in the case are in U.S. dollars unless otherwise noted.

IVEY

Ariff Kachra prepared this case under the supervision of Professor Mary Crossan solely to provide material for class discussion. The author does not intend to illustrate either effective or ineffective handling of a managerial situation. The author may have disguised certain names and other identifying information to protect confidentiality.

director used this meeting to grasp initial perceptions and thoughts of the bereaved family. The family had many choices including anything from a simple disposition to a traditional, full visitation service. With the help of the funeral director, the family made decisions on the elements of the funeral service, such as embalming, visitation, music, chapel, etc. As required by law, the funeral director reviewed the fee schedule with the family. The family then purchased merchandise such as caskets and urns. The family was then referred to a local cemetery, where they purchased a burial plot and any other related merchandise like vaults, markers, and headstones. After obtaining the family's legal authorization, the funeral director proceeded with the arrangements. Typically, a few weeks after the service, the funeral home made an after-care call to determine if the family needed additional support or had any bereavement-related concerns.

The following chart maps out the industry players that made up the funeral industry's business system:

Suppliers	Funeral Homes	Combination Facilities	Cemeteries
Caskets Embalming Related Items	Traditional Funeral Service Simple Services Cremations Pre-need Insurance		Burial plots Cremation niches Perform cremations Pre-need plots

Funeral Homes

Funeral homes did everything from selling pre-need insurance[2] to arranging a cremation, a simple burial and, more often than not, a traditional funeral service. Sources of revenue for a funeral home included professional services, facility and automotive rentals, and casket and urn sales. Expenses were made up of personnel, automotive equipment, promotion, business services, supplies, after-sale expenses and sundry items (See Exhibit 2). The funeral home was usually the customer's first point of contact. Whether the customer wanted a simple burial or a traditional funeral, the funeral home had the first opportunity to sell all related services and supplies.

Suppliers

Funeral home consolidators had consistently put a great deal of pressure on suppliers to reduce prices. This had a negative impact on the profitability of suppliers because they were very dependent on funeral homes. The potential threat to the casket producers and embalming suppliers was that as the funeral industry gave way to more and more consolidation, they would become increasingly dependent on a few large customers. With this dependence would come decreased margins and potential consolidation in the supply side of the industry.

---

[2]The consumer who wished to pre-plan and pre-pay for his or her funeral purchased pre-need insurance.

Cemeteries

The sources of revenue for cemeteries included the sales of at-need[3] and pre-need burial plots, cremation niches,[4] burial stones and plaques and professional services related to cremation and burial. Expenses consisted of personnel, maintenance of facilities, and sales and promotion (See Exhibit 3). Historically in Canada and the U.S., the vast majority of cemeteries had been privately owned. At the beginning of 1996, in Canada alone, there were over 10,000 private cemeteries. There were two key benefits of purchasing a cemetery. The first was that cemeteries offered a secure revenue stream for about 30 to 50 years. This revenue stream slowly began increasing as cemeteries concentrated on merchandising. The second was that cemeteries accrued pre-need revenues upon receipt, and used the money for investment purposes. This was a legal use of the funds, as long as 10 to 15 per cent of the revenues were invested in a perpetual care fund.[5] This represented a marked advantage over funeral homes, whose pre-need sales revenues had to be placed in trust until the time when the beneficiary passed away.

Combination Facilities

A recent development in the industry was the concept of combination facilities. Combination facilities afforded consumers the very attractive option of one-stop shopping, i.e., both the funeral home and the cemetery were located in one facility. The growth opportunities were vast in terms of combinations because industry statistics indicated that: "within six to eight years of opening, the average funeral home operating within a cemetery should perform the number of funerals approximately equivalent to 80 per cent of the number of interments at that cemetery." (The Death Care Industry, July 16, 1996, Darren Martin, TD Securities Inc.)

IMPORTANT INDUSTRY TRENDS

Consolidation

The North American funeral industry was very large and fragmented (See Exhibit 4 for industry structure). This made it ripe for consolidation. Consolidators felt that there were many opportunities for growth and profitability. With an increasing death rate (See Exhibit 6) and more funeral homes being typically family-run businesses, there was great potential for increased revenue generation and cost cutting.

One industry characteristic that directly affected consolidation was the succession crisis. Independent funeral homes needed to deal with the issue of succession, since the average age of a funeral home owner was older than 50. Most independently owned funeral homes were family

---

[3]Sales of at-need burial plots referred to sales that occurred when someone had died.

[4]When a body was cremated, the remains were usually stored in an urn. If the family chose not to scatter the ashes, the urn could be placed in the family home, buried in a cemetery or stored in a cremation niche. Usually, cremation niches were structures in cemeteries that allowed families to store the cremation remains of loved ones. Niches afforded family members an alternative to burying cremation remains while retaining the benefit of having a place where they could visit and remember the departed.

[5]A perpetual care fund was a perpetual annuity that ensured that cemeteries would always have funds for up-keep of the cemetery.

businesses. As with many family businesses, there was often no one who was interested in taking on the succession responsibility. Generally, only 30 per cent of family businesses made it to the second generation, and 10 per cent to the third generation.

Consolidators were typically the only buyers who had access to enough capital to make a market price offer to purchase a funeral home. Obtaining a fair price was crucial to funeral home owners because the equity in their business was, often, their only form of savings.

With issues like a succession crisis, and an increasing death rate, it would seem that there would be a number of new funeral facilities in the market. This was not the case because there were many barriers to entry associated with establishing new facilities. These included elements such as high fixed costs, lack of history in the local community, zoning regulations, and "not-in-my-backyard" protests.

Increasing Consumer Price Sensitivity

There were indications in the market that consumers were looking for lower priced products and services. In response to this demand, there was an increase in "no frills" funeral homes. "No frills" referred to companies who specialized in simple funerals, graveside services, limited or no visitation and frequently no embalming. Another reaction to the demand for lower priced products and services, was the casket shop. Most major cities had casket shops that exclusively sold caskets at prices much lower than those offered by the funeral home. These shops, although in their infancy, had the potential of decreasing casket sales revenues for funeral homes.

Pre-Need Funerals

Pre-need planning was gaining in popularity with consumers. This was because it afforded individuals peace of mind that, upon their death, their loved ones would not be faced with the often-difficult task of making funeral arrangements. In addition to emotional security, pre-need planning also offered financial security. It allowed individuals to determine which types of products and services they were willing to pay for when it came time for them to pass on. It also allowed them to lock into present-day prices.

Pre-need plans were usually financed through trust funds or the purchase of pre-need insurance. Money placed in trust was usually invested in bonds, stocks and other investments; these decisions were very strongly regulated. Money placed in insurance was typically placed with a third-party insurance provider who guaranteed a fixed rate of return, typically four to six per cent. The very conservative approach to investing pre-need dollars did not afford the seller any real opportunities for revenue generation. In fact, with every pre-need contract sold, there was a threat that when the contract came due, on average after 10 to 12 years, the amount of money available would not cover the at-need price of the service. Despite all of these risks, consolidators were very actively selling pre-need contracts.

Cremations

According to the CANA (Cremation Association of North America), cremation rates in the year 2000 would be 35.72 per cent and in the year 2010, they would be 41.80 per cent. The increasing rate of cremations could be attributed to the increasing income and education levels, immigration rates, environmental concerns and the perception of cost savings.

There were significant differences in the way that funeral homes treated cremations relative to traditional funeral services. A traditional service involved a casket, visitation, and a burial ceremony. Traditional cremations had typically been marketed with no visitation, an extremely simple casket, and an urn (See Exhibit 5).

Combination Facilities

Cemeteries had traditionally been considered as suppliers to funeral homes. They supplied burial plots, stones, plaques, etc. With an increase in cremations and combination facilities, cemeteries were very well poised to take a larger role than that of a simple supplier. This represented a threat to the traditional funeral home on many levels. First, the cemetery culture was a sales-oriented culture, i.e., they had been actively selling pre-need plots for decades and, therefore, had access to an extensive list of sales leads, if they decided to sell full pre-need funeral services. Second, with an increase in cremations, items such as crematory niches and cremation viewing facilities (a necessary part of many cultures) represented opportunities for potentially high margins. It was plausible that with increased combination facilities, cremations could become a solely cemetery phenomena. This would steal market share away from the funeral homes and then pose a barrier to entry for new funeral homes. In addition to all of this, combination facilities were able to offer real one-stop-shopping, a definite advantage to the consumer.

Cost Control

Consolidators maintained a cost advantage over independent funeral homes because they were able to take advantage of economies of scale. By using "clustered locations", consolidators were able to significantly reduce their operational costs. Clustering involved centralizing vehicle fleets, embalming operations and corporate management, in addition to buying supplies in bulk and sharing staff.

Competitors

Consolidators in the funeral service industry could be classified by size. The first group consisted of large public companies such as Service Corporation International (SCI), The Loewen Group (Loewen) and Stewart Enterprises (Stewart), whose current equity market capitalization and public float by company exceeded $1 billion. The second group consisted of small companies such as Arbor Memorial Services, Equity Corporation International and Carriage Services, whose current equity market capitalization and public float by company did not exceed $1 billion.

SERVICE CORPORATION INTERNATIONAL

SCI, located in Houston Texas, was the largest funeral service provider in the world with 2,795 funeral homes and 324 cemeteries. In 1996, SCI was expected to have an equity market capitalization of $6.04 billion and revenues of $2.4 billion. Establishments that it owned performed 9, 29, 14 and 24 per cent of the funeral services in North America, France, the UK and Australia, respectively. SCI was also active in the funeral service industries of Malaysia and Singapore. Finally, it was becoming active in the funeral industries of six European countries in addition to France and the UK.

SCI had initiatives in response to all the major industry trends. For example:

- SCI had the second largest backlog (1.5 years) of pre-need funeral services.[6] It also consistently tried to increase its pre-need revenue base. In 1995, 22 per cent of all funerals performed by SCI were pre-arranged. This was the highest percentage in the industry.
- SCI was increasing its presence in the area of combination facilities.
- In response to the potential threat of a more price-sensitive consumer, SCI started its own chain of discount operators called Family Funeral Care.

SCI was successful at leveraging its size through its aggressive use of clustering. At SCI, clustering drove the decisions on where to locate new homes and where to purchase existing ones. SCI was so committed to the concept of clustering that it had developed maps showing death rate projections by zip code and by the company's market share in different areas. Analysts believed that clustering was one of the key drivers of SCI's profitability. Although costs were an important element of operational management, sometimes equally as important, for a consolidator, was the facility with which it integrated new acquisitions. Of all of the large capital companies, SCI seemed to be the most aggressive in terms of integrating its existing acquisitions. This was clearly seen in the following comments made by Robert Waltrip, Chairman of the SCI Board of Directors:

> What many in this industry don't seem to understand or want to believe is that when we make a purchase, we have to introduce our way of doing business. You can't spend $100 million to buy a business of that size and just go on doing business the old way.

("Robert Waltrip Takes on His Critics," Mortuary Management, May 1993)

SCI's approach to integration was aggressive and detail oriented. Previous owners and managers were often asked to step aside. Owners who were retained, worked solely in public relations on a part-time basis. This allowed SCI to benefit from the owners' community presence and network. SCI used a decentralized approach to manage its network of homes. SCI had recently changed its organizational structure from eight regions to 17 regions. This was done to allow regional managers to be more in touch with their areas and to be able to make decisions in more proximity to their respective homes.

In terms of acquisitions, SCI tended to concentrate on urban homes. It prided itself on owning quality institutions. Like most industry players it retained the original names of its acquisitions to benefit from the goodwill. However, SCI claimed that goodwill was not the only factor that kept its customers coming back. Excellent service levels and quality personnel also played a key role in customer retention. SCI acquired many of its homes based on referrals from Provident. Provident was SCI's financial subsidiary. It lent money to independent funeral home operators. Provident played an important role in allowing SCI to keep its fingers on the pulse of the industry.

---

[6]A backlog of 1.5 years in pre-need funeral services was interpreted as follows: If all the company's pre-need funerals came due, the company would be able to run at full capacity for 1.5 years without performing any at-need services.

MR. LOEWEN AND THE LOEWEN GROUP

Ray Loewen

In 1961, Ray Loewen graduated from Briercrest Theological College before joining his father in the family funeral home in Steinbach, Manitoba. He left the family firm to purchase, along with his wife, Anne, their own funeral home in Fort Frances, Ontario, and subsequently another home in the Lower Mainland of B.C. Times were good and by 1975, Loewen owned a number of different funeral homes. He turned to politics to serve one term as the Social Credit MLA for Burnaby-Edmonds in the B.C. legislature. In 1979, he returned to his business career. More and more, the owners of funeral homes whose children were either unable or unwilling to take over the family business were searching for an answer to the question of their own succession. This represented an excellent opportunity for the Loewen Group. Loewen knew that by raising money on the stock exchange and using it to acquire these homes, while enabling local owner families to remain as active in the business as they would like, he could make Loewen Group a national presence. In 1987, fuelled by Loewen Group's first public offering, Ray Loewen acquired $24 million in funeral establishments and acquired its first U.S. property.

Mr. and Mrs. Loewen owned 15 per cent of the company's voting shares and, in his capacity as CEO and Chairman of the Board of Directors, Ray Loewen played an active role in guiding senior management. He took a real interest in the operations of the company and had a grass roots understanding of the business, given his background. This meant he was sensitive to the needs of funeral directors.

Mr. Loewen looked on his growing complement of employees as part of a family and felt they should all be able to participate in the company. This led to the introduction of "Sharing The Vision," an employee stock plan with employees receiving five free shares and being offered a stock purchase program. This reflected Mr. Loewen's vision of having a company in which every employee was a shareholder. When he described his management philosophy, he liked to use the analogy of an eagle's flight: one wing was the caregiving at the heart of funeral service, the other, fiscal responsibility. The eagle needed both wings to soar. Mr. Loewen was passionate about the Loewen Group and he counted on his management and employees for their full support.

Acquisitions Group

Since 1992, the acquisition growth rates for Loewen, SCI and Stewart had all been greater than 50 per cent (See Exhibit 6). Loewen attributed its position to four key competitive advantages. First and foremost, it had an acquisition group that was very skilled and very dedicated to identifying and closing the sale. Second, Loewen's Regional Partnership Program had often accounted for more than 50 per cent of its yearly acquisitions. This program allowed Loewen to capitalize on the skills and network contacts acquired through its acquisitions by partnering up with the previous owners. These owners helped Loewen initiate new acquisitions in return for a 10 per cent ownership stake in every successful referral. Loewen participated in about 20 of these types of partnerships. Third, Loewen had built a reputation for doing its utmost to satisfy the needs of sellers. Fourth, with its acquisition of Osiris Holdings, a large and successful cemetery management company, Loewen was building its in-house expertise in cemetery management.

Competition around acquisitions was not entirely price-based, since all major industry consolidators were amply capable of matching each other's price offers. Instead, competition was based on the more intangible nature of acquisitions. Loewen claimed it had one of the most customer-focused approaches and a genuine concern for sellers' needs. In every single acquisition, Loewen maintained the funeral home's name. It also strove to increase the brand equity of this name by offering excellent service, being involved in the community, and improving the facilities. When Loewen purchased a home, it tended to keep all employees in place. This allowed seamless service during the acquisition process and was in line with preserving the home's heritage and community appeal. Also, the salaries and benefits it introduced were usually an improvement over what had previously been offered. Owners and their families could remain active in the management of the business. In terms of capital gains and other financial issues, Loewen was extremely flexible. It did anything from paying a large cash portion up front, usually 75 per cent, to a share for share stock issue. In some cases it had even agreed to lease a home, although this was not common practice.

Given Loewen's penchant for smaller homes, it has a reputation as the "country bumpkin" of funeral home acquirers. This was a misnomer because like its competitors, Loewen also acquired large, urban funeral homes in the $10 million to $50 million range. However, given that these opportunities were not commonplace, Loewen had developed an infrastructure that allowed it to identify and purchase smaller, yet very profitable, homes in more rural areas.

As the number of acquisitions grew, Loewen became increasingly strategic in its expansion planning. This was explained by Mr. J. P. Gabille, Loewen's Vice President of Corporate Development: "We use many different criteria to evaluate a home. For example, we prefer larger operations, reputable operations, profitability, good staff, etc. Until about two or three years ago we just bought funeral homes that met our criteria. Now we are much more strategic, i.e., trying to build hubs, consolidating existing properties to create new, more high quality properties, building new homes to fill the gaps. We currently have 20 to 25 new homes in progress."

Loewen believed that its reputation as "the preferred acquirer" was a significant advantage in attracting high quality acquisitions. Loewen endeavoured to develop this image by paying competitive prices for homes and cemeteries, being very flexible in the integration of these establishments, and going the extra mile to satisfy the needs and concerns of sellers. Many independent funeral establishments indicated that they would prefer selling to the Loewen Group rather than to other consolidators, a position that saw many holding on until Loewen's 1995 Mississippi court case problems were resolved in early 1996. The company planned to sign or close a record number of acquisitions that year. However, for every funeral director that preferred Loewen Group, there seemed to be a funeral director that preferred SCI.

Operations Management

Mr. Harry Rath, VP of Eastern Canada, described how Loewen integrated its acquisitions: "Loewen does not have homogeneous operating guidelines for the various homes we own. We understand the importance of local culture and allow our homes a great deal of leeway in operations. We make one very important change, i.e., we impose the utilization of budgets[7] that can be agreed upon together, and we insist on regular accountability and encourage accountability. Our expectations are clear. We are also very interested in helping funeral homes achieve their goals, i.e., you don't only see us during budget time. For example, as VP Operations of Eastern Canada, I oversee 62 funeral homes,

---

[7]Once a home had been acquired, the use of Loewen's legal counsel and insurance provider was non-negotiable.

with the help of some regional managers. All my homes know me personally. I am available to them for guidance and assistance."

One of the challenges faced by Loewen was the balancing act between operational profitability and commitment to its corporate culture. Loewen paid close attention to cost control and efficiency improvement. However, with the pressures for continual growth and with the various events in the life of the company, Loewen found the balancing act more and more difficult to manage.

Marketing Orientation

In terms of pre-need, Loewen's unfulfilled prearranged funeral contracts amounted to $750 million. This equated to a backlog of just under 1.5 years of services. Loewen realized the importance of increasing its pre-need sales and hoped to be more aggressive in the future. At present, 16 per cent of all funeral services performed by the Loewen Group were pre-arranged. It was hoped that by 1997, Loewen would increase its pre-need funeral revenues by five to 10 per cent.

In terms of cremations, Loewen expected that by the year 2000, its cremation rate would jump from 26 per cent, in 1995, to 28.21 per cent. To deal with the industry's gradual shift towards cremations, Loewen had increased its acquisition of cemeteries and had developed a "Celebration of Life" program. This program allowed Loewen to sell cremations in such a way that they were almost as profitable and often more profitable than the traditional funeral service. Traditionally, cremations were treated in the same way as dispositions. No effort was made to provide families with visitation, a memorial service, a reception, etc. This was because funeral homes did not understand their cremation customers. When a customer chose cremation, he or she was not choosing a less dignified funeral service; he or she was only choosing not to be buried. Loewen's "Celebration of Life" program trained its funeral directors to sell cremations just like traditional funerals. Brian Falvey, Loewen's Celebration of Life program coordinator for Cape Cod, explained:

> The family had never had a cremation before . . .but they wanted to respect the mother's wishes . . .They also wanted to have some type of religious service and a final chance to say goodbye to her.

> (VISION Magazine, November / December 1996, The Loewen Group Inc.)

By explaining the Celebration of Life philosophy, Brian assured the couple that together they could tailor arrangements to include a private family viewing at the funeral home, followed by a religious service conducted by a local minister. Furthermore, he would personally supervise the burial of the cremated remains at an out-of-state family plot.

> They were surprised that all this could take place. Like many people, they didn't realize that these arrangements could be made in conjunction with a cremation.

> (VISION Magazine, November / December 1996, The Loewen Group Inc.)

Organizational Culture

> Stock at funeral home owner Loewen Group has risen nearly $5, to a recent 35¼, since a recent promotion that carried the message: Exercise, Eat Well, Stay HealthyXWe Can Wait.

> (Forbes, July 3, 1995.)

Loewen's organizational culture was truly captured in the above few lines. The key tenet of the Loewen culture was that employees believed that the company was doing something good, something beyond just making money. The Loewen Group insisted that they were not solely a funeral consolidator or a funeral service operator, they were both. This belief provided a strong sense of purpose to employees.

Shareholder Relations

From 1990 to 1994, when Loewen was experiencing high growth levels and good profitability, there was never a need for formal shareholder relations. However, with the loss of a major legal battle[8] causing share prices to fall from $41 to $18, shareholder relations became crucial. After this immense drop in share price, Loewen's financial people became very active and for two months they never stopped talking to investors. Their goal was to communicate the key message that Loewen's stock was undervalued and, with a little time, would be trading at its previously high multiples. These trips were very successful, as the market saw some active purchasing of Loewen stock and an increase in stock prices. Other methods by which shareholders were kept abreast of Loewen's activities included: a detailed annual report, Loewen's *VISION Magazine*[9] and conference calls between Mr. Loewen and the company's major shareholders. However, despite all of these tactics, the most important link to shareholders was that, notwithstanding any crises, Loewen maintained its acquisition pace and operational profitability.

Finance

Every year since 1990, Loewen had successfully raised funds from the public. Loewen had a very innovative financial group that regularly developed new types of issues that allowed increased fund raising and increased returns for potential buyers. For example, even after coming close to bankruptcy after the Mississippi trial, Loewen's financial people, with the assistance of Nesbitt Burns and RBC Dominion securities, designed a convertible preferred security with a seven-year term to raise funds for increased acquisitions. Funds were placed in trust to ensure that they would be used for acquisitions and not legal obligations. This financing tool helped Loewen raise US$200 million.

Another innovative tactic used by Loewen was a partnership with Blackstone Capital Partners II Merchant Banking Fund LP. This partnership allowed Loewen to make strategic acquisitions off the balance sheet. The first was Prime Succession Inc., a consolidator that had 16 cemeteries and 146 funeral homes in the U.S. Prime Succession was purchased for $295 million. Loewen paid $72 million and held 20 per cent of the shares, with an option to buy the remaining 80 per cent after four years. Until that time, the 80 per cent would be held by Blackstone. Loewen's holdings were primarily preferred shares and Blackstone's holdings were common shares. Its partnership with Blackstone allowed Loewen to make strategic deals, while leaving enough capital free to continue to make other acquisitions.

---

[8]The major legal battle in question was the Mississippi case. Details of the Mississippi case are provided later on.

[9]VISION Magazine was a publication that Loewen sent to all its funeral establishments, industry analysts, shareholders and other industry stakeholders. It allowed Loewen to explain what was going on in the company, from the perspective of an individual funeral home right up to major issues like the Mississippi case.

Competitive Rivalry

The two largest competitors in the North American market were Loewen and SCI. Nationally, they competed with each other in terms of acquisitions and regionally for market share. Increasing acquisitions and ensuring their successful integration were fundamental to the success of both companies. However, both Loewen and SCI approached acquisition and integration in different ways.

Business Activity	SCI	Loewen
Personnel	Almost all of the homes purchased by SCI were part of a clustering strategy. Clustering allowed the company to decrease operational costs by pooling and sharing resources among regionally proximate homes. Clustering saved personnel costs because it allowed homes to operate with a skeletal staff while being able to call upon floater employees for assistance.	It was part of Loewen's integration strategy not to make significant changes to the staffing levels of a newly acquired funeral home. The preservation of a funeral establishment's brand equity was very important to Loewen and it viewed personnel as a key component.
Facilities	Clustering allowed SCI to centralize functions such as embalming and preparing the body.	Loewen did not centralize its embalming or preparation facilities.
Automotive Equipment	Typically at SCI, every cluster shared one fleet of cars.	Loewen did not actively centralize its use of automobiles. However, some homes often shared automobiles.
Management	SCI offered a great deal of training and had a large number of managers available to assist homes with specific problems. From an organizational perspective, a home was about four management tiers away from the head office.	Training was an important component of Loewen's integration process. Funeral home managers worked closely with the Regional Vice Presidents to develop budgets together. Budgeting was done on an individual home level, taking into account factors in each home's microenvironment. All Regional Vice Presidents reported directly to the Head Office.

Business Activity	SCI	Loewen
Locations of Acquisitions	The driver behind SCI's growth strategy was clustering. Rarely were homes purchased that did not fit into one cluster or the other.	Loewen tended to acquire profitable homes that showed the potential for sustainable and/or increasing future profits and growth. It focused on smaller "mom & pop" operations with larger returns on investment. Loewen developed greater regional market share in some areas via strategic (large, urban) acquisitions.
Purchasing	SCI used a centralized purchasing program, both at the regional and national levels. Purchases of vehicles, caskets, cremation urns, grave markers were centralized at the national level.	Loewen often allowed funeral establishments to keep their suppliers intact, especially if relationships were profitable. However, Loewen had established large volume contracts for most of its supply needs.
Legal Counsel/ Insurance	Centralized	Centralized

These different approaches were very important to potential funeral home sellers. Funeral home sellers were not only interested in selling to the highest bidder, but typically had a number of criteria that had to be met before a sales deal could be signed. For example, funeral home owners were very concerned with:

- preservation of the funeral home's name and heritage
- job security of their managers and non-management staff
- fair staff remuneration
- maintenance of the home's community involvement
- the maintenance of a service to the community image as opposed to a corporate business image

Of these owners, those who were selling larger establishments involving stock trades were also concerned with issues related to:

- the company's acquisition growth rate
- historical and future growth in the stock price
- meeting industry trends head on
- company cost structures and profitability

See Exhibit 10 for a comparison of SCI and Loewen along some key financial indicators.

Strategy

Loewen's strategic direction had not significantly changed in the last few years. It was clearly and simply stated in its 1995 annual report as follows:

> The company capitalizes on these attractive industry fundamentals through a growth strategy that emphasizes three principal components (i) acquiring a significant number of small, family-owned funeral homes and cemeteries; (ii) acquiring strategic operations consisting predominantly of large, multi-location urban properties that generally serve as platforms for acquiring small, family-owned businesses in surrounding regions; and (iii) improving the revenue and profitability of newly-acquired and established locations. The first element of the Company's growth strategy is the acquisition of small, family-owned funeral homes and cemeteries. Management believes the Company has a competitive advantage in this market due to its culture and its well-known and understood reputation for honoring existing owners and staff. The final element of the Company's growth strategy is its focus on enhancing the revenue and profitability of newly acquired and established locations.

Cemeteries were going to play a major role in Loewen's strategy over the next few years. Loewen executives forecasted that from 1997 onwards, 30 to 40 per cent of all revenues would come from cemeteries.

THE FAMOUS MISSISSIPPI CASE

In 1990, Loewen made two major purchases in Mississippi. The first was an insurance company and funeral homes from the Riemann Family of Gulfport, Mississippi and the second was a Jackson-based funeral home from Wright & Ferguson funeral directors. A large funeral home operator in the Gulfport area was Jerry O'Keefe, who owned Gulf National Life Insurance Company and some funeral homes and cemeteries. Prior to Loewen's acquisition of the Wright & Ferguson funeral homes, Gulf National had an exclusive contract with Wright & Ferguson, to exclusively sell it's "burial insurance" as this product was defined in Mississippi. Gulf National also had a non-exclusive representation contract with Wright & Ferguson, to sell "pre-need" insurance (a different product than burial insurance) on behalf of Wright & Ferguson. O'Keefe commenced a court action, following Loewen's acquisition of Wright & Ferguson, claiming that since the Loewen acquisition, Wright & Ferguson had not been honoring the exclusivity agreement with respect to burial insurance. O'Keefe sued Loewen for breach of contract. In reply, Loewen's position was that it had at all times scrupulously honored the exclusivity contract with burial insurance; however, burial insurance had become out of date, and most funeral insurance being sold was of the pre-need variety, and Gulf National had no exclusivity provision with respect to pre-need insurance.

The parties subsequently entered into a settlement agreement settling the litigation, whereby Loewen agreed to sell to Gulf National its insurance company (purchased from Riemann) and O'Keefe would sell to Loewen, two of its funeral homes. The settlement agreement was clearly made subject to subsequent agreement on the valuation of the funeral homes; the valuation of the insurance company; mutually satisfactory design of a new insurance product; and mutually satisfactory agreement on a new agency representation agreement. A number of these "subject to" provisions were never satisfied, and the settlement agreement therefore did not complete. O'Keefe then amended his lawsuit to claim that Loewen breached the settlement agreement and acted in bad faith.

The litigation took place in Jackson, Mississippi, before judge and jury. With respect to the settlement agreement, the total value of the assets involved (the insurance company and two funeral homes) was approximately $6 million. Close to trial, O'Keefe hired Willie Gary, a renowned Plaintiff's contingency fee lawyer in the United States. Many people felt that, as a result, the case was not based on facts in law but rather on an emotional, "theatre of mind" approach to the jury.

The jury's verdict was in favor of O'Keefe for an amount of US$500 million which amounted to 20 times the damages stated by the Plaintiff in pre-trial motions. Loewen wished to appeal the result, but under Mississippi court rules, a pre-condition of the appeal was that Loewen post a full-cash bond in the amount of US$625 million. Accordingly, Loewen's lawyers began making preparations to voluntarily file for Chapter 11, since a filing in Chapter 11 would permit the appeal to go forward without the necessity of filing the $625 million bond.

In the result, the Company was able to settle with O'Keefe on an after-tax basis to the Company of US$85 million, consisting of a combination of cash, shares, and a promissory note.

The initial result of the bizarre jury award was to send Loewen's share price spiralling down from CDN$41.00 to CDN$18.00 per share. The process of dealing with the aftermath of the Mississippi jury award, and the consequent need to refinance the Company left management tired after a challenge that lasted many months. About six months after the settlement of the case, SCI announced its hostile takeover bid.

Options facing the Loewen Group

As Mr. Loewen heard the letter, sent by SCI's President, William Heiligbrodt, several thoughts ran through his head:

- Was the price being offered for Loewen shares a fair value?
- Was selling the Loewen Group in the best interest of shareholders and other stakeholders?
- Could the Loewen Group guarantee that dollar for dollar it would be able to generate a better return than SCI?

Exhibit 1:

L. William Heiligbrodt
President
September 17, 1996

Mr. Raymond L. Loewen
Chairman of the Board and Chief Executive Officer
The Loewen Group Inc.
4126 Norland Avenue
Burnaby, British Columbia, Canada

Dear Mr. Loewen:

As you know, I have tried to reach you several times since September 11. While your office has assured me that you received my messages, my calls have not been returned. In view of that, and in view of the importance of this matter, I am sending this letter.

I would like to discuss with you a combination of our two companies. The combination would involve a stock-for-stock exchange accounted for as a pooling which values Loewen Group at US$43 per share. We believe that this transaction can be structured in a manner that is tax-free to both companies and (except for a relatively nominal amount in the case of U.S. stockholders) to the U.S. and Canadian stockholders of Loewen Group.

I think you and your Board and stockholders would agree that our proposal is a generous one, resulting in the following premiums for Loewen Group stockholders:

- 48.9% above the price at which Loewen Group stock traded 30 days ago;
- 39.3% above the price at which Loewen Group stock traded one week ago; and
- 27.4% above the price at which Loewen Group stock is currently trading.

This represents an opportunity for your stockholders to realize excellent value, by any measure, for their shares. In addition, and importantly, since your stockholders would be receiving stock, they would continue to participate in Loewen Group's business as well as share in the upside of our business.

Thus, in essence, your stockholders would:

- continue their investment in our industry;
- get an immediate, and very significant, increase in the market value of their investment;
- get that immediate and substantial increase on an essentially tax free basis; and
- diversify their risk by participating in a much larger number of properties.

This is a "win-win" situation for you and your stockholders.

Finally, with respect to consideration, I would note also that our proposal is based on public information. After a due diligence review, we may be in a position to increase the consideration that your stockholders would receive.

We, of course, recognize that our businesses overlap in various locations. We have carefully reviewed this matter and are convinced that competition issues can be cured by selecting divestitures without impairment of the values that a combination would achieve for the stockholders of our two companies.

I would very much like to discuss any and all aspects of our proposal with you and your Board of Directors. We believe you and they will recognize the tremendous benefit to your stockholders of our proposal. Our proposal is conditioned upon approval of our Board and upon negotiation of mutually satisfactory agreements providing for a combination on a pooling basis.

We hope that after you meet with us, you will similarly determine that the transaction should be pursued. We look forward to hearing from you.

In view of the importance of this matter, we are simultaneously releasing this letter to the press.

Sincerely,

William Heiligbrodt
President

Exhibit 2: **Typical Income Statement of an Independent Funeral Home ($)**

	1986	1991	1992	1993	1996
Average "Regular Adult Funeral" Services & Casket	2766.26	3507.19	3663.49	3819.17	4287.14
Operation Cost per Adult Funeral	2015.75	2597.69	2717.2	2823.03	3160.33
Percentage of Operating Cost to Selling Price	72.87%	74.07%	74.17%	73.92%	73.72%
Casket Cost	469.99	606.04	627.7	652.18	729.68
Percentage of Casket Cost to Selling Price	16.99%	17.28%	17.13%	17.08%	17.02%
Profit Before Federal Income Tax	280.52	303.46	318.59	343.96	397.13
Percentage of Profit to Selling Price	10.14%	8.65%	8.70%	9.01%	9.26%

Using data from Federated Funeral Directors of America

Breakdown of Operational Expenses for a Typical Independent Funeral Home ($)

	1986	% of Rev.	1991	% of Rev.	1992	% of Rev.	1993	% of Rev.	1996	% of Rev.
Personnel	913.33	33.02	1209.51	34.49	1266.75	34.58	1347.55	35.28	1507.20	35.16
Cost of Facilities	602.78	21.79	789.55	22.51	811.81	22.16	830.13	21.74	919.32	21.44
Automotive Equipment	207.43	7.50	213.11	6.08	222.42	6.07	223.20	5.84	256.50	5.98
Promotion	118.48	4.28	146.72	4.18	157.10	4.29	159.12	4.17	173.06	4.04
Business Service	65.06	2.35	86.49	2.47	90.12	2.46	93.52	2.45	107.46	2.51
Supplies	59.51	2.15	74.69	2.13	79.35	2.17	83.08	2.18	92.32	2.15
After Sale Expenses	41.05	1.48	66.90	1.91	78.50	2.14	75.49	1.98	93.57	2.18
Sundry	8.11	0.29	10.72	0.31	11.15	0.30	10.94	0.29	10.90	0.25
Total Operating Expenses	2015.75		2597.69		2717.20		2823.03		3160.33	

Using data from Federated Funeral Directors of America

Exhibit 3: Typical Income Statement of a Cemetery

	$	%
Revenues		
Pre-Need Sales	$1,173,000	65.9%**
At-Need Sales	213,000	11.9%**
Other	395,000	22.2%**
	1,781,000	100.0%**
Cost & Expenses		
Cost of Sales	313,000	22.6%*
Selling	446,000	32.1%*
Cemetery Maintenance	259,000	14.5%**
G & A	215,000	12.1%**
	1,233,000	69.2%**
Cemetery Gross Margin	**$ 548,000**	**30.8%****

*   Percentage of P/N + A/N Sales
**   Percentage of Total Revenues

Exhibit 4: Ownership Distribution in the Industry

Funeral Homes

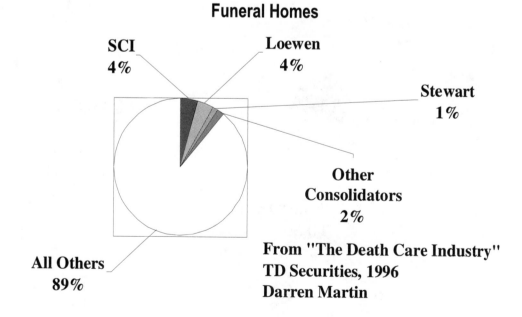

SCI
4%

Loewen
4%

Stewart
1%

Other
Consolidators
2%

All Others
89%

**From "The Death Care Industry"
TD Securities, 1996
Darren Martin**

Cemeteries

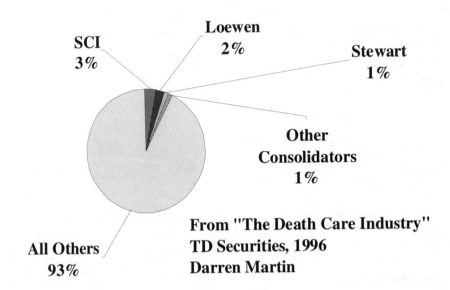

SCI
3%

Loewen
2%

Stewart
1%

Other
Consolidators
1%

All Others
93%

From "The Death Care Industry"
TD Securities, 1996
Darren Martin

Breakdown of Death Care Industry Revenue by Company in the United States and Canada

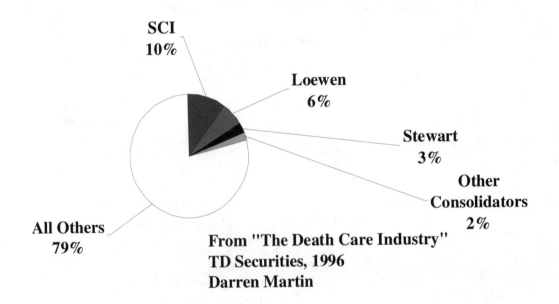

SCI
10%

Loewen
6%

Stewart
3%

Other
Consolidators
2%

All Others
79%

From "The Death Care Industry"
TD Securities, 1996
Darren Martin

Exhibit 5: **Typical Charges for a Funeral Service ($)**

Itemized Charges	Home1 Traditional Service	Home2 Traditional Service	Home3 Traditional Service	Average Traditional Service	Average Simple Cremation
Professional Services					
Basic Service	730	255	1,070	685	NA
Visitation	370	365	0	245	NA
Day of Service	300	275	0	192	NA
Documentation	130	155	145	143	NA
Embalming	60	150	285	165	NA
Other Preparation	50	0	0	17	NA
Facilities and Equipment					
Basic Facility	450	275	625	450	NA
Visitation	130	300	0	143	NA
Day of Service	200	0	0	67	NA
Preparation Room	90	110	150	117	NA
Retaining Room	140	0	0	47	NA
Motor Vehicles					
Initial Transfer	260	120	195	192	NA
General Purpose Vehicle	100	85	125	103	NA
Funeral Coach	205	195	195	198	NA
Total Charges	3,215	2,285	2,790	2,763	827
Casket	3,500	2,500	2,700	2,900	288
Urn					567
Total	**6,715**	**4,785**	**5,490**	**5,663**	**1,682**

Using Data from Consumer Funeral Home Information Packages, July 1996.

Exhibit 6: **DOLLAR VALUES OF ACQUISITIONS AS ESTIMATED BY LOEWEN (000's)**

	Loewen	SCI	Stewart
1992	83,200	203,774	33,962
1993	148,000	226,415	95,094
1994	265,000	815,094	178,868
1995	487,900	1,138,868	149,434
1996	1,154,600	498,113	201,509
1997E	600,000	498,113	249,057
1998E	840,000	647,547	336,226
1999E	1,680,000	874,189	470,717
2000E	3,780,000	1,223,864	682,540

Exhibit 7: **PROJECTED DEATH RATE**

Projected Annual Deaths: United States (millions/year)

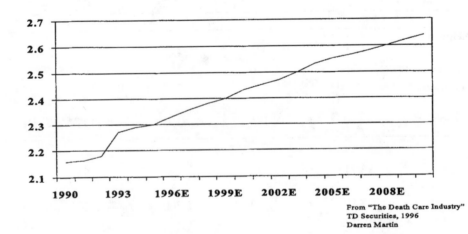

From "The Death Care Industry"
TD Securities, 1996
Darren Martin

Exhibit 8: **Income Statement** (US$000's)

Income Statement	1995	1994	1993	1992	1991	1990	1989	1988
Revenue								
Funeral	441,352	353,904	275,106	202,748	150,943	92,391	52,856	35,566
Cemetery	143,577	63,424	27,905	16,159	11,662	8,565	4,427	1,987
Insurance	13,564		0	0	0	0	0	0
Total Revenues	598,493	417,328	303,011	218,907	162,605	100,956	57,283	37,553
Costs and Expenses								
Funeral	258,872	210,471	166,782	123,044	90,861	55,237	29,759	20,557
Cemetery	103,726	48,003	21,111	12,155	8,657	5,152	3,152	1,240
Insurance	10,533	0	0	0	0	0	0	0
Cost of Goods Sold	373,131	258,474	187,893	135,199	99,518	60,389	32,911	21,797
Revenues - Costs of Goods Sold	225,362	158,854	115,118	83,708	63,087	40,567	24,372	15,756
Expenses								
General and Administrative Expenses	67,652	34,751	28,225	17,086	12,981	7,495	4,278	2,101
Depreciation and amortization	40,103	28,990	21,196	16,059	11,053	5,876	3,254	2,166
Total Expenses	107,755	63,741	49,421	33,145	24,034	13,371	7,532	4,267
Earnings from Operations	117,607	95,113	65,697	50,563	39,053	27,196	16,840	11,489
Interest on long-term debt	50,913	34,203	21,801	19,083	14,913	10,914	7,177	4,916
Legal Settlements	184,914	0	0					
Earnings (loss) before undernoted items	-118,220	60,910	43,896	31,480	24,140	16,282	9,663	6,573
Dividends on preferred securities of subsidiary	7,088	2,678	0					
Earnings (loss) before income taxes and undernoted items	-125,308	58,232	43,896	31,480	24,140	16,282	9,663	6,573
Total Income Taxes	-47,178	19,738	15,714	11,714	9,715	6,549	4,215	3,152
Net Income not incl. Equity/earnings from assoc.companies	-78,130	38,494	28,182	19,766	14,425	9,733	5,448	3,421
Equity and other earnings of associated companies	1,446	0						
Net Earnings (loss) for the year	-76,684	38,494	28,182	19,766	14,425	9,733	5,448	3,421
Basic Earnings (loss) per common share	-1.69	0.97	0.77	0.59	0.46	0.39	0.31	0.23
Dividend per Common Share	0.05	0.07	0.045	0.032	0.017	0	0	0
Dividend per Preferred Share	0	0	0	0	0	0.288	0.586	0.327
Number of Common shares at year-end (in thousands)	48,168	41,015	38,647	35,534	32,754	28,391	19,977	12,849
Common share price at year-end ($Cdn.)	34.38	36.75	33.25	19.63	15.63	12.5	9.31	5.31
Common share price at year-end ($U.S.)	25.31	26.5	25.38	15.5	13.38	10.63	n/a	n/a

Exhibit 9: **Balance Sheet** (US$000's)

	1995	1994	1993	1992	1991	1990	1989	1988
Current Assets								
Cash and term deposits	39,454	15,349	18,167	12,176	16,035	9,706	17,940	3,180
Receivables, ,net of allowances	115,953	70,547	51,684	37,211	27,451	25,063	10,574	5,882
Inventories	27,489	19,673	15,952	12,323	8,165	6,381	2,919	1,805
Prepaid Expenses	8,185	4,299	4,941	3,974	2,248	785	956	645
Total Current Assets	191,081	109,868	90,744	65,684	53,899	41,935	32,389	11,512
Prearranged Funeral Services	245,854	178,982	175,216	146,109	127,086	104,413	49,524	33,343
Long-term receivables, net of allowances	167,367	67,895	30,059	11,460	5,725	2,319		
Investments	86,815	78,269	3,749	1,338	915	921		
Insurance invested assets	97,024							
Cemetery property at cost	369,022	114,861	48,158	24,135	15,939	15,230	3,160	2,859
Property and equipment	551,965	426,038	346,244	284,654	216,851	159,438	79,417	52,442
Names and Reputations	424,944	314,599	199,514	126,156	87,547	72,982	25,363	17,910
Deferred Income Taxes	61,959							
Other Assets	66,949	35,763	19,977	15,575	10,530	6,881	2,845	4,091
Total Assets	2,262,980	1,326,275	913,661	675,111	518,492	404,119	192,698	122,157
Liabilities and Shareholders' Equity								
Current Liabilities								
Current indebtedness	38,546	3,700	4,435	3,558		5,404		
Accrued settlements	53,000							
Accounts payable and accrued liabilities	80,058	48,436	37,952	22,715	13,601	14,013	6,504	4,188
Income taxes payable				446	730		589	1,582
Long-term debt, current position	69,671	45,529	6,572	7,553	6,073	6,088	4,431	2,990
Total Current Liabilities	241,275	97,665	48,959	34,272	20,404	25,505	11,524	8,760
Long-term debt	864,838	471,125	335,405	239,162	187,780	141,072	61,280	44,613
Subordinated debentures						8,956	8,571	8,240
Other Liabilities	136,433	83,678	22,327	16,439	9,415	5,956	375	458
Insurance policy liabilities	84,898							
Deferred income taxes		8,686	5,864	2,812	1,413	385	1,364	1,485
Deferred prearranged funeral services revenue	245,854	178,982	175,216	146,109	127,086	104,413	49,524	33,343
Preferred Securities of Subsidiary	75,000	75,000						
Total Non-Current Liabilities	1,407,023	817,471	538,812	404,522	325,694	260,782	121,114	88,139
Shareholders' Equity								
Common shares	490,055	282,560	227,968	172,133	139,151	98,031	42,418	11,828
Common shares issuable under legal settlements	72,000							
Preferred shares							7,566	7,566
Retained earnings	36,439	115,492	79,867	53,382	34,651	20,720	11,275	6,414
Foreign exchange adjustment	16,188	13,087	18,055	10,802	-1,408	-919	-1,199	-550
Total Shareholders' Equity	614,682	411,139	325,890	236,317	172,394	117,832	60,060	25,258
Total Liabilities and Shareholders' Equity	2,262,980	1,326,275	913,661	675,111	518,492	404,119	192,698	122,157
Number of funeral homes	815	640	533	451	365	268	131	98
Number of cemeteries	179	116	70	38	23	21	7	5
Number of funeral services	114,000	94,000	7,900	64,000	52,000	34,000	22,000	18,000
Number of employees	10,000	7,000	5,000	4,000	3,000	2,000	1,000	1,000
Business acquisitions in millions	487.9	265.6	148	83.2	68.5	140.2	31.5	30.8

Exhibit 10:   **Key Financial Indicators**

	1995	1994	1993	1992	1991	1990	1989	1988
Gross Profit Margins on Funeral Homes for Loewen	41.4%	40.5%	39.4%	39.3%	39.8%	40.2%	43.7%	42.2%
Gross Profit Margins on Cemeteries for Loewen	27.8%	24.3%	24.4%	24.8%	25.8%	39.9%	28.8%	37.6%
Gross Profit Margins on Funeral Homes For SCI	25.3%	29.5%	29.4%	28.8%	28.7%	29.4%	28.2%	29.5%
Gross Profit Margins on Cemeteries for SCI	34.6%	32.1%	28.4%	24.4%	22.9%	20.0%	18.8%	19.7%
EPS for Loewen (US$)	-1.69	0.97	0.76	0.58	0.46			
EPS for SCI (US$)	1.70	1.43	1.17	1.07	1.00			
Growth Per Year in EPS at Loewen	-274.2%	27.6%	31.0%	26.0%				
Growth Per Year in EPS at SCI	18.9%	22.2%	9.4%	7.0%				
Share Price at Loewen (US$)	25.31	26.50	25.38	15.50	13.38			
Share Price at SCI (US$)	33.17	25.56	22.00	17.38	16.09			
Growth Per Year in Share Price at Loewen	-4.5%	4.4%	63.7%	15.8%				
Growth Per Year in Share Price at SCI	29.8%	16.2%	26.6%	8.0%				
Return on Sales for Loewen	-12.8%	9.2%	9.3%	9.0%	8.9%	9.6%	9.5%	
Return on Sales for SCI	11.1%	11.7%	11.5%	11.2%	11.4%	10.7%	9.0%	
Return on Total Asset for SCI	2.4%	2.5%	2.8%	3.3%	3.5%	3.6%	2.9%	
Return on Total Asset for Loewen	-3.4%	2.9%	3.1%	2.9%	2.8%	2.4%	2.8%	
Return on Equity for Loewen	-12.4%	9.4%	8.7%	8.4%	8.4%	8.7%	9.1%	
Return on Equity for SCI	9.3%	11.0%	11.7%	12.7%	11.9%	13.9%	8.4%	

Source: Annual Reports of the Loewen Group and Service Corporation International

MEUBLES CANADEL: LOOKING TOWARDS THE FUTURE

case 15

Ken Mark
Louis Hébert and
Mary M Crossan

INTRODUCTION

In less than 20 years, Canadel (www.canadel.com), based in Louiseville, Quebec, had become Canada's leading manufacturer of casual dining room furniture. Following the entry into the U.S. market in 1992, sales had multiplied eight-fold and were expected to reach $125 million in 2000. Canadel's top management team, the three Deveault brothers, Guy, Michel and Jean, were discussing recent results and future orientations of the firm. Some questions that surfaced included growth in existing and new markets, and competition from established industry giants and new startups. The Deveaults were determined to assess these opportunities and threats in the upcoming weeks.

IVEY

Ken Mark prepared this case under the supervision of Professors Louis Hébert and Mary Crossan solely to provide material for class discussion. The authors do not intend to illustrate either effective or ineffective handling of a managerial situation. The authors may have disguised certain names and other identifying information to protect confidentiality.

THE NORTH AMERICAN FURNITURE MARKET

With an estimated value of about US$100 billion in 2000, the global market for household furniture showed a wide range of consumer preferences in terms of style, design, uniqueness, quality and price. The United States was the world's biggest market (28 per cent of the world market) as well as the home base of most of the world's biggest manufacturers. Other major markets were Japan and Germany (15 per cent and 10 per cent respectively).

The Canadian market for household furniture was estimated to US$3.5 billion in 2000. After some difficult years in the early '90s, the Canadian market had registered annual growth above 10 per cent since 1996. U.S. exports of furniture to Canada, valued at US$1.4 billion in 1999, represented approximately 70 per cent of Canada's total import furniture market in 1997. The success of the U.S. furniture suppliers in Canada reflected the advantages that U.S. manufacturers enjoyed over Asian suppliers, including geographical proximity, common furniture designs, similar quality demands, tariff-free entry and similar channels of distribution.[1] In turn, Canadian producers exported just over Cdn$1 billion in to the United States (who absorbed over 90 per cent of total Canadian furniture exports).

THE CANADIAN FURNITURE INDUSTRY

The furniture industry in Canada included producers of household, office, hotel, restaurant and institutional furniture, with household furniture accounting for 45.1 per cent of the total industry shipments. Prior to the implementation of the Free Trade Agreement (FTA) between Canada and the United States in 1989, the Canadian household furniture industry was highly fragmented and included 1,157 establishments. The top 10 plants accounted for a relatively low 16.8 per cent of industry shipments, and the top 100 for only 61.9 per cent. By 1994, increased import competition, the elimination of tariffs under the FTA and sluggish domestic demand had led the number of establishments to fall by 50 per cent to 578. The top 10 establishments accounted for 21.7 per cent of industry shipments, while the top 100 had consolidated their share at 73.9 per cent. Still, in 1999, approximately 65 per cent of the industry was comprised of small plants with 20 or fewer employees, and less than 10 household furniture firms in Canada had more than 500 employees.[2]

The strong family ownership tradition in this industry had kept ownership private and had deterred consolidation, resulting in less than one per cent of firms being foreign controlled. The vast majority of firms were single-plant operations, counting a large number of small entrepreneurial firms and a small number of large firms. Market barriers to entry were still relatively low, but were becoming higher as the industry adopted more expensive production technologies. Small firms were usually short of capital, technology and management skills; specialized in one or few lines of furniture; and served a local or regional market. Larger firms usually kept abreast of technological

---

[1] U.S. Department of Commerce. Source: STAT-USA on the Internet, Publication Date – 1999-04-05. Accessed through www.strategis.gc.ca.

[2] Canada's 578 plants in 1994 employed 19,536 people, and generated $1.72 billion worth of shipments. The average plant employed 34 people and generated shipments valued at $3 million, compared with 52 employees and $11 million in shipments for the average factory in the overall Canadian manufacturing sector. By comparison, the U.S. industry had approximately seven times as many plants, 12 times the employees and 15 times the shipments of the Canadian industry. The average U.S. plant was twice the size of its Canadian counterpart.

changes, had professional management and accounted for the bulk of Canadian exports. These firms had diversified product offerings which encompassed various usages and the different sections of a typical house, from the dining room to the bedroom or the living room.

The disappearance of the last tariff barriers in 1993 was a turning point for the industry. The opening of the U.S. market, coupled with the growth of that market and the fall of the Canadian dollar compared to the American currency, created huge opportunities for Canadian firms. For the latter part of the 1990s, shipments of household furniture grew at more than 10 per cent annually — up to 19 per cent in 1998 — in large part due to exports. The largest firms were better equipped to take advantage of these opportunities. They had the resources to invest in new equipment and products and to develop distribution networks. Firms with more that 200 employees saw their share of the industry shipments go from 26 per cent to 42 per cent between 1990 and 1997.

The two largest Canadian firms in terms of revenue, Dorel Industries Inc. (www.dorel.com) and Palliser Furniture Ltd. (www.palliser.com) – both with sales around or over $500 million — had become international producers with plants in various locations in the world. Some of the largest firms were publicly owned: Dorel, Shermag (www.shermag.com); Bestar (www.bestar.ca); La-Z-Boy Canada Ltd., the largest foreign-owned company, generated the fourth highest revenue. Still, firms considered large in Canada were small relative to their international competitors; the largest U.S. manufacturer produced as much as the entire Canadian industry.

INDUSTRY STATISTICS

Some product specialization existed regionally: wooden furniture production was largely concentrated in the province of Quebec, while upholstered products were largely made in Ontario. Total furniture shipments from Quebec grew to Cdn$2 billion in 1999, 50 per cent of which was exported. Home furnishings accounted for Cdn$1.1 billion, among which wood furnishings accounted for Cdn$708 million.[3]

Despite its consolidation, the Canadian industry's productivity, as measured by value-added per employee, continued to trail that of its U.S. counterpart by about 20 per cent to 25 per cent. The higher productivity level was due in part to higher capital investment and to the larger scale of U.S. plants. Technology innovation in the household furniture industry, both in Canada and other countries, generally originated with machinery and equipment suppliers. Similarly, the industry depended largely on outside companies for research and development on materials, and there were no basic differences in the technologies used by most of the Canadian and U.S. household furniture industries.

For the Canadian industry, materials and supplies were the greatest cost factor (49.2 per cent of industry shipments), making the access to competitively priced inputs a critical success factor. Wages represented 21.1 per cent of industry shipments value in 1994, while capital expenditures accounted for 1.6 per cent, well under the 5.3 per cent average for Canada's overall manufacturing sector. Machinery and equipment costs were relatively modest in the furniture industry, but were growing. In both Canada and the United States, production workers made up about 85 per cent of the household furniture labor force, while management, administration and sales functions ac-

---

[3]Association des Fabricants de Meubles de Quebec – 1999 statistics – 2000-09-25. Accessed through http://lemeubleduquebec.com.

counted for the other 15 per cent. However, average annual salary costs of non-production employees were lower in Canada than in the United States (US$35,809 versus Cdn$40,845).

CANADEL'S EARLY DAYS

Located an hour's drive northeast of Montreal in Louiseville (population 8,000), Quebec, Canadel was a rapidly growing, privately owned, consumer-customized furniture assembler that specialized in designing, assembling, finishing and marketing casual dining furniture. Created in 1982, Canadel's sales had grown to over Cdn$103 million by 1999 (from $82 million in 1998), with expectations that they would hit $125 million in 2000. The region around Louiseville had been relying on a few large textile firms and furniture companies for employment, only to see them close their operations in the 1970s and 1980s. Compared to other regions in Canada, unemployment was extremely high, and the situation was unlikely to improve in the near future.

The three Deveault brothers had been involved in the furniture industry from an early age. Their father had started Yugo in 1975, a furniture company importing ready-made furniture from the former Yugoslavia. Unfortunately, he was caught in the North American recession of 1981 without access to financing and was forced to declare bankruptcy. The bankruptcy came as Guy was graduating from university in accounting and was preparing himself to formally join the company the following month. Jean was studying communications at University of Montreal while Michel, a business graduate from the Royal Military College of St-Jean, was based in Germany.

Hardened by this experience, in 1982, Guy started Canadel using his father's contacts and funds borrowed from friends and family. Michel joined him the following year. In its early years, the firm went through short periods of tight cash flow and the first profits were used to pay back debts and especially to repurchase minority shareholders, most often close friends or family members who had been convinced to invest amounts as small as $1,000. With limited financial resources, the young company relied on external suppliers for parts, as well as chairs, in order to limit investments in machinery and equipment. In 1985, Jean joined his two brothers to handle sales and marketing issues.

GROWING CANADEL

Between 1987 and 1991, the firm established itself as a supplier of high-quality furniture for the casual dining segment of the Canadian market. Canadel was among the very first manufacturers to foresee the potential of this middle-of-the-road segment. Traditionally, the dining furniture market had been more or less divided along two segments. First, there was the low-end "lunch corner" segment with their one table and four-chair sets for everyday usage and retailing for less than $800. Then, there was the formal dining room set, designed for special usage and typically for a formal room. Such a set could include eight to 10 chairs or more as well as, a buffet and would retail for more than $6,000. Yet, changes in lifestyle, families with fewer or no children and trends favoring open-space architecture in homes fuelled the demand for dining room furniture for everyday usage. During that period, Canadel progressively focused on that trend, while moving away from the lunch corner segment.

Building on the success of their casual dining line, with sales reaching Cdn$15 million in 1992, Canadel decided to enter the U.S. market. A personal friend introduced the Deveaults to a group of U.S.-based sales representatives whose employer was experiencing financial difficulties. The firm ended up, almost overnight, with a sales network in the eastern United States. By quickly securing a few large U.S. retailers, Canadel was able to substantially increase its revenue and drive more business to its network of suppliers which had been slowly built up over the years.

While focusing on the U.S. market for its growth, Canadel introduced in 1992 its "workshop concept" which consisted of a stand-alone display module, that allowed clients to visualize style, wood and color combinations for customized casual dining furniture. Whereas competitors often provided small, two-inch-square swatches of cloth and wood squares in an attempt to save on sample costs, Canadel's tabletop samples were made two-feet square. The workshop displayed pictures of 40 choices of furniture styles — tables, chairs and buffets, including different table and chair legs — 40 choices of colors, and extra combinations for wood types and finishes.

Marketing the workshop was quite a gamble. The Deveaults acknowledged that few retailers would be ready to cough up the $4,000 fee for the workshop. It was difficult to get stores to purchase the traditional booklet of wood samples and color combinations at Cdn$50. However, the discriminating price of the display enabled Canadel to "cherry-pick" the more valuable, high-volume retailers to receive the display, knowing that they would work harder to amortize their investment in the display. The marketing strategy purposefully targeted those large retailers, proving them with territorial exclusivity, even if this meant dropping smaller retailers. The volume generated by these larger accounts would justify the resources invested in relationship building, customer support and prompt delivery.

CANADEL IN 2000

By 2000, Canadel had established a strong position in this fast-growing segment, which now represented 50 per cent of the entire dining room market. Their products were priced between five and 10 per cent over similar quality non-customized furniture made in North America. The price differential increased at 20 per cent when compared to lower-quality imports from Asia. Through the years, Canadel had benefited from the increasing popularity of its line of buffets. Compared to an industry average of about one buffet sold per 10 dining sets, Canadel's ratio had reached three out of 10. A buffet added $1,500 to the $1,500 to $2,000 retail price of a typical "five-piece suite." About 20 per cent of all sales involved six or eight chairs, a proportion that increased during the excellent economic conditions of the latest years. The firm was also attempting to continue its upscale transition by moving up into the junior dining room segment.

Seventy-five per cent of sales were coming from the United States, 20 per cent from Canada and five per cent from international retailers located in Japan and Europe. Canadel employed 800 people directly, with another 750 in its subcontracting network. It could assemble and ship an estimated 2,000 tables, 8,000 chairs and 800 buffets per week.

CANADEL'S OPERATIONS

Canadel was essentially a "furniture assembler" as it relied on a large subcontractor network. Many of these subcontractors had long-time relationships with the firm. Since its early days, the firm had forged personal relationships with these subcontractors, even helping their former employees and business contacts – including their former account manager at the local bank – to start them up.

Using the workshop at the retail locations, customers would place orders for customized casual dining furniture, which would then be relayed to Canadel's head office. The orders would be sorted and manufacturing instructions forwarded to the suppliers, who would then produce to specifications and deliver the parts just-in-time. Each supplier specialized in producing a certain part of the product, and it was not uncommon to find five different suppliers providing parts for a single chair. Assembly, painting and finishing of the furniture was handled at Canadel's facilities, all located within a radius of 500 metres from their headquarters in Louiseville. Order turnaround time could be reduced to as low as two weeks. Although Canadel could produce an item from start to finish within this time frame, it promised a delivery window of between four to six weeks, still easily besting the industry average of eight weeks for customized furniture. On one occasion, the firm had been able to ship a special order for its largest customer within 48 hours.

In 1993, Canadel purchased a Beauce-based woodmill, Kennebec, for $1.5 million in order to centralize sourcing and to guarantee a continued supply of raw materials for its supplier network. The purchase came at an opportune time when wood prices were starting to creep upwards in 1994. While other manufacturers hastily reacted by raising their prices to retailers, Canadel held its prices steady for almost six months, even though the additional costs were eating into the company's bottom line. This gesture generated increased loyalty from their retailers. In turn, Canadel's credit conditions — net 30 days — were stringently enforced, even if this meant dropping some large and well-known retailers. Indeed, with Canadel, retailers did not have to carry inventories and were most often asking for significant deposits from customers.

A team of 50 representatives across North America served the retail markets, and although it controlled less of the "value chain" by relying on subcontractors, Canadel realized more of the "value added" through focusing on its core competency of furniture marketing and sales. Due to its unique system, Canadel achieved 45 inventory turns per year, versus the industry average of 15.

CANADEL'S NETWORK OF SUPPLIERS

Canadel drew its suppliers from the surroundings of Louiseville, a region known for its cottage industry of small wood furniture makers. The abundance of small, five-person shops provided a flexibility that would be hard to replicate elsewhere; within a 50-kilometre radius, there were 200 wood-furniture makers in its network. About 70 per cent of them were suppliers to Canadel.

These wood-furniture makers ranged from five- to fifteen-strong operations, achieving in the vicinity of $300,000 in annual sales. They were mostly shops that were owner-managed and operated, and had been in existence for several years. To expand beyond $200,000, these furniture makers would usually be forced to formalize their marketing and sales activities. With Canadel's steady stream of work, it became more viable for the company to concentrate on manufacturing, invest in specialized machinery and break through this sales ceiling without having to add marketing, sales or receivables capabilities. The firm's process allowed each parts supplier to specialize on certain elements and achieve significant economies of scale. Because customization was limited to choices outlined in the workshop concept, suppliers knew they would not face unpredicted furniture specifications in the form of oversized or undersized furniture requests or special customized instructions.

Canadel had a reputation for high-quality products in the furniture industry. The company held its suppliers to high-quality standards and worked with them to improve their processes. One of the key motivating reasons for suppliers to maintain a high quality standard was the benefit of regular payment. Paying suppliers on-time every Friday eliminated the uncertainty of cash flow and was important for them since many counted on Canadel for 80 per cent to 90 per cent of their volume. As a result, the rate of returns and repairs was 0.7 per cent of one per cent, mostly due to transportation damage. This rate was considerably lower than the 20 per cent defect rate for imported Asian-made furniture. Other manufacturing companies in United States and Canada experienced defect rates of three per cent to seven per cent, mainly because they were involved with all stages of manufacturing. Canadel was also known to extend aid to its suppliers beyond parts sourcing, going as far as to find buyers for their businesses if the owners were seeking to retire from the trade.

CANADEL'S ASSEMBLY OPERATIONS

Each facility had a distinct focus. Plants 1, 2 and 4 handled the assembly, painting and finishing of buffets, tables and stools, and chairs respectively. Plant 3 manufactured for Canadel's suppliers the wood panels that were used sample for table tops. Plant 5 hosted the central shipping dock, the warehouse and the headquarters. These factories transferred and tracked orders using a wireless network. The most recent addition, Plant 2, was about 100,000 square feet wide and had a reinforced structure that didn't require an internal support beam. The absence of this beam provided greater flexibility for the production layout. All manufacturing and assembly activities were controlled by a proprietary computer system developed in large part by a local software programmer. Development costs had been considerably lower than if a big-city consulting firm had been used.

On schedule, parts from each supplier were dropped off to the respective plant and sorted by order. Each order for a piece of furniture was then tracked by an order sheet entered into a computer system, which produced a UPC code to follow the order from entry to shipping. There were conveyer systems throughout the factory that transported the work-in-process to different stations. Because each piece of furniture could be assembled from five to 10 separate parts, three assembly lines ran in parallel, terminating at the painting station. For example, in the creation of a chair, the legs and the back would be assembled separately, but within two to four hours they would be put together and sent to the painting station. Once dried and packed, the furniture was sent to Plant 5, the central warehouse headquarters facilities.

There, the different pieces of furniture — for instance the chairs, the table and the buffet — were put together according to order slips and stored in specific aisles, awaiting shipping. In parallel, trucks assigned to specific regions awaited loading. The warehouse was really a cross-docking operations; products never sat on the floor for more than four days before being shipped.

Using a just-in-time (JIT) inventory system, Canadel never received more than two to three days of parts from its suppliers. Over the years, it had managed parts shortages by adjusting its production schedule, but the JIT process meant that the system was at risk of shutting down if parts did not arrive. Even a day's shortage would cause a "domino effect" of backed-up schedules. Therefore, time buffers were built into the assembly process, allowing human intervention to repair damaged parts, rush a set of orders, locate missing parts or tweak the process to accommodate the four- to six-week delivery promise. At any given time, there could be one of over 3,000 combinations of chairs or tables to manufacture, and experience had shown that allowing for flexibility and intervention in the system resulted in correctly shipped orders.

MANAGING CANADEL THREE WAYS

Canadel was managed jointly by the three Deveault brothers, who worked independently on their own projects: Guy on finance and strategy; Michel on operations, information technology, human resources and credit assessment; and Jean on sales and marketing. They would walk into each other's offices unannounced and get comments or resolutions to their outstanding issues in immediate fashion. Every month, they met on an informal basis and conferred with each other on the status of their latest projects.

Michel, Operations

By computerizing Canadel's operations, the Deveaults were able to track order processing and delivery status instantly. Even the warehouse managed order entry and processing using a wireless connection, providing instant feedback and control to management. Michel, aged 44, outlined that they used a combination of UNIX and a Windows NT operating system. "We don't need a graphical user interface here, for what we want to do. Too often, others seek perfection, to have the top of the line equipment. Here, we want a system that takes into account human error; and our system has to permit that. I fix the UNIX and NT issues myself!"

Jean, Sales and Marketing

"We took a single-page ad in our industry news magazine when we first launched in the United States," remarked Jean, aged 40. "It cost us US$13,000, but it announced that we had arrived." With its workshop concept, retailers were questioning some of the combinations that Canadel sought to offer to consumers, colors that ranged from lime green to pale pink. "Don't make the mistake of choosing for your customer," reminded Jean. "Let them choose their own damned colors. The same person who buys a 'fluo' green Volkswagen Beetle will also buy a table with this 'fluo' green top. In fact, these garish colors make up 20 per cent of our total sales."

Guy, Finance

"Canadel does not invest in expensive capital machinery," commented Guy, aged 42. "We want always to retain a high amount of liquid assets." Most of the firm's assets were short-term and the company had virtually no debt. Since casual dining furniture purchases were subject to consumer whim and fancy, they experienced a 15 per cent drop in sales after the March-April Nasdaq crash, with orders staying weak for six to seven weeks after that. "Our biggest fixed costs are ourselves," laughed Guy. Canadel generated $100 million in revenue on an asset base of $40 million.

Guy had specific return on investment targets. He strove to keep the firm debt-free and having a 200 per cent return on assets. Canadel was thus managed with an aversion to acquiring fixed assets or tying up cash resources in inventory.

CANADEL'S CULTURE

The Deveaults had maintained a very hands-on approach, and prided themselves on maintaining a small power distance between management and employees. All three brothers had an open-door policy, which they explained was very important — any employee could walk straight in and air a grievance. In fact, although this privilege had been used several times in the past few years, Michel indicated that it was this perception of openness rather than an actual face-to-face encounter with management that resulted in employee loyalty and diligence.

Even meetings were informal. A new IT manager had requested a meeting with Michel to discuss a matter. Stopping his work, Michel motioned to the surprised individual to sit down. The manager was used to the protocol of a fixed meeting time at other companies, but the brothers preferred this informal setting. Even Michael Hoff, their American sales manager, was known to have monthly strategy meetings that lasted not more than 15 minutes. The Deveaults did not have a secretary to manage their agendas —another aspect of their company's difference from other large competitors.

While the firm did not have formal management committee meetings, key issues and projects were typically discussed over lunch at a local restaurant on Fridays. Around the table, in addition to the Deveaults, one would find Guy Brassard, aged 40, in charge of purchase and supplies; Claude Lamarche, 50, the designer; Alain Thibeault, 34, the general manager of Kennebec; Yvon Dubé, 48, the human resources manager; and Benoît Laplante, 40, the plant engineer. With the exception of Laplante, all these individuals had been with Canadel for more than eight or 10 years. Besides reviewing key events of the current week and plans for the following week, the group acted as a sounding board, to brainstorm and discuss ideas and projects. One or two key suppliers were also regularly invited to join.

Canadel was well known for the company activities and parties offered to all its personnel. The brothers were readily accessible and seemed to be integrated within the small population of Louiseville. They remarked with satisfaction that they walked the same roads, shopped the same shops and drank at the same bars as their employees and suppliers. It was obvious that an effort was made not to distance themselves from those who worked around them. The Deveault brothers considered themselves part of the fabric of Louiseville and staunchly refused to entertain any thoughts of moving the company.

MANAGING PEOPLE

Canadel's hiring policy was unique to its field. The Deveault brothers preferred not to hire ambitious MBA graduates because they felt that these overachievers might not stay for more than two years. The brothers were uninterested in qualifications, preferring to have employees who had worked their way up from the shop floor, taking courses to improve their skills. This policy of promotion from within underlined the Deveaults wish to maintain control over the culture of the workplace at Canadel. Salary raises of seven per cent to eight per cent were considered for 2000, versus four per cent to five per cent in 1999.

"We're not just selling a product as a manufacturer," explained Guy. "It's also important to us the manner in which we do things." There was a rather successful salesperson who was told in no uncertain terms that if he did not change his attitude, he would be fired. "It's about liking what we do and having fun at it. If we do not like what we do, we'd stop and go do something else. The secret to Canadel is not the fact that we're in the furniture business — it's our system that we've come up with."

Canadel had a policy of customer satisfaction, but not at the expense of employee relations. There was an instance during the last few days leading up to Christmas 1999 (December 25) that the firm had fallen behind on a batch of unexpected, last-minute rush orders. Delivery before Christmas would have meant extra days spent on the road for their trucking staff. Instead of having their employees deliver the furniture on time, Jean made the decision to deliver the goods late in order to allow all employees to spend Christmas with their families. In his explanation to the irate customer, Jean shrugged his shoulders and proclaimed, "Madame, it's just furniture."

COMPETITION

Canadel was one of 70 main manufacturers in the Quebec wood household furnishings market alone (Quebec had a population of seven million people, a quarter of the Canadian population), but was generally perceived as being a class apart. There were actually 10,000 competitors in total, but most of the group were small custom furniture operations that could not compete on the same level. Canadel's return on capital invested was at least twice as high as the rest of the industry's, due in large part to their outsourcing strategy — their suppliers bore the brunt of capital investments in machinery. "We're not doing anything new," Guy mentioned, "Furniture making is almost as old as prostitution — we don't imagine we can make a chair more comfortable — everything has been thought of. What we're trying to do is to sell a product of decent quality to the general market."

Their success had nevertheless triggered several firms to mimic Canadel's approach. Some had adapted it for various furniture segment, for instance for living room furniture, but also dining room furniture. One of the largest imitators, located in the region, had went as far as copying Canadel products, the production systems, the workshop concept, and even brochures. So far, the presence of this imitator had been limited to the Quebec and had seen its sales grown over $10 million. However, according to rumors, this imitator had approached two of Canadel's U.S.-based customers, offering what was thought a significant price cut. Wondering whether other clients had been contacted, the Deveaults were conscious that they may have to consider such imitators as more of a threat in the near future.

In addition, some U.S. competitors had offered to purchase the firm, but the thought of giving up control and the remote possibility of moving its operations away from Louiseville did not interest the Deveault brothers. Jean casually mentioned that one can eat only three meals a day — what more can one want? Besides, because of the region's high unemployment, the brothers felt an obligation to keep operations in Louiseville.

LOOKING AT GROWTH PROSPECTS

The Deveault brothers were not worried about their rate of growth. "We will grow when we are ready to grow," stated Jean. Canadel was not a public company and was not bound to shareholder demands for a target growth level, even if it meant forfeiting sales of $10 million to $15 million yearly. Preferring to grow at their own pace, without incurring debt, meant that their operation could take more time to absorb new changes. "We always have several irons in the fire," mentioned Michel. "At any time, we will try something new and if it works, we'll go for it. If not, we'll just kill the project right there and then." They had ventured into bedroom furniture manufacturing, incubating this idea in a corner of their warehouse. They had also tried to use the workshop concept on metal furniture. Both ideas did not generate sufficient interest or return and were subsequently dropped.

"Our philosophy is to keep it simple. That's it, that's all," concluded Jean.

HARLEY-DAVIDSON, INC.

Robert M. Grant

Luis Escudero

Nicole Flavin

Juan Trevino

Chris Gergen and

Bart Quillen

> You've shown us how to be the best. You've been leaders in new technology. You've stuck by the basic American values of hard work and fair play...Most of all, you've worked smarter, you've worked better, and you've worked together...as you've shown again, America is someplace special. We're on the road to unprecedented prosperity...and we'll get there on a Harley.
>
> President Ronald Reagan, speech at Harley-Davidson
> plant, York, Pennsylvania, May 6, 1987

JULY 1998

Reporting on the company's second-quarter results, Harley-Davidson's president and CEO Jeffrey Bleustein expressed satisfaction at progress during the year:

> In addition to delivering another record quarter, we also achieved several significant milestones. We celebrated our 95th anniversary, introduced a new big twin engine, the Twin Cam 88, and announced plans to establish a motorcycle assembly operation in Brazil. These events

created a lot of excitement and are part of our strategy for continuing to grow the worldwide demand for Harley-Davidson motorcycles.[1]

The results for the first half of 1998 were indeed spectacular. Despite the substantial investments that the company had made in growth and development – including expanding sales and distribution outside the US, the new assembly plant in Kansas City, the acquisition of Buell Motorcycle Company and Eaglemark Financial Services – gross margins had widened to 34.3 percent, and net income had increased by 12.6 percent over the year-ago period. Harley-Davidson (H-D) was well on track to meet its production target of 148,000 bikes for 1998.

For Jeff Bleustein, his first few months as CEO had focused upon consolidating the achievements of his predecessors Rich Teerlink and Vaughn Beals, as well as promoting new growth initiatives. Compared with the difficult years between the 1981 management buyout and the 1986 flotation when H-D was fighting for survival in a hostile world, the 1990s had been a period of uninterrupted success. Harley had displaced Honda as worldwide market-share leader in heavyweight motorcycles and despite an almost three-fold expansion of capacity, demand for Harleys continued to outstrip production. Steady growth in net income, from $42m in 1990 to $174m in 1997, was reflected in spectacular shareholder returns: $100 invested in H-D stock at the 1986 initial public offering would have been worth $4,067 by the end of 1997, an annual rate of return of 40 percent. Bleustein wanted to maintain the growth trajectory: in his first year as CEO, he authorized increased investment in production capacity, new product development, and overseas market development.

Yet despite this run of outstanding success, Bleustein was reminded of the advice of Intel founder Andy Grove. In his recent book, *Only the Paranoid Survive*, Grove emphasized the need to be constantly wary of threats from competitors and new market and technological trends. Bleustein realized that H-D could not afford to be complacent. The company continued to face rivalry from well-established global players such as Honda, BMW, Yamaha, and Kawasaki. At the other end of the scale, in addition to established specialist manufacturers such as Ducati and Moto Guzzi, there had been an influx of newcomers to the heavyweight motorcycle market such as Triumph, Polaris, and Excelsior-Henderson. If the world economy were to weaken, would there be sufficient demand for these expensive leisure toys to support H-D's continued prosperity and growth? Although Bleustein felt a general sense of unease about the future, identifying in precise terms the threats that H-D might face, and how H-D's strategy might be amended to take account of these threats was less evident to him.

THE HISTORY OF HARLEY-DAVIDSON

Harley-Davidson, Inc. was founded in 1903 by William Harley and brothers William Davidson, Arthur Davidson, and Walter Davidson. At this time, a motorcycle was no more than a bicycle with a small motor attached to it. Harley's 1903 model was made in the Davidson family shed and had a three-horsepower engine. Prior to World War I, Harley competed with about 150 other US motorcycle manufacturers. In 1909 Harley introduced its first two-cylinder, V-twin engine, featuring

---

[1] Harley-Davidson reports record second quarter sales and earnings," Harley-Davidson press release, July 13, 1998 (www.harley-davidson.com).

the deep, rumbling sound for which Harley motorcycles are known today.[2] Henry Ford's assembly-line concept (1913) and wartime orders pushed Harley out of the small-scale craft shed and into an era of mass production. In 1921 a Harley motorcycle won the first race in which machines reached speeds of over 100 miles per hour. This same year, H-D's new model featured a front brake and the distinctive Harley tear-drop gas tank. During its first three decades the industry consolidated: in 1910 there were close to 150 motorcycle producers, by 1929, Indian, Excelsior, and Harley accounted for the majority of US motorcycle sales. The Great Depression killed Excelsior, and Indian closed in 1953, leaving Harley the sole American manufacturer of motorcycles. Exhibit 1 shows H-D's production over the century.

The post-war era was one of opportunity and problems. Post-war affluence and the rise of youth culture created a growing demand for motorcycles. However, this was satisfied primarily by imports. By 1959, Harley was still market leader with sales of $16.6 million,[3] but British imports amounted to about 30,000 bikes a year with BSA, Triumph, and Norton taking 49 percent of the US market.[4] In 1959, Honda entered the US market. The result was the rebirth of motorcycling in the US.

From 1960 to 1965, motorcycle registrations increased from under 600,000 to almost 1,400,000. The new motorcycle owners were not traditional motorcycle owners, and certainly not "The Wild Ones" portrayed by Marlon Brando in the 1953 gang-movie.[5] The new riders were students, office workers, and leisure riders, both men and women, who found the new lightweight two-wheelers produced by Honda, Suzuki, and Yamaha to be convenient, economical, and fun. Honda's 1963 advertising campaign featured the slogan: "You Meet the Nicest People on a Honda." By 1966, Honda accounted for 63 percent of the motorcycles sold in the US.[6] Initially, H-D benefited from the overall expansion in the motorcycle market induced by Honda. However, Honda soon moved up-market. In 1969 Honda introduced the CB750, a technically advanced, four-cylinder machine that severely dented the sales of H-D and Triumph in the heavyweight market.

Also in 1969, H-D was acquired by AMF, which proceeded to expand production capacity with the building of the York, Pennsylvania assembly plant. Boosting capacity to 75,000 units annually had disastrous consequences for product quality. A company audit in the mid 1970s revealed that more than half the cycles coming off the line were missing parts.[7] By the end of the 1970s, Honda had replaced H-D as market leader in heavyweight motorcycles in the US.

The Buyout

In 1981 H-D's senior managers, led by Vaughn Beals, organized a leveraged buyout. Harley emerged as an independent, privately owned company, but heavily laden with debt. The buyout coincided with one of the severest recessions of the post-war US economy and, especially troublesome for a highly leveraged business, a soaring of interest rates under the Fed's tight monetary policies. Registrations of heavyweight motorcycles fell during 1981 and 1982, and

---

[2] Ibid.

[3] Ibid.

[4] Boston Consulting Group, "Strategy alternatives for the British motorcycle industry," Her Majesty's Stationery Office, London, July 30, 1975; quoted in Richard T. Pascale, "Perspectives on strategy: the real story behind Honda's success," *California Management Review*, March 23 (Spring 1984): 47–72.

[5] Pascale, "Perspectives on strategy."

[6] Ibid.

[7] Peter Reid, "How Harley beat back the Japanese," *Fortune*, September 25, 1989.

Harley's own sales plummeted. By 1982 its sales of bikes were down by more than a third on 1979. During 1981 and 1982, Harley-Davidson lost a total of $60 million. Redundancies came thick and fast: 30 percent of the office staff were dismissed, with similar cutbacks among hourly workers. "I can remember when we used to have 2,700 people working here," recalled Ken Beaudry, vice-president of AIW Local 209 adjacent to Harley's Milwaukee engine and transmission plant. "Now we've got 535 members left."

Rebuilding Manufacturing

The company's first priority was to systematically rebuild production methods and working practices with a view to cutting costs and improving quality. The new Harley management team had visited several Japanese auto-manufacturing plants and carefully studied Toyota's just-in-time (JIT) system. After a visit to Honda's Marysville, Ohio plant in the following year, CEO Vaughn Beals commented: "We were being wiped out by the Japanese because they were better *managers*. It wasn't robotics, or culture, or morning calisthenics and company songs – it was professional managers who understood their business and paid attention to detail."[8] Tom Gelb, senior VP of operations, offered similar comments:

> I came away, as many others did, thinking "There's no magic." The plants weren't filled with robots, and the three I saw were surrounded by people watching them. There's no super-duper machinery that's different from ours. I did notice that the labor pace was greater than ours by 20 to 30 percent, but the real difference between US and Japanese management is in the staff – the manufacturing engineers, the accountants, the salaried workers.

The first few years after the buyout saw a revolution in Harley's production methods. Less than four months after the buyout, Harley management began a pilot JIT inventory and production-scheduling program called "MAN" (Materials As Needed) in its Milwaukee engine plant. The objective was to reduce inventories and costs and improve quality control. Within a year, all H-D's manufacturing operations were being converted to JIT: components and sub-assemblies were "pulled" through the production system in response to final demand. Production and component deliveries occurred when they were needed, where they were needed, and in the exact quantity needed.[9] Its adoption required a systematic rethinking and redesign of supply-chain management and manufacturing management. One result was much closer relationships with a smaller number of suppliers.

The new system of manufacturing and purchasing was accompanied by fundamental changes in job design and human resource management at plant level. During the early 1980s, the new management sought to redefine the responsibilities of manufacturing employees and transform their relationship with management. A key element was to give machine operators more responsibility, including responsibility for the preventive maintenance of their machines and participation in discussions about quality improvement. This in turn required investments in retraining.

The goal, stated Beals, was "to achieve cost and quality parity with foreign competition." However, the goal was to be achieved, not by automation, but by changes in working practices,

---

[8] Ibid.

[9] Ruth W. Epps, "Just-in-time inventory management: implementation of a successful program," *St. John's University Review of Business*, September 22, 1995.

organization, and attitudes. Rod Willis of *Management Review* summarized the changes in manufacturing management:

> Armed with the latest in Japanese manufacturing concepts – or as much as they could pry from their often tight-lipped competitors – Beals and his cadre of top managers returned to Milwaukee to reorganize Harley Davidson. The first big change was in plant management structure. The traditional American hierarchy of responsibilities was replaced with a system in which each employee from the line up has "ownership" in running an efficient operation. Each plant is assigned four to seven area managers each responsible for everything that takes place in his or her area. Staff jobs were cut throughout the company and divided among area managers and line workers. There are no corporate or plant heads of quality control. The area managers can't blame problems on staff failures, and line workers can't blame faulty equipment for productivity problems unless there are serious malfunctions. The chickens come home to roost.

By eliminating staff functions, the company obtained a shallower organizational chart and big cost savings. "Our biggest savings came from decreasing the number of salaried staff," said Beals. "That is where the greatest improvements in productivity have occurred...The presence of those service functions tends to emasculate the basic line with regard to authority, and that's what we are trying to avoid...All the line workers are responsible for inspecting and making basic adjustments to the machinery they use and managers should run their parts of the plant fully. It's a long-term transition to making each plant a profit center." Similarly, line workers, who were once given quotas and told to meet them, were given a voice in setting realistic quotas based on actual production capacity and needs. As a result, they felt a sense of ownership in meeting those goals. "In the past, line workers had to wait for a repairman to come and fix broken or malfunctioning machinery; now they can make most repairs themselves."

The revolution in manufacturing occurred without large-scale investment in new capital equipment. The high leverage and weak cash flows of the 1980s meant that the improvements in productivity and quality had to occur without the benefits of the latest computer-controlled machine tools and flexible manufacturing systems. The installation in 1987 of eight Japanese-built computer-controlled machining centers at a cost of over $1.5 million was a major investment for H-D. Even with these constraints, the improvements in all aspects of manufacturing performance were spectacular. The company reduced its inventory levels, lowered its setup and changeover times for machinery, and radically improved the quality of its products. Improved quality meant reduced costs in other areas: scrap, rework, supplier corrective action, downgraded end product, warranty costs, loss of future sales, recall costs, and return costs.

Product Development and Design

While management had decided to "play the game the way the Japanese play it" in terms of quality control and operations management, it decided to play a different game in terms of products and marketing. Harley abandoned all notions of becoming a broad-line competitor and concentrated its efforts into developing the big-bike niche. Although the heavyweight segment had traditionally been the preserve of Harley and the European manufacturers, by the 1980s it had become dominated by the Japanese. Moreover, the appreciation of the US dollar between 1980 and 1986 made it increasingly difficult for US manufacturers to remain price competitive. To give it time to develop its capabilities and market position in the heavyweight segment, the company sought (and won) a temporary five-year tariff on imported Japanese heavyweight motorcycles.

To build its position within the heavyweight segment, H-D's strategy was to exploit its traditional image while at the same time appealing to a more affluent, up-market customer base. In terms of product policy, this meant emphasizing the traditional Harley style, but improving the products to meet the needs of buyers who had neither the time nor the skill nor the inclination to maintain, rebuild, and upgrade their own bikes. Under the leadership of William G. ("Willy G") Davidson, grandson of one of the founders, H-D put greater emphasis on product styling, bringing back many of the design and stylistic features of former Harley models. Many managers today credit the company's survival during the early and mid-1980s to the innovations in paint, trim, chrome, and exhaust-pipe shaping that Willy G and his team introduced. Under Willy G's leadership, Harley introduced a number of new models, for the most part developed at minimal cost by combining modified components from its two most popular old models, the heavy Elektra Glide and the lighter Sportster. The new models took traditional Harley features and carefully adjusted the styling to appeal to the modern buyer. Says Willy G, "Every little piece on a Harley is exposed, and it has to look just right. A tube curve or the shape of a timing case can generate enthusiasm or be a total turnoff. It's almost like being in the fashion business."[10] The new bikes mimicked many of the cosmetic innovations with which Harley fans had traditionally customized their bikes after purchase. Even with its traditional appeal, it was essential for Harley to upgrade its product to meet the standards of performance, comfort, reliability, and ease of maintenance expected by the market in the 1980s. The developments were incremental and involved no major innovations. In 1984, Harley introduced its improved "Evolution" range of V-twin engines. The Gates Poly chain belt drive offered greater quietness and reliability in rear wheel drive. Other improvements have included redesigned engine mounts to reduce vibration, a new carburetor offering a smoother power delivery, an improved starter, and redesigned gear case, which helped Harley meet the 1986 Federal noise limit for motorcycles.

Increasing differentiation and widening market appeal meant more frequent new model introductions. However, to exploit economies of scale, key components were standardized. Thus, H-D based its model range around three engine types and four different frames.

Given the high level of brand loyalty among Harley owners, increasing market share meant capturing new customers, and new riders in particular. To this end, the 883cc Sportster, Harley's entry-level bike priced (in 1985) at below $4,000, played a particularly important role.

Marketing

Communicating the appeal of Harley ownership to a new breed of potential customers also presented a challenge to the company. As with all other aspects of H-D's turnaround strategy, the key was to achieve maximum bang for very few bucks. In the area of marketing, H-D's approach was to obtain wide-ranging exposure of the company, its products, and its heritage, while largely eschewing traditional mass advertising.

The key was to build upon Harley's identification with American values of independence, ruggedness, and dependability, while undermining Harley's association with rebellious, law-flouting motorcycle gangs. The company publicized widely its efforts and success in implementing TQM with articles in technical magazines such as *American Machinist*, *Quality*, and *Industrial Engineering*. President Reagan's visit to H-D's York plant created a torrent of publicity. To counter the antisocial image associated with motorcycle gangs, the new management put a heavy emphasis

---

[10] Ibid.

on patriotism, charity, and community involvement. Publicity events such as the Harley-sponsored rides to raise money for the Muscular Dystrophy Association, and its organization of a Los Angeles to Washington D.C. "Ride for Liberty" to raise donations for the restoration of the Statue of Liberty, not only promoted a favorable image, but generated substantial publicity for Harley-Davidson motorcycles.

By the beginning of 1988 it was apparent that Harley's attempts to extend its appeal to a whole new group of more affluent customers were making steady progress. Market research data showed that the median age of Harley customers was a little over 34 – much higher than the average for motorcycle customers as a whole. Their median household income was almost $40,000 and over half were married.

With solid gains in quality and reliability, H-D sought to win back sales to public authorities, most of which had been lost to its Japanese rivals. In 1987 Harley made sales of some 4,000 bikes to police departments and had chalked up some notable successes, including a switch by the California Highway Patrol from Honda to Harley.

It was not only in the motorcycle market that Harley-Davidson was able to exploit the strength of the Harley brand image. The Harley-Davidson name was licensed to suppliers of tee-shirts, jackets, underwear, jewelry, and toys. Although licensing income accounted for less than 1 percent of Harley's revenue from motorcycles and related products, it was almost all profit. In 1982, Harley began vigorously enforcing protection of its trademarks. From its own dealerships to tattoo parlors (where the Harley-Davidson logo was the most popular single tattoo design), Harley prohibited unauthorized use of its trademarks, and drove out bootleg products. The starting point was the major motorcycle trade shows. Initially Harley found that bootleg merchandise was so prevalent that legitimate Harley-licensed products were hard to find. The result was a rise in licensing income to Harley, plus tighter controls against the Harley name being used in connection with poor quality or pornographic products.

Central to H-D's marketing efforts was building the relationship between the company and its customers. If the appeal of the Harley motorcycle was the image it conveyed and the lifestyle it represented, then the company had to ensure that the experience matched the image. To increase H-D's involvement in its customers' riding experience it formed the Harley Owners' Group in 1983. Through HOG, H-D became involved in organizing charity events, and employees, from the CEO down, were encouraged to take an active role in HOG activities.

Distribution

Improving H-D's much-neglected distribution network was essential to the company's market objectives. Far too many of Harley's 620 US dealerships were poorly managed shops, operated by enthusiasts, with erratic opening hours, a poor stock of bikes and spares, and indifferent customer service. H-D began rebuilding its dealership network. Harley's dealer development program improved support for dealers while imposing higher standards of pre- and after-sales service, and requiring better dealer facilities. The dealers were obliged to carry a full line of Harley replacement parts and accessories, and to perform service on Harley bikes. Harley-Davidson placed a strong emphasis on training dealers to help them meet the higher service requirements, and encouraging dealers to better meet the needs of the professional, middle-class clientele that H-D was now courting.

Despite the tariff protection awarded by the Reagan Administration and the popularity of the models, Harley flirted with bankruptcy between 1984 and 1986. By 1987, however, after a period of stronger sales and a successful round of $49 million in debt financing (where Citicorp took a $10 million write-down on its original investment), Harley's financial condition stabilized.[11] Between 1986 and 1990, Harley's share of the heavyweight market grew from about 30 percent to over 60 percent, with demand outstripping production. During this time, management improved the quality and reliability of its product and also began to look at growth opportunities in retail clothing and sales abroad. In 1989, Harley established a subsidiary in the UK.

THE HEAVYWEIGHT MOTORCYCLE MARKET

In the 1990s Harley has experienced eight years of uninterrupted growth in the heavyweight motorcycle market (650+ cc). This market is comprised of three segments:

- Cruisers: *"big, noisy, low riding, unapologetically macho cycles"*[12] *with loud V-twin engines*
- Touring bikes: *large motorcycles with seats designed for long rides*
- Performance bikes: *built for superior handling and acceleration, they have lighter, stiffer frames, and require a more forward, crouched seated position*

Harley dominates the cruiser and touring segments of this market, capturing over 50 percent of overall heavyweight motorcycle sales in the US in 1997 (see Exhibit 2). Cruiser motorcycles are big, powerful machines with an upright riding position. Their design reflects the dominance of styling over either comfort or speed. For the urban males (and some females) in Los Angeles, New York, Paris, and Tokyo, the cruiser motorcycle is practical transportation in congested metropolises, but is primarily a statement of style. The cruiser segment has practically been created by Harley. Most of the bikes in this segment feature V-twin engines, many with cylinder capacities that exceed those of a small family car. Harley's major competitors include Japanese companies with models based upon traditional Harley design (Honda's Shadow range, Yamaha's Virago, the Suzuki Intruder, and Kawasaki's Vulcan).

Touring bikes include cruisers specially equipped for longer-distance riding (such as several Harley models) and bikes specially designed for comfort over long distance (including the Honda Goldwing and the bigger BMWs). These tourers feature luxuries such as audio systems, two-way intercoms, and heaters. In touring bikes, Harley is challenged by the greater smoothness and comfort of the multi-cylinder, shaft-drive BMWs and Goldwings.

Performance models are based upon racing bikes. These are high-technology, high-revving engines with a heavy emphasis on speed, acceleration, and race-track styling with minimal concessions to rider comfort. The segment is dominated by Japanese motorcycle companies, with a significant representation of European specialists such as Ducati and Triumph. H-D entered this segment in 1993 with its involvement in the formation of Buell Motorcycles, and with the acquisition of Buell in 1998 is now more heavily committed.

---

[11] Ibid.

[12] Gary Strauss, "Born to be bikers," *USA Today*, November 5, 1997.

COMPETITION

Although H-D was well established as the market-share leader in the US heavyweight market, in the global motorcycle industry it was only a medium-sized player. In the smaller sizes of motorcycle, it was the Japanese that dominated the US and the world markets. Outside of the US, H-D lagged behind Honda, Yamaha, and Kawasaki, even in the heavyweight segment. However, the conventional segmentation into lightweight, middleweight, and heavyweight does not clearly define H-D's market. H-D's strength lies not in the heavyweight motorcycle market, but in just one part of this: the *super-heavyweight* segment, comprising bikes with cylinder displacement of more than 850cc. In the 650–850cc range, the Japanese dominance is nearly as great as in the lightweight and middleweight markets.

As result of its single-segment focus, H-D produces a much smaller volume of bikes than its major competitors. The most striking comparison is between H-D and Honda: H-D's 150,000 bikes a year are dwarfed by Honda's 5 million. These volume differences have important implications for H-D's ability to access scale economies.

Compared to its competitors, H-D is also much less diversified. Honda, BMW, and Suzuki are important producers of automobiles. It seems likely that there are benefits from sharing technology, engineering capabilities, and marketing and distribution know-how between automobile and motorcycle divisions. In addition, sheer size confers greater bargaining power with suppliers.

H-D's smaller size and scale has important implications for its investments in technology. Because of the costs involved, H-D does not have a separate research function, and it lags far behind its competitors in the application of motor vehicle technology. To a great extent, it has succeeded in making a virtue out of necessity – its motorcycles not only look old-style, the technology is old-style, even the new Twin Cam 88 engine launched in 1998 in an era of multi-valve, liquid-cooled, overhead camshaft engines. The Twin Cam 88 is a 1450cc traditional V-twin with push rods and is air-cooled. By contrast, BMW's R1200C cruiser model launched in 1997 with a star role in the James Bond movie "Tomorrow Never Dies," features shaft drive; a multi-valve, fuel-injected engine; triple-disc, anti-lock brakes; and road-hugging cornering from its advanced suspension system and low center of gravity. In contrast to its Japanese rivals, who have focused upon applying the latest automotive technology to their new models, H-D has concentrated upon incremental refinements to its engines, frames, and gearboxes, whose basic design has remained fundamentally the same for the past 70 years. Unlike technological leaders such as Honda and BMW, H-D has been forced to outsource most of its technological needs. In 1997 it established a joint venture with Porsche AG to source and assemble motorcycle components. H-D was particularly interested in accessing Porsche's expertise in engine emission compliance.

Appendix 2 gives profiles of several competitors of H-D in the heavyweight motorcycle market, Exhibit 3 compares market shares, and Exhibit 4 shows price comparisons.

HARLEY-DAVIDSON IN THE 1990S

Brand Loyalty

Harley-Davidson has emerged as one of the archetypes of American style. The famed spread eagle signifies not just the brand of one of the world's oldest motorcycle companies, but an entire lifestyle that it is associated with. Harley-Davidson has been described as "the ultimate biker status symbol...a quasi religion, an institution, a way of life."[13] As a result, the "golden, all-American brand name" has earned a considerable following. In a recent annual report, Harley's Chairman and CEO Richard Teerlink wrote, "Most people can't understand what would drive someone to profess his or her loyalty for our brand by tattooing our logo onto his or her body – or heart...this indescribable passion is a big part of what has driven and will continue to drive our growth."

Tattoos, strong brand loyalty, and Harley's icon status have created a distinct marketing advantage for the company. Harley ran no domestic advertisements in 1996, but was ranked number 26 in the listing of the "World's Top 100 Brands" for that year.[14] In 1997, it spent a mere $1 million on advertising out of a total marketing budget of $20 million. Meanwhile, Harley cycles have been featured in ads for countless other products, providing millions of dollars worth of free advertising. For example, during the 1997 Super Bowl 100 Harleys were part of the half-time show, at no cost to the company. The brand is so strong that Harley closed down its branding department in 1995 citing it as unnecessary.[15]

Creating the Harley Owners' Group (HOG) was a crucial factor in building the brand image and consolidating the relationship between the company and its customers. HOG's web site describes the kind of emotion and atmosphere that the company is trying to deliver to customers through its HOG organization: "the feeling of being out there on a Harley-Davidson motorcycle links us like no other experience can. It's made HOG like no other organization in the world...The atmosphere is more family reunion than organized meeting." By becoming a HOG member, riders get a company pin and patch, a membership card, and a HOG atlas as well as a host of membership benefits including the *Hog Tales Magazine*, a bimonthly newsletter. The organization has also come to include the Ladies of Harley, "giving the women riders among us the recognition they deserve."[16] (Women now make up 12 percent of US Harley buyers.) When it first started, in 1983, the organization had 28 members. HOG currently has 365,000 members in 940 chapters throughout the world.[17] Run by Harley employees, HOG sponsors motorcycle events almost every weekend from April to November across the country.[18] Harley managers participate along with their spouses. Marketing chief Kathleen Lawler-Demitros explains, "We try to run our business by the maxim 'The sale begins after the sale.' HOG is one way we differentiate ourselves from our Japanese competitors."[19]

The loyalty and fervor of Harley owners is most evident from the participation in the rallies whose sole purpose is to celebrate the company and the bikes. When Harley turned 90 in 1993, more than 100,000 bikers from around the world rode into Milwaukee swelling total party crowd size to approximately 600,000. The celebration of the 95th anniversary in June 1998 was even bigger.

The involvement of H-D managers and employees in HOG and Harley rallies also provides opportunities for market research and continuous customer feedback. "We listen to our customers," says Jeff Bleustein. "We're building the motorcycles they are asking for."[20] Managers listen to

---

[13] Marc Ballon, "Born to be wild," *Inc*, November 1997, p. 42.

[14] Nicholas Korkham, *The World's Greatest Brands*, New York: Macmillan, 1996.

[15] Ibid.

[16] http://www.harley-davidson.com/experience/family/hog

[17] Ibid.

[18] Reid, "How Harley beat back the Japanese."

[19] Ibid.

[20] Lillie Guyer, "Escape roads," *Auto Week*, February 23, 1998.

customers directly through their own involvement with HOG events and Harley rallies. Harley's chief designer, Willy G. Davidson, and his wife have been going every year for twenty years to "Bike Week," an annual rally organized in Daytona Beach, Florida by the company for its customers. Asked about the design process at H-D, Willy G replied, "There is no manual, it's just drive and creative juices. We got input over a long time, from places like the Boot Hill Saloon and Sturgis, South Dakota about what our riders thought about the product."[21]

To continue growing its customer base and tap into a growing group of affluent baby boomers, H-D's marketing focus and target customer group have shifted. During the 1980s, the average Harley customer was 32 years old with a household income of $30,000. Today, the average customer is 44 years old with a household income of $72,000. Harley maintains an image of rebelliousness and non-conformity, but Harley riders have few associations with their Hell's Angel predecessors. HOG is a major supporter of the Muscular Dystrophy Foundation, and HOG members are the fourth-largest contributing group to the Jerry Lewis Telethon.

The dealers have played a central role in Harley's repositioning, growth, and fostering of customer loyalty. Forced initially by the company, over 500 of the 600 dealers in the United States have rebuilt, renovated, or substantially upgraded their stores. Dealers' showrooms have moved locations and gone from being gritty motorcycle shops to airy boutiques that feature a wide variety of items ranging from motorcycles to Zippo brand lighters. Recognizing that the dealers are the point of contact for the brand, Harley has also launched a $600,000 "Genuine Deal" campaign. The campaign is designed to build the Harley brand image, dealership loyalty, and dealership traffic. It is also geared to taking advantage of the growing parts and accessory business. Most parts and accessory sales occur during the first year of Harley motorcycle ownership, adding on average $3,500 in incremental retail sales.[22] As part of the Genuine Deal campaign dealers receive a Genuine Dealer promotion kit. The kit includes a television spot, three black-and-white small space ads, a radio ad, and a store-hours sign. The shift to selling clothing and collectibles as well as motorcycles and parts has been a major transition for many dealers.

Sales

The effectiveness of H-D's strategy, particularly the power of the Harley image, is evident in the fact that, despite a fourfold increase in production capacity, demand for Harley motorcycles continues to outstrip supply. Every motorcycle that H-D makes has already been sold long before it comes off the production line. For many models, would-be buyers must join a waiting-list. One result is that used bikes frequently sell at higher prices than new bikes; customers are willing to pay a premium to get a used Harley now rather than waiting a year or more before a dealer can ship the product. More generally, the rate of price depreciation of used Harleys is very low. Hence, the high price of the original purchase is mitigated by high resale values. At the same time, H-D has benefited not only from the appeal of its own products, but from the expansion of the market. While the overall motorcycle market in the US has seen little growth during the 1990s, the heavyweight segment has been an area of robust growth. Since 1993, registrations of heavyweight motorcycles in the US have grown at a rate of about 15 percent each year, with projected growth rates of 12–15 percent per year for the next decade. H-D's revenues and profits have also benefited from a shift in demand from the

---

[21] Tom Tucker, "Davidson clan member recalls Harley's U-turn," *Daytona Beach News Journal*, March 16, 1996.

[22] S. Eisenberg, "Harley-Davidson company report," Cibc Oppenheimer, October 14, 1997.

cheaper Sportster models to the more expensive models among the touring and custom ranges (see Exhibit 5).

Extending the Brand

For both H-D and its dealers, the proportion of revenue and profit contributed by the sales of parts, accessories, and "general merchandise" (clothing and collectibles) has grown over time (see Exhibit 6). During 1998, general merchandise were running close to 20 percent ahead of 1997, accounting for about 6 percent of total sales. Brand extensions include MotorClothes apparel and collectibles. Harley has also introduced a new line of denim products and the Spring MotorClothes line.

Only a small proportion of the clothing, collectibles, and other products bearing the Harley-Davidson trademark are sold through the H-D dealership network. Most of this business is a pure licensing operation where H-D's role is to sign the licensing agreements, collect the royalties, and ensure that the trademark is not devalued. The clothing bearing the Harley-Davidson logo has extended far beyond motorcycle apparel. For example, Nice Man Merchandising supplies children's clothing under the Harley brand. A giftware company is licensed to supply Harley holiday bulb ornaments, music boxes, and a Road King pewter motorcycle replica. In Europe, L'Oreal licensed the Harley name for a line of cologne. The first Harley-Davidson Cafe is in midtown Manhattan. The cafe is styled after a Hard-Rock Cafe and contains a gift shop serving up a gamut of Harley gift items including leather-clad Harley Barbie dolls. A second Harley Cafe recently opened in Las Vegas.

Eaglemark Financial Services

Eaglemark Financial Services was launched in 1993 with minority investment by H-D, and was later acquired. It was established to provide financial services to H-D dealers and customers, helping them to do business with H-D. It offers wholesale and retail financing, extended service contracts on Harley bikes, motorcycle insurance, and dealer insurance. More closely linked to its core motorcycle business has been H-D's expansion into financial services. Consumer finance is a critical service for any company selling big-ticket consumer durables. Prior to the formation of Eaglemark, H-D offered financing through Ford Motor Credit. In 1997, Eaglemark launched the Harley-Davidson Chrome VISA card.

In the first half of 1998, Eaglemark earned an operating income of $8.9 million, about 6 percent of H-D's total operating income, and up from $5.6 million a year previously.

Operations and Purchasing

Facilities

At the heart of H-D's business is its Milwaukee head office and nearby plants. The Milwaukee plants are responsible for engines and components. Under AMF's ownership the York, Pennsylvania assembly plant was opened. To alleviate the continuing pressure on capacity (since the 1986 IPO, H-D's motorcycle output has tripled), the Kansas City plant was opened in 1998. This plant will concentrate upon manufacturing Sportster models. Together with the Buell Motorcycle operation (see below), H-D's output will be close to 150,000 units in 1998. All plants are unionized. Exhibit 7 gives information on H-D's facilities.

European headquarters, based in Windsor, England, manages H-D Motor Company's activities in European, African, and Middle Eastern markets. The European heavyweight market is the largest worldwide, 18 percent bigger than the US. In the Asia-Pacific region the major markets are Japan and Australia/New Zealand. In "Other Asia," H-D's sales are primarily in Malaysia, Singapore, Thailand, and Hong Kong. Japan has a wholly owned subsidiary that services its 35 dealers. Three independent distributors service 55 Australian dealers.

Purchasing and supplier management

A large proportion of the final price of a Harley motorcycle is accounted for by the cost of bought-in components. Because H-D is unable to purchase in the volumes of rivals such as Yamaha and Suzuki, and does not possess the additional clout that Honda and BMW enjoy because of their big automotive operations, purchasing is a critical and problematic area for H-D. Purchasing managers are at senior levels within the H-D management structure. Says Garry Berryman, H-D's director of purchasing, "If purchasing is at a second or third tier level then it is too deep in the organization to have the early influence that it needs. In the 1990s, Harley made organizational changes to ensure that purchasing would be directly represented in the same group that wrestles with all the company's high-level strategic issues."[23]

In 1992, Harley extended its program of quality improvement to encompass its suppliers. It established a supplier advisory council (SAC) to expose supplier executives to the best practices of other suppliers in the Harley network.[24] Says Berryman, "Through the SAC, we're able to take some of the entrepreneurial aspects of our smaller, privately held suppliers and inject that enthusiasm, spirit, and energy into those that may be larger, publicly held companies." In this way, the SAC not only serves to improve purchasing efficiency, but also provides a forum to share information, ideas, and strategy. The SAC, says Berryman, is a way "to leverage the successes that occur in one area across the broader organization."[25] The SAC is made up of 16 suppliers, representing a cross-section of Harley's more than 400 OEM suppliers. Each SAC member contacts 9–12 other first-tier suppliers to get their input on various issues under review: costs, quality, scheduling, and strategy. The primary goal of the SAC is to spread best practices within Harley's supplier base and to improve the quality of Harley's own practices. Says Berryman, "The knowledge, leadership, and intelligence represented in our supplier council brings our capabilities well beyond what we could do with internal resources." Increased communication and coordination with suppliers is viewed as instrumental in improving Harley's new product development process. Says Leroy Zimdars, Harley's director of purchasing development, "We want suppliers to be deeply involved, at an early stage, in new product development. We'll use the SAC as a sounding board for how the supply base accepts the new structure, and we can react to it. The input is very candid, due to the close relationship between the SAC and the rest of the supply base."

Organizational Structure and Employee Empowerment

Following the management buyout of 1981, H-D's new management group systematically rethought management–employee relationships, employee responsibilities, and organizational structure. The result was a transformation in employee commitment and job satisfaction. "What other company has employees who tattoo the company name on their bodies? Or offers not just a job but a lifestyle?" observed an assembly-line worker at Harley's Milwaukee plant. Harley has a no-lay-off policy, 12 weeks of paid maternity leave, and unlimited sick days for salaried staffers.

---

[23] Ann Millen Porter, "One focus, one supply base," *Purchasing*, June 5, 1,1997.

[24] Kevin R. Fitzgerald, "Harley's supplier council helps deliver full value," *Purchasing*, September 5, 1996.

[25] Porter, "One focus, one supply base."

The process of management innovation continued when Harley's new Northland Plant went on-line in Kansas City in January 1998. The plant's management structure and working methods reflected the company's desire to make further advances in employee commitment and self-management. "I'm not aware of anybody anywhere doing anything that emulates this," says plant chief Karl Eberle.[26] In contrast to the traditional layout of Harley's other plants, the Northland Plant does not have a management space that oversees floor production from a glassed-in office upstairs. Instead, the plant manager and other administrators work in a "bullpen area" on the floor and in the center of the 330,000 square foot building.

In an effort to engage and motivate the entire plant workforce, management developed a novel operating structure different from anything else within the company. The structure comprises three types of teams:

- Natural work groups – *every worker belongs to a work group, with 8–15 people per group*
- Process operating groups – *comprised of representatives from each work group, there are four process operating groups; each oversees one of the plant's four operating divisions: paint, assembly, fabrication, and engine production*
- Plant leadership group – *a 14-member committee, responsible for governing the facility; comprised of the plant manager, the presidents of both unions representing the plant workforce, four elected representatives from the process groups, an elected representative from maintenance, and six administrators*

Harley is betting on this less hierarchical, team-based structure to improve employee motivation and accelerate the learning process at its new plant. Says plant chief Eberle, "We recognize there is a tremendous benefit – financially, psychologically, quality-wise, output-wise – to be gained by engaging the workforce."[27]

Harley Headquarters: from Hierarchy to Teams

The movement toward a flatter, more team-based organizational structure is also evident in recent changes occurring in Harley's overall corporate structure. "In our new organization," explains Clyde Fessler, VP for business development, "the Harley-Davidson Motor Company has been divided into three broad, functional areas called Circles. They are: the Create Demand Circle (CDC), the Produce Product Circle (PPC), and the Provide Support Circle (PSC). Each Circle is composed of the leaders representing the functions within it. The flexibility of the organization extends even to the decision of which functional areas are identified within a given circle. It is quite possible that Circle definitions may shift from time to time, depending on the demands of the business."[28] Like the team structure developed for the new Kansas City plant, each Circle operates as a team with the leadership role moving from person to person, depending on what issue is being addressed. Individual Circles meet once a month, and all three Circles meet together quarterly.

Overall coordination is provided by the Strategic Leadership Council (SLC), which is made up of individuals nominated by each of the three Circles. Explains Fessler:

---

[26] Stephen Roth, "Harley's goal: unify union and management," *Kansas City Business Journal*, May 16, 1997.
[27] Ibid.
[28] Clyde Fessler (H-D VP for Business Development), "Rotating leadership at Harley-Davidson: from hierarchy to interdependence," *Strategy & Leadership*, July 17, 1997.

The role of the SLC is to resolve issues that have not been settled previously by consensus in Circle meetings. Leadership of the Council also rotates, shifting to the Circle representative who "owns" the topic being discussed...The Circle format is especially valuable in that it facilitates systems thinking in our strategy implementation. If the marketing function plans to focus on a specific product, the Circles provide an opportunity to get feedback from manufacturing about timing and availability. If the manufacturing function needs to shut down its operations to upgrade equipment, the Circle structure allows all the affected functions to be involved in the decision. We have now been working with this organizational design for three and a half years. And we would probably all agree that the shift from hierarchy to Circles has not been easy – practicing consensus decision-making never is. However, defining the roles and responsibilities of each functional Circle and each Circle member has brought clarity, which in turn stimulates dialogue, trust, and eventually, non-threatening confrontation...Collaborative interdependent teams may not be able to move as quickly as the single decisive leader in a hierarchy, but they can be more innovative and resourceful and, ultimately, more effective in today's complex business climate.[29]

International Marketing

A key part of H-D's growth strategy is expanding its sales outside of the US and Canada. Europe is the focal point of H-D's overseas ambitions, simply because it is the largest heavyweight motorcycle market in the world. "A few years ago," says Harley CEO Bleustein, "our prime focus was the domestic market, and the rest was gravy. That view had to change. If our growth is to continue, Europe will have to play a significant part." Europe is also a huge challenge for H-D. Unlike in the US, H-D has never had a major position in Europe and it must fight to take market share from the market leaders: BMW, Honda, Kawasaki, and Yamaha. Harley launched its first large-scale European advertising campaign in the summer of 1998. The direct-response ads ran in style-conscious magazines such as *GQ* and *Esquire* in Europe with the intention of building up data on European potential customers and enhancing H-D's existing customer base.

A critical issue for international marketing is the extent to which the products and the Harley image need to be adjusted to meet the needs of overseas markets. Harley's image is rooted in American culture, and thus seems central to their appeals to European and Asian customers. "The US and Harley are tied together," says Hugo Wilson of Britain's *Bike* magazine, "the guy who's into Harleys here is also the guy who owns cowboy boots. You get a Harley and you're buying into the US mystique."[30] At the same time, the composition of demand and the customer profile is different in overseas markets. The European motorcycle market differs significantly from the American market in that 70 percent of the heavy motorcycle market is for performance bikes (such as the popular Japanese high-power, lightweight, racing-style bikes), while the touring/cruiser bikes such as those Harley makes account for only 30 percent. European buyers tend to be knowledgeable and highly style conscious. Also, European roads and riding style are different from the US. As a result, Harley has modified its 1998 models to the needs and tastes of its European customers. The US Sportster, for example, has a straight handlebar instead of curled buckhorns and a new suspension system to improve cornering. The name has also changed to the "Custom 53." The Harley Softail has also received a new look, becoming the "Night Train." As in the US, Harley management regards the after-sale value of biker clubs and events as a critical differentiator for its product. The biggest Harley gathering ever planned was for June 20, 1998 in Austria, when some 10,000 European Harley owners were expected to gather in celebration of the company's 95th anniversary.

---

[29] Ibid.

[30] Marco R. della Cava, "Motorcycle maker caters to the continent," *USA Today*, April 22, 1998.

The European heavyweight market grew strongly during the mid- to late 1990s, especially in Italy, where a new customer base of Italian youth has driven sales. "Sales to those 25 and younger are about 3% among the world's motorcycle manufacturers," says Carlo Talamo, owner of 40 Numero Uno Harley Stores scattered around Italy. "In Italy [the youth market] is 37%."[31] However, despite growing sales, Harley has found it difficult to increase its market share significantly in Europe. The high price of Harleys and the rising value of the US dollar during the late 1990s have given Japanese and European manufacturers a competitive edge.

Buell Motorcycle Company

Harley regards Buell as an important extension of its market position and a potential market winner in Europe. Founded by ex-Harley engineer Erik Buell in the 1980s, Buell Motor Co. produces bikes that synthesize the comfort and style of a Harley cruiser with the high-performance attributes of a sports bike. Harley purchased a 49 percent stake in Buell in 1993, and more recently gained majority ownership. Buell bikes use Harley engines and other components, but mount them on a lighter, stiffer frame. The superior handling and acceleration of Buell models are appealing to the European market, where customers are younger and tend to put greater value on sporty performance and a cheaper price tag.

In the US, the Buell bikes are also targeted for a younger, more price-sensitive and performance-oriented market. In the US, the typical Buell customer is seven years younger and the price tag is about $10,000 compared to an average Harley price of $15,000.[32] To appeal to this younger segment, Harley has been using slogans such as "Pull Some Gs" and "Different in Every Sense" to advertise Buell bikes.[33] In addition, the company formed the Buell Riders Adventure Group (BRAG) modeled after HOG. Buell produced 4,462 units in 1997 and plans to increase that number to 5,500 by the end of 1998.[34]

LOOKING AHEAD

As he examined in detail the budget projections for the third quarter of 1998, Bleustein considered the remarkable achievements of H-D over the past decade and a half. From 40,000 bikes a year, H-D had grown to produce over 150,000 bikes in 1998, with capacity rising to 200,000 units per year. Yet even with expanded output and a big price premium over rival machines produced by Japanese competitors, H-D still faced a waiting-list for most of its models.

Did H-D really need to worry about competition? A Harley was a Harley. All the market research pointed to the improbability of Harley customers buying a look-alike Japanese machine, even if it was cheaper and embodied more advanced technology. And yet, the competitive situation was changing. In Europe, Harley was a relative newcomer – it was BMW, Triumph, Ducati, and Moto Guzzi which represented motorcycling tradition. In the US, H-D faced a new breed of competitor, US manufacturers such as Polaris and Excelsior which directly challenged H-D with retro-styled big bikes that also sought to recreate American motorcycle nostalgia. As H-D expanded its market share from a single segment – the US super-heavyweight market – it inevitably was

---

[31] Ibid.

[32] "Harley battles to stay on top of US biker revival," *Financial Times*, April 22, 1998.

[33] Chris Reidy, "Wheels are in motion for area Harley dealer," *Boston Globe*, April 24, 1998.

[34] "Harley battles to stay on top of US biker revival."

drawn into competition with companies that possessed greater size, resources, and technological capabilities than H-D. Indeed, the Buell subsidiary represented a direct attack upon the performance bike market long dominated by the Japanese.

Apart from competition, there was also the question of whether the market for heavyweight motorcycles would continue to grow. The demand for Harley bikes had been remarkably resilient to downturns in the general economy. However, the world seemed to be moving into a new era of economic uncertainty. Warnings of global recession were hardly encouraging to any company that sold a leisure product costing up to $20,000 a unit. But the risks were not simply from a deteriorating economy. H-D, Bleustein reminded himself, was in the business, not of selling motorcycles, but of selling a lifestyle. Would this lifestyle have the same appeal in the decade of the 2000s as in the 1990s?

Appendix 1: Harley-Davidson, Summary of Financial Statements, 1994–1998

	1994	1995	1996	1997	1st half 97	1st half 98
Net sales	1,159	1,350	1,531	1,762	871.2	983.7
Gross profit	358	411	490	586	288.5	327.4
Operating Income						
Motorcycle and related products					135.5	154.3
Financial services	—	3.6	7.8	12.4	5.6	8.9
Selling, admin., engineering					(4.6)	(5.2)
Total income from operations	153.6	180.8	228.4	270.0	136.4	158.0
Interest income	1.7	0.1	3.3	7.9	3.7	1.4
Other income/(expense)	1.2	(4.9)	(4.1)	(1.6)	2.0	(1.8)
Income before taxes	156.4	176.0	227.6	276.3	142.1	157.7
Provision for income taxes	60.2	64.9	84.2	102.2	52.6	57.5
Net Income	104.3	112.5	166.0	174.1	89.5	100.1
Earnings per share (diluted)	$0.62	$0.73	$0.94	$1.13	$0.59	$0.66

Balance sheets	1994	1995	1996	1997	June 1997	June 1998
Assets						
Current assets						
Cash and cash equivalents	59.3	31.5	142.5	147.5	144.5	154.5
Finance receivables, net	—	169.6	183.8	249.3	237.7	346.1
Accounts receivable, net	143.4	134.2	141.3	102.8	198.7	91.3
Inventories	173.4	84.4	101.4	117.5	101.4	131.5
Other	20.1	20.3	44.0	43.0	40.9	44.6
Total current assets	405.6	337.2	613.1	704.0	644.1	724.1
Property, plant, equipment	262.8	284.8	409.4	528.9	454.1	562.0
Total assets	739.2	1,000.7	1,230.0	1,598.9	1,453.4	1,746.1

Continued ...

Continued ...

Liabilities & stockholder's equity

Current liabilities

Current portion of finance debt	18.2	2.7	8.6	90.6	56.3	126.0
Accounts payable	64.0	102.6	100.7	106.1	117.4	294.5
Total current liabilities	216.3	233.2	251.1	361.7	324.4	420.4
Finance debt	0	164.3	258.1	280.0	250.0	280.0
Other long-term liabilities	89.7	108.6	70.3	62.1	70.0	63.3
Post-retirement benefits	n.a.	n.a.	65.8	68.4	67.2	70.2
Total stockholders' equity	433.2	494.6	662.7	826.7	741.7	912.1
Total liabilities & stockholders' equity	739.2	1,000.7	1,230.0	1,598.9	1,453.4	1,746.0

Cash flows	*1994*	*1995*	*1996*	*1997*	*1st half 97*	*1st half 98*
Operating activities – net cash flow	80.8	169.1	228.3	309.7	100.6	166.7
Capital expenditures	(94.7)	(113.0)	(178.8)	(186.2)	(76.3)	(69.1)
Investing activities	(96.6)	(187.8)	(213.8)	(406.5)	(138.7)	(177.4)
Financing activities	(2.6)	(10.5)	96.5	101.8	40.1	17.7

Source: Harley-Davidson financial statements (www.harley-davidson.com).

Appendix 2: **Harley-Davidson's Competitors**

Excelsior Henderson Motorcycle Manufacturing Company (Excelsior)

In the early 1990s two brothers, Dave and Dan Hanlon, bought the trademarks to a pre-war motorcycle manufacturer, Excelsior and Henderson. Formed in 1876, Excelsior Supply Co. was one of the top three US motorcycle manufacturers at the turn of the century along with Indian Motorcycle and Harley-Davidson. Its motorcycle was the first to break the 100mph barrier. However, the company was liquidated during the Depression (1931). Over 60 years later, the Hanlon brothers are trying to resuscitate its image by manufacturing, marketing, and selling cruisers and touring bikes under the Excelsior brand name. The Hanlons feel that the Excelsior brand "evokes an authentic American motorcycling heritage and lifestyle"[35] and will be able to create a mystique similar to that associated with the Harley name.

The Hanlons have developed a prototype of a retro-style cruiser with the latest technology and accessories, such as electronic fuel injection, a four-valve cylinder, and an overhead cam engine. The Super X, the inaugural model, is "reminiscent of the classic American heavyweight cruiser" and will be sold through independent dealers at a sticker price between $17,000 and $20,000 (a price comparable to the high-end Harley "Fat Boy"). The first bike will be produced during the first quarter of 1998 with 5,500 orders already awaiting delivery. It is estimated that the company will

---

[35] "Excelsior Henderson selects J. D. Edwards to provide smooth ride to growth," *Business Wire*, March 24, 1998.

need to sell 5,000 bikes per year to achieve break-even. Excelsior is projecting sales of $5.4 million in 1998 and $284 million in 2002.

Excelsior is a development-stage company with no revenue recorded to date and a reported net loss in 1997 of $5.9 million and a $2.5 million loss in 1996. Construction of the company's new administrative and manufacturing facility in Belle Plain, MN, was financed through a 1997 $28 million IPO and a $1.7 million State of Minnesota equipment financing bond. The facility will manufacture 20,000 bikes per year by 2003 and will include a motorcycle heritage museum. Since neither of the two brothers is experienced in motorcycle manufacturing and sales, the Hanlons have formed a top management team, which includes VP of Manufacturing and Operations Allan Hurd (a former production engineer at Triumph who assisted in the rejuvenation of that brand), and VP for Sales and Marketing Dave Auringer, who created the Sea-Doo dealership network. Auringer has already singed up 36 independent dealers (some of whom are Harley-Davidson dealers) with promised margins of 25 percent.[36] Dealers are already carrying Excelsior merchandise and accessories such as leather jackets and T-shirts which generated $100,000 sales in 1997.

Polaris

A leading snowmobile, ATV (all-terrain vehicle), and personal watercraft maker since the 1950s, Polaris will launch a new cruiser, the Polaris Victory, in the spring of 1998. With a retro look and new technology, Victory will target the high-margin, high-growth cruiser market dominated by Harley. Victory will have the biggest available V-engine (1507cc), overhead cams, and electronic fuel injection. High-tech engineering has also "eliminated some of the noise and vibration associated with a Harley."[37] The Victory will be positioned to compete with technologically advanced Honda, Suzuki, Kawasaki, and Yamaha cruisers, even though its price of $13,000 places it above most Japanese models. Polaris says that the plan is to "compete with Japanese on price, quality, and technology." The company stresses its "made in the USA" appeal to attract customers away from these foreign competitors and is counting on its previous experience making personal watercraft and ATVs to beat the competition. According to CEO Wendel, "We met these guys in snowmobiles and ATVs and we beat their asses off."[38] Polaris does have past success with taking on Japanese competitors. In the early 1990s, Polaris entered the personal watercraft and the ATV markets, both dominated by Japanese competitors – Kawasaki and Honda respectively. Since then, Polaris has gained the number two market share in ATV sales (37 percent of Polaris' 1996 revenue), and challenged Kawasaki's dominance of the personal watercraft market by gaining significant market share and brand recognition.

With $1.2 billion in revenues (1996) and 45 percent profit margins, Polaris is a very efficient and aggressive company with high-tech manufacturing capabilities and a wide distribution network of 2,000 dealers. Over 600 dealers have been selected to offer the Victory, and the company is counting on cross-selling opportunities with its other vehicles (28 percent of Polaris customers already own a motorcycle).[39] Aside from its distribution network, the company is also leveraging its engineering and manufacturing capabilities. Engineering of the new cruiser was performed in-house,

---

[36] "Motorcycles," *The Orlando Sentinel*, November 13, 1997; and Ballon, "Born to be wild."

[37] Macario Juarez, "City business to help debut American Harley rival," *Albuquerque Tribune*, December 18, 1997.

[38] Paul Klebnikov, "Clear the roads, here comes Victory," *Forbes*, October 20, 1997.

[39] Ronald Ahrens, "Harley faces competition from Polaris bike," *Star Tribune*, December 20, 1997.

lowering development costs, and production and assembly will take place at two plants that have extra capacity. As a result, the Victory was developed on a $20 million budget, and Polaris will reach break-even at 4,000 motorcycles per year (3 percent of the current cruiser market).

Polaris anticipates becoming a significant player in the motorcycle market in a few years by developing a line of touring, cruiser, and performance bikes with projected sales of $500 million by 2003. The company will limit production to 3,000 Victory cruisers this year, but will move to expand capacity to 40,000–50,000 per year.[40] Polaris is known as an efficient, low-cost manufacturer. Despite a decline in sales in 1996, the company reported its ninth year of increased earnings primarily due to cost-cutting measures and new engine-sourcing arrangements.[41]

BMW

Even though BMW sold ten times more cars than motorcycles in 1996, the company is committed to supporting and developing its line of bikes. In 1996 motorcycles contributed DM 1 billion to the company's DM 60 billion revenues.[42] BMW Motorcycles will celebrate its 75th anniversary in 1998 and its bikes have led the way to technical innovation, pioneering such things as advanced suspension systems, anti-lock brakes, and fuel injection.[43] Because of these technological innovations, BMW motorcycles have lower operating costs than the competition. In a recent comparison of Kawasaki and BMW touring bikes, the California Police Department estimated an operating cost of 1.9 cents per mile for the Kawasaki model tested, compared to an operating cost of 1.7 cents per mile for the BMW model tested.[44] The company has always been associated with a high technical and quality standard, and its motorcycles are also known for reliability, safety, and comfort. BMW is repositioning its motorcycle brand to build on this reputation but at the same time disassociate motorcycles from its luxury cars.[45]

BMW offers a full line of performance and touring bikes, and recently it has introduced its first cruiser, the R1200C. The motorcycle was introduced in 1997 as part of the latest James Bond movie, "Tomorrow Never Dies," and became BMW's best-selling bike in its first model year.[46] R1200C includes the latest technological innovations and safety features; however, it departs from the retro look favored by other producers. In creating the bike, BMW assumed that in the future "high performance cruisers will replace retro-look customs with a sportier look and feel."[47] The R1200C would be the first in this category. At a price of $23,600, the cruiser will be priced $2,000 above a comparable Harley model. However, the BMW motorcycle can command a premium due to its unsurpassed features such as anti-lock disc brakes (the only motorcycle to have this technology), superior acceleration performance, and a liquid-cooled engine (which allows the bike to idle in traffic and hot weather).[48] Half of R1200C buyers are those who already own a Harley, and the other

---

[40] Strauss, "Born to be bikers."

[41] James Miller, "Spotlight on: Polaris Industries," *Anchorage Daily News*, March 15, 1998.

[42] http://www.bmw.com

[43] Richard Truett, "Motorcycling has long run in the BMW family," *The Orlando Sentinel*, March 5, 1998.

[44] John O'Dell, "Giving chase: BMW wants to break Kawasaki's and Harley's hold on the police market," *Los Angeles Times*, September 21, 1997.

[45] "BMW in control with Bond bike cruiser," *The San Diego Union Tribune*, March 14, 1998.

[46] Truett, "Motorcycling has long run in the BMW family."

[47] Adrian Blake, "Two motorcycle giants celebrate anniversaries," *The Toronto Star*, April 11, 1998.

[48] O'Dell, "Giving chase"; and *The Evening Post* (Wellington), November 21, 1997

half are those who own a Japanese motorcycle. BMW will introduce a new cruiser model in 1998 and a new touring model in 1999.[49]

Honda

Honda Motor Co. has been manufacturing motorcycles since 1948 and entered the US market in 1959, first with cheaper, lightweight bikes, before quickly moving into the higher-priced segments such as performance and touring bikes. Today, it is the world's largest motorcycle manufacturer, with 5,198,000 bikes produced in 1997 (vs. 54,000 made by BMW and 132,000 made by Harley).[50] The company holds 27 percent of the total US motorcycle market, a close second to Harley-Davidson. (See Exhibit 3 for US market share data.) Honda is a superior engineering company and its motorcycles have traditionally been "on the leading edge of technology."[51] Its performance bikes have dominated motorcycle racing for decades and are associated with the world's greatest racers. In the early 1970s the company also had great success with street and touring bikes with the introduction of the style-setting CB750K0 in 1969 and the Goldwing, the world's first long-distance touring bike, in 1975.[52] Honda's motorcycles are technically superior to most of the competition, and are offered at a lower price owing to the company's scale and efficient distribution advantages. In 1998, Honda plans to revise its line of ten motorcycles to celebrate its 50th anniversary in the motorcycle business.[53]

Smaller competitors

Ducati,[54] a "highly regarded but underfunded [Italian] company" attracts customers by leveraging its legendary reputation for high-performance stylish motorcycles. Traditionally, the company has concentrated on the performance segment of the market and sells about 4,000 of these motorcycles in the US each year. However, in 1998 Ducati is expanding into the touring bike market in an effort to double its sales.

Triumph,[55] a British manufacturer, began motorcycle production in 1902. By 1909 the company was producing 3,000 bikes per year and by the 1950s became one of the world's most renowned motorcycle brands (in part thanks to its appearance as Marlon Brando's bike in the classic movie "The Wild One"). However, by the 1970s the company faced financial problems and was forced to liquidate in 1983. Primarily due to the efforts of its current head John Bloor, the company revived in the early 1990s and began development and production of new models. In 1996 the company produced 50,000 bikes (touring, cruisers) and unveiled plans to introduce a new performance motorcycle. The company's most popular model (25 percent of production capacity) is a cruiser, Thunderbird. Thunderbird's styling is similar to that of the 1960s Triumph model with the same name and the bike is positioned to capture a part of the lucrative heavyweight cruiser market.

---

[49] Jean Halliday, "BMW bikes get 'bridge' print ad effort for spring," *Advertising Age*, March 30, 1998.
[50] http://www.honda.com; http://www.bmw.com; and Exhibit 1
[51] Blake, "Two motorcycle giants."
[52] Ibid.
[53] Ibid.
[54] Valerie Morris, "Ducati's market challenge," *Business Unusual*, CNN, April 17, 1998.
[55] http://www.georgian.net/rally/triumph

Big Dog Motorcycles,[56] produces high-end, customized cruisers for prices that often exceed those of comparable Harleys (between $18,000 and $26,000). The company produces 300 bikes per year and primarily sells to customers who do not want to "buy a Harley and put thousands of dollars in it to get it up to real world standards."

Other Japanese competitors

Several Japanese companies followed Honda's example and entered the US motorcycle market in the 1970s. Yamaha, Suzuki, and Kawasaki began with sales of small, lightweight motorcycles and moved into the "heavyweight" segments of cruisers and touring bikes. Most compete on technological innovation and low price driven by the economies of scale of these large companies. However, while these companies had great success in gaining share in the overall motorcycle market (see Exhibit 3), they have captured only 25 percent of the cruiser market, where the Japanese product competes less effectively against the "Made in the USA" Harley mystique.

Exhibit 1: Annual Production of Motorcycles by Harley-Davidson

1901	*1903*	*1913*	*1920*	*1933*	*1936*	*1948*	*1953*
3	150	12,904	28,189	3,700	9,812	31,163	14,050

1966	*1975*	*1981*	*1986*	*1987*	*1988*	*1989*	*1990*
36,310	75,403	41,586	36,700	43,300	50,500	58,900	62,500

1991	*1992*	*1993*	*1994*	*1995*	*1996*	*1997*	
68,600	76,500	81,700	95,500	105,104	118,800	132,300	

Source: www.harley-davidson.com

Exhibit 2: Harley-Davidson's Motorcycle Registrations, 1993–1997

	1993	*1994*	*1995*	*1996*	*1997*
United States	132,800	150,400	163,100	178,500	205,400
Harley-Davidson	63,400	69,500	77,000	79,936	93,491
Market share (650+ cc)	47.7%	46.2%	47.2%	44.8%	45.5%
Europe	218,600	201,900	207,200	224,688	250,293
Harley-Davidson	13,200	14,400	15,400	15,300	15,300
Market share (650+ cc)	6.1%	7.1%	7.4%	6.8%	6.1%
Japan/Australia	35,700	39,100	39,400	37,417	58,880
Harley-Davidson	6,700	7,600	7,900	8,200	9,700
Market share (650+ cc)	18.7%	19.4%	20.1%	21.9%	16.5%

Source: www.harley-davidson.com

---

[56] http://www.bigdogmotorcycles.com

Exhibit 3: **Market Shares in Heavyweight Motorcycles, 1997 (%)**

	North America	Europe	Japan/Australia
Harley-Davidson	48.3	6.1	16.5
Honda	18.6	25.0	30.1
Kawasaki	10.6	10.7	20.2
Suzuki	10.5	17.2	8.7
Yamaha	5.8	17.2	13.9
BMW	2.4	12.6	4.0
Other	3.8	11.2	6.6

Source: Harley-Davidson *Annual Report*, 1997.

Exhibit 4: **Heavyweight Motorcycles: Price Comparisons, 1998**

Manufacturer and model	Engine	Price ($)
H-D XLH 800 Sportster	V-twin, air-cooled, 840cc	5,845
H-D XL 1200S Sportster	V-twin, air-cooled, 1203cc	8,395
H-D DynaWide Glide	V-twin, air-cooled, 1340cc	14,775
H-D Bad Boy	V-twin, air-cooled, 1340cc	14,925
H-D Heritage Softtail Classic	V-twin, air-cooled, 1340cc	15,157
H-D FLSTS	V-twin, air-cooled, 1340cc	16,995
Honda Shadow ACE 750	V-twin, OHC, 745cc	6,299
Honda Pacific Coast	V-twin, liquid-cooled, 800cc	8,699
Honda Shadow Aero	V-twin, liquid-cooled, 1099cc	9,695
Honda Shadow ACE Tourer	V-twin, liquid-cooled, 1099cc	10,999
Suzuki Maurauder	V-twin, liquid-cooled, OHC, 805cc	5,999
Suzuki Intruder	V-twin, air-cooled, 1462cc	9,899
Kawasaki Vulcan 800	V-twin, 8-valve, OHC	7,999
Kawasaki Vulcan Classic	V-twin, air-cooled, 1470cc	11,590
Yamaha 750 Virago	V-twin, OHC, 749cc	6,499
BMW F650	Liquid-cooled, double OHC, 652cc	7,490
BMW R1200 Cruiser	Horizontal-twin, 1170cc	12,990
Polaris Victory V92C	V-twin, 4-valve OHC, 1507cc	13,595

Source: www.motorcycle.com

Exhibit 5: **Harley-Davidson Shipments 1997–1998**

	Jan.–June 1997	Jan.–June 1998
Motorcycle shipments		
United States	48,211	52,650
Export	18,614	19,585
Motorcycle product mix		
Touring	20.9%	24.4%
Custom	54.7%	53.5%
Sportster	24.4%	22.1%
Buell motorcycle shipments		
United States	1,118	1,287
Export	989	1,520

Source: Harley-Davidson quarterly results (www.harley-davidson.com).

Exhibit 6: **Harley-Davidson's Sales Of Parts, Accessories, And General Merchandise, 1986–1997 ($ million)**

	1986	1990	1991	1992	1993	1994	1995	1996	1997
Parts and Accessories	35.7	80.2	94.3	103.6	127.8	162.0	192.1	210.2	241.9
General merchandise	9.4	29.8	36.0	52.1	71.2	94.3	100.2	90.7	95.1

Source: Harley-Davidson financial statements (www.harley-davidson.com).

Exhibit 7a: **Harley-Davidson facilities, 1997**

Location	Function	Total employment
Wisconsin		2,400
Milwaukee	Corporate Headquarters, parts/accessories sales, R&D	
Wauwatosa	XL Engine/Transmission production, Product Development Center	
Menomonee Falls	FL Engine/Transmission production	
Franklin	Parts/Accessories Distribution Center	
Tomahawk	Fiberglass parts production/painting	
Pennsylvania		2,600
York	Final assembly plant, parts and painting	
Missouri		350 by 1998
Kansas City	Manufacturing, painting	

Source: Harley-Davidson *Annual Report*, 1997.

Exhibit 7b: **Comparative Financial Data for Harley-Davidson, Polaris, and Excelsior ($ million, except per-share data)**

	Harley-Davidson		Polaris		Excelsior	
	1996	1997	1996	1997	1996	1997
Assets						
Current assets						
Cash	142.50	147.50	5.8	1.2	9.40	24.20
Trade receivables	141.30	102.79	36.2	42.6	0.00	0.00
Finance subsidiary receivables	183.80	293.33	0.0	0.0	0.00	0.00
Inventories	101.39	117.48	122.9	139.4	0.00	0.00
Other	44.14	42.96	28.5	34.1	0.01	0.11
Finance receivables (net)	154.26	249.35	0.0	0.0	0.00	0.00
Property and equipment (net)	409.43	528.87	93.5	98.0	0.23	13.40
Intangible assets (net)	40.90	38.70	24.4	23.5	0.14	0.20
Other	82.26	77.96	40.4	45.8	0.23	10.20
Liabilities						
Current liabilities	251.10	361.69	161.4	191.0	0.41	3.30
Long-term debt	250.00	280.00	35.0	24.4	0.00	13.70
Other	136.17	130.54	0.0	0.0	0.00	0.00
Shareholders' equity	662.72	826.67	155.3	169.2	9.60	31.20
Sales	1,531.20	1,762.60	1,191.9	1,048.3	0.00	0.00
COGS	1,041.10	1,176.40	928.1	785.8	0.00	0.00
Gross profit	490.10	586.20	263.8	262.5	0.00	0.00
SG&A	224.35	262.91	138.1	142.7	1.41	3.9
R&D	37.30	53.30	28.3	26.7	1.27	2.60
Operating income	265.75	323.29	97.4	93.1	(2.68)	(6.50)
Non-operating expenses:						
Interest expense (income)	(3.30)	(7.87)	4.3	2.8	0.00	0.00
Taxes	84.20	102.20	35.0	36.8	0.00	0.00
Other expenses (income)	(18.52)	1.57	(4.20)	(11.80)	(0.17)	(0.63)
Net income	203.37	227.39	62.3	65.3	(2.51)	(5.87)
Net income per share	$1.10	$1.15	$2.24	$2.45	$(0.43)	$(0.65)

Sources: www.harley-davidson.com; www.polarisindustries.com; http://sec.gov

Exhibit 7c: **Comparative Financial Data For Honda and BMW ($ million)**

	Honda		BMW	
	1996	1997	1996	1997
Balance sheet data				
Assets				
Current assets				
Cash	2,894	2,035	437	451
Trade receivables	3,077	2,525	299	443
Finance subsidiary receivables	9,187	11,261	—	—
Inventories	4,442	4,395	1,084	1,186
Other	5,293	5,458	2,689	2,900
Property and equipment (net)	8,353	8,387	2,419	2,662
Intangible assets (net)	—	—	55	41
Other	532	536	2,717	3,041
Liabilities				
Current Liabilities	14,577	14,516	4,393	4,816
Long Term Debt	5,918	6,153	36	35
Other	2,095	1,956	1,346	2,146
Shareholders' equity	11,190	11,971	3,927	3,727
Income statement data				
Sales	41,477	45,383	18,269	20,200
COGS	29,406	31,336	11,633	12,966
Gross profit	12,071	14,047	6,636	7,234
Other operating income	—	—	584	491
SG&A	7,148	8,119	6,833	7,219
R&D	2,007	2,211	n.a.	n.a.
Operating income	2,916	3,717	386	506
Non-operating expenses				
Interest	222	194	—	—
Taxes	1,282	1,760	212	351
Other expenses (income)	(351)	(212)	(138)	(105)
Net income	1,763	1,975	313	260

See Exhibit 7.C for comparable figures for H–D.

Exchange rates used:
  Yen/Dollar 1996: 124.08yen/$
  Yen/Dollar 1997: 130.10yen/$
  DM/Dollar 1996 and 1997: 1.77DM/$

Sources: http://www.honda.com and http://www.bmw.com

WORKBRAIN CORPORATION[1]

case 17

Trevor Hunter and

Mary Crossan

> It's almost as if I had another eye added to my head. This person would give me insight to see different perspectives, yet at the same time be part of the company. I don't like the term "outsider" but, really, it's like adding a new function to the business that allowed me to think in new directions.
>
> David Ossip, President and CEO of Workbrain Corporation

Introduction

Eric Green, the newly hired vice-president, Corporate Development at Workbrain Corporation, looked at his offer letter (which was one half page long) and wondered how his role would evolve. There was no job description in the letter, and the president of the firm had given him some far-reaching and abstract goals. The position had been described to him as one that would mainly

---

[1]Some of the information in this case is taken from internal Workbrain documents authored by Daniel Debow, Matt Chapman, Eric Green and other members of the Workbrain management team.

IVEY

Trevor Hunter prepared this case under the supervision of Professor Mary Crossan solely to provide material for class discussion. The author does not intend to illustrate either effective or ineffective handling of a managerial situation. The author may have disguised certain names and other identifying information to protect confidentiality.

involve developing external partnerships with some emphasis on the internal development of the firm. However, from Green's perspective, there were many issues that needed to be handled both on the internal and external sides of the business. At the time, the Workbrain sales team was in the process of securing a major client, there were some growth goals that needed to be achieved and there were no organizational protocols for making a sale in place. There was little time to organize his new office.

Eric Green

Eric Green had recently graduated from an MBA program in Fontainebleu, France. Having practiced both corporate law and been a management consultant, he had several years of corporate experience behind him, yet when he graduated he had entrepreneurial aspirations. It was through the process of trying to start his own business that he was made aware of Workbrain.

> A couple of my friends and I had worked together in cyber-entrepreneurship class and we had put together a business plan that we were quite excited about. After school, we came back thinking we would shop it around to see what we would find.
>
> In the course of doing that I called a friend of mine who had been involved in the Internet for five years in Toronto who I figured would be a good person to run it by. He referred me to David Ossip saying that David was a strong technology guy and could probably shed some light on the industry. He also suggested that David was starting a company and that I might want to look at it.
>
> I went to the (old) Workbrain website and it didn't look that interesting. My friend called me later and said that David wanted me to call him and he felt I would be a good fit with his company. I thought he would want me to be an implementation consultant and that was not what I was looking to do. I was looking for business development, with a more strategic focus. When I finally met with David we didn't talk about my business plan at all because what he told me about the company was a very powerful and compelling story. It was almost too good to be true; he was looking for somebody to do exactly what I wanted to do, and it was in a company at the exact stage of development that I wanted, in the industry I wanted.

Green's role was very loosely defined and there were high expectations of him. He was given a lot of responsibility but also a lot of autonomy to make the decisions he needed to make and David Ossip was completely on his side. Ossip described the role and the type of person he wanted to fill it:

> The individual I was looking for was someone who was very bright, who was a quick thinker, someone who could push the organization and really push me into growing it and who would be able to communicate the vision to the other people in the organization.
>
> I also wanted someone who could function as a recruiter to get other very bright people into the company. I needed a person who would be able to work out how we were going to get the right people we needed into the corporation, and how we were going to come up with an environment to keep them.
>
> Also, we had to define what these people would be doing. Because we were a new company, a lot of the time we would have to hire people before we had active projects and we had to make sure that they would be busy and productive even though they might be (in consultants' terms) on the beach.

I wanted someone who could come in and think in almost textbook terms of how we could scale the business up and build an infrastructure while the rest of us were focused on more operational kinds of functions. It was right up front that I thought about this position.

Ossip did not have to sell Green on the job. Green knew Ossip's track record and was confident in his abilities. Although the job was not well defined, Green felt that the way it was presented to him, this job would offer him the challenges he wanted:

> He described the role as both external development and internal development. I knew coming in that I would be wearing many different hats. On the external side I would be helping with the strategy, the marketing side and forming alliances. Since we knew that we wanted to partner with consulting firms, my background made me a good fit. On the internal side, I would be managing the strategic growth of the company, which was of interest to me since some of my experience was applicable to that as well.
>
> When I first joined the company we were in the middle of an RFP (request for proposal) development for a large client that we were pitching and it was a good opportunity to get involved right away. I was helping to draft documents about a system that I didn't really know. At the time I was the only person in the company who didn't have a technical background.

Workbrain

Workbrain was founded in 1999 by a group of former employees of a leading supplier of client-server labor management systems, headed by president and CEO David Ossip. Years earlier, Ossip had founded this previously very successful company that had specialized in time and attendance management.

Ossip possessed a combination of technical, industry and management experience that he turned into a successful business that was eventually purchased by a larger firm. When he sold the firm and began thinking about starting a new company, he was able to gather together a trusted group of former colleagues to form the management team out of which the concept for Workbrain was born.

The members of the Workbrain management team all had extensive contacts in various industries and were recognized for their firm's expertise. At the time of Green's arrival, Workbrain was not very large. Table 1 presents a list of all the employees and their roles. As can be seen, at the time, every employee was also a senior executive.

Table 1: **Employees and their Roles**

Name	Role
David Ossip	President and CEO
Martin Ossip	Executive Director
Ezra Kiser	VP and GM, US Operations
Scott Morrell	VP Technology
Raymond Nunn	VP Operations
David Stein	VP Sales
Eric Green	VP Corporate Development

The firm had secured US$5.5 million in start-up capital from investors. The main activities in the small offices they rented were either the preparation of the RFP or the development and testing of the system.

From his knowledge of the industry, Ossip recognized that an opportunity existed in the form of the millions of routine employee transactions that took place to track and manage hourly or "blue-collar" workforces (e.g., time-clock entries, employee scheduling, overtime allocation, etc.). Exhibit 1 presents the competitive position of Workbrain in relation to its indirect competitors. Several firms had developed automated systems to manage the activities of so-called "white-collared" or professional workers (e.g., expense reports, travel schedules, etc.); however, there were no firms that focused directly on the "blue-collar" workforce. Considering that in the United States alone, it was estimated that there were 64 million "blue-collar" workers,[2] there was clearly an opportunity. The market was generally broken out on a "per seat" basis, which referred to a per employee calculation. Therefore, the market size calculation was found by taking the number of employees in target companies multiplied by the dollar value per seat. The enterprise software industry generally priced its software between US$100 to US$300 per seat.

Workbrain's main product was an e-business application suite that combined workforce management, workplace administration and workplace community process automation.

The market in which Workbrain operated was highly competitive, yet the other firms all could be described as indirect competitors. There were no other firms that had workforce management products specifically designed for the large "blue-collar" workforce. Those "blue-collar" workforce management systems that were available were either "shrink-wrapped systems" that were "optimized for smaller organizations with less complex hourly labor rules," or were "based on older client-server technologies" that were more difficult and costly to deploy.

A direct comparison with the workforce management industry leader, Kronos Inc. (which had an estimated 50 per cent of the market), revealed that more than 75 per cent of the company's installed base used UNIX and DOS-based applications that meant they had limited Internet functionality.[3] Internet functionality was the basis of Workbrain's product and was in line with industry analysts who predicted that much of the workforce management would soon be web-based. The low implementation cost, flexible architecture and Web-based ease of operation gave Workbrain a strong competitive advantage.

Once the product was installed, managers of Workbrain's clients could more effectively automate hourly employee processes such as time and attendance tracking, activity-based costing and employee scheduling. At the same time their clients' employees could, in turn, request shift changes, vacations, and overtime, administer their benefits claims and carry out a host of other value-added, third-party transactions. In short, the product allowed Workbrain's clients to better manage their workforce through real time information transfer and analysis, while also providing the hourly employees more control over their activities and access to information that they needed to better perform their jobs and make their lives away from work easier, all through web-based technology.

There were clear benefits to the clients in that the system would significantly reduce a number of administrative costs and payroll charges. It was estimated that form-processing costs ranged

---

[2] U.S. Bureau of Statistics.
[3] Hambrecht & Quist, 1999

between \$36 and \$175 per submitted form[4] when one included the time spent filling in, submitting, approving and auditing employee-related forms. For a facility employing 500 or more employees these costs would add up quickly. In addition, automated time and attendance systems reduced input errors and misrepresented working times that, on average, resulted in a loss equivalent to one per cent to six per cent of total payroll costs.[5] Improved labor analytics allowed managers to perform robust scenario analyses to determine impacts of potential labor policy changes and union contract terms on their firm's financials.

Ossip discussed one of the many examples of how a client could decrease costs by using Workbrain's product:

> Forms for any type of business process can be created and defined in real-time. This is just one of the many business objects embedded in our system. For example, if a company wanted to create something like a new safety glove requisition form project from scratch, that required access passwords and security for every employee, the cost could easily reach \$100 000 to get it started. When our system is installed, it would be a five-minute job. To send out a new type of process form, the new form is created first. Since everyone has a mailbox with complete messaging service built in, the new report is just a business object that is then messaged out to everyone. Our system allows companies to create a data store that can be uploaded (things like procedure manuals, ISO checklists, etc. can be accessed). We make it more convenient for the employees to access the information they need to do their jobs.

Employees were presented with a number of services and functions designed to enhance their work and personal lives through a web-based interface allowing them to contact their managers through any Internet access portal. Beyond directly work-related functions, a worker would be presented with email, and a business-to-employee "concierge" service through which they could take salary cash advances, make travel arrangements, and take advantage of e-procurement systems. These employee services would be provided through various alliances with partner firms who would gain direct access to many regular users with each additional contract. David Ossip described the product as follows (Exhibit 2 presents a screen shot of one of the Workbrain web pages):

> The first level of contact is the employee self-service access, through kiosks onsite or from other Internet portals. Below that are the workforce management systems, which are our expertise – time and attendance plus labor analytics, shop floor data capture, attendance control, scheduling, etc. (Exhibit 3 presents a graphic of the concept) We believe that provides the client with an information layer that benefits them. In between the Workbrain transaction servers we can design different types of business objects that can either be provided by us or by other companies.
>
> If an employee wants to see her/his pay, there is a pay stub viewer. The employee can see the pay stub before it's printed. For benefit administration an employee can change the benefit plan to see different scenarios (this could be provided by a partner like Wattson Wyatt or Mercer Consulting in the form of additional modules). Another module might be incentive calculators, where an employee gets points based on things that are accomplished which can then be used to purchase things.
>
> The vision is the end-to-end total solution. We want to own the "blue-collar desktop." It is completely web-based so it can be accessed from any web portal. They can log-on, check their

---

[4]American Express & AMR Research, 1997
[5]American Payroll Association

time, do their schedule and at the same time they can use these other business objects that we have provided for them.

Our advantage is that our competitors only do one facet of the solution (i.e., the workflow automation or the workforce management) but they can't do the full end-to-end solution. We provide a very different viewpoint because all we are trying to do is make it friendlier. We believe that in the long run, in order for companies to retain people, they have to make the workplace more friendly or less frustrating to do things. That is what we are selling. That is the vision. It is not just our time and attendance management expertise that gives us our advantage. Our comprehensive approach (we view ourselves as consultants) the thoroughness of our proposals, and the quality of our work is what sets us apart.

It was clear that Ossip placed a high level of importance on the recruitment of alliance partners. Exhibit 4 presents Workbrain's strategy for alliances. The product was seen as a "win-win-win" situation for the client, their employees and the partners since it brought everyone together in a virtual marketplace where job-shifts, benefits, processes, products and services were exchanged in one arena.

Along with cutting-edge technology, there were two other keys to success that Ossip recognized: alliances and people, both of which fell under Green's responsibility. Exhibit 4 presents the firm's strategies for ensuring that these keys were in place. Distribution and content were the two important components to their strategy that alliances gave Workbrain.

The Challenge

Workbrain was armed with what seemed like an industry-leading product, and highly skilled people to implement and service the systems and able salespeople to find clients. The key now was to develop an organization that would allow Ossip to bring his vision to reality and that job fell to Eric Green.

One of the first things I did was to put together an organizational chart that described who did what. It only had about five boxes. I tried to get an idea of all the internal activities that went on in the company such as legal, accounting, operations, technology, and who owned what. There seemed to be no real definition of roles. It seemed as though everyone was just working on this RFP and everything was directed towards a client focus at that point.

David didn't necessarily think in terms of organizational structure. I don't think that was really his interest. I think he was very much product-driven. He really loved the technology. He loved playing around with the coding. I guess I was the one who was supposed to be focusing on the internal growth and managing that growth.

One of the major things I did was really push the recruiting forward. More than once I was referred to as the "fluffy" guy; it became a bit of a joke where people would say that if it was not selling or coding, then it was fluffy. For example, on my first day they were interviewing a candidate for the position of Director of Human Relations. I met with him and we really didn't click. At the end of the day we met to discuss whether we should make him an offer. Everyone was very nonchalant about it and David liked him because he saw an immediate need to hire someone for the HR position — which is a credit to David because a lot of entrepreneurs just don't think HR is important. I didn't want to talk out of turn but I really didn't feel he was right for the job for a few reasons. I left that day afraid that I had insulted some people, but we couldn't afford to make hiring mistakes, especially at that stage in the company's life. On the one hand there was a sense of urgency that we needed to fill roles and get people doing things, but if we made mistakes, it would have been a lot harder to correct them.

One of the things that seemed to be like a black hole was the whole selling process because David Stein, VP Sales, was used to doing almost everything. He is technical. He's a great salesman. He's very smart. He can do the documentation. He can do everything. He felt that all he needed to do was hire people like himself, but people like him were impossible to find. He had a very unique skill set. I put together charts and documents to visually communicate what it was that I wanted to get across. It helped David Stein separate some of the issues that he may have been co-mingling. I wanted him to create an organizational structure to allow him to understand the type of people he needed to hire and what skills they needed to possess. It put some clarity around what his organization needed to look like.

I was stressing recruiting, but it was really more strategic thinking. I was getting them (the senior managers) to realize that there were a lot of complimentary skill sets out there. They didn't have to find every skill resident in one person. I think that since these guys worked in small companies where a few people did a lot of different things, especially in an industry where a person's experience is very industry-related, some people had to take a leap of faith that we could hire someone with general skills rather than industry-specific knowledge.

Another thing that was a bit concerning was that compensation seemed to be somewhat ad hoc. Salary levels and difficult compensation packages that included options were not really well thought out. I had to determine how much a VP or an analyst should be paid. I felt that we couldn't hire anyone until we really understood or knew what we were going to offer them in compensation.

Another important task was to develop job descriptions. We had to ask a lot of questions. What would this person be doing? What skills were we looking for and where could we find them? We needed to build processes to answer these questions. To do this we needed to start from the job descriptions and really think about what needed to get done and what each department was responsible for and who was going to do what.

There was one watershed moment where it seemed to me that it all became clear to everyone. I had been under the assumption that everyone had been working with the same vision and the same growth plan, that to me was represented by the business plan that was put together before I was hired. To me, the business plan was the company. What I later learned was that due to time constraints, some of the technical and implementation team had not been as involved in the planning process as they should have. There was some resentment that they had not been a part of it because some of them were founders of the firm. There was a disconnect about where they thought the company was going that had manifested itself in the way they were thinking about hiring.

At a meeting of the senior managers, which David Ossip could not attend, the department heads were discussing projects on the horizon, the expected value, and how many people they felt were needed for each project. I felt that we needed to hire about ten implementation people. They came out with numbers like 2.3 people for a project. I felt this was wrong and that it indicated that there was an assumption that we would grow using internally generated cash — I felt that we needed to get big fast. I suggested that the business would come but we needed to build up the infrastructure, which to me was the people.

There was definitely a lot of cynicism from the guys who came from a different environment who were not in this new economy, dot.com kind of thinking. To them it seemed ridiculous to hire people with nothing to do right now. I thought we had a lot to do. There was a lot of infrastructure to be developed for every group. All the materials and processes had to be developed because we were starting from scratch. We needed to get up to speed before we could take on another project and to me that seemed like a lot of work. People needed to be convinced that there was work to do that was not immediately realizing value or revenue.

At the conclusion of that meeting I think a lot of us were quite frustrated and I realized that a lot of those guys had never even seen the business plan. They weren't really quite sure what the vision was.

When David came back he saw that I was really frustrated. He called everyone into a meeting and walked everyone through the vision as he saw it and how the company should grow. This wasn't going to be a company that would grow using internally generated cash; we needed to build quickly. This is what we were promising investors. We were supposed to be 170 people by September 2001 and we had clear revenue targets. We couldn't do that by building incrementally. When David heard about the 2.3 people thing, he reiterated that we should not be thinking that way. We needed to get everyone on the same page and he said specifically that I was here to do that. Because I came from a big company, I thought like a big company and that's what we needed to be and, although I was pulling people in a different direction, that was the way we had to go.

That stands out in my mind as a real turning point in the company. It's not as if it changed overnight, but that started the sequence of events that started to get everyone on the same page. What was encouraging the whole time was that David had taken the step to hire someone like me in the first place because his last company didn't have anyone like me. To me that meant that as tough as this stuff might be to sell internally to get people thinking a certain way, I had his buy in.

It wasn't my vision. These guys had it before I got here. It disappeared for a little while under the bulk of the work that we had. I think that for the guys that came from the previous company it was a bit of a mind shift on a couple of fronts. On the product front, they had to stop thinking only in terms of time and attendance functionality and think more broadly, remembering that this was just one process within the system, and what we were building was a platform for all sorts of processes. Secondly, they had to stop thinking in terms of incremental growth and think more big bang. We were going to be up to 60 people after only eight months in business; that meant that we needed to think big. We needed big company processes. We needed to hire people dedicated to hiring and we needed to act like a big company. We needed to develop our infrastructure to support what we thought we were *going* to be. The people who came from the last company just had to get their heads around it.

In its first months of existence, Workbrain was on pace to exceed its revenue goals. However, the firm still needed to develop the crucial partnerships and client relationships that were required to secure investors in its next round of funding. With this success came more challenges in maintaining the vision, cementing and creating new processes and mental models within the firm. As divisions grew, the roles of the managers would have to be altered and new divisions would need to be created. As the firm grew, how could the culture Ossip espoused be maintained? The firm was staffed with and pursued highly talented, and thus much sought-after, people. How could they be retained? The task of answering these questions lay on the shoulders of Eric Green.

Exhibit 1: Competitive Positioning of Workbrain

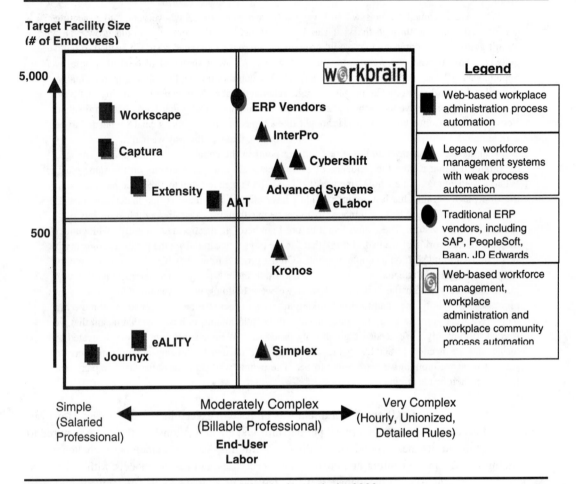

Source: Company reports and Web sites; Workbrain Analysis, 2000

Exhibit 2: **Screen Shot of the Workbrain System**

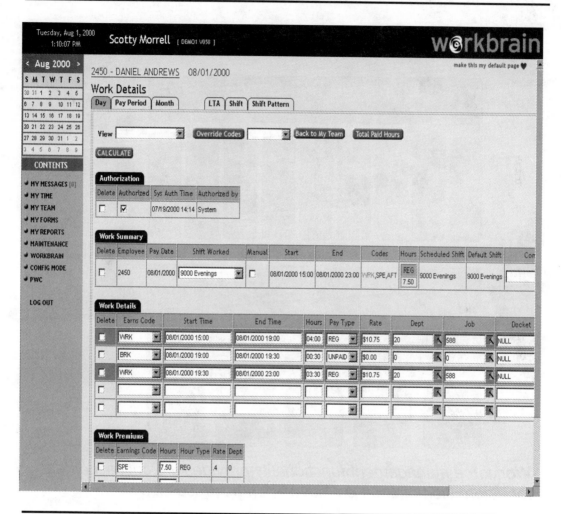

Source: Workbrain Corporation, 2000

Exhibit 3: **Graphic of the Workbrain Concept**

Workbrain eProcess Automation Platform

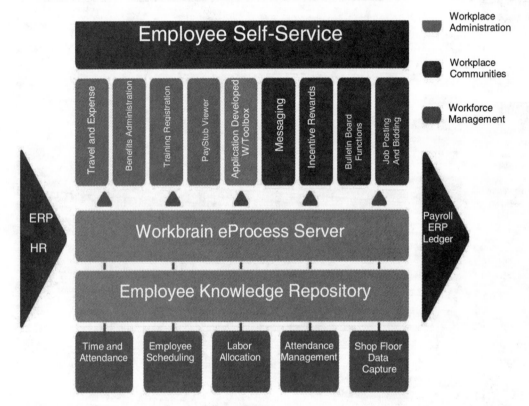

Workforce management functionality provides the critical content for automation of other employee-centric processes

Source: Workbrain Corporation, 2000.

Exhibit 4: **Workbrain's Alliance and Recruiting Strategy**

Alliance Strategy

Workbrain recognizes that strategic alliances and partnerships are critical to the company's success, enabling the company to scale revenues quickly, leverage its resources and focus on software development. Accordingly, Workbrain will partner with best-in-class companies to establish and enhance its market position.

Partnership opportunities fall into four categories:

Sales and Marketing Partners. Channel partners who will sell and co-market Workbrain solutions. The value to Workbrain would include expanded distribution and business scalability. As well, the value-added sales approach taken by some of these partners will position Workbrain as part of a broader business process redesign solution, potentially leading to higher prices and faster sales cycles. Value to partners would include a percentage of product sales and the ability to offer a broader set of solutions to clients. Such partners would include:

- Systems consultants and management consultants with strong technology capabilities (e.g., PriceWaterhouseCoopers, Andersen Consulting, A.T. Kearney/EDS, Origin, Cambridge Technology Partners)
- HR consultants with technology practices (e.g., Watson Wyatt, AON)
- Enterprise software vendors (e.g., PeopleSoft, JD Edwards, SAP)
- Application Service Providers (e.g., Corio, US Internetworking)

Implementation Partners. Systems integrators and consultants who will lead and support the implementation of Workbrain solutions. As in the case of sales and marketing partnerships, implementation partners will help increase the scalability of Workbrain by not limiting the company's execution capacity. These partners will derive value by earning software configuration fees, systems integration fees, software development fees (e.g., designing additional modules to leverage the system's workflow infrastructure), and training fees. It is expected that in most cases, these partners will also have sold the Workbrain solution to the client. This group would, therefore, include the systems integration firms and the ASPs outlined above.

Solution Partners. Hardware and software vendors whose products will be bundled with Workbrain to offer a more complete solution to clients. The benefits to Workbrain would include an enhanced value proposition and expanded solution portfolio, as well as a co-marketing channel. Solution Partners would derive value through hardware and software sales, as well as new and/or strengthened customer relationships. This group would include:

- OEMs, including makers of PCs and servers (e.g., Dell, Compaq), Internet appliances (e.g., Netpliance), wireless devices (e.g., Palm, Research in Motion), and data capture devices (e.g., Synel Industries)
- Enterprise software vendors (e.g., PeopleSoft, JD Edwards, SAP)
- E-business software vendors and service providers (e.g., Ariba, Icarian, Healtheon/WebMD, RewardsPlus)

Commerce Partners. Providers of goods and services who will enhance the value of the workplace community aspect of the Workbrain solution. These partnerships are fundamental to Workbrain to execute its vision to be the gateway for hourly employees to the outside world. By providing the 'sticky' content for hourly workers (e.g., payment and schedule information), Workbrain can build a large user base that would be attractive to other companies seeking to acquire customers. Transaction fees would be shared between the client, Workbrain, and the Commerce Partner. This group of partners would include:

- Incentive management administrators (e.g., Maritz)
- B2E aggregators (e.g., Perksatwork.com, employeesavings.com)
- B2C vendors (e.g., Expedia.com, Citibank, E-trade, Paymybills.com, Amazon.com)

Workbrain is currently developing training and alliance programs to ensure that partners work effectively with Workbrain in executing all aspects of its strategy.

Rapid market penetration is key to Workbrain's long-term success. Although it is anticipated that in the longer term, the majority of software sales will be derived from channel partners, Workbrain is committed to building a strong direct sales force that will build market presence and complement our Sales and Marketing Partners.

Human Resources Strategy

Workbrain management recognizes that in today's competitive labor market, the ability to attract, develop, retain and inspire exceptional people is the single most important key success factor in building a great company. Workbrain's growth philosophy, therefore, focuses on excellence in recruiting, workplace environment and compensation policies.

Recruiting. Workbrain is growing rapidly in Toronto and Atlanta by aggressively recruiting both experienced industry professionals and new graduates. Workbrain is looking primarily for results-oriented employees who understand the implementation needs of complex projects. Accordingly, the company's recruiting resources are focused on attracting experienced project managers from the industry segments that Workbrain serves. Workbrain management is leveraging their industry relationships to identify, recruit and train these sales and technology leaders with strong client contacts. Undergraduate, MBA, and IT recruiting is being conducted in conjunction with innovative human resources firms. Incentive compensation for *all* Workbrain employees recognizes their contribution to the firm's recruiting strategy.

Workplace Environment. Workbrain management is intensely focused on creating an inspiring place to work, where risk-taking, results, creativity, and fun are all valued and rewarded. Responsibility is distributed to allow employees to make a real impact and to create uniquely stretching jobs. Cutting-edge productivity technologies and workplace amenities (including on-site health club memberships), flexible work hours, a relaxed workplace, and a genuine respect for work/life balance are all part of Workbrain's work environment.

Compensation. All Workbrain employees receive highly competitive cash and equity-based compensation and best-in-class benefits, including health and dental insurance, continuing education, and a broad variety of employee perquisites.

Source: Workbrain Corporation, 2000

THE LONDON FREE PRESS (A): STRATEGIC CHANGE

case 18

Detlev Nitsch and
Mary Crossan

Phil McLeod had been appointed as the new editor of the London Free Press (LFP) in November, 1987, with a mandate to make changes. Like most other North American daily newspapers, the LFP had been gradually losing readership, and its share of advertising revenues in the community was shrinking. Despite its ability to remain profitable, McLeod thought that it was not living up to its potential, especially since it was the only daily newspaper in London. He feared that there were ominous signs of a continuing decline in market share, which could only mean still lower profits in the future.

McLeod had been hired from the Toronto Star and put in charge of LFP's newsroom and editorial department to do whatever was necessary to reverse this trend. Now, in 1991, he wondered if it would be possible to stop the slow decline of the newspaper or if its shrinkage was an inevitable consequence of broader trends in the information industry and Canadian society.

Ivey

Detlev Nitsch prepared this case under the supervision of Professor Mary Crossan solely to provide material for class discussion. The author does not intend to illustrate either effective or ineffective handling of a managerial situation. The author may have disguised certain names and other identifying information to protect confidentiality.

THE NEWSPAPER INDUSTRY

Newspapers obtained revenues from two sources: from readers, who paid for papers through regular subscriptions or on a single copy basis, and from advertising clients, who hoped to expose their messages to as many members of a community as possible. Conceptually newspapers could be seen as a medium that attracted readers with its editorial content, and in turn delivered those readers to advertisers as potential purchasers.

Advertising sales accounted for about three-quarters of a typical paper's total revenues, but these amounts were closely linked to the paid circulation of the paper. Advertisers' willingness to pay a given rate depended on the size of the audience they could expect to reach with their messages. The price advertisers paid for space in a newspaper was usually based on a combination of 1) total circulation, and 2) penetration, expressed in terms of the percentage of total households reached.

McLeod saw newspapers as having two basic functions: gathering information, and packaging it for resale. Information came in two varieties: public "news"; and private, or advertising information. The news information-gathering function could be further broken down by source:

1. A paper's own reporters gathering local news.
2. Staff reporters responsible for news from distant locales. Many larger newspapers had "bureaux" staffed by their own people in important cities around Canada and the rest of the world, so they could have proprietary access to any information these reporters uncovered.
3. Exchange arrangements through the corporate umbrella—for example, LFP had a contractual link with Southam News that enabled it, for a fee, to tap into this large organization's worldwide network of news sources. This also allowed papers access to news developed initially for other media.
4. Wire services. Canadian Press (CP), American Press (AP), and Reuters were examples of news agencies that existed solely to provide news on a fee basis to anyone who was willing to pay for it. In some cases (CP for example), the agency was a co-operative owned by newspapers.

The LFP was fairly typical of daily newspapers in that approximately 60 per cent of its space was allocated to advertising (paid messages), with the "newshole," or editorial content, occupying the rest. Of the 40 per cent of the available space dedicated to the newshole, 60 per cent was purchased from wire services or other sources. McLeod estimated that approximately 30 per cent of his $10-million editorial budget was spent on purchased news; one-third of the balance was devoted to re-working or repackaging these stories for publication, and the rest was spent on maintaining the LFP's in-house news-gathering apparatus.

As advertisers became more sophisticated, they were no longer merely interested in a newspaper's raw circulation figures, but rather in its ability to reach those most likely to purchase their products. Electronic media in particular were often able to target very narrow market segments with a high degree of precision. Television programming was being geared to ever-smaller segments of the population, as cable and satellite proliferation expanded the choices available to consumers. With sophisticated demographic market research data, programmers could produce and schedule shows designed to appeal to specific groups, and have relatively high confidence that their target would be reached. This was attractive to advertisers because they could spend their advertising budgets more efficiently, avoiding messages sent to members of the community who were not potential customers. In contrast, daily newspapers were seen as a rather blunt instrument, with potentially broad mass-market coverage but little ability to ensure that a given message had reached its target segment.

Past Performance, Future Outlook

Newspaper companies had enjoyed a very profitable history in North America: at the beginning of the 1980s they boasted a median 9.6 per cent profit margin, compared to a median of less than five per cent for Fortune 500 Industrials. Even though, depending on commodity prices, newsprint accounted for anywhere from 20 to 25 per cent of total costs, newspapers' return on sales ranged from 14 to 18 per cent, while industrials averaged six per cent. In 1991, U.S. newspaper companies enjoyed a resurgence in the stock market, outperforming index averages by a large margin (Exhibit 1). This followed several years of sluggish performance during which consolidation and downsizing were the norm in the industry.

Despite this evidence of good performance potential, there were several signs that indicated a long-run trend to declining circulation, reduced revenues and smaller profit margins. Exhibit 2 shows the decline in profitability of a typical North American newspaper company.

Newspapers' level of penetration, or market share as a percentage of households reached, was dropping for newspapers all across North America. In the U.S., 124 copies of daily newspapers were sold for every 100 households during the 1950s. By the 1970s, the comparable figure was 77, with the drop attributable in part to a decline in the number of two-newspaper households. The Canada-wide circulation growth rate, at 1.7 per cent, was also well below the growth rates of the adult population (2.1 per cent) and of households (3.0 per cent) during the 1970s, even though it still outpaced the growth of total population (1.0 per cent). Similar trends seemed to apply to London, where McLeod had noted that the LFP was losing about a percentage point per year in penetration, down to below 60 per cent in the early 1990s.   *losing audience*

While the total circulation of daily newspapers was still increasing, other indicators such as average daily circulation and penetration levels suggested that newspapers were losing readers, and were thus becoming less attractive as an advertising medium. As recently as 1973, daily newspapers had attracted 30.5 per cent of total Canadian advertising expenditures, compared to television in that year with 13.4 per cent. In fact, until 1977, daily newspapers held a larger share of ad revenues than radio, television, and weekly newspapers combined. But the long-run trend since 1972 showed a gradual decline in the newspapers' share, while television and other media continued to gather strength. Daily newspapers still had the largest share of total advertising revenues, but this share was gradually shrinking, (Table 1).

Breaking total advertising revenues down into national and local categories yielded further insights into the differing strengths of the competing media. For example, in 1973/74 daily newspapers received 19.8 per cent of their advertising revenues from national accounts. The corresponding figure for television was 73.9 per cent, which shifted upward to 75.3 per cent by 1980, while the dailies' proportion fell to 18.7 per cent. This suggested that newspapers' heavy reliance on local retail and classified advertising was, if anything, increasing.

PROB/ISSUE

Table 1: Canadian Advertising Expenditures Per Cent Share of Total, by Medium (estimates)

Medium	1973	1989 (Estimates)
Daily Newspapers	30.5	22.8
Catalogues, Direct Mail	20.6	21.9
Television	13.4	15.6
Radio	10.8	8.3
Weekly Newspapers	5.1	6.9
Magazines	2.4	3.1
Other	17.2	21.4

Source: Maclean Hunter Research Bureau

Demographics of Readership: Long-Run Implications

A 1986 study of newspaper readers showed that most readers were in the over-35 age category, and that 75 per cent of people in their 20s did not regularly read the paper. In the past, there had been some support for the notion that newspaper-reading habits grew as individuals aged. Cross-sectional studies had turned up much the same data decade after decade, as young non-readers in an early study evolved into 50-year old newspaper aficionados 30 years later.

But McLeod feared that times had changed, and that these non-readers would be difficult to turn into loyal newspaper customers in the future. The current crop of young adults was the first who had been raised in an age in which television was accepted as a legitimate news source. Unlike previous generations, these people believed and trusted what they saw on the small screen, and did not feel the need to see it in print. The public's familiarity and comfort level with television had grown over time, aided by the medium's presence on the scene of historic events such as the 1963 assassination of U.S. President Kennedy, and the first moon landing in 1969. Also, McLeod admitted that television had proved competent in areas where newspapers were once thought to have a competitive advantage: background and analysis. Network news and news-only cable TV channels were increasingly supplying high-quality, in-depth coverage of important events, with a timeliness and sense of immediacy that newspapers could not match.

Television's new-found strengths might make it impossible for newspapers to attract the current group of younger people. This meant that the expected shift in preference, from television to newspapers as people aged, might not take place this time. Thus the old assumption that readership would stay more or less constant over time appeared to rely on a "no change" scenario which did not fit reality.

Some evidence suggested that, by 1991, newspaper readership was recovering from its precipitous decline. Gross circulation was actually up by 32 per cent from 15 years before, while population had only risen 16 per cent. Also, the proportion of Canadian adults reading newspapers had increased from 63 per cent to 68.5 per cent. However, McLeod thought that these numbers were misleading because they focused on overall total circulation instead of daily averages, and they ignored the fact that new newspaper formats had begun to penetrate the market. The gross circulation statistic compared present total readership with comparable figures before the "tabloid era" in many major Canadian centres. Tabloids were new and very different newspapers, adding 700,000 new readers who were, arguably, in a different category than traditional ones. Also, 14 new Sunday editions had been started in the past seven years, contributing another 1.5 million new readers to the circulation total, but not raising the daily average circulation. Thus, while total circulation was up, daily average circulation per newspaper was still in decline across the country (Table 2).

Table 2: ### Daily Circulation Averages (1990 to 1991)

Vancouver Sun	Down 5.5%
Montreal Gazette	Down 5.2%
Ottawa Citizen	Down 4.0%
Kitchener Record	Down 3.7%
Kingston Whig-Standard	Down 3.7%
London Free Press	Down 3.6%
Calgary Herald	Down 3.4%
Calgary Sun	Down 2.5%
Toronto Sun	Down 2.4%
Hamilton Spectator	Down 2.4%
Toronto Star	Down 2.2%
Edmonton Sun	Down 1.3%
Edmonton Journal	Down 0.6%
Windsor Star	Even
Vancouver Province	Up 2.6%

Source: LFP internal documents

On this basis, circulation was being outpaced by population growth in virtually every market in Canada. Among other things, this had also placed increasing pressure on the sales function. The London Free Press in 1990 had to sell 81,364 new subscription orders to maintain its average daily home delivery at 85,646 in the city of London. In the previous year, the home delivery average had been slightly higher but only 63,000 new orders had to be sold.

A recent study conducted in the United States and Canada had suggested three main reasons why readers were abandoning newspapers:

1.   No time:
   • your paper is hard to read
   • I really don't have any time
   • you don't make it clear why I should make time

2.   No news:
   • I saw it all on TV; you gave me nothing new
   • insufficient insight, understanding, depth

3. No interest:
- Nothing for me in the paper
- I don't share your idea of what is new or important
- You don't care about what I care about—in fact you often belittle the things my friends and I enjoy

The same study had reconfirmed that one of the causes of newspapers' decline in importance to readers was the fact that other media, principally television, had made news more easily consumable by the public. Comparing statistics over time exposed a trend away from newspapers on virtually every dimension, (Table 3).

Table 3: COMPARISON OF TELEVISION AND NEWSPAPERS

Percentage of respondents who responded positively to each question

	1986	1991
Main source of international news:		
Television	63%	73%
Newspapers	21%	16%
Main source of national news:		
Television	69%	75%
Newspapers	19%	16%
Main source of local news:		
Television	41%	43%
Newspapers	34%	35%
Most believable:		
Television	no data	30%
Newspapers	no data	24%
Most accurate:		
Television	no data	33%
Newspapers	no data	19%
Most likely to be fair:		
Television	no data	33%
Newspapers	no data	19%

Source: Environics, reproduced in LFP internal documents

Industry Consolidation Trend

The competitive dynamic among newspapers in Canada had changed gradually over the years. In the past, newspapers had competed as a collection of geographically-dispersed individual markets. While there had been virtually no competition between cities, there had often been intense rivalry among papers within cities. But by the 1980s, cities with two or more dailies had become a rarity

(Table 4). Even in the few locations that still had more than one daily, the papers tended to be positioned in fairly well-defined niches, such as Toronto's Globe and Mail, Sun, and Star. Through consolidation and attrition, the industry had evolved into a series of local newspaper monopolies.

Table 4: **Major Newspapers with Circulation (1991)**

City	Newspaper	Daily Average Circulation
Calgary	Herald	125,000
	Sun	76,000
Winnipeg	Free Press	154,000
Regina	Leader-Post	68,000
Hamilton	Spectator	135,000
Edmonton	Journal	137,000
	Sun	69,000
Vancouver	Province	185,000
	Sun	221,000
Victoria	Times-Colonist	77,000
Winnipeg	Free Press	154,000
Halifax	Chronicle Herald	97,000
Waterloo	K-W Record	75,000
London	Free Press	115,000
Ottawa	Citizen	178,000
Toronto	Star	544,000
	Globe and Mail	311,000
	Sun	272,000
Windsor	Star	86,000
Montreal	Gazette	163,000
	Journal de Montreal	293,000
	La Presse	205,000
Quebec City	Journal de Quebec	102,000
	Le Soleil	99,000

Source: Canadian Advertising Rates and Data, March 1994

Consolidation had also led to domination of the Canadian industry by a few national or regional chains. Advantages to group ownership were: 1) shared resources, including pooled information services from abroad; and 2) the owner's deep pockets, which enabled a chain newspaper to weather temporary downturns in its financial performance, and gave it access to capital for major investments in technology.

The two largest chains, Southam and Thomson, together controlled 58 per cent of the English-language circulation in Canada. Southam, with 17 of the total 95 Canadian English dailies, had 33.5 per cent of overall circulation, while Thomson, with 36 papers, had 24.5 per cent. These percentages did not, in themselves, suggest that the newspaper market had taken on the characteristics of a monopoly. But by avoiding head-to-head competition among papers in individual cities, the chains' newspapers had managed to enjoy local monopolies and high profits.

Threat to the Public Interest? – No!

Critics of industry consolidation favoured some form of government intervention to help support financially troubled newspapers and to preserve competitive rivalry. Arguing out of concern for the public interest, they cautioned that in single paper monopolies, readers' opinions would be manipulated by selective reporting and by opinion masquerading as objective journalism. Further, since advertisers would have no alternative outlets for their print messages, they would be at the mercy of greedy newspaper owners, and would become the victims of price-gouging and other undesirable tactics.

Those who saw no problem with the demise of direct competition maintained that newspapers in monopoly markets were able and willing to sustain a high level of journalistic quality, because their resources were not eroded through needless duplication and price competition with rivals. A section of the 1981 Royal Commission on Newspapers suggested that there was no evidence of declining quality or journalistic integrity as a result of industry consolidation. Publishers in single-newspaper towns were characterized as being able to "afford excellence," while still having to compete with other media for advertisers' dollars.

Neither was the trend to group ownership of newspapers seen, by these observers, as a threat to editorial independence. Publishers of chain newspapers frequently made mention of their freedom from interference by their corporate bosses. In support of this contention they cited the fact that some of Canada's most respected papers were being run at a loss by large chains (for example, Thomson's Globe and Mail), implying that high quality standards were not being eroded in pursuit of corporate profitability.

Even the Supreme Court of Canada had indirectly supported the position that the public interest was not threatened by industry consolidation. In ruling on a 1977 case brought under anti-combines legislation, the court held that "the Crown was unable to prove, as the law requires, that a single owner of the [only] five dailies in New Brunswick would be detrimental to the public." In reaching this conclusion, the Court noted the Irving chain's success in increasing the circulation of all five papers, the fact that capital investment had been made in them, and that money-losing papers had been subsidized to enable them to continue operating.

Social Role of Newspapers

In Western society, the press had long been viewed as an expression of the right of free speech, and as one of the pillars of democracy. Independence from government and other interference was held to be absolutely essential if editorial quality and integrity were to be preserved. The press was seen as the "watchdog" charged with informing the public about the activities of the state.

There was a sense that the press had a larger role in society than that of other commercial enterprises. Some observers and industry insiders had concluded that newspapers have higher ideals than just making money, and responsibilities beyond simply keeping shareholders happy. While admitting that, at some level at least, financial viability was important, many people nevertheless felt that newspapers had an altruistic mission to present the complete truth, and that the naked pursuit of larger profits would put their editorial objectivity at risk. Newspapers were thus seen to be driven by both a service ethic and a market ethic.

Partly as a result of this extra commercial role, a mystique had arisen about journalism which led to the belief, among many reporters, that journalists alone were competent to judge what stories the public should see in print, and in what form they should be presented. Among many traditionalists, journalistic quality (as defined by them) should be emphasized over the pursuit of mere profit. Papers which "sold out" in order to target a larger audience were seen to be pandering to the whims of an unsophisticated public whose members often did not know what was good for them.

McLeod saw the notion of newspapers' "altruistic mission" as a self-serving rationalization. He felt it was invoked to support the idea that maintaining the existing editorial process was more important than the consumption of the product, thus providing a rationale for preservation of the status quo. The result, he thought, was that newspapers had lost touch with their communities. By refusing to respond to readers' needs, under the pretext of preserving journalistic integrity, papers were becoming increasingly irrelevant to many potential readers. Print journalism's insular mentality, bred of a grandiose view of its role in society, its professional arrogance, and its past success, had isolated it from those on whom it depended for its survival.

Evidence about the relative profitability of different editorial approaches was equivocal, in any event. Observers could point to successful and unsuccessful examples at both ends of the "quality" continuum. For example, the Globe and Mail, widely perceived as a high-quality paper, was operating at a loss, while other quality papers such as the Washington Post and the New York Times were earning money. At the tabloid end of the spectrum, the Toronto Sun was a financial success, while USA Today was still struggling to break even. It seemed that, for all the criticism levelled at papers which tried to boost circulation by appealing to a larger and, arguably, less discriminating mass market, this "sell-out" tactic was no guarantee of profits. There seemed to be profitable market niches for newspapers following either strategy.

THE LONDON FREE PRESS

The London Free Press was the only daily newspaper in London, Ontario, a southwestern Ontario city of approximately 300,000. It was part of the Blackburn Group Inc. (BGI), which was made up of businesses in the communication and information fields. Begun in 1849, The Free Press had been owned and operated for five generations by the Blackburn family of London, and maintained a strong tradition of community service.

As communications technology evolved, so did the organization's activities in various media. An AM radio station was started in 1922, and in 1953 television was added to the Blackburn empire[1]. An FM radio station completed the growing conglomerate's coverage of the available "instant media."

In addition to these holdings, BGI had also launched Netmar Inc. in 1974, and purchased Compusearch in 1984. Netmar published and distributed weekly newspapers, shopping guides, and

---

[1] The TV Station was sold in 1993 because the Blackburn Group felt it no longer fit the news focus of its other holdings, and because it needed substantial new investment to stay competitive in the entertainment field.

advertising flyers in Ontario and Alberta. Compusearch, based in Toronto, was a North American leader in market information and analysis.

In 1991, BGI established Blackburn Marketing Services Inc. (BMSI), an investment and management company formed to develop a portfolio of businesses in the direct marketing area. BMSI had made inroads into the U.S. market through acquisitions and mergers with American market research organizations.

BGI and its operating subsidiaries were private companies, and had been run under Blackburn family control since their founding. The LFP had the longest history, and was the most "legitimate" in terms of traditional journalistic values. Blackburn's senior management were proud that they had been able to maintain both the financial health of the paper and its high journalistic quality while creating a work environment that was described as caring and paternalistic.

The LFP had up-to-date production facilities, and its distribution system was described by McLeod as leading-edge, given the current state of technological development. Minimizing printing and distribution costs was an ongoing effort at the LFP, but any gains made in this area would be incremental. For true strategic impact, McLeod thought he had to focus on the revenue generating side of the profit equation. This placed the onus for change on the editorial department.

Organization

The LFP, like most newspapers, was organized along functional lines. The principal departments were advertising, production, administrative, and editorial. The editorial department of approximately 130 employees was headed by McLeod, and divided into sections that corresponded to the principal sections of the newspaper. Staff were assigned to sports, entertainment, business, political, or local/regional sections on a more or less permanent basis, under the leadership of a senior editor who was in charge of that part of the paper.

Exhibit 3 presents a chart showing the organization of editorial staff within sections of the paper. In operation, it worked as follows: For a typical local news event, a reporter was sent into the field by a senior editor to gather the facts, and to write the story. The piece was then turned over to a copy editor, who would check spelling and grammar, alter its length, or make other changes. After this step, the graphics people took over, adding pictures, diagrams, or maps as required, and physically re-working the story to fit into the page layout that was being planned for that edition. Again, the original story could be changed to meet space restrictions.

McLeod saw several weaknesses in this system. For example, a typical reporter might be assigned to cover local news, and be routinely sent to cover regular meetings of some special-interest group. This reporter might return with a story about a particularly colourful and lively meeting, at which members expressed various forms of outrage and stated their political positions for the record. The story would run in the newspaper, suitably headlined with attention-getting phrases, and the responsible section editor would feel that the job of covering local news had been accomplished. However, the only "outrage" felt might be on the part of the 20 people attending the meeting, and the significance of the event for the greater community could be non-existent. Without probing more deeply into the reasons behind the meeting, and investigating the possible consequences on a level that went beyond the narrow interests of a particular group, the LFP might not be reporting anything meaningful to readers. Many reporters' roles had been created in response to a specific need in the past, but were maintained today, McLeod had decided, more out of habit than for the intrinsic "newsworthiness" of the material that was ultimately written. When making decisions about how to deploy limited reporting resources to the best possible effect, the test of community relevance was often not applied.

Another problem was that, throughout the traditional process, there was little or no communication between the various production stages. Because the printing schedule of the LFP dictated that the presses start rolling at midnight, the latter steps in the process were often not done until evening, while the original story may have been written that morning. By the time the editors and graphics people first saw the story, its original author could be home in bed, with no opportunity for input or influence over how it would finally appear in the paper.

The lack of a perceived connection with the community was symbolized by the LFP's physical premises as well. With only one access door, the building itself was not easy for the public to enter. Once inside, they faced a forbidding security checkpoint, a symbolic barrier between the public and the reporters who chronicled their lives. At the same time, McLeod remarked on the fact that none of the editorial staff had a view of the outside from their work area. The lack of a visual link to the city of London reinforced the inward-directed focus of those who purported to be writing about issues and events that were important to the community.

The organization structure also isolated departments within the newspaper from one another. Each section was conceptually and editorially an independent entity, and there was little communication or sharing of information among them. McLeod thought that this arrangement had led, on occasion, to stories falling through the cracks because they did not fit neatly into one of the pre-defined categories. An example of this occurred when a major World Wrestling Federation (WWF) event was scheduled to be held in London. The match was to be held at the London Gardens, which was the biggest arena in the city, and frequently the venue for major music concerts and sports events. The London Free Press often reported on these activities in the next day's edition, and it had been informed by the WWF's sophisticated publicity department about the major wrestling stars who would be making a rare appearance in London. The most popular and biggest money-making wrestlers were more accustomed to appearing in places such as New York's Madison Square Garden or the Fabulous Western Forum in Los Angeles than in a relative backwater such as the 8,000 seat London Gardens.

As it happened however, the sports section of the LFP declined to cover the WWF event because they felt that professional wrestling was not a true "sport", but more a form of staged entertainment. The entertainment editor meanwhile assumed that, since wrestling billed itself as a sport, and its participants were "athletes", the sports section would be reporting on it. The lack of communication between sections, and the fact that professional wrestling could not be neatly pigeonholed as either "sport" or "entertainment", led to neither section covering what was, for many London residents, a major news item.

Strategic Response

To halt further declines in readership, a major makeover of the LFP was undertaken in 1989, to give it a different look and make it more contemporary, "breezy", and attractive to readers. In what was seen in the trade as a major departure from tradition, the front page was redesigned. The number of stories it contained was reduced in favour of making it more of a road map for the contents of the inside pages. More colour was used, in conjunction with other cosmetic changes designed to make the paper look more user-friendly and less boring.

These changes, while hardly revolutionary to the eye of an average reader, were perceived by some members of the editorial staff as an abandonment of its tradition of editorial excellence. They interpreted the emphasis on readability and graphic attractiveness as an effort to lure readers with pretty pictures and colourful presentation. In the detractors' opinions, an emphasis on the quality of writing was being supplanted by less meaningful priorities.

The increased use of graphics meant that, for the first time, charts, maps, and graphs were incorporated into stories right from the outset, as opposed to being added as an afterthought on a "space available" basis. One group which felt threatened as a result was the staff photographers, who saw their work competing for space with that of the graphics designers. Another unhappy group was the reporters. They felt their pre-eminent position in the LFP newsroom being eroded, since now much of what they wrote might be captured in a chart or graph. While this had always been the case to a certain extent, graphics and pictorial summaries of key story points were now intended to be an integral part of the creation of an article, to be included in the process right from the start. Reporters thought that their influence over how a story would be presented would now have to be shared with others, who often might have little training in journalism.

Results

Reader response to the changes was mixed. Evidence favouring and criticizing the changes was gathered from focus groups, and was revealed in letters to the editor. From these sources, it became clear that some readers were upset with the new look of the paper and found it disconcerting that items they were interested in were relocated to unfamiliar sections. On the other hand, some reported that they liked the new format, and saw it as a step towards making the paper more readable. While it was difficult to draw quantitative conclusions from this, McLeod estimated that the split "for" and "against" the redesign was about 50-50.

Circulation for 1990, the first full year of operation with the new format, was down three per cent from the year before. However, London was just beginning to feel the effects of a recession at that time, and this made it difficult to disentangle the effect of the change from broader economic trends. The question of how much circulation would have dropped without a change remained impossible to answer.

At the same time as changes in the appearance of the LFP were being implemented, a drive to unionize the newsroom was successfully completed. Though professing considerable philosophical discomfort with their decision, supporters of the unionization effort had decided that this was the only way they could combat what they saw as unilateral and wrong-headed action by the paper's management. In what many saw as a result of the unhappiness of editorial staff about the new direction the LFP appeared to be taking, they voted to go on strike in early 1990. The strike was settled after a few weeks, during which the paper was put together by managerial staff, but unresolved ill feelings remained.

Package versus Content

McLeod had come to believe that, while a newspaper's packaging was closely linked to its content, the two "must become disentangled in our minds" in order for progress to be made. He had changed the package, following the tradition of consumer goods marketers. Now perhaps something a little more substantive was in order.

In order for readers to see the LFP as an important source of information, the content of the paper would need to reflect their wishes more closely. But changing the content would not be easy. As McLeod put it, a newspaper is like a sausage factory:

You can put as many good ideas as you want into the front end of the machine, but unless that machine has been retooled to think and act in new ways, it will always turn out more or less the same thing. In other words, whatever goes in, sausages come out. Perhaps sausages with better texture or taste, less fat and fewer calories, but sausages nevertheless.

McLeod felt that the changes would require a substantial "rewiring of our heads", and would be risky because they conflicted with traditional attitudes about journalism. More stories needed to be written about topics that readers were actually interested in, and they needed to be covered in greater depth. At the same time, McLeod no longer believed that each piece in the paper had to be written, edited, and laid out in the final few minutes before the press deadline. "While I wouldn't know the details of the stories, I can tell you two days in advance what 80 per cent of our paper is going to look like," he said. "If we know, broadly, what the subject matter is going to be, why can't we do a better job of background and analysis on those stories we already know are going to be in the paper?"

Potential Resistance

Opposition to any proposed changes could be high. McLeod was risking criticism for tampering with the natural order of the way newspapers were run, because of the strong entrenched culture that existed in the profession. According to one view, he might be allowing the process of producing a newspaper to be unduly tainted by customer influence.

On a more personal level, the changes might shake many staffers' strongly held beliefs about how newspapers should be produced, and about the role of journalism in a society. Some reporters thought that the atmosphere in the newsroom was already poisoned because of a strong polarization between those in favour of and those opposed to change. Some, who were suspicious of any attempts to solicit their opinion, were guarded about their comments regarding the organizational changes. While these individuals expressed deep concern over the future of the newspaper, they felt alienated, disenfranchised, and devalued because of the changes that had been implemented or proposed. Some had gone for stress counselling to help them deal with the effects.

Opponents also felt that a sacred trust established by the late Walter Blackburn was being violated. The LFP had, until recently, been regarded as a writer's paper because of the consistently high quality of its journalism, as judged by other journalists. There was a strong tradition of editorial freedom, and the reporters had become accustomed to being treated as highly trained and valued professionals. Some feared that, with change, their skills would be devalued in favour of "People" magazine-style writing, which could be executed by relatively unskilled individuals.

One reporter commented:

> Management should be trying to involve people, rather than alienating them. Many of us are deeply concerned about what's going on, but management isn't paying any attention. We've been left behind in this whole thing; nothing coming from us has been listened to. Many people feel disenfranchised, devalued. There's a high level of distrust here, and an adversarial climate. In fact, the environment is so poisoned, I'm worried that what I say to you [that is, the case writer] might be used against me.

There was also resistance to what some saw as the "scourge of MBAs." Market research reports which suggested declining profits and an unsustainable future for the newspaper had been shared with the staff, but they were dismissed by dissidents as mere spreadsheet manipulation. The report authors were characterized as pinstriped automatons bent on forcing higher short-term profits out of a venerable institution by squeezing out its lifeblood. Opponents of change pointed out that none of the blue suit crowd's forecasts ever came true anyway, and saw the doom and gloom scenarios, with their accompanying recommendations, as a stratagem that allowed the MBAs to increase their own consulting revenue.

Scepticism and mistrust was further fuelled by the fact that McLeod's own managerial style was sometimes less than tactful, especially when he was challenging some of journalism's sacred cows. A typical comment about a proposed story might be: "Who cares?", which was intended to mean: "Do our readers feel strongly about this story, or does the way we've presented it give them a reason to care?" However, some reporters, not accustomed to thinking this way, might misinterpret the remark as a personal criticism or as a lack of confidence in their writing ability.

McLEOD'S POSITION

Although he felt strongly that change was needed, McLeod was in a quandary about what form it should take, the urgency with which it should be implemented, and what support or resistance the changes might encounter. BGI management had hired McLeod from the Toronto Star with the expectation that he would be a change agent. The culture of the Star, of which McLeod was a product, was perceived as much less family-like and paternalistic than the LFP. This was partly because it operated in a much more competitive market, but also because of the long tradition of Blackburn family influence on the way the London paper was run. The Blackburn legacy implied that employees would be cared for during difficult periods in their personal and professional lives, and would not be treated as interchangeable chattels or disposable factors of production. McLeod's arrival on the scene, with his outsider's background and perspective, was a signal to some that these traditions might be consigned to history, to be replaced by a much more impersonal bottom-line focus.

Previous editors had also tended to put high-quality journalism at the top of their agenda. As a result, the LFP was widely perceived, both internally and by outsiders, as a "writer's paper." Any change which threatened these priorities would meet with stiff opposition. BGI executives were willing to support any reasonable initiative—Phil McLeod's challenge lay in choosing the right one and avoiding the most serious pitfalls.

Exhibit 1: Year-End Newspaper Results—1991 Stock Market Performance

	GAIN(**)
A.H. Belo (NYSE - BLC)	30.4%
Dow Jones (NYSE - DJ)	23.7%
Gannett (NYSE - GCI)	11.4%
Knight Ridder (NYSE - KRI)	17.7%
McClatchy (NYSE - MNI)	21.9%
Media General (ASE - MEGA)	17.2%
Multimedia (NASDAQ - MMEDC)	9.8%
New York times (ASE - NYTA)	68.8%
Times Mirror (NYSE - TMC)	47.5%
Tribune (NYSE - TRB)	37.7%
Washington Post (NYSE - WPO)	23.5%
Average Gain	28.6%
Standard & Poors	
- 400 Industrials	6.2%
- 500 Composite	10.3%

Source: Company Reports, Alex Brown & Sons estimates

Exhibit 2: Thomson — North American Newspapers ($ million)

	1988	1989	1990	1991
Revenues	981	1081	1158	1142
Operating Profit	306	317	282	228
Operating Margin	31.2%	29.3%	24.4%	20.0%

Source: Company Reports, Alex Brown & Sons estimates

Exhibit 3: **Partial Organization Chart circa 1987**

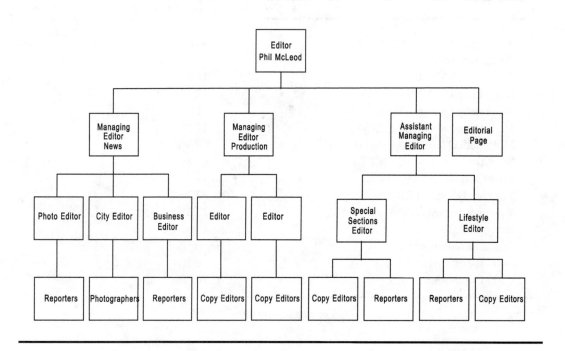

Source: Philip McLeod interview

FIRST BANK DIRECT

Joseph N. Fry

Late in August 1996, senior management of the Bank of Montreal (the Bank, BMO) were reviewing the development of the Bank's direct banking services and, specifically, plans for the pilot launch of a comprehensive direct banking venture in Calgary in mid- October under the name of First Bank Direct. An air of urgency had been added to the discussions by recent announcements from Vancouver City Savings, a relatively small but progressive credit union, and ING, the giant Dutch insurance group, that they were each preparing to launch "virtual banking" concepts, and by rumours that the Royal Bank, another of Canada's large financial institutions, was considering a similar move.

THE BANK OF MONTREAL

The Bank of Montreal group of companies ranked third (as measured by total assets) in 1995 among Canadian chartered banks and ninth in scale among North American banks. The Bank was unique among Canadian banks in the extent of its involvement in the United States, through its

IVEY

Joseph N. Fry prepared this case solely to provide material for class discussion. The author does not intend to illustrate either effective or ineffective handling of a managerial situation. The author may have disguised certain names and other identifying information to protect confidentiality.

Harris Bank operating unit, and in Mexico, through a 20 per cent stake in Bancomer, a large Mexican bank. In the fiscal year 1995, the Bank marked its sixth consecutive year of earnings growth and of return on equity above 14 per cent. The fiscal year 1996 promised to be a banner year for the Bank and for its Canadian competitors as well. There were expectations that the earnings of a number of banks, including BMO, would, for the first time, exceed $1 billion.

THE CHANGING ENVIRONMENT OF BANKING

In spite of the record earnings there was a distinct sense of concern among senior management in the Bank, and throughout the industry for that matter, that the current prosperity of the industry was masking basic changes in the banking environment and slowing the pace of adaptation to new realities. This view was reflected, for example, in an address by Matthew Barrett, CEO of the Bank, to bank executives in June 1996, in which he highlighted six drivers of change: globalization; the democratization of information; demographic patterns; alienation; the new workplace; and the restructuring of the financial services industry. Excerpts are presented below:

> **Globalization** . . . The financial services industry . . . (has been) . . . in many, although not all, ways the leader in economic globalization. Major banks are competing at home and abroad with rivals whose competitive advantages are hard to match. They are fighting back by investing heavily in technology, by upgrading their human resources, by adopting sophisticated techniques for the management of risk, and by seeking economies of scale and a global presence through mergers, acquisitions and alliances. Often they are trying to do all these things at once. Not all will succeed.

> **Democratization of Information** . . . Far more information is more readily accessible to far more people than ever before. Few, if any, sectors are more affected by this revolution than the financial services industry. It is not simply that banks have become utterly dependent on vast computer and communications networks. Information technology has brought a massive shift in power to the customer and thereby made banking far more competitive and responsive.

> A dynamic spiral has been set in motion whereby new technology creates new products and new standards of service; customers welcome these, quickly take them for granted, and demand the next wave of greater convenience and choice. Perhaps more important, abundant information is eroding the bankers' traditional arbitrage that sprang from superior knowledge of the available means and opportunities for lending and investing money. To keep ahead or even abreast of their customers' rising expectations and complex demands, banks are being forced to train staff to far higher levels of expertise than ever before. Paradoxically, while information technology is eliminating many traditional human careers in banking, it is greatly increasing the value of others. It follows that banks that fail to invest in people will not be with us long.

> **Demographics** . . . Shifting (demographic) patterns are . . . reinforcing the effects on financial institutions of the democratization of information. In the short and medium term they are moving banks from an emphasis on lending products to one on savings products, and from transaction-based customer relationships to more complex partnerships. Products and services are being redesigned to meet the higher expectations of a more educated, experienced and diverse customer base...In the longer term, banks will evolve into essentially professional institutions, whose core product is advice, backed up by access to capital, processing capability, and skill at marshalling and analyzing information . . .

Alienation Sweeping . . . (social and economic) . . . discontinuities have left many people in North America and around the world increasingly alienated from their social and political institutions, or even actively hostile to them . . . Such a mood will breed protest movements, internal withdrawal, and attempts to return to a real or imaginary past when life was simpler . . . Since banks are among the most conspicuous institutions in any modern society, they are prime targets and can expect rather more than their fair share of public resentment. Given the degree to which banks everywhere are subject to regulation, this is grounds for serious concern, and nowhere more so than in Canada. Banks are among the few institutions present in every part of this country and a tenacious Canadian myth paints them as a protected and monopolistic cartel.

The New Workplace . . . For those awake to (trends in the workplace) . . . a secure career is more and more perceived to flow from constant investment in oneself . . . A lifetime may see service with many different employers, but the true employers will always be the employees themselves. Increasingly the employees are entrepreneurs, in partnership with a larger entrepreneur who supplies the framework for their skills.

The implications for large commercial banks are potentially nothing less than earth shattering. They have tended to be textbook models of the traditional corporation: strongly hierarchical, bureaucratic, rule-based and driven from the top down. The real and continuing need for stability, prudence and customer confidence has legitimized the hierarchy, and indeed tends to validate all established procedures simply because they have stood the test of time thus far . . . Adopting the new model of the workplace, while retaining the old model's advantages of continuity and employee loyalty, will amount to a revolution in banking . . .

Restructuring All these trends together are bringing about a sweeping restructuring of the world's financial services industry . . . and all the more rapidly because many developed country markets suffer from over-capacity in traditional distribution channels.

Canada, in particular, is over-banked. We have too many major banks, so that none of them is large enough to compete globally. They, in turn, have too many branches, which saddle them with high distribution costs. This situation is aggravated by the rapid growth of alternate, low-cost, convenient distribution channels such as ABMs, telephone banking and soon the Internet, too. So-called niche players X specialized, focused non-banks X are capturing an increasing share of their chosen markets, while political pressures prevent the banks using their costly branch networks to compete effectively. Those same pressures will delay a major restructuring of the Canadian industry, but no serious observer doubts that it will come sooner or later. Some branches will close, others will be transformed as new distribution channels grow in importance. Expect to see major mergers between Canadian banks, or yes, even between Canadian and U.S. banks. We are living in the last years of the Big Five, and of the street corner with up to five different bank branches competing head to head."

Notes on Technology

New technologies were creating new channels of distribution for the handling of traditional banking transactions. These technologies offered dramatically lower costs. According to McKinsey consultants: "It is roughly 40 to 50 per cent cheaper to process a cash withdrawal at an ATM than at a branch teller window, up to 90 per cent cheaper to deal with an electronic payment, and 70 per cent cheaper to employ an automated telephone response unit." (1) A further illustration of the economics of typical transactions is given in Table 1.

Table 1: **Example Transaction Costs by Channel**

Transaction Type	Channel	Cost Per Transaction ($)
Withdrawals	Branch	2.00
	ABM (Bank-Owned)	.40
	Other ABM	.75
Deposits	Branch	2.00
	ABM	2.00
Bill Payments	Branch	2.00
	Telebanking - Agent	1.25
	Telebanking - AVR[*]	.40
	ABM	.40
	Direct Debit	.04
	PC	.04
Account Transfers	Branch	2.00
	Telebanking - Agent	1.25
	Telebanking - AVR	.40
	ABM	.04
	PC	.04

*AVR: Automatic Voice Response

Source: Bank of Montreal, Industry Sources.

The new technologies, in tandem with relaxed legislation and more knowledgeable customers, were also facilitating the entry of new competitors into traditional bank markets. For example, in the U.S., "four main product areas—mortgages, savings, personal loans and credit and life insurance—account for almost 65 per cent of total industry profitability. A number of companies focusing on these areas have recently emerged, notably Countrywide in mortgages, AT&T, GM, Ford, and many others in credit cards, and mutual fund companies such as Vanguard specializing in high return money market funds in deposits." (2).

A good example of parallel developments in Canada was in mutual funds. According to CIBC Wood Gundy Securities: ". . . investors dissatisfied with low interest rates have flocked into mutual funds in force, applying pressure on banks to sweeten the rates offered to clients . . . since 1992, Canadian bank deposits have increased by 38 per cent while mutual fund assets under management have jumped 160 per cent. Mutual fund assets in Canada represent approximately half the amount of bank deposits, while in the U.S. they are equal to bank deposits. Consequently, we believe that the mutual fund growth will continue." (3) And to pursue this potential, mutual fund companies were moving to offer bank-like services, such as cheque-writing privileges on money market accounts, and in the case of Trimark Mutual Fund's purchase of Bayshore Trust, integrating forward into the ownership of trust companies.

But there was even more to the new technology. It also offered unique opportunities for capturing customer information, storing and assembling it, and "mining" it to create new and specifically targeted marketing strategies. This was not yet common. According to McKinsey: "Few providers have yet developed a significant sales capability through these channels, especially for complex products, but things are likely to change rapidly in the next decade with growing acceptance of electronic and remote channels among younger consumers." (4). There was little question, however, that sophisticated marketing, based on sophisticated customer databases, was just around the corner.

THE BANK'S BUSINESSES

The Bank managed its operations through four operating groups, each with its own distinct market, product and geographic mandate. These units were the:

1. Personal and Commercial Financial Services group (PCFS) which provided financial services to individuals and commercial businesses in the Canadian market.
2. Corporate and Institutional Financial Services (CIFS) which provided financing, treasury and operating services to large corporate and institutional customers throughout North America and selectively abroad.
3. Harris Bank (HB) which provided banking, trust and investment services to individuals, as well as small and mid-market businesses in the Chicago area; corporate banking services throughout the Midwest United States; and trust, cash management, investment management, and private banking card services throughout the United States.
4. Investment Banking (IB) included Canada's largest investment dealer, Nesbitt Burns, and offered full-service brokerage, mutual funds, investment management, discount brokerage and various planning and advisory services to corporate, government, institutional and private clients in Canada and the United States and selectively in other markets.

The operating groups were provided with technology, transaction processing and professional services by two support groups—Operations, and Corporate Services. The relative scale and contribution of the operating groups to the Bank as a whole are summarized in Table 2.

Table 2: **1995 Net Income And Average Assets By Operating Group ($ millions)**

	PCFS	CIFS	HARRIS	IB	OTHER	TOTAL
Net Income	571	301	213	55	(198)	986
Average Assets	54,493	42,514	22,229	22,068	2,811	144,115

Source: Bank of Montreal Annual Report, 1995.

PCFS

PCFS was the Bank's traditional core business, and notwithstanding significant diversification moves by the Bank in the past 15 years, still its largest operating group. It was this group that, arguably, had been facing and would continue to face the brunt of changes in the industry environment.

PCFS had been responding to these changes with a wide range of initiatives. It had adopted a community banking structure under which bank executives in 230 communities across Canada were given the authority to take significant decisions to meet the unique needs of each local community. It had invested in new technology, including the expansion of its ABM network and telephone service channels, the development and initial introduction of Pathway, a software product that put a range of information about the Bank's products at the fingertips of sales representatives, and extensive employee training. These kinds of investments had helped PCFS to improve its revenues, earnings and productivity (Table 3), to maintain its position with respect to facilities (Table 4), and to improve its market share (Table 5).

Bank executives took some satisfaction in these results. But there was also a sense that they were achieved by doing the same things better rather than transforming the thrust of the Bank. As Ron Rogers, vice-chairman and head of PCFS put it: "Even if we continue to run full out, even if we stick with the strategies that made us the success we are today, we are not going to increase our rate of growth. We flatline—and that is a danger sign flashing bright red." Tony Comper, president and chief operating officer, spoke about the Bank as a whole: "We can't do the job by 'keeping on keeping on' and hoping that our competitors won't rise to the challenge either."

The task set by senior management for PCFS, and for the Bank generally, was one of reinvention and reinvention in a hurry. As Tony Comper put it: "We must reinvent our relationship with customers. Which means we must reinvent our relationships with the employees we count on to create and nurture our relationships with customers. Both of which require us to reinvent our business processes and tools — in other words, the way we do business . . . (and to change fast we must) . . . become very adept at continuously re-shaping our corporate structure . . . (at making) . . . fundamental and ongoing realignments to increase sales origination and efficiency. In some cases we need to reorganize by line of business rather than geography, which is the only way to operate efficiently from an enterprise-wide perspective. Right now, for example, we provide cash management services through CIFS and Harris Bank. We need to integrate them. And the same can be said for our credit, debit, and smart card lines of business." Matthew Barrett added a note of impatience: "We have a beaver on top of our coat of arms, but in many ways a tortoise would be far more appropriate."

Table 3: **BMO PCFS Financial Record ($ millions except as noted)**

As at or for the year ended October 31	1996[E]	1995	1994	1993	1992
Net interest income	2,281	2,234	2,139	1,914	1,881
Other income	640	608	581	578	529
Provision for credit losses	123	88	108	140	144
Non-interest expense	1,736	1,752	1,666	1,552	1,534
Income before taxes	1,062	1,002	946	800	732
Income taxes	452	431	416	344	308
Net income	610	571	530	456	424
Average assets	57,870	54,539	50,892	49,277	46,412
Average current loans	52,764	49,380	45,050	42,770	39,231
Average deposits	53,159	50,723	47,893	46,492	44,040
Full-time equivalent staff (number)	15,782	16,363	17,233	17,162	17,165
Expense-to-revenue ratio (%)	59.4	61.6	61.2	62.3	63.7

Source: BMO Annual Reports, Internal Files.

Table 4: **BMO PCFS: SELECTED FACILITIES COMPARISONS**

	BMO		Royal		CIBC		TD		BNS		NA	
	1992	1996	1992	1996	1992	1996	1992	1996	1992	1996	1992	1996
Branches*	1176	1148	1471	1262	1464	1352	895	910	1081	1137	643	614
ABMs**	1293	2017	3828	4215	2596	3032	1663	1991	1190	1526	482	713

* Excludes: Corporate/Independent Business Centres/Student Loan Centres/Private Banking, etc. (e.g., Royal Trust's 99 branches are excluded).

** ABMs: Automated Banking Machines

Source: Bank Annual Reports, BMO Internal files

Table 5:   **BMO PCFS: Market Share By Selected Business Lines**

	Bank Market* (%)	
Product/Service	**1992**	**1996**
Total Personal Deposits	13.9	14.4
Personal Loans	14.3	15.0
Residential Mortgages	12.9	14.4
Small Business Loans	14.0	16.0

* Bank Market includes credit unions and trust companies.

Source: BMO Annual Reports, Internal Documents.

DIRECT BANKING

Direct banking, virtual banking, branchless banking, multimedia banking, whatever the term, referred to a wholly new form of banking created by clustering previously separate technical developments. Its features were described by McKinsey consultants as follows:

> A multimedia bank looks nothing like a traditional financial institution. It need have neither branches nor tellers . . . it gives customers easy access to a wide variety of financial services— credit cards, bill payment, insurance, investments, and brokerage—in a single integrated account. It offers products from many different providers: a bond fund from Fidelity, a credit card from Visa, a mortgage from Countrywide.
>
> Consumers communicate with the multimedia bank through a range of devices including phones, PCS, faxes and ATMs. All the information on their accounts is automatically downloaded and updated in real time as the transactions take place.
>
> The advantages over conventional banking are numerous. Clearly, multimedia banking offers customers real convenience. It also gives financial institutions the opportunity to use information residing in the new integrated accounts to carry out highly tailored marketing. But the most compelling—and least understood—advantage derives from cost.
>
> The multimedia bank . . . (avoids) . . . both the expense of branches and, in the long run, the processing costs associated with paper transactions. By carefully targeting its customers and service offerings, a phone-based direct bank can secure a 30 percentage point cost advantage over traditional banks, thus redefining cost-effectiveness for the entire industry (Table 6).
>
> The savings come from three sources:

- A smaller, leaner staff with a greater focus on marketing. To serve a customer base of one million, a multimedia bank will have a total headcount of 2,000 compared with approximately 3,000 to 3,500 for a traditional bank. Despite paying higher wages to its more skilled employees, the multimedia bank will have a total salary bill less than half that of its conventional rival.

Table 6: **Traditional Retail vs. Multimedia: Comparative Business Models**

EXPENSE CATEGORY	Expense/Revenue (%)	
	Large Retail	**Multimedia**
Salaries	25	9
Rent	11	2
Transaction Related	10	8
Systems/Communication	4	5
Marketing/Advertising	3	4
Other	12	5
Total	**65**	**33**

Source: John H. Ott, Jack M. Stephenson, Paul K. Weberg, "Banking on Multimedia," The McKinsey Quarterly, 1995, Number 2, p. 97.

- Occupancy costs that are 80 per cent lower than for a traditional institution. The multimedia bank will have centralized customer service and processing centers located in low rent areas, in direct contrast to the geographically dispersed retail bank operating a high cost branch network largely in urban areas.

- Lower transaction processing costs, due to the lower volume of cash, cheques, and personal transactions. As technology continues to develop, the economic advantage of the multimedia bank will grow. With the introduction of electronic cash, processing costs should decline even further.

- Through its emphasis on electronic payment, the multimedia bank will also acquire many opportunities to capitalize on information . . . (enabling) . . . highly customized marketing approaches and a flurry of new product innovation . . . finally, the multimedia bank will reduce transaction times and expand the number of consumer access options available 24 hours a day. (5)

Experience with Direct Banking

The traditional banks had adopted two modes of entry for introducing direct banking services, commonly referred to as complementary direct banking and standalone direct banking.

Complementary Direct Banking: Under complementary direct banking, traditional banks offered "extended telephone service and ATM access and mimicked many of the attributes of direct banks, but positioned . . . (these services) . . . under the core brand of the parent bank as a supplement to the branch system. Often, . . . (these services) . . . are priced at premiums to branch-based transactions, creating incentives curiously at odds with the underlying economics." (6)

Complementary direct banking was the dominant practice in the industry in North America and in Europe. The banks were clearly fearful of the consequences of a standalone approach for their traditional systems and had chosen what McKinsey called a "wait and see" response. Under this approach banks "take marginal costs out of the branch system while focusing the bulk of marketing and other activities on supporting the branches . . . and they make ad hoc investments in new distribution systems like phones or PCS, and participate in industry alliances and consortia without taking a clear leadership role." (7)

McKinsey goes on to note that the "wait and see" approach seems "at first sight conservative. . . (but) . . . actually is far more costly than it seems. It actually layers on additional costs as channels multiply and the cost of complexity rises . . . (and) . . . it overlooks the cost-reduction and skill-building programs that are required to compete in the new environment . . . (and it risks) . . . lockout as key alliances are formed and the industry consolidates." (8)

A further limiting consequence of layering in new direct bank channels was that it typically failed to realize the potential for consolidating customer information. Most banks had built their formidable information systems to facilitate transactions and capture revenues and costs by products, services, branches and other organizational entities, <u>but</u> not by customer. The reality of millions of customers, multiple product and organizational entities and complex systems constituted an enormous barrier to reworking the systems to track and assemble information by customer. But this was quite feasible from a fresh start if the direct banking services were handled on a standalone basis.

Standalone Direct Banking: Standalone direct banks sought to build a separate entity—internally, in terms of organization, and externally in terms of independent services and brand identity. Several European banks had moved in this direction and it also tended to be favored by U.S. banks for expansion outside their established territory. Wells-Fargo was using a standalone concept, for example, to reach out to small and medium business accounts outside their branch coverage in the U.S. and was attempting to secure approval to move into Canada.

There appeared to be a tremendous opportunity with standalone banking to pick off and target specific customer segments and to try to capture their business across a wide range of traditional banking services. There was a rule of thumb in the industry, for example, that about 20 per cent of retail customers accounted for 120 to 140 per cent of retail profitability. These customers were an obvious target for new standalone entries.

Midland's First Direct[1]

Perhaps the most successful example of standalone banking was in the United Kingdom—Midland Bank's First Direct. (9) First Direct was launched in October 1989. At the time, telephone banking was largely untested and a completely new idea to the public at large. Midland proceeded on the premise that a viable alternative to branch banking had to put the customer first and that this would require an autonomous banking service with its own systems, culture and operating philosophy. It set a young development team to work on what would become an independent person-to-person banking service available over the phone, 24 hours a day, seven days a week, 365 days a year.

First Direct engaged in very heavy introductory promotion, with a television budget alone estimated at £6 million. By the end of its first year it had enlisted over 60,000 customers. By 1994 First Direct broke even with approximately 450,000 customers, and in 1995 announced its first full year of profitability with over 500,000 customers and a growth rate of over 10,000 customers per month.

---

[1] This section is drawn from Virginie Lagoutte, "The Direct Banking Challenge," Middlesex University, April 1996.

By 1996 First Direct employed about 2,000 full-time equivalent workers and offered checking accounts, credit cards, savings products, mortgages, personal loans, brokerage, travel and insurance services. Customer satisfaction was high; 87 per cent of First Direct customers were extremely/very satisfied with their service compared with an average of 51 per cent for high street banks. Customers, split roughly evenly between male and female, were predominantly in the age range of 25 to 44 and from the higher socio-economic categories. In common, these customers reported that they valued speed and efficiency and human contact and interaction. Among new customers, about 73 per cent came from Midland's competition and 41 per cent reported that word-of-mouth was critical to their decision.

First Direct handled about 26,000 telephone calls a day with an average duration of three minutes. To support this requirement First Direct operated a dedicated call center with some 330 miles of cabling in a totally flexible, open plan environment, purposely built to adapt to new technology. Banking representatives (BR) each worked with a Davox intelligent terminal which allowed them to access several systems simultaneously, providing a total picture of the caller's personal details, business with the bank and previous transactions. By 1992, First Direct was working to develop special software that would build customer profiles identifying characteristics such as price, service and time sensitivity and even to forecast the next major product purchase that the customer was going to make.

Five years after the launch of First Direct, the four other leading retail banks in the U.K. had moved to offer telephone and other direct banking channels. These, however, were add-on units, designed to remove the need for a branch visit for standard transactions, rather than clones of Midland's unique branded operation. The Bank of Scotland had launched a similar direct bank, but the major banks had yet to launch standalone competitors.

The official view inside Midland was that the traditional branch system and First Direct were partners, providing service in a different, albeit similar, market. Further, they emphasized that First Direct was not about cutting costs, but about finding a better way to serve customers. Nevertheless, Midland had had to defend First Direct against complaints that it was skimming the bank's most profitable customers, and magnifying job losses in the conventional structure.

FIRST BANK DIRECT

In Canada, through to the summer of 1996, BMO and the major Canadian banks had adopted, implicitly at least, the complementary direct banking strategy. New access channels and services had been and were being offered as technology permitted, but always within the context of the traditional branch systems. At BMO, however, there had been a growing concern that this approach was not moving costs down fast enough and that it was not proving particularly effective in building revenues (as compared to sustaining them). For some time a line of thought had been developing that the Bank should move in the direction of a more comprehensive direct banking initiative. Specifically, work had been proceeding on the development of a new and distinct business entity that would offer its customers an integrated range of direct banking services while operating under the umbrella of the PCFS infrastructure and side-by-side with the traditional system.

The new initiative was to be called First Bank Direct, an extension of the Bank's existing brand line-up, and plans had been laid for a pilot launch in Calgary in mid-October. Then, as PCFS refined the marketing and operational aspects of the new business, and as results justified, the concept would be rolled out across the country. The recent announcements by ING and Vancouver City Savings of their intentions to launch "virtual" banks and the rumors that the Royal Bank was considering a similar move were focusing increasing attention on the First Bank Direct project. Was this a sufficient response to a changing environment and impending direct bank competition?

References

1. Lenny Mendonca and Gordon D. McCallum, "Battling for the Wallet." <u>The McKinsey Quarterly</u>, Number 2, 1995, p. 76-92.
2. Ibid. p. 80.
3. CIBC Wood Gundy, "The Canadian Chartered Banks," August 23, 1966.
4. Op. Cit. (1), p. 85.
5. Brian A. Johnson, John H. Ott, Jack M. Stephenson, and Paal K. Weberg, "Banking On Multimedia." <u>The McKinsey Quarterly</u>, Number 2, 1995, p 94-106.
6. Ibid., p. 100.
7. Ibid., p. 100.
8. Ibid., p. 98.
9. Ibid., p. 100.

VISIONING AT
XEROX CANADA

Nick Bontis and
Mary Crossan

On June 15, 1994, Diane McGarry, Chairman, CEO and President of Xerox Canada, asked Bryan Smith, a consultant working for the company, if he would join her outside the conference room for a brief tête-à-tête. They had been meeting with her leadership team[1] since eight o'clock that morning to craft the organization's new vision statement.

It was now past eleven-thirty and the "visioning" session was scheduled to end at noon. During the previous three and a half hours, some progress had been made, but Smith felt that more time would be needed to give the decision its due process. Smith suggested that they extend the allotted time into the afternoon or postpone the session. However, McGarry was hesitant to delay the final selection of the vision statement because it was very important to her. As they both returned to the conference room, McGarry contemplated her next move.

---

[1]Consisting of 23 senior managers (many of which were McGarry's direct reports).

Ivey

Nick Bontis prepared this case under the supervision of Professor Mary Crossan solely to provide material for class discussion. The author does not intend to illustrate either effective or ineffective handling of a managerial situation. The author may have disguised certain names and other identifying information to protect confidentiality.

XEROX CORP.

Xerox Corp. was a global player in the document processing market. Its activities encompassed the designing, manufacturing, and servicing of a complete range of document processing products. Xerox copiers, duplicators, electronic printers, optical scanners, facsimile machines, networks, multifunction publishing machines and related software and supplies were marketed in more than 130 countries.

Xerox Corp. had won many accolades in the United States, Australia, Belgium, Brazil, Canada, Colombia, France, Hong Kong, India, Ireland, Japan, Mexico, the Netherlands and the United Kingdom, reflecting its prestigious standing in the business world. In 1980, Fuji Xerox won the Deming Prize, Japan's highest quality award. The major U.S. award was the Malcolm Baldrige National Quality Award, which Xerox Business Products and Systems won in 1989. Then in 1992, Rank Xerox won the first European Quality Award. The pursuit of these awards often incited organizations to participate in the visioning process. Vision statements were a critical element in the evaluation process.

XEROX CANADA

Although Xerox Corp. controlled its Canadian subsidiary from a regulatory perspective, it often allowed the smaller organization enough latitude to pursue its own initiatives (this included developing its own vision statement). The Parent considered its Canadian subsidiary as a laboratory for strategic experiments. With this unofficial mandate, the Canadian operation had developed a solid reputation for the implementation of various employee-inspired programs. Xerox Canada was also known for its publicly displayed corporate ideals. A senior manager described the company's situation this way:

> Our company is very well known and respected in the business community for integrating its various "corporate concepts"[2] . In fact, CEOs of other large multinational enterprises often marvel at the way we are able to harmonize our numerous strategic initiatives into a coordinated effort. They often sit in our boardroom and just admire the programs we proudly display on our walls. Many of these strategic initiatives are sponsored by our parent company in Stamford, Connecticut, while others are independently developed by our own employees here in Canada.

One of the main themes in Xerox Canada's philosophy deals with "satisfied customers." To further improve service to its customers, Xerox Canada announced an organizational restructuring that would create special customer business units in order to maintain closer ties with the marketplace. This restructuring was McGarry's responsibility.

McGarry's Arrival in Canada

McGarry was promoted to the top position in Canada in October 1993 because she was recognized as a team player who prided herself on open communication. Her leadership skills and risk-taking attitude were exactly what Xerox Canada needed during this restructuring period. In the first 60 days in her new position, she visited 14 cities across Canada and talked to thousands of employees,

---

[2]Including Xerox's signature, philosophy, priorities, cultural dimensions (see Exhibit 1*).*

customers, and suppliers in order to "get to know Canada." She came back from this trip with a better understanding of the company, the domestic market, Canada's economy and its government. McGarry's most important mandate since her arrival in late 1993 was to bring this restructured design to life and make it work in Canada.

While the restructuring took place, Xerox Canada employees continued to develop and support innovative strategic initiatives. Many of these programs, including the new employee evaluation system, went on to become world-wide initiatives that eventually helped shape the culture and the values of the whole organization.

Employee-Inspired Initiatives

A commitment to community involvement was basic to the company's business philosophy. Xerox Canada contributed $1.3 million in 1994 to charities and non-profit organizations across Canada. About 65 per cent of the contributions were focused on projects which support INFORMATION TECHNOLOGY LITERACY which includes the Xerox Aboriginal Scholarships program for aboriginal students studying programs which could lead to a career in information technology. The remaining funds were focused on community programs such as the United Way, matching employee gifts to post-secondary institutions, and the Xerox Community Involvement Program (XCIP). The XCIP offered financial support to community organizations in which employees volunteer on a regular basis.

In addition to its sense of community involvement, Xerox Canada shared the public's concern about the environment and integrated that concern into its business activities. The company was dedicated to protecting the environment as a responsible corporate citizen. In its marketing materials, Xerox described itself as setting standards for its products that went beyond many government requirements for health, safety and environmental protection in the countries in which it operated. The company was proud to communicate its commitment to the philosophy of sustainable development, which meant meeting the needs of the present without compromising the needs of future generations.

Another very successful program that symbolized the progressive culture of the organization was a new collaborative, performance-feedback process: COMIT (Communication of Objectives and Measurements and ensuring our success through Inspection and Teamwork). COMIT's objective was to extend beyond Xerox Canada's standard business results by incorporating its five key priorities with eight new cultural dimensions (see Exhibit 1 for details). Senior management hoped the union of these 13 elements would allow the COMIT process to affect the behaviours of the employees and to create a more empowered and dynamic organizational culture. Although Xerox Canada could be criticized for its overzealous pursuit of these and other programs, which went above and beyond its operational duties, the company never ignored its pledge of boundless service to its customers. In the 1994 Annual Report, Diane McGarry stated:

> We focus on what will make a difference for our customers—anticipating their needs, satisfying and exceeding all their expectations, and creating relationships that will serve them into the next century.

During the restructuring period, McGarry also familiarized herself with the most recently developed employee-inspired initiatives to get a better sense of what important issues interested the employees of Xerox Canada. The following describes three more employee-inspired programs developed at Xerox Canada:

XEROX CHEZ MOI—in this work-from-home or work-from-anywhere program, nearly 750 staff "telecommuted" as part of a work-at-home experiment that began company-wide in March, 1994. Reaction so far was favourable. Employees claimed that they got double and triple the work done without normal office interruptions.

KEEPING CUSTOMERS FOREVER—the objective of this program was to get customers and keep them forever. The advent of CBUs provided for a system that allowed service employees to build loyal and long-term relationships in which customers felt satisfied.

XEROX FLEXPLACE—ninety percent of surveyed employees said that being able to balance the needs of both family life and the needs of the business was a key factor in the satisfaction of an employee. This program offered a wide range of flexible work arrangements, including the opportunity for men to nurture new babies while on a parental leave.

As the restructuring continued and new initiatives were launched, the Parent watched over McGarry closely. This prompted her to re-examine not only her contribution to the organization, but the contribution of every other employee as well. The genesis of the visioning process had emerged. Senior management felt that a new vision statement would convey the ideals of the corporation, encompass present attitudes, and continue to align employees in their operational activities and in their innovative efforts.

THE VISIONING PROCESS

By mid-1994, Diane McGarry's leadership transition into Xerox Canada was running smoothly. Business performance was favourable (see Exhibit 2) and customers and employees alike were supporting new developments in the organization. Furthermore, corporate insiders predicted that Xerox Canada was slowly becoming the jewel of the Xerox Corp. empire worldwide.

As Xerox Canada moved comfortably into the latter half of the 1990s, McGarry believed that a vision statement for the company should be developed to help integrate all of the company's diverse activities. Previous vision statements for Xerox Canada were not widely known throughout the organization and had been practically forgotten by most employees since McGarry's arrival in Canada. Although McGarry recognized that Xerox Canada already had several important "corporate concepts" such as the signature (THE DOCUMENT COMPANY), the philosophy, five priorities and eight cultural dimensions (see Exhibit 1), she believed that it was imperative to synthesize a vision statement for the company that would coordinate all of the concepts, initiatives and activities of the organization. This was considered a critical exercise early in her tenure and one she felt would prove to be highly insightful.

McGarry invited her leadership team to Niagara-on-the-Lake for a two-day corporate retreat. The first scheduled item on the program was a four hour session to create the new vision statement.

McGarry also brought in a management consultant, Bryan Smith, who had prior experience with visioning with several other large corporate clients.[3] Smith had also done some prior consulting with Xerox Canada and was, therefore, somewhat familiar with the company's history.

Several weeks prior to the meeting, McGarry asked each team member to review the company's earlier vision statements. Approximately 90 per cent of the team members had been through a visioning process at least once in their careers. The last time any of the participants had been through this process was during David McCamus' tenure in the early 1990s. Bryan Smith also played a significant role during McCamus' tenure and had earned a solid reputation for himself amongst the senior managers by running several successful workshops and joint projects. Current members of Xerox Canada's leadership team were already familiar with Smith's work and respected his contributions. McCamus' team had developed the following vision statement during the early 1990s:

> Our raison d'être is to create a dynamic growth oriented business by providing superior customer satisfaction through quality products and innovative services supported by an inspired team of skilled individuals.

When Richard Barton took over the leadership position from McCamus in 1991, he personally developed a vision statement which was subsequently confirmed by his management team at a meeting in August 1991. This statement was printed on the 1992 COMIT documents for all employees:

> We will know we have reached the desired state of Xerox when the Document Company is the leader in providing Document services that enhance business productivity.

Now that McGarry was in charge, she felt that it was necessary not only to create a new vision statement, but to seek input from her direct reports and their subordinates. She wanted this to be a team effort. The first task she had her team accomplish was to seek feedback from Xerox Canada's largest customers on what their needs were. The following describes some of the comments received from customers:

- we want someone with skill, expertise, resources and the creativity that is needed to take cost out of operations, and add speed and quality;
- we want someone to identify what our needs are, recommend solutions, and work every step of the way to ensure success;
- we need software that will allow us to access information and respond far more quickly than we could in a paper-based environment.

As the visioning session approached, McGarry's team reflected on the organization's recent accomplishments and carefully considered the values that motivated the employees to work each and every day. At the start of the visioning session, the team members collectively selected the criteria that they would use to help guide the process. The three chosen criteria ensured that the statement would be: i) clear; ii) motivating; and iii) inspiring. The brainstorming session

---

[3]In fact, he had published an article on the topic: Smith, Bryan. (1989). Vision: A Time to Take Stock Business Quarterly. Autumn. pp. 80-84.

commenced once the criteria were set. Each participant was asked to write down three words on a flip chart to help spark the brainstorming process. At this point, the tone of the session was very positive and there was a tremendous amount of energy and excitement in the conference room. Soon after, the participants were asked to create and write down one vision statement that included their three key words.

Eventually, twenty-four individual statements (one from each member of the leadership team plus McGarry) were posted around the room on flip charts. Participants were asked to read out their own statements twice while emphasizing the key words. The whole group cheered after each participant was finished. Smith then facilitated the session by grouping the statements together and removing duplication.

JUNE 15, 1994, 11:32 A.M.

McGarry had allotted four hours for the whole visioning process. Each of the participants had brainstormed ideas all morning and it was becoming increasingly difficult to select the "one statement." After three and a half hours, they had only narrowed it down to about half a dozen possibilities (see Exhibit 3 for the final statements). Many participants became discouraged as time elapsed and the tone of the session turned 180 degrees as their energy drained away. Although the morning had started off with a bang, now there were concerns that the rest of the two-day retreat would be consumed by this visioning process. Other planned activities risked being cancelled.

By 11:32 a.m., McGarry was becoming concerned with the team's progress. She asked Smith to join her outside the conference room for a brief private meeting. She told Smith that she was hesitant to extend the session past noon because she realized that continued discussion of the vision statement would preclude work on other scheduled initiatives. However, she recognized that the visioning process deserved a dedicated commitment by the whole group and a concerted amount of time and effort. Furthermore, Smith suggested that it was going to be very difficult to assimilate all the agreed-upon suggestions thus far into one coherent statement within the next half-hour. On the other hand, Smith also knew that time pressure could facilitate the creative process. McGarry returned to the conference room with Smith and spoke to her team.

Exhibit 1: **Xerox Canada's Priorities, Philosophy and Cultural Dimensions**

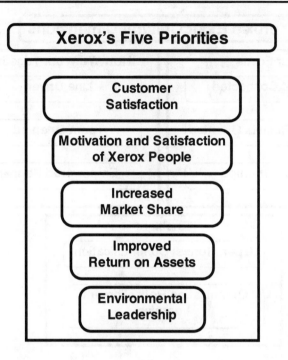

Xerox's Five Priorities

- Customer Satisfaction
- Motivation and Satisfaction of Xerox People
- Increased Market Share
- Improved Return on Assets
- Environmental Leadership

Xerox's philosophy is stated as: *"We succeed through satisfied customers. We aspire to deliver quality and excellence in all we do. We require premium return on assets. We use technology to develop product leadership. We value our employees. We behave responsibly as a corporate citizen."*

Exhibit 1 continued

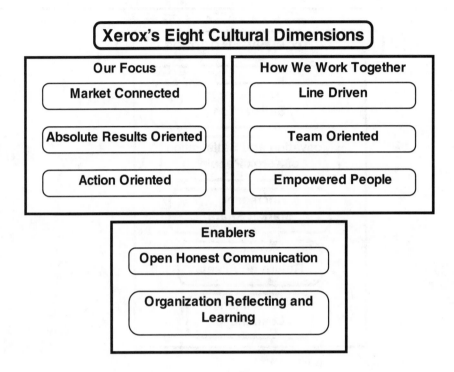

Xerox's Eight Cultural Dimensions

Our Focus	How We Work Together
Market Connected	Line Driven
Absolute Results Oriented	Team Oriented
Action Oriented	Empowered People

Enablers

Open Honest Communication

Organization Reflecting and Learning

Exhibit 2: Historical Business Performance (Dollars In Millions)

Operational Highlights	1994	1993	1992	1991	1990
Revenues: Sales	767.1	722.3	656.7	651.1	641.9
Revenues: Service and Rental	302.9	310.3	307.1	281.2	274.3
Revenues: Finance	101.7	112.1	115.5	119.0	122.8
Total Revenues	1,171.7	1,144.7	1,079.3	1,051.3	1,039.0
Net Earnings	88.8	25.8	61.1	39.5	35.7
Total Assets	1,601.3	1,706.8	1,717.5	1,686.9	1,904.8
Shareholder's Equity	670.7	676.3	610.9	578.0	569.3
Cash Flow from Operations	182.3	95.1	35.4	317.4	139.1
Number of Employees	4,315	4,775	4,802	5,017	5,059
Return on Equity	13.4%	3.9%	10.4%	6.8%	6.4%

Source: Company reports

Exhibit 2 continued

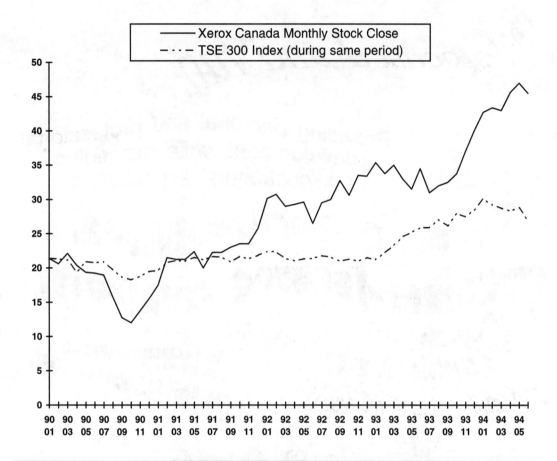

Note: Monthly close stock prices of XXC.B on the TSE.

Source: Casewriter's Illustration (data taken from Bloomberg)

Exhibit 3: **Final Remaining Vision Statements**

Fast, focused and fun.

Providing personal and professional
development while exceeding
our customers' expectations.

Xerox, a market-driven,
customer-focused company.

To maintain 15% growth
and 20% return on equity.

TO boldly go where no
company has gone before!

TO PROVIDE OUR CUSTOMERS WITH
INNOVATIVE PRODUCTS AND SERVICES
THAT FULLY SATISFY THEIR NEEDS.

Employee energy and quality work
keeps customers for life.

MERCK & CO., INC. (A)

David Bollier and
Kirk O. Hanson
Adapted by Stephanie Weiss

In 1978, Dr. P. Roy Vagelos, then head of the Merck research labs, received a provocative memorandum from a senior researcher in parasitology, Dr. William C. Campbell. Dr. Campbell had made an intriguing observation while working with ivermectin, a new antiparasitic compound under investigation for use in animals.

Campbell thought that ivermectin might be the answer to a disease called river blindness that plagued millions in the Third World. But to find out if Campbell's hypothesis had merit, Merck would have to spend millions of dollars to develop the right formulation for human use and to conduct the field trials in the most remote parts of the world. Even if these efforts produced an effective and safe drug, virtually all of those afflicted with river blindness could not afford to buy it. Vagelos, originally a university researcher but by then a Merck executive, had to decide whether to invest in research for a drug that, even if successful, might never pay for itself.

River Blindness

River blindness, formally know as onchocerciasis, was a disease labeled by the World Health Organization (WHO) as a public health and socioeconomic problem of considerable magnitude in over 35 developing countries throughout the Third World. Some 85 million people in thousands of

This case was adapted by Stephanie Weiss from a monograph "Merck & Co. Inc." by David Bollier, under the supervision of Kirk O. Hanson, President of The Business Enterprise Trust and Senior Lecturer at the Stanford Graduate School of Business.

tiny settlements throughout Africa and parts of the Middle East and Latin America were thought to be at risk. The cause: a parasitic worm carried by a tiny black fly which bred along fast-moving rivers. When the flies bit humans—a single person could be bitten thousands of times a day—the larvae of a parasitic worm, *Onchocerca volvulus*, entered the body.

These worms grew to more than two feet in length, causing grotesque but relatively innocuous nodules in the skin. The real harm began when the adult worms reproduced, releasing millions of microscopic offspring, know as microfilariae, which swarmed through the body tissue. A terrible itching resulted, so bad that some victims committed suicide. After several years, the microfilariae caused lesions and depigmentation of the skin. Eventually they invaded the eyes, often causing blindness.

The World Health Organization estimated in 1978 that some 340,000 people were blind because of onchocerciasis, and that a million more suffered from varying degrees of visual impairment. At that time, 18 million or more people were infected with the parasite, though half did not yet have serious symptoms. In some villages, close to fly breeding sites, nearly all residents were infected and a majority of those over age 45 were blind. In such places, it was said, children believed that severe itching, skin infections and blindness were simply part of growing up.

In desperate efforts to escape the flies, entire villages abandoned fertile areas near rivers, and moved to poorer land. As a result, food shortages were frequent. Community life disintegrated as new burdens arose for already impoverished families.

The disease was first identified in 1893 by scientists and in 1926 was found to be related to the black flies. But by the 1970s, there was still no cure that could safely be used for community-wide treatment. Two drugs, diethylcarbamazine (DEC) & Suramin, were useful in killing the parasite, but both had severe side effects in infected individuals, needed close monitoring, and had even caused deaths. In 1974, the Onchocerciasis Control Program was created to be administered by the World Health Organization, in the hope that the flies could be killed through spraying of larvacides at breeding sites, but success was slow and uncertain. The flies in many areas developed resistance to the treatment, and were also known to disappear and then reinfest areas.

Merck & Co. Inc.

Merck & Co., Inc. was, in 1978, one of the largest producers of prescription drugs in the world. Headquartered in Rahway, New Jersey, Merck traced its origins to Germany in 1668 when Friedrich Jacob Merck purchased an apothecary in the city of Darmstadt. Over three hundred years later, Merck, having become an American firm, employed over 28,000 people and had operations all over the world.

In the late 1970's, Merck was coming off a 10-year drought in terms of new products. For nearly a decade, the company had relied on two prescription drugs for a significant percentage of its approximately US$2 billion in annual sales: Indocin, a treatment for rheumatoid arthritis, and Aldomet, a treatment for high blood pressure. Henry W. Gadsden, Merck's chief executive from 1965 to 1976, along with his successor, John J. Horan, were concerned that the 17-year patent protection on Merck's two big moneymakers would soon expire, and began investing an enormous amount in research.

Merck management spent a great deal of money on research because it knew that its success, ten and twenty years in the future, critically depended upon present investments. The company deliberately fashioned a corporate culture to nurture the most creative, fruitful research. Merck scientists were among the best paid in the industry, and were given great latitude to pursue intriguing leads. Moreover, they were inspired to think of their work as a quest to alleviate human disease and suffering worldwide. Within certain proprietary constraints, researchers were encouraged to publish in academic journals and to share ideas with their scientific peers. Nearly a billion dollars was spent between 1975 and 1978, and the investment paid off. In that period, under the direction of head of research, Dr. P. Roy Vagelos, Merck introduced Clinoril, a painkiller for arthritis; a general antibiotic called Mefoxin; a drug for glaucoma named Timoptic; and Ivomec (ivermectin, MSD), an antiparasitic for cattle.

In 1978, Merck had sales of US$1.98 billion and net income of US$307 million. Sales had risen steadily between 1969 and 1978 from US$691 million to almost US$2 billion. Income during the same period rose from US$106 million to over US$300 million. (See Exhibit 1 for a 10 year summary of performance.)

At that time, Merck employed 28,700 people, up from 22,200 ten years earlier. Human and animal health products constituted 84 per cent of the company's sales, with environmental health products and services representing an additional 14 per cent of sales. Merck's foreign sales had grown more rapidly during the 1970s than had domestic sales, and in 1978 represented 47 per cent of total sales. Much of the company's research operations were organized separately as the Merck Sharp & Dohme Research Laboratories, headed by Vagelos. Other Merck operations included the Merck Sharp & Dohme Division, Merck Sharp & Dohme International Division, Kelco Division, Merck Chemical Manufacturing Division, Merck Animal Health Division, Calgon Corporation, Baltimore Aircoil Company, and Hubbard Farms.

The company had 24 plants in the United States, including one in Puerto Rico and 44 in other countries. Six research laboratories were located in the United States and four abroad.

While Merck executives sometimes squirmed when they quoted the "unbusinesslike" language of George W. Merck, son of the company's founder and its former chairman, there could be no doubt that Merck employees found the words inspirational. "We try never to forget that medicine is for the people," Merck said. "It is not for the profits. The profits follow, and if we have remembered that, they have never failed to appear. The better we have remembered it, the larger they have been." These words formed the basis of Merck's overall corporate philosophy.

The Drug Investment Decision

Merck invested hundreds of millions of dollars each year in research. Allocating those funds amongst various projects, however, was a rather involved and inexact process. At a company as large as Merck, there was never a single method which projects were approved or money distributed.

Studies showed that, on the average, it took 12 years and US$200 million to bring a new drug to market. Thousands of scientists were continually working on new ideas and following new leads. Drug development was always a matter of trial and error; with each new iteration, scientists would close some doors and open others. When a Merck researcher came across an apparent breakthrough—either in an unexpected direction or as a derivative of the original lead—he or she would conduct preliminary research. If the idea proved promising, it was brought to the attention of the department heads.

Every year, Merck's research division held a large review meeting at which all research programs were examined. Projects were coordinated and consolidated, established programs were reviewed and new possibilities were considered. Final approval on research was not made, however, until the head of research met later with a committee of scientific advisors. Each potential program was extensively reviewed, analyzed on the basis of the likelihood of success, the existing market, competition, potential safety problems, manufacturing feasibility and patent status before the decision was made whether to allocate funds for continued experimentation.

The Problem of Rare Diseases and Poor Customers

Many potential drugs offered little chance of financial return. Some diseases were so rare that treatments developed could never be priced high enough to recoup the investment in research, while other diseases afflicted only the poor in rural and remote areas of the Third World. These victims had limited ability to pay even a small amount for drugs or treatment.

In the United States, Congress sought to encourage drug companies to conduct research on rare diseases. In 1978 legislation had been proposed which would grant drug companies tax benefits and seven-year exclusive marketing rights if they would manufacture drugs for diseases afflicting fewer than 200,000 Americans. It was expected that this "orphan drug" program would eventually be passed into law.

There was, however, no U.S. or international program that would create incentives for companies to develop drugs for diseases like river blindness which afflicted millions of the poor in the Third World. The only hope was that some Third World government, foundation, or international aid organization might step in and partially fund the distribution of a drug that had already been developed.

The Discovery of Ivermectin

The process of investigating promising drug compounds was always long, laborious and fraught with failure. For every pharmaceutical compound that became a "product candidate," thousands of others failed to meet the most rudimentary pre-clinical tests for safety and efficacy. With so much room for failure, it became especially important for drug companies to have sophisticated research managers who could identify the most productive research strategies.

Merck had long been a pioneer in developing major new antibiotic compounds, beginning with penicillin and streptomycin in the 1940s. In the 1970s, Merck Sharp & Dohme Research Laboratories were continuing this tradition. To help investigate for the new microbial agents of potential therapeutic value, Merck researchers obtained 54 soil samples from the Kitasato Institute of Japan in 1974. These samples seemed novel and the researchers hoped they might disclose some naturally occurring antibiotics.

As Merck researchers methodically put the soil through hundreds of tests, Merck scientists were pleasantly surprised to detect strong antiparasitic activity in Sample No. OS3153, a scoop of soil dug up at a golf course near Ito, Japan. The Merck labs quickly brought together an interdisciplinary team to try to isolate a pure active ingredient from the microbial culture. The compound eventually isolated—avermectin—proved to have an astonishing potency and effectiveness against a wide range of parasites in cattle, swine, horses and other animals. Within a year, the Merck team also began to suspect that a group of related compounds discovered in the same soil sample could be effective against many other intestinal worms, mites, ticks and insects.

After toxicological tests suggested that ivermectin would be safer than related compounds, Merck decided to develop the substance for the animal health market. In 1978 the first ivermectin-based animal drug, Ivomec, was nearing approval by the U.S. Department of Agriculture and foreign regulatory bodies. Many variations would likely follow: drugs for sheep and pigs, horses, dogs, and others. Ivomec had the potential to become a major advance in animal health treatment.

As clinical testing of ivermectin progressed in the late 1970s, Dr. William Campbell's ongoing research brought him face-to-face with an intriguing hypothesis. Ivermectin, when tested in horses, was effective against the microfilariae of an exotic, fairly unimportant gastrointestinal parasite, Onchocerca cervicalis. This particular worm, while harmless in horses, had characteristics similar to the insidious human parasite that causes river blindness, Onchocerca volvulus.

Dr. Campbell wondered: Could ivermectin be formulated to work against the human parasite? Could a safe, effective drug suitable for community-wide treatment of river blindness be developed? Both Campbell and Vagelos knew that it was very much a gamble that it would succeed. Furthermore, both knew that even if success were attained, the economic viability of such a project would be nil. On the other hand, because such a significant amount of money had already been invested in the development of the animal drug, the cost of developing a human formulation would be much less than that for developing a new compound. It was also widely believed at this point that ivermectin, though still in its final development stages, was likely to be very successful.

A decision to proceed would not be without risks. If a new derivative proved to have any adverse health effects when used on humans, its reputation as a veterinary drug could be tainted and sales negatively affected, no matter how irrelevant the experience with humans. In early tests, ivermectin had had some negative side effects on some specific species of mammals. Dr. Brian Duke of the Armed Forces Institute of Pathology in Washington, D.C. said the cross-species effectiveness of antiparasitic drugs are unpredictable, and there is "always a worry that some race or subsection of the human population" might be adversely affected.

Isolated instances of harm to humans or improper use in Third World settings might also raise some unsettling questions: Could drug residues turn up in meat eaten by humans? Would any human version of ivermectin distributed to the Third World be diverted into the black market, undercutting sales of the veterinary drug? Could the drug harm certain animals in unknown ways?

Despite these risks, Vagelos wondered what the impact might be of turning down Campbell's proposal. Merck had built a research team dedicated to alleviating human suffering. What would a refusal to pursue a possible treatment for river blindness do to morale?

Ultimately, it was Dr. Vagelos who had to make the decision whether or not to fund research toward a treatment for river blindness.

Exhibit 1: 10-Year Summary of Financial Performance

Merck & Co., Inc. and Subsidiaries
(Dollar amounts in thousands except per-share figures)

Results for Year:	1978	1977	1976	1975	1974	1973	1972	1971	1970	1969
Sales	$1,981,440	$1,724,410	$1,561,117	$1,401,979	$1,260,416	$1,104,035	$942,631	$832,416	$761,109	$691,453
Materials and production costs	744,249	662,703	586,963	525,853	458,837	383,879	314,804	286,646	258,340	232,878
Marketing/administrative expenses	542,186	437,579	396,975	354,525	330,292	304,807	268,856	219,005	201,543	178,593
Research/development expenses	161,350	144,898	133,826	121,933	100,952	89,155	79,692	71,619	69,707	61,100
Interest expense	25,743	25,743	26,914	21,319	8,445	6,703	4,533	3,085	2,964	1,598
Income before taxes	507,912	453,487	416,439	378,349	361,890	319,491	274,746	252,061	228,555	217,284
Taxes on income	198,100	173,300	159,100	147,700	149,300	134,048	121,044	118,703	108,827	109,269
Net income **	307,534	277,525	255,482	228,778	210,492	182,681	151,180	131,381	117,878	106,645
Per common share **	$4.07	$3.67	$3.38	$3.03	$2.79	$2.43	$2.01	$1.75	$1.57	$1.43
Dividends declared on common stock	132,257	117,101	107,584	105,564	106,341	93,852	84,103	82,206	76,458	75,528
Per common share	$1.75	$1.55	$1.42 1/2	$1.40	$1.40	$1.23 1/2	$1.12	$1.10	$1.02 1/2	$1.02 1/2
Gross plant additions	155,853	177,167	153,894	249,015	159,148	90,194	69,477	67,343	71,540	48,715
Depreciation	75,477	66,785	58,198	52,091	46,057	40,617	36,283	32,104	27,819	23,973
Year-End Position:										
Working Capital	666,817	629,515	549,840	502,262	359,591	342,434	296,378	260,350	226,084	228,296
Property, plant, and equipment (net)	924,179	846,784	747,107	652,804	459,245	352,145	305,416	274,240	239,638	197,220
Total assets	2,251,358	1,993,389	1,759,371	1,538,999	1,243,287	988,985	834,847	736,503	664,294	601,484
Stockholders' equity	1,455,135	1,277,753	1,102,154	949,991	822,782	709,614	621,792	542,978	493,214	451,030
Year-End Statistics:										
Average number of common shares outstanding (in thousands)	75,573	75,546	75,493	75,420	75,300	75,193	75,011	74,850	74,850	74,547
Number of stockholders	62,900	63,900	63,500	63,500	61,400	60,000	58,000	54,300	54,600	53,100
Number of employees	28,700	28,100	26,800	26,300	26,500	25,100	24,100	23,200	23,000	22,200

* The above data are as previously reported, restated for poolings-of-interests and stock splits.

** Net income for 1977 and related per-share amounts exclude gain on disposal of businesses of $13,225 and 18¢, respectively

THE BODY SHOP
INTERNATIONAL

case 22

Christopher A. Bartlett
Kenton Elderkin and
Krista McQuade

> Business people have got to be the instigators of change. They have the money and the power to make a difference. A company that makes a profit from society has a responsibility to return something to that society.
>
> Anita Roddick, founder and managing director of The Body Shop

"Let's face it, I can't take a moisture cream too seriously," Anita Roddick was fond of saying, "What really interests me is the revolutionary way in which trade can be used as an instrument for change for the better." This heretical statement by the head of the fastest-growing company in the cosmetics industry reflected her habit of going against the tide of the industry's established practices.

The Body Shop did not advertise, avoided traditional distribution channels, spent as little as possible on packaging, and used product labels to describe ingredients rather than to make miraculous claims. Its products were based on all-natural ingredients, and were sold in refillable, recyclable containers. But the most unconventional of all, was The Body Shop's strong social message. As Roddick explained: "There hasn't been an ethical or philosophical code of behavior for any business body ever, and I think it's going to have to change."

This case was prepared by Professor Christopher A. Bartlett and Research Associates Kenton Elderkin and Krista McQuade with an additional contribution by Myra Hart, as the basis for class discussion rather than to illustrate either effective or ineffective handling of an administrative situation. Reprinted by permission of Harvard Business School.

From a single storefront in 1976, The Body Shop had grown to 586 shops by 1991, trading in 38 countries and 18 languages. Worldwide retail sales from company stores and licensees were estimated at $391 million. Along the way, The Body Shop was voted U.K. Company of the Year in 1985, and U.K. Retailer of the Year in 1989. In addition, Roddick had been the Veuve Cliquot Businesswoman of the Year in 1985, and Communicator of the Year in 1987. In 1988, she was awarded the prestigious Order of the British Empire by Queen Elizabeth (who herself was rumored to use The Body Shop's Peppermint Foot Lotion).

ANITA RODDICK: THE ENTREPRENEUR

The world of business has taught me nothing. . . I honestly believe I would not have succeeded if I had been taught about business.

Anita Roddick

Born to Italian-immigrant parents, Roddick (née Perella) grew up working in the family-owned café in Littlehampton, West Sussex. Trained in education, she taught briefly in a local elementary school before accepting a position as a library researcher for the *International Herald Tribune* in Paris. Next, she moved to Geneva, where she joined the United Nations International Labor Organization to work with issues of Third World women's rights. With money saved, she traveled throughout the South Pacific and Africa, developing a fascination along the way for the simplicity and effectiveness of the beauty practices of the women she encountered.

Returning to England, she met Gordon Roddick, a Scots poet and adventurer who shared her love of travel. The birth of two daughters forced the Roddicks to settle down, and the couple decided to convert a Victorian house in Brighton into a hotel. In 1976, however, they sold their business so Gordon could fulfill a lifelong dream of riding on horseback from Buenos Aires to New York City—a journey that would take up to two years. Anita agreed to the plan ("Gordon never was a boring man") and, at 33, undertook to support the family. She had an idea for a shop.

With a £4,000 bank loan (approximately $6,000), Roddick developed a line of 25 skin and hair care products based on natural ingredients. Sourcing exotic ingredients like jojoba oil and rhassoul mud from a local herbalist, she prepared the first product batches on her kitchen stove and packaged them in the cheapest containers she could find—urine-sample bottles. Handwritten labels provided detailed information about the ingredients and their properties. A local art student designed her logo for £25. The Body Shop name—a tongue-in-cheek inspiration Anita took from auto repair shops she had seen in the United States—turned out to be a potential liability when she located her first shop in a small storefront near a funeral parlor. When her new neighbor's lawyer threatened to sue unless she changed her shop's name, Roddick took the story to the local newspaper. The curiosity inspired by the subsequent article assured that her first day of business, March 27, 1976, was an unqualified success.

Roddick gradually developed a loyal clientele. Some found the natural products less irritating to sensitive skin; others liked their novel aromas and textures; and many just enjoyed the relaxed, honest shop environment. As the sole employee, Anita formulated new products, ran the store, purchased supplies, kept the books, and constantly tried to draw attention to her business. (In one successful ruse, she sprinkled strawberry essence along the street leading to her door, in an attempt to lure customers by the pleasing aroma.)

After a successful summer, Roddick exchanged a half share in her fledgling business for a £4,000 investment by a local businessman, funding the opening of a second store. In April 1977, when Gordon returned (his horse had died in the Andes), he hit upon the idea of franchising as a way to continue expansion despite limited capital. When the first two franchises in nearby towns both succeeded, the Roddicks began receiving calls from other interested parties. The business began to take off.

Founding Concepts and Practices

From the beginning, the company was an extension of Anita Roddick's personal philosophy and convictions. Although these were not formalized early on, her intense involvement in the growing organization shaped its operations. Yet she freely acknowledged she "didn't have a clue about business matters," and from the early days, Gordon managed the financial and administrative aspects.

Roddick's first goal for the company was simple: survival. To make her original selection look larger, for example, she offered each product in five sizes—creating a choice much appreciated by her customers. Due to a cash flow that prevented her buying more bottles, she created a refill service at a 15% discount. This service subsequently appealed to a new generation of environmentally-conscious consumers. Detailed labeling information had originally been necessary because of the products' unfamiliar ingredients, but later seemed totally in tune with a consumer awareness movement. Even the trademark Body Shop green color—now so politically correct— was chosen originally because it was most effective in concealing the damp that showed through the walls of the first store. Roddick recalled:

> There was a grace we had when we started—the grace that you didn't have to bullshit and tell lies. We didn't know you could. We thought we had to be accountable. How do you establish accountability in a cosmetics business? We looked at the big companies. They put labels on the products. We thought what was printed on the label had to be truthful. I mean, we were really that naïve.

In addition to the products, Roddick also strove to create a unique environment in her stores— one of honesty, excitement, and fun. Rather than become overly sophisticated, she focused on the elements of what she called trading: "It's just buying and selling, with an added bit for me, which is the magical arena where people come together—that is, the shop," she said. "It's all just trading."

Building on the Foundation

The Body Shop experienced phenomenal growth through the 1980s, expanding sales at a rate of 50% yearly (see Exhibit 1). In April 1984, when the stock was floated on London's Unlisted Securities market, it opened at 95 pence and closed that afternoon at 165 pence. In January 1986, when it obtained a full listing on the London Stock Exchange, the stock was selling at 820 pence and had become known as "the shares that defy gravity."[1] By February 1991, the company's market value stood at £350 million ($591 million).

---

[1]The Roddicks retained 30% of the equity, Ian McGlinn, the source of the original £4,000 investment, held another 30%, and an additional 7% had been distributed to franchisees.

The products and the stores had also evolved, but had remained true to the original concepts. Entering a Body Shop anywhere in the world, the customer experienced brightly-lit, open spaces, trimmed in dark green, with a black-and-white tiled floor. Neat stacks of black capped, green labeled plastic bottles lined wall shelves, their monotony broken by pyramids of brightly colored soap bars or displays of natural loofah back scrubbers, potpourri, and T-Shirts. Cards in front of each display offered information about products with simple and descriptive names like Orchid Oil Cleansing Milk, Carrot Moisture Cream, and Seaweed and Birch Shampoo. A self-service perfume bar featured natural oils that could be used either as perfume, or added as scents to a selection of non-perfumed lotions. The whole experience, in Roddick's vision, was designed to be "theater, pure and simple."

Products were priced more expensively than mass merchandised cosmetics, but well under exclusive department store lines. Sales staff were trained to be friendly and knowledgeable, but never overbearing. Stacks of pamphlets provided information on a range of topics, from "Hair, Who Needs It?," to "The Body Shop Approach to Packaging," or "Against Animal Testing." In one corner, a giant Product Information Manual described each product in detail. Noticeably lacking, for a cosmetics retail company, were any photographs of models with beautiful hair and perfect skin. Roddick was fond of saying that her concept of beauty was Mother Theresa not some bimbo: "There are no magic potions, no miracle cures, no rejuvenating creams. Skin care products can do nothing more than cleanse, polish and protect. That's it. End of story."

THE BODY SHOP APPROACH

It turned out that my instinctive trading values were dramatically opposed to the standard practices in the cosmetics industry. I look at what they are doing and walk in the opposite direction.

Anita Roddick

As she built her business, Roddick developed most of the Body Shop's unique operating practices and management policies to respond to opportunities she perceived. From product development to human resource management, The Body Shop had been described as "innovative," "daring," and even "radical." But there was no question it was successful. (See Exhibit 2)

FRANCHISING

The company's explosive international growth was driven by its franchising program, and by early 1991 there were 586 shops worldwide (see Exhibit 3). Of these, only about 10% were company owned, but these served the important role of testing new products and marketing concepts, and sensing customer interests and trends. By appointing a head franchisee in each major national market, Roddick was able to concentrate on the development of new product lines and the company's global vision, rather than worry about the complexities of administration or personnel management. The franchise contract was for 5-10 years, and involved an investment of £150,000 to £250,000 ($270,000-$450,000). The start-up cost included shop fittings, opening day stock, a percentage of the location's rent (The Body Shop chose the sites and maintained the lease), and a licensing fee of between £5,000 and £25,000 ($9,000 to $45,000) for The Body Shop name. Typically, it took a franchise two to three years to become profitable (see Exhibit 4).

Roddick felt that one reason why the cosmetics industry had become exploitive was that it was dominated by men who traded on women's fears. She felt business practices could be improved substantially "if they were guided by 'feminine principles'—like love and care and intuition," and openly acknowledged a preference for women as franchisees:

> What is wonderful about the company is that 90% of the people running the shops are female, have no formal business training, and yet are brilliant retailers and brilliant business people. . . . This business is run by women. Policy decisions are made by women, all the words are written by women, product development is controlled by women. So our customer, our female customer, believes that we have a covert understanding of women. It gives us an extraordinary edge. It's The Body Shop's secret ingredient.

Anita Roddick kept strict control over the franchising process—no small task with over 5,000 applicants at any one time. The process, which involved a personality test, a home visit, and an assessment of the candidate's business acumen and attitude towards people and the environment, took as long as three years. Roddick liked to conduct the final interview, and was known for asking unexpected questions. ("How would you like to die?" "Who is your favorite heroine in literature?") Her objective was to ensure that The Body Shop image and the principles it was based on, were not diluted through franchising. "We choose as franchisees only people who are passionate about our product and our ideas," she explained. Once selected, the candidate was required to undergo extensive training on product knowledge, merchandising, and store operations.

Cathy Stephensen was, in many ways, a typical franchisee. Selected from over 2,000 unsolicited inquiries from would-be franchisees in her large urban center, she had given up a secure, twenty year career in financial and investment management in order to run a Body Shop. She reflected on her decision:

> I was interested in issues of motivation, social responsibility and particularly in the concept of a corporation that could do good as well as do it profitably. . . . I didn't have a list of franchise or business opportunities. It was The Body Shop or nothing. I think that was the case with a lot of franchisees.
>
> I sense that the store does make a difference in people's lives, and I feel really good about that. . . . I don't think you become a Body Shop franchisee for the money. You do it because you believe in the principles. Somehow you think it will all work out alright in the end. That's very much the common profile [of Body Shop franchisees.]

Product Development and Production

Believing that the cosmetics industry had a lot to learn from the skin and hair care practices of women all over the world, Roddick spent two to four months of every year travelling to remote corners of the world, with an anthropologist. In Sri Lanka, she saw women rubbing their faces with the skins of freshly-cut pineapple, producing a fresh, clean look. Later, she learned that pineapple had an enzyme which acted to remove dead cells from the surface of the skin. This was translated into The Body Shop's Pineapple Face Wash. In the Polynesian islands, she saw women rubbing an untreated extract from the seeds of the cocoa plant into their hair to make it shine. Cocoa butter was then incorporated into a number of products, making The Body Shop one of the world's largest importers of this raw material. In Ghana, she discovered Shea-butter oil, a product extracted from an African tree nut; in Hawaii, she learned of anfeltia conccina, a seaweed extract incorporated into her Seaweed and Birch Shampoo; in Japan, she picked up tsubaki oil, extracted from camellias.

Even back in England, Roddick would approach anyone, "from taxi drivers, to shop assistants, to your mother-in-law" to inquire about personal care habits. She wrote the chairman of Quaker Oats, in Chicago, to ask about the cosmetic properties of oatmeal. He sent her a formula for a protein extract which she discovered could be used in a range of products such as eye shadow and soap. After reading about huge stockpiles of powdered milk in U.K. warehouses, she telephoned the Milk Marketing Board for information, a conversation which resulted in The Body Shop's Milk Bath. Instead of market research, The Body Shop relied on direct customer ideas and feedback obtained through the widely used suggestion boxes located in each outlet, and six staff members cataloged and replied to ideas submitted.

Initially, product development had been driven by samples brought back in Anita's back pack, and the creativity of the herbalist she had worked with since the startup. Testing had been done on staff volunteers, and because ingredients had been used for centuries, risks were minimal. Eventually, the company employed an outside academic to test for toxicity and effectiveness, and finally, by 1990 established a formal research department. There was some debate about the extent to which The Body Shop's products were "natural," and the company acknowledged using some synthetic preservatives, ingredients derived from petrochemicals, and artificial colors.

Although over 70% of Body Shop products were supplied by outside contractors, the company hoped to increase its in-house manufacturing from 30% to 50% by the early 1990s. Most of its production occurred in Wick, West Sussex, where the company had 320,000 square feet of production and warehouse space.

Marketing

As a cosmetic retailer, The Body Shop defied most accepted marketing practices. In an industry where 30 cents on every dollar of sales was typically devoted to advertising, the company had no marketing or advertising department. It made no elaborate claims or promotions. And the products still packaged in plain plastic bottles were never "sale" priced. Said Roddick:

> (The cosmetics industry) makes its money through packaging and advertising, which together are eighty-five percent of its costs. Charles Revlon, the founder of Revlon said, 'In the factory we make cosmetics, in the store we sell hope." And he's right. The cosmetics industry is a dream machine.

Roddick recognized the value of publicity, however, and by 1980 had hired a PR consultant. She openly courted the press, and by her own estimate, generated £2 million worth of free publicity in a year. She was a natural for the role: "The press like us. I'm always available. I'm loud-mouthed and quotable."

Because the stores represented the company's primary marketing tool, Roddick used regular visits by regional managers to keep tight control over layout, literature, window displays, and operating style. The company's Write Stuff Department—five writers and six graphic designers—created The Body Shop's constantly changing brochures and displays. In 1990 when The Body Shop was nominated to the U.K. Marketing Hall of Fame, Roddick insisted her approach was only common sense:

"The trouble with marketing is that consumers are hyped out. The din of advertising and promotion has become so loud, they are becoming cynical about the whole process. What we have tried to do is establish credibility by educating our customers. . . . It humanizes the company, and makes customers feel they are buying from people they know and trust."

Organization and Human Resources

As The Body Shop grew, so too did Roddick's recognition of the need to maintain the enthusiasm and commitment of her employees, 75% of whom were women under thirty:

> Most businesses focus all the time on profits, profits, profits . . . I have to say I think that is deeply boring. I want to create an electricity and passion that bonds people to the company. You can educate people by their passions, especially young people. You have to find ways to grab their imagination. You want them to feel that they are doing something important. . . I'd never get that kind of motivation if we were just selling shampoo and body lotion.

Roddick constantly worked at communications within the company. Every shop had a bulletin board, a fax machine and a video player through which she bombarded staff with information on topics ranging from new products, or causes she supported, to reports on her latest trip or discussions of "dirty tricks in the cosmetics industry." The in-house video production company, produced a monthly multi-lingual video magazine, *Talking Shop*, as well as training tapes and documentaries on social campaigns.

Roddick also encouraged upward communication through a suggestion scheme to DODGI (the Department of Damned Good Ideas), through regular meetings of a cross section of staff, often at her home, and through a "Red Letter" system which allowed any employee to bypass management and communicate directly with a director. But she was equally aware of the power of informal communication, and unabashedly tapped into the grapevine by planting rumors with the office gossips. She explained the motivation behind her intensive communications:

> What's imperative is the creation of a style that becomes a culture. It may be forced, it may be designed. But that real sense of change, that anarchy—I tell Gordon we need a Department of Surprises—we do whatever we must to preserve that sense of being different. Otherwise, the time will come when everyone who works for us will say The Body Shop is just like every other company.

Roddick took advantage of her travel to visit stores regularly. Appearing in jeans and carrying a knapsack, she typically told stories, joked about embarrassing moments in her travels, described new products or projects she was working on, and listened to employees' concerns. She encouraged employees to "think frivolously" and "break the rules," and tied bonuses to innovative suggestions. She also introduced a system of two-way assessment, asking staff to evaluate their managers' effectiveness. She detested bureaucracy and kept meetings short by requiring participants to stand through them. Roddick explained:

> I tend to encourage separateness and eccentricity. . . . For me, the bottom line is keeping my company alive in the most imaginative, breathless, honest way I can. I don't think in all the years I've been running this business there has been one meeting, except for the end-of-year results, where profit has been mentioned.

Extending the family feeling, the company built a £1 million day care facility at its Littlehampton headquarters. The charge for this service was staggered by salary level and free day care slots were offered to social service organizations. In 1986, a training center in London and began offering courses on the company's products and philosophy, problem hair and skin care, and customer service. Soon, however, there were sessions on topics as diverse as sociology, urban survival, aging and AIDS. Any employee of the company or its franchisees could sign up, and all courses were free. "You can train dogs," explained Roddick. "We wanted to *educate* and help people realize their own potential."

THE BODY SHOP PHILOSOPHY

All the Body Shops around the world form part of a whole that is held together by a common bond. It is underwritten by a common philosophy. This is the strong foundation on which a thriving and successful international company has been built.

Anita Roddick

As The Body Shop became increasingly successful in a period often characterized as "The Decade of Greed," Roddick kept pushing herself and others to define the appropriate role for their growing corporation. Going public did not seem to reduce the company's quirkiness as some had predicted. Indeed Roddick seemed little concerned about the investment community's view of The Body Shop, and routinely referred to investors in the stock as "speculators:"

Most are only interested in the short-term and quick profit; they don't come to our annual meetings and they don't respond to our communications. As far as I am concerned, I have no responsibility to these people at all.

Indeed, in her view, The Body Shop's stock flotation marked a very different historic watershed:

Since 1984, the year The Body Shop went public, as far as I am concerned, the business has existed for one reason only—to allow us to use our success to act as a force of social change, to continue the education of our staff, to assist development in the Third World, and above all, to help protect the environment.

Environmental Consciousness

Long a critic of the environmental insensitivity of the cosmetics industry ("Its main products are packaging, garbage and waste" she claimed), Roddick found in this area a natural focus for her redoubled commitment to a social agenda. Within months of the public stock issue, she entered into an alliance with Greenpeace, and began campaigning through the shops to "save the whales." The link was natural since several Body Shop products were based on jojoba oil, a plant-based product that she argued could be substituted for the oil from sperm whales widely used in the cosmetics industry. When several franchisees expressed concern that the campaign was becoming "too political," she dismissed their protests.

Within a couple of years, disagreements with Greenpeace led Roddick to switch her primary allegiance to Friends of the Earth, jointly promoting awareness campaigns on acid rain, recycling, and ozone layer depletion. Again, she turned over display windows to posters, and distributed literature through the shops. Simultaneously, she set up a four person Environmental Projects Department not only to coordinate the campaigning, but also to ensure that the company's own products and practices were environmentally sound. In addition to using biodegradable packaging and refilling 2 million containers annually, the company expanded its use of recycled paper, substituted reusable cases for cardboard shipping boxes, and offered refunds on returned packaging. It also banned smoking in all its offices and shops, and provided bicycles at low prices to over 350 headquarters employees.

Feeling frustrated with the bureaucracy of Friends of the Earth, in 1987 Roddick decided that The Body Shop should define and implement its own environmental and social campaigns. She enjoyed the freedom of being able to pick her own issues, and respond rapidly to crises.

Community Activity

About the same time, Roddick was looking for ways to become more active at the local level. As she put it, "We had to neutralize the corrupting effect of our wealth by taking positive steps to ensure we remained a humane and caring company." She set up a Community Care Department and began talking to franchisees about having every shop commit to a local need, and supporting it by allowing staff time off to work on the project. Most responded positively, and soon shops worldwide were working with disabled centers, AIDS support groups, and homeless programs. But Roddick still fretted that some were not imaginative enough, and some "malingerers" remained uninvolved:

> If a shop didn't have a project and said, in effect, it didn't give a damn about the community, it was usually the franchisee speaking, not the staff. . . . If they absolutely refused to become involved, there was not much I could do—other than to make quite sure they did not get another shop.

As she launched into the social and environmental projects, Roddick became sensitive to some associated risks. First, she didn't want to make potential customers feel guilty or overwhelmed by the campaigning. Second, she saw a risk that staff could become so enamored with the causes that they neglected their "trading" role. But the biggest risk was that the company's motivations would be questioned. An article in *Marketing* noted: "There are times when Roddick's thirst for publicity seems almost insatiable. She has associated herself with every conscience-raising exercise from Third World development to a cheap condom campaign to curb the spread of AIDS." Her response to such criticism varied from defensive to dismissive:

> A poster to stop the burning of the rain forest creates a banner of values, it links us to the community, but it will not increase sales.
>
> To cynics, altruism in business is disarming. But the bottom line is, you keep your staff—and good staff are hard to keep, especially in retail.
>
> The absolute truth is that nothing of what we do is undertaken with an eye to our "image" . . . If there is a single motivation for what we do, it is, in the words of Ralph Waldo Emerson, "to put love where our labor is."

Trade Not Aid

Her regular travels made Roddick acutely aware of the huge development needs that existed in the

Third World; but her experience with the ILO in Geneva convinced her that aid programs were not the answer. In 1987, she launched a "Trade Not Aid" policy with the objective of "creating trade to help people in the Third World utilize their resources to meet their own needs". Eventually, she hoped to trade directly with those who grew or harvested all the raw ingredients The Body Shop used. By 1991 two major projects had been initiated.

During a visit to southern India in 1987, Roddick visited a group of farm communities set up by a British expatriate to train poor and homeless boys. Impressed, Roddick agreed to make Boys Town the primary supplier of Footsie Rollers—serrated pieces of acacia wood sold by The Body Shop as foot massagers. A price was calculated using first world wage rates—four times the local norm. The boys were paid local wages, with the balance being deposited in a trust account for each worker to receive as he left to start an independent life at the age of 16. Retail profits from the Footsie Rollers funded the boys' healthcare and education.

Returning home, she raised the money required to open a new village, and in 1989 returned to India to set up The Body Shop Boys' Town, with facilities to house and employ 85 boys. This led to other contracts to produce soap bags, woven baskets, Christmas cards, and silk-screened T-shirts. Over the next three years, The Body Shop proudly reported that 3,000 jobs were created as the impact of the programs' spread into surrounding communities. By 1990, Roddick had plans to establish Boys Town Trusts in Mexico, Africa, and Thailand.

On a trip to Nepal, Roddick found entire villages unemployed as a result of a government limit on the harvest of the lokta shrub—the traditional source of material for their handmade paper. Seeing the possibility of setting up another Trade Not Aid project, she brought in an expert who found alternative sources of paper fiber—water hyacinth, banana tree fiber, and sugar cane. Roddick then committed The Body Shop to an order for bags, notebooks, and scented drawer liners that allowed a large family paper factory to convert to the new production. In June 1989, this company bought the land needed for another papermaking factory that employed 37 people. A portion of The Body Shop's profits were used to replant the area and another ten percent went to the Nepal Women's Association.

Some ventures, however, resulted in frustration, failure, and even occasional disillusionment. The Boys Town project, for example, ended in what Roddick described as "a cruel deception," with work being sub-contracted to local sweatshops at a fraction of the price The Body Shop was paying. The contract was canceled and relationships severed. A textile project in Bangladesh and a sponge sourcing venture in Turkey were also aborted due to various supply problems. Yet Roddick remained committed to Trade Not Aid, and was pursuing projects in Somalia, Malaysia, Philippines, and Kenya.

The Soapworks Project

In 1989, Roddick turned the principles of her Trade Not Aid campaign to what she termed "Britain's own third world." A visit to the depressed Glasgow suburb of Easterhouse, a 55,000-person slum with 37% unemployment, resulted in the decision to locate a new 33,000 square foot soap factory in the town, almost 400 miles from the company's other facilities. She explained:

> It certainly would have been more conventional to set up the Soapworks factory near Littlehampton. But it's more fun, more motivating, and better for morale to do it here. It's not economic in terms of transport, but it's easier to inculcate our ideas here.

Eight months and £1 million later, Soapworks opened, staffed by 16 of the community's chronically unemployed. After two weeks training, they returned to Easterhouse on Littlehampton wages—a third higher than local rates. By 1991, the payroll had reached 100, and eventually Soapworks was expected to provide a third of The Body Shop's worldwide soap needs. Once the factory became profitable (expected in 1991), 25% of after-tax profits were to be placed in a charitable trust for the purpose of benefitting the community.

Although the project was highly praised by public officials and was widely reported by the press, a few Easterhouse residents felt that The Body Shop had a patronizing and even exploitative attitude about Soapworks. When Roddick referred to the community as a location "where angels fear to tread," for example, one observer remarked, "To hear her speak . . . you might think The Body Shop was the only industrial employer in Easterhouse. But as you can see, her plant is on a small industrial estate surrounded by several busy factories." In typical fashion, Roddick's response was, "Cynics—up yours!" She hoped that she would inspire other firms worldwide to establish similar projects. In her view, "The Body Shop will have failed by 50% if we don't provide a role model for other companies."

Political Involvement

In the late 1980s, The Body Shop's social and environmental activities became increasingly political. Although the company had long required suppliers to vouch that their ingredients had not been tested on animals in the past five years, in 1989 it escalated its activities in this area. In response to a 1989 EC draft directive proposing that all cosmetics be tested on animals, Roddick mounted a massive media blitz and began a petition in her shops. With five million supporting signatures, the petition was influential in the bill's eventual withdrawal.

Critics within the industry claimed that her cruelty-free platform was a marketing ploy. Indeed, they claimed that most base cosmetics ingredients—including many used by The Body Shop—had originally been tested on animals. Roddick responded:

> Although we recognize that, realistically, most existing ingredients used in the cosmetics industry have been tested on animals by someone, somewhere, at sometime, we make sure that no animal testing is carried out by us or in our name.

Roddick's environmental concerns also became more political in nature as she became committed to the protection of the rain forests. After a visit to Brazil to attend a rally protesting the construction of a dam which would flood 15 million acres of rain forest, Roddick returned to England to take action. She held a franchisee meeting where she raised £200,000, initiated a "Stop the Burning" poster campaign, and organized a petition which collected 1 million signatures in four weeks. Followed by a small media army, Roddick and 250 of her staff marched on the Brazilian Embassy in London and tried to deliver the sacks of protest letters to the Ambassador. Several franchisees expressed concern about such high profile political activity, and one wondered if The Body Shop was going into the "rent-a-mob" business.

The Body Shop also began associating itself with several other organizations such as Amnesty International and FREEZE, the anti-nuclear weapons group. It was this latter campaign that finally brought a strong reaction from several franchisees who felt that Roddick should not be speaking for them on such issues.

> My first reaction was "if you support nuclear weapons, what the hell are you doing in one of

my shops?". . . . But then I realized I did not necessarily have the right to speak for The Body Shop on every issue. . . . I accepted that principle— and completely ignored it. I have never been able to separate Body Shop values from my own personal values.

Profit with Principle

Roddick acknowledged that she was on a mission to create "a new business paradigm"—one in which companies accepted the responsibility that came with their economic power and became engines of social change. To implement her vision, however, she recognized she had to overcome two major impediments. Externally, she rejected the pressures of shareholders and the financial community to focus companies on profits to the exclusion of other objectives:

> The responsibility of business is not to create profits but to create live, vibrant, honorable organizations with real commitment to the community. . . . I certainly believe that companies should not be evaluated solely on their annual report and accounts.

Equally threatening to Roddick was the growing complacency among employees as The Body Shop became larger, more widespread and more successful:

> What worries me now is that within the company there is an umbrella of corporate goodness which some people are hiding under, saying "I work for The Body Shop, therefore I am sincere, good, caring, humane, and so on." It really depresses me. . . . We talk about being lean and green, but I can see a fat cat mentality creeping in: paper being wasted, lights left on after meetings. What it comes down to is arrogance.

THE U.S. MARKET CHALLENGE

> It was Gordon's view that while the United States offered The Body Shop the greatest potential for growth, it also represented the greatest potential for disaster."
>
> Anita Roddick

In 1988, with over 200 stores in 33 countries, The Body Shop finally entered the $12 billion U.S. cosmetics market by committing to a 50,000 square foot production and warehouse facility in Morristown, New Jersey. Under the direction of a British expatriate, who was previously the president of Unilever's fragrance subsidiary, twelve company-owned shops were opened on the East Coast. Total investment exceeded £10 million. In mid-1990, the company began franchising, and by year's end, 37 shops had been opened. Anita Roddick explained the delay: ". . . We wanted to wait for two years to see how we would do. . . . We don't advertise. We've never never gone into shopping malls, and we were terrified of those. The question was, "Were we good enough?" By 1990, U.S. sales were £5.8 million, or 7% of total revenues. Due to the high cost of the initial infrastructure, however, the U.S. operations were still running at a loss.

Challenges of the U.S. Market

Whether these initial losses would continue or indeed, whether stores remained open, depended on how the company dealt with a different set of challenges. First, environmental concern had been less of a public issue in the United States during the 1980s, and it was not certain that The Body

Shop's strong image and unfamiliar practices would appeal to them. A 1990 Price Waterhouse report commented:

> The link between common ideals and store loyalty is not yet proven . . . Some customers may be willing to pay $3.00 for a bar of soap, knowing that some of the money is going to a worthy cause. Others will be turned off to a company that uses its profits to support such a bold political agenda. The diversity of the U.S. market, in terms of consumer values and demand, and the vocal nature of dissident groups may make it difficult for The Body Shop to find a solid platform on which to build a business.

Roddick learned how difficult it was to transfer her values even within her organization. It was hard to recruit staff who embraced Body Shop values and could fit into what she called "our quirky, zany, organization." "I thought our values were global," she said, "and that our image and style were so strong that they would be easily transferrable across the Atlantic. I was wrong."

She was also amazed by how constrained business was in a country that epitomized the free enterprise system. The Food and Drug registrations, the various state and city regulations, and the lawyers horror stories all made Roddick nervous about her decision. Under warnings about product liability and the likelihood of litigation, for example, she was advised not to offer a refill service in the United States. Lawyers also convinced her to drop her "Against Animal Testing' logo on products for fear of retribution by the cosmetics industry. "They really put the frighters on us," she said, "We felt we had to modify our trading practices drastically."

Furthermore, some experts questioned whether The Body Shop's resistance to advertising would limit growth in the communications-intensive U.S. market. Price Waterhouse calculated that The Body Shop's target of 1,500 shop openings by 1995 implied sales of $685 million, equivalent a 17% share of the top third of the cosmetics industry where it competed. Analysts predicted that this would be a difficult challenge without advertising. David Altschiller, chief executive of the New York advertising agency handling the $10 million Liz Claiborne fragrance account, commented: "It's very hard to cultivate awareness and familiarity among consumers here without media advertising. Many highly successful European concepts have fizzled . . . when they're plunked down unadulterated in the American market." Roddick acknowledged, "There's no example of anyone doing what we're doing in America and making it work. . . . I think I have to become slightly more eccentric and slightly more theatrical to get my point across."

Finally, The Body Shop's global success had not gone unnoticed in the cosmetics industry. Betting that the "green consumer" population would continue to grow, many leading firms were introducing "natural" lines, and revamping the look and the marketing pitch of their products. Revlon was marketing "New Age Naturals"—a line of cosmetic products with names like Peppermint Skin Toner and Almond and Walnut Scrub. In 1990, Estée Lauder created Origins, a product line based on plant oils and extracts. It sold them in recycled (and recyclable) containers, and emphasized that no animal testing had been carried out on its ingredients within six years. Lauder planned to market this line in stand-alone stores, the first of which was scheduled to open in Cambridge, Massachusetts in mid-1991. And Leslie Wexner, founder of the hugely successful retailer, The Limited, had opened 42 Bath and Body Works shops. *Business Week* reported that Roddick was so concerned about the shops which looked "astonishingly like Body Shops" that her lawyers were discussing the concern with The Limited. "People think we're a flaky New Age company," Roddick declared. "But my God, we defend ourselves like lions."

* * * * *

In early 1991, observers wondered whether The Body Shop could maintain its phenomenal growth. They pointed to the fact that sales in the United Kingdom, which represented 67% of the company's total, had grown by only 1%, after inflation and new store openings had been removed from the 1990 figures. The price of "the shares that defy gravity" seemed to reflect some of the uncertainty the company faced in its markets (see Exhibit 5). Some analysts felt that the company had outgrown its historical strategy, organization, and even its leadership. Could the company adequately defend itself against the wave of new competition without resorting to advertising, they wondered? Should it—indeed, could it—adjust its organizational and cultural values? And how would it survive the eventual change of leadership?

At least the last question seemed to be one that concerned the Roddicks. Commented Anita:

> Leadership of a company should encourage next generation not just to follow, but to overtake. . . . The complaint Gordon and I have is that we are not being overtaken by our staff.

Announcing the 1990 results, Gordon added:

> The thing we now have to do is reduce the dependence of the business on Anita and Gordon. You can either create a structure where the business is unable to do without you because you hang on to all the bits, or you can create a structure where they are pleased to see you, but they can do without you. That is our aim.

Exhibit 1: **Key Financial Data for The Body Shop, 1984-1991 (in £'000)**

Fiscal Year[a]	1984	1985	1986	1987	1989	1990	1991
Turnover	4,910	9,362	17,394	28,476	55,409	84,480	115,599
of which:							
Overseas	20%	21%	22%	25%	25%	33%	37%
Profit before taxes	1,044	1,929	3,451	5,998	11,232	14,508	20,037
Dividends	75	150	300	605	1,439	1,558	2,261
Shareholders' funds	812	1,683	3,445	6,587	23,477	25,992	65,149
Outstanding shares ('000)	na	80,000	80,000	80,397	84,908	85,306	90,133
Number of outlets							
United Kingdom	45	66	77	89	112	139	173
Overseas	83	102	155	186	255	318	406
Total	128	168	232	275	367	457	579

[a]In 1988, The Body Shop changed its fiscal year. Fiscal years 1984-1987 are based on a reporting period from October 1 to September 30. Fiscal years 1989-1991 are based on a reporting period from March 1 to the last day of February. Thus, the last three fiscal years report activity from 10 months of the prior calendar year.

Financial data for the period 10/1/87 to 2/28/88 are not included in this exhibit.

Source: Body Shop Annual Reports

Exhibit 2: **The Body Shop Performance versus U.K. Industry Segment Standards (December 31, 1990)**

	The Body Shop	Industry[a] Lower Quartile	Industry Median	Industry Upper Quartile
Return on Capital	43.6%	3.1%	16.5%	41.2%
Return on Total Assets	20.2%	-.9%	6.8%	14.2%
Pretax Profit Margin	17.2%	0.0%	4.8%	10.5%
Sales/Total Assets	117.9%	111.8%	159.7%	192.9%
Average Remuneration	£10,424.5	£6,740.7	£9,000.0	£12,269.2
Sales/Employee	£66,782.6	£32,927.6	£50,483.9	£99,252.1

[a]Industry comparison against U.K. Chemical Industries Manufacturing: Perfumes, Cosmetics and Toilet Preparations. Category includes perfumes, hair preparations, bath salts, shampoos, toothpastes, and other toilet preparations.

Source: ICC Online, Ltd., *Financial Datasheets*, November 5, 1990

Exhibit 3: **Worldwide Shop List (March 1991)**

	No. of Shops	Overseas History First Shops Opening In:	
Antigua	1	1978	Belgium (Brussels)
Australia	31		
Austria	5	1979	Sweden (Stockholm)
Bahamas	4		Greece (Athens)
Bahrain	1		
Belgium	4	1980	Canada (Toronto)
Bermuda	1		Iceland (Reykjavik)
Canada	87		
Cyprus	1	1981	Denmark (Copenhagen)
Denmark	5		Finland (Tampere)
Eire	5		Eire (Dublin)
Finland	11		
France	3	1982	The Netherlands (Leiden)
Germany	28		France (Paris)
Gibraltar	1		
Grand Cayman	1	1983	Australia (Melbourne)
Greece	14		Cyprus (Limassol)
Holland	23		Germany (Cologne)
Hong Kong	7		Singapore
Indonesia	1		Switzerland (Zurich)
Italy	22		UAE (Dubai)
Japan	1		
Malta	1	1984	Hong Kong (Tsjmshatsui/Kc)
Malaysia (E)	3		Italy (Catania/Sicily)

Continued ...

	No. of Shops	Overseas History First Shops Opening In:	
Malaysia (W)	7		Malaysia (Kuala Lumpur)
New Zealand	3		
Norway	13	1985	Bahamas (Nassau)
Oman	2		Bahrain (Manama)
Portugal	5		Norway (Oslo)
Qatar	1		
Saudi Arabia	6	1986	Austria (Vienna)
Singapore	6		Kuwait (Safat)
Spain	17		Oman (Muscat)
Sweden	30		Portugal (Lisbon)
Switzerland	18		Spain (Madrid)
Taiwan	3		
UAE	1	1987	Antigua (St. John's)
USA	39[a]		Saudi Arabia
			Malta (Sliema)
			Bermuda (Hamilton)
OVERSEAS	412		
UK & Channel Isles	174[b]	1988	USA (New York)
GRAND TOTAL	586		Gibraltar
			Taiwan (Taipei)
[a]Franchise 23, Company 14			
[b]Franchise 133, Company 41		1989	New Zealand (Wellington)
		1990	Indonesia
			Japan (Tokyo)
		Number of Countries we trade in: 38	
		Number of Languages we trade in: 18	

Source: The Body Shop Press Office

Exhibit 4: Franchise Financial Projections, Year 1

Store Sales	100.0%
Total Cost of Goods Sold	55.8
Gross Profit	44.2
Employee Costs	23.6
General Administration, Marketing	16.4
Interest Expense	2.7
Total Expenses	42.7
Net Income	1.5%

Exhibit 5: **The Body Shop's Stock Price Movement, 1984-1990**

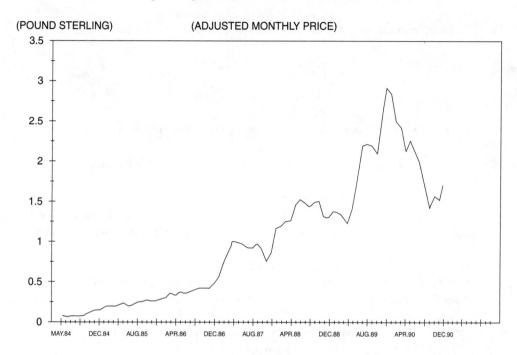

Source: Interactive Data Corp.

Adjusted Six-Monthly Closing Price[a]		
June 84 £0.058	June 87 £0.971	June 90 £2.11
Dec. 84 £0.143	Dec. 87 £0.865	Dec. 90 £1.80
June 85 £0.189	June 88 £1.526	
Dec. 85 £0.258	Dec. 88 £1.297	
June 86 £0.349	June 89 £1.780	
Dec. 86 £0.476	Dec. 89 £2.923	

[a]Adjusted for five 2 for 1 splits

APPENDIX: The Body Shop: A Timeline of Key Events and Milestones

1976   First shop opens in Brighton (March). Second shop opens in Chichester (November).

1977   First franchises granted

1978   First franchisee outside the United Kingdom—in Belgium

1984   The Body Shop goes public on the U.K. unlisted securities market in April

1985   Anita Roddick selected as the Veuve Cliquot Business Woman of the Year

1986   SAVE THE WHALE campaign launched with Greenpeace
        New £4 million headquarters and 320,000 square foot warehouse and production facility
        opened Environmental Projects department and Body Shop training school established

1987   FRIENDS OF THE EARTH campaign launched
        Jacaranda, the company's own independent video company, is established
        Named Company of the Year by the Confederation of British Industry (CBI)

1988   Queen awards Anita Roddick the Order of the British Empire (OBE)
        The first U.S. branch of The Body Shop opens in New York
        Soapworks, a 33,000 square foot soap factory, opens in Easterhouse, Scotland

1989   The Body Shop is voted Retailer of the Year
        "STOP THE BURNING" rainforest campaign launched

1990   AGAINST ANIMAL TESTING campaign is launched.
        The first Body Shop opens in Tokyo
        Among many 1990 awards are the Queen's Award for Export, U.K. Hall of Fame
        Marketing Award, the Animalia Award for animal protection, the U.K. Environmental
        Management Award, the International Women's Forum Award, and the U.S. Environmental
        Protection Agency's Environmental Achievement Award

LAIDLAW: THE RESIGNATION OF JAMES R. BULLOCK[1]

case 23

Joseph N. Fry

On December 23, 1999, the board of directors of Laidlaw Inc. announced that the company's chief executive officer (CEO) James R. Bullock, had been asked to resign and that John R. Grainger, the company's chief operating officer, would be taking his place. Peter Widdrington, Laidlaw's chairman, explained that the leadership change was the result of the board's frustration with the company's performance for several months: "We just felt the performance of the company was not what it should have been. We just didn't seem to be clicking."[2] Further, he noted that the leadership change was "consistent with the company's new direction of divesting . . . (certain operations) . . . to strengthen its balance sheet and to take full advantage of further growth opportunities in the North American bus transportation sector."[3]

---

[1] This case has been written on the basis of published sources only. Consequently, the interpretation and perspectives presented in this case are not necessarily those of Laidlaw or any of its employees.
[2] Paul Waldie, "New CEO tries to reassure Laidlaw Shareholders," National Post Online, December 22, 1999.
[3] Laidlaw press release, December 20, 1999.

IVEY

Bullock, 55, was frustrated too.

The fact of the matter is that the company has had a tough year. I acknowledge that and the board feels, I guess, that they need to do something and they've done it . . . (but) . . . I don't agree with the decision and they are going to have to explain to the shareholders and others why this change will make a difference. I don't think the strategy, as annunciated by the board (Monday) evening . . . is any different than what the company has been pursuing.[4]

The market seemingly reserved judgement: Laidlaw's stock hovered slightly above $5.00[5] down from a 52 week high of $10.50 and a peak of $16.60 in early 1998.

(handwritten margin note: Problem)

BACKGROUND

Michael De Groote of Burlington, Ontario entered the solid waste (garbage) services business in 1969 under the Laidlaw name. At that time the solid waste industry was very fragmented, with many small local operators servicing limited geographic areas. The entrepreneurial De Groote saw the opportunity for consolidation and set out to acquire and integrate local solid waste businesses, first in Canada and then in the United States. Later, in the 1970s, he began to apply the same approach to the fragmented school bus business. Further acquisitions took him into the hazardous waste business. In the 1980s, he moved further afield, acquiring a 29 per cent interest in ADT Limited, a company providing electronic surveillance systems for industries and households, and a 29.5 per cent interest in Attwoods PLC, a company involved in the waste management business in the United States and Europe. The ADT and Attwoods investments were carried on Laidlaw's books at values, respectively, of $892 million and $287 million.

At the time of De Groote's retirement in 1990, Laidlaw's revenues and operating profits had grown, respectively to $1.74 billion and $478 million. The company's average return on equity (ROE) over the prior five years had been 20.4 per cent, and its five-year growth in earnings per share had been 26.7 per cent. De Groote had assembled what appeared to be a well positioned, diversified business, which was regarded by analysts as having "excellent growth prospects, particularly in waste management."[6]

A Questionable Heritage

Appearances were deceiving, however, as Donald K. Jackson, Laidlaw's incoming CEO, would soon find out. The recession of the early 1990s stalled growth in the operating businesses; in the next three years, revenues plateaued and operating profits slipped. But the real hit came from extraordinary charges required to write down the ADT and Attwoods investment by some $736 million pre-tax, plus an additional $225 million to restructure the waste management business. Furthermore, the company was engaged in a tax dispute with the U.S. Internal Revenue Service for claims going back to 1986. (These claims were ultimately settled by Laidlaw in 1998 by a payment of about $160 million.) By 1993, Laidlaw's shares were trading at half of their 1990 level and in October 1993, Jackson resigned. He was replaced by Bullock.

(handwritten margin notes: PMF 1, PMF, PMF, Goals?, Write off of assets)

---

[4] Op.cit., National Post Online, December 22, 1999.
[5] All dollar figures are in US$.
[6] Wood Gundy Research Report, December 20, 1990.

A Fresh Start

Bullock came to Laidlaw after a twelve-year tenure as president and CEO of the real estate development and investment business, Cadillac Fairview Corporation. He was not a stranger to Laidlaw, having served on the company's board since 1991. On taking over, he announced that he intended to focus on the growth of Laidlaw's three businesses — solid waste management, hazardous waste management, and transportation services — and on the North American market, where each business had a relatively small market share. As time passed and circumstances changed, he moved to divest the waste management businesses and to increase Laidlaw's concentration on existing and new transportation businesses. Throughout this transition, Bullock built on Laidlaw's experience as an industry consolidator. He saw consolidation in this way:

> Sound strategy for growth, provided you are able to meld the acquired parts into an organization more effective at service delivery than the sum of its parts . . . (you should think) . . . of the consolidation of service businesses as an investment in infrastructure, because that's what you are buying. You're buying market positions, bus companies that have been there for 30 years, ambulance companies that have been there for 30 years and that is the quickest and most effective way for us to grow.[7]

Corporate Management

The corporate structure through which Bullock chose to work was one that was common among highly diversified companies. There was a clear distinction between the roles of the corporate office and the various business units. The corporate office focused on entry into new businesses, major acquisitions and the approval and monitoring of business unit initiatives and plans. The business unit heads were responsible for developing business level strategies, plans and budgets and for achieving their approved performance targets. The businesses also took the lead in proposing "tuck under" acquisitions which would help to build their business base. Business unit management was rewarded on the basis of business unit results. Once a year, at the time of the Laidlaw annual meeting, the business heads met to exchange experience and progress. Otherwise, they operated quite independently from one another.

The following pages review Laidlaw's operations and performance by business for the period of Bullock's tenure.

SOLID WASTE MANAGEMENT

The solid waste management business encompassed the collection, transport, disposal via recycling and incineration or landfill of residential and commercial solid waste. In 1996, the company served about 400 municipalities in North America, representing about 4.1 million households and approximately 260,000 industrial and commercial customers. To fulfil these contracts, Laidlaw operated about 2,900 collection vehicles and 31 landfill sites.

Laidlaw's revenues of $763 million ranked it as the third largest competitor in the solid waste industry, behind WMX Technologies ($4.7 billion) and Browning Ferris ($4.3 billion). But revenue

---

[7]J.R. Bullock, Address to Raymond James and Associates conference, March 16, 1998.

growth in recent years had been minimal, reflecting the difficulty of finding economic acquisitions in an industry that had been going through consolidation for over 20 years. This slow growth also indicated the natural limits of internal programs to streamline the business and to focus it on its strongest markets. The performance of the business through 1996 is given in Table 1.

In late 1996, Laidlaw sold the solid waste business to Allied Waste Industries for $1.6 billion. Bullock explained the decision to sell,

> In the (solid waste) industry, there are many companies, large and small, all competing for growth by acquisition. Our growth would therefore be very expensive. The barriers for new entrants into this low-tech business were, and remain, very few. We believed there were better opportunities for Laidlaw in its other far-better-positioned businesses. [8]

Table 1:   Waste Management Business Results 1993-96 ($Millions)

	1996*	1995	1994	1993**
Revenues	763	795	750	756
Operating Income	91	106	84	61
Operating Margins (%)	11.9	13.3	11.2	8.0
Identifiable Assets	828	745	NA	NA
Op.Inc./Id.Assets (%)	11.0	14.2		

*   Laidlaw's fiscal year ends August 31.
** Excluding a $225 million pretax restructuring charge taken in 1993.

Source: Laidlaw Annual Reports.

HAZARDOUS WASTE MANAGEMENT

The hazardous waste industry encompassed the transportation, disposal, recycling and destruction of industrial waste, waste water treatment, and disposal site remediation. When Laidlaw entered this business in the 1980s, it was with high hopes, founded on growing social concerns about industrial pollution and expectations of a parallel development of the political will necessary to do something about it. In fact, the hazardous waste industry turned out to be a very difficult place to operate. The same early optimism about the industry prompted competitors to increase capacity as well. Then, as the early 1990s recession hit, the industry found itself caught in a price and cost squeeze with surplus capacity on the one hand, and regulatory red tape that was pushing up treatment and disposal costs on the other.

After some early rapid growth in the 1980s based on acquisitions and internal development, Laidlaw's revenue growth tapered off in the 1990s. The only increases in the 1990s were due to acquisitions, most notably a $263 million acquisition in December 1994 which was expected to add about $300 million in annualized revenues. The results for the hazardous waste business through fiscal 1997 are given in Table 2.

---

[8] J.R. Bullock, Address to Investors Conference, March 3, 1997.

A Staged Retreat

Despite establishing a position as North America's largest hazardous waste operator, Laidlaw's profitability was far from satisfactory, leading the company to initiate the first step in what eventually became a three-step progression toward divestment. In January 1997, Laidlaw engineered a reverse takeover of Rollins Environmental Services under which it received $400 million in cash, and the equivalent of $600 million in Rollins shares and securities, leaving Laidlaw with a 67 per cent interest in Rollins. Rollins, renamed Laidlaw Environmental Services Inc., (LESI) continued to trade on the New York Stock Exchange. At this point, Laidlaw's stated intentions, in spite of the industry's "less than satisfactory financial performance," were to "continue to grow (LESI) by making selected acquisitions and by capturing increased market share."[9]

Table 2: **Hazardous Waste Management Business Results 1993 to 1997 ($Millions)**

	1997	1996	1995	1994	1993
Revenues	710	716	642	518	512
Operating Income	68*	62	62	46	52
Operating Margins (%)	9.5	8.7	9.7	8.8	10.1
Identifiable Assets	1,547	1,418	1,389	NA	NA
Op.Inc./Id.Assets (%)	4.4	4.3	4.5		

* Excluding a restructuring charge of $332 million pretax.

Source: Laidlaw Annual Reports.

In what became the second step of the divestment process, in mid-1998 LESI acquired the Safety-Kleen Corp. by way of a tumultuous takeover battle. In the end, the transaction cost $2.2 billion, financed with $1.5 billion in cash, and the balance through issuance of LESI shares. The result was a reduction in Laidlaw's ownership of LESI to about 35 per cent, with shares and securities now valued on Laidlaw's balance sheet at $738 million. At the time, it was Laidlaw's view that there was "substantial opportunity for Safety-Kleen's value to appreciate, (and) we expect to hold this interest for some time."[10]

In September 1999, however, Laidlaw announced that it intended to sell its now 44 per cent interest in Safety-Kleen (created by conversion of pay-in-kind debentures created in the earlier transaction). The sale would be subject to procedures established by an independent Safety-Kleen board committee, but Laidlaw believed that it would be able to sell its 43 million shares at a premium to the then-current $14 trading price of Safety-Kleen, yielding over $600 million. Up to the time of Bullock's resignation, however, there had been no announcements of a transaction, and Safety-Kleen's stock had fallen to under $11.

---

[9] Laidlaw Annual Report, 1997.
[10] Laidlaw, Annual Report, 1998.

AMBULANCE AND EMERGENCY SERVICES

In the early 1990s, about 75 per cent of the industry revenues in the $7 billion U.S. ambulance service industry were based on the non-emergency transport of patients among treatment facilities and back and forth between hospital and home. Most of these transfers were paid for on a fee-for-service basis by Medicare, Medicaid, insurance companies and private payers. The balance of industry revenues came from 911-type emergency response contracts held with municipalities. The industry was highly fragmented, but in the first throes of consolidation. The consolidation was being led by and the largest firm in the business, American Medical Response (AMR), located primarily in the eastern United States, and by the second largest, CareLine, located in Florida and California. The consolidation of the industry, in Laidlaw's view, was being driven by the increasing cost of more sophisticated technology and training, the retirement of owners who had built the local firms, and the demands from health maintenance organizations for integrated providers to meet the needs of their expanding regional membership bases.[11]

Growth by Acquisition in Ambulance Services

In January 1993, Laidlaw entered the ambulance service business by acquiring National Medical Transport Services, the third largest ambulance service provider in the United States. Bullock explained Laidlaw's approach:

> We saw the ambulance business as more or less an extension of our passenger service operations. It had similar contracting characteristics; it required fleet management and dispatch communications and it carried people. Our strategy as a consolidator ... was to purchase high quality ambulance service providers in major markets, use them as local platforms onto which we could add other providers, reduce administration, rationalize dispatch facilities and bring to bear economies of scale in the purchase of vehicles, supplies and insurance.[12]

By 1996, a program of more than 50 acquisitions, including CareLine, had generated annualized revenues of over $600 million.

Then, in 1997, Laidlaw more than doubled its position in healthcare services through the $1.2 billion acquisition of AMR. Bullock explained this move, which came close on the heels of the solid waste business disposition:

> This move takes Laidlaw beyond transportation into the broader emergency health care industry. Transporting patients will still dominate our health care activities; however, with our geographic coverage and our communications centres in most major U.S markets we will be uniquely positioned to plan and coordinate a broad range of healthcare activities within health maintenance organizations and the wider American healthcare system. This acquisition has put us in an unassailable position in terms of expanding the health care side of Laidlaw's business. It begins to take us into a number of related fields linked to emergency patient transport — physicians and nursing services and emergency room department management.[13]

---

[11] Laidlaw, Annual Report, 1997.

[12] J.R. Bullock, Address to Donaldson, Lufkin, Jenrette Conference, September 15, 1997.

[13] J.R. Bullock, Address to Raymond James and Associates Conference, March 3, 1997.

Growth by Acquisition in Emergency Department Services

There were about 5,000 emergency departments in the United States, and 80 per cent outsourced their management and staffing. About 25 per cent of this market was provided by national physician practice organizations; the balance was provided by regional or small local groups. Laidlaw moved quickly to build on the foothold provided by AMR. In September 1997, the company announced the $418 million acquisition of EmCare Holdings of Texas, a physician practice management organization with annual revenues of $260 million, derived largely from contracts with 153 hospital emergency departments. A month later, the acquisition of Spectrum Emergency Care Inc., for $94 million, added 185 contracts and brought the total number of physician practices under Laidlaw management to 3,800, and service coverage to about 4.9 million patient visits a year. In early 1998, Bullock expressed management's enthusiasm for this field:

> Emergency department management will be the faster growing unit of our patient services business. We see no impediments to doubling the size of this service during the next two-to-three years, through acquisition of established high quality physicians groups and by winning contracts from hospitals in new markets.[14]

The Health Care Bubble Bursts

In the late 1990s, the federal Health Care Financing Administration (HCFA), under pressure from runaway health costs and the Balanced Budget Act of 1997, had started to tighten access to medical services and to change reimbursement policies. In the ambulance industry, for example, this was leading to a stricter interpretation of medical necessity and the HCFA was consequently cutting payments for ambulance services and retroactively clawing back payments for services provided in the past. Meanwhile, insurance companies, which had been engaging in costly market share battles in health care, began their own push on access and remuneration. The changing conditions were creating confusion in the market and, ominously for ambulance service companies, a significant shift from full service ambulance towards less costly wheelchair van transfers.

By mid-1998, these new economic realities were forcing AMR management to accelerate its cost reduction programs and to exit under-performing contracts. Laidlaw acknowledged that AMR was under margin pressure, but argued that progress was being made to develop new definitions and payment schedules in the industry and that AMR was "in an excellent position for long term stable growth and in a position to benefit from the increasing health care demands of an aging population."[15] The AMR situation continued to deteriorate, however, and in March 1999, Laidlaw took a $370 million restructuring charge to reflect the deterioration of its assets in the business, particularly goodwill, and to cover severance and other charges associated with reducing AMR's employee base by approximately 10 per cent.

The new access and remuneration pressures also applied to Laidlaw's fledgling Emergency Department Management business. By mid-1999, Laidlaw's revenues in this business were down 10 per cent from a year earlier, reflecting churn in contracts; as well, operating profits were off by over 40 per cent, reflecting costs to convert physicians from contract to employee status and lower

---

[14] J.R. Bullock, Address to Raymond James and Associates Conference, March 16, 1998.

[15] Laidlaw, Annual Report, 1998.

pricing on new and renewal contracts. While the circumstances were not as dramatic as those in ambulance services, they were still a major disappointment relative to expectations.

The results for the health care business are included in Table 3.

Table 3: Health Care Services Business Results 1994 to 1999 ($Millions)

	1999	1998	1997	1996	1995	1994
Revenues	1,490	1,659	957	464	206	130
Operating Income	(263)*	174	79**	56	20	12
Operating Margins (%)	(17.7)	9.5	8.7	12.1	9.7	9.2
Identifiable Assets	***	3,016	2,332	786	NA	NA
Op.Inc./Id.Assets (%)	NA	5.8	3.4	7.1		

* Including restructuring charges of $370 million pretax.
** Including restructuring costs of $35 million pretax.
*** Including a $1,003 million provision for anticipated loss on sale.

Source: Laidlaw Annual Reports.

Divestment

In September 1999, Laidlaw decided to throw in the towel. The company announced that it intended to divest its health care service businesses for a proposed $1.5 billion. In the process, it made a $1 billion provision to write down the book value of its health care assets in anticipation of its loss on the sale. Of the whole health care episode, Bullock confessed, "We thought we were entering a business that was aligned with many of the skill sets associated with our bus business . . . We now realize it was quite a different business, and particularly with its challenge associated with reimbursement."[16] It was not clear at the time of Bullock's resignation that Laidlaw would be able to sell the business for the proposed price.

PASSENGER SERVICES

Laidlaw's passenger service operations encompassed school bussing services and intercity and tour bus operations. School bussing had long been the dominant business in this segment, although new initiatives by Laidlaw in the late 1990s were broadening the passenger services base. Most notably, in 1997 Laidlaw acquired Greyhound Canada, and in 1999, Greyhound in the United States. As a result, in 1999, the company split passenger services for reporting into Education Services and Transit and Tour Services.

Education Services

In the late 1990s, there were almost 450,000 school buses on the roads of North America. About two-thirds of these were run by school boards, the balance by private operators on contract to school boards. Conversion from public to private transit had long been a goal of the private operators, and

---

[16] Paul Bagnell, "Laidlaw's Rough Ride," *Financial Post,* September 25, 1999, p C3.

indeed over the past decade, they had increased their share of the vehicles in service by about 10 per cent. The industry was highly fragmented, with 5,000 operators and only two with revenues over $100 million.

Laidlaw had been the principal consolidator in the school bus industry. Under James Bullock, the company had made three major acquisitions for a cumulative total of about $700 million, and various smaller ones to increase its fleet from approximately 22,000 vehicles in 1994 to 40,000 in 1999. The next largest operator in the industry had 10,000 buses; the next nine businesses operated a total of about 20,000 buses, and the balance of the industry fleet was scattered widely. The performance of the school bus (education services) business is summarized in Table 4.

Laidlaw felt it was in an excellent position in the education services business with unmatchable economies of scale in operations and capital acquisitions. In 1999, the company forecast internal growth rates of five to six per cent, based on the conversion of public operators and better pricing. This, they added, would be augmented as opportunities arose (by acquisitions) to tuck acquired operators into Laidlaw's established base.

Table 4: Education Services Business Results 1994-99 ($Millions)

	1999	1998	1997	1996	1995	1994
	Education Services Only			*Education, Tours and Transit*		
Revenues	1,327	1,227	1,132	1,115	873	730
Operating Income	163	164	136	116	93	82
Operating Margins (%)	12.3	13.4	12.0	10.4	10.6	11.2
Identifiable Assets	1,647	1,581	1,527	1,482	NA	NA
Op.Inc./Id.Assets (%)	9.9	10.4	8.9	7.8		

Source: Laidlaw Annual Reports.

Transit and Tours Business

Up to 1995, Laidlaw had operated a relatively small coach business, providing regional intercity and tour services, handling it more or less as an appendage to the school bus business. Then the acquisition of the Mayflower Company in the United States, although primarily to boost the school bus business, gave Laidlaw a significant position in the private sector operated municipal transport market. The company built on this opportunity and by 1997, held the leadership position in the market, providing service to 202 municipal transit systems.

In 1998, Laidlaw entered the national intercity coach business by acquiring Greyhound Canada for about $75 million. With the subsequent $650 million acquisition of Greyhound U.S. in March 1999, Laidlaw became the principal provider of intercity transit in North America. The company was optimistic about the future where it saw growth opportunities through revitalization of the bus business to provide better passenger and package service, and through acquisitions in the regional tour business where there were an estimated 6,000 individual operators.

A summary of the results for the Tours and Transit businesses is given in Table 5.

The Arrival of Competition

Laidlaw was not alone in sensing opportunity in the transportation business. Other consolidators were at work. Starting in 1994, Coach USA had built a fleet of 9,500 vehicles and revenues of over $800 million through 70 acquisitions of charter, tour and municipal transport businesses. Then in June 1999, Coach USA was acquired for $1.2 billion cash by Stagecoach Holdings PLC, a U.K.-based consolidator with revenues of about $1.7 billion and operations throughout the world. In Stagecoach's view, the Coach USA investment was a beachhead from which it intended to accelerate consolidation in the United States.

Table 5: **Transit and Tour Services Business Results 1997 to 1999 ($Millions)**

	1999	1998	1997
Revenues	935*	444	250
Operating Income	71	32	16
Margins (%)	12.3	13.4	12.0
Identifiable Assets	1,401	348	229
Op.Inc./Id.Assets (%)	NA	9.2	7.0

* Includes only 5 months of anticipated $900 million annualized revenues from Greyhound U.S.

Source: Laidlaw Annual Reports.

On the heels of the Stagecoach announcement, another British firm, FirstGroup PLC, completed two acquisitions in the United States. The first was the relatively small $13 million acquisition of a 1,000-bus operator in New England in June 1999. The second purchase, in September 1999, was much more significant — the $964 million acquisition of the Ryder Transportation subsidiary of Ryder System Inc. Ryder Transportation encompassed three business units: (1) Ryder School Transportation, the second largest school bus operation in the United States, with revenues of $582 million and operating profits of $62 million from a fleet of slightly more than 10,000 buses, (2) Ryder ATE, the second largest provider of public transit services and revenues of $197 million and (3) Ryder MLS, the largest public fleet maintenance provider in the United States, with revenues of $142 million.

THE CORPORATE PICTURE

A summary of Laidlaw's consolidated income and balance sheet position as of August 31, 1999, taking into consideration the pending announcements of its intention to sell its health care businesses and Safety-Kleen investment, is presented in Exhibit 1. Commenting on the results and the consequent fall in Laidlaw's stock price, Bullock wrote that "As a shareholder like you, I look back on fiscal 1999 with some frustration. The year has been operationally extremely challenging and our stock price performance was clearly unrewarding."[17] However, Bullock remained

---

[17] Laidlaw Annual Report, 1999.

optimistic about Laidlaw's prospects. He outlined his expectations for a new, more focused Laidlaw:

> We will realize in excess of $2 billion in proceeds from the sales of the ambulance operations, emergency department services and Safety-Kleen, within the current fiscal year.
>
> Proceeds will be used to retire about $1 billion of bank debt, reducing total debt by one-third; the cash balance, $1 billion plus, will be reinvested in the growth of our continuing businesses.
>
> As a result Laidlaw will be a bus passenger service business with revenues in the $3 billion neighborhood, cash to spend and a debt-to-equity ratio of less than one to one.
>
> I would also point out that the reinvestment of the cash on our balance sheet will obviously add further value in due course.
>
> The company is now a much more simplified story, a pure bus industry play, more easily understood and, therefore, more saleable to investors.[18]

Exhibit 1: Laidlaw Summary Financial Statements ($Millions)

	1999	1998
Revenue*	$ 2,262	2,056
Operating Income*	268	272
Net Income *	166	268
Net Income	$ (1,119)	346
Earnings per Share* ($)	0.50	0.81
Earnings per Share	(3.39)	1.05
Current Assets	$ 564	449
Net Assets (Disc. Ops.)	1,617	2,791
Long Term Inv. (mainly Safety-Kleen)	781	984
Property and Equipment	1,481	1,008
Goodwill (net)	1,212	740
Other	99	31
Total Assets	$ 5,754	6,003
Current Liabilities	$ 486	435
Deferred liabilities	242	188
Long Term Debt	3,113	2,290
Shareholders Equity	1,913	3,090
Total Liabilities and Sh. Equity	$ 5,754	6,003

* From continuing operations.

Source: Laidlaw Annual Reports

---

[18]J.R. Bullock, Presentation to Nesbitt Burns, September 21, 1999.

NEWELL COMPANY: THE RUBBERMAID OPPORTUNITY[1]

case 24

Joseph N. Fry

In October 1998, the board of directors of the Newell Company was considering a proposed merger with Rubbermaid Incorporated to form a new company, Newell Rubbermaid Inc. The transaction would be accomplished through a tax-free exchange of shares under which Rubbermaid shareholders would receive Newell shares valued at approximately $5.8 billion at a ratio which represented a 49 per cent premium on Rubbermaid's current stock price. At the time of the transaction the annual revenues of Newell and Rubbermaid were, respectively, about $3.2 billion and $2.4 billion. If approved, the agreement would mark a quantum step in Newell's growth, but, equally, it would pose a formidable challenge to the company's demonstrated capacity to integrate and strengthen its acquisitions.

---

[1]This case has been written on the basis of published sources only. Consequently, the interpretation and perspectives presented in this case are not necessarily those of Newell Company or any of its employees.

IVEY

Joseph N. Fry prepared this case solely to provide material for class discussion. The author does not intend to illustrate either effective or ineffective handling of a managerial situation. The author may have disguised certain names and other identifying information to protect confidentiality.

NEWELL: RIDING THE ACQUISITION TIGER

In 1998, the Newell Company had revenues of $3.7 billion distributed across three major product groupings: Hardware and Home Furnishings ($1.8 billion), Office Products ($1.0 billion), and Housewares ($.9 billion). Over the past ten years the company had achieved a compound sales growth rate of 13 per cent, an earnings per share growth rate of 16 per cent and an average annual return on beginning shareholder equity of 21 per cent. These results were consistent with Newell's formal goals of achieving earnings per share growth of 15 per cent per year and maintaining a return on beginning equity of 20 per cent or above. Further financial details on Newell are given in Exhibit 1.

Acquisitions

Acquisitions were the foundation of Newell's growth strategy. Given the relatively slow growth of the product markets in which it chose to operate, Newell's corporate goal for internal growth was only three per cent to five per cent per annum — with internal growth being defined as the growth of businesses that Newell had owned for over two years. Actual internal growth in the past five years had averaged about five per cent per annum. This put a premium on acquisitions if Newell was to meet its aggressive growth targets. Indeed, over $2 billion of its current sales were the result of over 20 acquisitions made since 1990.

Newell's approach to acquisition was both aggressive and disciplined. Its targeted acquisition candidates were generally mature businesses with "unrealized profit potential" which further passed a number of screening criteria, including having a:

- strategic fit with existing businesses—which implied product lines that were low in technology, fashion and seasonal content and were sold through mass distribution channels.
- number one or two position in their served markets and established shelf space with major retailers.
- long product life cycle.
- potential to reach Newell's standard of profitability, which included goals for operating margins of 15 per cent, and Sales, General and Administrative costs at a maximum of 15 per cent.

The size of the acquisitions varied. In 1996, Newell made one acquisition for $46 million cash, in 1997, three material acquisitions for $762 million cash and in 1998 to date, four material acquisitions for about $413 million cash. Once acquired, the new companies were integrated into the Newell organization by means of an established process that had come to be called "newellization."

Newellization

Newellization was the profit improvement and productivity enhancement process employed to bring a newly acquired business up to Newell's high standards of productivity and profit. The Newellization process was pursued through a number of broadly applicable steps, including the:

- transfer of experienced Newell managers into the acquired company.

- simplification and focusing of the acquired business's strategy and the implementation of Newell's established manufacturing and marketing know-how and programs.
- centralization of key administrative functions including data processing, accounting, EDI, and capital expenditure approval.
- inauguration of Newell's rigorous, multi-measure, divisional operating control system.

[handwritten: Potential Problem when integrate]

Newell management claimed that the process of newellization was usually completed in two or three years.

Continuing Operations

A summary of Newell's product groups and major lines is outlined in Table 1. These products were, for the most part, sold through mass merchandisers. In 1997, Wal-Mart accounted for 15 per cent of Newell's sales; the other top ten Newell customers (each with less than 10 per cent of Newell sales) were Kmart, Home Depot, Office Depot, Target, J.C. Penney, United Stationers, Hechtinger, Office Max and Lowe's. International sales had increased from eight per cent of total sales in 1992 to an expected 22 per cent in 1998 as Newell followed customers and opportunities into Mexico, Europe and the Americas.

Table 1: Newell Product Lines, 1998

Housewares	Hardware and Home Furnishings	Office Products
Aluminum Cookware and Bakeware	Window Treatments	Markers and Writing Products
Glassware	Home Storage	Office Storage
Hair Accessories	Picture frames	
	Hardware	

[handwritten: CRITICAL VP]

Newell's fundamental competitive strategy, which applied to all of its operations, was to differentiate on the basis of superior service to its mass merchandise customers. For Newell, superior service included industry-leading quick response and on-time, in-full delivery, the ability to implement sophisticated EDI tie-ins with its customers extending to vendor-managed inventories, and the provision of marketing and merchandising programs for product categories that encompassed good, better and best lines.

Organization

[handwritten: Potential Proble]

Newell centralized certain key administrative functions such as data management (including order-fulfillment-invoice activities), divisional coordination and control, and financial management. Otherwise, the presidents of the company's 18 product divisions were responsible for the full scope of manufacturing, marketing and sales activities for their product lines and for the performance of their businesses.

[handwritten: makes integration easy]

Divisional coordination and control were facilitated by the fundamental similarities of the Newell businesses. These similarities made it possible for corporate level management to develop a common pool of managers and know-how that could be transferred relatively easily from one division to another. The business similarities also made it possible for corporate management to apply a common set of detailed operating standards and controls across the businesses, and to play a knowledgeable role in reviewing divisional progress and plans. Corporate management held monthly reviews (called brackets meetings) with divisional presidents to track multiple operating and financial measures and to ensure that appropriate attention was given to items that were off budget. As a result, divisional management operated in a goldfish bowl under high pressure, but they were paid very well for meeting their targets.

Outlook

In Newell's view, the company's adherence to a highly focused strategy had established a sustainable competitive advantage for the corporation and this, coupled with abundant acquisition opportunities and internal growth momentum, would support the continuing achievement of its financial goals.

RUBBERMAID: A FALLEN ICON

Rubbermaid was a well known, and, for several decades, a renowned manufacturer of a wide range of plastic products ranging from children's toys through housewares to commercial items. From 1986 through 1995 Rubbermaid was ranked among the top 10 in Fortune's list of America's most admired companies, including the No. 1 spot in 1993 and 1994. But by March 1998 Rubbermaid had fallen to No. 100. After a wonderful run of growth and profitability, extending as far back as the 1960s, the company had clearly hit a rough patch.

Rubbermaid earned its early reputation by setting aggressive goals for 15 per cent growth in revenues and profits and then, by and large, meeting its targets. Under the intense and very personal management of Stanley Gault, an ex-senior executive at General Electric and CEO and chairman of Rubbermaid from 1980 to 1991, the company was pressed to broaden its product line through development and acquisition and to meet demanding operating targets. From propitious beginnings Rubbermaid became a ubiquitous brand and a Wall Street darling — with sales and profits, respectively, at the end of Gault's tenure of $1.7 billion and $162 million.

Rubbermaid's earnings momentum continued into the early years of Gault's successor, Wolfgang Schmidt, but the good times were to be short-lived. In 1994 Rubbermaid was hit by a doubling of plastic resin prices.[2] The company's clumsy reactions to this shock revealed a number of accumulating problems. Fortune enumerated them in a 1995 article[3]:

- Customer relations: Rubbermaid angered its most important retail buyers with the heavy-handed way it has passed along its ballooning costs. Some are so angry that they have given more shelf space to competitors…
- Operations: Although it excels in creativity, product quality, and merchandising, Rubbermaid is showing itself to be a laggard in more mundane areas such as modernizing machinery, eliminating unnecessary jobs, and making deliveries on time…
- Competition: It has been slow to recognize that other housewares makers — once a bunch of no-names who peddled junk — have greatly improved over the past half dozen years. The

---

[2] Materials accounted for between 45 and 50 per cent of Rubbermaid's net sales.
[3] Lee Smith, "Rubbermaid Goes Thump," Fortune, October 2, 1995.

premium prices that Rubbermaid charges over its rivals have grown too large, and customers are turning away.

- Culture: The company's extraordinary financial targets…seem unrealistic — and straining to reach them is proving increasingly troublesome. Some of the friction between Rubbermaid and its customers can be traced to Rubbermaid's voracious appetite for growth.

Rubbermaid's profits peaked in 1994 at $228 million. In 1995 sales were up eight per cent but the company took a restructuring charge of $158 million pre-tax and net earnings fell to $60 million. The restructuring charges were taken in anticipation of a two-year program designed to reduce costs, improve operating efficiencies and accelerate growth. In 1997, Rubbermaid reported[4] that the realignment activities were substantially complete and that the company "has or initiated closure of all nine locations slated for closure in the plan, completed the associated reductions, and achieved the estimated annual savings of $50 million anticipated in the 1995 program." Unfortunately, this action did not have a material effect on sales, which remained essentially flat, and operating profits, which dipped somewhat, as detailed in the financial summary given in Exhibit 2. Thus, early in 1998, Rubbermaid announced another restructuring charge, which it estimated would reach at least $200 million pre-tax, to fund a program that would include centralizing global procurement and consolidating manufacturing and distribution worldwide.

Rubbermaid Lines of Business

In 1998, Rubbermaid manufactured and sold over 5,000 products[5] under four key brand names:

- Rubbermaid: a wide range of household utility products encompassing five categories (Kitchen, Home Organization, Health Care, Cleaning, and Hardware/Seasonal) and 23 product lines.
- Graco: children's products in six product lines focusing on baby strollers and related items.
- Little Tikes: juvenile products, with 11 product lines focusing on toys and furniture.
- Curver: a European-based home products business with revenues of $180 million, acquired at the beginning of 1998.

Rubbermaid's international sales and operations had been growing in recent years as it followed its customers abroad. The Curver acquisition increased foreign sales, including exports from the United States, to about 25 per cent of total revenues, helping the firm along the path to its goal of 30 per cent by 2000.

Rubbermaid Strategy

Rubbermaid's strategy reflected an uneasy balance of not necessarily consistent ambitions. The 15 per cent growth goals of the past had disappeared from public statements, but there was no question that the company remained aggressive in its goals and optimistic about its prospects. To achieve its aims Rubbermaid relied on a multi-faceted competitive strategy. It wanted, at once, to be a company with a:

---

[4] Rubbermaid Annual Report, 1997.

[5] In 1997 Rubbermaid had sold its Office Product business to Newell for a $134 million pretax gain, which it promptly offset by a one-time charge of $ 81 million for asset impairment related to acquisitions.

- strong consumer franchise based on unique product features, quality and rapid innovation, and on brand recognition and aggressive advertising. Rubbermaid had, for example, set a goal that 10 per cent of each year's sales should come from new, high value products and it had reduced new product time to market from 20 plus months in the 1980s to six months currently, with a goal of four months by 2000.
- low-cost sourcing, production, and fulfilment base. The company was in the process, for example, of cutting product variations by 45 per cent and consolidating its supplier base from 9,000 to less than 2,000 vendors.
- reliable and efficient supplier to mass merchandisers. Rubbermaid was moving, for example, to scheduling manufacturing by customer order and to just-in-time service and continuous replenishment of its best selling items.

There was a tension at work behind these aims. In its 1996 Annual Report Rubbermaid noted that its market was at a point of inflection, in which the control of information was shifting from mass marketers to individual consumers. In this context Rubbermaid claimed that it would strike a new balance in its strategies, to continue to lead in innovation while becoming a low cost producer. Similarly, in its 1997 Annual Report, the company noted that in a squeeze of higher costs and lower retail prices it was making bold moves to become the low-cost producer, while retaining world-class quality and innovation. Finally, another "point of inflection": in his 1997 Letter to Shareholders, Wolfgang Schmidt promised that, "with the initiatives of the past two years and the opportunities ahead, we are at the inflection point from which we can combine our financial strength and innovation capabilities with a more favorable cost climate to generate stronger shareholder returns."

THE OUTLINE OF A DEAL

Newell's appetite for all of Rubbermaid might have been whetted with its $247 million acquisition of Rubbermaid's Office products division in 1977, adding about $160 million of annualized revenues to Newell's developing office products line of business. Whatever the stimulus, talks soon began on a total combination of the two firms.

Negotiations led to a provisional agreement under which Rubbermaid shareholders would receive 0.7883 shares of Newell common stock for each share of Rubbermaid common stock that they owned. Based on Newell's closing price of $49.07 on October 20, 1998 this represented $38.68 per Rubbermaid share or a premium on 49 per cent over Rubbermaid's closing price of $25.88. Under this arrangement Newell would issue approximately 118 million shares of common stock to Rubbermaid shareholders. Rubbermaid shareholders would end up holding approximately 40 per cent of the combined company. The transaction represented a tax-free exchange of shares and would be accounted for as a pooling of interests. A simple pro forma of the results, the transaction is given in Exhibit 3.

Newell management forecast[6] that, as soon as the transaction was completed, they would begin the "newellization" process and improve Rubbermaid's operating efficiencies to achieve 98 per cent on-time and line-fill performance and a minimum 15 per cent pretax margin. They also expected

Goal

---

[6] Newell press release, October 21, 1998.

revenue and operating synergies through the leveraging of Newell Rubbermaid's brands, innovative product development, improved service performance, stronger combined presence in dealing with common customers, broader acquisition opportunities, and an increased ability to serve European markets. They forecast that by 2000 these efforts and opportunities would produce increases over anticipated 1998 results of $300 million to $350 million in operating income for the combined company.

Exhibit 1: Selected Financial Information for Newell Company, 1996-1998 ($000)

	To End Q3/98	12/31/97	To End Q3/97	12/31/96
Net sales	**$2,650,263**	**$3,336,233**	**$2,395,037**	**$2,972,839**
Cost of products sold	1,786,640	2,259,551	1,631,253	2,020,116
Selling, general & administrative expenses	404,882	497,739	365,123	461,802
Goodwill amortization and other	40,502	31,882	22,872	23,554
Operating Income	418,239	547,061	375,789	467,367
Interest expense	43,966	76,413	54,363	58,541
Other, non-operating, net	(213,373)*	(14,686)	(12,862)	(19,474)
Profit before tax	587,546	485,334	334,288	428,300
Income taxes	250,740	192,187	132,373	169,258
Net Income	**$336,806**	**$293,147**	**$201,915**	**$259,042**
Current assets	1,767,370	1,433,694		1,148,464
Property, plant and equipment	834,486	711,325		567,880
Trade names, goodwill, other	2,001,862	1,559,594		1,342,086
Total Assets	**4,603,718**	**4,011,314**		**3,058,430**
Current liabilities	1,061,675	714,479		665,884
Long-term debt	912,650	786,793		685,608
Other non-current liabilities	243,862	285,241		206,916
Convertible preferred securities	500,000	500,000		
Shareholders' Equity	1,885,531	1,725,221		1,500,022
Total Liabilities & Shareholders' Equity	**4,603,718**	**4,011,314**		**3,058,430**
Approx. common shares outstanding (000)	173,000	163,300		162,000
Earnings per share (fully diluted)		$1.80		$1.60
Stock Price $High/Low	$54/37	$43/30		$33/25

* Primarily gain from sale of Black & Decker holdings.

Source: Company Financial Reports

Exhibit 2: **Selected Financial Information for Rubbermaid, 1995-1998 ($000)**

	To End Q3/98	12/31/97	To End Q3/97	12/31/96	12/31/95
Net sales	$1,936,829	$2,399,710	$1,825,416	$2,354,980	$2,344,170
Cost of products sold	1,383,564	1,748,424	1,327,990	1,649,520	1,673,232
Selling, general & administrative expenses	353,805	416,641	314,229	432,063	402,586
Operating Income	199,460	234,645	183,197	273,397	268,352
Interest expense	27,795	35,762	28,463	24,348	10,260
Restructuring Costs	73,740	16,000	16,000		158,000
Other, non-operating, net	(23,749)	(51,032)	(49,729)	4,046	4,457
Income taxes	42,586	91,370	77,717	92,614	35,863
Net Income	$79,088	$142,536	$110,746	$152,398	$59,772
Current assets	952,841	816,204		856,720	
Other assets	445,995	399,716		475,346	
Property, plant and equipment	784,228	707,974		721,914	
Total Assets	2,183,064	1,923,984		2,053,980	
Current liabilities	802,231	567,084		742,841	
Long-term debt	152,556	153,163		154,467	
Other non-current liabilities	171,302	153,385		142,992	
Shareholders' equity	1,056,885	1,050,262		1,013,700	
Total Liabilities & Shareholders' Equity	2,183,064	1,923,984		2,053,980	
Approx. common shares outstanding (000)		149,900		151,000	158,800
Earnings per share (fully diluted)		$0.95		$1.01	$0.38
Stock Price $High/Low		$30/22		$30/22	$34/25

Source: Company Financial Reports.

Exhibit 3: **Simple Pro Forma Financial Information for NewellRubbermaid, EndQ3-1998 ($000)**

	Newell Q3/97-Q3/98	Rubbermaid Q3/97-Q3/98	Simple Pro Forma NewellRubbermaid Q3/97-Q3/98
Net sales	**3,591,459**	**2,511,123**	**6,102,582**
Cost of products sold	2,414,938	1,803,998	4,218,936
Selling, general & administrative expenses	537,498	456,217	993,715
Goodwill amortization and other	49,512		49,512
Operating Income	589,511	250,908	840,419
Interest expense	66,016	35,094	101,110
Other, non-operating, net	(215,197)*	48,688	(166,509)
Profit before tax	738,692	167,126	905,818
Income taxes	310,554	56,239	366,793
Net Income	**428,138**	**110,887**	**539,025**
Balance Sheet as of End Q3/98			
Current assets	1,767,370	952,841	2,720,211
Property, plant and equipment	834,486	784,228	1,618,714
Trade names, goodwill, other	2,001,862	445,995	2,447,857
Total Assets	**4,603,718**	**2,183,064**	**6,786,782**
Current liabilities	1,061,675	802,231	1,863,906
Long-term debt	912,650	152,556	1,065,206
Other non-current liabilities	243,862	171,302	415,164
Convertible preferred securities	500,000		500,000
Shareholders' Equity	1,885,531	1,056,885	2,942,416
Total Liabilities & Shareholders' Equity	**4,603,718**	**2,183,064**	**6.786,782**
Approx. common shares outstanding (000)	173,000	150,000	291,000
Earnings per share (fully diluted)	$2.47	$0.74	$1.85

* Primarily gain from sale of Black & Decker holdings.

Source: Estimates based on Company Financial Reports.

LABATT – FEMSA: AMIGOS FOR GROWTH?

case 25

David Ager and
Joseph N. Fry

In May 1994, George Taylor, president and chief executive officer of John Labatt Limited (Labatt), was reviewing the preliminary terms of a proposal under which Labatt would enter into a partnership with Cerveceria Cuauhtémoc Moctezuma (FEMSA Cerveza) of Monterrey, Mexico. A successful agreement with FEMSA Cerveza, in the face of contending overtures from Philip Morris/Miller Brewing of the U.S., would represent a major recommitment of Labatt to its brewing roots and a significant improvement of its position in the North American brewing industry. Appendix A presents a brief description of Philip Morris/Miller Brewing.

JOHN LABATT LIMITED

Founded in 1847 in London, Ontario, by John Kinder Labatt, Labatt was one of Canada's oldest companies and largest brewing concerns. For over a century the company had focused, with

IVEY

David Ager prepared this case under the supervision of Professor Joseph N. Fry solely to provide material for class discussion. The author does not intend to illustrate either effective or ineffective handling of a managerial situation. The author may have disguised certain names and other identifying information to protect confidentiality.

significant success, on developing its brewing operations in Canada. In the early 1960s, however, the decision was taken to diversify the company and seek growth in other areas as well. This was marked in 1964/65 by a company reorganization under which Labatt became a holding company for four main subsidiaries: Labatt Breweries of Canada; General Brewing Corporation (U.S. brewing operations); Labatt International (international property operations); and Labatt Industries (bio-technical interests). This was the first of several corporate reorganizations that the company would undergo over the next 25 years as it pursued an aggressive acquisition and development strategy in Canada and the U.S. In addition to beer assets, Labatt acquired subsidiaries involved in the processed foods, dairy, and packaging industries, as well as the Toronto Blue Jays baseball club, the Toronto Argonauts football club, a stake in the Skydome stadium, sports networks, and a company that specialized in rock concert promotion.

By 1989 Labatt reported consolidated revenues of $4.8 billion and net profits of $141 million on an asset base of $2.8 billion and described itself as a broadly based North American food and beverage company. Consolidated financial statements for 1988 – 1994 are presented in Exhibit 1, and segmented financial results for the same period are presented in Exhibit 2.

Then, in 1990, Labatt changed direction. The company, which was having difficulty supporting and achieving acceptable returns in its agriculture and food related businesses, decided to dispose of them and concentrate on its brewing, and broadcast and entertainment businesses. The 1990 annual report put it this way:

With the increasing globalization of its core businesses, John Labatt's long-term objective is to concentrate on fewer, larger businesses and to grow internationally.

By 1994 the divestiture program had, for the most part, been completed and consolidated results showed revenues down to $2.3 billion while earnings had increased slightly to $155 million. The business comprised two segments: brewing, and sports and entertainment. Brewing accounted for about 74 per cent of the company's revenues and 80 per cent of its profits.

Labatt's Brewing Business

Labatt was a national brewer in Canada and had significant operations in the United States, the United Kingdom and Italy. Segmented financial information for these operations is presented in Table 1. Context for these numbers is provided in the following review of trends in the North American brewing industry and of Labatt's current position in each of its geographic markets.

Table 1: **Segmented Financial Data From Labatt's Brewing Division (Millions of Cdn $)**

Net Sales	EBIT		Net Assets Employed			
	1994	1993	1994	1993	1994	1993
Labatt Canada	$1,245	$1,241	$ 283	$ 239	$ 495	$ 534
Labatt's USA	$ 228	$ 180	$ 4	$ 5	$ 74	$ 67
Tariff	--	--	$ (4)	$ (8)	--	--
Birra Moretti	$ 134	$ 130	$ (1)	$ (3)	$ 203	$ 180
Labatt UK	$ 74	$ 42	$ (2)	$ (8)	$ 110	$ 75

Source: John Labatt Limited 1994 Annual Report

THE EVOLUTION OF THE NORTH AMERICAN BREWING INDUSTRY (POST 1980)

In the late 1970s, brewing in North America was a regional business, with international borders creating three separate national markets. Nine independent national brewers dominated the markets:

In Canada: Labatt Breweries (a subsidiary of John Labatt Limited), Molson Breweries (a wholly owned subsidiary of Molson Group of Companies), Carling O'Keefe Breweries of Canada Limited (a wholly owned subsidiary of Foster's Brewing Group Limited—a division of Elders IXL Limited of Australia).

In the United States: Anheuser-Busch,
Miller Brewing Company (a subsidiary of Philip Morris Companies Inc.), Adolph Coors Company.

In Mexico: Cerveceria Cuauhtémoc (a wholly owned subsidiary of Fomento Económico Mexicano, S.A. de C.V. a division of Valores Industriales S.A.), Cerveceria Moctezuma, Cerveceria Modelo S.A. de C.V.

By 1994 the structure of the industry had changed significantly through mergers that consolidated competition in Canada and Mexico, and by alliances and ownership arrangements that crossed the national borders. The resulting relationships among the major breweries, as of 1994, are summarized in Exhibit 3. The major events in this evolution were as follows:

1980

Labatt enters a licensing agreement with Anheuser-Busch to brew and market Budweiser, Busch's prime U.S. brand, in the Canadian market. In 1983 Carling-O'Keefe enters into a similar agreement with Miller for Miller's key brands and in 1985, Molson follows suit with an agreement with Adolph Coors.

1985

In Mexico, Valores Industriales S.A. acquires Cerveceria Moctezuma, and in 1990 combines this property with Cerveceria Cuauhtémoc to form FEMSA Cerveza, a division of its Fomento Económico Mexicano, S.A. de C.V. (FEMSA) group.

1988

Molson enters a distribution joint venture which, among other things, imports and distributes Cerveceria Modelo beers in Canada.

1990

Molson Breweries and Carling O'Keefe merge to form Molson Breweries with the Molson Group of Companies and Foster's each carrying a 50 per cent ownership.

1992

Philip Morris Companies acquires a 7.9 per cent interest in FEMSA, the parent of FEMSA Cerveza, from Citicorp.

1993

Anheuser-Busch acquires a 17.7 per cent stake in Grupo Modelo, for an estimated US$447 million, and carries an option to increase its stake to as much as 50 per cent.

Miller acquires a 20 per cent interest in Molson Breweries for US$273 million or about 6.9 times earnings before interest, taxes, depreciation and amortization (EBITDA). As part of the transaction Miller acquires exclusive marketing rights to Molson brands in the U.S. Molson retains the right to brew and sell Miller brands in Canada.

The introduction of "ice" beers touches off a storm of legal battles. Labatt claims ownership of a fundamental ice brewing technology and insists that terms such as "ice beer" can be used only for beers brewed using this technology. This claim is widely ignored by other brewers, including Anheuser-Busch. Labatt sues Busch, Molson and Miller for trademark infringement. Busch counter sues.

1994

Coors signs an agreement with Labatt for the ice brewing technology. Coors also goes to court to seek early termination of its license agreement with Molson's, which technically requires a ten year notice of termination. Coors also launches an antitrust suit against Miller, claiming the Miller's 20 per cent stake in Molson will substantially lessen competition in the U.S. beer market.

LABATT IN CANADA

The Canadian market was of critical importance to Labatt. About 75 per cent of its brewing revenues and virtually all of its earnings were delivered by the Canadian business. This was of some concern to the company since demand in Canada was flat, competition for market share was intense, and the role of government in regulating the industry and buffering it from foreign competition was increasingly uncertain. Labatt was well aware of the view of some international investors that the profitability of the company's brewing operations was the product of a contrived, unsustainable, Canadian brewing environment, made all the more uncertain by separatist political developments in Quebec.

Demand

The aggregate demand for beer in Canada had been relatively stable at around 21 million hectolitres (hL) for several years. Little, if any growth was anticipated for reasons including demographic changes, taste shifts away from alcoholic beverages, high prices due in large part to very heavy taxes, and regulatory constraints on marketing and distribution. Key aspects of the Canadian brewing industry are summarized in Exhibit 4.

Competition

In 1994, the Canadian market was dominated by two companies: Labatt, with a 44.2 per cent share and Molson, with a 48.9 per cent share. In recent years, a number of local and micro brewing businesses had emerged to serve regional and specialty tastes but these together amounted to less than five per cent of the market.

Competitive activities among the breweries were constrained by government regulation of pricing and distribution and, to a lesser extent, by advertising and promotional practices. In this context competition focused on product and brand differentiation. New product introductions such as "Ice Beer" and "Dry Beer" were common, and although they gave some advantage to the first mover, they were usually quickly copied. In the same way, heavy spending on brand advertising and clever new advertising approaches often cancelled out, yielding no significant and sustainable change in market share. The relative share positions of the two majors had been stable although Labatt had slowly gained market share at the expense of Molson. Since 1990, the year that Molson acquired Carling O'Keefe, its market share had fallen from 52.2 per cent to its current level of 48.9 per cent, while Labatt had increased its market share from 42.0 per cent to 44.2 per cent.

The Canadian breweries operated at a substantial cost disadvantage relative to their U.S. counterparts. As a result largely of geography and provincial regulation, the Canadian brewing industry consisted of a series of small- and medium-sized production plants across the country. The average brewery size in Canada was estimated at 1.24-million hL, much smaller than the average size of a U.S. brewer that was estimated at 3.0-million hL. Supplies such as malting barley were purchased in the U.S. on the open market, whereas Canadian brewers had to purchase at a (premium) price set by the Canadian Wheat Board. As a consequence, Canadian breweries operated under the continuing threat of U.S. entry, which to this point, had been limited in two ways: (1) by tariffs and by provincial non-tariff measures such as packaging requirements and minimum pricing requirements, and (2) by the alliances between the major Canadian and U.S. breweries under which "Can-Am" brands were produced in Canada with license fees going to the U.S. brand owners. But this still left second tier U.S. brewers with a thirst for the Canadian market.

Government

Government involvement in the brewing industry, and particularly at the provincial level, was a traditional "given" of life in Canada. This grew from the desires of various governments to achieve several, not necessarily consistent objectives such as controlling the sale of an alcoholic beverage, maximizing tax revenues, and ensuring local employment.

In recent years, however, international developments and consumer pressures had started to modify traditional policies. For decades, brewers had been required to brew beer within a province in order to list it for sale there. This requirement was eliminated as a result of several complaints launched by U.S. brewers and adjudication by the General Agreement on Tariffs and Trade (GATT) panel, which ruled that inter-provincial trading policies in Canada were inconsistent with international trading policies. As a result of this change, Labatt breweries closed three of its 12 breweries between 1992 and 1994, although it maintained its domestic sales volume at approximately 8.3 million hL.

Further, under the Canada-U.S. Free Trade Agreement, tariffs on brewing products shipped between the two countries were to be reduced to zero per cent by 1998. This agreement had been reached despite repeated protests on the part of the industry and a one-day strike by brewery workers who were convinced that without pre-1988 tariff protection the Canadian industry would cease to exist.

The government, however, still held some good cards. The traditional method of distribution of beer in Canada was through government owned or regulated outlets. The exceptions were Quebec and Newfoundland, which allowed sales through corner stores as well. Control of distribution provided some degree of control over supply and suppliers. Complaints had been made, for example, by some prospective U.S. exporters about the difficulty of gaining distribution access and meeting distribution requirements. In time, this leverage on the industry might diminish with popular demand for wider distribution and government policies of privatization. Alberta, for example was in the process of privatizing its retail system for alcoholic beverages. But other provinces such as Ontario, which had also considered the idea, did not seem to be rushing in this direction.

Another area of government control was pricing, in which it was common to have regulations requiring minimum prices and distribution mark-ups and uniform prices across a jurisdiction. While serving domestic political purposes, these policies also had the effect of constraining low price competition from the U.S. Naturally, these policies were under attack by elements of the U.S. industry and their maintenance was subject to substantial political uncertainty.

LABATT IN THE USA

While Labatt had actively exported its portfolio of brands to the U.S. since the early 1960s, it was not until 1987 with the acquisition of the Latrobe Company (Latrobe) that it established a brewing presence in the U.S. Latrobe brewed the premium brand *Rolling Rock* which had, since Labatt's purchase, steadily grown from a regional beer to a niche premium brand distributed throughout the U.S.

Beer Demand in the U.S.

The U.S. beer market, estimated at 237 million hL in 1994, represented the largest single beer market in the world. Overall demand was static but significant opportunities were emerging as consumers traded up to premium beers that offered something different, something that was not mass-produced and was more full-bodied in taste. These emerging demands were being met by a plethora of specialty beers and imports. Key aspects of the U.S. brewing industry are summarized in Exhibit 4.

Competition

The maturation of the U.S. mass market for beer had turned the industry into a gruelling battleground for market share. Three brewers accounted for nearly 80 per cent of the market: Anheuser-Busch (46 per cent), Miller (23 per cent), and Coors (11 per cent). While there were several smaller brewers operating throughout the U.S., they operated on a regional basis because they lacked both the production capacity (minimum 26 million hL) and the financial resources (Anheuser-Busch spent in excess of US$300 million in 1993) to support a national brand.

Imports accounted for 4.4 per cent of beer sales in the U.S. Heineken of the Netherlands was in the top position, accounting for 29.4 per cent of imports. Canada was second at 25.8 per cent, followed by Mexico at 18.4 per cent. The top three imported brands in the U.S. were Heineken (2.7

million hL), Corona Extra (1.2 million hL), and Molson Golden (0.62 million hL). The import segment was expected to experience volume growth of 5.5 per cent in 1994.

The microbrew segment of the U.S. brewing industry that had at one time been considered insignificant, was expected to experience a 50 per cent growth in volume in 1994. Although this segment accounted for less than two per cent of the entire U.S. industry, with overall beer sales showing little growth, the four largest U.S. brewers had begun to aggressively enter the micro segment through the purchase of significant stakes in microbrewers and through the development of "micro-style" brands.

Labatt and FEMSA Cerveza's combined sales volumes in the U.S. for all their brands represented approximately 2.7 million hL[1] in 1994.

Supply and Distribution

In the U.S., the brewing infrastructure of plant locations and distribution systems was a function of market size, geography, and transportation costs, not of state legislation. Breweries could ship product across state lines. The average new brewery built in the United States was in the eight to 10 million hL size.

Government

Unlike in Canada, governments in the U.S. influenced prices only to the extent that excise and sales taxes were levied on beer. Wholesale and retail prices were set by the members of the distribution and retail network in response to market conditions and supply. While beer could be shipped across state lines, 27 states had packaging and labelling requirements that favoured U.S. producers and discriminated against imported products.

LABATT IN THE UNITED KINGDOM

The six largest brewers in the United Kingdom (U.K.) controlled over 75 per cent of the domestic market. Brewers had vertically integrated to include not only beer production but also wholesale and retail outlets for beer distribution. This arrangement allowed brewers to control the products that were for sale and their prices. The result was that independent suppliers faced difficulties in distributing and selling their products.

Labatt first entered the U.K. in 1988 when it began marketing its Canadian draught products through Greenall Whitley pubs. By 1993, Labatt U.K. held interests in partnerships and joint ventures owning approximately 300 pubs. In all, Labatt brands were marketed through approximately 12,000 pubs, in addition to sales through outlets for off-premise consumption. However, the trading environment in the U.K. was difficult and was expected to remain so; total industry volume in the U.K., for example, had declined one per cent in 1993. Labatt's strategy was to continue to focus its activities on augmenting its strong brand franchises and building a solid pub estate. Labatt had yet to earn an operating profit from its U.K. activities, recording losses of $2-million and $8-million in 1994 and 1993 respectively, although the company was confident that the coming year would reflect improvements.

---

[1] A Winning North American Brewing Partnership, John Labatt Limited, July 1994.

LABATT IN ITALY

Labatt International, a division of Labatt Breweries, began operating in Italy in 1989 when it acquired a 77.5 per cent interest in a joint venture with Birra Moretti S.p.A. of Italy. Birra Moretti, in turn, acquired Prinz Brau S.p.A., another Italian brewery, which was integrated to form the fourth largest brewing group in Italy. In 1992, Labatt acquired the 22.5 per cent minority interest in Birra Moretti to achieve full ownership.

Despite poor industry growth, nationwide discounting by competitors, deepening recession, and successive upsets in Italy's political, economic and industrial environments, Labatt had continued to make sales volume gains in Italy, although earnings had been negative in 1994 and 1993. Its main strategy was to establish a premium position for its brands rather than compete on price simply to gain volume. The company believed that this strategy, which was driven by creative advertising and promotional programs, was proving to be successful, and expected its first operating profit from its activities in Italy in the coming year.

FOMENTO ECONÓMICO MEXICANO, S.A. de C.V. (FEMSA)[2]

FEMSA was a sub-entity of Valores Industriales, S.A., more commonly known as VISA. VISA, Mexico's fifth-largest publicly traded company, was founded in 1890 as Cerveceria Cuauhtémoc. Through the years the brewery expanded into other industries, and in 1936, VISA was created as a holding company to manage the portfolio of enterprises. FEMSA was the result of a consolidation of VISA's food-related activities and was organized into four divisions: Beer, Retail, Coca-Cola FEMSA and Packaging.

The brewing division of FEMSA was a consolidation of two Mexican brewers: Cerveceria Cuauhtémoc and Cerveceria Moctezuma. FEMSA management had proved itself in the mid-1980s when, in the midst of a general economic collapse in Mexico, it had acquired Cerveceria Moctezuma, a Mexican brewer that was experiencing significant financial and operational difficulties. At the same time, however, Grupo Modelo S.A. de C.V. (Modelo), known internationally for its Corona brand, began to compete aggressively on the basis of price. Although FEMSA lost market share to Modelo, by the end of the 1980s both Modelo and FEMSA emerged as the key competitors in the Mexican beer market. FEMSA's accomplishment, and its ability to absorb Moctezuma, led some analysts to suggest that FEMSA's management's experience might be a hidden corporate asset.

Recent Financial Developments

In October 1991, FEMSA's parent Grupo VISA, acquired Bancomer, one of Mexico's largest financial services companies, from the Mexican government for an estimated US$2.8 billion[3].

---

[2] Information for this section is taken from: Annual Report 1993, Fomento Económico Mexicano, S.A. de C.V.; A Winning North American Brewing Partnership, John Labatt Limited, July 1994 (this public document was provided to all Labatt's shareholders and was reported widely in Canada's press); Laboy, Carlos, Special Report: The Mexican Beer Industry, Bear Stearns & Co Inc, New York: February 16, 1994; and Siempre Los Mejores, Edición Especial, Diciembre 1993.

FEMSA was called upon to increase debt significantly to help fund this move. Proceeds from the sale of 49 per cent[4] of Coca-Cola FEMSA, S.A. de C.V. and the sale of 60 per cent of Aguas Minerales, the company's mineral water division, had been used to help pay down the debt. In addition FEMSA issued US$300 million worth of five-year Eurobonds at 9.5 per cent. At the end of fiscal 1993 the company's long-term debt totalled N$2,345-million or US$752.7-million. Of this amount N$1,844-million or 78.6 per cent was denominated in U.S. dollars and German marks[5].

By 1994, the company remained very heavily indebted and was believed to be talking to prospective foreign partners over arrangements, similar to that with its Coca-Cola division, for its packaging and beer subsidiaries. Philip Morris, holder of eight per cent of FEMSA stock, and its subsidiary Miller Brewing, were known to be interested in the beer business.

The chairman of the board of FEMSA, in the 1993 annual report, stated that the company would:

> Continue to pursue our objective of identifying and carrying out strategic joint ventures that will improve our position in the industries and markets where we operated and will open new opportunities for growth.

Exhibit 5 presents financial data for FEMSA for fiscal 1992 and 1993 and segmented financial information for the period 1991 to 1993.

FEMSA CERVEZA AND THE MEXICAN BREWING INDUSTRY

Demand

The Mexican beer market, which was estimated to be 41 million hL in size in 1994, was almost twice as large as Canada's. Unlike the Canadian and U.S. brewing industries, the Mexican beer market had grown in excess of six per cent per annum through the 1980s and early 1990s and was expected to continue to grow at the same rate in the foreseeable future. Improving economic conditions, a young population and lower per capita consumption rates were all factors in this expectation. Key aspects of the Mexican brewing industry are summarized in Exhibit 4.

Competition

The Mexican beer market was essentially a duopoly shared by FEMSA Cerveza (49 per cent) and Grupo Modelo, S.A. de C.V. (Modelo) (51 per cent)[6]. FEMSA had enjoyed a dominant position in the northern and southern regions of the market, while Modelo (known internationally for the Corona brand) had led in the central and Metropolitan Mexico City markets..

---

[3] Poole, Claire, "The Resurrection of Don Eugenio," Forbes, February 17, 1992, p. 106.

[4] Thirty per cent was resold to Coca Cola International and 19 per cent was distributed in a public offering.

[5] Annual Report 1993, Fomento Económico Mexicano, S.A. de C.V., p. 65.

[6] Laboy, Carlos, Special Report: The Mexican Beer Industry, Bear, Stearns & Co. Inc., New York: February 16, 1994, p. 1.

Although FEMSA was considered to be more aggressive than Modelo in expanding its brand portfolio and in the growing non-returnable segment of the market, these moves had yet to improve aggregate market share. Table 2 presents Mexican domestic beer shipments and Mexican beer exports by company.

Table 2: Mexican Domestic Beer Shipments (millions of hL)

	1993	1992	1991	1990	1989	1988
FEMSA	19.1	19.1	18.9	18.7	18.3	15.9
Modelo	20.7	20.0	20.0	18.4	18.1	15.1
TOTAL	39.8	39.1	38.9	37.1	36.4	31.0

Source: ANAFACER

Mexican Beer Exports (millions of hL)

	1993	1992	1991	1990	1989	1988
FEMSA	0.65	0.60	0.68	0.69	0.61	0.70
Modelo	1.85	1.75	1.37	1.41	1.46	1.90
TOTAL	2.50	2.35	2.05	2.10	2.07	2.60

Source: ANAFACER

Over 95 per cent of FEMSA's exports, primarily under the Tecate and Dos Equis brand names, were destined for the U.S. Wisdom Import Sales Co. was acquired by FEMSA in 1986 and was the company's exclusive importer in the U.S. Wisdom distributed FEMSA products throughout the country, although its strength lay in the U.S. south and southwest. FEMSA Cerveza's sales from exports totalled US$56.8-million in 1993, up six per cent from 1992. Export earnings were of particular importance to FEMSA as a hard currency offset to import requirements.

Production and Distribution[7]

FEMSA and Modelo operated production facilities spread throughout the country. FEMSA's production facilities ranged in size from 0.36 million hL to 6.0 million hL, whereas Modelo's ranged in size from 0.5 million hL to its plant in Mexico City that had a production capacity of 11.1 million hL. Between 1988 and 1993, FEMSA had invested US$950-million as part of a capital expenditure program designed to modernize its manufacturing and distribution facilities[8].

The most significant barrier to entry in the Mexican beer market was its distribution system. The nature of the retail system and the prevalence of returnable presentations required far-reaching distribution capabilities. FEMSA and Modelo distributed their product to over 348,000 retailers in Mexico, many of whom (in excess of 80 per cent) had exclusive arrangements with one producer or

---

[7] This section is taken from: Laboy, Carlos, "Special Report: The Mexican Beer Industry," Bear, Stearns & Co. Inc, New York: February 16, 1994, p. 22 - 24.

[8] Annual Report 1993, Fomento Económico Mexicano, S.A. de C.V., p. 6.

the other. Each company also operated its own chain of retail outlets (FEMSA's chain of 700 outlets operated under the name of OXXO). Supermarkets accounted for less than five per cent of total industry sales.

FEMSA's distribution network consisted of 274 wholly-owned distribution centres which operated a fleet of 3,100 trucks and moved 73 per cent of the brewery's volume. In addition, the company's product was also delivered to retailers through 122 franchised third-party distribution outlets which operated 1,500 trucks. Modelo operated in much the same way as FEMSA, with 88 per cent of its product being distributed through 82 majority-owned distributors and the remainder through third-party distributors. In total, Modelo claimed to operate a fleet of 6,379 trucks and service vehicles.

The preceding distribution characteristics made it unlikely that domestic or foreign competitors would be able to independently penetrate the market in a meaningful way in the near future.

Government

The primary influence of the Mexican government on the brewing industry was in the form of pricing controls. Price wars between the two brewers throughout the 1980s and then the inclusion of beer as food in the *Pacto de Solidaridad Económica (Pacto)*[9] introduced in December, 1987, had resulted in real producer beer prices being fixed at levels about 35 per cent below pre-price-war levels. Most recently there had been a modest improvement in the real price of beer.

The number of retail outlets authorized to sell beer was regulated by the Mexican government through licenses which were granted to beer producers which, in turn, authorized specific dealers to carry their products under their permits. This practice further reinforced the closed nature of the Mexican beer distribution system.

CONSIDERATIONS IN A LABATT-FEMSA PARTNERSHIP

In a series of discussions with FEMSA management Labatt management had formulated a provisional approach to link the two companies. It called for Labatt to purchase a 22 per cent interest in FEMSA Cerveza for $720 million (US$510 million), with an option to acquire an additional eight per cent position within three years. Further, it called for a cooperative approach in exchanging skills and experience and jointly exploiting the U.S. market. The parameters of this approach had been set by a valuation[10] that Labatt thought was reasonable, a share position that was meaningful and within the capacity of Labatt to finance, and the need to establish a relationship with FEMSA Cerveza managers that would be of value to all parties in the future. Labatt understood that Philip Morris/Miller and perhaps other suitors were also interested in FEMSA Cerveza, but were of the view that Labatt's cooperative approach and provisions for partnering in operations were of significant interest to the FEMSA executives.

---

[9] The Pacto was an agreement among government, industry and labour which froze wages, prices and the exchange rate. It was designed to fight against inflation.

[10] This valuation was reported to be consistent with valuations derived from trading and initial public offering (IPO) multiples of Latin American brewers and consumer products companies believed to form FEMSA-Cerveza's "peer" group and it was believed to be consistent with the price paid by Anheuser-Busch for its 17.7 per cent stake in Grupo Modelo.

The corporate structure envisaged in the approach is presented in Exhibit 6. Under this structure:

- FEMSA would continue to hold 51 per cent of FEMSA Cerveza, and 19 per cent of the division's equity would be earmarked for sale at an appropriate time in the Mexican and international equity markets.
- FEMSA would appoint the chairman and Labatt the vice-chairman of FEMSA Cerveza; the board would comprise 11 FEMSA nominees, five Labatt nominees and two public members. The current FEMSA Cerveza chief executive officer would retain his position, although he would now be advised by a six-person management committee consisting of three FEMSA and three Labatt members.
- In Mexico, the partners would jointly select the best portfolio of U.S. and imported brands for market development. All of Labatt's Canadian, U.S. and European brands and brewing technology would be made available to FEMSA Cerveza. Labatt would also bring its brand management skills to Mexico, where Labatt executives believed the company's experience in "pull" marketing in diverse cultural markets would produce significant results.
- In the U.S., Labatt USA and Wisdom (FEMSA's U.S. import company) would be merged into a U.S. specialty beer company. Labatt would hold a 51 per cent position in this entity, FEMSA would hold 30 per cent, and the remaining 19 per cent would go to additional partners when appropriate.

The merged entity would be managed jointly by both companies and would give each company access to the other's wholesaler and distribution networks (Labatt had traditionally been strong in the U.S. northeast, and FEMSA in the U.S. south and southwest). Both partners would work together to seek and develop additional quality, specialty brands that would complement their own brands in order to achieve faster growth in the U.S.

- In Canada, Labatt would position a portfolio of FEMSA Cerveza's brands throughout the country, aiming to become the leading Canadian importer of Mexican beer.

If the partnership proposal was successful, plans were to finance it through cash on hand of $300 million, drawdown of a bank loan facility by $300 million, and issuance of commercial paper of $100 million. The bank loan facility would be new and involve a revolving extendable facility at floating rates with a minimum term of three years, and could be drawn in U.S. or Canadian dollars.

Labatt management thought that one of the important considerations in the investment was the currency risk of both the Canadian dollar and the Mexican peso. Historically, Mexico had been subject to significant inflation and currency devaluation. For this reason, in putting together its proposal, Labatt assumed that inflation in Mexico would be 5 per cent higher per annum than U.S. inflation and that the peso would devalue by 5 per cent per annum.

POLITICAL DEVELOPMENTS IN MEXICO

On January 1, 1994, the day that the North American Free Trade Agreement (NAFTA) took effect, Indian peasants in the southern state of Chiapas had risen in armed rebellion. Led by the Zapatista

National Liberation Army (EZLN), the Indians claimed that they had been cheated of their land, denied basic services and had had their culture eroded. Many people claimed that the roots of the rebellion lay in poverty, racial discrimination and the failure of regional and social policy. Others claimed that Guatemalan guerrillas were behind the situation and were using it to destabilize Mexico.

On March 23, shortly after the uprising in the state of Chiapas appeared to have been brought under control, Luis Donaldo Colosio, the presidential candidate for the PRI party, was shot at a rally in Tijuana. In the days that followed, many stories emerged in the press suggesting that the assassination might have been conceived by ultra-conservatives within the PRI party who were allegedly opposed to the economic and political reforms that Colosio was promising to continue if he were elected[11].

On March 28, Ernesto Zedillo, Mexico's former education minister, accepted the presidential candidacy for the PRI. Many people in the country questioned the political skills and abilities of Zedillo because of the previous bureaucratic positions he had held and the limited time available for him to prepare for the position of president. This widespread concern gave rise to speculation that one of Mexico's two other national political parties might be elected to power, although neither had any experience in running the country. Presidential elections were scheduled for August, 1994.

Many investors were concerned with events in Mexico: Chiapas, bombings in Mexico City, kidnappings, and the assassination of the presidential candidate. By April 1994, the peso had been devalued to 8 per cent below its January level and interest rates had been raised to 18 per cent, double the figure of two months before.

Appendix B contains economic data on Mexico and a brief discussion of the country's political and economic history.

CONCLUSION

As he worked through the various aspects of the proposal to partner with FEMSA, George Taylor continued to ask himself the same question. Was it or was it not a sound move in furthering Labatt's future as a global brewer?

Appendix A: PHILIP MORRIS/MILLER BREWING DESCRIPTION

Philip Morris Companies Inc. was the world's largest consumer packaged goods company. Tobacco products which accounted for 43 per cent of Philip Morris' operating revenues in 1993 and 1992, food products, beer, and financial services and real estate represented the company's significant segments. Philip Morris owned Kraft Foods, the second largest food business in the U.S. after ConAgra, and Miller Brewing, the world's third largest beer producer after Anheuser-Busch and Heineken. A summary of Philip Morris' segmented results for the most recent three years is presented below:

---

[11] "Mexico's whodunit," The Economist, New York: October 15, 1994, p. 53.

Consolidated Operating Results (US$ millions)

(Year Ended December 31)

	Operating Revenues			Identifiable Assets[12]		
	1993	**1992**	**1991**	**1993**	**1992**	**1991**
Tobacco	25,973	25,677	23,840	9,523	9,479	8,648
Food	30,372	29,048	28,178	33,253	32,672	31,622
Beer	4,154	3,976	4,056	1,706	1,545	1,608
Financial Services and Real Estate	402	430	384	5,659	5,297	4,538
Other				1,064	1,021	968
TOTAL	60,901	59,131	56,458	51,205	50,014	47,384

	Operating Profit (US$ millions)		
	1993	**1992**	**1991**
Tobacco	4,910	7,193	6,463
Food	2,608	2,769	2,016
Beer	215	258	299
Financial Services and Real Estate	249	219	178
Less: Unallocated Corporate Expenses	395	380	334
OPERATING PROFIT	9,449	7,587	10,059

Miller Brewing was the second-largest brewer in the U.S. The brewer's primary brands were: Miller Lite, which was the largest selling reduced calories beer and second largest selling beer in the United States in 1993; Miller High Life; and Miller Genuine Draft which was one of the fastest growing premium beers in the U.S. Based on the company's estimates of beer shipments in the U.S., and the industry's sales of beer and brewed non-alcoholic beverages, Miller reported that its share of the industry had remained relatively stable since 1991, as per the following:

	1994[13]	1993	1992	1991
Miller's Share of the Industry	22.7%	22.2%	21.4%	22.2%

Source: Philip Morris Companies Inc. Annual Report 1993

---

[12]Identifiable assets are those assets applicable to the respective industry segments.

[13] Estimate based on year-to-date figures.

Appendix B: MEXICO'S ECONOMY - HISTORICAL PERSPECTIVE

Before it joined the General Agreement on Tariffs and Trade (GATT) in 1986, Mexico was an inward-looking country. The protection of domestic industry was the main principle underlying all government economic policy. If a product could be manufactured in Mexico, it was, even if it was more expensive and of lower quality than similar products available internationally. The Mexican government implemented several economic policy tools to ensure the achievement of this goal. High tariffs (often over 100 per cent), restrictions on foreign ownership and investment, import permits, and export requirements, succeeded in dampening foreign interest in Mexico.

From 1958 to 1970, Mexico thrived. The country's gross domestic product (GDP) grew at an average annual rate of approximately 6.8 per cent, with GDP per capita growth of 3.2 per cent annually. Consumer price inflation over the same period averaged only 2.9 per cent per year. The ratios of public-sector deficits and public external debt to GDP were low and stable, and real interest rates were positive. During this period neither the current-account deficit nor the balance of payments exceeded 3 per cent of GDP.

According to the statistics, all should have been well in Mexico. Unfortunately, this was not the case. Wealth in the country was very unevenly distributed. To correct this inequity and to reduce the widespread poverty in Mexico, President Echeverría (1970-76) and his successor, President López Portillo (1976–82) attempted to increase the country's economic growth by pursuing a policy of higher government expenditure. In theory, such a policy would:

> Permit a more plentiful "trickle down" to those on the lowest incomes; higher public expenditure, and, in particular, higher welfare spending and transfer payments, would soften the rigours of an inegalitarian system.[14]

Increased government spending throughout the 1970s and early 1980s was financed through foreign borrowing. The discovery of the large Capecha oil fields in the State of Chiapas in the late 1970s allowed the government to intensify its expenditures by borrowing more furiously from foreign banks that were ready and anxious to lend money to Mexico because they anticipated rising oil revenues for the country.

When oil prices began to fall in the early 1980s, the Mexican economy was destabilized with large increases in inflation and the current account deficit. Under pressure from the international financial community, the Mexican government responded with severe import restrictions and high domestic interest rates.

In 1982, investors, anticipating a devaluation of the currency, moved out of pesos into more stable currencies. This put strains on the government as it used foreign currency reserves to maintain the country's fixed exchange rates. Oil prices softened further, the global recession peaked, interest rates increased, and private capital in international markets disappeared. On August 15, 1982, the Mexican government announced that it was no longer able to meet its interest obligations on its US$88 billion foreign debt. The government signed an agreement with the International Monetary Fund (IMF) that rescued the country, but forced it to introduce a program of economic reforms. Public expenditures were reduced, taxes were increased and some small public

---

[14] The Economist Intelligence Unit, "Mexico: Country Profile," (New York: Business International Limited, 1992), p. 10.

service enterprises were closed. Exchange controls were abolished, and the currency was devalued by over 100 per cent. Prices for public services and administered prices (for foodstuffs) were brought into line with production costs or international prices. The group who suffered most was Mexico's middle class. Real wages fell and savings were all but wiped out. Unlike Mexico's elite class, this group did not have the luxury of investing abroad in order to insulate their savings from currency devaluations.

The debt crisis of 1982 forced Mexico to abandon its inward-looking policies of protection and state regulation in favour of new policies that stressed a more outward-focused development strategy that would be led by the private sector.

The results from 1983-85 showed a resumption in real growth and a decrease in inflation from over 90 per cent in 1982-83 to approximately 60 per cent in the following two years. The public sector deficit as a share of GDP was halved. The fall in the real exchange rate stimulated export growth and reduced the level of imports from US$25 billion in 1981 to US$9 billion 1983. From 1985-87, real GDP fell to 3 per cent and inflation accelerated to over 130 per cent. Oil prices softened and Mexico neared crisis once again. A new debt repayment plan was introduced by the IMF that tied Mexico's debt repayment schedule to the health of the country's economy.

Upon assuming office on December 1, 1988, President Carlos Salinas de Gortari introduced the first of what was to become a series of pacts among government, labour and employers' organizations. The intention of these pacts was to reduce inflation without causing a recession. These pacts used publicly controlled prices, minimum wages and the nominal exchange rate as the tools to eliminate the economic distortions that had led to inflation in the past. Fiscal and credit policies were tightened and a more equitable tax system was introduced. Tariffs were reduced, as was the number of products subject to import licenses. Another significant element of the government's strategy to curb inflation was a reduction in the money supply growth rate. In 1982, when foreign capital disappeared, the Mexican government borrowed from domestic banks. After 1988, government borrowing was done predominantly through bonds.

In 1989, the Salinas government introduced its National Development Plan (1989-94), which committed the government to the liberalization of foreign trade and investment policies. These changes were intended to force Mexican enterprises to introduce stricter efficiency standards and new technologies in an effort to render Mexican products more competitive in domestic and world markets. The government sought foreign investment as a means of complementing domestic capital in this plant modernization process. It introduced a new tax policy that protected the lowest income groups without adversely affecting public finances. Finally, it introduced subsidy policies that were intended to increase the purchasing power of the needy.

The Salinas government appeared to have ushered in a new era of improved performance of the Mexican economy. Inflation fell from 52 per cent in 1988 to approximately 7 per cent in the first seven months of 1994. Most of the fall was attributed to the government's wage and price restraints and its trade liberalization policies that culminated in the North American Free Trade Agreement (NAFTA) which came into effect on January 1, 1994. The public sector deficit was reduced from 12.5 per cent of GDP in 1988 to a surplus of 0.1 per cent of GDP in 1993. A reduction in interest rates through the liberalization of markets and lifting of interest controls and cash reserves had also had a positive influence on the economy.

The country's current account deficit, fuelled by growth in imports which led to a merchandise trade deficit (1993 US$13 billion, 1994 estimated at US$18 billion) was expected to be US$27.8 billion or 8 per cent of GDP in 1994. While foreign capital inflows had acted to cover the shortfall, the bulk of these inward flows had been in the form of portfolio investment, money going to both the stock market and to government securities such as Treasury Certificates (CETES), both of which were intrinsically volatile and were required to offer high rates of return in order to continue to attract capital inflows and avoid capital outflows.

Purchasing Power Parity Estimates of GNP

Country	PPP estimates of GNP per capita United States = 100		Current International dollars[15]
	1987	**1992**	**1992**
Mexico	31.6	32.4	7,490
Canada	91.0	85.3	19,720
United States	100	100	23,120

Source: World Development Report 1994: Infrastructure for Development, The World Bank

---

[15] The "international dollar" has the same purchasing power over total GNP as the US dollar in a give year.

Exhibit 1: **John Labatt Limited Consolidated Statement of Earnings**[16]
(Millions of Canadian dollars)

Year Ended April 30	1994	1993	1992	1991	1990	1989	1988
Net Sales	2,321	2,135	3,837	4,760	4,681	4,857	4,611
Operating Costs	2,085	1,896	3,562	4,602	4,450	4,661	4,390
Earnings before Interest, Income Taxes and Restructuring Charges	292	274	301	199	264	263	295
Income Taxes	85	64	37	50	72	57	85
Earnings before share in Partly Owned Business	151	130	93	108	159	129	142
Net Earnings	155	(70)[17]	101	109	169	135	141

John Labatt Limited Consolidated Balance Sheet[18]
(Millions of Canadian Dollars)

ASSETS

Year Ended April 30	1994	1993	1992	1991	1990	1989	1988
Current Assets	1,102	1,187	1,634	1,234	1,184	1,227	964
Fixed Assets less Depreciation	813	784	1,027	1,257	1,181	1,002	992
Other Assets	621	597	520	647	581	528	582
TOTAL ASSETS	2,536	3,020	3,320	3,138	2,946	2,757	2,538

LIABILITIES

Year Ended April 30	1994	1993	1992	1991	1990	1989	1988
Current Liabilities	721	932	836	913	628	683	736
Non-Convertible Long-term Debt	610	630	646	416	544	533	482
Deferred Income Taxes	86	141	90	133	130	143	162
Convertible Debentures and Shareholders' Equity	1,119	1,317	1,748	1,676	1,644	1,398	1,158
TOTAL LIABILITIES	2,536	3,020	3,320	3,138	2,946	2,757	2,538

Source: John Labatt Limited, Annual Reports 1988 - 1994.

---

[16] Over the period 1988 to 1993, John Labatt divested itself of several of its businesses. This explains the significant drop in net sales over the period.

[17] In 1993, John Labatt incurred a loss from discontinued operations of C$ 203 - million as a result of provisions for estimated future liabilities from businesses sold in prior years, and a provision to write down the assets of its U.S. dairy business.

[18] Over the period 1988 to 1993, John Labatt divested itself of several of its businesses. This explains the significant drop in net sales over the period.

Exhibit 2: **Segmented Financial Results John Labatt Limited**

	1994	1993	1992	1991	1990	1989	1988
Net Sales (Millions of C$)							
Brewing	1,769	1,672	1,564	2,043	1,920	1,818	1,633
BS&E[19]	630	--	--	--	--	--	--
Entertainment	--	546	374	--	--	--	--
Dairy	--	--	2,110	--	--	--	--
Food	--	--	--	3,327	3,354	3,606	--
Agri Products	--	--	--	--	--	--	2,450
Packaged Food	--	--	--	--	--	--	1,024
Earnings Before Interest, Restructuring Charges and Income Taxes (Millions of C$)							
Brewing	260	218	181	109	174	157	140
BS&E	32	--	--	--	--	--	--
Entertainment	--	56	58	--	--	--	--
Dairy	--	--	62	--	--	--	--
Food	--	--	--	90	90	106	--
Agri Products	--	--	--	--	--	--	91
Packaged Food	--	--	--	--	--	--	64
Capital Expenditures (Millions of C$)							
Brewing	103	191	122	104	98	78	77
BS&E	20	--	--	--	--	--	--
Entertainment	--	12	5	--	--	--	--
Dairy	--	--	45	--	--	--	--
Food	--	--	--	87	108	160	--
Agri Products	--	--	--	--	--	--	71
Packaged Food	--	--	--	--	--	--	61
Net Assets Employed (Millions of C$)							
Brewing	960	1,146	799	727	717	516	527
BS&E	308	--	--	--	--	--	--
Entertainment	--	283	140	--	--	--	--
Dairy	--	--	629	--	--	--	--
Food	--	--	--	1,319	1,233	1,110	--
Agri Products	--	--	--	--	--	--	657
Packaged Food	--	--	--	--	--	--	651
Stock Price	**1994**	**1993**	**1992**	**1991**	**1990**	**1989**	**1988**
High	26.25	30.38	27.88	26.00	27.50	24.38	29.75
Low	20.50	24.25	22.25	18.38	20.50	20.63	20.13
Dividend Record (C$ per share)	0.82	3.82	0.795	0.77	0.73	0.685	0.62
Dividend Record (millions of C$)	88	344[20]	83	84	73	50.6	45.5
Dividend as % of Net Profits	56.8	NA	82.2	77.1	43.2	37.5	32.4

Source: John Labatt Limited, Annual Reports 1988 – 1994

---

[19] BS&E is an abbreviation for the Broadcast, Sports and Entertainment division.

[20] Large dividend payout to shareholders as a result of the sale of Labatt's food-related assets.

Exhibit 3: North American Brewing Alliances 1994

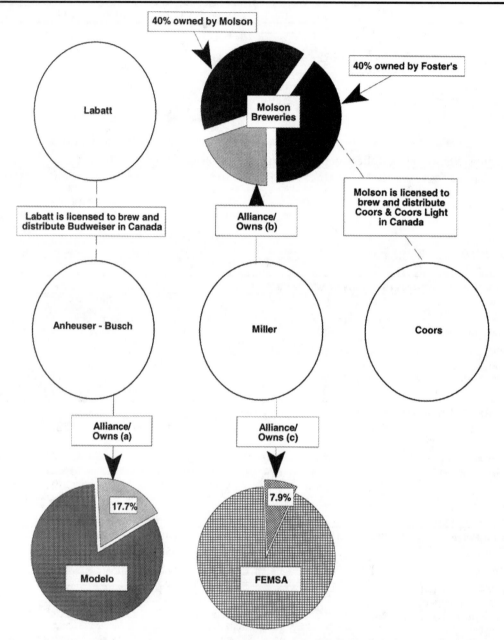

Exhibit 4: Key Aspects of the North American Brewing Industry

	CANADA	UNITED STATES	MEXICO
DEMAND			
Market size (millions hl)	21	237	41
Market growth	Flat	Flat	+6.0%
Per capita consumption (litres)	78.3	87.4	44.2
COMPETITION			
Market structure	Duopoly	Mass market	Duopoly
Market share (major brewers)	Labatt Breweries (44.2%) Molson Breweries (48.9%)	Anheuser-Busch (46%) Miller Brewing (23%) Coors Brewing (11%)	FEMSA Cerveza (49%) Modelo Cerveza (51%)
Market share (imports)	2.9%	4.4%	Less than 1%
National vs regional brands	Both	Focus on national	Both
Avg. brewery size (millions hl)	1.24	3.0	3.90
Market strategy	• Limited price competition • Some new product introduction	• Price competition • Some niche-targeted products	• Price competition • Controlled distribution system • Some market segmentation and limited attempts to use marketing to develop brand awareness
DISTRIBUTION			
Characteristics	• Owned stores or regulated retail outlets except in Québec (grocery stores were permitted to sell beer) and Newfoundland (corner stores and privately owned liquor stores were permitted to sell beer)	• In most states beer was distributed through a free enterprise system based on wholesalers and distributors, with supermarkets as the main retail outlet	• Beer was sold through government authorized retail outlets. Distribution was most significant barrier to entry in the Mexican brewing industry. FEMSA and Modelo distributed their products to over 348,000 retail outlets throughout Mexico of which over 80 per cent had exclusive arrangements with one of the two brewers. FEMSA and Modelo operated distribution fleets of 3,100 and 6,400 vehicles respectively
GOVERNMENT			
Bottle/can ratio	80:20	30:70	78:22
Tax (per cent of retail price)	53	18	22 to 25
Involvement in the industry	• Where beer could be sold and imposed constraints on pricing such as minimum price mark-ups, minimum allowable prices and uniform pricing throughout a province. Provincial governments regulated the sale of beer	• Packaging and labeling requirements in some states that favoured U.S. producers	• Pricing controls through PACTO, an agreement between business, labour and governments that limited wage and price increases. The government also regulated the number of retail outlets permitted to sell beer through licenses that it granted to beer producers who, in turn, authorized specific dealers to carry their products

Exhibit 5: Financial Statements, Fomento Económico Mexicano, S.A. de C.V. and Subsidiaries (Millions of New Pesos (N$), Millions of US$)

CONSOLIDATED INCOME STATEMENT

Year Ended December 31	1993		1992	
	N$	US$	N$	US$
Sales	7,571	2,430	7,090	2,275
Gross Profit	3,515	1,128	3,122	1,002
Operating expenses:	2,718	872	2,382	764
Income from operations	777	249	710	227
Income tax, tax on assets and employee profit sharing	348	111	359	115
Income before extraordinary items	243	78	289	93
Net income for the year	684[21]	219	552	117

CONSOLIDATED STATEMENT OF FINANCIAL POSITION

Year Ended December 31	1993		1992	
ASSETS	N$	US$	N$	US$
Current Assets:	1,895	608	1,832	588
Investments and Other Assets:	21	6	42	13
Property, Plant and Equipment:	7,981	2,561	7,711	2,474
Other	226	72	139	44
TOTAL ASSETS	10,123	3,247	9,724	3,119

Year Ended December 31	1993		1992	
LIABILITIES	N$	US$	N$	US$
Current Liabilities:	1,226	394	1,718	551
Long-Term Liabilities:	2,345	753	2,679	860
Other Liabilities:	437	139	453	146
Stockholders' Equity:	6,115	1,963	4,874	1,564
TOTAL LIABILITIES AND STOCKHOLDERS' EQUITY	10,123	3,249	9,724	3,121

Source: Annual Report 1993, Fomento Económico Mexicano, S.A. de C.V.

NOTE: Mexican peso figures for 1992 and 1993 have been restated in US dollars using 1993 average annual exchange rate, because 1992 figures were restated in terms of the purchasing power of the Mexican peso as of 1993 yearend. This practice was commonly referred to as 'Accounting for Change Price Levels.'

---

[21] In 1993 the sale of Coca-Cola FEMSA shares resulted in N$353 - million gain that was recorded as an extraordinary item.

Exhibit 5: **Segmented Financial Information, Fomento Económico Mexicano, S.A. de C.V. (Millions of Average New Pesos (N$), Millions of US$)**

	1993		1992		1991	
	N$	US$	N$	US$	N$	US$
Sales						
Tbrewing	4,089	1,312	4,072	1,306	4,077	1,308
Retail	1,061	340	872	279	737	236
Coca-cola Femsa	1,838	589	1,601	513	1,468	471
Packaging	1,214	389	1,104	354	1,056	339
Operating Profit						
Brewing	449	144	443	142	438	140
Retail	20	6	31	10	25	8
Coca-cola Femsa	277	88	247	79	230	73
Packaging	187	60	156	50	142	45
Cash Flow from Operations						
Brewing	379	121	504	161	459	147
Retail	14	4	30	9	25	8
Coca-cola Femsa	245	78	181	58	199	63
Packaging	194	62	175	56	171	54
Total Assets						
Brewing	6,542	2,099	6,196	1,988	5,950	1,909
Retail	396	127	366	177	230	73
Coca-cola Femsa	1,384	444	1,172	376	1,024	328
Packaging	1,440	462	1,327	425	1,268	407

Source: Annual Report 1993, Fomento Económico Mexicano, S.A. de C.V.

NOTE: Mexican peso figures for 1991, 1992 and 1993 have been restated in US dollars using 1993 average annual exchange rate, because 1991 and 1992 figures were restated in terms of the purchasing power of the Mexican peso as of 1993 yearend. This practice was commonly referred to as 'Accounting for Change Price Levels.'

Exhibit 6: **Envisaged Labatt/FEMSA Partnership Structure**

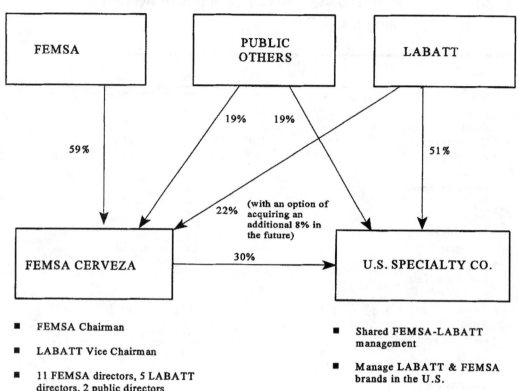

- FEMSA Chairman

- LABATT Vice Chairman

- 11 FEMSA directors, 5 LABATT directors, 2 public directors

- Current FEMSA Cervesa CEO, retains leadership role

- CEO advised by 6 member management committee (3 FEMSA, 3 LABATT)

- LABATT-FEMSA management interchange program

- Shared FEMSA-LABATT management

- Manage LABATT & FEMSA brands in the U.S.

- Utilize LABATT USA and Wisdom existing management & distribution network

- Utilize LABATT USA's and Wisdom's national wholesaler and distribution presence

- Jointly seek other brands for portfolio

Source: <u>A Winning North American Brewing Partnership</u>, John Labatt Limited, July 1994

TROJAN TECHNOLOGIES INC.: THE CHINA OPPORTUNITY

case 26

Ruihua Jiang
Pratima Bansal and
Paul Beamish

In August 1999, Sarah Brown, senior market associate of Trojan Technologies of London, Ontario, reflected on the water shortages anticipated in developing countries as a result of their explosive economic growth. Trojan sold water disinfection equipment, and Sarah's job was to find new areas for growth. China was particularly intriguing because it had as much water as Canada but 40 times the population, and its economic boom would further stress current water resources. Given Trojan's high growth expectations, China offered an enormous opportunity. Sarah knew little of China: how decisions were made for water disinfection equipment, whether Trojan's patents would be protected, what level of resources would be required, etc.. Her task in new market development was to

IVEY

The Richard Ivey School of Business gratefully acknowledges the generous support of The Richard and Jean Ivey Fund in the development of this case as part of the RICHARD AND JEAN IVEY FUND ASIAN CASE SERIES.

Ruihua Jiang prepared this case under the supervision of Professors Pratima Bansal and Paul Beamish solely to provide material for class discussion. The author does not intend to illustrate either effective or ineffective handling of a managerial situation. The author may have disguised certain names and other identifying information to protect confidentiality.

determine if Trojan should enter China, and if so, when, where and how. Ralph Brady, the vice president of New Business Development, wanted to see her recommendations within the month.

TROJAN TECHNOLOGIES INC: MORE THAN "LIGHT IN A PIPE"

An Overview of Trojan

Located in London, Ontario, Canada, Trojan Technologies Inc. started with a staff of three in 1977. Its original technology was based on a pioneering patent on an ultraviolet (UV) water disinfection system. The idea was simple — often referred to as "light in a pipe" — but its implementation embodied complex engineering, science and technology. Banks of UV light tubes were installed inside an open water channel constructed of either concrete or metal. As water flowed through the channel, the high-intensity UV light destroyed the DNA structures of the microorganisms in the water so the risk of disease would be eliminated.

There were two major applications of UV technology. One was to disinfect the wastewater discharged into receiving waters. Applications included primary, secondary and tertiary treatment for industrial, commercial and municipal waste treatment processes. The other was to disinfect incoming clean water. Applications included household drinking water supplies, municipal drinking water treatment plants, industrial product and process water requirements, and commercial applications (See Exhibit 1).

As UV technologies became more accepted as an environmentally responsible and cost-effective replacement for the widely used chemical disinfection methods, Trojan had posted an annual compound revenue growth rate of 27 per cent since 1989, and 36 per cent since 1994. In 1998, Trojan was a TSE 300 company, employing about 400 employees, with annual sales reaching almost $70 million. As a world leader in ultraviolet water disinfection technology and the world's largest supplier of ultraviolet disinfection systems for municipal wastewater applications, Trojan now had some 2,000 UV systems in operation around the world, treating in excess of six billion gallons of water per day.

In 1998, the company approved a five-year strategic plan, which projected a continued growth rate of at least 30 per cent for the following five years. By 2003, the annual sales were expected to reach over $300 million and total employment more than 1,000.

To achieve the goal, Trojan was actively looking for growth opportunities. Trojan decided to increase its investment in the clean water market. Currently, 95 per cent of Trojan's business was in the wastewater market. The clean water business' five per cent contribution was marginal. However, recent research results showed that UV could destroy giardia and crytosporidium in municipal drinking water supplies, which further enhanced its competitiveness in the clean water market. Giardia and crytosporidium are responsible for waterborne outbreaks causing diarrheal infections, and are resistant against chlorine.

In the same year, Trojan obtained the exclusive worldwide licence for an innovative photocatalytic technology used in air treatment applications. The Air 2000 system using the technology won the 1998 Environmental Technology Innovator Award in the U.S., and had similar features to Trojan's UV water systems, i.e., they were both more environmentally-positive and cost-effective substitutes for current treatment technologies.

Trojan was also looking to expand geographically, especially to new markets with legal regulations and standards regarding discharging water and clean water. One potential market being evaluated was Asia, especially the world's most populous country — China. Trojan made a breakthrough sale of a \$4.5-million System UV4000™ water disinfection unit to Hong Kong in 1999, after a few smaller installations there. In the same year, Trojan shipped seven industrial clean water units to Mainland China through a Chinese-owned company in the U.S. Sales had also been made to Thailand, Indonesia, the Philippines, Taiwan and Korea.

The Product Market

Water disinfection was usually the last step in water treatment, following other physical, chemical or biological purification processes, killing the organisms, viruses, bacteria in the effluents from primary and secondary treatment. Three water disinfection methods were commonly known: ozone, chlorine, and UV. Chlorine was the most commonly used in the world, accounting for over 80 per cent of the market. Chlorine offered a residual disinfection effect that lasted after treatment point, and could prevent the growth of algae and slime in pipes and tanks, a feature that was important when the water supply and sewage systems were dated and leaking. However, chlorine could combine with the residual elements in the treated water and create new environmentally harmful and potentially carcinogenic compounds which often resulted in facilities installing dechlorination equipment to reduce chlorination by-products. Also, chlorine must be handled and transported cautiously as spills were toxic. Therefore, it was under considerable scrutiny in Europe and North America.

In contrast to the traditional chlorination method, UV technology had the advantage of being environmentally positive. It did not add anything to the water or change its chemistry, nor did it use dangerous additives or leave chemical residues harmful to plant and marine life. It was also more efficient, treating water instantly. Chlorination required contact time so large contact tanks needed to be constructed. The relative capital cost of UV and chlorine depended on the cost of labor and land, the size of the facility and the need for dechlorination equipment. Generally, operating and maintenance costs were lower for UV, offering a better net present value in the life of the equipment (see Exhibit 2). The major ongoing costs of UV units are the electric power consumption and lamp replacements. The UV units also required limited space for installation, which was important to large metropolitan areas, where land costs could be high. The Water Environment Research Foundation funded research in 1995 to compare UV and chlorination. The research confirmed the environmental and economic advantages of UV technology, and predicted that, as existing chlorine facilities concluded the end of their useful life, many would be replaced with UV systems.

For both the wastewater and clean water market, roughly four segments could be identified: (1) the municipal; (2) the industrial; (3) the commercial (dealing with the discharges from and the water supplies for office buildings, hotels, restaurants, shopping malls, etc.); (4) the residential. Trojan could supply products for all the four segments in both clean and wastewater markets. However, the municipal wastewater market was the most important revenue source for Trojan. A UV disinfection system typically accounted for about four per cent of the total cost of a municipal water treatment plant.

Trojan had about 80 per cent of the world's UV wastewater treatment market. Trojan's 1998 annual report estimated "that only 5% to 10% of municipal wastewater sites in North America use

UV-based technology . . . (and) of the approximate 62,000 wastewater treatment facilities operating worldwide, only 2,500 currently utilize UV disinfection systems".

Trojan's UV units vary considerably in price. A small residential unit could range from $200 to $1,000. Commercial and industrial units could be as high as $100,000, while municipal units could cost several million dollars. The cost of the unit would depend on the volume and the quality of water (both in and out).

International Presence

Most of Trojan's sales were made through its 90-plus agents scattered around the world. The agents worked on commission. By leveraging their relationships with major project design and contractor companies in their territories, these agents could influence the type of disinfection technology that was used in the project. When the customer, such as the municipal government, made the decision, it was important that the customer be familiar with UV technology. In Hong Kong, for instance, Trojan initially sold a few small installations, which convinced the government officials to install a larger system because of the advantages of UV systems.

So far Trojan's development had been focused in North America and Europe. Because of the greater interest in and financial resources for environmental protection, this area accounted for 80 per cent of the world's total water treatment market, of which North America had about 55 per cent, and Western Europe about 24 per cent. Although industry experts estimated that the annual growth rate for these developed areas would slow down to less than five per cent in the coming years, replacement of chlorine systems would fuel growth in UV. However, as these markets matured, competition was escalating and profit margins thinning. Furthermore, technology regulations and customer preferences could change rapidly in these markets. In addition to their London, Ontario head office, Trojan had branch offices in The Hague, Netherlands, California, U.S.A., Australia and UK. In 1998, out of a total of 1,975 wastewater installations worldwide, 1,526 were in the U.S., 227 in Canada, 64 in Europe, 34 in South America, 82 in Asia, and 34 in Australia and New Zealand.

Human Resources

UV systems required very little maintenance. Usually one Trojan staff person was enough to help with the installation and the training of local staff. Trojan's London staff could often assist in maintenance of the units through verbal instructions. Only occasionally would on-site repair be required.

Currently, the company did not have personnel experienced with the Chinese water disinfection market and Chinese business practices. There were five engineers working in the R & D department, however, who were originally from Mainland China. None of them had a business or marketing background and none of them were in management positions.

Competitive Pressure

As the pioneering leader in ultraviolet water treatment technologies, Trojan had been able to thrive with the growing demand for the UV technology without facing much competition. However, the market had become increasingly competitive in the past two years. On June 29, 1999, the company announced lower than expected earnings for the fiscal year, citing competitive pressures, increased product development, and patent litigation as reasons behind the earnings disappointment. The next day its share price plummeted from $38.80 to $27.10. Trojan's main competitors in UV technology were Wedeco in Germany, and Infilco Degremont and Calgon Carbon in the U.S. To Trojan's knowledge, none had entered China. However, Trojan also faced competition from manufacturers of chlorine-based disinfection systems, where numerous companies existed. The most powerful players were the full-service water treatment companies, who could provide a complete set of services from consulting, to design, to installation and maintenance.

The company had responded to the competitive challenge with a series of strategic moves. One was to accelerate the development of next-generation technologies; the other was to launch a comprehensive cost engineering program. The strategic moves, together with the patent litigation discussed in detail below, would nevertheless incur increased costs for the short term.

Trojan had also made some significant investments recently. In 1998, Trojan acquired Sunwater Limited of U.K. and spent $2.8 million in purchasing a 39-acre property for future expansion. Additional capital expenditures were expected in support of company growth. In the same year, Trojan issued 700,000 common shares for gross proceeds of $21.7 million. In 1998, the net debt equity ratio stood at 0.53:1, compared to 0.20:1 in 1997.

Exhibits 3 and 4 provide the financial statements of Trojan Technologies Inc.

Intellectual Property Protection

Trojan was built on patented technologies. As a high-tech enterprise, Trojan spent heavily on research and development. The management believed that continued development of proprietary, state-of-the-art technologies were critical to maintaining a competitive edge in an increasingly competitive environment. However, direct and indirect imitation of its patented technologies would seriously hurt its business and damage the return on its investment in R&D.

The raw materials for the UV systems were concrete channels, metal reactors, pipes, UV lamps, and electronic components. Many of the components were made of stainless steel and manufactured in a Trojan subsidiary in London, Ontario. These parts were all standard and easily available. The single most important input were the patented ballasts. These circuits were designed for each unit and ensured superior effectiveness and reliability of the UV lamps. As well, Trojan offered unique knowledge by custom-designing each unit to the quality and volume of water at the site.

Trojan's management was constantly on the watch for any possible loss of intellectual property. In January 1999, Trojan initiated patent infringement action in the U.S., accusing Calgon Carbon Corporation, Calgon Carbon Canada, Inc. and the City of Hinesville, Georgia of infringing Trojan's U.S. Patent for a fluid purification device based on its System UV4000™ technology. The action intended to seek damages and an injunction against further infringement and also showed Trojan's determination to defend its patent rights in the world.

THE CHINA OPPORTUNITY

The Environmental Protection Market in China

China's economy had been growing at double-digit speed since its 1979 reforms. However, the development had come at the cost of the environment. By taxing environmental resources such as air, land and water, its economic growth was constrained. China's population was 1.2 billion and was expected to grow to 1.5 billion by 2020 at the current rate. Already, 60 million were without sufficient clean water for their needs. Arguably, the additional people would further tax water resources which would mean further deterioration of coastal and inland waters so that drinking water and water needed for industrial processes would become increasingly scarce. The failure of the government to respond quickly and responsibly could lead to devastating social and economic outcomes.

Recognizing the constraints imposed by a deteriorating environment on sustainable development, the Chinese government put environmental protection onto its agenda as a key issue. By the year 2000, an aggregate investment of US$34 billion, almost one per cent of China's GNP, was anticipated in order to control national pollution. The investment in environmental protection would continue well into the next century. Exhibit 5 presents the forecasted investments in environmental protection and demand for equipment in China from 2001 to 2010. The forecasted ten-year annual growth rate of the industry would be 23 per cent, way above the annual GNP growth. Priority in environmental protection for the next few years would go to four areas: development of urban sewage treatment systems; equipment to curb air pollution; solid waste disposal; and monitoring equipment.

Even though the size of the market was growing, corporate profits were not. While the annual output for the environmental protection industry increased by 721 per cent from 1988 to 1993, the average profit margin decreased from 22 per cent to 13 per cent, and to 8.5 per cent in 1997. The environmental protection industry in China was heavily concentrated in the densely populated coastal areas, due to the higher level of industrialization and commensurate pollution in these areas. The trend would most likely continue for the next decade, because these areas would remain financially better off and better endowed with advanced technologies and human resources in science and research. China had recently designated a few Environmental Industry Parks, encouraging foreign direct investments in the industry. Exhibit 6 identifies the output in the environmental protection industry by province for three years, i.e., 1988, 1993, 1997.

Water Resources and Water Treatment in China

The per capita water resource in China was only one-quarter of the world average. By 1997, about 400 of China's 668 cities were suffering from water shortages, of which more than 100 had serious water shortages and poor quality water supply. Underground water resources were overexploited. Ninety per cent of the urban water resources were seriously polluted; about 50 per cent of the drinking water supplies in major cities were below the national standard.

Water pollution resulted from two major sources: industrial wastewater and sewage water. Industrial wastewater could be effectively reduced through cleaner production processes. However, municipal wastewater would increase with the rise of living standards. The average per capita water usage in China had already increased from 162 litres in 1986 to 208 litres in 1996. The average percentage of municipal wastewater in the total wastewater discharge was around 40 per cent in China. However, in rich coastal cities like Shanghai and Guangzhou, the percentage was already close to 50 per cent and still on the rise.

About 82 per cent of China's wastewater was discharged into water bodies without any treatment, seriously contaminating the water resources of the country, and resulting in epidemic diseases and deteriorating aquatic life. The National Environmental Agency had required that by 2000, 74 per cent of the industrial wastewater and 25 per cent of the sewage water be treated before being discharged into receiving waters.

Therefore, one priority in water treatment in China had been the construction of urban water treatment plants. Urban water treatment facilities were growing in number faster than industrial wastewater facilities. Yet, of the 668 cities existing in 1997, only 123 cities had a total of 307 urban water treatment plants. Moreover, the majority of the country's 17,000 towns did not have any sewage and water treatment facilities. Therefore, the potential demand of the municipal segment would be significant in the coming years.

The Water Treatment Industry in China

In 1997, there were 2,558 manufacturers of the water treatment systems. More than 80 per cent of the companies were small enterprises with limited resources and low technological strength. Most of the domestic-made products were 10 to 20 years behind current world technology levels. Many were being made by village and township enterprises. Experts believed that 70 to 80 per cent of the domestic-made water treatment equipment were below acceptable international standards.

Water disinfecting equipment was among the products most in demand. However, the most widely used disinfection method was chlorination. Ultraviolet disinfection was a new idea to China. The cost of chlorination was roughly $200 per ton of water treated in China. One major cost of UV was electricity, which cost about $.10 per kilowatt hour in China.

A large proportion of the water treatment projects, especially the costly municipal water plants, received foreign funding. The environmental sector had absorbed more than US$3.3 billion in foreign funds by 1999. Foreign capital from various sources like the World Bank, the Asian Development Bank, United Nations Development Program, as well as bilateral government organizations and multi-lateral international organizations made up a substantial contribution to the environmental projects. The majority of the bilateral government loans made it clear that 60 per cent of the loan total must be used to purchase equipment from designated sources. Even when no such conditions were attached, foreign-made equipment was preferred for advanced technology and quality, or sometimes for other obscure considerations (e.g., foreign trips desired by the city officials). As a result, the municipal water treatment market was dominated by imported products, although the imports were usually three to six times more expensive than the domestic products. The U.S. Department of Commerce estimated that the percentage of imports of the total demand for wastewater treatment equipment had risen from 2.7 per cent in 1992 to 37.7 per cent in 1996. The government had, however, repeatedly called for the development of a domestic water treatment industry.

The project design market of water treatment plants was still dominated by domestic players. Since the engineering design market of China was not yet open to foreign competition, almost 98 per cent of the water treatment project design market in China was dominated by the "big eight institutes". The "big eight institutes" referred to the five institutes of civil engineering design affiliated to the Ministry of Construction and the institutes of civil engineering design in Beijing, Tianjing and Shanghai.

The Legal Environment and the Decision-Making Process

China's legal framework regarding environmental protection was quite advanced relative to other developing countries. Environmental policy had been written into the country's constitution since 1983, and the Environmental Protection Law was released in 1989. Standards for air, surface water, and noise had been established. The National Environmental Protection Agency (NEPA) was the leading government institution for developing policies, laws, and regulations related to environmental protection. Approximately 2,300 Environmental Protection Bureaus (EPBs) or Environmental Protection Offices (EPOs) existed at every level of local government, setting

standards, monitoring the environment, conducting inspections, and issuing punishments for violations (usually in the form of fines). In addition, most EPBs and EPO's at the provincial level had in-house research institutes.

The legal framework for environmental protection in China was similar to that developed in the West. However, the implementation of the policies was considerably different. The levels of bureaucracy were deep and the project approval process lacked transparency. The involvement of numerous decision-makers made it difficult for firms to identify the person that had the power to make a binding decision.

The Municipal Segment

Theoretically, municipal governments had the power to determine what to do in building a water supply or treatment plant in their city. However, assistance in funding, foreign exchange, fuel, or transportation services might have to come from the central government, and therefore, approvals from higher levels were necessary. Large projects would always require feasibility studies submitted to both the Ministry of Construction and NEPA for approval. Frequently, contracts were awarded after a bidding process. However, the selection of the winning bid was not always based on business considerations. Personal contacts with the key people could influence the bidding process. The key decision-makers, however, varied from place to place.

In the coastal areas, different ways of building and maintaining water treatment facilities were being explored. Among them were long-term contracts, build-operate-transfer forms (in which a firm would build the facility, operate it and collect fees for a predetermined period before transferring it to the government), and turnkey projects (a foreign operator would build the project which would be turned over to the local authority for maintenance).

The Industrial and the Commercial Segments

The decision making for industrial and commercial facilities was decentralized. The government environmental agencies were in charge of stipulating standards, issuing permits, and conducting inspections. Although approvals from higher level authorities were always necessary, unless they had a vested interest, usually decisions made by the managers of the businesses would be honored. Contracts would be awarded through a bidding system. Again, the bidding processes were not transparent, and the final decision could be based on many non-business factors.

The Residential Segment

More than 90 per cent of urban families had access to running water, which was purified to some extent, but never clean enough for drinking. At home, people would boil water before they drank it. The demand for small, under the sink, household water purification products was weak, largely because of the lack of penetration of this type of equipment into the Chinese household market.

Urban real estate developers often installed sewage systems for residential buildings, and sometimes also installed sewage treatment facilities. The decisions for procuring suppliers lay with the developers, given the fact that all equipment was inspected and approved by environmental agencies.

Problems of the Chinese Environmental Market

The environmental protection market in China was not a well developed, orderly market with normal and healthy market competition. Problems abounded. Some issues were common to the whole Chinese market, which was in the painful process of changing from a command to a market economy.

First, there was an issue of local protectionism. Many local governments restricted products made outside their areas to protect their tax revenues. Some even required permissions for the sale of non-locally-made products. Second, corruption led to unfair competition. Bribery or abnormally high commissions were sometimes necessary to make sales. The bidding process was often not transparent, creating opportunities for corruption. Last but not least, there was a lack of respect and protection for intellectual property. Despite all the protection laws, violations of intellectual property happened with alarming frequency. It was not unusual for good products to not succeed because of competition from cheaper and inferior imitations. The water treatment market was no exception. One CEO of a Beijing water treatment company commented that one could not afford to go after all the imitators. However, he pointed out that quality, reputation and financial strength were still essential to stay in the market, especially the municipal water treatment market.

THE DECISION

There was little doubt that China offered enormous market potential and a strong need for water disinfection. Furthermore, selling environmental products in developing countries offered significant sustainable growth opportunities for Trojan. However, a number of issues complicated the decision so that Sarah was not sure if, when, how, and where Trojan should enter the Chinese market.

The contrast between the image outside of Sarah's window and her image of China was startling. As her gaze moved to the glass of crystal clear water on her desk, she recognized the enormous value of clean water and China should not be without it. The question was whether Trojan would be one of the companies that provided it.

Exhibit 1: **Applications of Trojan's UV Systems**

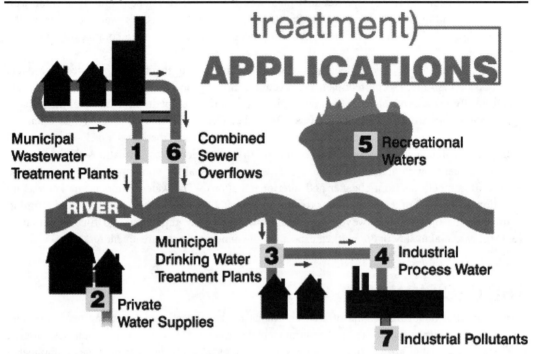

1. **Municipal Wastewater Treatment Plants**

    System UV4000 – 10 million gallons per day and up or 37,800 cubic meters per day and up

    System UV3000 – 1 million gallons per day to 30 million gallons per day or 3,780 cubic meters per day to 113,400 cubic meters per day.

2. **Private Water Supplies**

    Aqua UV Units - 2 to 12 gallons per minute or 5.5 to 45 liters per minute

3. **Municipal Drinking Water Treatment Plants**

    System UV8000 – 20 to 2000 gallons per minute or 75 to 7,500 liters per minute

4. **Industrial Process Water**

    System UV8000 – 20 to 2,000 gallons per minute or 75 to 7,500 liters per minute

5. **Recreational Waters**

6. **Combined Sewer Overflows**

    System UV4000 – 10 million gallons per day and up or 37,800 cubic meter's per day and up

7. **Industrial Pollutants**

    System UV3000 PTP - up to 1 million gallons per day or up to 3,780 cubic meters per day

    System UV3000 – 1 million gallons per day to 30 million gallons per day 3,780 cubic meters per day to 113,400 cubic meters per day

    AIR2000 - for remediation of contaminated air, soil and groundwater

Source: The company website of Trojan Technologies Inc., http://www.trojanuv.com, August 1999

Exhibit 2: **Comparison of UV and Chlorination**

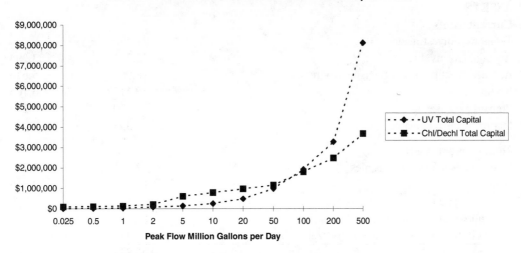

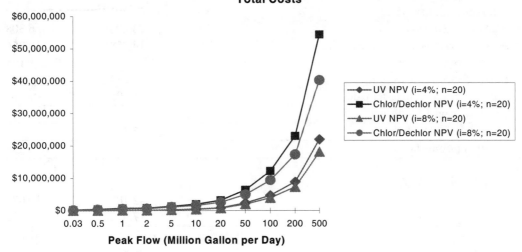

Source: Trojan Technologies Inc.

Exhibit 3: Consolidated Balance Sheets as at August 31 1998	(in CDN$000)	
	1998 $	**1997 $**
ASSETS		
Current assets		
Temporary investments	21,730	--
Accounts receivable	32,266	23,294
Accrued revenue on contracts in progress	18,965	5,618
Inventory	12,117	6,105
Prepaid expenses	320	254
Income taxes receivable	393	--
Total Current Assets		
Investments in other companies	2,191	2,236
Capital Assets	16,367	12,866
Patents, trademarks and licence (net of accumulated amortization of $825,117 ($650,637 in 1997))	1,512	729
Goodwill (net of accumulated amortization of $25,231)	984	--
	106,845	51,102
LIABILITIES AND SHAREHOLDERS' EQUITY		
Current Liability		
Bank Indebtedness	23,296	6,308
Accounts payable and accrued charges	14,258	10,356
Income taxes payable	--	1,108
Deferred income taxes	2,224	1,300
Current portion of long-term debt	1,195	--
Total Current Liabilities		
Long-term debt	6,407	--
Deferred income taxes	282	338
Shareholders' Equity		
Share capital	42,108	19,070
Retained earnings	17,075	12,622
	59,183	31,692
	106,845	51,102

Exhibit 4: **Consolidated Statements of Income and Retained Earnings for the year ended August 1, 1998 (in CDN$000)**

	1998 $	1997 $
Sales	69,852	51,150
Cost of goods sold	40,586	30,156
Gross margin	29,266	20,994
EXPENSES		
Administrative and selling expenses	13,560	10,415
Research and development, net	3,318	3,184
Interest and bank charges	1,183	210
Amortization	1,807	982
	19,868	14,791
Operating income	9,398	6,203
Other income		
Interest income	51	248
Income from equity investment	935	698
Income before special charge and income taxes	10,384	7,149
Special charge	2,650	--
Income taxes	2,571	2,414
Net income	5,163	4,735
Retained earnings, beginning of year	12,623	7,888
Share issue costs, net of taxes	(712)	--
Retained earnings, end of year	17,074	12,623
Earnings per share		
Basic	0.67	0.62
Fully diluted	0.67	0.61

Exhibit 5: Ten-year Forecast for the Chinese Environmental Market (2001 to 2010, US$ billions)

Year	2001	2002	2003	2004	2005	2006	2007	2008	2009	2010	Total
Investment Amount	*58.5*	63.5	68.5	74.0	79.9	86.4	93.2	100.6	108.8	117.9	851.3
Market Demand	23.4	25.4	27.4	29.6	32.0	34.6	37.3	40.2	43.5	47.2	340.6

Exhibit 6: Distribution of Chinese Environmental Industry (Annual Production Output, US$ billions)

Year	Country Total	Eight Provinces, Municipalities with Highest Annual Production in Environmental Industry							
1988	3.8	Jiangsu 0.899	Liaoning 0.472	Shanghai 0.36	Shandong 0.188	Jilin 0.182	Hunan 0.155	Zhejiang 0.136	Beijing 0.130
1993	31.2	Jiangsu 4.734	Zhejiang 4.448	Liaoning 2.606	Tianjing 2.435	Guangdong 2.287	Shanghai 1.781	Anhui 1.311	Hubei 1.273
1997	52.17	Jiangsu 9.755	Zhejiang 7.263	Shandong 3.914	Tianjing 2.848	Guangdong 2.845	Shanghai 2.425	Sanxi 2.21	Henan 2.16

GURU.COM: POWER FOR THE INDEPENDENT PROFESSIONAL

Ken Mark and
Mary Crossan

> There's a new movement in the land — as fast growing as it is invisible. From coast to coast, in communities large and small, citizens are declaring their independence and drafting a new bill of rights. Meet some of the 25 million residents of Free Agent, U.S.A.
>
> Dan Pink, Author, *Free Agent Nation*

Introduction

With only a small team of people and a big vision, Guru.com believed it was on the brink of a huge opportunity. They intended to transform the global labor market by creating the world's largest online marketplace for independent professionals (IPs) — freelancers, consultants, "knowledge

IVEY

workers" and "hired guns." Affectionately known internally as "gurus," independent professionals were one of the fastest growing segments of the North American workforce.

In August 1999, one month into the launch of its preview site (version 0.5), Guru.com was preparing for its first major release, scheduled for November 1999. Their goal was to build a home on the Web for independent professionals, providing the essentials for running a guru business. Jon and James Slavet, co-founders of Guru.com believed that catering to the needs of gurus was the key to achieving market leadership and revolutionizing the traditional contingent staffing business. Turning to a recent hire, Jennifer Tyler, Jon and James wanted her opinion on Guru.com's product strategy.

JENNIFER TYLER

Jennifer Tyler was brought into Guru.com as one of its first team members in July 1999. Having graduated from the Ivey Business School in 1995, Tyler joined Monitor Company where she focused on developing emerging technology strategies for clients. Tyler recognized the IP trend and brought an intimate knowledge of the market to this early stage team — she developed a similar concept and strategy for a company who was in a market closely aligned with Guru.com's. Tyler believed that focusing on the IP market was a tremendous opportunity and believed that Guru.com's approach, focusing on attracting the gurus, was going to allow them to capture market leadership. Tyler commented on her initial thoughts about the business:

> I saw Guru.com as a tremendous opportunity to catalyse the emerging freelance market. I had explored many approaches to the business, and felt strongly that focusing on the guru would allow us to achieve market leadership. For most traditional companies finding the talent was the toughest part. Pulling together a fragmented population like independent consultants would be incredibly valuable. Guru.com had a vision for connecting with people, speaking their language, empowering the independent professional. It was energizing at a personal level, and I believed the approach would differentiate the business.

OVERVIEW OF THE TRADITIONAL STAFFING INDUSTRY

In 1946, William Russell Kelly, anticipating a post-Second World War business and industrial boom, moved to Detroit and founded the Russell Kelly Office Service. The firm, a service bureau that sent its employees to fill in for vacationing or sick employees, set the standard for the newly-created staffing industry, and coined the term "Kelly Girls" to identify their staff, most of whom were female secretaries.[1]

Kelly set the mould for the temporary staffing business, which remained relatively unchanged through most of the 1970s and 1980s. Temporary staffing was typically used for clerical and administrative work. However, the downsizing trend in the late 1980s, coupled with the technology boom in the 1990s dramatically changed the way that companies worked with contingent staff. Instead, companies relied on outside expertise to guide their companies through uncharted territory,

---

[1]Laabs, Jennifer L; "Father Of The Staffing Industry — William Russell Kelly — Dies"; <u>Workforce</u>; Costa Mesa; March 1998; Volume 77, Issue 3.

and to bring in knowledge that didn't exist within the corporate walls and to help projects move at a speed that was not possible using internal resources alone.

The staffing industry was broken down into three categories — temporary staffing agencies who hired workers and outsourced them to companies in return for a fee (usually a markup on the consultants hourly rate), talent matchmakers who received a bounty for matching freelance independent professionals with companies who required their specialized services, and independent consultants that relied primarily on their personal networks to find work for themselves.

There were basically two classifications of temporary workers whom the staffing industry counted on: agency-dependent contract employees, and independent professionals. In the agency-dependent model, the agency located the assignment, recruited the contractor, negotiated with and billed the client. The agency also withheld applicable taxes from the contractor's regularly scheduled payroll cheque, with the difference between the client bill rate and the contractor pay rate (minus taxes) being the agency's revenue. Alternatively, IPs were personally responsible for managing the entire process from sourcing work to billing clients and managing taxes (see Exhibit 1).

THE RISE OF THE GURU NATION

According to Guru.com, the independent professional phenomenon was a fundamental socio-economic shift in the American workforce. By 1999, there were an estimated 25 million independent workers in the United States.[2] Within this group, an estimated eight million were considered highly skilled independent professionals, or IPs. In addition to the existing group of IPs, it was thought that there were still a large number of professionals-to-be; people on the cusp of going "guru." This potential market included "moonlighters" and work-at-home parents.

There were a number of factors fuelling the rise of "gurudom." Affected by corporate downsizing in the 1990s, entrepreneurship tendencies were on the rise, while career-long allegiance to big corporations was fading into American corporate history. Hyper-competitive companies were increasingly looking to selectively hire "expertise" for short stints as a way to outsource their workload, thus improving profitability and "speed to market." In addition, information technology was making tremendous strides as a powerful enabler and equalizer for IPs. And an increased awareness and concern for balancing career with personal interests was leading people to choose careers with more flexibility.

The result was that proven IPs were a new breed of American worker — non-traditional, highly skilled, and able to garner astronomical fees for much sought after advice. While millions of people were benefiting from this trend, and enjoying the freedom of shaping their own careers, the transition to this new way of work came with some challenges. Guru.com's initial research indicated that gurus faced a number of hurdles in their pursuit of an independent lifestyle. These included: accessing professional community, generating a steady flow of consulting projects, and managing business logistics. Guru.com aimed to focus on solving these problems for gurus, through a combined online and offline strategy.

opportunity

---

[2]U.S. Bureau of Labor Statistics.

The Creation of Guru.com

The founding members saw dramatic changes in the market and an opportunity to revolutionize the way that independent professionals connected with the clients that needed to hire them. James and Jon Slavet, together with Al Yau co-founded Guru.com in April 1999. From Guru.com's Website:[3]

Jon Slavet, Co-CEO

In the three-ring circus that is Guru.com, Jon Slavet waves the baton. As co-CEO, he manages Guru.com's marketing, sales, and business development teams. From 1997 until 1999, Jon worked at E! Online in Los Angeles as vice-president responsible for advertising sales, business development, and international content syndication. As a senior executive for strategic development at Wired Ventures, Jon built a great department and sold lots and lots of ads. He has also worked as director of corporate sales for National Public Radio in New York. Jon graduated with honors from Dartmouth College.

James Slavet, Co-CEO

James Slavet develops the strategies that power Guru.com's growth. Today, he oversees Guru.com's financing, human resources, operations, product and engineering teams. Previously, he was a member of the launch team at Drugstore.com. Before that, he served as manager of business development at Wired Ventures. James has also worked in marketing and operations for Vivid Studios, a San Francisco Web development firm, and as a strategy consultant with Monitor Company. He graduated from Brown University and has an MBA from Harvard Business School.

Al Yau, vice-president of Product Management

Al Yau knows how to run a tight ship. As a manager of business development at Peoplesoft, he helped the company migrate its software from a client/server architecture to the Internet. At Sun Microsystems, he identified acquisition targets and learned to appreciate casual dress. He also worked as an associate at McCown DeLeeuw & Co., a private equity investment firm, and in the mergers and acquisitions group at Goldman Sachs. As a former U.S. Army Airborne Ranger, Al can go for very long periods without food. He graduated from Stanford University with a degree in industrial engineering and has an MBA from Harvard Business School.

All three believed that the Internet was the perfect platform on which to build an online contractor-professional marketplace. Jon commented on this opportunity,

> We'd tried to get expert help on projects in our past lives and found it was a really difficult process. You relied on your personal network and hoped you found a good person. Also, a lot of our friends had left corporate America and gone off on their own, so we knew about the frustrations of the guru. With the Web, we figured we had a perfect opportunity to streamline this process.

While the experience and network of the founding team members was strong on the business side, they recognized the challenge of building a technology company without engineering or product experience under their belts. Jon continued,

---

[3]www.guru.com/content/about/about_team.jhtml (January, 2001).

GOAL

We are determined to pull together the right set of resources to make the business successful. Our top priority in the summer of 1999 is our investor network — bringing in experienced Internet angels to back the company and to give us advice. We also need technology experts. It is going to be incredibly difficult to find a talented engineering lead given the tightness in the market. So we made the decision to outsource development of the Web site.

Marketing is our strength. We know we can build a brand that is compelling to the gurus. The challenge for us is to build a product that can back up our promises. We are pulling together a team of people that have a strong connection with the IP trend — non-traditional trendsetters with a touch of irreverence.

The early team has set the voice and culture for the company, and it is a company that the gurus can identify with. We can't create a corporate-style company when our customers are trying to free themselves from that environment.

James concluded,

Our strength is that the brand has connected with gurus in terms of engendering trust — even from the first day. Our model is focused on helping gurus achieve independence and it is important that our product reflected that commitment.

VP

In August 1999, backed by US$3 million of angel funding, the team wanted to draft out a list of priorities, particularly related to the product. The vision was compelling, but turning the vision into a successful product was no small task. The next round of investors would also want clarity around what Guru.com was going to build and how they planned to generate revenue. The stakes were higher now, with Guru.com in discussions for US$10 million to US$15 million in their first venture round with firms such as Greylock and Kleiner Perkins. Guru.com's first step was to analyse the market.

GURU CHARACTERISTICS AND NEEDS

> I work in my robe
> While all my friends toil away
> In starched monkey suits.

> Guru haiku submitted by Michelle Goodman, writer, Seattle, WA

In addition to being a large, rapidly growing market, IPs were a highly attractive target group for many reasons. According to the U.S. Bureau of Labor Statistics, IPs were ahead of the rest of North American households on every measure of income, technology optimism and education. They were generally a higher-skilled demographic and they appeared to have significant unmet needs (see Exhibits 2(a) and 2(b)). Tyler commented on the initial customer findings,

I was overwhelmed with the positive response we received — with only the promise of what was to come. Customers would write to us telling their stories about how we had given them the motivation and support to venture out on their own and how the site we were creating was going to be a cornerstone for them in building their independent careers. It raised the bar, putting a lot of pressure on the product team to deliver what our customers envisioned and needed.

Early research on the market, combined with feedback from the preview site helped to develop the team's understanding of the guru (see Exhibit 3). Three primary needs were identified: finding

VP

work, accessing community and managing day-to-day business logistics. Guru.com next looked at hirers and their needs.

HIRER CHARACTERISTICS AND NEEDS

> I know where the creative people hang out, and where the techies hang out, and I go there to network and recruit candidates. I don't care where these people go, if they are using Toiletbowl.com, I'll go to Toiletbowl.com.

> Corporate user, Guru.com Focus Group, August 1999

Guru.com's target corporate customers were companies with a high demand for project-based workers. These companies ranged from small to mid-size businesses with fewer than 500 employees, to large corporations such as Microsoft. The defining characteristic of these companies was their need for specialized workers on a project basis. It was thought that as companies increasingly moved to an outsourced model and felt heightened pressure to find resources in high demand areas such as Web development without paying astronomical placement fees, there would be an increasing demand for the services offered by Guru.com.

The outsourced labor market was growing at six per cent annually, and professional and technical outsourcing was growing at 24 per cent, four times faster than the broader market. These businesses relied heavily on professional/technical outsourcing to access essential skills while limiting overhead expenses. Furthermore, outsourcing allowed these companies to focus full-time human and financial resources on their core competencies. The use of outsourced expertise could also provide substantial personnel cost savings versus hiring full-time employees. These savings could be achieved through lowered training and benefits costs, plus the ability to smooth out labor expenses during volatile operating periods. In this bull market,[4] traditional staffing firms were continuing to increase rates, garnering a 30 per cent to 50 per cent markup on the contractors' fee (see Exhibit 4).

At present, staffing agencies had a stronghold on the hiring companies, with long-term contracts and onsite resources to keep each other's competitors at bay. Jon and James thought their best chance was to attract the talent — who were typically hard to find and highly fragmented in terms of geography.

THE COMPETITIVE LANDSCAPE

In August 1999, Guru.com believed that there was no brand that embodied the guru movement, or effectively delivered on the core needs of independent professionals and the corporate hirers who depended on them. Thus, although there were many different online competitors, Guru.com believed that no one firm dominated this nascent online market. Tyler stated,

> There were a number of companies that were trying to create a marketplace for independent work — but they were all limited by the constraints of their core business strategy, which usually didn't put the independent professional first. Guru.com was the first company in the space to

---

[4]In 1999, the American economy was enjoying a period of expansion unrivalled since the 1950s.

approach the problem from a blank slate — our whole business was about the independent professional, which gave us a huge advantage.

Their competitive analysis revealed the following two charts (Table 1 and Table 2). Both map out Guru.com's competition, strengths and weaknesses, and market positioning:

Table 1:

Category	Value Proposition	Sample Competitors
Online career sites	• Job matching • Heavy orientation towards full time positions • Limited: no community, tools, content or commerce	• Monster.com (Talent Market) • HotJobs.com • Dice.com • Headhunter.net
Professional service automation (PSA) companies	• Focus on enterprise software customers • Tools focus — migrating enterprise applications to the Web • Limited: no community, content	• Opus360 • Niku • Evolve • Portera
Staffing agencies	• Job matching • Agency model (high fees on signed deals, recruiters) • Heavy offline infrastructure • Online access to agency-sourced jobs • Basic tools for independents such as billing, 401Ks • On-site services and dedicated account reps	• Aquent (MacTemps) • Manpower • Adecco and Olsten
Independent professional job sites	• Job matching • Typically focused on a specific vertical, such as IT • Limited / no community, content, or commerce	• eWork • IC Planet • Brainpower

From Guru.com's perspective, there was no effective service that provided: (1) a place for gurus of all types to band together to share knowledge and experiences, and (2) tools, services and tips for gurus that are needed to run their businesses more efficiently and profitably. From the corporate users perspective, Guru.com also held the promise of a much-needed solution — a place to locate talent. Guru.com's analysis had revealed that hirers employed a variety of methods for finding and hiring gurus and drastic measures were often used to find and recruit these people (see Exhibit 5).

Table 2:

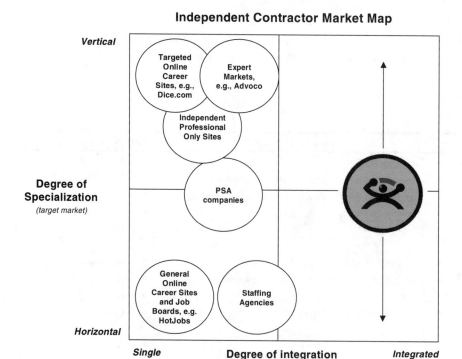

Independent Contractor Market Map

GURU.COM LAUNCHES ITS PREVIEW SITE IN JULY 1999

Against the advice of investors who advised Guru.com to wait until it had a more robust product, the Guru.com team launched a preview site in July 1999 to begin spreading the word about Guru.com's service and acquiring customers.[5] According to James,

> It has no functionality — there is some content aimed at IPs and a place for people to pre-register for our service, but we decided not to do project matching at this stage.

Tyler added,

> Our initial site, which was entirely content-driven, was getting a huge response from the guru community. We figured that we'd keep bringing in the gurus and then start acquiring hirers.

---

[5]In this first version, gurus could sign up with Guru.com by filling out a registration form.

THE GURU.COM STRATEGIC APPROACH

Now that they had a "placeholder" site that was beginning to sign up hundreds of IPs per week, Guru.com's next step was to build a functional Web site.

The brand was to be guru-centric. With the goal to create the largest database of independent professionals, customer acquisition would focus on gurus initially, with hirer acquisition following not far behind. The goal was to establish a 10:1 (guru:hirer) ratio in key markets such as San Francisco, Boston and New York by the end of the year. Guru.com's revenue model would be based on project posting, with hiring companies paying a fee to post projects on Guru.com. Additional revenue would come from online advertising and offline events. Upon reviewing the business model, Tyler commented,

> We are building something new and different, but we can look to other markets for proxies. For example, Monster has built a successful business on project postings for full-time positions. This gives us, and our investors, confidence that we could use a similar model to build a marketplace for contract work.
>
> As for focusing on gurus or hirers, it is a classic 'chicken and egg' scenario. Without the gurus, the hirers wouldn't take us seriously. Without the projects, the gurus wouldn't be interested.

James added,

> The staffing industry has changed and the difference between Guru.com's product and traditional staffing industries is that our product will be automated and boundary-free — there will be no physical locations. To start, there won't be much screening, vetting, handholding — it'll be low touch. But we won't have the mark-ups that temp agencies charge.

The Guru.com version 1.0 Product

Working with a small technical development company, Guru.com started to build its first major product (Version 1.0).

The product goals were to provide:

A place for gurus of all types to band together to share knowledge and experiences;
Access to "hot," exclusive gigs for all types of gurus;
Tools, services and tips for gurus to run their businesses more efficiently;
Content to provide advice and perspective on issues that are relevant to gurus and to generate lively discussion within the community; and
A place for corporate hirers to find top quality gurus.

Implementing the plan

To achieve these goals, Guru.com planned to launch a series of online products that covered four major areas: project matching, community, tools and services, and commerce. The first release would establish a basic project matching system, and to build on the existing content infrastructure to enhance its community features. They planned to roll out tools and commerce products within six to nine months from the initial release.

Release	Timing	Focus
1.0	Nov 1999	Project matching and community
1.5	Dec 1999	Added project matching functionality
2.0	Mar 2000	Tools and services offering, commerce phase 1
3.0	Jun 2000	Full commerce offering

Version 1.0 — Project matching and community

Project matching features

The cyclical "feast and famine" nature of the guru's workload would be the first issue addressed. To help generate a steady flow of consulting projects, Guru.com planned to provide IPs with a variety of methods to increase their access to quality projects. These key features would include:[6]

Guru Profiles: Guru Profiles would serve as a vibrant showcase through which gurus could highlight their skills and expertise — a résumé on steroids.

Gig Postings: The gig posting system would allow hirers to easily create project postings via a simple to use, modular interface. Postings would be accessible to all gurus via the Guru.com project database. A basic messaging system would allow gurus to easily apply for projects by sending a link to their Guru Profile and a brief message.

Guru Search: Searching and browsing capabilities would be provided to allow hirers to quickly locate gurus that matched their project requirements. Hirers would be able to conduct searches based on key criteria such as skills, availability and location. Additionally, hirers would be able to specify attributes and request notification new gurus that met their criteria on an ongoing basis.

Gig Search: Gurus looking for new clients or projects would be able to proactively seek out new work by searching the Guru.com project database. Through an easy-to-use, searchable database, gurus would be able to identify interesting opportunities posted by hirers or other gurus. Gurus would have the option to specify target project characteristics and receive notifications of postings that met these criteria.

Response Management: Guru.com planned to build an online response management system to give hirers the ability to manage responses from candidates.

Community features

Community at Guru.com would extend far beyond the typical confines of chat rooms and message boards. Thus, content, community, tools and services, commerce, and jobs would be tightly integrated. Guru.com intended its community to drive the creation and flow of content, giving Guru.com access to a perpetual source of granular, timely, relevant, low cost material:

---

[6]From Guru.com's 1999 business plan.

<u>Relevant and timely content</u>: Content would be provided to give guidance and generate discussion within the Guru.com community. Features included Guru Guides, which provided how-to instructions on topics of interest to gurus, Guru Portraits, which showcased interesting gurus, cartoons to provide comic relief, and special features to provide more in-depth coverage of key topics.

<u>Interactive community forums</u>: Moderated community forums, led by Guru.com community leaders, would provide gurus with the opportunity to voice opinions and share knowledge relevant to the entire guru community. Guru.com also planned to rely upon topical experts to answer specific questions from users and to post responses. For example, Dan Pink hosted a forum, answering questions from gurus across a range of topics from how to moonlight to how to protect your intellectual property. Experts were recruited to host community channels in five major areas: workstyle, tax and finance, legal, tech and gear, and lifestyle.

Future Web site features proposed

These were the features that Guru.com proposed for their future Web site versions (1.5 and higher). Although they would have liked to include these features in version 1.0, Guru.com recognized that their time and financial resources were not unlimited (from Guru.com's Business Plan).

<u>Quality control</u>: Guru.com planned to pursue a variety of methods to ensure that both gurus and hirers received quality leads. Guru.com would create a feedback loop through which customers could rate their experience with a contractor and vice versa. In addition, gurus and hirers would have access to credit and background check information through a Guru.com partner.

<u>Collections services</u>: Collecting from non-paying clients was another major problem for gurus. Guru.com planned to offer services via partners to help gurus collect on unpaid invoices.

<u>Time and expense management</u>: Guru.com was considering offering Web-based time and expense tools to ease the burden for gurus of tracking hours and invoicing clients. They had not determined whether they would buy or build this product.

<u>Rate advice</u>: Once they had achieved a critical mass of data in the system, Guru.com would consider offering a rate advisor to provide gurus with aggregate information about market rates for relevant projects and skill levels.

<u>Project management tools</u>: Guru.com was considering offering gurus and hirers access to shared workspace for file sharing and collaboration.

<u>Commerce</u>: Through partnerships with leading e-commerce vendors, and the ability to leverage an aggregated buying model, Guru.com planned to provide access to discounted products and services through a store targeted to independent professionals. Product areas under consideration included:

- Insurance and financial and retirement planning services
- Tax and legal services
- Computer hardware and software
- Communications products and services
- Continuing education, training and certification programs
- Industry research, conferences and events
- Office equipment and supplies
- Business gifts and greetings

Recommendation time

As Tyler started to think about Guru.com's product strategy, her extensive consulting experience prompted her to link product with business strategy. Was focusing on the guru the best place to start? Were they making the right choices about prioritizing the product features? Tyler commented,

> We have to make some tough choices. We don't have a lot of time because competitors have started to launch their products, the customers are getting restless, and we've only got a small team to build this product. We've also got aggressive goals, but we can't build it all at once. If we choose to build a bit for the gurus and a bit for the hirers, we'll end up with a lot of nothing. I think we're starting in the right place, but we've got a long way to go.

Exhibit 1: **Traditional Staffing Industry**

Overview

- Six per cent annual growth overall; 24 per cent growth in professional and technical markets
- 7,000 firms in industry with 17,000 locations
- Top 10 firms control 29 per cent of US$72 billion industry (Manpower Inc., Adecco Staffing Services, Interim Services, Norrell Corp, Kelly Services)
- 100 firms with revenues exceeding US$100 million
- 90 per cent of firms offer training programs

Examples

Company	Type	Focus	Financial performance	Other
Roth Staffing Company	Traditional temporary staffing service	75% of demand was for clerical or secretarial workers 25% of demand was for higher-skilled workers Company focused on driving volume of placements	Achieved US$74 million in 1998 20% revenue growth from 1994 to 1998 Expected to approach US$240 million in sales by 2003	Roth placed 5,000 temporary workers in 1999 65 offices in seven states

Robert Half International	Traditional temporary staffing service	Focused on high-priced financial and accounting talent	Achieved US$1.3 billion in 1997 43% CAGR from 1995 to 2000	Market capitalization US$5 billion
Aquent (formerly MacTemps)	Talent matchmaker	Focused on creative and technical talent	US$100 million in 1998, expected to top US$190 million in 2000	Offices in nine countries 110% money-back guarantee Offers additional services such as training and factoring

Sources:

U.S. Bureau of Labor Statistics

Davidson, Linda; "Maximize the return on temp staff investments"; <u>Workforce</u>; Costa Mesa; November 1999; Volume 78, Issue 11

Welles, Edward O, "Number 1 company: The People Business;" <u>Inc</u>; Boston; Oct 19, 1999; Volume 21, Issue 15.

www.aquent.com

Exhibit 2(a):   **Guru Characteristics And Needs**

They are affluent and high spending — IPs are twice as likely than corporate employees to earn more than $75,000 per year. According to a Guru.com survey, a large percentage of this population spends between 10 per cent and 15 per cent of their annual income on business related products and services.

They are "connected" — Independent professionals are highly connected, with nearly 90 per cent of the market owning a computer for business purposes (Freelance Centre Survey) and a large percentage of the online population using high-speed Internet connections.

They are experts working in high demand job categories — In addition to being concentrated in large metropolitan areas,[7] over 85 per cent of Guru.com's user base has expertise in the Web, IT, creative, sales, marketing and public relations, and management consulting categories — areas of high corporate demand. Furthermore, these professionals are experienced in their fields, with many having worked independently for more than five years.

They adopt this workstyle by choice — Contrary to popular belief, independent professionals actively choose the solo workstyle, consciously rejecting the confines of corporate life. According to industry surveys, less than 10 per cent of independent consultants cited downsizing as the reason

---

[7]50 per cent of Guru.com's user base was located in one of 10 major metropolitan areas. These included Austin, Boston, Chicago, Dallas, DC, Houston, LA, NY, Seattle, and SF.

for going solo.[8] Gurus cited flexibility and freedom as their primary reasons for wanting to go solo (Guru.com survey and focus groups), and 76 per cent said that their quality of life improved dramatically after becoming an independent (U.S. Bureau of Labor Statistics).

Exhibit 2(b): **Needs**

While they enjoyed the freedom of shaping their own careers, gurus faced three major challenges:

Generating a steady flow of consulting projects

Gurus cited their biggest challenge as being the ability to maintain a steady flow of quality jobs. Moreover, they do not currently have effective mechanisms for marketing themselves and sourcing jobs. For most, the process of finding clients is at best a "word-of-mouth" proposition — 80 per cent cited their personal network or referrals as their primary source of jobs (Guru.com survey) — an often inefficient channel. Additionally, they reported that current online sites do not deliver the type and quality of projects that match their needs and qualifications — often being contacted by companies looking for full-time candidates. The typical guru has a limited marketing budget and would rather focus on doing the work they love. The combination of tight project deadlines and operating a small business leaves scarce time for networking and lead generation.

Accessing professional community

> I just read about you today via *The Industry Standard*, and I must say, I'm impressed. I'm spreading the news about your site, as I think it has real promise in building the community we home-based workers need.
>
> Wendy J., User Feedback, August 1999

Isolated (70 per cent work from home, according to industry surveys) and without effective means to collaborate with their peers, independent professionals had a high need for finding and teaming with a professional community. They rated this solitude one of the top dislikes of their profession. In focus groups conducted by Guru.com, gurus suggested that they wanted to find ways to collaborate with each other to learn, to share experiences, and to form virtual project teams, however, they did not have an effective way to do this.

Managing business logistics

> Freelancers need tools. Providing links as a first step is good, but I think the real sticky business, where the margins are, is in providing mission critical services to these independent virtual companies. Financial tools and banking partnerships . . . [or] partnering with Office Depot for supplies and discounts. From my research, there is a definite need for such services.
>
> Marc L., User Feedback, July 1999

---

[8]Penn Schoen & Berland's survey.

The day-to-day hassles of running a solo business prevented gurus from focusing on working with clients and honing their expertise. These administrative tasks were also listed as a top dislike of their profession. Almost all participants in Guru.com's focus groups reported having problems collecting fees from clients. Additionally, the process of completing quarterly tax reports and dealing with legal contracts and business forms was considered tedious.

Gurus independently manage the details of running a business, and they often lacked the time, expertise, and operating leverage to do so efficiently. Gurus lack purchasing power, and often make purchase decisions in an information vacuum. Major products and services purchased by gurus included: computer hardware and software, telecommunications, office equipment and supplies, business gifts, travel and entertainment, insurance, legal advice, tax and financial planning services, magazines and books, industry research, conferences and networking events, continuing education and career certification. With respect to many of these categories gurus expressed a strong desire to be able to purchase at a discount.

Exhibit 3: **Selected Customer Feedback**

- How did you know so well what we need? I have been on for ten minutes and all I can do is mumble Yes!!! Yes!!! Yes!!! — Gene Russell
- What a terrific idea! I'm excited about the potential for your new site. Keep up the great work — I'll be around for the long term. — Deborah Mayfield
- Great work! Finally, a Web site worth surfing. Hope you will continue to provide insightful and helpful hints. I wish you all the best and please continue with the great Web site. Although still in its infancy stage, I can see a huge potential for it. — Steven C, Strategy Consulting Guru, Boston
- I love your Web site! I have been procrastinating over starting a financial consulting biz targeting women and you have given me the inspiration to go for it! I have made you my homepage. — Nia Barrameda, Soon-to-be Virtual CFO, LA
- This is too cool! I'm tap dancing in my living room. Go guys! — Louise Marchildon
- Funny. I always thought of myself as a whore, a mere utensil at the hands of the highest bidder, a body, an overglorified typist. And whenever I met someone under social circumstances I inevitably ended up labeled as a guru. But I never thought of myself as one — until this morning when I found your site. I love your site. It's new think for the new world I live in. — Erick Calder
- Your site is chock full of useful info and I love the tasty tidbit sidebars. Fast. Easy. Useful. Entertaining — that's Guru.com. Keep up the good work and continue practicing those pushups — the better to carry our guru banner onward into the battle for freedom and fun! — Juliet McCleery
- All I can say is, "Finally" — Suzanne Petrizzi Wilson

Exhibit 4: Hirer Characteristics and Needs

Hirer Needs

Although these companies covered a broad range of industries and varied widely in terms of size and revenue, their core needs with respect to finding, hiring and working with independent professionals were fairly similar. Guru.com also believed that most companies would be price insensitive.

Sourcing quality candidates

How am I finding developers? I'm wandering the halls at MIT.

David Kelly, Founder, Net Startup

Consistently, the feedback received from corporate managers through focus groups and interviews was the tremendous challenge associated with finding qualified candidates. Word-of-mouth, temporary staffing agencies, and online sites were all mentioned as channels used to find candidates. However, all were deemed inadequate. Word-of-mouth was the most frequently cited method of sourcing candidates, but was also considered to be highly inefficient and limited. Many communicated frustration with the process of using temporary staffing firms, due to high fees and an inability on the part of these firms to deliver qualified candidates. Furthermore, managers communicated dissatisfaction with most online sites because of their inability to deliver a manageable set of qualified candidates.

Time sensitive versus price sensitive

Research found that hiring managers were relatively insensitive to price when it came to finding quality candidates. Managers were typically under significant time pressure to find contract resources, and would sacrifice cash to find qualified people in a timely manner. Moreover, they were frequently forced to use unsatisfactory channels, such as temporary staffing agencies, when faced with a tight situation. As quoted by one focus group member, "There is a love, hate relationship with agencies. I'll turn to them in a tight situation, but I'd prefer not to use them due to the cost, hassle and their general inability to deliver the high level candidates that I need."

Support on the legal requirements of hiring independent contractors

Heightened by concerns generated from the recent Microsoft ruling, hiring managers increasingly recognized their need for guidance with respect to the requirements of hiring and managing independent contractors. Most hiring managers were unclear about the differences between freelancers and independent contractors and did not have adequate resources, outside of consulting an expensive legal firm, for getting clear information about the technical distinctions and their responsibilities as employers. Furthermore, hiring managers reported that it was sometimes difficult for them to confirm that an independent professional was a qualified independent contractor.

Exhibit 5: **Competitive Landscape**

Guru.com considered its primary competitors in the space to be:

Professional services automation (PSA) software companies (i.e., Evolve Software (EVLV), Opus360 (OPUS), and Niku (NIKU)). These companies were developing enterprise software for automating professional services firms such as MarchFirst (MRCH). Each of them had developed an online strategy to source additional resources for their clients and to boost their potential valuations (at the time, enterprise software companies needed to have an Internet strategy in order to garner attention in the public markets). It was thought that PSA software companies would be at a disadvantage due to a lack of focus, as their core business was servicing the corporate customer side with enterprise software applications.

Major online career sites (i.e., Monster.com): Online career sites such as Monster.com and HotJobs were mass classifieds businesses focused primarily on full-time job placement and international expansion. They were not building the content, community, tools or commerce features to provide a home for gurus, and their brands didn't target solo professionals. Vertically focused job sites such as Dice.com were also included in this segment. Some of these companies were making efforts to target the independent professional market (e.g., Monster's Talent Market — eBay style bidding on independent professionals), however, their products and brand positioning were failing to address the core concerns of high-end independent professionals.

Temporary staffing firms (i.e., Manpower): Guru.com viewed their business as disintermediating the staffing industry, which was based upon marking up placement services 30 to 50 per cent. Temporary staffing firms were focused on consolidating the temporary staffing industry for W-2 employees, rather than building Web-based solutions for independent professionals. However, many were hiring expensive management consultancies to study the impact of the Web on their core businesses. Some companies in this market, such as Aquent (formerly MacTemps), were attempting to launch online businesses. However, the legacy of an agency model remained, which served as a disadvantage for these players. Due to their reliance on the agency model (and its associated margins), corporate and guru reluctance to use staffing agencies, and their limited Internet capabilities, these companies were not viewed as a strong competitive threat.

IP focused job sites: A series of startups were emerging to serve job seeking independent professionals, such as eWork and eLance. Again, these companies appeared to lack the ability to integrate interesting and relevant content with community, commerce and gigs. These were typically new entrants, therefore, it was important to keep a close watch on movements in this area. However, at the time, these competitors were not viewed as a major competitive threat.

WESTMILLS CARPETS LIMITED

Joseph N. Fry

"We are in quite a pickle with Westmills, and in dire need of a rescue program," said Derek Mather, senior vice-president of Canadian Enterprise Development Corporation Ltd. (CED), a venture capital company with a major equity position in the Calgary-based carpet manufacturer.

> Our losses are continuing and the prospects for early relief are poor since the market is soft and our operations disorganized. The banks are very nervous. Garry Morrison, whom we groomed for a year, has just resigned after two months as president. Harry Higson, his predecessor, is filling in on a stopgap basis, but neither Harry, the board, nor the banks want this to continue for more than a few weeks. The balance of the management team look promising, but are as yet untested.
>
> As shareholders, we (CED) have to sort out our options and position on this investment, but the matter, for me, is a personal one as well. I've just been asked to step in as president, at least until we are in position to hire a new man. I'd appreciate your views on where we go from here.

THE CANADIAN CARPET INDUSTRY

The carpet industry in Canada, as it is presently known, had its beginnings in the late 1950s with the introduction of carpet tufting technology from the United States. Tufting was a low cost, flexible

IVEY

process for producing carpets of various qualities and styles. The new production capability coincided with expanding affluence in the Canadian marketplace and a prolonged boom in residential construction. Carpet sales grew dramatically in the 1960s and early 1970s reaching a volume of 74 million square metres in 1975.

The growth of the Canadian market slowed in 1976 and 1977 with total sales of 76.5 million 78.6 million square metres respectively. Nevertheless, Canadian consumption at 3.4 metres per capita was approaching that of the United States.

Between 85 per cent and 90 per cent of Canadian sales were domestically produced. Imports were limited to the less price sensitive segments of the market by a tariff of 20 per cent plus $.375 per square metre.

CARPET MANUFACTURE

A tufted carpet was made in three principal sequential production steps: the tufting itself, dyeing and finishing. Equipment and process flexibilities were such that in each step there were a number of design options (Figure 1). By pursuing combinations of these options, carpet mills, within the constraints of their particular equipment configuration, could produce a variety of carpet lines. A major mill might produce over 25 different products and each of these would be produced in 10 to 15 different colours. This capacity for diversity had the effect of complicating both manufacturing operations and the nature of competition in the industry.

As noted in Figure 1, there were a variety of construction possibilities open for the design of carpets for particular functional and/or aesthetic purposes. A level loop pile design made with relatively coarse nylon yarn might be developed for a heavy-traffic commercial application, for example, or a plush, cut pile design of fine yarn might be produced for a high fashion location. Different carpet designs implied different materials, costs and processing efficiency. The actual design decision was thus a mixture of craft, science and economics, as aim was taken at a particular target product market and a balance was struck between fashion, function and production costs.

The value added in carpet manufacture was relatively low in relation to the total value of the finished product. Purchased materials typically amounted to 75 per cent or more of total costs, plant labor five per cent and general overhead 20 per cent. Production scheduling was a critical function in carpet mills the challenge was to maintain customer service on the one hand and avoid excessive inventories, with their built-in working capital demands and fashion risks, on the other hand.

Carpet Marketing

The Canadian carpet market was comprised of three major segments: retail, residential contract and commercial contract. An approximate division of the market into these categories is given in Table 1.

Table 1: **The Canadian and Western Canadian Carpet Markets by Segment – 1977**

	Retail	Residential Contract	Commercial Contract	Total
	(estimated volume in million square meters)			
Canadian Market	51.0 (65%)	14.0 (17.8%)	13.4 (17.2%)	78.5
Western Canadian	8.8 (40.2%)	7.6 (34.7%)	5.5 (25.1%)	21.9

Source: Canadian Carpet Institute, Case writer's estimates.

Retail Market

The typical retail customer was a homeowner purchasing a relatively small amount of carpet for first-time or replacement installation. The rough order of importance of purchase criteria in the retail market was generally cited as color, style (texture), price, dealer service and guarantees. There was a very low awareness of brand names in the market, with perhaps only Harding (a carpet manufacturer) and DuPont (a fibre supplier) having any significant recognition. Similarly, consumers had very little knowledge of the technical characteristics of carpets and the variables that would influence wear and care.

The retail market was serviced by a wide variety of outlets including department stores, specialty floor covering dealers, promotional carpet warehouses, furniture stores and home decoration centres. These outlets, depending upon their volume, their proximity to the mill and the manufacturer's distribution strategy, were in turn supplied directly from the mill, by mill-owned distributors or by independent distributors. The approximate proportions of the retail market serviced by mill-direct, mill-owned distributor and independent distributor were for Canada 35 per cent, 45 per cent and 20 per cent respectively, and for western Canada 25 per cent, 40 per cent, and 35 per cent. The trend in the previous decade had been for the mills to seek greater control of their distribution by implementing mill-direct or mill-owned distribution programs.

Residential Contract

This market consisted of home/apartment/condominium builders and mobile home manufacturers. It was serviced directly or through contract dealer/installers. Builder preferences tended toward basic carpet styles at price points below those popular in the retail and commercial markets. Order sizes were quire large and price competition was severe, with orders switching on differentials as low as five to 10 cents a metre. Assuming price and style competitiveness, service elements and particularly the dependability of delivery were important in maintaining mill/account relationships (Table 2).

Table 2: **Ranking of Channel Service Aspects by Segment**

Service Item *	Retail	Residential Contract	Commercial Contract
Speed of delivery	2	4	
Delivery when promised	1	1	1
Update of samples	4		3
Complaint handling	3	2	
Notification of price changes			4
Regular representative contract		3	2

* Original lists contained many additional items such as mill warranties, co-op advertising, salesperson personality, etc.

Source: Westmills research files

Commercial Contract

The commercial market consisted of new and replacement installations in offices, hotels, retail outlets, schools, etc. The majority of commercial business was controlled by specialty installation firms that purchased directly from the mills. Unlike residential contract sales, the product was usually specified for particular project by architects and interior designers on the basis of information from many sources (building owner, project manager, architect, etc.) The most popular styles were patterned multicolor carpets with specific wear characteristics for the intended use.

Competitive Structure

There were 28 firms engaged in the manufacture of tufted carpet in Canada in 1977. These firms could be divided into three categories on the basis of their scale, scope of activities and degree of integration in marketing and manufacturing.

Group 1

This group consisted of firms with sales of $20 million or more, wide product lines and, in most cases, yarn spinning and substantial captive distribution operations. Operating results for the five firms in this group are summarized in Table 3. Together these firms accounted for somewhat less than 50 per cent of the carpet market.

Group 2

This group consisted of approximately eight firms with sales ranging from $10 to $20 million. They were generally somewhat more specialized than the Group 1 firms in product line or geographic market coverage. Most were private firms or divisions of U.S. manufacturers, with the result that specific financial data are not available.

Group 3

The balance of the industry consisted of small firms specializing in particular product, channel or geographic markets. Firms with sales as low as $2 million were apparently viable operations. Such firms might use pre-dyed yarns exclusively in order to limit operations to tufting and minimal finishing.

Table 3: **Summary Performance of Major Carpet Firms ($000 000)**

		1977	1976	1975
Harding Carpets	Sales	$73.0	$74.5	$58.7
(as of Oct.31)	Profit before tax	(.2)	3.0	2.1
Celanese Canada	Sales	$37.6	$39.0	$47.7
Carpet Division	Profit before tax	(5.5)	(4.1)	.9
(as of Dec. 31)				
Peerless Rug	Sales	40.0	37.8	32.4
(as of Feb. 28)	Profit before tax	.6	.9	(.7)
Peeters Carpets	Sales	22.0 (est.)	22.0	20.0
Westmills	Sales	21.7	23.1	21.7
(as of Aug. 31)	Profit before tax	(1.5)	(2.4)	(.7)

Source: Corporate Financial Reports

As the total market grew in the 1960s and early 1970s, entry had been relatively easy. By 1977, there was substantially more capacity in the Canadian industry than was justified by current demand. Excess capacity, coupled with a fragmented industry structure and the dynamics of style obsolescence, had led to fierce competition, price-cutting and a deterioration of industry profitability.

Style competition was a major aspect of rivalry in the industry, stemming from a heterogeneous and fashion-conscious market on the one side and flexible manufacturing on the other. The benefits of design innovations were frequently short-lived; however, as other manufacturers "knocked-off" the popular styles. The time lag before a new innovation could be imitated by competitors was as short as six to nine months. With lasting product advantages difficult to achieve, success in specific markets often turned on price and a mill's ability to deliver high quality and excellent service.

WESTMILL'S BACKGROUND

Westmills Carpets Limited was incorporated in February 1966 in Kelowna, British Columbia. The company was (and remained through 1977) the only carpet manufacturer in the west. The intention was to capitalize on the fast-growing mass housing markets in British Columbia and Alberta through the manufacture of a relatively narrow range of tufted carpet products. Westmills commenced production in September of 1966 and by 1969 had sales of $2.4 million.

Early Growth

After some start-up difficulties, Westmills capitalized on the emerging popularity of shag carpet to fully establish it operations. Growth accelerated and facilities were expanded. In 1970, a distribution center was opened in Winnipeg. In 1971, the Kelowna distribution facility was enlarged and sales were commenced in Ontario. In 1972, the capacity of the Kelowna plant was almost doubled.

The pace of activity increased even further in 1973 as the company moved to become a national manufacturer and distributor. "We felt we were an awfully clever carpet company," Derek Mather recalled, "and that we might as well be clever on a national scale."

In January 1973, Westmills acquired Globe Mills of Meaford, Ontario in a move to reduce its dependence on outside yarn suppliers. In February, Westmills was converted to a public company. "This provided additional equity money for the company and an opportunity for the original investors to realize a profit," Mather explained. Financial statements for Westmills from 1973 onward are given in Exhibits 1 and 2.

Later in 1973, Westmills acquired the assets of Centennial Carpets in Trenton, Ontario. Further, to expand the company's marketing base, major exclusive distributors were appointed in Quebec and Ontario. By the end of 1973, Westmills had manufacturing plants in Kelowna, Meaford and Trenton and distribution facilities in Vancouver, Calgary, Winnipeg and Trenton.

"In retrospect it was overconfidence, but we felt awfully good about ourselves at that time," said Mather. Markets remained buoyant in early 1974. In Kelowna, however, the company was becoming entangled in changing political jurisdictions with different views and rules affecting plant effluent. Since this posed uncertainties and constraints on operations and expansion, a decision was made to move all dyeing operations to Calgary. This transfer to a purchased 13,000 square foot plant was initiated during the year. Distribution in Calgary continued to be handled through a separate 8,000 square foot facility. The fiscal year (to August 31, 1974) closed strong, with the company booking record sales and profits.

Decline

In the last quarter of 1974 the carpet market across Canada turned soft and Westmills' fortunes started to sag. For the first time, the company faced significant price and style competition and found itself overextended.

In 1975, the Kelowna plant was completely closed and all manufacturing equipment was moved to Calgary for installation on an ongoing basis in 1975 and early 1976. The Trenton manufacturing facility and distribution center were also closed. Sales volumes were maintained near $22 million, but gross margins slipped from 23.4 per cent in 1974 to 16.5 per cent in 1975 and a before-tax loss of $715,000 was incurred (Exhibit 1).

Market remained soft in 1976 and Westmills further consolidated facilities and attempted to reduce costs. The Winnipeg distribution center was closed; now all carpet manufacturing and distribution was handled out of Calgary. Cost reductions were hampered by the need to re-establish production with an untrained labor force earning in most cases $1.50 more per hour than workers in eastern mills; quality declined, deliveries became erratic, inventory grew and market credibility slipped. In fiscal year 1976, the company experienced a before-tax loss of $2.4 million.

Mather explained,

"Through this period we (the board) were slow to realize that there was something fundamentally wrong with the company and the way it was being run. The market problem, withdrawing from carpet manufacture in the east, and the plant relocation from Kelowna to Calgary, all confused our perception of the real situation."

Management Changes

As poor operating results continued, the Westmills board moved to strengthen management. Mather commented,

"Harry's (Harry Higson, the president) difficulty was in building a team; he couldn't develop strong men around him. As a result, he was working under tremendous pressure and his health was beginning to suffer. The scale of operation wasn't for him and he realized it. But improving management meant going outside. There was no one in a functional job that was near strong enough to step up."

Mr. Garry W. Morrison was hired as executive vice president in late 1976. Morrison, aged 32, was an American citizen and now a Canadian landed immigrant. He held a B.Sc. in Textile Technology, an MBA, and had had seven years of management experience with U.S.-based Riegel Textile Corporation. At Riegel, Morrison had moved quickly through management ranks. Just prior to moving to Westmills, he had been a significant figure in the turnaround of a Canadian division of Riegel. His initial job at Westmills was to back up Harry Higson, but it was generally assumed he would become president in the not too distant future.

Morrison set out to learn the business, address some of the more pressing issues and recruit a second echelon of management.

Operating Changes

From January through August 1977, steps were taken to improve Westmills' financial condition, to cut operating costs and to bolster the product line. The vacant Trenton and Kelowna plants were sold; the former for $915,000 cash and the latter for $200,000 cash plus mortgage receivable for $1 million. The cash proceeds were used to reduce Westmills' long-term indebtedness to its banks and the mortgage was assigned to the banks as additional security. Inventories were reduced by fiscal year end to about $4.3 million in an attempt to reduce the pressure on interest costs and working capital levels. Salaried and hourly personnel were cut and more stringent guidelines were introduced for administrative, travel and other expenses. Five new high-end commercial carpet lines and six new residential lines were designed and prepared for introduction in the fall selling season. This brought the total Westmills product range to 34 lines.

Management Additions

In August 1977, Mr. J. William Ford joined Westmills as secretary-treasurer and chief financial officer. Ford, aged 33, was an American citizen and a Canadian landed immigrant. He was also married to a Canadian. He had known and worked with Garry Morrison at Riegel's Canadian subsidiary. Bill Ford's background included undergraduate and graduate studies in management at Virginia Polytechnic and Clemson University; service with the U.S. Army, including combat experience and decoration in Vietnam; and experience in senior financial positions in two Canadian-based textile companies. Ford explained his move to Westmills:

"Garry didn't pull any punches in describing the situation, but we'd been through a difficult turnaround before and I knew I could work with him. It seemed like a great challenge and opportunity."

At the time, Higson and Morrison were also engaged in negotiations with David Hirst, which would lead to Hirst joining Westmills as vice president of manufacturing in January 1978. Hirst, aged 54, was born in Yorkshire and educated in the U.K. at Batley Technical College (Textile Engineering) and Bradford Technical College (Cloth Manufacture). He had moved to Canada in 1957 and worked in a variety of carpet mill plant supervisory and general management positions. Hirst was well known in technical circles in the industry and highly regarded for his capability in carpet design and particularly for designing around equipment constraints. Prior to committing to Westmills, David Hirst had visited Calgary to review the operation and recalled;

"It was clear to me that there were also significant opportunities to improve productivity and quality. I welcomed the challenge."

A third senior manager was also hired by Westmills in this period to assume the top marketing position. By the time of the case, however, it was apparent that this appointment was not working out and that the marketing/sales function would have to be covered by James W. Hamilton, the current general sales manager. Hamilton, aged 36, had 18 years' experience in sales and sales management in the floor covering business. He had started with Westmills in 1971 as a contract sales representative in Vancouver and shortly thereafter had been moved to Toronto to "open up" the east for Westmills. This he had done very successfully and after a short sales management stint with another company had been persuaded by Harry Higson to come back to Calgary and address the now apparent sales problems in the west. He had been general sales manager since mid-1976. Jim Hamilton knew the grassroots workings of the carpet business and had a reputation as a top-flight sales representative and sales manager.

For fiscal year 1977, however, there were no miracle cures. The year closed with another significant loss having to be booked this time about $1.5 million pre-tax. Working capital was at a perilous level and the banks were becoming increasingly uneasy about their position. Now the financial, as well as operating foundations of the business, were deteriorating and the very survival of the firm was coming into question.

THE RECOVERY PLAN

Through the latter part of the 1976-77 fiscal year, Westmills had been working on a recovery plan, which took form at the beginning of the 1977-78 period. The essence of the plan was to reduce the company's product/market base somewhat, but maintain or improve volume by achieving greater penetration in the commercial and retail markets in western Canada. At the same time, steps would be taken to relieve financial pressure through the sale and leaseback of the Calgary plant. Projections for the 1978 fiscal year, which management regarded as conservative, are given in Exhibits 3 and 4. Significant parts of the new plan follow.

Marketing

In late 1977, Westmills distributed carpets through nearly 3,000 accounts across Canada, but primarily in the west. Geographic, customer type and product type segments, and Westmills share therein, are given in Table 4.

Table 4:   **Westmills' Position in the Canadian Market, 1976 (Volumes in million of square metres)**

	Western Market			Eastern Market	Total
	Retail	**Residential Contract**	**Commercial Contract**	**All Segments**	**Total**
All Product Volume	8.8	7.6	5.5	56.6	78.5
Westmills					
Volume	.51	1.76	.25	.80	3.32
Share (%)	5.8	23.1	4.6	1.4	4.2
Solid Color					
Volume	4.4	4.6	1.8	N/A	10.8
Westmills					
Volume	.40	1.41	.20	N/A	
Share (%)	9.1	30.6	11.1	N/A	18.6

Source: Company and case writer estimates

Under the plan for 1977 to 1978, sales in the west were to be emphasized. Representation would be maintained in Quebec, but at a minimum level. There was some anticipation of better results in Ontario through a new sales agency arranged by Garry Morrison. This latter activity had been debated in the company as not fully consistent with the western focus, but Morrison had prevailed, arguing that the incremental volume was essential.

Segment and Product Emphasis

Westmills' traditional market in the west had been residential contracts. The new carpet lines mentioned previously had been developed as part of a program to increase Westmills' retail and commercial market penetration. Most were multicolored lines developed from pre-dyed acrylic/nylon blends. The reasons for emphasis on pre-dyed yarns in the new products were market preferences and the limitations if Westmills' post-tufting coloring capabilities. It should be noted that many dealers in the west serviced more than one and perhaps all three segments, although most had a particular emphasis in their trade. It was also true that certain carpet styles could suitably be used by purchasers in one or more of the segments. The ultimate market mix of a mill could thus be only roughly estimated.

As a complement to the new product lines, Westmills was readying a foam backing application process in the Calgary plant. Foam-backed carpet accounted for about 20 per cent of carpet sales by volume and was particularly popular in lower-price print and multicolor styles. Since foam-backed carpet was easier and less expensive to install than conventional jute-backed carpet, it had a specific advantage in the "do-it-yourself" market and in certain residential contract applications. Westmills intended, at least initially, to put foam backing on selected current solid color lines to build volume at minimum incremental investment.

Promotion

Westmills' sales force numbered 23 representatives, each covering a specified geographic territory or, in the major cities, a specific accounts list. The sales representatives were paid a guaranteed minimum of $16,000, plus a commission which varied from one to three per cent of sales, depending on the carpet line. Each sales representative had a $200 per month car allowance and a travel and entertainment budget. The average gross earnings of the sales force were about $30,000. No changes were anticipated in the size or nature of the sales organization, although certain specific personnel adjustments were foreseen.

A major promotional expense was the cost of samples, sample kits, "waterfalls," etc., for use by the sales reps, in trade showrooms and in retail stores. While as much of the sample cost as possible was recovered from the trade, the net cost of sampling a new line was in the order of $50,000. Overall, sampling expense in 1976-77 was about $420,000. Only incidental amounts were spent on media advertising.

Delivery and Customer Service

Westmills' 8,000 square foot Calgary distribution center housed the majority of the finished goods inventory, as well as the customer service and shipping departments. This facility had never operated to management's satisfaction and was believed to be the weak link responsible for mounting customer complaints about late or mistaken delivery. There were plans for 1977-78 to reduce the space used by half, to relocate personnel to the plant (making changes and reductions in the process) and to ship more goods directly from the plant. One objective of the move was to reduce finished goods inventory by $1 million.

Manufacturing

Westmills' manufacturing costs had recovered somewhat from the effects of relocation and the coincident plateauing of sales. Efficiency had improved through 1976-77, but costs were still about 20 per cent higher than those incurred by similar mills in the U.S. (after adjustments for differences in input costs).

A consultant hired by Westmills noted that the high costs in the plant were due to production scheduling problems, low equipment utilization (in dyeing) and inappropriate equipment utilization (in finishing). The production process, in short, was not as yet running in a smooth and balanced fashion. Regarding quality, the consultant commented,

> Off quality in manufacturing is approximately double what one would expect . . . Part of this may be due to operational reasons . . . some must be attributed to attempts to utilize substandard fibres and blends in the carpet yarns (creating problems at Globe, as well as Calgary) . . . some is due to the high personnel turnover in Calgary.

While identifying these problems, Wilson noted that if Westmills could achieve "U.S. level" costs it would be competitive with any mill in Canada and could dominate the west in the demand segments which fit its yarn and carpet production capabilities.

The 1977 to 1978 plan anticipated the following changes.

1. Reduce plant direct labor.
2. Shift the product line to achieve greater utilization of Globe Mills' spinning capacity, and have Globe seek external contracts.
3. Implementing more stringent quality control, with the goal of reducing "second" yardage from seven to 4.5 per cent.
4. Change certain dye and chemical formulations to cheaper equivalently effective materials.
5. Eliminate a 4,000 square foot warehouse currently housing raw materials and off-quality or slow-selling goods.

The aggregate savings were forecast to be slightly more than $1 million on a volume base equivalent to 1976 to 1977. Morrison wrote, "We are performing major surgery on our operations to reduce their size to conform with sales volumes dictated by the marketplace." Westmills would still retain the capacity, however, to produce about 4.6 million metres of carpet, provided there were no unusual product mix demands.

Finance

As part of the recovery plan, Westmills was pursuing financial arrangements that would "reduce long-term debt, improve working capital and generally put us in a better situation financially." The main elements of this plan were the sale and lease-back of the Calgary plant and the discounting and sale of the Kelowna mortgage.

Discussions with potential purchasers of the Calgary plant indicated that a $3 million price might be acceptable, with a lease-back based on an eight to 10 per cent capitalization rate. It was probable that one year's lease cost in advance would have to be maintained in a trust account. Negotiations were underway, with an anticipated closing in January or February 1978. Other discussions regarding the mortgage on the Kelowna property indicated that the mortgage might be sold for something in the order of $900,000 cash. It was anticipated that this, too, would close early in the new year.

THE CRUNCH

As Westmills moved through January and February of 1978, it became increasingly apparent that events were not unfolding as anticipated. Sales were substantially below forecast and losses were accumulating at a distressing rate (Exhibits 3 and 4). Garry Morrison had left the company to be replaced on an interim basis by Harry Higson. The company's plight became well known in the industry and it was losing credibility as a continuing supplier. Management was working, as Jim Hamilton put it, somewhere between desperation and chaos.

Westmills, seen from outside, was on the verge of collapse. Within the company the difficulties were recognized, but there was resilience in management's attitude that offered at least the possibility of continuity and survival. The question they were asking was not whether, but how. An assessment by various managers of their areas of operation follows.

Marketing   Jim Hamilton

The problems Jim Hamilton was facing in the marketplace were, in simple form, credibility product and reliability in quality and delivery. "Right now," he said, "we have a terrible image in the market."

Credibility

Hamilton commented,

> Most of our accounts have been real good and have tried to support us; but they have heard rumors of us folding and they are really very concerned about the availability of goods. Some have come to us saying they just have to protect themselves by adding other suppliers. Others just won't do business with us; they say we are too shaky. Naturally, our competitors are taking as much as they can and have kept prices real keen.

Product

The new product programs had not met expectations. The foam-backed solid-color carpets had encountered market and salesperson resistance and took an inordinate time to run in the plant. The new multicolor retail lines had been based on yarn imported from the United States; the depreciation of the dollar had sharply increased materials costs, forcing Westmills into a non-competitive situation. No Canadian supplier had the capacity to supply on a reliable basis. Further, there was resistance at the retail level to purchasing samples and inventories at least in part because of Westmills' uncertain position. It was too early to evaluate the contract lines as the selling cycle in this market was considerably longer.

In spite of these difficulties, as Hamilton notes, "We have a good basic line in solid-color goods, particularly for residential contract. We make a good solid color fabric. What we don't have are reasonable upgrades to cover the higher price points."

Quality/Delivery Reliability

Good intentions to the contrary, Westmills was not living up to its promises to customers. The "mechanics" of order processing, commitment, scheduling, production and shipping were in Hamilton's words the "worst ever." He commented, "We are missing delivery dates and we are having quality problems; we have had to issue a pile of credit notes for problems we have created. I have a 4,000 square foot warehouse full of seconds to dispose of. How do I do this without upsetting the market?"

As a result of the foregoing, Hamilton was having trouble with sales-force morale. "There has been a tendency in this company to treat salesmen as a necessary evil anyway," he noted, "and now we aren't giving them product and service. How am I supposed to keep good men?"

Manufacturing   David Hirst

In the plant, Hirst was confronted with problems of morale, production scheduling and control, and product quality. His first test was immediate: on the very day he arrived in Calgary for work (having moved his family across the country), Garry Morrison had announced his resignation as president, to the surprise of all.

Morale

There was a bad morale problem in the plant, David Hirst noted, stemming from inadequate direction and control of work and further instability rising from concerns that there was "every possibility . . . (we) . . . may not be there tomorrow."

In his first weeks at the plant, Hirst had had a chance to assess his supervisory staff and was quite pleased, with the exception of one or two areas where he anticipated making changes. But overall, he felt he could build on the strengths and experience of these people and that the problems being experienced were more the result of the context they had been working in than of particular personal shortcomings. In light of this assessment, Hirst felt his first priority was to earn the respect of the plant personnel, establish that one person was in control and from this foundation isolate and address the operating problems.

Production Scheduling

The production scheduling of Westmills had fallen into progressive disarray as market pressures, new-product development, quality problems and financing difficulties had accumulated, driving operations into a vicious circle of deterioration. Hirst commented, "We are dealing in chaos . . . the tufters are being scheduled on the spot by telephone calls, slips of paper that people walk in with . . . there is no way we can operate efficiently like this . . . sales and customer service just don't see the costs . . . how can they make the promises they do?" Such were the difficulties of co-ordination between sales, customer service, manufacturing and delivery that one sales representative had recently verified that an order he had placed for 2,500 square metres of carpet had, quite simply, been lost.

The key to manufacturing efficiency in a carpet plant, Hirst pointed out, was proper scheduling and integration of equipment loads through the entire production process. This was quite impossible in the current circumstances and it was essential, as he put it, "to reduce the interference factors."

Quality

The sources of product quality problems were not all known but there appeared to be three principal contributing factors: the quality of the incoming yarns from Globe Mills, certain product designs, and deficiencies in training and experience in Calgary.

The limitations of Globe Mills had not been fully appreciated or considered in some product designs, with the result that it was stretching its capabilities to make certain yarns. Hirst, among others, agreed that Globe did a good job on yarns within its range and that the core problem was one of not balancing capabilities and efficiency in Globe and Calgary when designing fabrics.

Certain product designs, as well, were ill fitted to the Calgary plant. An internal memo commented that one of the new multicolor lines "makes our inadequacy in the multicolored area only too evident."

On training and experience, Hirst noted that "Calgary is not exactly a textile center and there is little access to trained workers." Westmills was thus forced to hire in a booming resource-based economy with the attendant high wage-rates and worker mobility. Substantial progress had been made in developing a stable workforce, but it was clear from the kind of problems arising from the plant floor that a great deal of training and experience was yet necessary.

Hirst weighed the circumstances.

> Sure we have problems. We have limitations in our equipment in Meaford and Calgary. But, with the exception of multicolor, we can produce volume and quality and make carpets that sell. We can do more than has been done with what we have now. I guess, coming from Yorkshire, if that's all you have, use it well. The job can be done . . . I have no reservations.

Control and Finance   Bill Ford

In early 1978, Bill Ford was working to improve the quality and use of the company's information systems and at the same time doing battle day-to-day for cash to meet immediate obligations.

Information Systems

On arriving at Westmills, Ford had reviewed the control and financial systems and found that "a lot of good things had been started, but they were still in a half-finished state." The computer facility had been applied to the financial side of the business for such tasks as payroll and receivables accounting and financing reporting. These areas, he felt, were in pretty good shape.

The problems lay more in the lack of development and use of operating and cost accounting systems. Here there were shortcomings in most areas, from order entry through manufacturing cost control to inventory control. The general framework for a workable system was in place but the actual work being done was not up to a reasonable standard in either effectiveness or efficiency. The matter was further complicated by a lack of understanding and communication between accounting and the line managers and supervision. "There was a problem of attitude and capabilities both inside and outside the accounting department," Ford noted, "and it has been necessary to change some personnel and segment the general and management accounting functions." Work was proceeding to improve the control system, but in the prevailing circumstances progress had been fairly slow.

Cash Flow

Westmills' cash position in early 1978 was so tight that Bill Ford was personally monitoring all receipts and approving all disbursements. The noose was drawing tighter every day.

On the receipts side, sales were down and collections were becoming more difficult. To prop up sales, credit had been granted in questionable circumstances. Difficulties with deliveries and quality claims had led to a flurry of credit notes being granted in the field, which meant a very complicated reconciliation of accounts. Some accounts were deferring payment until such matters were clarified; others, sensing weakness, were simply being very slow to pay. On the payables side, suppliers were getting tougher about terms and some had put Westmills on COD for orders incremental to existing balances.

Ford described the situation: "I'm in daily discussions with the banks. They are very sceptical and very close to pulling the plug. If they did now, my guess is that they might end up 10 to 15 per cent out of pocket. They have asked for a meeting within the next few days."

Derek Mather and CED

Derek Mather, aged 45, had started his business career as an investment analyst for Sun Life Assurance Co. In 1962, he had joined CED as an investment officer and was currently senior vice president. In his time at CED, Mather had been involved in the recruiting and screening of new corporate ventures and the monitoring of venture investments. He had been a member of Westmills' board of directors since 1967. These jobs, he pointed out, had not brought him into direct operating management.

> I see my own involvement as a dubious solution . . . a solution with many flaws. Although I've been on the board for many years, I don't know the industry from a technical standpoint, nor do I know the market particularly well. I don't have the high level of skills in the business, which I think financial people, considering an investment, would demand.

The countervailing problem at the moment was the expected difficulty of finding an experienced and credible presidential candidate. Mather commented, "I don't think we've got a hope of finding a guy like that in this present environment. I think whatever solution we are able to work out at this time . . . and by that, I mean the next few days . . . will be a patchwork solution . . . if we were to go out and try to hire a new man we'd just be wasting our time." He continued, "It may be, from a banker's point of view that if CED is prepared to supply additional equity capital and personnel, then that degree of shareholder commitment would be impressive."

CED was currently Westmills' major shareholder, holding approximately 40 per cent of the 1,100,984 common shares issued and $402,000 worth of the $1.144 million in unsecured convertible debentures (convertible to common shares at $2.50). Westmills common stock was currently trading on the Toronto Stock Exchange at from $.70 to $.90.

On CED's future involvement, Mather and Gerald Sutton, CED's president, were of one mind: within reason, CED must stick with the investment and do what is necessary to revive the company. Sutton explained, "We took Westmills public and in so doing reduced our holdings, recapture our initial investment and made a profit. Under the circumstances we can't just withdraw from this situation; we have a moral responsibility to the public." Mather added, "The business community in the west knows we started this company . . . we can't have them say we walked away when times got tough."

Figure 1: **Main Steps in Tufted Carpet Manufacture**

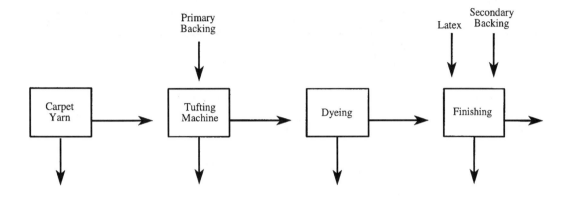

MAJOR VARIABLES

1. Material, i.e., Nylon
polyester,
polypropeline,
acrylic fibres

1. Construction i.e.,
level *loop*, hi lo
loop, shag, cut and
loop, cut pile

1. Process i.e., piece
dyeing, roller or
screen printing,
"Millitron" spray
jet.

1. Backing i.e., Jute,
woven or nonwoven
synthestic, foam
rubber

2.Yarn form i.e., spun
staple, bulked
continuous filament

2. Gauge Spacing of
needles across
width of machine

3.Thickness. Of both
individual filaments
and yarn.

3. Stitches per inch.
The number of
tufts per inch
counting
lengthwise

4. Color approach.
Use of pre-dyed,
variable dye affinity,
or plain yarn.

4. Pile weight

Exhibit 1: **Consolidated Operating Results for Fiscal Years Ending August 31 (000's)**

	1977	1976	1975	1974	1973
Net sales	$21,678	$23,056	$21,725	$22,823	$14,407
Costs of Sales	17,886	19,594	17,506	17,098	10,622
Depreciation	712	660	638	347	188
Total	**18,598**	**20,254**	**18,144**	**17,445**	**10,810**
Gross Margin	3,080	2,802	3,581	5,378	3,597
%	14.2%	12.1%	16.5%	23.4%	25.0%
Marketing expenses	2,625	2,478	2,141	3,063	1,933
Administration	876	900	610	--	--
Financing					
Long-term	756	681	597	309	133
Short-term	308	514	333	156	37
Extraordinary costs	--	635	615	--	--
Total	**4,565**	**5,208**	**4,296**	**3,528**	**2,103**
Net Income before tax	(1,485)	(2,406)	(715)	1,849	1,494
Income tax	(305)	(361)	(309)	798	651
Net income	(1,180)	(2,045)	(405)	1,051	842
Extraordinary items	314	--	96	96	--
Net Profit	**(866)**	**(2,045)**	**(309)**	**1,147**	**842**

Source: Company Document

Exhibit 2: **Consolidated Balance Sheets For Fiscal Years Ending August 31 ($000s)**

	1977	1976	1975	1974	1973
Current Assets					
Cash	$--	$--	$--	$77	$169
Accounts Receivable	3,880	3,871	4,506	3,480	2,337
Inventories	4,584	6,198	5,316	6,033	3,857
Prepaid expenses	253	227	169	168	173
Income Taxes recoverable	--	--	354	--	--
	8,717	10,296	10,345	9,757	6,536
Current Liabilities					
Short-term borrowings	4,497	4,230	2,576	2,463	421
Accounts Payable, accrued liabilities	2,458	2,796	3,421	3,279	2,164
Income and other taxes	195	255	236	231	519
Current portion, LT debt	470	402	397	653	442
	7,620	7,683	6,630	6,626	3,546
Working capital	1,097	2,613	3,715	3,131	2,990
Net fixed assets	6,644[1]	7,811	8,075	7,841	3,887
	7,741	10,424	11,790	10,972	6,877
Long-term debt[2]	4,989	6,500	5,461	4,459	1,873
Deferred income taxes	408	713	1,074	948	586
Shareholders' equity:					
Common stock	3,362	3,362	3,362	3,362	3,362
Retained earnings	(1,018)	(151)	1,893	2,203	1,056
	7,741	10,424	11,790	10,972	6,877

Source: Company documents.

[1]Includes mortgage receivable for $1,000,000 on sale of Kelowna plant
[2]The structure of the long-term debt as of August 31, 1977 was as follows:

9.5% First mortgage on land and buildings; payment $9,000 per month, including interest.	*$1,017,950*
Term bank loans at 1.5% over prime; payments $30,000 per month plus interest.	
Secured by assignment of mortgage receivable plus a charge on land, buildings and equipment	*$1,556,000*
12% Series A debentures, due 1980; payments $22,000 per month including interest.	
Secured by charge on land, buildings and equipment ranking with bank term loan	*$1,444,775*
12% Convertible, redeemable unsecured debentures. Series A and B.	
Semi-annual interest	*$1,441,000*
	$5,459,725
LESS: Current portion of long-term debt	*470,705*
	$4,989,020

Exhibit 3: **Forecast Profit and Actual Experience, 1977-78 ($000s)**

	Recovery Plan Pds. 1-6	Forecast FY 1978	Estimated Actual Pds. 1-6
Square metres (000)	$1,550	3,340	1,230
Net Sales	10,217	22,138	7,966
Cost of Sales	8,712	18,611	6,888
Gross Margin	1,505	3,527	1,078
Per cent Net Sales	14.7%	15.9%	13.6%
Marketing	968	2,029	893
Administration	412	871	432
Finance – interest	415	777	461
Total	**1,795**	**3,677**	**1,786**
Operating income (loss)	(290)	(150)	(708)
Taxes recoverable	(96)	(201)	(106)
Income (loss before extraordinary items)	(194)	51	(602)
Extraordinary Items:			
Sale of mortgage (net)	(48)	(48)	--
Sale of plant (net)	892	892	--
Income tax recovery	356	356	--
Net Profit (loss)	**$1,006**	**$1,251**	**$(602)**

Exhibit 4: **Balance Sheet Forecasts and Actual Experience, 1977-78 ($000s)**

	Recovery Plan End Period 6	Forecast End 1978 FY	Estimated Actual End Period 6
Current Assets:			
Accounts receivable	$4,750	$4,500	$4,191
Trust account	300	300	--
Inventories:			
Raw material	1,600	1,600	1,355
Work in process	650	650	1,087
Finished goods	1,425	1,176	1,947
Total inventory	3,675	3,426	4,389
Prepaid expenses	225	316	156
Total current assets	**8,950**	**8,632**	**8,736**
Mortgage	--	--	1,000
Net fixed assets	3,691	3,495	5,427
Total	**$12,641**	**$12,127**	**$15,163**
Liabilities & Shareholders' Equity			
Bank indebtedness	5,501	4,507	5,701
Accounts payable	1,847	2,198	1,943
Taxes payable	225	214	220
Current portion:			
Long-term debt	--	--	470
Current liabilities	**7,573**	**6,919**	**8,334**
Long-term debt	1,441	1,441	4,785
Deferred taxes	278	173	302
Shareholders' Equity			
Common shares	3,362	3,362	3,362
Retained earnings	(13)	232	(1,620)
Total	**$12,641**	**$12,127**	**$15,163**

PROVINCIAL PAPERS INC. (A)

case 29

Sheree Jackson and
Joseph N. Fry

In mid-July 1993, Ian Ross, recently elected director and Chairman of the Board of Provincial Papers Inc. (Provincial), met with the two independent directors of the company to inform them that Provincial's CEO was leaving the company. Provincial was a coated paper manufacturer located in Thunder Bay, Ontario. The company had just been created as an independent entity by way of an employee buyout from its former parent, Abitibi-Price, Inc. (Abitibi). Ross described the situation:

> We need to remedy this problem quickly. We are facing a crisis! Our operations are losing $2 million a month and some of our key managers have left, including the people heading our marketing and sales and finance activities. The coated paper industry is over-supplied and market prices are depressed. Our customers are uneasy and our competition is spreading the news of our troubles.

The directors agreed on the need for immediate action, but there didn't appear to be any internal candidates for the CEO position. A traditional executive search for an outsider would be problematic and, in any case, would probably take up to four months. As the discussion continued it became increasingly apparent to Ross that the directors were looking at him as the solution.

IVEY

Ross was no stranger to turnaround situations. He recalled his experience in the early 1980s when he led a near-bankrupt boxboard mill out of difficulties and set up the basis for what was now the $700-million Paperboard Industries Corp. But he wondered if it would be wise to step into the CEO's position at Provincial. (See Appendix A for a further description of Ian Ross' background).

INDUSTRY BACKGROUND

The following section describes some characteristics of the pulp and paper industry that are particularly relevant to the Provincial situation.

Pulp and Paper Categories

Wood pulp was the primary raw material in the production of paper products. There were two basic processes for manufacturing wood pulp. The first, mechanical or thermomechanical pulping, consisted of physically grinding pulp logs. Mechanical pulping provided higher yields of pulp per unit of raw wood fibre than the alternative of chemical pulping, but the pulp was generally less suited for paper products of high brightness and permanence. Chemical pulping represented the vast majority of the world's capacity. This process removed most of the undesirable lignins and extractives from raw wood fibre during a series of chemical-intensive "cooking" phases. The advantages of chemical pulp were that it was much stronger, easier to bleach (whiten), and papers produced from it were less likely to lose their brightness over time. The disadvantage of chemical pulp was its cost – chemical pulp mills were more expensive to build and lower in yield than their mechanical counterparts.

Paper products were usually classified into four general categories: newsprint, printing and writing paper, packaging and converting paper, and tissue paper. The largest category by value was printing and writing paper, which itself consisted of four sub-groups: coated and uncoated groundwood papers, made from mechanical pulp, and coated and uncoated freesheet papers, made from chemical pulp.

The Coated Paper Business

Coated paper was manufactured by adding layers of coating materials to a base sheet of uncoated paper. Coating facilitated printing and enhanced the optical properties of the paper, such as gloss and brightness. Typically, there was more value added in the manufacturing of coated paper than in other paper types since the process involved a greater investment in technology and facilities and a higher reliance on operating skill and experience. Coated paper, as a consequence, was usually sold at higher prices than other types of paper, but these prices were a function of market forces and provided no guarantee of higher margins.

Coated groundwood paper was used in applications such as mass-market magazines, newspaper inserts, catalogues and direct mail advertising. Coated freesheet paper was used in specialty magazines, catalogues, books, brochures, annual reports, labels and so forth.

The coated paper business was a global market. In this respect the role of European producers was of particular note. To keep their facilities loaded in periods of slack demand, EEC producers sold product into international markets, and particularly Canada. Trade barriers made it difficult for North American producers to respond in kind.

There had been no announcements of new facility additions in the fine paper industry for several years. Overall industry capacity had increased, however, since every mill worked constantly to increase machine speeds and efficiencies. These increments were material over time, but other than this, there were no expectations of major steps in capacity within the three or four years that it would take to build and bring a new facility on line.

Commodity Coated Paper Producers

Coated paper producers could be divided into two categories: commodity producers and specialty producers. Provincial's production consisted of approximately 90 per cent commodity paper and 10 per cent specialty paper.

Commodity paper producers manufactured paper in large volumes with broadly agreed upon standardized specifications by grade of, for example, weight and finish, and little product differentiation between producers. Typically, commodity producers sold to large customers with high volume requirements, for example, for magazine and catalogue publishing. Commodity producers tended to be price-takers, selling on the basis of quoted list prices. During periods of excess supply, prices were essentially determined by the cost structure of the lowest-cost producers.

Given the commodity coated paper market structure, manufacturers in this sector concentrated on cost, consistent quality and reliable supply. They sought advantages in pulp supply, in the scale and efficiency of their operations and in product and customer focus.

Specialty Coated Paper Producers

Specialty producers manufactured paper with specific attributes to meet the needs of customers in specific market niches. Specialty producers tended to be smaller than their commodity counterparts and to operate smaller paper machines.

Given the structure of the specialty market, producers in this sector focused on unique customer needs, technical depth and flexible production. These activities protected the specialty producers to some extent from the large commodity producers whose mills were designed for higher speed, longer run economies.

Industry Slump

Trends in the coated paper business were consistent with broader trends in the pulp and paper industry. In this larger context, for the past four years the profitability of the pulp and paper industry in North America had been in cyclical decline. A <u>Pulp & Paper Week</u> survey of 19 leading Canadian forest product companies showed a net loss of $750 million for the nine months ending Sept. 30, 1992. And more specifically, the coated paper markets in Canada were in oversupply as a result of imported European coated groundwood paper and excess North American coated freesheet capacity.

There were some signs, however, that industry fundamentals might improve. A recent decline in the Canadian dollar was making Canadian pulp and newsprint increasingly competitive abroad. There were reports that newsprint prices in the U.S. were stabilizing in response to higher consumption and improved market pulp demand. One industry expert stated that the U.S. economy seemed to be recovering more strongly than anticipated, and that this upswing would positively affect the Canadian industry. Other positive influences in the industry were the continued strength in the wood products sector, extensive cost reduction efforts by producers, and an increase in market pulp prices. These positive developments, however, had yet to offset the depressed paper prices facing Canadian mills. From 1990 through 1992, for example, the average selling price for coated freesheet paper had declined 15 per cent.

COMPANY BACKGROUND

Provincial manufactured fine, coated paper for the commercial printing, label, book publishing and magazine markets. The company's three paper machines were located at a single paper mill in Thunder Bay, Ontario, on the northern shore of Lake Superior.

Provincial's aggregate annual capacity was approximately 166,000 tons. As such, it was a relatively small player in the coated paper industry. Repap, its main domestic competitor, had a capacity of approximately 1,000,000 tons, while its major U.S.-based competitors, Consolidated Paper, S.D. Warren, and International Paper had capacities of 1,348,000, 1,334,000 and 680,000 tons, respectively. By rank, Provincial was the thirteenth-largest producer of coated groundwood paper and the ninth-largest producer of coated freesheet paper in North America.

A flow chart of Provincial's operations is presented in Exhibit 1 and serves as an outline for the following narrative.

Suppliers

Provincial purchased its fiber requirements from several suppliers. Groundwood logs, which served as furnish for Provincial's thermomechanical pulping mill and accounted for about 25 per cent of the company's pulp requirements, were purchased from Abitibi under a new twenty-year supply agreement. The price for these logs was set annually by negotiation or, failing agreement, arbitration.

Provincial purchased hardwood and softwood pulp from mills run by Canadian Pacific, Kimberly-Clark and Champion. Both Canadian Pacific (Thunder Bay, Ontario) and Kimberly-Clark (Terrace Bay, Ontario) represented local sources of pulp, providing the mutual advantage of low transportation costs. Provincial's major suppliers of de-inked recycled pulp, which comprised roughly 10 per cent of its pulp requirements, were Superior (Duluth, Minnesota) and Ponderosa (Wisconsin).

Provincial's operating problems and financial difficulties had resulted in late payments to its pulp suppliers. Accounts payable were approximately 120 days compared to an industry norm of 60 days. Recent problems in the forest products industry were resulting in greater caution on the part of suppliers in providing credit to their customers. In particular, two of Provincial's key suppliers, Canadian Pacific and Kimberly-Clark, had recently lost money through customer bankruptcies and their credit departments were not about to extend Provincial's terms. In fact, with the widespread news of its losses, Provincial management was having a difficult time trying to maintain existing credit terms.

Production Facilities

Provincial's mill was built in 1918, and over the years had undergone a number of expansions, renovations and refurbishments. For example, over the eight-year period from 1985 to 1993, Abitibi had invested more than $60 million to upgrade fixed assets.

Although Provincial's machines were old, they produced quality paper at efficient rates. The company's three paper machines were known respectively as machines No. 5, 6, and 8. The No. 5

machine first came on line in 1923, and was rebuilt in 1965. This machine had been idle since 1990. The No. 6 paper machine first came on line in 1927 and was subsequently rebuilt in 1984 and 1988. This machine was used primarily for the production of groundwood paper. The No. 8 machine came on line in 1966 and had undergone a major rebuild in 1989. This machine was capable of producing both groundwood and freesheet paper, although it was currently being used for freesheet paper only.

Employees

The Provincial workforce was highly skilled, stable and mature. Prior to the buyout arrangements discussed later, there were approximately 800 employees of whom about 90 per cent were members of one of the following four unions:

1. Communications, Energy, and Paper Workers Union (CEP); two locals.
2. International Union of Operating Engineers (IUOE)
3. International Brotherhood of Electrical Workers (IBEW)
4. Office and Professional Employees' International Union (OPEIU)

Relations between the unions and management at Provincial had varied over time but for the most part could be characterized as formal or distant. The stresses of the buyout negotiations and subsequent operating pressures had not improved this situation.

Non-unionized employees were broken down by function as follows:

	Executive	Sales & Marketing	Operations	Finance & Admin.	Engineering & Product Services	Develop	Temp.
# of employees	7	8	25	12	10	2	8

Products

Provincial produced a wide range of high quality coated groundwood and coated freesheet products as reflected by the scope of its approximately 240 product stock-keeping units (SKUs). This product variety had accumulated over time as new products had been introduced to meet evolving customer needs and old products had been retained to service remaining demand. To provide competitive customer service across this product line, Provincial had to make frequent grade changes on its paper machines and hold substantial finished goods inventories in a Toronto warehouse. On the other hand, given its struggles to sustain revenues and machine loading, the company had been very reluctant to cut lines and to turn down orders, whatever their significance.

Provincial also had approximately 200 products at various stages of research and development. These reflected a push by management in recent years to shift the revenue base of the business toward specialty papers. The wide variety of development products put pressure on operations, however, as schedules were modified to accommodate experimental production runs.

Customers

Provincial sold to over 100 commercial printers and paper distributors. Product distribution was handled either directly from the mill to the end user/distributor, or from the warehouse in Toronto to end user/distributor. Three or four major customers purchased approximately 30 per cent of the mill's output directly.

Approximately 60 per cent of Provincial's sales were to customers located in Canada and the remaining 40 per cent were to customers in the United States, although several of Provincial's Canadian customers also sold their printed products, in turn, to end-users in the United States.

With the widespread news of Provincial's losses, customers were beginning to question the company's credibility as a continuing supplier.

Sales Force

Provincial's eight-member sales force was responsible for developing and maintaining strong customer relationships. Representation was geographically dispersed through account managers located in Toronto, Montreal, Winnipeg, Chicago, and Cincinnati, and supported by a six-person customer service department located in Thunder Bay. The vice-president of Sales, who had 14 years of sales experience, was one of the managers who had just left the company.

PROVINCIAL AND ABITIBI

Prior to the 1993 buyout, Provincial had operated for over 60 years as a wholly owned subsidiary of Abitibi, one of the world's largest newsprint producers and a major producer and marketer of other groundwood-based paper. In 1992, Abitibi's revenues were over $1.6 billion.

Provincial had been a troubled holding for Abitibi for some time and in recent years had been running up significant operating losses as summarized below.

	1990	1991	1992
Tons Sold (000's)	140.5	98.8	122.4
Sales	$145.7	$95.1	$107.6
Operating Loss	$(26.3)	$(40.7)	$(35.6)

Abitibi's Turnaround Efforts

In spite of Provincial's troubles over the years, Abitibi had felt that as Canada's only full-line coated papermaker it had considerable prospects, and it had invested in the company and had worked to improve its performance. Abitibi had restructured mill management at Thunder Bay, for example, and had worked with Provincial to achieve cost reductions and quality improvements and to intensify marketing efforts, including new product launches. In the early 1990s these efforts had yet to bear fruit and Provincial was turning out to be only one of the thorns in Abitibi's side. Depressed market conditions were hurting Abitibi's pulp and newsprint businesses as well, and after a strategic review the company decided to divest its non-core assets. Provincial, Abitibi's only coated paper operation and an increasing source of operating losses, was put up for sale.

The Search for a Buyer

For Abitibi, sales was a clear preference over shutdown because the latter would involve significant environmental clean-up and employee severance costs. As part of the preparations for sale, Provincial was incorporated as a separate company.

After several unsuccessful attempts to sell Provincial to industry or financial buyers, Abitibi initiated buyout discussions with employee representatives in November 1992. The company's employees were aware of its difficult circumstances. Many of them feared that significant job losses would occur if the economy and company did not turn around. Given the potential impact of the situation for the city of Thunder Bay and more generally for northern Ontario, Abitibi and the Union leadership invited the provincial government to join in the discussions. This was not an unprecedented step. The Province of Ontario had recently played an active role in negotiating similar deals. In one, the employees of the Spruce Falls newsprint and groundwood mill in Kapuskasing purchased the business from Kimberly-Clark. In another, the employees at Algoma Steel in Sault Ste. Marie had acquired 60 per cent of Algoma's equity in return for significant wage concessions.

THE EMPLOYEE BUYOUT

In December 1992 discussions for a possible sale of Provincial to the employees began. The parties involved in negotiating the agreement were the unions (represented by two locals of the CEP, and one local of each of IBEW, IUOE, and OPEIU), the mill management, Abitibi, and the Government of Ontario. A group called the Management Committee was formed to represent members of the management group during the buyout negotiations. This committee consisted of the seven members of the senior management team. A Union Coalition was formed with a similar purpose to the Management Committee, but to represent the unionized employees. The Union Coalition group was made up of one representative from each CEP local and one representative from each of the other three unions. Negotiations were facilitated by the Ministry of Economic Development, Trade and Tourism and took place throughout December and into January 1993.

The buyout negotiations proved to be difficult and the talks collapsed frequently. By February 1993, however, an agreement had been reached on the basic structure of a transaction and a memorandum of understanding was signed. This preliminary agreement was the basis for further intense negotiations in March and April 1993. One consequence of these negotiations was that the president of Provincial was removed from the leadership of the buyout team with the agreement of both the Management Committee and the Union Coalition. His successor, a former general manager in the business, took over to complete the negotiations and became CEO of the new Provincial on June 1, 1993, only to leave a few short weeks later.

The 800 employees voted almost 90 per cent in favor of the mill purchase. On May 31, 1993, an agreement to sell Provincial to its employees was ratified by the union locals and approved by the Government of Ontario and the Board of Directors of Abitibi. The mill plant and equipment, with a 1993 net book value of $93.4 million, was purchased for $1. Further, to assist the company in establishing normal banking relationships and to provide it with the flexibility necessary to ensure long-term viability, the provincial government provided a five-year, $6.5 million loan and an $11.5 million loan guarantee.

As a result the starting balance sheet of the new Provincial was as follows:

Balance Sheet - as of June 1, 1993		
ASSETS		
Current Assets		
Cash	$	12,000,000
Accounts Receivable		17,000,000
Inventory		14,000,000
Fixed Assets		1
TOTAL ASSETS		43,000,001
LIABILITIES		
Current Liabilities		
Accounts Payable		18,000,000
ODC Term Loan		6,500,000
Total Liabilities		24,500,000
SHAREHOLDERS' EQUITY		
Retained Earnings		18,500,001
TOTAL LIABILITIES AND SHAREHOLDERS' EQUITY		43,000,001

Details of the Buyout Agreement

Under the buyout agreement Provincial was wholly owned by its employees, with 75 per cent of the shares going to unionized employees and 25 per cent to non-unionized management and staff. Each of these employee groups held their ownership interests through separate classes of shares of Provincial Papers Holding Inc., which in turn held 100 per cent of the shares of Provincial Papers Inc. The affairs of Provincial Papers Inc. were to be supervised by a seven-member board of directors, comprised of two union representatives, two non-union representatives and three independent directors. A diagram of Provincial's corporate structure is set out in Exhibit 2.

Although the buyout saved 700 jobs, 100 union and 12 non-union jobs were eliminated during the restructuring agreed in the negotiations. In addition, the company's union and management employees agreed to a wage rollback of 20 per cent. Under the agreement, these new wage rates were to remain constant until February 1998. These sacrifices represented annual wage savings of $6.5 million.

To help Provincial develop the infrastructure of an independent business, Abitibi agreed to a Transitional Services Agreement with Provincial for the provision of management support services, including support with respect to management information systems, supply management, treasury functions, and credit management and distribution. Over the term of the agreement, Provincial reimbursed Abitibi for the hourly costs incurred by Abitibi's employees to the extent that they were engaged in the performance of environmental services, assistance on employment matters, and the provision of other services for Provincial's benefit. The services provided by Abitibi were to be gradually phased out, with the final phase ending in the fall of 1995.

Abitibi assumed ongoing responsibility for certain pre-existing environmental issues at the Company, but not for issues relating to ongoing business operations subsequent to the sale to the employees. Abitibi also retained responsibility for all Provincial employees who were subject to workers' compensation or short-term disability relief at the time of the transaction.

Ross' Decision

Ian Ross was elected as one of the three independent directors of the new Provincial Papers business — after a selection process that included questioning and approval by both the Management Committee and the Union Coalition — and shortly thereafter, at the inaugural meeting of the board, he was also elected chairman. Then, on the heels of this appointment, Provincial's new CEO informed Ross that he would be leaving the company. For Ross the situation had taken an unexpected turn. In short order he was going to have to decide whether he should take on the CEO role at Provincial.

Appendix A   Ian Ross's Experience

Ian Ross had over 20 years of experience in the forest products industry, including involvement in the creation of Paperboard Industries Corporation (PIC) in the early 1980s and its development into Canada's largest integrated paperboard producer, with sales of over $700 million and strong operating profits. Ross served as president and chief executive officer of PIC from 1986-1990.

In addition to his involvement with Provincial, Ross was chairman of Telular Canada Inc., a publicly traded wireless communications company. Earlier he had served in the 1980s as director of SHL Systemhouse Inc., one of Canada's largest high tech companies, and of the Ontario Development Corporation. Ross had been a member of the Law Society of Upper Canada since 1968.

Exhibit 1: **Flow Chart of Operations**

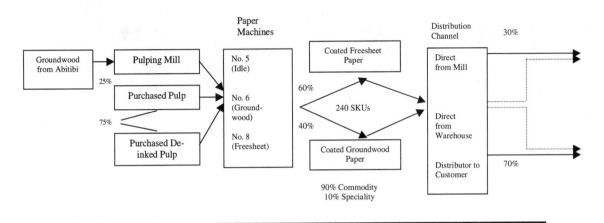

Exhibit 2: **Corporate Organization Chart**

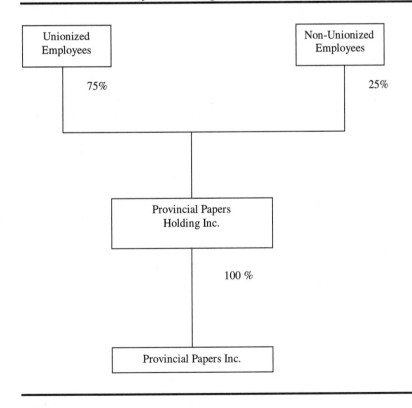

WELLINGTON INSURANCE (A)

case 30

Julian Birkinshaw and
Mary M. Crossan

Murray Wallace, the newly appointed President and Chief Executive Officer (CEO) of Wellington Insurance, realized that he needed to take action swiftly. It was late January 1988, and Wallace had held the post of CEO for less than a month. In that time he had made a comprehensive assessment of Wellington's operations, and had concluded that the company was in a very poor state of health. A consultant's report described Wellington as "a company without hope." It was Wallace's job to prove the consultant wrong.

Wallace had been offered the job of CEO several months earlier by Trilon, the parent company of Wellington. Through his experience as a Wellington board member, and an initial assessment of Wellington's competitive position, he concluded that the best course of action was to sell Wellington. Trilon's board did not take his advice, having committed themselves to maintaining a portfolio of diversified financial services. They asked Wallace to take the job, beginning on January 1, 1988. Despite the need for a sustained long-term change at Wellington, quarterly reporting to Trilon also created a sense of urgency in Wallace's task.

IVEY

Julian Birkinshaw prepared this case under the supervision of Professor Mary Crossan solely to provide material for class discussion. The author does not intend to illustrate either effective or ineffective handling of a managerial situation. The author may have disguised certain names and other identifying information to protect confidentiality.

There were multiple problems at Wellington, not least of which was the low morale of the employees. Wallace was aware that a number of change programs had been implemented over the years, with very little apparent success. As a result he realized that any initiatives he came up with would probably be seen as "just another change program." He began to consider what action he could take that would have a positive impact on the attitudes of the employees.

THE GENERAL INSURANCE INDUSTRY

The basic principle of insurance was to share the losses of few amongst many. It was originally conceived in the shipping industry, through the formation of syndicates of ship-owners that each contributed a "premium" to a common fund that would be used in the event of an accident. The last hundred years, however, had seen a rapid rise in individual prosperity, and in particular the ownership of cars and houses, such that most insurance became directed towards consumers. Commercial ventures made up the minority.

There were two principal types of insurance: Life insurance, which protected the policyholder's health and life; and General insurance, which protected the policyholder's possessions. A critical difference from the insurance companies' point of view was that life insurance usually included a guaranteed payout (on death) while general insurance made payments only to the minority who incurred material loss. Life insurance was the larger industry with 1987 Canadian revenues of $41 billion, compared to $17 billion for general insurance. The combined figures represented 0.6 per cent of the Gross Domestic Product (GDP).

The primary function of the general insurance company was to calculate an appropriate premium for every risk, such as damage to the policyholder's automobile or theft from the home, so that the income received in premiums was larger than the outlay in claims (called underwriting). A secondary role was to invest the policyholders' premiums until claims were made. This provided a relatively predictable return to counterbalance the erratic returns from risk sharing. A third aspect of the general insurance company's work was loss reduction and prevention: through its experience in dealing with a large number of claims, the insurance company was ideally placed to educate the consumer on how to avoid accidents, deter theft, and reduce loss.

Performance measures for general insurance firms were designed to reflect the distinction between underwriting and investment. The key measures are presented in Table 1:

Table 1: **Key Financial Ratios in General Insurance**

Earned Loss Ratio	The percentage of total premiums paid out as claims. A figure of 70 indicated that for every $1 in policy premiums collected $0.70 was paid out in insurance claims.
Total Expense Ratio	Earned Loss Ratio
Combined Ratio	The earned loss ratio plus the total expense ratio. A figure of less than 100 indicated that the company had made a profit on its underwriting activities.

Investment income was usually quoted as a dollar sum rather than a percentage, and was added to the underwriting profit (loss) to arrive at the total profit. Thus a combined ratio of 108 on total premiums of $1 million represented an underwriting loss of $80,000. If the investment income for the year were $100,000 the company would still make a profit of $20,000.

Business Functions in General Insurance

A general insurance company was typically organized into three main functional areas.

Underwriting

Whenever a new customer required insurance, or its established customers' policies were up for renewal, the underwriters calculated an appropriate premium based on the previous history of the individual, age, sex and so on. For commercial customers (i.e., businesses) premiums were based on industry statistics and an assessment of the business facilities.

Claims

Whenever a claim was made, such as an automobile accident or a theft, the claims department worked with the customer and his or her broker to ensure satisfactory payment. Damage would be assessed by an appraiser, either over the telephone or in person. The adjuster would do the rest of the work: ensuring the policy was valid, arranging any legal documentation, and arranging payment.

Marketing and Sales

This function was responsible for the product: the coverage offered, its price, the commission rate (to brokers), any special features, and the segment of the market it targeted. Marketing employees worked with brokers and with the general public to increase awareness of product features.

Every insurance company also had a number of other functions, including capital investment, actuarial work, legal work, and accounting, but these typically involved much smaller numbers of staff.

THE CANADIAN GENERAL INSURANCE INDUSTRY

The Canadian industry had 350 licensed companies in 1988. The top eight held less than 40 per cent of the market and no single company held more than seven per cent. In addition there were a number of mutual companies (in which the shareholders were policyholders), and four government-owned auto-insurance companies. $4 billion of the $17 billion 1987 revenues were attributable to the government-owned companies. Only 40 per cent of the market was held by Canadian-controlled firms. The rest was held by multinational insurance companies such as Zurich and Royal Insurance. There were no significant multinational Canadian companies.

The industry was heavily regulated to ensure that companies had both the capital reserves and expertise to fulfil their obligations to policyholders. Entry requirements were, however, considered to be straightforward. Foreign acquisitions of Canadian companies were typically not restricted, except in Quebec where foreign ownership was limited to 25 per cent.

Market Segments

The market for general insurance was divided into six sectors. Automobile insurance was by far the largest, accounting for $5.5 billion out of the private-sector total premiums of $11 billion[1], and was generally the least profitable as well. Property insurance accounted for $3.8 billion of the total, with the remainder being taken up by the various specialty lines: liability, surety and fidelity, boiler and machinery, and marine and aircraft. Most insurance companies and brokers distinguished between "personal lines" and "commercial lines." Personal lines were just written in auto and property; commercial lines were written in all six areas. The major difference between the two was the high level of individual attention needed for commercial assessments. Typically, each business would be assessed through a personal visit by an underwriter, whereas individuals were assessed according to a prescribed formula.

The prevailing wisdom in the industry was to offer a broad range of products across most or all sectors. Automobile insurance, in particular, was offered by nearly all companies because of its predominance, and because there were opportunities to cross-sell into property. A number of companies had opted for a more focused strategy. Cigna specialized in commercial lines only, and Pilot had deliberately restricted its operations to Ontario, with a focus on personal automobile within that. Evidence suggested that a focused strategy could be effective if well executed, but was inherently more risky than the full-line alternative.

Product Characteristics

Most consumers viewed insurance as a commodity. In the automobile and property sectors every insurance company offered similar coverage, and claims were infrequent enough that speed of payment and service were hard to compare. Attempts had been made to differentiate products by branding or by special features, but these were quickly copied. Furthermore, there was no cost to the customer for transferring business to another company, and contracts were renewed annually or bi-annually. The consequence was that there was little company loyalty, and in periods of price fluctuations many customers changed company. A further concern to the industry was the inelasticity of demand. Insurance purchases were often legislated (e.g., liability insurance) and usually bought grudgingly. A lower price, for property insurance for example, did not encourage customers to buy more insurance. For any individual company, however, volume could be substantially affected by price because it was being achieved at the expense of competitors. A low price strategy, for example, would likely have the effect of increasing sales but with a corresponding drop in quality. Companies did not just want customers: they wanted customers who were unlikely to make claims. The opposing strategies of increasing sales and weeding out the high-risk businesses represented an ongoing dilemma for insurance companies.

There was some potential for differentiation in the niche lines such as surety and fidelity or boiler and machinery because there was a considerable amount of direct contact with the customer. High quality service was rewarded through word-of-mouth referrals so that reputation, rather than price alone, became a source of competitive advantage. These niches were too small to be the focus of the business, but represented a profitable sideline for any company that could secure a position.

---

[1] Note that the private sector revenues of $13 billion (1987) consisted of $11 billion premiums and $2 billion investment income.

Industry Characteristics

While the barriers to entry were moderate, the costs of exiting the insurance industry were substantial. Companies were liable for up to seven years for claims, and often the reserved sums of money were insufficient to pay for future costs. Thus, a company exiting the industry could expect several years of future expenses, with no revenues against which to offset them. The result was an industry with far too many players, all competing on price. Profitability was low, and the consolidation among players, long anticipated in the industry, had not happened. As one analyst commented: "If you can't make a decent return on revenues of $200 million, you think twice about expanding to $400 million." Evidence in the Canadian market suggested that significant economies of scale were attainable up to about $300 million revenues. Only two players were substantially larger than $300 million and both reputedly had organizational difficulties. However, it was not known whether these difficulties stemmed from the additional complexities of running a larger business, or whether they were attributable to a lack of strategic focus.

Size did, however, confer advantages of a different sort on the multinational insurance companies. By operating in multiple jurisdictions these companies had a certain amount of flexibility in deciding where they would realize profits. A poor performance in Canada, for example, could effectively be smoothed over as long as money was being made elsewhere. This cross-subsidization allowed the multinationals to take a very long-term perspective on their portfolio of operations. The multinationals were also better positioned to pick up the commercial business of multinational customers, such as liability insurance for international trade.

The general insurance industry had typically been very cyclical, with changes in income from year to year as high as 10 per cent of sales. At its peak the industry had excess capital; therefore, insurance companies cut prices or extended coverage to gain market share. This resulted in lower premiums, a reduced capital base and a reduced profit margin. After a number of years of lean profits the major players would push up their prices again to reasonable levels, only to begin price-cutting again. In recent years the upturns had become shorter and the downturns more severe, with the effect that underwriting profits had become something of a rarity. Exhibit 1 shows average industry income for the period 1977 to 1987.

The Broker System

The brokerage industry was highly fragmented with upwards of 3,000 competitors in Canada. They ranged in size from the two-person personal lines broker, with maybe 1,000 customers, up to the big multinational broker interested only in commercial lines for large corporations. A small minority of insurance companies, such as State Farm and Allstate, had tied brokers who were obliged to sell that company's products. All the rest were independent, and saw themselves as agents acting in the best interests of their clients. The depressed state of the insurance industry was hitting the tied broker companies particularly hard, as they were obliged to maintain their brokers regardless of volume. It was rumoured that Allstate's Canadian business was for sale.

Independent brokers typically dealt with several insurance companies and selected policies for their clients according to the client's specific needs. The decision was usually made on the basis of price, but brokers were free to recommend insurance companies with which they had a good relationship, or which provided exceptional service. They were also free to push their worst business (i.e., most risky) towards less-favoured companies. Broker commissions varied from 10 per cent to 25 per cent depending on the segment and on the precise arrangement with the insurance company.

Most independent brokers felt very strongly about retaining their independence. They saw objectivity and freedom of choice as their major services to the customer, and viewed with suspicion or outright rejection any attempt by insurance companies to tie them in to certain products. Nonetheless, insurance companies used a variety of tactics to gain preferential status with their brokers. Some worked on providing swift, efficient claims services; some competed on price or commission; others offered a "contingent profits" scheme whereby the broker received a share in the company's profits over a certain dollar amount. The dividing link between creating a strong relationship with brokers, and encroaching on their independence, was very fine.

The traditional way of doing business in general insurance was to manage the combined ratio, as investment returns were fairly standard across companies. Most companies achieved this through careful underwriting, maintenance of steady relations with brokers, and careful attention to costs in the management and administrative side of the business. One way of ensuring that costs were kept down was to operate with a "centralized" structure, whereby most functions stayed at head office and only those who had frequent contact with customers (e.g., appraisers) positioned themselves in the field. The disadvantage of this approach was that customer responsiveness suffered. Claims could not be assessed quickly, and brokers reported dissatisfaction in dealing with their insurers by phone rather than in person. Some companies had regional sales and marketing offices to alleviate this concern, but most viewed cost control as more important.

The low-cost strategy used by most competitors was responsible for the vicious price-cutting that had damaged the industry's profitability. Some observers thought that opportunities existed for innovative companies to differentiate themselves and break out of the price war, but this had not occurred. Insurance was a very "old fashioned" industry and competitors tended to preserve the status quo.

Trends in the Industry

The underwriting side of general insurance (as measured by the combined ratio figure) was an erratic but persistent money loser in the period 1978-1988, and it was only the booming equities market that had sustained the industry. Ten per cent annual increases in premiums had been necessary to counter the increasing number of claims and inflation, but now consumers were pressuring governments to legislate lower increases. Nowhere was this problem more acute than in Ontario, where the Liberal government had recently put a rates freeze on the automobile insurance market. Insurers were already losing money in this sector, and were pressuring the government to consider a "no-fault"[2] insurance package that would stabilize and reduce claims.

The Canadian insurance industry was not expecting to be severely affected by the anticipated Free Trade Agreement with the U.S. American insurance companies were generally much larger than their Canadian counterparts (up to $3 billion in revenues), but this was thought to give them very little advantage: because each state had its own set of regulations, the full scope of insurance activities was duplicated in each one. Furthermore, the Canadian market had been open to foreign competition for years, with American and European companies outnumbering Canadian in the top

---

[2] No fault insurance was intended to reduce the number of questionable damages claims by making each insurance company pay all the costs of its client, regardless of fault. It was expected to lower insurance costs at the expense of the legal profession.

ranks. The trend in recent years, in fact, had been the exit of a number of American players, who saw the Canadian market as unattractive. They were in a position to use their continuing American revenues to offset the exit costs from Canada.

Further changes in the insurance industry were anticipated if recent policy proposals to break down the traditional barriers among financial institutions went through. The current laws required separate institutions for insurance companies, banks, trust companies and securities firms (the "four financial pillars"). If these laws were relaxed, diversified financial institutions were expected to form. The consequence for the general insurance industry was expected to be a shakeout in which the successful companies were bought up by the major banks, and the less-successful driven out of business. Change at the retail end was also expected, as the broker industry would be duplicating the service of the traditional branch network. Analysts were unsure how this conflict of interests would be resolved. Some saw the insurance broker as a dying breed, unable to compete with the efficient coverage of a retail bank branch network. Others argued that brokers would always retain their competitive advantage over banks. As one broker commented: "You can call me at three in the morning when you've just been burgled, and I'll do my job. Try doing that with a bank."

WELLINGTON INSURANCE AND TRILON CORPORATION

Wellington Insurance had been in existence since 1840 under a number of different names. In 1982 it was purchased by Fireman's Fund Insurance Co, an American general insurance company owned by American Express, and became known as "fireman's Fund Insurance Company of Canada." It wrote property and automobile insurance to individuals (about 300,000) and to small or medium-sized businesses (about 40,000). Operations spanned Canada, but about 50 per cent of the company's business was in Ontario. In 1984 the Company's premium volume was $166 million, or about two per cent of the national market, making it the fourteenth largest general insurer in Canada.

In January of 1985, the company was bought by Trilon Corporation for $143 million and renamed Wellington Insurance. Trilon was part of Edward and Peter Bronfman's business empire. It had been set up as a management company to oversee the Bronfman's financial services interests. Trilon already had strong positions in life insurance (London Life), trust service (Royal TrustCo), and Real Estate brokering (Royal LePage). The purchase of Fireman's Fund of Canada gave it access to the general insurance industry as well. Trilon's management recognized that these businesses, along with investment banking, were complementary to one another. Trilon expected to generate synergies through cross-selling, integrated broker networks, and a consistent approach to customer service. The possibility of future deregulation in the financial services industry was a further rationale for Trilon's acquisition strategy.

The Trilon Business Strategy

Under CEO George Collins (Wallace's predecessor), Wellington's objective had been to reach Trilon's target return on equity of 15 per cent, a significant increase over the 1985 figure of 9.4 per cent. There were two main thrusts to the strategy: overhead reduction, and broker partnerships.

The overhead reduction program was implemented through a massive re-centralization in November of 1985. Staff levels in each branch office were cut by 40 to 80 per cent. In London, Ontario, for example the numbers were reduced from eight down to four. Those functions that could easily operate over the phone, such as underwriting, were centralized in Toronto, and all other functions began to report back to supervisors based in Toronto rather than spread through the regions.

Staffing costs were significantly reduced through this strategy, but parts of the business started to suffer. The first problem was a backlog in the claims area, as the reduced number of adjusters struggled to keep up with the new claims. This had the immediate effect of damaging customer service and also broker confidence. "There were people out there who never got their car looked at in two or three weeks," commented one employee. "And when they did it was with a different adjuster each time."

A further consequence of the understaffing was in underwriting: "We had such a backlog that there was no underwriting being done. Work was being processed, but we didn't know what we had on the books. There were many high-risk policies that got through." One employee estimated that a backlog of 40,000 pieces of paper had accumulated by 1987.

The second major thrust was a partnership strategy with brokers called "Partnership Pact." The logic was to create partnerships with a select number of brokers so that the interests of both could be better served. Wellington would buy a 25 per cent stake in each broker's business, and the broker would give a minimum of 25 per cent of his or her business to Wellington. Wellington was to receive preferred status in its chosen segments, and in return profits for that business would be split between the broker and Wellington. Long term it was hoped that the brokers would stock other Trilon products such as life insurance and investment plans.

The Partnership Pact strategy never got off the ground. It met with considerable resistance from the Canadian Federation of Insurance Agents and Brokers Associations Agents and Brokers Association (CFIABA). They valued their independent status, and thought that Wellington's proposal was a departure from "virtually all that Federation sees as being an independent agent."[3] The scheme was quickly dropped, but the relationship with brokers had been soured. Their loss of confidence in Wellington was manifested in a loss of business as Wellingtons market share dropped from 2.1 per cent to 1.5 per cent in two years.

The State of the Insurance Industry in 1987

At the same time as Wellington's self-imposed problems, the entire general insurance industry was going through its worst downturn ever. Over-capacity in the industry, in terms of number of competitors, had led to severe price-cutting, while claims continued to rise. In 1985 the industry had a combined loss on underwriting of $1.2 billion, a new record. Only strong investment returns prevented a negative return on equity. At the same time, the Ontario automobile insurance industry was going through a crisis. All insurers were incurring heavy losses, but the government had frozen rate increases. Steps were being taken to bring in a no-fault scheme, which would lower claims, but for the period since 1985, all auto insurers in Ontario had been badly hit. Wellington was amongst the worst hit, with 40 per cent of its total business in the Ontario auto segment. For the period 1985-1987 it achieved combined ratios of 123.7 per cent, 108.9 per cent and 117.9 per cent respectively. Exhibits 2, 3 and 4 summarize Wellington' performance for the period 1981-1987.

---

[3] Conrad Speirs, President CFIABA, at the 1985 Independent Brokers Association of Ontario convention.

⸢ THE APPOINTMENT OF MURRAY WALLACE

Towards the end of 1987 Trilon decided that changes were necessary at Wellington Insurance, and appointed Murray Wallace to take over as the new President and CEO on January 1, 1988. Wallace was a senior executive at Royal Trust, a sister company, but had considerable experience in the insurance industry through a period as the president of Saskatchewan's government insurance business. His mandate was to do whatever it took to turn the company around. Trilon had a target return on equity of 15 per cent for all its operating companies. However, Wallace understood that financial targets were really only one measure of a successful turnaround. Equally important was a fundamental change in the way the company operated so that brokers regained their respect for Wellington and staff regained control of internal operations.

Assessment of Internal Operations ⼂

The Wellington that Murray Wallace took control of was a very traditional, bureaucratic organization (see Exhibit 5). It had six levels of management, most at the vice-president level. They were distributed through eight centres, but with the vast majority at head office in Toronto. The structure was primarily functional, so that staff belonged to claims, underwriting or sales and rarely communicated with each other. Each manager was responsible for a certain business portfolio, and had strict limits on his or her signing authority. Large claims, for example, had to be referred several steps up the ladder before they could be processed.

The organization was complicated by the fact that each sales group (responsible for a certain region) also had functional staff, such as adjusters or claims managers. These people were accountable both to their region manager and also to the appropriate functional vice-president. They had to ensure that their actions met with the approval of both managers. As a result, processing was often very slow. Furthermore, each region was centralized, so that the few "field" offices such as London, Ontario, still had to refer back to head office for critical functions such as underwriting. London office staff commented that they would spend hours every day discussing claims or premiums by phone with their supervisors in Toronto. They thought that the dual reporting lines, and the lack of face-to-face contact with managers, were detracting from their ability to serve their customers.

Staff morale was described by John Carpenter, the new Chief Operating Officer (COO), as "deplorable." The backlog in claims, the recent staffing cuts, and the rigid structure had all taken their toll on employee motivation, so that a feeling of demoralization had set in. Carpenter commented: "We had some good people, but they were constrained by the structure. There was no focus on the company." Another employee added that the commitment to the company was missing: "If anybody had got a job elsewhere at that point, they would have gone."

Other aspects of the organization also contributed to the malaise. Promotion was based largely on years in the company rather than on performance; salaries were adjusted on a seniority basis, so that there was no reward for creativity or initiative; and training programs were effectively non-existent. The hierarchical nature of the business was underlined by the physical layout of the building. Each executive had a mahogany-walled suite with a separate dining room, while the rest of the employees were segregated by functional area in an open-plan arrangement. Wallace realized that change at Wellington would hit senior management the hardest. They had the most to lose, and would certainly be expected to resist any move that threatened the security and comfort of their privileged position.

Another critical area of concern was information processing. "The systems to provide timely and reliable information were not in place," observed Carpenter. This had the effect that management did not know which segments or geographical regions were losing money, and also handicapped the claims and underwriting staff in their regular activities.

A final concern became apparent as Wallace began to explore Wellington's financial statements in more detail. In simple terms the company was under-reserved. The previous management had not set aside enough income to cover likely future claims, so that short-term earnings were inflated but long-term earnings damaged. Wallace realized that the shortfall in reserves, estimated at around $15 million, would have to be made up over the following seven-year period.

Wallace's Recommendations

The insurance industry, like much of the financial services sector, had resisted change for a long time. Wallace was convinced that the time was ripe for some new thinking. Product offerings were all very much the same between companies, but he was sure that Wellington could differentiate in one crucial way: customer responsiveness. "There is a real sense of 'this is the way things have always been done' in this industry. Brokers and customers don't know what it means to get good service. They have never dealt with a company that will bend over backwards to help them." Wallace believed that Wellington could avoid the worst effects of the cyclicity in the industry, and extract a premium price, if an effective customer-oriented operation were put in place. "Brokers should be recommending Wellington because it turns around claims in record time, not because it is the best price," said Wallace.

Wallace was also impressed by the focused strategies of companies like Pilot and Lloyd's non-marine. These companies had achieved strong results by specializing in certain product segments and geographical areas. Wellington had traditionally been a full-line competitor, but could feasibly reduce its volume to focus its scope of operations in this way. A third possible strategic direction that Wallace foresaw was to push for a short-term turnaround, and then sell the company. This would not be easy either, but represented a less drastic shift than the re-alignment demanded by a differentiation or focus strategy.

One of Wallace's first actions as CEO was to meet with Wellington brokers from across the country. Samples of their comments are listed in Exhibit 6. The process underlined Wallace's belief in a customer service-based strategy, and also drew his attention to the notion of a decentralized organization. Under this structure, all key functions would be grouped together in the field, in close proximity to brokers and customers. Rather than deferring to a central unit for underwriting and claims servicing, each unit would be self-contained and autonomous. Wallace's major concern about a decentralized structure was that no company was using that organizational form. The most successful companies in the industry, in fact, operated with well-managed centralized structures.

The biggest headache for Wallace was the apparent lack of concern for the company's problems among the staff. The company had been through so many changes of ownership that they saw Wallace's appointment as "just another change." Wellington's results were poor, but the company was still turning a small profit. As one manager commented: "Most employees had been doing the same thing for 15 years. They were not interested in any new ideas."

The picture was not all gloom, however. With Trilon as the parent company, Wellington had access to capital, experienced managers and a commitment to long-term profitability. Changes would not have to be compromised for short-term results. In addition, Wallace concluded that the company had some well-respected products, and a lot of good people. In an industry noted for its lack of innovation and dynamism, Wallace predicted that any company, Wellington included, could steal a march on its rivals with some creative management.

Thriving on Chaos

Wallace had developed a clear management philosophy through extensive reading and his own management experiences. His greatest influence was management guru Tom Peters, author of the bestselling *In Search of Excellence* and a number of other books. In particular, Peters' most recent book, *Thriving on Chaos*, detailed a number of strategies for change along the lines of customer responsiveness, empowerment and leadership. Table 2 lists some of the key prescriptions. Wallace found the ideas appealing, and in his previous job at Royal Trust he had begun to put some of them into practise. Wallace wondered if it would be possible to implement the *Thriving on Chaos* prescriptions at Wellington.

Table 2: **Thriving on Chaos Prescriptions**

Creating Total Customer Responsiveness	Achieving flexibility by empowering people	A new view of leadership at all levels
Specialize/create niches	Involve everyone in everything	Develop an inspiring vision
Provide top quality	Use self-managing teams	Manage by example
Provide superior service	Listen/celebrate/recognize	Practise visible management
Achieve extraordinary responsiveness	Spend time lavishly on recruiting	Defer to the front line
Become obsessed with listening	Train and retrain	Delegate
Make sales and service forces into heroes	Provide incentive pay for everyone	Pursue horizontal management
Launch a customer revolution	Simplify/reduce structure	Evaluate everyone on their love of change
	Re-conceive the middle manager's role	Create a sense of urgency
	Eliminate bureaucratic rules	

Exhibit 1: **Canadian General Insurance Industry Aggregate Results 1977-1987**

Year	Underwriting Income	Investment Income	Net Income	Average Combined Ratio
1977	$20m			
1978	$69m			
1979	-$163m			
1980	-$513m			
1981	-$890m	$937m	$160m	111.4%
1982	-$562m	$1054m	$456m	108.5%
1983	-$328m	$1119m	$741m	104.5%
1984	-$916m	$1255m	$362m	111.7%
1985	-$1260m	$1350m	$383m	114.0%
1986	-$555m	$1509m	$1004m	105.2%
1987	-$535m	$1706m	$1165m	104.8%

Source: Canadian Underwriter 1977-1987

Exhibit 2: **Wellington's Market Performance 1981-1987**

Year	Ranking in Canada (market share based)	Market share % (on net premiums earned)
1981	15th	1.68%
1982	12th	2.42%
1983	14th	2.28%
1984	14th	2.13%
1985	18th	1.75%
1986	19th	1.52%
1987	19th	1.55%

Source: Canadian Underwriter 1981-1987

Exhibit 3: **Wellington Key Financial Performance Data 1977-1987**

Year	Sales (i.e., net premiums)	Costs (i.e., claims)	Earned Loss ratio	Total Expense ratio	Combined Ratio	Under-Writing income	Invest-ment Income	Net Income
1977	$123m	$73m	59.7%					
1978	$124m	$79m	63.7%					
1979	$125m	$90m	71.8%					
1980	$127m	$102m	79.0%					
1981	$131m	$104m	79.3%	38.9%	118.2%	-$24m	$24m	$0
1982	$162m	$120m	74.0%	36.1%	110.1%	-$16m	$27m	$11m
1983	$168m	$126m	74.8%	33.3%	108.1%	-$13m	$34m	$21m
1984	$167m	$143m	85.5%	33.7%	119.2%	-$32m	$26m	-$6m
1985	$157m	$135m	85.7%	38.0%	123.7%	-$37m	$41m	$4m
1986	$163m	$125m	77.0%	31.9%	108.9%	-$15m	$53m	$38m
1987	$172m	$145m	84.0%	33.8%	117.9%	-$31m	$51m	$20m

Source: Canadian Underwriter 1977-1987

Exhibit 4: **Wellington's Business Segmented By Line And Province, 1987 (A): Segmented by product line**

Line	Net prem. earned $000	Net claims $000	Earned loss ratio
Property - personal	$45,012	$27,336	60.7%
Property - commercial	$17,573	$12,099	68.8%
Property - total	$62,585	$39,435	63.0%
Automobile - liability	$50,120	$59,234	118.2%
Automobile - personal acdt.	$7,658	$5,976	78.0%
Automobile - other	$47,412	$35,688	75.3%
Automobile - total	$105,190	$100,898	95.9%
Boiler and Machinery	$3	$17	566.7%
Fidelity	$173	-$49	-28.3%
Liability	$3,416	$4,078	117.8%
Surety	$164	$168	102.4%
Marine	$846	$523	61.8%
Total for 1987	$172,422	$145,070	84.1%

(B): Segmented by province

Province	Premiums earned ($000)	Province	Premiums earned ($000)
Newfoundland	$911	Manitoba	$2,451
PEI	$1,271	Saskatchewan	$59
Nova Scotia	$14,128	Alberta	$14,278
New Brunswick	$1,752	British Columbia	$18,790
Quebec	$18,496	Yukon & NWT	$37
Ontario	$100,249	Total	$172,422

Source: Canadian Underwriter, May 1987

Exhibit 5: **Simplified Organization Chart, 1987**

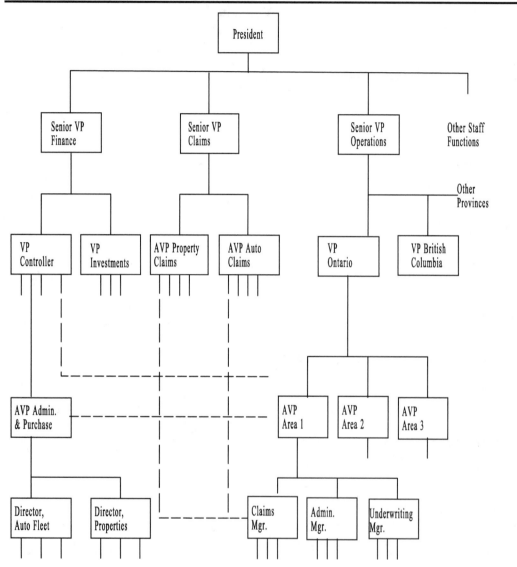

Source: Company Interviews

All area-based functional managers report to a) Regional VP and b) functional manager/VP. Profit responsibility is held by both operations managers (for a geographic portfolio) and functional managers (i.e. For all auto claims)

Exhibit 6: Broker Comments

These comments were collected from brokers in January 1988, on a trans-Canada tour by Murray Wallace.

"First class products, good prices, but your service. . . ."

"It sure would be nice to get our policies within a reasonable time."

"I wish you'd get the policy right the first time, most of the time anyway."

"I don't want to talk to a different person every time I call."

"I do expect a return phone call when I leave a message."

"It would be so much easier for me if you had an office right here in town."

"I want to deal with the person who makes decisions."

SILENT WITNESS ENTERPRISES LTD.

Adam Fremeth and
Charlene Nicholls-Nixon

As Rob Bakshi, president and CEO of Silent Witness, entered the lobby of his new corporate offices his eyes were drawn to a framed poster hanging adjacent to the reception desk; it read "*Innovation, the best way to predict the future is to create it*". The caption strongly reflected Bakshi's personal views. The company which he had founded 14 years earlier had re-conceptualized the role of video technology in the security surveillance industry. Bakshi had created a new market niche by developing novel applications of VCR-based video recording technology that were easier to use, offered better performance and were priced below existing systems based on CCTV (closed circuit television) technology. His innovative and aggressive entry into the CCTV market had earned the company recognition as one of Canada's fastest growing businesses in 1995, 1996, 1997 and 1998, and placed the firm in a competitive arena dominated by industry giants Sony and Panasonic. In 1999 the company received an award for Excellence in Product Innovation from the Security Industry Association and the BC Export Award for being one of British Columbia's top export companies.

On October 6, the company released its 1999 annual report. The results were quite impressive. Revenues were $34 million at year-end, up from $22 million in 1998 and $13 million in 1997 (see Exhibits 1 to 3 for the historical financial statements). Bakshi was projecting revenues of $250 million by 2005. This was an ambitious goal, but he was confident that it was attainable. There were so many new and emerging opportunities to exploit Silent Witness's unique camera technology. The

Ivey

Adam Fremeth prepared this case under the supervision of Professor Charlene Nicholls-Nixon solely to provide material for class discussion. The author does not intend to illustrate either effective or ineffective handling of a managerial situation. The author may have disguised certain names and other identifying information to protect confidentiality.

issue was how to prioritize among these opportunities. For example, should the company focus on entering new markets with existing technology, or should it concentrate on developing and patenting new technology before pursuing additional markets? In Bakshi's mind, as important as these considerations was the need to develop the organizational capabilities that would enable Silent Witness to reach and sustain its growth targets. What kind of systems did he need to put in place to manage the increasing complexity of the firm's growing operations, while at the same time nurturing the "outside the box" thinking and the quest for innovative applications that had made Silent Witness successful in the first place?

Bakshi felt some sense of urgency to address these issues. He had just returned to his Surrey, B.C. office from a large security trade show in Las Vegas. He was both flattered and astonished by the fact that three of his competitors had just unveiled clones of Silent Witness products at the trade show. Bakshi had not expected to see imitations for at least six to eight months.

CCTV INDUSTRY OVERVIEW

CCTV camera surveillance systems were most commonly used to (a) protect against inventory shortage and (b) monitor and protect personnel and assets in the workplace, at home, and in public places. For example, most retail bank outlets used CCTV systems to monitor the actions of both their customers and employees in order to prevent fraud or theft.

Technology

The traditional CCTV system was composed of a number of different components that were integrated to form a CCTV system. These components included a camera, a lens, a monitor, a camera enclosure, a mount, and a multiplexer. Within these component categories, numerous options existed. For example, there were many different types of cameras: indoor, outdoor, low light, high-resolution, and special applications. Each of these camera types had to be fitted with a specific lens. Again, there were a variety of options in terms of angle width and distance capabilities. Thus, numerous configurations existed in the design of a CCTV security system.

There were many barriers to the adoption of traditional CCTV systems, including: limitations to recording duration and the need to constantly change and store video tapes, complexity of installation and proliferation of cables. Digital technology had eliminated many of these barriers. With digital technology, the surveyed image could now be transmitted via ISDN lines to a number of different monitors and subsequently be integrated with computer technology. Moreover "plug and play" capabilities, which Silent Witness had pioneered, made it possible to integrate many security applications into a single product that was easier to use.

Consumer Segments

The consumer market was generally segmented into two groups: Security and Non-security (see Exhibit 4). The security segment, the more traditional of the two, was focused on using CCTV to prevent crime or vandalism. This group could be further separated into public, commercial and residential buyers. Each of these groups had its own individual purchasing preferences. The public consumer was generally a city council, police department, or public institution that was looking for a method to deter crime and observe the public domain. The commercial market was composed of banks, casinos, department stores, and/or industrial manufacturers that used surveillance systems to protect their assets or inventory and to collect evidence in the event of a crime. Finally, the residential market was made up of household consumers who were looking to complement their current alarm system with a more advanced component that could act as additional protection against crime. Although the public and commercial markets accounted for the greatest amount of revenue in 1999, the residential market was expected to grow exponentially in the next five years.

The non-security market, which included all other uses of surveillance systems, was at the earliest stages of development. Some examples of non-security uses of CCTV technology included traffic control on busy roadways and Internet-based real time images. The list of potential applications was endless and limited only by one's imagination. For this reason, the non-security segment was expected to grow dramatically in the immediate future. However, because of the uncertainty associated with the nature and direction of new product development initiatives, specific growth estimates were not available.

The market for CCTV products had grown rapidly in the late 1990s. In 1999 revenues grew by approximately 12 per cent, and this trend was expected to continue into 2000 and beyond. The growing popularity of CCTV surveillance systems was attributed to their ability to provide a high level of security without the expense of security guards. A British study discovered that areas monitored by CCTV could deter crime by as much as 80 per cent. In fact, the United Kingdom was the most progressive country in its use of CCTV, with more than 150,000 cameras monitoring city streets and public places. Market growth had also been driven by the litigious culture in the United States which had created a heightened demand for surveillance products that could be used as evidence in civil or criminal court cases. The American CCTV market size was estimated to be as large as $2.5 billion in 1999 and could grow to as large as $3.5 billion by 2002.[1]

Distribution

Due to the complexity of the systems, most CCTV consumers made their purchases from a security products installer. These installers determined the client's needs and then prescribed adequate products for them. They were responsible for installing the system and servicing it when needed. Therefore, most manufacturers had little understanding of their product's final users. Installers were usually small to mid-sized regionally based companies that would generally be focused on installing traditional alarm systems, but offered CCTV systems as a component of their product offering. Many of the mid-sized installers also acted as the distributors for a number of different manufacturers' products, while the smaller installers would purchase the systems wholesale from a larger distributor. Most large distributors were multinational corporations that carried a wide line of products from hundreds of different manufacturers.

Two of the largest American distributors of CCTV systems were ADI and Richardson Electronics. ADI, a television cable company, had diversified into security products distribution. The company, which carried many different product lines, had annual revenues of approximately $100 million in 1999.[2] Richardson Electronics was a distributor of electronic products and components. Its principal products were semiconductors, electron tubes and security systems. Richardson had earned $321 million in revenue in 1999 and had diversified its holdings into a number of more defined operating units.[3]

---

[1] Peter Quitzau. Institutional Investment Report, Cannaccord Capital. March 26, 1999.
[2] ADI Annual Report found at www.adilink.com
[3] Richardson Annual Report found at www.cctvnet.com

Recent innovations in camera and digital technology had led to the development of CCTV systems that were easier to install and use than traditional products. This led to speculation that direct retailers would become a primary source of sales in the future. Such a development would have significant implications for the role of installers and distributors in the CCTV industry.

COMPETITIVE ENVIRONMENT

The CCTV industry was fragmented and competition within the industry was fierce. Hundreds of security equipment manufacturers competed for the sale of CCTV products. These CCTV manufacturers also faced competition from traditional security products, such as alarms and security guards (see Exhibit 5 for a list of competitors). The proliferation of competitors within this segment of the security industry had been triggered by the significant growth rates projected over the next decade and the ease of entry into the marketplace.

A number of large Japanese companies, such as Sony, JVC and Panasonic, offered generic CCTV products as part of a much larger product offering. These companies had the benefit of large research and development groups that could create innovative CCTV components. However, these large multinationals were not focused on any individual aspect of the CCTV product. As a result, they had not changed their product design for some time and were often slow to react to the market dynamic.

Numerous small- to mid-size companies, including Ultrak, Vicon, Pelco and Silent Witness, focused solely on CCTV products. These competitors each specialized in different areas of the CCTV market, and shared many of the same distributors. For example, Ultrak offered a completely integrated security system that included CCTV, alarms, and access control made up of numerous components. Vicon manufactured a wide range of CCTV systems and components targeted at the large public consumer segment. Pelco, which focused on cloning many of the leading CCTV innovations, attempted to differentiate itself by developing an extensive consumer education program.

Many of these and other mid-sized competitors offered "me-too" solutions which matched the design of the popular products, but lacked their quality and durability. In most cases, they established their production and assembly in developing countries where they were able to realize significant savings. Currently, Sony had 25 per cent of the market, while Panasonic had 25 per cent, Pelco had 20 per cent, and Silent Witness held four per cent. These market shares changed frequently, as many of the smaller companies had been successful at creating greater brand awareness over the past three years.

Increasingly, alliances were being formed between the large Japanese companies and the small to mid-size competitors. The Japanese manufacturers saw these partnerships as a means of speeding up their new product development efforts, while the small and mid-sized companies sought access to financial and technological resources. For example, Pelco had recently announced a research agreement with Sony to attempt the development of the next generation of CCTV systems. This relationship allowed Pelco to use Sony's proprietary Pan-Tilt-Zoom technology in its camera systems.

Five factors were critical to success in the CCTV industry: innovative technology, speed to market, effective distribution, reliable customer service, and ability to educate the consumers about the benefits of the product. The CCTV market was fast-paced; if a player in the industry developed a new concept that was well received in the marketplace, it was inevitable that it would soon be copied, unless it was protected with proprietary technology.

COMPANY BACKGROUND

Silent Witness was a classic entrepreneurial success story. The company's 14-year history had been marked by many ups and downs. It was Rob Bakshi's visionary thinking and his deep personal commitment to the venture that had kept the company going. As a result, Bakshi had made himself and his investors wealthy. The company went public in 1987 with a stock price of $1.25/share. In 1996 the company effected a "one new for two old" consolidation which ended up setting the stock price at $1.35. By 1999, Silent Witness's shares were trading for $12 (see Exhibit 6 for chart detailing the stock's performance).

Silent Witness was located in Surrey, British Columbia, a suburb of Vancouver. All functional areas operated out of a 27,500 square foot office space in a small, but growing, commercial park. The company's physical facilities had recently been expanded to include an adjacent building. Future growth would likely involve moving parts of the organization across the street into another facility. Currently, Silent Witness employed about 114 people, but this number was rising daily and was expected to reach 130 by July 2000.

The Launch of Silent Witness (1985-1988)

Founded in 1985 by Rob Bakshi and Bob Galbraith, Silent Witness was created to develop a system of on-board computers for buses, truck fleets and automobiles. The original product functioned in a manner similar to the "Black Box" used on airplanes. It monitored the vehicle's speed, RPM, brakes, turn signals, etc.

Rob Bakshi and Bob Galbraith had developed the original product concept in the mid-1980s while working together at the BC Attorney General's office. Galbraith, an ex-RCMP officer, was the chief coroner and Bakshi, a graduate in Commerce and Computer Science, was his Information Systems consultant. Galbraith had been called in to investigate the circumstances surrounding a police fatality. The death was the result of an accident involving two police cars. The dead officer was being blamed for the accident. His widow had pressured the police for further investigation. However, Galbraith did not have sufficient evidence to make a final conclusion.

Galbraith had been discussing this problem with Bakshi. Bakshi suggested the possibility of developing a product capable of monitoring police vehicles, so that in the future they would have the benefit of understanding how the cars were being driven prior to an accident. As they were having this discussion, a Special Investigator stopped by the office. Bakshi and Galbraith had asked him what he thought of the idea. The Investigator had replied that he thought the concept was a great idea and that it would act like a "silent witness". When the two partners formed their company, they adopted the name.

For the first three years, Silent Witness focused on developing the market for its "Black Box" product named the SW100. The market for this product was virtually untapped and provided an opportunity for the company to realize (actually there were no sales until 1988/1989) revenue growth. In 1987, Silent Witness made an Initial Public Offering on the Vancouver Stock Exchange with the condition that an outside president would be brought in to manage the company. Bakshi was considered "too young" to be the president and Galbraith did not want to leave his chief coroner's position. This infusion of equity capital was intended to complete the development and market the product. However, by 1988 Silent Witness still had not made any substantial advancements in this area and Bakshi was getting frustrated with the lack of progress. At this point Bakshi called for the president's resignation but instead, he was forced to resign by the board of directors. The company floundered in his absence and was close to insolvency by 1991.

Reviving Silent Witness (1991-1995)

After leaving the company, Bakshi still remained the majority shareholder and a director. As time passed, he became increasingly concerned about the company's lack of progress and deteriorating financial performance. In late 1991 Bakshi, with help from Galbraith and other shareholders, regained control of the company through a hostile takeover. He returned with the goal of implementing a winning strategy that would allow the company to once again realize growth through the introduction of new products. Thus, he assumed direct responsibility for the product development function, leaving the senior management of the company to Galbraith and others.

Although Bakshi was not an engineer by training, he had a keen ability to envision new product opportunities. In early 1992, Silent Witness obtained all rights to a school bus video system. The first product introduced under his direction was a new, redesigned School Bus Surveillance system, named the SW200-VS. Launched in 1992, the SW200 used the state-of-the-art V30 enclosure and off-the-shelf camcorder technology which was modified and installed in a box so that when the ignition was turned on, the device would start recording. In its first year, sales of the SW200 increased from $1 million to $3 million.

A New Direction (1995-1996)

In spite of the success of the SW200, Bakshi knew that there was room for further improvements. School bus districts complained that the two-hour recording capabilities of the machine were too restrictive. Yet, the only way to lengthen the recording period was to move to a VCR-based system, which could record up to eight hours. To do this, however, involved designing a camera that could interface with a specially designed VCR for mobile applications. Bakshi was assigned the task of developing such a system. At the company's insistence, Bakshi and his wife headed to Hawaii so that he could take a working vacation to develop the new product.

> I didn't take any material with me. Developing a camera for school buses was not a challenge, but I wanted this product to do more. I wanted this camera to be so innovative that it would take Silent Witness into the mainstream CCTV industry. I had been studying the CCTV market for months but I could not pinpoint its weaknesses. I spent the first six of our seven-day vacation with my wife sightseeing and resting. The last day I was there, I just got up, and everything became clear to me. I knew exactly what I was going to do. So I sat out on the porch and I wrote page after page after page after page; the whole design was done. I realized that in the last 20 years, the security camera really hadn't changed. You had your Sony, Panasonic and Toshiba. They would make cameras; somebody else would make lenses. Some other American company would make housings for them. Somebody else would make power supplies, cabling and brackets, and everything else. So an installer would have to integrate all of these components into one, and every time something didn't work, you know, the installer had to go back to the lens guy or the camera guy or the box guy to try to figure it out. I also realized that camera technology had progressed at an alarming rate but the industry had been slow to adapt. For example, the CCD (Charged Coupled Device) used to capture the image on a camera had shrunk in size from 1/2" to 1/3". Therefore, the

cameras had shrunk in size and price, yet delivered almost the same quality of picture. But the industry was using these small inexpensive "board cameras" for covert applications. They would hide them in teddy bears or exit signs or smoke detectors. Since there was no way to use these smaller cameras in the professional market, the "body cameras" remained as the only choice for installers.

Bakshi envisioned a new paradigm in electronic surveillance; a small high-end security camera that was easy to use right out of the box. This product with plug and play capabilities would be the most innovative product on the market. The major benefit would be its ease of use and customization capabilities. The current CCTV systems on the market were large, box-shaped systems that were overpriced and difficult to operate. These cameras could not be customized and were impractical for the large and untapped small business and residential markets. Bakshi believed that the disadvantages of the current CCTV cameras provided a gap in the market that could be filled with an innovative line of video cameras.

Bakshi approached the senior managers with this new concept in early 1995; however, they did not share his enthusiasm for this product. Management had doubted both the market potential for the product and Bakshi's ability to develop and integrate the necessary technology. "The last thing this market needs is another security camera," said one senior officer. Bakshi persisted. He was successful in amassing $50,000 to finance the development of this new product. Bakshi knew all along that the total development cost would probably be $150,000 to $200,000. He had accepted the lesser amount hoping that once senior management had committed to the project, they would have difficulties stopping it midstream. However, as the bills continued to escalate, senior management gave notice that they would order a shut down of the initiative. At the eleventh hour, Bakshi received a call for bids from a school bus manufacturer in Savannah, Georgia. The company wanted surveillance systems for 365 buses. Armed with a good idea, but without the benefit of a completed prototype, Bakshi flew the company's sales manager and an engineer to Savannah to introduce his new product concept, the V60.

> . . . in order to win the bid, I had the electronics ready but I didn't have the enclosure ready, because the mould takes time. So, I bought an off-the-shelf box from Radio Shack and put the electronics into it. Our people were able to install and operate the system successfully. We also showed them a computer-generated color picture of the camera that was under development and promised to deliver them on time. The customer was sold on the technology and gave us an order of about $700,000. I then approached Ultrak with this concept. This was a company that had sales over $100 million in the CCTV industry and had mobile applications. I went and had a meeting with the CEO. I showed him the color photograph that I had generated from the computer, and I sold him on the concept. So, he agreed to buy, I think it was 2,000 units. Before a single prototype was made we had about $1.7 million worth of contracts in hand. So the product never went into prototype. It went straight from conception into production.

The introduction of the V60 spearheaded a major change in both the direction of the company and Bakshi's role in it.

Taking Control (1996-1999)

Although the company kept growing in sales, it never made any profits. As a result, the company raised more capital through share issuance. In the spring of 1996 the company was over $800,000 into the line of credit and the bank was becoming unfriendly. At this time, the company's president was fired. Bakshi, as a major shareholder and board member, had taken a proactive role in this change. With the firing of the president, Bakshi assumed the position of president, CEO and chairman of the board of Silent Witness.

Bakshi's first initiative as president and CEO was to bring in cash. A private placement was done mostly by the insiders and about $700,000 was raised so that the bank could be appeased. The next step for Bakshi was to determine why the company was under-performing financially. In the fiscal year 1995 Silent Witness realized a net loss of $500,000 on sales of $5.6 million. This desperately concerned Bakshi. He knew that it would be impossible to operate a leading company with such inefficiencies. Bakshi created a number of accounting control systems while eliminating many frivolous expenses (including liberal use of company cars and corporate credit cards). All of the senior management was replaced and many money-losing programs were shelved. Now, the soul-searching began. Bakshi needed to define the company's core competencies and establish its mission.

STRATEGY

Under Bakshi's leadership, R&D was considered the most integral part of the organization. Silent Witness would focus on developing its own products instead of relying on suppliers for technological advances. To this end, Bakshi established the goal of launching a new product in each fiscal quarter and allocated seven per cent of revenues to the development of new technologies and applications.

His commitment to R&D was reflected in the new company motto, *Innovative CCTV Solutions*. Bakshi insisted that the motto be used in all promotional material. He believed it reflected the focus on cutting edge technology that Silent Witness would need in order to become a major player in the CCTV market. He also felt that it would help the consumer recognize Silent Witness in the increasingly competitive marketplace.

Product Development

The cornerstone of Bakshi's new strategy was the V60 CCTV system. The V60 camera used state-of-the-art closed circuit technology with picture-perfect video image quality encased in a rugged die cast enclosure that would hold up under the most rugged conditions. It could be installed almost anywhere because it was quite small, weighing only 2.6 lbs.

Due to its compact size and exceptional durability, the V60 was suitable for almost any condition; it was the polar opposite of the current CCTV products in the marketplace at the time of its launch in 1996. The V60 began to make a big impact in the school bus market. The company also private labelled it for Ultrak's mobile division. But, its acceptance in the general security market fell far below expectations. Its benefits were not fully appreciated; this was a new paradigm and people resisted change. Moreover, the V60 was perceived to be overpriced.

Through extensive marketing efforts, the V60 had garnered significant praise within the industry press; in 1996 it was the highest rated product ever in *Security Installer*, one of the most esteemed industry journals. The company also quickly launched other derivatives of the V60: the Night Hawk, able to see in total darkness up to 40 feet; the Arctic Hawk, able to operate in –45C; the Desert Hawk, able to work in extremely hot environments. Each of these new products received a tremendous amount of media attention. Within two years, the V60 had grown about 30 permutations. By 1999 the company had established itself as a market innovator, selling approximately 70,000 V60 types of cameras. A further development that had resulted from the company's success was the move from the Vancouver Stock Exchange to both the Toronto Stock Exchange in 1998 and a listing on the Nasdaq SmallCap Exchange in 1999.

Perhaps the greatest benefit of the V60 was that it gave Silent Witness the ability to leverage its technology into many other products. Following the success of the V60, Silent Witness introduced eight more cameras that used similar technology, but focused on different niches within the CCTV marketplace. The R&D group was the driving force behind the development of all the products that followed the V60 and the hybrid cameras that Silent Witness was now able to offer. The group, which had grown rapidly in the last three years, now had 18 engineers working in it. Further growth of this department was only inhibited by the company's ability to attract experienced engineers to work in the organization. This was an industry-wide problem in Canada, but was amplified in the suburban area of Surrey, B.C.

Production and Operations

All production was outsourced to approximately 100 suppliers, who provided a number of different components. The three largest suppliers represented 44 per cent of the company's costs of goods sold. The major components of the system included the camera, the lens, the integrated circuit and the enclosure. These parts were all designed by Silent Witness to be used specifically in their products. The company's suppliers performed all manufacturing functions. Bakshi did not see manufacturing as a competence that the company would ever develop. Their focus was on designing and marketing camera systems. The only production functions that were performed in-house related to the assembly and packaging of the final goods. The assembly area, one of the larger divisions of Silent Witness, employed approximately 40 individuals.

Each of Silent Witness's products focused on a different segment of the CCTV market. As a result, each camera within the product line offered a number of different options that would be specified by the installer or distributor. These options included different lens focal lengths, temperature requirements, color, light sensitivity, power supply and resolution. Each product configuration was assigned its own stockkeeping unit (SKU). The proliferation of hybrid products at Silent Witness had "ballooned" to approximately 1,200 SKUs.

Marketing and Sales

In Bakshi's new organization, marketing and sales were consolidated into one group. Previously, the marketing and sales functions had been divided along product lines: Security Distribution and Mobile Products (devices for school buses). However, sales in the Mobile Products division were not growing as fast as in the Security Distribution division. Bakshi had decided that it would be more efficient to amalgamate the two groups. The focus for this department would be to increase market share by pursuing new customers and by enhancing responsiveness to customer demands. Silent Witness employed a direct sales force of 10 employees who worked throughout North America and Europe. The company's sales were divided into 75 per cent security distribution and 25 per cent mobile division. The U.S. produced most of the sales for the mobile division and about 70 per cent of distribution sales. Canada produced about seven per cent and the U.K. produced about 12 per cent. Growth in the two markets was expected to be 30 per cent and 10 per cent in security distribution and mobile divisions, respectively, with the greatest potential for new sales coming from distribution in the U.S. and Western Europe.

The company utilized a network of over 50 distributors and 300 to 400 dealers and installers; this network consisted of large security companies or systems installers that offered a complete line of security products (see Exhibit 7 for a list of the distributors carrying Silent Witness products). One large distributor represented 20 per cent of Silent Witness's total sales in 1998. The development of a broad distribution network was critical to success in the CCTV market. Although Silent Witness had a large network of distributors, Bakshi felt that the company should concentrate on expanding this network. Silent Witness also employed a number of telemarketers who were responsible for soliciting potential customers and informing them of the benefits of a Silent Witness CCTV system. The company's marketing efforts were focused on building brand image through trade shows and advertisements in industry journals. Currently, Silent Witness had no sales or marketing efforts targeted at the residential or small business consumer.

PREPARING FOR FUTURE GROWTH

Bakshi's goals for Silent Witness involved taking the company from an annual sales level of $34 million in 1999 to $250 million in revenue and a net income of $30 million by 2005. This would mean capturing a 12 per cent share of the North American market.

In order to achieve these growth objectives, Bakshi believed that Silent Witness would need to undergo significant strategic changes throughout 1999. The most critical development was the shift away from the focus on "*Innovative CCTV Solutions*" to a more broadly defined business definition based on "*The Evolution of Cameras.*" Under the former, Silent Witness had created value by combining innovations in camera technology with novel configurations of the components involved in CCTV systems. In contrast, Bakshi's new vision meant that the company would no longer be concerned with the *components* involved in a CCTV system; instead efforts would be focused on developing the best *cameras* in the world.

SWC-40: The New Paradigm

The driving force behind Bakshi's new vision for the company was the recent development of the SWC series of cameras. Research on the SWC-40 was initiated in late 1997, and the product was launched in the summer of 1999. Industry insiders who had difficulty categorizing the SWC-40 predicted that it would represent the new standard for the industry. Traditional surveillance systems were impractical and uneconomical for home or non-security use. In contrast, the SWC-40 had the potential to operate in these untapped markets by offering a low priced, turnkey surveillance camera that was easy to use and could complement a traditional electronic security alarm. The SWC-40 retailed for US$995, while equivalent and older camera systems would cost between US$2,000 and US$3,000.

The SWC-40 was an 'all-in-one CCTV solution.' It comprised a high-performance security CCTV camera, a digital video recorder, a still image camera, a motion detector, an intelligent light compensation system, and the ability to integrate with an alarm system. This product was complemented with a remote control that was capable of arming and disarming the system and an enclosure that was weather-sealed and vandal-proof. However, the real breakthrough with this new product was its use of digital video motion detection, compression and storage technology, which eliminated the need for a motion detector or VCR and the need to change tapes and keep the tape heads clean. These capabilities meant that it was now practical to maintain surveillance of low-traffic areas that would not normally warrant full coverage with a time-lapse VCR. Moreover, unlike current products, the SWC-40 was so simple to install and easy to use that the services of an installer were unlikely to be required.

The SWC series of cameras was focused on the residential and small business users. These segments had yet to see significant adoption rates for CCTV surveillance systems. The major reason for the low adoption rate was the expense involved in installing a CCTV system in a home or small business, thus providing an untapped market for the SWC-40. Furthermore, currently no other competitors were capable of providing a simple, "out of the box" CCTV system at a reasonable price. Most competitors, still focused on catching up to Silent Witness's previous technology, were not ready for the market shake-up that these new cameras would create. The potential market size in the U.S. alone was massive, with approximately 102 million households. However, adoption rates were uncertain, but were thought to parallel the adoption rates of traditional alarm systems in the home and for small business use.

The company planned to distribute the SWC-40 through its conventional distribution network of security installers and system providers. However, management foresaw alternative distribution opportunities through retail stores or direct sales via the Internet. Understanding the new consumers, and the associated distribution channels, would be a challenge for Silent Witness; it was an area that would require significant marketing effort. Management believed that the success of the SWC-40 would depend upon the company's ability to gain early acceptance into the retail distribution chain and to convince the final consumer that the SWC-40 was an easy-to-use tool that was effective in deterring crime.

Non-security applications represented another possible market for the SWC-40. A wide range of possibilities existed. For example, the SWC-40 could be installed on hills at ski resorts to show interested skiers what the current conditions looked like. Management believed that as information continued to become more important and easier to attain, the demand for surveillance cameras would grow exponentially. The possibilities were endless and the SWC-40 provided a good solution for this growing niche, with its simplicity and low cost. Bakshi could not determine the potential market for this product, but stressed the importance of the inroads that it had made into the early stages of the non-security surveillance market.

CHALLENGES

Since its inception in 1985 Silent Witness had had four different CEOs and three separate management transitions. The most recent transition occurred in the summer of 1999 when four of Bakshi's top managers left the company, either voluntarily or involuntarily, because they would not follow his lead in the re-designing of the organization. Included was Bakshi's own brother-in-law.

The current senior management team at Silent Witness was a mix of new and old faces. Those who had been around for some time included Tom Gill, the CFO and COO, Darren Jarvis, the production and purchasing manager, and Rob Bakshi, the CEO, while the new members of the team included Dean Lumb, product manager, Coleen Hunter, HR manager, John Francis, director R&D, and John Jennings, director of marketing and sales. The majority of these new employees had had a professional relationship at a telecommunication company before coming to Silent Witness. Bakshi had hired these managers because of their previous experience working for a rapidly growing organization in a highly competitive environment. His hiring decisions were also based on the belief that these individuals supported his vision for the company's future and had the skills needed to move the company forward in this direction.

Each department within Silent Witness faced a unique set of challenges as a result of Bakshi's ambitious growth goals. The growth projections that would stretch the company's existing capabilities in a number of critical areas would require the development of new competencies in order to realize Bakshi's vision.

1. Operations

Darren Jarvis, the operations manager, was a five-year veteran at Silent Witness, making him one of the company's most seasoned managers. Until recently, the production and purchasing department involved a relatively simple process. However, with recent and anticipated growth the Operations department was becoming much more complicated.

Just three years ago Silent Witness had only around 100 SKUs; currently it was operating with approximately 1,200. The proliferation of SKUs arose from the many different customization options that consumers were permitted in adapting the company's 12 different base models to their individual needs. This diversity created complexity throughout the organization. The greatest challenges were in the operations department where it was necessary to account for the purchasing, assembly, and distribution of 1,200 different product configurations.

The sheer number of SKUs strained the abilities of the purchasing area to make precise buying decisions and the ability of the assembly line to ensure total quality satisfaction. The anticipated growth of the product line made it inevitable that, if there were no significant changes, the number of SKUs would only continue to grow.

A further challenge facing the Operations department was the formalization of their processes. Until recently this department was very flexible with few policies or rules about how things were to be completed. However, with the growth of the organization and proliferation of products, the operations department was compelled to regulate their processes, starting with the adoption of a Materials Requirement Planning System (MRP) that required greater documentation and attention to details. The system was intended to improve the efficiency and accuracy of the assembly process. Adhering to these procedures changed the time required to perform many standard activities. For example, in the past the process of making a revision to a product manual involved a quick decision and about thirty minutes' work by an astute employee. Now the process involved six steps (including sign-off by committee) that took significantly more time.

2. Research and Development

The key to Silent Witness's past success had been the ability to develop innovative CCTV products that filled an unmet need. A key challenge facing the organization was how to sustain innovation while dealing with the increasing pressures for formalization and efficiency in the existing core products.

Bakshi had recently hired John Francis to head up the R&D function. He believed that Francis had the experience and drive needed to revolutionize camera technology and establish Silent Witness as an industry leader. A major challenge he faced was attracting talented people to staff the growing department. The best and brightest engineers were continually attracted away from Canada to more lucrative opportunities in the United States. Unless Francis was able to attract people with the right technical abilities to Silent Witness, the company would have a difficult time growing the needed critical mass in the R&D department.

Another challenge facing the R&D department was how to counteract imitation by competitors. Although management knew that imitation was inevitable, they had not expected that it would be done so quickly. The products introduced by competitors at last month's security trade show used Silent Witness's V60 technology, but Bakshi and his team believed they were still about two years behind the SWC-40 technology. Silent Witness had not been able to use patents or trademarks to protect its designs, and as a result, there was nothing stopping competitors from launching their own versions of the product. Thus, the R & D department was under increasing pressure to design products that could be patented.

To this end, Bakshi had been exploring the possibility of developing a "Universal Platform" that would serve as the base technology for all of the company's cameras. Exploiting digital and computer technology, the platform would consist of a single integrated circuit that could be customized to support different product configurations. As a result, the company would be able to offer a wide range of product configurations with virtually no effect on the number of SKUs, since the platform could be programmed to perform functions currently offered only by combining various camera components in different configurations.

No research had yet been dedicated to this concept, but the R&D manager was convinced he could develop this technology. If this "Universal Platform" could be developed, it would represent a paradigm shift to CCTV cameras and would simplify the process involved in purchasing and assembly. Furthermore, if the technology was successful and properly protected, it had the potential of launching Silent Witness far ahead of the competition.

A further challenge facing the R&D department was the availability of funds to support their research efforts. Because the revenue benefits of R&D were not realized until one to two years after the initial investment was made, there was a sizeable gap that needed to be financed. Recently, cash accessibility had not been a problem at Silent Witness. The company had made an Initial Public Offering (IPO) in 1987 and had made its last offering in 1996. Tom Gill, the company's CFO, did not foresee any more public offerings in the near future.

Becoming a $250 million company would require a significant amount of capital to be spent on continued R&D. This was particularly important considering that Silent Witness's past success had come from its position as a technology leader. As a result, senior management was considering some less typical routes of attaining the needed R&D, such as acquiring a large share of a small R&D company with expertise in camera technology. This investment, which would be less costly than developing the technology in-house, could provide similar results. The company was also holding some preliminary discussions with a large Japanese manufacturer. However, this company had yet to agree to relinquish its latest technology to Silent Witness.

3. Customer Needs

Silent Witness relied upon 50 companies to distribute and install its products. Since the company did not have direct contact with the end-users of its systems, it was difficult to develop a clear understanding of what consumers liked or disliked about its products and how they might react to any new features or changes to the product line. This problem was exacerbated by the fact that distributors and installers kept their customer lists highly confidential and would not provide Silent Witness with any customer information.

Absence of direct customer contact also made it difficult for Silent Witness to assess the needs of residential and small business consumers. Because the company had never focused its efforts on this segment of the security marketplace, it did not really understand the needs of these consumers.

Bakshi tried to address this issue by hiring a product manager whose primary responsibility would be to build knowledge of customer needs. Dean Lumb, the new product manager, did not have direct industry experience. However, he had been successful in the role of product manager with a local telecommunications company.

4. Human Resources

Historically, Silent Witness was characterized by an extremely open and flexible corporate culture. Employees were attracted to the entrepreneurial spirit that was prevalent throughout the organization and the lack of rules and strict processes. With the growth and continued expansion of the organization it was becoming clear that greater formalization would be inevitable. This trend had already become apparent in the Operations department.

Bakshi and the senior management team were concerned about what such a change would mean for Silent Witness, in terms of the company's ability to reach the market first with innovative new products, a capability that had been pivotal to the company's past success.

In an attempt to generate the capabilities needed to manage the formalization of Silent Witness, Bakshi hired Coleen Hunter, an experienced Human Resources manager who had been a former colleague of Dean Lumb in the telecommunications business. It was her job to effectively establish formalization within the organization and act as a facilitator across the different departments. After her first two months at Silent Witness, Hunter had already hired 12 new employees. She had also discovered a few gaps in the organization as a result of its rapid growth. For example, one new employee had gone without a promised salary adjustment for nine months. The employee had expressed his frustration; however, no action had been taken to correct his salary. Hunter resolved the problem immediately, but she was concerned that such miscommunication could hamper the firm's performance.

With projected growth of close to 600 per cent in six years the workforce at Silent Witness would grow exponentially. While greater formalization in the recruiting, selection, training and compensation functions would be required, it was inevitable that the managers of the company would have to learn to alter their management styles.

In order to ensure that all the managers, new and old, were working towards executing the new direction for the organization, Bakshi had implemented a strategic planning initiative. Bakshi, with the help of an external consultant, was pushing for more focused strategies in the functional departments. The desired result of this strategy was to improve planning and create a more forward-looking organization. Bakshi wanted an organization in which his senior management team would spend 80 per cent of their time planning and exploring new technology and growth opportunities, and 20 per cent of their time on operational matters.

ESTABLISHING PRIORITIES

Bakshi's new goals were aggressive, but he was confident that the new vision and strategy would permit the name 'Silent Witness' to become synonymous with top surveillance cameras in the world. His concern now was to establish priorities and an action plan for addressing the issues the company faced in moving forward.

Exhibit 1: **Consolidated Income Statements Years ended July 31**

	1999	1998	1997	1996	1995
Revenue	$34,045,027	$21,689,607	$13,402,606	$8,321,174	$5,605,239
Cost of Sales	$16,437,775	$11,864,847	$7,850,661	$4,757,480	$3,359,632
Gross Margin	$17,607,252	$9,824,760	$5,551,945	$3,563,694	$2,245,607
Selling Expenses:					
Sales and Marketing	$4,753,859	$3,627,476	$2,621,041	$1,550,943	$1,215,632
General and Administrative	$2,859,642	$1,450,817	$1,256,893	$1,560,265	$1,534,550
Service	$611,076	$392,280	$92,794		
Research and Development	$1,794,703	$821,711	$501,788	$289,389	$283,574
Amortization	$504,917				
Other Expenses			$1,023	$1,230,268	
Earnings (loss) before income taxes	$7,083,055	$3,532,476	$1,078,406	($1,067,171)	($788,149)
Income Tax:					
Income tax expense	$2,704,188	$1,350,569	$400,000		($205)
Utilization of loss carryforwards		($40,000)	($400,000)		
Net Earnings (loss)	$4,378,887	$2,221,907	$1,078,406	($1,067,171)	($787,944)

Source: 1999 Annual Report

Exhibit 2: Consolidated Balance Sheet at July 31

ASSETS	1999	1998	1997	1996	1995
Current Assets:					
Cash	$ 5,516,795	$ 4,337,351	$ 1,288,344	$ 57,760	$ 24,814
Accounts Receivable	7,016,718	3,979,459	2,853,697	1,854,487	2,701,826
Short-Term Investments	1,116,076				
Inventory	3,905,913	2,004,596	1,214,889	1,232,129	743,697
Prepaid Expenses	286,922	238,220	91,738	93,081	63,522
Total Current Assets	17,842,424	10,559,626	5,448,668	3,237,457	3,533,859
Capital Assets	1,862,952	982,603	402,607	359,084	258,353
Investment	-	-	-	1,023	1,023
Deferred Share Issue Costs	441,762	-	-	-	155,372
Incorporation Costs	-	5,358	5,358	5,358	5,358
TOTAL ASSETS	$ 20,147,138	$ 11,547,587	$ 5,856,633	$ 3,602,922	$ 4,190,010
LIABILITIES AND SHAREHOLDERS' EQUITY					
Current Liabilities:					
Accounts Payable and Accrued Liabilities	$ 4,872,829	$ 3,129,377	$ 2,368,934	$ 1,089,606	$ 799,256
Income Tax Payable	2,580,473	724,587	-	-	-
Warranty Reserve	312,847	155,000	-	-	-
Loans Payable	-	12,861	25,723	38,584	80,334
Bank Indebtedness	-	-	-	294,133	704,362
Current Portion of Capital Lease Obligations	5,795	5,077	14,282	22,161	11,002
Total Current Liabilities	7,771,944	4,026,902	2,408,939	1,444,484	1,594,954
Capital Lease Obligations	3,198	8,993	14,070	23,453	23,202
Due to Shareholders	-	-	-	-	45,317
Shareholders' Equity:					
Share Capital	7,066,791	6,585,374	4,716,519	4,459,522	3,783,903
Retained Earnings (deficit)	5,305,205	926,318	(1,282,895)	(2,324,537)	(1,257,366)
TOTAL LIABILITIES AND SHAREHOLDERS' EQUITY	$ 20,147,138	$ 11,547,587	$ 5,856,633	$ 3,602,922	$ 4,190,010

Source: 1999 Annual Report

Exhibit 3: **Annual Financial Results**

(Annual Revenue (000's Canadian Dollars)

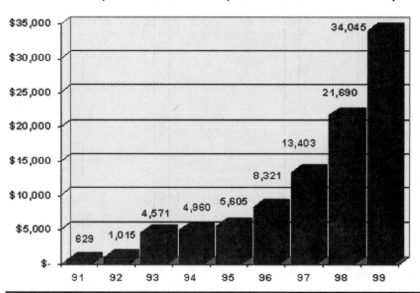

Source: Silent Witenss Web site

	**F1994	**F1995	F1996	F1997	F1998	F1999
Revenue	4,960	5,605	8,321	13,403	21,690	34,045
Net Income	(211)	(787)	(1,067)	1,078	2,222	4,379
EPS Basic	(0.07)	(0.20)	(0.25)	.22	.41	.71

**During Fiscal 1996, the company changed its method of accounting for costs related to research and development, patents and trademarks and licenses. These costs, which were formally deferred, are now being charged to operations as they are incurred. This change has been applied retroactively.

Source: 1999 Annual Report

Exhibit 4: **U.S. Market Size and Segmentation**

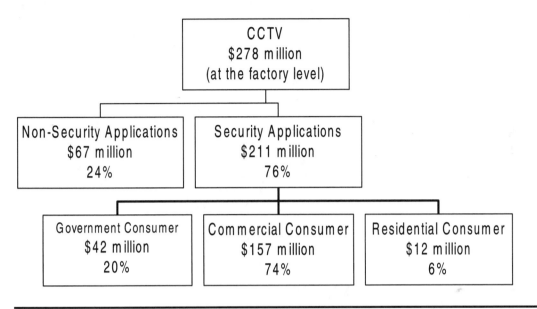

Sources: Multiple Public Sources

Exhibit 5: **Analysis of Competitors in the Security Products Industry**

Company	Revenue (millions)	Net Income (millions)	R&D Budget (millions)	Market Cap. (millions)	Product Focus
SILENT WITNESS (Can. $)	$ 34.0	$ 4.4	$ 1.8	$ 73.0	CCTV CAMERAS
Checkpoint Systems	$ 357	$ 5.7	NA	$ 287.7	Security Alarm Mfg.
Honeywell	$ 8,300	$ 519.1	$ 481.9	$ 8,200.0	Diversified Technologies
ITI Technologies	$ 103	$ 12.2	$ 7.97	$ 207.8	Security Alarm Mfg.
Johnson Controls	$ 1,200	$ 316.2	$ 346.0	$ 3,600.0	Facility Management
JVC	$ 7,823	$ (68.7)	$ 344.3	NA	Electronics
Panasonic	$ 63,670	$ 113.0	$ 4,166.5	$ 53,280.0	Electronics
Pelco[1]					CCTV Systems
Pittway	$ 1,300	$ 32.5	NA	$ 1,095.0	Alarm Mfg. & Distributor
Sensormatic	$ 1,018	$ 38.1	$ 25.8	$ 753.0	Sercurity Systems
Sony	$ 57,109	$ 1,504.0	$ 3,127.6	$ 72,442.5	Electronics
Ultrak	$ 195	$ 3.5	NA	$ 80.0	Security Alarm Mfg.
Vicon	$ 72	$ 5.6	$ 2.2	$ 32.2	CCTV Systems

[1] Pelco is a privately operated company, but is the most comparable to Silent Witness.

Sources: Multiple Public Sources

Exhibit 6: Stock Performance of Silent Witness on the TSE (SWE)

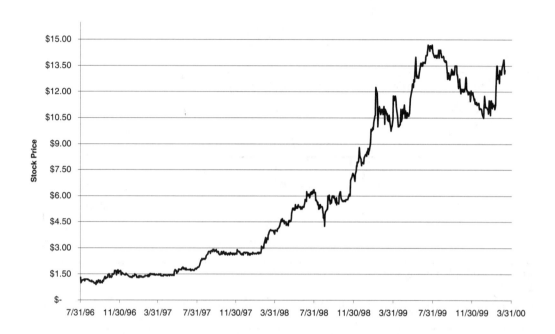

Exhibit 7: List of Major North American Distributors

Canada
1) ADI
2) Burtek Systems Inc.
3) E.B. Horseman & Son
4) Electroquip
5) Nedco

United States (Southern)
1) ADI
2) A1 Alarm Supply
3) Alarm Products Distributors Worldwide Inc.
4) Grand Central Engineering & Security, Inc.
5) International Security & Trading Corp
6) Northern Video Systems Inc.
7) Richardson Electronics
8) Scope Ltd.
9) Shields Electronic Supply Inc.
10) Silmar Electronics Inc.
11) William B. Allen Supply

United States (Eastern)
1) ADI
2) AFY Security Distributors Inc.
3) Alarm it Distributors
4) Alarm Warehouse
5) Alarmax Distributors Inc.
6) Elcor International Inc.
7) Meadowlands Electronics
8) Royal Systems
9) Seacoast Security

United States (Central & Western)
1) ADI
2) Alarm Center
3) Anicom Inc.
4) Audio Video Innovator
5) Dealer Connection
6) Dee Electronics
7) Diamond Pacific Inc. Electronic Customer Dist.
8) Mid State Distributors
9) Northern Video Systems Inc.
10) Pam Distributing
11) Richardson Electronics
12) Sprint North Supply
13) Tri Ed Distribution Inc.
14) Video Security Specialists
15) William B. Allen Supply

Source: Silent Witness Web site: http://www.silent-witness.com, December 1999.

SABENA BELGIAN WORLD AIRLINES

case 32

Mary M. Crossan and
Barbara Pierce

On July 3, 1990, Carlos Van Rafelghem, Chairman of Sabena Belgian World Airlines suffered a massive stroke and never recovered consciousness. For months he lay in a coma. When it became obvious that Van Rafelghem would not return to his position, the Belgian government began to search for a suitable replacement. Jean Luc Dehaene, the Belgian Deputy Prime Minister and Minister of Communications knew that finding a suitable replacement would be a difficult assignment. He described his task as seeking out a "rare bird." Given the unfavourable condition of the global airline industry and the difficulties Sabena was experiencing due to months of interim leadership, it seemed obvious that the person hired to replace Van Rafelghem should already have proven himself in the airline industry.

Rumours of potential candidates had been rampant; the Belgian press speculated for months as to possible successors. The much anticipated announcement of the new Chairman for Sabena Belgian World Airlines caught the entire nation by surprise. On November 9, 1990 the government announced that Pierre Godfroid, Vice President of European Operations for the U.S. based Campbell Soup Company, would be the new head of the Belgian national air carrier. Dehaene, in making the

Ivey

main issue

announcement, explained that the government felt Godfroid's skills in industrial restructuring would more than outweigh his lack of direct involvement in the airline business. It would fall to Godfroid, a man with no experience in managing an airline, but with skills in restructuring, to find a way to ensure the continued survival of Sabena; a clearly troubled airline, in clearly troubled times.

PIERRE GODFROID

Godfroid, born in Antwerp, was a 56 year old Belgian of Flemish descent. He had been trained as a lawyer but in his early career he worked primarily as an investment banker. In the late 1970s he rescued France's leading catalogue sales company from bankruptcy. By doing so he developed the reputation as a highly competent turnaround manager. In 1981 Godfroid joined Continental Foods, a major European food distribution company and became its President in 1982. While head of Continental, he assumed a leadership role in the European food distribution industry eventually becoming president of the Fédération de l'Industrie Alimentaire, the industry's trade association. In 1984, Continental was acquired by the Campbell Soup Company and after the takeover, Godfroid remained with the company to successfully integrate Continental into Campbell's worldwide operations.

Personal Preference

Godfroid accepted the job at Sabena because he felt that the challenge of saving the company was one he simply could not turn down. He knew that the risk of failure was great but the personal rewards of success would be equally significant. If things could be turned around for Sabena, the transformation would establish a model for other state run businesses trying to make the transition from public to private enterprise. There was potential for the impact he had on Sabena to be felt well beyond the borders of one struggling company.

Resource

Resource

Godfroid strongly believed that business success was the result of competent leadership and "good people." Leadership set the direction and tone for individual employees to follow but it was their competence, applied within a framework established by the leader, which produced positive results. "I only believe in people they make the difference." He felt that the right kind of people were those with a simple approach; people who were not pretentious, who saw what needed to be done and went ahead and did it. He stated that, "Success comes to those who are willing to take the greatest risks." He was willing to tolerate mistakes in the belief that the problems they caused would be more than offset by the learning that accompanied failure. Godfroid had little tolerance for bureaucratic ritual or unnecessary paperwork; direct, hands-on control, was not of primary importance.

SABENA'S HISTORY

Founded in 1923, Belgium's Sabena Airlines, was one of the oldest air carriers in the world. The Belgian people were very proud of the fact that their country had a national airline whose roots could be traced back to the early days of aviation. They believed that a national airline was necessary to ensure Belgium remained connected to the rest of the world. Over the years Sabena had developed air connections throughout Europe and to a lesser extent to North America, but the airline played its most crucial role in the development of Belgium's colonial ties to Africa. The routes which carried wealthy colonists between Africa and Europe linked Belgium to its colonies and at the same time allowed the airline to prosper in spite of Belgium's relatively small domestic market. What was good for the development of the country was good for the development of Sabena.

On a number of occasions, Sabena aircraft had been directed to African trouble spots to air lift Belgian nationals in emergency situations. The airline was seen as a lifeline to the home country and its ability to respond in a crisis increased the perception among Belgians that the airline was an important component of their national sovereignty.

The airline's dependence on African routes, eventually, resulted in long run problems when the ties between Belgium and its African colonies were broken. In 1963, after the colonies achieved independence, the government of Zaire, the former Belgian Congo, ended Sabena's monopoly on routes to Europe. It later expelled the company from domestic air services altogether. The loss of these routes, together with the fact that the company had neglected development of more lucrative routes to North America and Asia while its competition had not, almost resulted in the company's collapse. However, the Belgian government, cognizant of the air line's historical position and its importance as a source of employment (over 12,000 Belgians worked for the airline), continued to support Sabena during the tough times. As long as the company did not lose too much money, there were strong political forces keeping it afloat.

INDUSTRY ENVIRONMENT

In 1990, the European airline industry consisted of over 20 national and private carriers of varying size and profitability. Most of these carriers were wholly owned or significantly supported by their home governments and they enjoyed a strong hold on their national markets (Exhibit 1). Smaller independent regional and charter airlines had emerged and were positioning themselves for smaller niche or under-serviced markets. However these start-up airlines were not perceived to represent significant competition because of their size and the limited nature of their services.

According to the International Civil Aviation Organization, the world's airlines transported over 1.1 billion passengers in 1989; however there was growing concern that some markets were beginning to mature and growth would slow (Exhibit 2) in future years. In addition, industry profits were extremely variable. While some major airlines were doing extremely well, (Singapore, Delta and AMR) others were on the brink of bankruptcy (Texas Air, Pan Am and TWA). As noted in Exhibit 3, Sabena was the 34th largest airline in the world on the basis of revenues and the 44th on the basis of passenger miles in 1989.

FIXED COSTS

The basic operating economics of an airline hinged upon high fixed costs. Once the airline set its routes, established flight frequencies, and decided on the type of aircraft, most of its costs were in place. Every passenger represented contribution and the airline was under great pressure to fill the planes. Exhibit 4 provides the cost structure for a typical commercial airline. Since fuel costs were about the same for a full plane as an empty one, and the number of flight crew depended on the type of aircraft not the number of passengers, the only true variable expenses were services like ticketing and customers' meals. Most airlines used some form of product differentiation to attract customers, preferably high yield customers such as business travellers and first class passengers.

A UNIFIED EUROPE

In the fall of 1990, a number of changes and potential changes were facing the European airline industry and uncertainty was the most accurate way to describe the state of affairs. A key unknown was the impact of a unified Europe, planned for 1992. No one was sure what impact this new political alignment would have on the airline industry, but companies were beginning to position themselves to take advantage of the anticipated freer borders and the reduced regulatory environment. The European Commission, the regulatory body for European aviation, was seeking greater powers to ensure a competitive environment for post 1992. It was particularly concerned about a potential rise in predatory practices on the part of dominant carriers. For example, such airlines could flood the market with capacity or frequencies, charge fares below a carrier's fully allocated costs, or grant override commissions and other benefits to travel agents and frequent flier programs which locked in customers to one airline. The Commission was exploring ways in which it could encourage open competition so the consumer would benefit from increased services and lower costs. At the same time it was trying to determine the best way to intervene so that the industry would avoid the pitfalls evident in the post deregulation environment of the United States. European airlines, having had the advantage of watching the U.S. experience realized that deregulation would inevitably lead to fierce competition and likely result in industry consolidation. There was developing concern among industry officials that, in a deregulated environment, many of the smaller airlines could not survive in their current configuration. There was also uncertainty as to whether the European Commission would be given the appropriate power to intervene to protect the more vulnerable airlines.

ALLIANCES

The potential for industry consolidation seemed even more certain given the emerging trend to privatize national airlines. Many governments were no longer willing, and in many cases, no longer able, to prop up unprofitable operations. With reduced fiscal support and regulatory protection from home governments, airlines were beginning to realize that they could not continue to depend on their governments for preferential treatment. Governments had little to offer in support of their flag carriers. Many of the smaller airlines, seeing the handwriting on the wall, were not waiting to be taken over but were investigating the possibility of joining with competitors in some form of operational alliance. For example, in the spring of 1990, Austrian Airlines joined Finnair, Swissair and SAS in a European alliance created to serve an expanded market in Eastern and Southern Europe, North Africa, the Middle East and India. Sabena had been holding talks with a number of airlines and had recently received a firm proposal to join with British Airways and KLM to develop a European hub in Brussels. However these alliance relationships were new and untested and industry analysts wondered about the long term stability of such arrangements.

The independent competitors were fighting such alliances preferring to see the collapse of the smaller carriers. Alliances captured landing rights within existing operations and did not free up slots for expansions or new entrants. The start up operations were dependent upon access to existing slots because the current European airport infrastructure did not allow for the creation of new and expanded airline operations. Most governments did not have the money to build new airports or even to improve existing facilities. A special report for the International Air Transport Association found that capacity at 10 major European airports would be seriously restricted between

1995 and 2000 without major improvements and a total of 27 major Western European airports would be unable to accommodate traffic demand by the year 2000 without significant enhancements. This meant that airlines with existing slots had a valuable commodity to bargain with, in alliance negotiations.

THE GULF CRISIS

Another major uncertainty facing the airline industry concerned the impact of the Persian Gulf Crisis on airline operations. Since tensions began to mount in the summer of 1990, oil prices had increased significantly resulting in increased airline fuel costs. At the same time, passenger travel declined as people concerned about the unstable conditions delayed or cancelled travel plans. How long would the crisis last and how would it be resolved? How long would the tensions last and would there be any lasting repercussions? Would the oil prices decline when the situation stabilized? The little profitability that remained in the industry was being squeezed out by this unforseen event.

SABENA BELGIAN WORLD AIRLINES

Sabena had always operated as an instrument of the Belgian government and reflected many of the hallmarks of a government run bureaucracy. The organization functioned more like a public authority staffed by civil servants than a competitive airline. Under these conditions, the priority was not necessarily what was best for Sabena as a competitive business but rather what was seen as best for the people of Belgium. For example, it was not unusual for purchasing decisions to be made, not on the basis of the least cost alternative, but on the basis of other more politically important criteria.

The government saw the airline as a source of employment and did what it could to maximize the number of people working at Sabena. If this meant that the company lost money, then the government encouraged the airline to protect employment and covered losses until profitability improved. Systems to improve efficiency were given lower priority especially if their implementation resulted in job losses. As a result, the airline was seriously overstaffed and operated with probably the worst efficiency of any airline in Europe. Internal studies had shown that the airline did not have a good image among consumers and was not known for the quality or consistency of its service.

The company had 16 directors, many of whom were appointed because of the need to accommodate Belgium's various political parties, labour unions and linguistic factions. Staffing selections as well were influenced by the need to ensure balanced representation among Belgium's linguistic factions.

The airline operated out of Zaventem Airport, 30 km outside of Brussels and controlled most of the landing rights and runway slots. Access to Zaventem was one of Sabena's most valuable assets since the airport was strategically located near the centre of Western Europe (see Exhibit 5 for map). Many felt that Zaventem would make an ideal hub location if the European airlines decided to replicate the American approach to airline operations.

Management at Sabena

When Godfroid took over many of those in management positions had been appointed to their posts for political reasons and did not necessarily have appropriate work experience or managerial competence. It was not unusual for managers to act in the interests of the people who appointed them rather than the interests of the corporation which employed them. Skilled individuals who rose through the ranks to attain leadership positions in the company found it difficult to function among less motivated or competent colleagues. Some left in frustration because of the amount of political interference and their inability to function in a true management role. Most of the current senior managers had either an aeronautics or engineering background and saw technical concerns as the focus of their efforts. The planes and equipment were of excellent quality and well maintained, but management had much less appreciation for marketing and customer service requirements.

The management structure at Sabena was multi-layered and hierarchical with management clearly separate from workers. There were no accurate organizational charts or job descriptions. This meant that the organizational units within Sabena developed as separate fifedoms reflecting the unique relationships developed among managers and workers within the unit. There was little co-ordination at the management level except in crisis situations and it was not uncommon for open hostility to break out as one set of managers blamed another if problems arose.

There was a similar lack of competence at the supervisory level. Because of rigid compensation rules it was difficult to reward individual performance or to provide increased wages to employees who exceeded maximum levels in specified wage categories. It was common practice, therefore, to create special supervisory positions or to promote individuals to existing supervisory positions to justify a pay raise. This meant that a large number of supervisors were in these positions for administrative reasons rather for their ability to manage people. Such supervisors did not see themselves as management's representatives in their relations with hourly workers. It was not uncommon for them to provide weak leadership on the floor and to provide poor implementation of management direction.

Management did as little as possible to communicate directly with the workers, preferring instead to instruct through written communications and memos. There were those who suggested that management was afraid of the workforce and avoided face to face confrontations whenever possible. Management treated the workers as machines which were not expected, or encouraged, to think for themselves. When an employee had a work related problem, it was presented to a supervisor for a solution. Employees took no initiative beyond their limited responsibilities. Each worker performed his or her specific job unconcerned about the functioning of the whole. They took little or no pride in the outcome of their work. This attitude, coupled with ineffective supervision, meant that a significant amount of pilfering, work avoidance and shirking took place. Absenteeism was running at 9% per day.

Employer/Union Relations

The unions in Belgium were extremely powerful and dominated every aspect of Belgian life. They were established, not on the basis of job function or industry designation but rather on political affiliation. There were three unions, all of which were represented at Sabena; Socialist (30% of Sabena workers), Christian Democrats (30%) and Liberals (10%). In the past, unions had dominated management at Sabena. Industrial relations were strained and when the unions disagreed with management actions, strikes were a common occurrence. Human Resource (HR) managers at

Sabena had not kept up with trends in HR management. They preferred to continue to manage according to the existing status quo, which was unquestionably adversarial. Under this approach both management and unions had clearly defined "roles" and ongoing relations followed well established rules of the "game." The workers held a trump card, however, in that if they didn't like what they were told by management, their unions would complain to the politicians, who in turn would direct the Chairman to comply with the union demands.

Management was tightly bound by the terms and conditions of collective agreements. Workers were hired and trained to carry out very specific and limited functions. If there was no work available, workers would wait until appropriate work was found. Workers at Sabena were paid well, earning significantly more and working significantly less than workers in private industry. In addition to high wages, the level of employee benefits provided workers in Belgium approached 31% of their salary, significantly more than was required in the countries of competitor firms.

The workers at Sabena knew that they had well paid and secure employment. Wage increases were based on length of service. Pay hikes were automatically awarded for each year of continuous service, for a period of up to 33 years. As long as the worker continued on the payroll, he or she was guaranteed an increase in wages regardless of productivity or performance. It was almost impossible to fire anyone and there was virtually a no lay-off policy. If attempts were made to lay off workers, the union would intervene with the government and the Chairman would be directed to back down.

Corporate Restructuring

Van Rafelghem felt that the lack of management accountability had been a major source of reduced profitability. To resolve this problem he divided the company up into semi-autonomous subsidiaries or divisions. His plan was to hold each division accountable for the management of the assets under its control and to establish clear profit centres to monitor results. There were 12 of these subsidiaries established (airlines, flight school, catering, techniques (airline maintenance and repair), real estate, tourism, finance) each reporting to a holding company referred to as Sabena S.A.. Among these subsidiaries, Sabena World Airlines (SWA) was the largest and most important. The Chairman and Vice-Chairman of Sabena S.A. held the same positions in each of the 12 subsidiaries but after that, there was much duplication of administrative functions. This was not perceived as a problem because employment, not efficiency, was the government's key priority. In fact, the restructuring had a positive effect in that it resulted in the creation of a number of new managerial positions.

Although the intent to decentralize and introduce divisional accountability had merit, problems arose because of the lack of complementary integrating mechanisms to focus the subsidiaries on common purposes or goals. Immediately upon establishing the subsidiaries, boundaries were drawn between divisions and co-ordination became an almost impossible task. Although the change was intended to increase accountability, every time a problem occurred, individual divisions would pass the buck claiming the trouble was the fault of another division. Instead of solving problems, more problems were created. The fragmentation of management effort directed at internal problems diverted the company's attention from the truly important environmental challenges facing it.

Splitting Sabena up into smaller subsidiaries had, unfortunately, taken place before the completion of information systems to track corporate results in line with the new divisions. Although a great deal of effort had been directed at developing information and accounting systems, the company was not capable of sorting out data in meaningful ways to assist in identifying responsibility and the MIS systems were of no help in resolving jurisdictional disputes.

Financial Position

The Belgian state owned 53% of Sabena's shares with the remainder belonging to regional governments or state run investment funds. In the past, the Belgian government had only asked that the company be marginally profitable. It was willing to absorb small losses from time to time, as long as Sabena provided a maximum number of jobs for the Belgian economy. By 1990, however, the state was beginning to grow concerned about the company's steady stream of losses. Like many countries, Belgium was beginning to feel the effects of deficit financing and the country was experiencing a worsening debt problem. Political pressure was beginning to build to bring the national debt under control. The government was not sure how much longer it could tolerate the continuing drain of Sabena's poor financial results. Sabena expected to post a loss of BFr 3 billion (US$98 million) to BFr 4 billion in 1990, its worst performance in 15 years. In addition it was facing a capital expenditure over the next ten years of BFr 100 billion to pay for new planes on order. It was clear that the poor financial results were showing no signs of reversal. In fact, the losses were escalating at such an alarming rate that the company's equity had all but disappeared (Exhibit 6).

Van Rafelghem had been working on establishing a joint venture with British Airways (BA) and KLM . He was hoping to interest the two carriers into buying into SWA. Both would purchase a 20% equity share leaving Sabena (the Belgian government) with 60% ownership. The intent of the venture would be to establish a European hub at Brussel's Zaventem airport. This would allow these airlines to use the underutilized Zaventem airport to link secondary destinations throughout Europe. Interest in this alliance had cooled, however, because of anti-trust concerns among other competitors and Sabena's fears about its loss of autonomy under this arrangement. However, the hub idea had merit in and of itself and there were some who felt that Sabena should consider going it alone or consider interesting other more appropriate airlines in a Brussel's hub arrangement.

After Van Rafelghem's stroke, Sabena's Deputy Chairman Pahault stepped in to take over but, he was in no position to effectively replace Van Rafelghem. The Deputy Chairman position had been established as one of convention to appease Belgium's main linguistic factions. The tradition had been that if the Chairman was of Flemish descent, the Vice Chairman would be French and vice versa. In this case, since Van Rafelghem was Flemish, so Pahault, of French descent, had been appointed as Vice Chairman. Much of the knowledge about the company and how it functioned however, resided only with Van Rafelghem and it was inaccessible as long as he lay in a coma. Some even speculated that establishment of Sabena S.A. had been a masterful feat of financial engineering intended to increase equity through the creation of goodwill. Regardless of Van Rafelghem's intent, it was clear that the situation Pahault inherited was a company very near bankruptcy; immediate action was critical. Recognizing the financial crisis the company faced, Pahault brought in a group of McKinsey consultants to try and straighten out its financial position and to identify cost saving measures to get Sabena's costs under control. In their report, McKinsey suggested that to ensure its survival Sabena either drastically downsize its operations to become a low cost regional carrier or it find the funds to invest in the development of a European hub (estimated to be in the neighbourhood of $250 million U.S.).

GODFROID'S TASK

In offering him the position Dehaene had asked Godfroid to help with the transformation of Sabena from public to private enterprise. The government requested that he prepare a business plan by February 1, 1991 outlining his program for raising new capital and reorganizing the airline. The government was willing to release its control of the company reducing its level of ownership from 53% to 25%, allowing for a much needed infusion of new equity from private sources. To avert bankruptcy, Sabena would need to improve its profitability dramatically and to attract new partners from the private sector. Godfroid had just under two months to come up with a plan to achieve these objectives. What direction should he take the airline and how should he manage this mammoth undertaking? Was Sabena worth saving or would it inevitably be swallowed up by a larger and stronger competitor? Godfroid knew he had to set his direction soon since there was little time to waste.

Exhibit 1: European Airlines

Airline	Country
Aer Lingus	Ireland
Air France	France
Air Malta	Malta
Alitalia	Italy
Austrian Airlines	Austria
British Airways	Great Britain
CSA Czechoslovakian Airlines	Czechoslovakia
Finnair	Finland
Iberia	Spain
Iceland air	Iceland
JAT Yugoslavian Airlines	Yugoslavia
KLM	Netherlands
Lufthansa	West Germany
Luxair	Luxemburg
Malev Hungarian Airlines	Hungary
Olympic Airlines	Greece
Sabena	Belgium
SAS	Sweden
Swissair	Switzerland
TAP - Air Portugal	Portugal
Turkish Air	Turkey

Exhibit 2: **Selected RPK Forecasts (billions)**

DOMESTIC MARKET	1989 RPK	Forecast Average Annual Growth Rate 1990 - 2000
U.S.	505.1	5.1
Western Europe	52.2	6.3
Asia-Pacific	70.5	6.3
Total Domestic	627.8 out of total Domestic Market: 981.5	

Between Europe and	1989	1990	1991	1993	1995	2000
Intra-Europe	67.8	72.6	77.7	88.9	100.4	125.7
North America	168.2	178.9	190.0	213.1	237.2	303.3
South America	19.8	21.2	22.7	25.7	28.9	37.8
Africa	34.9	37.0	39.2	43.8	48.8	62.9
Middle East	35.9	37.3	38.8	42.0	45.4	55.2
Asia [1]	33.2	39.4	45.9	58.9	70.9	101.6

[1] Does not include the Indian subcontinent.

Source: Boeing Commercial Airplane Group

Exhibit 3: **Top 50 Airline Companies: Rank By Revenues**

RANK BY REVENUES				1989 REVENUES		PROFITS		TRAFFIC	
1989	1988	Airline Company	Country	U.S. $ Millions	% Change from 1988 (U.S.)	$Millions	Rank	Billions of Passenger Kms.	Rank
1	2	AMR	U.S.	10,589.5	20.0	454.8	3	118.5	1
2	1	UAL	U.S.	9,914.5	10.0	324.2	6	112.3	2
3	4	Japan Airlines [1]	Japan	8,509.0	17.4	157.3	10	54.4	8
4	5	Delta	U.S.	8,089.5	17.0	460.9	2	55.9	3
5	7	British Airways [1]	Britain	7,529.1	12.5	309.5	7	90.2	6
6	6	Lufthansa	W. Germany	6,941.2	3.0	56.8	22	57.9	12
7	3	Texas Air	U.S.	6,768.7	(21.0)	(885.6)	47	81.3	4
8	10	NWA	U.S.	6,553.8	16.0	355.2	5	73.7	5
9	9	USAIR Group	U.S.	6,257.3	9.6	(63.2)	41	54.4	9

Continued …

10	8	Air France	France	6,216.9	4.4	132.0	12	37.0	11
11	11	All Nippon [1]	Japan	4,858.4	9.7	60.2	19	26.0	16
12	12	Scandinavian Airlines	Sweden	4,567.3	3.5	N.A.	--	15.3	26
13	13	Trans World	U.S.	4,507.3	3.4	(298.5)	45	56.4	7
14	15	Hanjin Group	South Korea	4,243.6	13.7	69.6	18	17.9	23
15	14	Pan Am	U.S.	3,794.4	(8.9)	(336.6)	46	46.6	10
16	16	Alitalia	Italy	3,734.2	14.6	(168.1)	44	20.8	21
17	17	Swissair	Switzerland	3,174.5	1.7	103.3	16	15.8	25
18	20	Air Canada	Canada	3,104.3	11.8	125.8	13	26.3	15
19	18	Iberia	Spain	3,015.5	4.9	52.5	25	21.1	20
20	19	KLM [1]	Netherlands	2,938.9	4.1	184.2	8	24.0	17
21	21	Qantas [2]	Australia	2,655.1	18.1	144.3	11	26.6	14
22	22	Singapore [1]	Singapore	2,295.8	15.9	494.7		28.9	13
23	24	PWA	Canada	2,252.9	27.7	(47.3)	40	23.7	18
24	23	Cathay Pacific	Hong Kong	2,212.6	14.4	425.2		22.1	19
25	25	Saudia	Saudi Arabia	1,910.1	12.5	(140.0)	43	16.3	24
26	26	Varig	Brazil	1,862.1	21.6	10.4	39	13.9	28
27	28	Ansett Transport [2]	Australia	1,743.9	32.7	108.0	15	7.7	42
28	27	Thai International [3]	Thailand	1,683.8	17.9	182.1		18.7	22
29	29	Japan Air System [1]	Japan	1,418.3	12.7	12.2	36	7.3	43
30	30	Air Inter	France	1,356.5	9.5	18.3	32	8.5	39
31	34	China	Taiwan	1,246.4	20.3	115.6	14	10.5	33
32	31	Garuda	Indonesia	1,232.6	11.6	N.A.	--	12.9	29
33	33	Hudson Investments	Britain	1,211.6	11.6	11.7	37	6.9	45
34	36	Finnair [1]	Finland	1,160.9	13.5	18.3	33	9.2	35
35	32	Sabena	Belgium	1,146.9	4.9	18.0	34	6.8	46
36	37	Air New Zealand [1]	New Zealand	1,108.7	9.0	46.6	26	10.6	31
37	38	LTU	West Germany	1,094.4	13.6	N.A.	--	9.8	34
38	35	UTA	France	1,058.1	3.2	38.1	28	5.6	48

Continued …

39	39	Southwest	U.S.	1,031.7	22.6	71.6	17	15	27
40	43	Australian [2]	Australia	1,013.8	27.9	57.4	21	6.1	47
41	45	America West	U.S.	1,004.2	29.5	20.0	31	12.7	30
42	40	Alaska Air Group	U.S.	929.2	14.1	42.9	27	7.1	44
43	49	S. African Airways [1]	S. Africa	912.2	(9.3)	55.9	24	9.0	37
44	44	Aer Lingus	Ireland	899.5	14.5	56.2	23	3.4	49
45	∃	Austrian	Austria	850.5	9.7	11.6	38	2.4	50
46	42	Olympic Airways	Greece	*785.0	*(2.2)	*(123.1)	42	8.1	40
47	47	Mexicana	Mexico	764.3	2.0	13.7	35	10.5	32
48	48	Air India [1]	India	745.4	1.2	28.1	29	9.0	36
49	∃	El Al	Israel	713.6	7.3	24.2	30	7.7	41
50	∃	Malaysian [1]	Malaysia	712.8	14.0	59.0	20	9.0	38

* Estimate
[1] *Figures are for fiscal year ended March 31, 1989*
[2] *Figures are for fiscal year ended June 30, 1989*
[3] *Figures are for fiscal year ended September 30, 1989*
[4] *Figurers are for fiscal year ended October 31, 1989*
Note: *All figures converted to U.S. dollars using the average official exchange rate during each company's fiscal year.*

Source: Labich, Kenneth, "America Takes on the World", Fortune, September 24, 1990, p. 52.

Exhibit 4: Airline Operating Cost Distribution—International Civil Aviation Organization Airlines – 1988

Direct Costs		**Indirect Costs**	
Fuel 14.5%		Ticketing and Sales	17.6%
Maintenance	11.6%	User fees, Station expense	14.1%
Flight Operations	11.4%	Passenger Service	10.4%
Depreciation	7.8%	General/Admin.	8.9%
		Landing Fees	3.7%
Total	**45.3%**	**Total**	**54.7%**

Source: Boeing Commercial Airplane Group <u>Current Market Outlook</u>, February 1990

Exhibit 5: **British Airways Plan for a Brussels Hub**

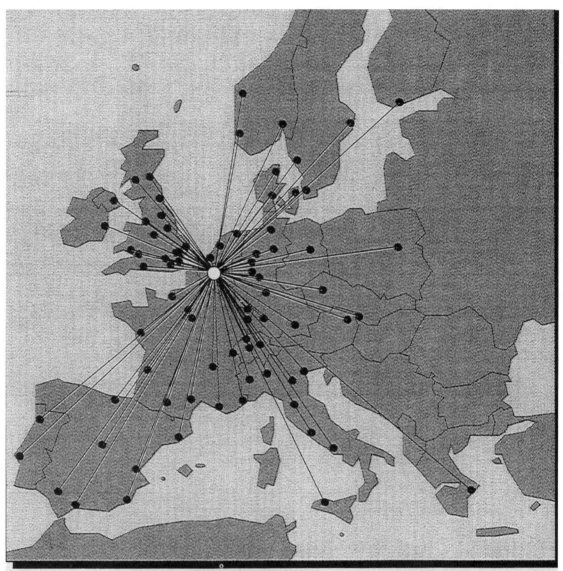

British Airways told the British MMC it plans to link 75 cities in Europe by 1995 through a hub-and-spoke network at Brussels if its proposed 20% stake in Sabena World Airlines is approved.

Source: Aviation Week & Space Technology, May 14, 1990.

Exhibit 6: **Financial History of Sabena 1984-1990 (billion BFr)**

	DEBT*	EQUITY
1984	17.0	2.4
1985	19.3	4.8
1986	23.5	10.5
1987	25.4	10.7
1988	25.9	9.0
1989	31.2	7.5
1990	43.4	0.1

* Does not include debt owed to the Belgian Government

THE GE ENERGY MANAGEMENT INITIATIVE

case 33

Joseph N. Fry and
Julian Birkinshaw

In August 1992, Raj Bhatt, business development manager for GE Canada, met with executives from GE Supply, a U.S.-based distribution arm of GE. The purpose of the meeting was to discuss new business opportunities in Energy Efficiency, an industry that focused on the reduction of energy usage through the installation of energy-efficient technologies. Bhatt had recently gained pre-qualification for GE Canada to bid in a $1 billion program to install energy-efficient technologies in all Federal Government buildings. He was confident that GE's expertise in lighting, motors, appliances and financing was sufficient to win at least some of the contracts. Furthermore, he saw the program as a stepping stone to building a new GE business to service the Energy Efficiency needs of a range of clients.

The GE Supply executives informed Bhatt that they had already established a position in the U.S. Energy Efficiency industry, through a joint venture with a new Energy Service Company (ESCo), and had retained the services of a full-time consultant to develop the business. They were interested in the Federal Buildings program that Bhatt had been working on, but felt that it would be

Ivey

Joseph N. Fry and Julian Birkinshaw prepared this case solely to provide material for class discussion. The authors do not intend to illustrate either effective or ineffective handling of a managerial situation. The authors may have disguised certain names and other identifying information to protect confidentiality.

more efficiently run as a division of GE Supply, rather than as a locally managed Canadian venture. The meeting posed a dilemma for Bhatt. He was encouraged by the level of interest that already existed for Energy Efficiency within GE, but at the same time held certain misgivings about folding the Federal Buildings program into GE Supply's nascent business. Specifically, he was concerned that a lot of interesting Energy Efficiency opportunities existed in Canada, which a U.S.-focused business would not be in a position to exploit. Bhatt left the meeting uncertain how to proceed.

GENERAL ELECTRIC (GE)

GE, with $60 billion dollars in revenues in 1991, was among the top ten industrial corporations in the world. From the early days of Thomas Edison, it had grown to be a diversified 54-business corporation by the early eighties. With 400,000 employees and a very strong corporate planning division, it exemplified the traditional strategic planning oriented corporation of the 1970s.

In 1980, Jack Welch, the incoming CEO, made a series of sweeping changes. The corporate planning department was eliminated, layers of management were eliminated and the concepts of empowerment and customer focus became the new drivers behind GE's activities. GE's many businesses were restructured into 13 autonomous groups (GE Aerospace, Aircraft Engines, Appliances, Communications and Services, Electrical Distribution and Control, Financial Services, Industrial and Power Systems, Lighting, Medical Systems, Motors, Plastics, Transportation Systems and NBC) which were further subdivided into a number of operating divisions. In the course of a series of divestments, acquisitions and amalgamations, Welch declared that a major criterion for holding on to a business was that it was number one or number two worldwide in its chosen industry.

Each business group worked from a U.S. head office and was charged with global responsibility for its operations. This move, which by-passed the traditional country organizations, was intended to give priority to the global demands of the businesses, rather than to national interests. International operations, which accounted for about 25 per cent of GE's revenues, were structured under a vice chairman, international, but the reality under a so-called direct-connect model was that the operating authority in each country was held by the relevant global business unit. Typically, this meant that general management roles in country operations were eliminated and that business leaders or functional managers of specific businesses reported to their headquarters in the U.S., rather than through their country organization. For example, the marketing manager of GE Lighting's Canadian operations reported directly to the GE Lighting group headquarters marketing manager in Cleveland, Ohio.

GE Canada

The shift to global management had a major impact on GE's Canadian business. In the 1970s, GE Canada operated as a "miniature replica" of its parent company; most businesses and all functions were represented in Canada, and typically a full line of products was made, primarily for the Canadian market but with some exporting possibilities. The Canadian CEO was fully responsible for the profitability of the Canadian operating divisions. This changed dramatically under direct-connect structure implemented in the late 1980s.

In 1992, Matthew Meyer, CEO of GE Canada, had a vastly different role from his predecessors. With all operations reporting straight to their U.S. divisional bosses, Meyer was directly responsible only for the activities of a very small number of employees. He had vice-presidents in finance, environmental affairs, legal, human resources and government affairs. These managers were responsible for all the uniquely Canadian issues that cropped up, such as new legislation, tax accounting, government grants and so on. In addition, there was a small business development group, consisting of three managers. Traditionally, this group had been involved in feasibility studies and new market development for the business units in Canada. Following the shift to a 'direct-connect' structure, the role had become primarily one of looking for opportunities to leverage the strengths of Canadian activities on a global basis. They were also concerned with identifying new business opportunities in Canada. Bhatt, one of the business development managers, explained:

> Canada is a relatively small marketplace. Consequently, most U.S.-based business leaders have a limited awareness of the opportunities here because they have either a U.S. or a global focus. The role of business development is to attempt to identify investment or market opportunities here that they might find valuable.

There was some discussion among business development managers over the extent to which they should actively 'sell' business opportunities to the GE businesses. Some felt that a proactive strategy of promoting Canadian opportunities was appropriate; others preferred to investigate only those cases where business development's involvement had been solicited. The recent decision to promote the vice-president of business development, but not replace him, added further to the uncertainty over the group's role.

Raj Bhatt

Bhatt was only 29. He had worked at GE for just one year, following a successful period at Northern Telecom and an MBA at the University of Western Ontario.

> Business development is quite a challenging experience. There are lots of good opportunities in Canada, but it is sometimes difficult to achieve the level of interest and buy-in necessary to attract the appropriate attention. The Oakville lighting plant, a global manufacturing mandate, is a planned $144 million investment and is certainly our biggest success so far, but there have been a lot of ideas that failed to materialize.

The business development manager typically held that post for only two years, after which he or she was expected to take a line position in one of the businesses. Bhatt had been given a number of attractive options, but had turned them down because he was afraid that his involvement was critical to a number of projects. Specifically, he was concerned that the Energy Efficiency business opportunity he had championed up to now would die because no one else had the knowledge of, or the enthusiasm for, that particular opportunity.

ENERGY EFFICIENCY

Energy Efficiency covered the multitude of ways that energy usage could be optimized, including conservation, use of efficient appliances and off peak usage. Energy Efficiency was originally conceived in the early 1970s as a response to rising oil prices. It recently saw a resurgence due to the environmental movement and the increasing need for cost competitiveness in the late eighties. Although strongly motivated by public opinion and government pressure, Energy Efficiency initiatives were usually sponsored by the energy supply utilities. They recognized that they could more effectively keep their investment down by reducing demand than by building expensive new power stations. There were also obvious benefits to consumers (in reduced costs) and to the environment.

The growth in utility-sponsored programs for Energy Efficiency was responsible for the formation of many Energy Service Companies (ESCos). These companies aimed to meet the demands and needs of their customers by utilizing these programs. Under the most common arrangement (called a performance contract), the ESCo would install energy efficient technologies at no upfront cost to the client. The costs would be recouped from the savings realized. Such an arrangement could be very lucrative, but the ESCo bore all the risk in the event that the promised savings never materialized.

The ESCo Industry in Canada

The Canadian ESCo industry was among the most advanced in the world. Both Federal and Provincial governments had active energy-management programs to promote 'green' issues, and had targeted Energy Efficiency as a critical industry. Ontario Hydro and Quebec Hydro had budgets for Energy Efficiency of $800 million and $300 million respectively, in comparison to the Cdn$1.5 billion budget for all U.S. utilities combined.

As a result of the utilities' involvement, the Canadian ESCo industry was growing very rapidly; 1989 revenues of $20 million had grown to $100 million by 1992, and one estimate put the total market potential in the billions of dollars. Three major segments could be identified, each accounting for approximately one third of the total volume. They were Commercial, which consisted primarily of office buildings, hospitals and other public buildings; Industrial, which consisted of factories and production plants; and Residential, which consisted of single-family dwellings. So far the commercial sector had been the most rewarding to ESCos, largely due to the similarities between (for example) one hospital and another. Industrial also had potential, but required knowledge of the specific process technology used in each case.

Over the past decade, the ESCo industry in Canada had experienced mixed fortunes, as companies struggled to understand the dynamics of the market. Lack of technical and risk management experience, flawed contracts, lack of financial strength and energy price collapses had all led to very low levels of profitability among major players. The recent upsurge of interest in Energy Efficiency, however, had pushed the industry onto a more steady footing. Furthermore, a shakeout had occurred, leaving between five and 10 serious competitors in Canada.

ESCo Strategies

ESCos saw themselves as undertaking three useful functions with commercial and industrial customers. First, they could undertake energy audits of client sites and advise what forms of energy management were most appropriate. Second, they could engineer and provide access to a wide range of energy-efficient technologies that would normally be hard to get hold of. Third, they could install new energy-efficient equipment, under a performance contract or similar. In the Canadian industry, there were several hundred consulting engineers that participated in energy audits, but only seven "full-service" ESCos that undertook all three functions.

Of the three functions, programs such as performance contracting offered the greatest potential return to ESCos, but also the highest degree of risk. Following an installation, it took between five and ten years before the financial benefits were realized. ESCos were paid at the time of installation by their financing partners, who recovered their costs over the lifetime of the project, but in the event that the project was badly estimated, the shortfall in revenue would have to be made up by the ESCo. Access to capital at a reasonable cost was thus critical. Some ESCos had parent companies with deep pockets. The audit and supply functions, while less lucrative, were important elements of the ESCo's business because they established legitimacy in the eyes of the customer. Many commercial clients were extremely sceptical of the estimated energy savings provided by ESCos, but if they agreed to an energy audit, there was a greater likelihood they could be sold on the merits of an installation. The credibility of the guarantee provided by the ESCo was thus of great importance.

THE GE ENERGY MANAGEMENT INITIATIVE

The Initial Opportunity

As GE Business Development Manager, Raj Bhatt received a communication from the Federal Government inviting ESCos to seek to be pre-qualified for the implementation of performance contracts in 50,000 federal buildings in Canada. The program had a potential total value of $1 billion, which was to be split into a number of smaller contracts. Bhatt was struck by the potential fit between GE's areas of expertise and the requirements of the program. ESCos had to be able to provide energy-efficient lighting, motors and controls and provide financing for the project; GE was a leading supplier of many of the required products and had a large financing division. Unlike rival firms that would have to form consortia between electrical and financing companies, GE could do many things in-house.

Bhatt submitted a proposal for the Federal Buildings program and, along with a number of other consortia, achieved "pre-qualification", meaning the right to bid on subsequent contracts that fell under the Federal Buildings umbrella. This success underlines the magnitude of the opportunity that GE was facing in the ESCo industry. Rather than limiting GE's involvement to the one-off federal Buildings program, Bhatt thought there was potential for an ongoing GE business to meet the expected surge in demand for energy management services. He began to think through the best way of proceeding.

The GE Canada Executive Meeting

Bhatt's first move was to meet with the GE Canada executive group and get their reaction to his idea for an Energy Management Business. Attending were Matthew Meyer, chairman & CEO, Mike Kozinsky, vice-president of finance; and Scott Larwood, vice-president of government relations. Larwood had already been heavily involved in the Federal Buildings program and was in favour of Bhatt's proposal.

Bhatt:	GE Canada is very well positioned to start an Energy Management business. We have a broader range of relevant products and services than any other ESCo, and the Ontario and Quebec Hydro programs are among the most advanced in the world.
Kozinsky (Finance)	But this is a systems business. We have never been very good at systems implementation.
Bhatt:	I realize that we may have to find partners. We are working with a small ESCo on the Federal Buildings project which will do all the installation work. We can identify suitable future partners as things progress.
Kozinsky:	But what is our experience in being a prime contractor? This seems to be very different from any business we have been involved with before.
Larwood: (Government Relations)	That's not quite true. The Apparatus Technical Service (ATS) business in Power Systems manages service contracts, and there is a lot of project experience in the States.
Meyer: (CEO)	But there seems to be a considerable risk here. What happens if we pull down a load of asbestos when we're changing a lighting system? GE is an obvious target for legal action.
Kozinsky:	And you stated earlier that there is some downside financial risk if the performance contract does not yield the expected savings.
Bhatt:	True, but the estimates are conservative. The overall financial projections are very promising, and involve very little upfront cost. Apart from the salaries of three or four employees, most costs are on a contract-by-contract basis.
Meyer:	Have you given any thought as to how this business would fit into the GE structure?
Bhatt:	One of the strengths of GE Canada is that it already taps into all the different businesses. I would like to see the Energy Management business based in Canada, and drawing from the other GE businesses as required.

Bhatt received a lot of questioning and cautioning on various aspects of the proposal, but there was consensus at the end that the project was worth pursuing. Meyer recommended that Bhatt investigate the level of interest in the U.S. businesses and at the corporate level before any formal proposal was put together.

The GE Supply Opportunity

In discussion with U.S. colleagues, Bhatt discovered that three U.S. divisions were attempting to establish their own ESCo-like initiatives. Two of them were at about the same stage of development as Bhatt. The third, GE Supply, which was a division of the GE Industrial and Power Systems Group, was more advanced. They had been working with an ESCo for a number of months, and had retained a well-connected consultant to advise them. Up to now, the ESCo had assumed all the risk, with GE providing their name, their products and some servicing expertise, but the division was planning to create a joint venture with the ESCo in the near future.

On hearing about the GE Supply initiative, Bhatt went to Connecticut to visit the GE Supply executives to discuss their respective plans. Present at the meeting were Bhatt, Doug Taylor, CEO of GE Supply, and Fred Allen, manager of the Energy Management business.

Taylor: (CEO)	Last week we signed a formal alliance agreement with Wetherwell Inc. to run for 18 months. We are now actively looking for contracts.
Allen:	But the U.S. market requires some education. How is the market in Canada?
Bhatt:	There is a very promising opportunity that we are working on right now. Basically, the Federal Government is looking for bidders on a $1 billion program, and we have already gained pre-qualification.
Allen:	That beats anything we've got down here. I think there could be some real opportunities for us to work together. We have gained quite a lot of experience over the past 12 months, and combined with your market, we could have a winning combination.
Bhatt:	I am certainly interested in exploring opportunities. How do you see a Canadian Energy Management business fitting with your business?
Taylor:	We could manage the Canadian business out of our office here.
Bhatt:	That causes me some concern. The business relies on close coordination with utilities and government bodies, and a strong local presence would definitely be necessary. I must admit, we considered that management of at least part of the business should be in Canada. The opportunities in Canada are unmatched.
Taylor:	Well, there is some strength to your argument, but I don't see why this business should not fit the normal model.

PROCTER & GAMBLE CANADA (A): THE FEBREZE DECISION

case 34

INTRODUCTION

"Should we agree to launch this product with the proposed U.S. funding? That would mean that we have to promise revenues above and beyond what our modelling analysis suggests." It was mid-March 1999 and Lynn Mepham, marketing director of new business development for Procter & Gamble (P&G) Canada, was pondering her situation in Toronto, Canada. She concluded: "If we are going to launch this year, have to make a decision before the end of this month."

IVEY

Ken Mark prepared this case under the supervision of Professor Rod White solely to provide material for class discussion. The author does not intend to illustrate either effective or ineffective handling of a managerial situation. The author may have disguised certain names and other identifying information to protect confidentiality.

THE HISTORY OF PROCTER & GAMBLE

William Procter & James Gamble created a family partnership in 1837 that would eventually lead to the development of a multinational corporation with US$38 billion in sales in 1999. With over 300 well-known brands such as Tide, Crest, Pringles, Pampers, Pantene and Always, and a presence in over 140 countries, P&G was considered one of the world's premier companies engaged in the development, manufacturing and marketing of consumer goods.

Organization 2005

During 1998, P&G's senior management in Cincinnati made the decision to implement Organization 2005, a comprehensive overhaul of the entire organization. On the top level, it meant that instead of being organized into four different groups based upon geographic location, P&G would now be organized along the lines of seven Global Business Units (GBUs), each representing a brand category, and eight Market Development Organizations (MDOs).

With the reorganization, the responsibility for all brand strategy, development of brand equities, innovation pipelines, package design and financial targets would be transferred to the GBUs (four of which were based in Cincinnati, one in Latin America, one in Belgium and one in Japan). To augment the brand strategy work performed by the GBUs, the local MDOs would build on that foundation by developing innovative marketing capabilities, and by tailoring P&G's global plans to fit local channels, retailers and consumers.

With overall brand strategy, equities and advertising coming from the GBU, the Canadian MDO organization would be freed up to focus resources on enhancing the marketing strategy through the use of customer-specific plans, and additional marketing tools such as public relations, professional marketing initiatives, endorsement projects, trial ideas, in-store promotions, sampling executions, etc. Profit responsibility would largely shift from the country unit to the GBUs, as MDOs became more focused on driving revenue and revenue growth.

Lynn Mepham

After completing her MBA in finance at York University, Lynn Mepham joined Procter & Gamble in 1988 and worked in several different product sectors such as paper, laundry and beauty care.

Mepham was the marketing director for new business development. She had been described as direct and fair, and she was a strong proponent of approaching business issues with discipline to incorporate both solid data analysis and intuition into plans. Mepham was known to be decisive and did not like prolonged discussions or long meetings.

Just as hard-driving outside of work, Mepham had finished the New York City Marathon in 1997 and was training for an Ironman-distance triathlon.

THE FEBREZE PROJECT

Febreze was an innovative new household product launched in the United States in late 1998. It used a unique cleaning formula to eliminate odors from fabrics (see Exhibit 1). This one-step odor cleaning system (contained in a spray-bottle) eliminated common odors such as pet, smoke, cooking and musty smells. This product provided a new set of benefits for the consumer. No comparable products were yet on the market. And, because the United States had just concluded retail trade presentations, it was too early to tell whether Febreze would be a success in the United States. Mepham, as marketing director of new business ventures, had to evaluate the situation and decide if and when this new product would be launched in Canada.

Mepham was still undecided about launching Febreze. In December 1998, she requested a market analysis, a move that was consistent with P&G's standard practices. P&G's Canadian market research department (MRD) had used its proprietary sales modelling analysis tool, the volume model, to evaluate this opportunity. The volume model had a good track record for predicting the success of product initiatives. It used internal and external inputs such as reach and frequency of each brand's television media plan, 'samples dropped' numbers, and predicted competitive reactions. It then compared the prediction against the record of previous initiatives at P&G.

With the U.S. data she had, Mepham knew that Febreze was basically a Cdn$5.5 million annual revenue idea with a predicted payout of 42 months on the investment (using a 20-year net present value in the volume model). These results would not warrant committing resources for a dedicated launch. To put things into perspective, most of P&G Canada's previously approved new brand launches involved projects that would generate more than Cdn$9 million in annual revenue.

Post-analysis management debate dismissed Febreze as a small idea; $7.5 million in annual revenue was the middle point of the volume model, meaning that there was a plus or minus 30 per cent volume swing (as low as $5 million or as high as $9 million). P&G Canada was not very excited about this new project; with fewer resources (marketing/sales personnel, investment) it had to focus on bigger initiatives. Febreze seemed small when contrasted with volumes of brands like Tide, which achieved over $400 million in revenue on an annual basis. So why would P&G Canada expend resources on Febreze versus investing efforts on Tide, Pampers, Crest or Dryel & Swiffer (two new high-volume potential new brands)? Mepham commented:

> It is not as if we cannot launch Febreze with current resources. We can. But we have tremendous pressure to avoid failure. To boot, our president, Yong Quek[1], has a reputation of doing well on new initiatives; going ahead would put the onus on us to deliver strong results on this project.

Uncertainties Surrounding Febreze

The volume model predicted that Febreze would be a relatively small business opportunity, but the model could not take into account the various new MDO marketing tools that might be deployed for the launch. Thus, the success of the Febreze project beyond the predicted volume would depend to some extent on how quickly the new MDO capabilities could be developed and used in the launch. Furthermore, Febreze was a brand with new benefits, and P&G would be creating a new product category for consumers. However, the once innovative P&G organization had not created a new product category in over a decade.

Last, there were career implications for Mepham if this project did not meet its goals. Historically, with respect to career progression at P&G, it was better to under-promise and over-deliver on a project's goals.

---

[1] Quek had announced that he would be stepping down as P&G Canada's president on July 31, 1999.

Because of these uncertainties, only two people had been assigned to this project: a marketing director (who also handled seven other brands) and an assistant brand manager in Canada. While the U.S. new business development organization encouraged more staffing in Canada, internal debate had resulted in a delay in any project staffing until February 1999.

The plan called for total spending of Cdn$7 million to launch Febreze, but this would make sense only if Canada delivered $10.1 million in revenue, over $2.5 million more than the volume model predicted as the middle point. To deliver this target, P&G Canada had to rely on GBU support, as well as new MDO tools (public relations, event marketing, endorsement, etc.) for which it had just started to develop capability.

Mepham commented:

> Do we go for it? Again I ask, who is going to sign up for this? Do we have the capability to deliver volume with these new 'communication tools' which we have not relied on in the past? And how would I gauge if $7 million is enough to fund the various projects and achieve the desired results? How would we value the effects of PR or grassroots promotions, neither of which we did in the past? Our volume model does not take that into account, so are we willing to bet our evaluations on this?

Mepham felt she had three options available to her:

1. Invest the full $7 million and promise results behind it.
2. Go small and exceed expectations by spending only a portion of the $7 million and delivering results against the amount spent.
3. Wait another four to six months for the U.S. launch, giving Canada the opportunity to assess U.S. results and better evaluate the opportunity for Febreze in Canada.

In order to have an early fall launch and avoid the Christmas season a decision was required within the next two weeks.

Mepham concluded:

> I guess it comes down to how much organizational effort we put behind Febreze. Remember that we sign up for our volume targets on our Work & Development Plan (W&DP), the same plan which ranks us against our peers in the organization, who are working on other projects. In the old organization, it was frowned upon when we took a risk and failed. We are being told that in the 'new' world, failure is acceptable if the risk taken was reasonable. Can we take that at face value? We have to decide upon this in the next two weeks.

Exhibit 1: **Febreze Product**

Source: Company files

NESTLÉ-ROWNTREE

case 35

James C. Ellert
J. Peter Killing and
Dana G. Hyde

Wednesday, April 13, 1988, 10.30 a.m.

"Our offer to help remains open, Mr. Dixon, and I urge you to reconsider our proposals. Please keep in touch." Mr. Helmut Maucher, Managing Director of Nestlé S.A., replaced the receiver and shook his head regretfully as he looked out from his office over Lake Geneva. On receiving the news of Jacobs Suchard's dawn raid on Rowntree plc, Mr. Maucher had called Mr. Kenneth Dixon, Rowntree's Chairman, to offer Nestlé's help and renew Nestlé's earlier proposal to purchase a stake in Rowntree.

Rowntree had been an attractive takeover target for some time, and Mr. Maucher and his colleagues had often discussed the possibility of making a bid. However, it was clear that Rowntree would aggressively contest any takeover attempt and, as Nestlé had never engaged in a hostile takeover, Mr. Maucher had done nothing more than initiate talks with the British-based confectioner. But as he prepared for the meeting with his Comité du Conseil that afternoon, Mr. Maucher worried about Rowntree falling into the hands of one of Nestlé's major competitors.

THE CHOCOLATE INDUSTRY

"Confectionery" was conventionally divided into "chocolate" confectionery and "sugar" confectionery. "Chocolate" confectionery included products made with chocolate; "sugar" confectionery included boiled sweets, toffees, chewing gum and other gums and jellies. Chocolate consumption represented a stable 54 per cent of the total volume of confectionery consumption in the major world markets between 1982 and 1987.

Markets

In value terms, more chocolate was consumed than any other manufactured food product in the world. In 1987 the population of the world's eight major markets consumed more than 2.7 million tonnes of chocolate (the equivalent of over 100 billion Kit Kats), with a retail value of over $19.5 billion (Exhibit 1). In volume terms, chocolate consumption in the eight major markets represented 61 per cent of total world chocolate consumption in 1987. Average per capita consumption in these markets was 4.3 kg per annum, with an annual per capita expenditure of $31. Between 1982 and 1987, volume growth averaged 2.8 per cent per annum in the eight major markets. Future growth was estimated at 2.2 per cent per annum for the next five years, with some variations across individual markets (Exhibit 2).

Product Types

Within chocolate confectionery there were three major product types[1]:

Blocks: generally molded blocks of chocolate, with or without additional ingredients (Hershey's Chocolate Bar, Nestlé Cailler, Suchard's Toblerone);

Countlines: generally chocolate-covered products, sold by count rather than weight (Mars' Mars Bar and Snickers, Rowntree's Kit Kat and Smarties);

Boxed chocolates: included assortments (Cadbury's Milk Tray, Rowntree's Black Magic) and also products such as Rowntree's After Eights.

A few manufacturers had succeeded in branding block chocolate, but in many markets block chocolate was considered a commodity product. Each manufacturer's range included a standard variety of block chocolate (milk, dark, white, etc.), and additional ingredients (nuts, fruit, etc.) sold in standard sizes (usually 100g and 200g). Block chocolate was sold mainly through grocery outlets, where it was displayed by manufacturer's range; all of the Nestlé block chocolate products would be grouped on one section of the store shelf, with the other manufacturers' ranges displayed in adjacent sections.

In constrast to block chocolate, countlines comprised a wide range of branded products, which were physically distinct from each other in size, shape, weight, and composition. Countlines had wider distribution than the other two product types, with a higher proportion sold through non-grocery outlets including confectioneries, news agents, and kiosks.

Boxed chocolates comprised a wide range of individually branded products, although in some markets boxed chocolates were marketed under the manufacturer's name, and displayed by manufacturer's range. Because boxed chocolates were regarded as a "gift/occasion" purchase, sales were very seasonal. Approximately 80 per cent of sales took place at Christmas and Easter, a high

---

[1] Product definitions varied widely by country. For the purposes of this case, British product definitions have been used.

proportion through grocery outlets; steady sales through the remainder of the year were made through non-grocery outlets.

The popularity of the three product types varied by market. In 1987, for example, Europe consumed approximately twice as much block chocolate and four times as many boxed chocolates as North America. The British and French together accounted for about 70 per cent of European boxed chocolate consumption; North Americans consumed 44 per cent of the world's countline consumption, followed by the British at 20 per cent.

At 7 per cent average annual growth between 1982 and 1987, countlines was the fastest-growing segment of the world chocolate market. Block chocolate sales showed an average annual volume increase of 1 per cent over the same period, while sales of boxed chocolates had declined by an average of 1 per cent per year. By 1987 countlines represented 46 per cent of the world chocolate market by volume, up from 38 per cent in 1982; block chocolate had declined to 30 per cent from 33 per cent, and boxed chocolates to 24 per cent from 29 per cent. In addition to growing demand for countline products, future growth was expected from "indulgence" products such as chocolate truffles, and from specialist branded chocolate retailing.

Industry Structure and Performance

In 1987, there were six major producers in the world chocolate industry: Mars, Hershey, Cadbury-Schweppes, Jacobs Suchard, Rowntree and Nestlé. With individual world market shares ranging from 18 per cent (Mars) to 4 per cent (Nestlé), these six companies accounted for 50 per cent of the total world volume of chocolate confectionery. With the exception of Jacobs Suchard and Nestlé, countline production represented the largest proportion of the chocolate confectionery portfolios of the major confectionery producers (Exhibit 3; additional detail on the product segment and geographic positioning of each company is outlined in Exhibits 4, 5 and 6).

The next tier of competitors included Ferrero, George Weston Ltd., Nabisco, and United Biscuits, each of which sold 2 per cent or less of the total world volume of chocolate confectionery. The remainder of the market was supplied by a large number of smaller (largely national) companies.

The major industry competitors had healthy rates of profitability. Because Mars was a privately held U.S. company, it did not publish sales and profit figures. For the other major competitors, trading profit on sales averaged 9.3 per cent over the five-year period ending in 1987; trading profit on assets averaged 16.1 per cent, and the rate of return on stockholders' equity averaged 16.1 per cent (Exhibit 7; Exhibits 8–12 provide additional financial information for these companies).

Over the past five years, several major producers had acquired a number of smaller, national chocolate companies. Between 1986 and 1988 Jacobs Suchard acquired six confectioners, including E.J. Brach (the third largest confectioner in the U.S., behind Mars and Hershey), Van Houten (Holland), and Cote d'Or (a famous Belgian chocolatier, which Nestlé had also considered acquiring). In 1987 Hersey purchased the Canadian confectionery assets of RJR Nabisco. In early 1988 Cadbury acquired Chocolats Poulain, a famous French chocolatier, and Nestlé was negotiating the purchase of Buitoni, an Italian food group which included the leading chocolatier Perugina.

Business System

Chocolate was made from kernels of fermented and roasted cocoa beans. The kernels were roasted and ground to form a paste, which was hardened in molds to make bitter (baking) chocolate, pressed to reduce the cocoa butter content, and then pulverized to make cocoa powder, or mixed with sugar and additional cocoa butter to make sweet (eating) chocolate. Sweet chocolate was the basic semi-finished product used in the manufacture of block, countline, and boxed chocolate products.

Average costs for a representative portfolio of all three product types of sweet chocolate could be broken down as follows:

Raw material	35%
Packaging	10
Production	20
Distribution	5
Marketing/sales	20
Trading profit	10
Total	100% (of manufacturer's selling price)

For countline products, raw material costs were proportionately lower because a smaller amount of cocoa was used. For boxed chocolates, packaging costs were proportionately higher.

RESEARCH AND DEVELOPMENT
Research and development (R&D) generally focused on making a better chocolate, and on developing new products, although one executive related, "there is never really anything brand new in the confectionery market, just different ways of presenting combinations of the same ingredients." There were minor differences in R&D across the product types, although R&D in the countline segment tended to emphasize applied technology.

RAW MATERIALS
The major ingredient in chocolate confectionery was cocoa, followed by sugar and milk. Although Jacobs Suchard claimed to benefit from large purchase hedging, some manufacturers purchased cocoa supplies as needed at the spot price quoted on the major cocoa exchanges, while others purchased cocoa a year or two in advance to obtain the "best price" and to ensure long-term supplies. Between 1977 and 1988, the international cartel of cocoa producers had fallen into disarray; the price of cocoa had fallen by 50 per cent ($US terms), and surplus cocoa stocks continued to accumulate.

Industry practice was for manufacturers to absorb raw material price changes internally to smooth extreme changes in consumer prices. However, Mars had made an unprecedented move in taking advantage of the falling cocoa price to stimulate volume demand. The company held the price of its Mars Bar and increased the product weight in the late 1970s by 10 per cent, and then by another 15 per cent in the early 1980s, enabling Mars to gain market share.

PRODUCTION
In general, it was difficult to sustain a competitive advantage based on manufacturing process, or on product features due to the lack of proprietary technology. However, some manufacturers had developed countline products which were difficult to duplicate (e.g., Rowntree's After Eights and Kit Kat). The major manufacturers tried to be low-cost producers through increased scale economies. Scale economies were more easily achieved in the production of block chocolate and countlines (both relatively capital intensive), and less easily in the production of boxed chocolates (which was more labour intensive). While minimum efficient scale varied by product, most major producers were moving toward fewer and more concentrated production plants, some dedicated to one or two products.

DISTRIBUTION Confectionery had the widest distribution of any consumer product. In the U.K., for example, wholesalers serving thousands of small "Confectionery-Tobacco-Newsagent" (CTN) outlets accounted for 50 per cent of total confectionery sales, with multiple grocery stores accounting for 30 per cent, and department stores and multiple confectionery stores the remainder. While distribution patterns and the balance of power between manufacturers and distributors varied across markets, retail concentration was on the increase. Canada and Western Europe (in particular the U.K., France and West Germany) were noted for high levels of retail concentration. Manufacturers' trading margins in these countries averaged 8–12 per cent, compared to U.S. averages of 14–16 per cent.

In general, European multiple retailers tended to stock narrower ranges of competing products than their U.S. counterparts. As one industry executive commented, "In Europe you pay more of a premium to get shelf space in a store. In addition, many of the (multiple) retailers stock only the leading brand and the Number Two. If you are third, you lose visibility, and this damages brand reputation."

MARKETING Consumers displayed considerable brand loyalty. As one industry executive explained, "Most people have a 'menu' of products they like and know. They will buy a new product perhaps once or twice, but the tendency is to go back to the 'old familiars,' the popular established brands." The most popular brands of chocolate were over 50 years old; Mars Bar, for example, was introduced in 1932, and Kit Kat in 1935.

In 1987 the six largest producers spent over $750 million per year on chocolate advertising. In recent years, manufacturers had dramatically increased their overall level of marketing spending, particularly with respect to launching new products. By 1988 one manufacturer estimated that new products, which generally had a much shorter life span than established brands, would have to generate at least $25 million in sales over the first two years to cover product development and marketing costs. Manufacturers therefore tended to focus on brand extensions into new product segments and particularly into new geographic markets.

MAJOR COMPETITORS

Mars

With the world's best selling chocolate bar, and other famous global brands such as Snickers, M&Ms, Twix and Milky Way, Mars was the world leader in chocolate confectionery. In 1987 confectionery was estimated to account for $4 billion of Mars' $7 billion total turnover of confectionery, pet food and electronics products.

With 38 per cent market share, Mars dominated the world countline sector, with particular strength in North America and Europe (Exhibit 4). In 1987, Mars held the largest share of the European chocolate market, and was a close third to Cadbury Rowntree in the U.K. (Exhibit 5). Like Rowntree and Cadbury, Mars spent approximately £25 million annually on advertising in the U.K. In 1987 Mars was one of the top 30 U.S. advertisers ($300 million), and had five of the top ten best-selling chocolate bars in the U.S.

The 1986 introduction of Kudos, a chocolate-covered granola bar, was Mars' first new product in over ten years. Since 1986, however, Mars had mounted a major effort to acquire and develop new products, particularly those which would capitalize on the Mars brand name. Recent product launches included a Mars milk drink and Mars ice cream.

Mars' strategy was consistent across all brands: produce high quality, technologically simple products at very high volumes on automated equipment dedicated to the production of either "layered" (Mars, Snickers) or "planned" (M&Ms, Maltesers) products; and support the brands with heavy marketing spending and aggressive sales organizations and retailing policies. The company's future strategy focused on building and strengthening Mars' global brands. In 1987, for example, Mars had dropped Treets, a £15 million U.K. brand, and repositioned Minstrels under the Galaxy label, both in order to strengthen the 1988 launch of M&Ms into the U.K. market.

Hershey Foods

Founded as chocolate company in 1893, by 1987 Hershey was a diversified food group with total turnover of $2.4 billion. More than 90 per cent of that turnover was in the U.S. (Exhibit 6); confectionery accounted for 66 per cent of total turnover and 80 per cent of trading profit. Although Hershey was a quoted company, it could not be taken over easily because 77 per cent of the company's voting stock was owned by a charitable trust.

Hershey's strength was in block chocolate in North America, where it held a 62 per cent market share. With Hershey's Chocolate Bar, Reese's Peanut Butter Cup and Hershey's Kisses all in the 1987 U.S. "top ten," Hershey was second only to Mars in the U.S. chocolate market. Hershey also produced major Rowntree brands under licence in the U.S.

Between 1981 and 1987, Hershey had increased its advertising and promotion spending from 8.5 per cent to 11.5 per cent of total turnover to "consolidate market share." Hershey's chocolate production was concentrated in Hershey, Pennsylvania, which supplied export markets in Japan, South Korea and Australia. The company also licensed some production in the Far East, Sweden and Mexico, normally under joint venture agreements.

Hershey's corporate strategy was to reduce exposure to cocoa price volatility by diversifying within the confectionery and snack businesses. The company had expanded into branded sugar confectionery, pasta products and ice cream restaurants, largely through acquisitions. By 1987, only 45 per cent of Hershey's sales came from products composed of at least 70 per cent chocolate, down from 80 per cent in 1963.

Cadbury Schweppes

Cadbury Schweppes plc was founded in 1969 with the merger of the Cadbury Group plc and Schweppes Ltd. In 1987, confectionery represented 43 per cent of Cadbury's total turnover of £2,031 million.

With 7 per cent of the world chocolate market and brands such as Dairy Milk, Creme Eggs, Crunchie, Flake and Milk Tray, Cadbury was a major world name in chocolate. Cadbury was the market leader in Australia, and three Cadbury brands (Mounds, Almond Joy and Peppermint Patties) were in the U.S. "Top 20." However, Cadbury's main business was in the U.K., where it held 30 per cent of the market, and had five of the top ten best-selling chocolate products. In 1986 and 1987, Cadbury had launched nine new U.K. brands.

During the late 1970s, Cadbury expanded overseas, and diversified within and beyond the food sector. However, with the appointment of Mr. Dominic Cadbury as Chief Executive in 1983, Cadbury Schweppes embarked on a more focused product and market strategy. Mr. Cadbury announced a restructuring of the Group "to concentrate resources behind (our) leading beverage and confectionery brands in those markets which offer the best opportunities for their development."

Major divestments were made, involving secondary activities in the food and nonfood sectors, and the assets of some under-performing core businesses. Acquisitions were made to strengthen the mainstream branded product lines, and to gain access to new geographic markets. The acquisition of Chocolats Poulain, for example, provided Cadbury's first manufacturing facility in Europe. In January 1987, General Cinema Corporation (which controlled the largest U.S. Pepsi bottling operation) announced the acquisition of an 8.5 per cent shareholding in Cadbury Schweppes and, in November 1987, increased that holding to 18.2 per cent. While General Cinema was less than half the size of Cadbury in market capitalization, industry observers speculated that the company was planning a leveraged buyout of Cadbury Schweppes.

Jacobs Suchard

Controlled by the Jacobs family and based in Zurich, the Jacobs Suchard Group was formed in 1982 in a reverse takeover by Jacobs (a West German coffee company) of Interfood, the parent company of the Suchard and Tobler chocolate firms. In 1987, Suchard's principal businesses were still coffee and confectionery, which accounted for 57 per cent and 43 per cent respectively of Suchard's 1987 turnover of SF6.1 billion.

Europe was Suchard's largest market, accounting for 83 per cent of 1987 turnover. However, Jacobs Suchard operated in more than 20 countries, represented by subsidiaries and licensees, and exported its products to over 100 countries. The Group also had substantial operations in the trading of raw materials for coffee and chocolate production.

Jacobs Suchard held 23 per cent of the European block chocolate market. Leading brands included Toblerone, Suchard, Milka and Cote d'Or. Developing and expanding its portfolio of global brands was of primary importance to the Group; as Mr. Klaus Jacobs, the entrepreneurial Chairman of the Board, stated, "We firmly believe that global brands are the wave of the future." An increasing number of Jacobs Suchard's brands were marketed globally, under the sponsorship of global brand managers.

Since 1984 Suchard had been concentrating production of individual brands in fewer and larger plants in an effort to gain absolute cost leadership. In 1987, European production of chocolate and confectionery took place in 17 plants; Suchard planned to reduce this number to 7 by 1991, as improvements were made in its cross-border distribution system.

Rowntree

Rowntree was founded in York in 1725 by a cocoa and chocolate vendor who sold the business to the Rowntree family in 1862. In 1970, Rowntree merged with John Mackintosh & Sons, Ltd., a British confectioner nearly half the size of Rowntree. In 1988, Rowntree's headquarters were still in York and, with 5,500 workers, the company was by far York's largest employer. Many of the traditions of the Rowntree family, including a strong concern for employee and community welfare, had been preserved; many of the current employees' parents and grandparents had also worked for Rowntree.

In 1987, Rowntree was primarily a confectionery company (Exhibit 13), with major strengths in the countline and boxed chocolate segments. Rowntree's major market was the U.K. where, with a 26 per cent market share, it was second only to Cadbury. Rowntree's Kit Kat was the best-selling confectionery brand in the U.K. (where 40 Kit Kats were consumed per second), and number five in both the U.S. and Japan. Kit Kat was part of a portfolio of leading global brands; many of these brands—Kit Kat, Quality Street, Smarties, Rolo, Aero, Black Magic—were launched in the 1930s; After Eights in 1962; and Yorkie and Lion in 1976. Since 1981 Rowntree had launched seven new brands in the U.K., including Novo, a chocolate cereal bar.

In 1987 Rowntree operated 25 factories in nine countries and employed 33,000 people around the world, including close to 16,000 in its eight U.K. operations. Group turnover was £1.4 billion, with the U.K. and Ireland accounting for 40 per cent of total turnover (Exhibit 14).

Rowntree was headed by Mr. Kenneth Dixon, age 58, who had been with Rowntree for 32 years, and was appointed as Chairman and Chief Executive in 1981. In the words of a long-time senior Rowntree executive, "Mr. Dixon fostered a real sense of positive change in the company."

During the late 1970s, Rowntree's operating performance had shown significant deterioration (Exhibit 15). To reverse this trend, Mr. Dixon initiated a long-term program to improve the efficiency of the U.K. core business, and led diversifications into related businesses, principally through the acquisition and development of brand names. Mr. Dixon also delegated more responsibility to the operating levels of the company, while maintaining a central brand and product strategy.

Branding was the essence of Rowntree's strategy. According to Mr. Dixon, "The fundamental idea which drives Rowntree is branding, the creation of distinct, differentiated, positively identifiable and market-positioned goods. Rowntree seeks to build brands by marketing products and services at competitive prices, positioning them accurately in the markets they serve, and giving them clear identity and character."

In the 1960s, Rowntree granted Hershey a long-term license to manufacture and sell Rowntree products in the U.S. With its expansion into continental Europe underway at the time, Rowntree believed that it lacked the resources to develop an effective marketing presence in both continental Europe and the U.S. In 1978 the agreement with Hershey was renegotiated, giving Hershey rights in perpetuity to the Kit Kat and Rolo brand names in the U.S., which would be retained by Hershey in the event of a change in Rowntree ownership. Rowntree was still free to enter the U.S. market with its other brand names. In 1987 royalties from this agreement contributed about £2 million toward Rowntree Group profits.

Between 1982 and 1987, Rowntree invested nearly £400 million to upgrade manufacturing facilities, and develop high-volume, product-dedicated equipment for several of the company's leading global brands, including Kit Kat, After Eights and Smarties. Products produced on this equipment had a consistent formulation, and were sold all over the world; the Hamburg After Eights plant, for example, shipped to 16 countries. By 1987 Rowntree's investment program for rationalizing capacity was well underway. The associated productivity gains were expected to continue to accumulate over the next few years.

In 1987 Rowntree's £100 million investment in continental Europe was still showing modest financial returns. Rowntree had entered the continental European market in the 1960s, establishing production facilities at Hamburg, Dijon, Elst (Holland) and Noisiel (France). Although advertising and promotion spending (as a percentage of sales) was double that of the U.K., volume growth had not met Rowntree's expectations; as one manager explained, "Kit Kats go well with a cup of tea, but not with wine and beer!"

The trading margin on the Continental European business had inched up very slowly, from 1.0 per cent in 1985 to 3.7 per cent in 1987. However, in early 1988 Rowntree believed that the long-term brand building strategy was finally beginning to pay off, with Lion Bar the second-best selling chocolate bar in France and with more After Eights sold in West Germany than in the U.K. Between 1983 and 1987, Rowntree spent nearly £400 million on acquisitions (Exhibit 16). The acquired companies expanded the company's presence in some traditional businesses, and also provided new activities, particularly in the area of branded retailing of specialist confectionery products. The retail shops acquired by Rowntree were viewed not as outlets for Rowntree brands, but rather as acquisitions of brands in their own right. Because of these acquisitions, a significant stream of Rowntree's profits were being earned in North America. While Rowntree had hedged its foreign exchange risk exposure on the balance sheet, it took a long-term view with respect to foreign exchange risk exposure on the income statement. The resulting transactions exposure concerned some financial analysts.

By 1987 Rowntree's capital investments were beginning to pay off. Over the past five years, the number of U.K. personnel had been reduced from 19,700 to 15,600, and productivity improvements were running at 9 per cent per annum. Trading margins had nearly recovered to the high level previously achieved in 1977, and Rowntree executives were confident that 1988 trading margins would continue to show improvement.

In a highly competitive U.S. market, Rowntree's snack food acquisitions were not generating trading margins consistent with other company activities (Exhibit 13). In January of 1988, Rowntree announced its intention to divest its major snack food businesses to concentrate on confectionery, retailing, and U.K. grocery activities where the potential to develop distinct consumer brands was considered more promising.

Although Rowntree's overall operating performance continued to improve, the company's common share price performance between 1986 and early 1988 was weaker than that achieved by the Financial Times "All Share" and Food Manufacturing Indexes on the London Stock Exchange (Exhibit 17). In early 1988, London's financial analysts published mixed opinions regarding Rowntree's immediate prospects (Exhibit 18). Mr. Nightingale, Rowntree's Company Secretary, recalled, "For years we have been trying to get the value of our brands reflected in our share price, but without much success. As a consequence, there have always been takeover rumours."

Nestlé

The Nestlé Group grew from the 1905 merger of the Anglo-Swiss condensed Milk Co., a milk processing firm founded in 1866, and Henri Nestlé, a Swiss infant food company founded in 1867 in Vevey. In 1988 the Nestlé headquarters were still in Vevey, and the Group operated 383 factories in 59 countries. In 1988 Nestlé employed 163,000 people, 10,000 in the U.K.

Nestlé was the world's largest food company, and the world's largest producer of coffee, powdered milk, and frozen dinners. In 1987, drinks, dairy products, culinary products, frozen foods, and confectionery products accounted for 79 per cent of Nestlé turnover of SF35.2 billion; other food products accounted for 18 per cent, and non-food products 3 per cent. Only 2 per cent of the Group's turnover came from sales within Switzerland. The 20 companies acquired between 1983 and 1985 (at a total purchase price of $5 billion) added new brands of coffee, chocolates and fruit juice to Nestlé's lineup of strong world brands such as Nescafé, Stouffer's, Maggi and Findus. In

1985 Nestlé increased its U.S. presence through the $2.9 billion purchase of Carnation and, in early April 1988, was finalizing the $1.3 billion purchase of Buitoni-Perugina.

This series of acquisitions had been spurred by Mr. Helmut Maucher, age 60, who joined Nestlé as an apprentice in 1948, and who was appointed Managing Director of Nestlé S.A. in 1981. Under Mr. Maucher's direction, Nestlé had cut costs and divested less profitable operations, including the $180 million Libby's U.S. canned food business.

Mr. Maucher explained Nestlé's approach to acquisitions. "At Nestlé we are not portfolio managers. Acquisitions must fit into our corporate and marketing policy. In other words, they must strengthen our position in individual countries or product groups, or enable us to enter new fields where we have not so far been represented. Acquisitions are part of an overall development strategy. That's why we cannot leave acquisition decisions purely to financial considerations. Of course, you must have some figures to evaluate an acquisition, but more important is the feel you have about why you can do with the brands."

Mr. Maucher was a strong believer in the importance of a long-term outlook. On his appointment as Managing Director, he had banned monthly 25-page reports and quarterly profit and loss statements in favour of a monthly one-page report, which highlighted key numbers such as turnover, working capital and inventories. As Mr. Maucher explained, "With quarterly reports all managers care about is the next three months, and they manage for the next quarter instead of for the next five years." For this reason, Mr. Maucher was reluctant to list Nestlé's shares on any stock exchange which required the disclosure of quarterly reports.

Nestlé entered the chocolate market in 1929 with the purchase of Peter-Cailler-Kohler, a Swiss chocolate group originally founded in 1819. Since 1981, confectionery sales had represented approximately 8 per cent of annual turnover, and in 1987 confectionery was Nestlé's fifth largest business. Nestlé's main product strength was in block chocolate, where it held 15 per cent and 14 per cent respectively of the European and American markets (Exhibit 4). Nestlé's leading brands included Milkybar in the U.S. and Crunch in the U.K. Recent research into the new generation of chocolate and confectionery products had produced "Yes," a pastry snack product, and "Sundy," a cereal bar.

As a result of Nestlé's market-oriented organization structure, Nestlé's block chocolate products were generally produced and positioned according to the tastes of local markets. For example, Nestlé's white block chocolate products, often produced in the same plants as coffee and other food products, were made from several recipes and marketed under several brand names. In the U.K., Nestlé's white chocolate brand, "Milkybar," was positioned as a children's chocolate, whereas in the U.S., it was called "Alpine White" and was oriented toward the "female indulgence" market. "Block chocolate is a traditional product with traditional tastes," Mr. Maucher explained. "A local market orientation is particularly important, because this kind of chocolate must taste the way you got it as a child from your grandmother, whether you are French or Italian or German, and so on. This is true for the traditional chocolate products, not so much for the new generation of products such as countlines."

During the 1970s, Nestlé's confectionery operations had been among the smaller and often relatively less profitable businesses in the company. However, Mr. Maucher saw opportunities in the confectionery business: "The key success factors in confectionery are technology, quality, creativity, and marketing skills, and Nestlé has all of those. If Nestlé cannot be successful at this business, then there is something wrong with Nestlé!"

NESTLÉ–ROWNTREE

In the early 1980s, Mr. Maucher made confectionery a strategic priority. Nestlé increased investment in research and development, and acquired two small U.S. confectionery companies. Nestlé then began to analyze the possibilities for significant expansion in the world confectionery market. "It will take 25 years to develop a major stake in this industry," Mr. Maucher said, "so we are looking at acquisitions to accelerate that development." According to Mr. Ramon Masip, Executive Vice-President in charge of the European market, "For some time we have discussed making a 'big move' into the confectionery business, and Rowntree has always been the number one choice."

"We have always seen Rowntree as a 'perfect fit,'" Mr. Masip continued, "because its strengths would complement Nestlé's." Rowntree's strong position in the growing countlines segment would complement Nestlé's strength in block chocolate. In addition, Rowntree's strong position in the non-grocery outlets such as CTNs would complement Nestlé's strong contacts with the multiple grocery retailers. Rowntree also held a stronger position in the U.K. and in some markets in continental Europe.

Although Nestlé was interested in Rowntree's recent success in launching new products such as the Lion bar, "We are much more concerned with the brands that Rowntree already has in the market!" Mr. Masip exclaimed. Rowntree's strong, well-established world brands were the key reason for Nestlé's interest. "There are very, very few companies in the world with their brands and with their skills in this particular business," Mr. Masip concluded.

Nestlé believed that, should the opportunity to acquire Rowntree arise, additional operating synergies could be achieved in research and development, administration and the sales force. With the potential acquisition, it was estimated that substantial savings—perhaps 5–15 per cent of Rowntree's fixed overhead expenses—could be realized from combining the two companies' operations.

November 1987

In November of 1987, Mr. Maucher and Mr. Masip met in Paris with Mr. Dixon and Mr. Masip's counterpart in Rowntree, Mr. Guerin. The proposal for this meeting had stemmed from quiet discussions between Messrs. Masip and Guerin regarding possible Nestlé-Rowntree cooperation in continental Europe. For over a year, Mr. Maucher had wanted to arrange a meeting with Mr. Dixon to discuss possible forms of cooperation between Nestlé and Rowntree. In fact, some of Mr. Maucher's external financial advisors had advised him to take a position in Rowntree stock, but Mr. Maucher had always replied, "That is not our policy. We do not do anything behind any company's back and, as I have told Mr. Dixon, we will not do anything that would be perceived as unfriendly to Rowntree."

The Paris meeting in November 1987 began with Mr. Dixon advising Mr. Maucher, "Nestlé does not appear to be interested in confectionery, and Rowntree is prepared to buy Nestlé's confectionery business on a worldwide basis." Mr. Maucher exclaimed, "We propose just the opposite!" The ensuing discussion explored possibilities for cooperation in production, marketing, distribution, or in various geographic markets, in order to optimize the situation for both companies. To facilitate development of long-term commitment and cooperation, Mr. Maucher suggested purchasing a 10–25 per cent stake in Rowntree.

After a lengthy and amicable discussion, Mr. Dixon promised to examine Nestlé's suggestions and take them to the Rowntree Board for consideration. According to Mr. Dixon, Rowntree had already considered cooperation with several parties as a basis for market development, particularly in Europe, but "we felt at Rowntree that we could proceed on our own and would prefer to do so." After making this reply to Mr. Maucher in February 1988, he added, "Unfortunately, any sort of association with a company of your size can only have one ending, and at this time we don't feel we need to make that kind of commitment to anyone." Mr. Dixon, responding to Mr. Maucher's grave concerns regarding the persistent takeover rumours, admitted, "This does not mean that we do not recognize there is a risk."

April 13, 1988

At 8:30 on the morning of Wednesday, April 13, 1988, Rowntree was advised that there was significant activity in the trading of Rowntree shares. By 9:15 a.m., Jacobs Suchard held 14.9 per cent of Rowntree plc. While the firm had made no contact with Rowntree, Suchard had begun acquiring Rowntree stock in mid-March, and by April 12th held just under 5 per cent of Rowntree shares. At the start of trading on the London Stock Exchange on April 13th, Suchard's intermediary telephoned major institutional holders of Rowntree shares, offering a 30 per cent premium on the opening share price of 477p[2] if they sold immediately. The shareholders did not know to whom they were selling their shares, but in less than 45 minutes Suchard increased its holding to 14.9 per cent, the maximum allowable under the City Code[3] for such a transaction. When the news of Suchard's raid reached the markets, Rowntree's share price jumped to over 700p.

In what was later described as a "tactical error" by some City observers, on the morning of April 13th, S.G. Warburg issued the following press release on behalf of its client, Jacob Suchard:

> We have acquired a 14.9% investment stake in Rowntree. The stake is a strategic investment in that Rowntree is a company with a great potential based on its excellent global brands. We intend to acquire not more than 25%, at a maximum price of 630p. As you know, we are only permitted to take our holding to 15% today. We hope to buy the remaining 10%, but at no more than the price we are currently offering. This is not a prelude to a full bid and there is no intention of increasing the holding beyond this 25% figure for at least a year although we reserve the right to do so if there is a full bid from a third party in the meantime.

Exercising its interpretive responsibility, the City Takeover Panel swiftly ruled that Warburg's statement prevented Suchard from purchasing any further Rowntree shares for the next 12 months, provided that the Rowntree share price stayed above 630p, unless a full bid for control came in from another party during that time period.

Reaction from the City of London Financial Community

After years of persistent rumours of a Rowntree takeover, Suchard's move ignited speculation on potential counter-bidders. Hershey was identified by City analysts as a leading candidate; purchasing Rowntree would make it second only to Mars in world confectionery. Other rumoured candidates included RJR Nabisco, Philip Morris, Unilever and United Biscuits.

As external financial advisor to Rowntree, Mr. David Challen, a Director of J. Henry Schroder Wagg, was encouraged by the Takeover Panel's ruling. As he explained, "The ruling puts Jacobs in a box. Provided that Rowntree's share price stays above 630p, he cannot purchase additional shares

---

[2] 2 1£ = 100 pence (p).
[3] Refer to Exhibit 19 for a description of the City Code rules which regulated takeover activity in the U.K.

for at least a year. This gives Rowntree the necessary time to prepare an effective takeover defence." Mr. Challen argued that it would be "madness" for another bidder to enter the battle now, as the new bidder would be restricted to accumulating shares (beyond 15 per cent) at the price of its initial offer. However, the entry of another bidder would free Suchard to bid above this price to accumulate more shares. In the scenario predicted by Mr. Challen, Suchard would ultimately emerge with 30 per cent of the shares and be poised to make an offer for the remaining shares. The second bidder would be restricted by the City Code to accumulating 15 per cent of the shares and would always be behind Suchard in share accumulation terms. Thus the second bidder would face a "mega disadvantage" in gaining effective control. Mr. Challen concluded that the situation facing Rowntree was not urgent: "The real challenge for Rowntree is to keep the stock price above 630p so that Suchard cannot accumulate more shares."

Mr. Peter St. George, a Director of County Natwest (Nestlé's financial advisor), recalled discussions with Nestlé in the summer of 1987 regarding a possible takeover bid for Rowntree: "We were in a raging bull market then; paper, not cash, was king; and the takeover bid premium required to purchase Rowntree could not be justified on the fundamentals. Besides, any takeover attempt would have been viewed as hostile by Rowntree."

County NatWest had approached Nestlé in early 1988, advising a raid on Rowntree. "Since the October 1987 crash, the world had changed," Mr. St. George explained. "Share prices had fallen to reasonable levels where one could justify paying takeover premiums. The market no longer wanted paper; cash was king now, and Nestlé had cash. However, Mr. Maucher demurred, stating that hostile raids were not in Nestlé's style."

"Suchard's raid put Rowntree 'in play,'" Mr. St. George concluded. "We contacted Nestlé as soon as we heard the news and encouraged them to make a counter bid for Rowntree. We advised them to act quickly and go into the market with a credible price to test (the fundraising capability of) Jacobs Suchard. We cautioned Nestlé, however, that a successful bid would require a substantial premium on the current Rowntree share price." (See Exhibit 19 for a description of the size of recent takeover bid premiums; Exhibit 20 contains financial market reference data.)

Rowntree's Reaction

The dawn raid came as a complete surprise to Rowntree, and reaction was swift. Mr. Dixon stated in a press release that morning:

> Rowntree does not need Jacobs. We regard the acquisition of a stake by Jacobs as wholly unwelcome and believe that the price at which Jacobs acquired its shares is wholly inadequate for obtaining a major stake in the Group. Rowntree has one of the best portfolios of brand names of any confectionery company in the world, far better known than Jacobs' own. We do not believe that it is in the interests of Rowntree, its shareholders, or its employees that a Swiss company with nothing like the breadth of Rowntree's brands should have a shareholding in the Group. Jacobs may need Rowntree, but Rowntree does not need Jacobs.

Nestlé's Reaction

Suchard's dawn raid also came as a surprise to Nestlé. Mr. Maucher's first reaction was to contact Mr. Dixon; in his telephone phone call that morning Mr. Maucher said, "I am sorry that what I warned you about has happened. I repeat our offer to help." He urged Mr. Dixon to reconsider Nestlé's earlier proposal to acquire a stake in Rowntree.

Mr. Dixon thanked Mr. Maucher for his offer of help, but replied that he did not expect Suchard to make any further moves in the short term. "According to the Takeover Panel, Jacobs cannot move for 12 months," he told Mr. Maucher, "and while I know that Suchard will try to become more involved with Rowntree, we have no intention of having any form of cooperation with Suchard. We fully intend to remain independent. It is our hope and belief that the situation will calm down and that nothing more will come of it." However, Mr. Dixon promised that he and his Board would nonetheless consider Mr. Maucher's proposal.

Mr. Maucher concluded the discussion by saying, "Our offer stands, and I hope you will reconsider and keep in touch. However, I fear that because of Suchard's move your independence is now an illusion. I must now feel free to act in Nestlé's best interests."

Average Currency Equivalents, 1983–88

	1 Swiss Franc equals		*1 British Pound equals*		*US$1 equals*	
1983	$0.48	£0.31	SF 3.23	$1.55	SF2.08	£0.65
1984	0.43	0.32	3.13	1.34	2.33	0.75
1985	0.41	0.32	3.13	1.28	2.44	0.78
1986	0.56	0.38	2.63	1.47	1.79	0.68
1987	0.67	0.41	2.44	1.63	1.49	0.61
1988*	0.71	0.39	2.57	1.83	1.41	0.55

(SF = Swiss Franc; $ = U.S. Dollar; £ = British Pound)
* As of April 1, 1988.

Source: Schweizerische Nationalbank.

Exhibit 1: **Major Chocolate Confectionery Markets Consumption and Expenditure Per Capita, 1987**

	*Chocolate Consumption (000 tonnes)**	*Chocolate Expenditure (US$ millions)*	*Population Mid-1987 (millions)*	*Per Capita (kg/annum)*	*Expenditure Consumption per Capita ($/annum)*
U.S.	1,189	5,202	243.8	4.9	21
U.K.	455	3,480	56.9	8.0	61
W.Germany	409	3,387	61.2	6.7	55
France	233	2,750	55.6	4.2	49
Japan	157	1,867	122.1	1.3	15
Canada	101	464	25.9	3.9	18
Italy	106	1,813	57.4	1.8	32
Australia	80	576	16.2	4.9	36
Total	2,730	19,539	639.1	4.3	31

* One metric tonne = 1000 kilograms.

Sources: UNIDO Handbook of Industrial Statistics, Vienna, 1988; World Bank; National Trade Associations; Trade Estimates.

Exhibit 2: Actual and Forecasted Chocolate Consumption in Major Markets

	Consumption (000 tonnes)			Compound Average Annual Growth Rate (per cent)	
	1982 Actual	1987 Actual	1992 Forecast	1982–87	1987–92
U.S.	1,003	1,189	1,364	3.5%	2.8%
U.K.	411	455	469	2.0	0.6
W. Germany	401	409	412	0.4	0.1
France	192	233	251	3.9	1.5
Japan	148	157	166	1.2	1.1
Italy	83	106	127	5.0	3.7
Canada	99	101	106	0.4	1.0
Australia	63	80	95	4.9	3.5
Above 8 Markets	2,400	2,730	2,990	2.6	1.8
Rest of World	1,495	1,740	1,990	3.1	2.7
Total	**3,895**	**4,470**	**4,980**	**2.8%**	**2.2%**

Sources: Joint International Statistics Committee of IOCCC; Euromonitor; United Nations Industrial Statistics Yearbook; IMEDE.

Exhibit 3: Chocolate Product Portfolios of Major Confectionery Companies, 1987

	Mars	Hershey	Cadbury	Rowntree	Suchard	Nestlé	Others
Tonnes (000s)	800	400	320	300	220	190	20240
World Market Share	18%	9%	7%	7%	5%	4%	50%
Companies' Turnover by Product Type:*							
Block	1%	46%	46%	11%	81%	73%	29%
Countline	99	54	36	55	8	17	32
Boxed	—	—	18	34	11	10	39
Total	100%	100%	100%	100%	100%	100%	100%

* For example, countline sales represented 99% of Mars' total chocolate confectionery turnover in 1987; block chocolate sales represented 1 per cent of Mars' total chocolate turnover.

Sources: International Chocolate Workshop, Vevey, 1988; Trade Estimates; IMEDE.

Exhibit 4: **Market Shares of Major Competitors by Product Type and Region, 1987**

	Total Market	Percentage Market Shares						
		Mars	Hershey	Cadbury	Rowntree	Suchard	Nestlé	Others
North America:								
Block	280	—	62%	16%	2%	3%	14%	3%
Countline	898	53%	23	5	2	—	1	16
Boxed	112	—	—	11	17	1	5	66
Total	1,290	53%	29%	8%	2%	—	4%	18%
EEC:								
Block	541	1%	—	9%	4%	23%	14%	49%
Countline	611	49	—	8	19	2	1	21
Boxed	437	—	—	7	14	4	2	73
Total	1,589	19%	—	8%	12%	10%	6%	45%
Rest of World:								
Block	521	—	2%	10%	1%	9%	4%	74%
Countline	544	4%	1	4	6	1	3	80
Boxed	526	—	—	3	4	1	1	91
Total	1,591	1%	1%	6%	4%	4%	3%	81%
World:								
Block	1,342	1%	14%	11%	2%	13%	10%	49%
Countline	2,053	39	10	6	8	1	2	34
Boxed	1,075	—	—	6	9	2	2	81
Total	4,470	18%	9%	7%	7%	5%	4%	50%

* In tonnes (000s).

Sources: International Chocolate Workshop, Vevey, 1988; Trade Estimates; IMEDE.

Exhibit 5: **European Chocolate Market Shares by Major Competitor, 1988**

	Mars	Suchard	Rowntree	Ferrero	Cadbury	Nestlé	Others
U.K.	24%	2%	26%	2%	30%	3%	13%
Austria	4	73	—	—	—	5	18
Belgium	6	82	2	5	—	3	2
France	11	13	17	6	8	10	35
Italy	1	—	—	4	—	5	60
Netherlands	23	—	13	—	—	—	64
Switzerland	9	17	—	—	—	17	57
W. Germany	22	15	3	6	—	8	36
Total	17%	13%	11%	10%	8%	9%	32%

Source: Henderson Crossthwaite.

Exhibit 6: **Percentage Breakdown of Total Turnover by Region for Major Confectionery Competitors, 1987**

	Nestlé	*Rowntree*	*Jacobs Suchard*	*Cadbury Schweppes*	*Hershey*
Europe	43%	61%[1]	83%[2]	63%[3]	—
N. America	29	29	17	18	> 90%
Asia	13				
Oceana	2	4		19	< 10%
Others	3	6	1		
Total	100%	100%	101%[4]	100%	100%

[1]U.K. and Ireland = 40% of total turnover.
[2]West Germany and France = 58% of total turnover.
[3]U.K. = 47% of total turnover.
[4]Does not add up to 100% due to rounding errors.

Source: Company accounts.

Exhibit 7: **Operating Financial Performance of Major Competitors, 1983–87**

	1987	*Average 1982–1987*		
	Confectionery Turnover as % of Total Turnover[1]	*Total Trading Profit[2] as % of Total Turnover*	*Total Trading Profit[2] as % of Average[3] Assets*	*Net Income[4] as % of Average[3] Shareholders' Equity*
Hershey Foods	76	14.7	15.8	17.2
Cadbury Schweppes	43	7.5	20.5	17.1
Rowntree	76	8.3	25.5	16.8
Jacobs Suchard	57	5.9	12.3	16.3
Nestlé	8	10.2	14.3	13.1

Note: As a measure of relative risk, the "beta" values for the common stocks of publicly traded confectionery companies generally clustered around a value of 1.0.
[1]Turnover = Net sales.
[2]Trading profit = Operating profit before interest and taxes.
[3]Average of beginning and end of year.
[4] Net income after tax but before extraordinary items.

Source: Company accounts.

Exhibit 8: **Hershey Foods Corp.—Selected Financial Data, 1984–87**

		1984	*1985*	*1986*	*1987*
A	**Financial Statement Data ($millions)**				
1	Turnover (Sales)	1848.5	1996.2	2169.6	2433.8
2	Gross Profit	578.7	640.4	716.2	821.7
3	Trading Profit	222.8	244.8	270.6	294.1
4	Net Income	108.7	120.7	132.8	148.2
5	Depreciation	45.2	52.4	59.0	70.6
6	Liquid Assets	87.9	110.6	27.6	15.0
7	Current Assets	385.3	412.3	393.4	484.9
8	Fixed Assets	727.3	785.1	962.9	1160.3
9	Total Assets	1122.6	1197.4	1356.3	1645.2
10	Current Liabilities	203.0	195.3	222.2	299.8
11	Long-term Liabilities	258.7	274.2	406.2	513.0
12	Stockholders' Equity	660.9	727.9	727.9	832.4
B	**Per Share Data ($)**				
13	Earnings	1.16	1.19	1.42	1.64
14	Dividends	0.41	0.48	0.52	0.58
15	Stock Price (Average)	11.60	15.00	22.80	29.30
16	Price-Earnings (Average)	10.00	9.70	16.10	17.90
17	Equity Book Value	7.00	7.70	8.10	9.20

Source: Company accounts.

Exhibit 9: Cadbury Schweppes PLC—Selected Financial Data, 1984–87

		1984	*1985*	*1986*	*1987*
A	**Financial Statement Data (£ millions)**				
1	Turnover (Sales)	2016.2	1873.8	1839.9	2031.0
2	Gross Profit	746.8	683.0	739.9	853.8
3	Trading Profit	154.4	113.0	140.4	180.6
4a	Net Income[1]	72.5	47.8	76.1	112.1
4b	Net Income[2]	65.1	41.9	102.0	110.7
5	Depreciation	55.9	54.7	60.4	63.3
6	Liquid Assets	36.6	47.1	177.4	139.9
7	Current Assets	710.7	618.9	723.4	795.5
8	Fixed Assets	627.5	594.0	555.4	603.5
9	Total Assets	1338.2	1212.9	1278.8	1399.0
10	Current Liabilities	531.2	479.3	536.7	688.7
11	Long-term Liabilities	288.3	262.6	278.9	233.6
12	Share Capital & Reserves	518.7	417.0	463.2	476.7
B	**Per Share Data (pence)**				
13	Earnings[1]	15.7	9.3	14.3	19.1
14	Dividends	5.9	5.9	6.7	8.0
15	Stock Price (Average)	137.0	153.0	170.0	238.0
16	Price-Earnings (Average)	8.7	16.5	11.9	12.5
17	Equity Book Value	112.0	92.0	87.0	83.0
18	Employees (000s)	35.5	33.8	27.7	27.5

[1] Earnings before Extraordinary Items.

[2] Earnings after Extraordinary Items.

Source: Company accounts.

Exhibit 10: **Jacobs Suchard Group—Selected Financial Data, 1984–87**

		1984	1985	1986	1987
A	**Financial Statement Data (SF millions)**				
1	Turnover (Sales)	5111	5382	5236	6104
2	Gross Profit	1104	1156	1304	1955
3	Trading Profit	244	265	338	471
4	Net Income	120	150	191	265
5	Depreciation	84	092	103	128
6	Liquid Assets	230	788	1470	705
7	Current Assets	1390	2008	2920	2206
8	Fixed Assets	666	674	832	886
9	Total Assets	2056	2682	3752	3092
10	Current Liabilities	796	843	1417	1120
11	Long-term Liabilities	483	487	885	829
12	Shareholders' Equity	777	1352	1450	1143*
B	**Per Share Data (SF per bearer share)**				
13	Earnings	351.0	353.0	414.0	503.0
14	Dividends	150.0	155.0	160.0	165.0
15	Stock Price (Average)	5028.0	6101.0	7324.0	8228.0
16	Price-Earnings (Average)	14.3	17.3	17.7	16.4
17	Employees (000s)	10.6	9.3	10.0	16.1

* It is normal accounting practice for Swiss companies to write off "goodwill" when acquiring businesses. Nestlé wrote off SF3.2 million of shareholders' equity on its purchase of Carnation in 1985. Jacobs Suchard reduced equity by SF1.1 million in 1987 due to depreciation of goodwill.

Source: Company accounts.

Exhibit 11:   ## Nestlé S.A.—Selected Financial Data, 1984–87

		1984	1985	1986	1987
A	**Financial Statement Data (SF millions)**				
1	Turnover (Sales)	31,141	42,225	38,050	35,241
2	Gross Profit	11,301	14,926	13,603	13,616
3	Trading Profit	3,206	4,315	3,671	3,651
4	Net Income	1,487	1,750	1,789	1,827
5	Depreciation	1,004	1,331	1,157	1,184
6	Liquid Assets	6,168	3,853	5,619	6,961
7	Current Assets	16,407	15,236	15,820	16,241
8	Fixed Assets	8,067	9,952	9,275	8,902
9	Total Assets	24,474	25,188	25,095	25,143
10	Current Liabilities	7,651	8,858	8,119	7,547
11	Long-term Liabilities	3,834	5,092	4,775	4,939
12	Shareholders' Equity	12,989	11,238*	12,201	12,657
B	**Per Share Data (SF per bearer share)**				
13	Earnings	480.0	515.0	526.0	537.0
14	Dividends	136.0	145.0	145.0	150.0
15	Stock Price (Average)	5,062.0	7,400.0	8,600.0	9,325.0
16	Price-Earnings (Average)	10.5	14.4	16.4	17.4
17	Employees (000s)	138.0	154.8	162.1	163.0

* It is normal accounting practice for Swiss companies to write off "goodwill" when acquiring businesses. Nestlé wrote off SF3.2 million of shareholders' equity on its purchase of Carnation in 1985. Jacobs Suchard reduced equity by SF1.1 million in 1987 due to depreciation of goodwill.

Source: Company accounts.

Exhibit 12: **Rowntree plc—Selected Financial Data, 1983–87**

		1983	1984	1985	1986	1987
A	**Income Statement Data**					
1	Turnover (Sales)	951.9	1156.5	1205.2	1290.4	1427.6
1a	Cost Of Sales	617.9	739.0	759.4	790.2	837.1
2	Gross Profit (1–1a)	334.0	417.5	445.8	500.2	590.5
2a	Fixed Overhead Expenses	265.6	328.3	350	400.5	465.8
2b	Other Operating Income	4.2	4.6	6.0	6.0	5.4
3	Trading Profit (2–2a+2b)	72.6	93.8	101.3	105.7	130.1
3a	Interest	12.2	19.3	22.0	21.7	18.0
4a	Profit After Tax	46.3	58.0	60.7	66.2	87.9
4b	Extraordinary Items	13.5	11.5	16.5	11.3	0.0
4c	Net Profit After Tax	32.8	46.5	44.2	54.9	87.9
5	Depreciation (£m)	28.6	36.2	39.1	43.7	51.0
B	**Balance Sheet Data (£ millions)**					
6	Liquid Assets	25.1	55.7	41.8	69.2	96.7
6a	Debtors (Receivables)	145.9	171.1	178.7	208.5	214.9
6b	Stocks (Inventories)	159.1	172.9	170.2	176.9	163.2
7	Current Assets	330.1	399.7	390.7	454.6	475.1
8	Fixed Assets	359.7	408.5	403.1	475.1	463.2
9	Total Assets	689.8	808.2	793.8	929.7	938.3
10	Current Liabilities	217.8	229.3	242.4	310.2	270.1
11	Long-term Liabilities	123.0	186.3	177.0	228.1	259.6
12a	Preferred Stock	2.7	2.7	2.7	2.7	2.7
12b	Share Capital & Reserves	346.3	389.9	371.7	388.7	405.9
C	**Per Share Data (pence)**					
13	Earnings*	31.0	36.0	34.8	35.0	40.8
14	Dividends	9.8	11.0	12.2	13.6	15.5
15a	Common Stock Price (High)	258.0	392.0	450.0	545.0	590.0
15b	Common Stock Price (Low)	200.0	212.0	337.0	363.0	367.0
16	Average Price-Earnings*	7.4	8.4	11.3	13.0	11.7
17	Equity Book Value (12b/19)	233.0	243.0	214.0	206.0	189.0
D	**Other Data**					
18a	Employees, U.K. (000s)	19.7	18.9	17.7	16.4	15.6
18b	Employees, World (000s)	31.2	32.4	32.0	32.5	33.1
19	Ordinary Shares (000,000s)	149.5	160.6	173.9	188.7	215.0
20	Cash Flow (4a+5)	74.9	94.2	99.8	109.9	138.9
21	Capital Expenditures (£m)	59.9	59.9	71.5	76.2	82.5
22	Business Acquisitions (£m)	159.6	3.3	34.2	189.9	14.2
23	Asset Divestitures (£m)	4.0	3.1	4.5	4.2	5.2

* Earnings based on line 4a (net profit after tax but before extraordinary items) minus preferred dividends. Average of high and low stock prices.

Source: Company accounts.

Exhibit 13: **Rowntree plc—Breakdown by Activity, 1987 (£ millions)**

	Turnover	Percent of Total Turnover	Trading Profit	Percent of Total Trading Profit	Trading Margin
Confectionery	1088.5	76.2%	101.0	77.6%	9.3%
Snack Foods	191.8	13.4	14.5	11.1	7.6
Retailing	97.3	6.8	8.1	6.2	8.3
Grocery (U.K.)	50.0	3.5	6.5	5.0	13.0
Total	1427.6	100.0%	130.1	100.0%	9.1%

Source: Company accounts.

Exhibit 14: **Rowntree plc—Breakdown by Region, 1987**

	Turnover	Percent of Total Turnover	Trading Profit	Percent of Total Trading Profit	Trading Margin
U.K. & Ireland	566.4	40%	61.7	47%	10.9%
Cont'l Europe	300.4	21	11.0	8	3.7
North America	416.1	29	41.0	31	9.8
Australasia	57.1	4	4.7	4	8.2
Rest of World	87.6	6	11.7	9	13.4
Total	1427.6	100%	130.1	100%	9.1%

Source: Company accounts.

Exhibit 15: **Rowntree plc—Operating and Financial Performance, 1976–81 (£ millions)**

	1976	1977	1978	1979	1980	1981
Turnover	340.90	469.20	562.70	601.30	629.80	688.00
Trading Profit	36.80	46.90	51.70	46.60	44.80	48.00
Net Profit[1]	16.90	30.40	34.40	27.20	17.50	29.10
Average[2]	194.90	246.80	332.50	396.60	412.50	448.60
Average Owner's[2] Equity	77.30	120.60	182.30	218.40	231.80	278.90
Trading Margin per cent	9.60	10.00	9.20	7.80	7.10	7.20
Trading Profit/Assets per cent	18.90	19.00	15.60	11.80	10.90	10.70
Turnover/Assets	1.83	1.66	1.47	1.46	1.52	1.38
Net Profit/Equity per cent	21.80	25.20	18.90	12.50	7.60	10.30

[1] Net after-tax profit attributable to ordinary common shares.
[2] Average of beginning and end of year.

Source: Company accounts.

Exhibit 16: **Rowntree plc—Major Business Acquisitions, 1983–87**

Company	Location	Primary Area of Business Activity	Year of Purchase	Purchase Price (£m)
Tom's Foods	U.S.	Snack foods	1983	£138
Laura Secord	Canada	Branded retailing	1983	19
Original Cookie Co.	U.S.	Branded retailing	1985	32
Hot Sam	U.S.	Branded retailing	1986	14
Sunmark	U.S.	Branded confectionery	1986	154
Gales	U.S.	Honey products	1986	1
Smaller Acquisitions	U.S., U.K., France, Australia	Snack foods, Confectionery, Branded retailing	1983–87	29
				£399

Source: Company Accounts.

Exhibit 17: **Rowntree plc—Share Price Performance, 1980–87**

Rowntree Share Price Performance compared to the Financial Times' Market and Food Manufacturer's Price Indexes on the London Stock Exchange (01/01/80 to 31/21/87, weekly).

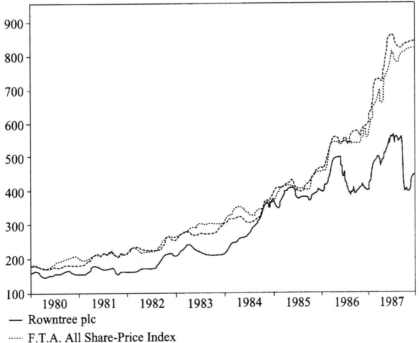

— Rowntree plc

····· F.T.A. All Share-Price Index

---- F.T.A. Food Manufacturer's - Price Index (Marked)

Source: Financial Times.

Exhibit 18:   **Stockbrokers' Comments on Rowntree**

Name of Broker	Date of Report	Forecast of 1988 Trading Profit (£m)	Summary of Major Comments and Recommendations
County Natwest	01/21/88	125	• Sell—Dollar weakness limits prospects for 1988.
BZW	01/25/88	127	• Decision to sell snack food business correct but unable to give final verdict until consideration is known.
County Natwest	01/26/88	125	• Surprise disposals, but good move.
BZW	02/24/88	127	• Buy—Current rating of shares is not expensive with absence of bid premium.
Warburg Securities	03/17/88	128	• Hold—Core business performed well but reversal in snacks and slowdown in retailing leaves strategy looking threadbare.
Hoare Govett	03/17/88	127	• Overvalued in short term. Longer term outlook remaining clouded by current divestment/acquisition plans.
BZW	03/17/88	129	• Hold—Lower consideration for disposals than expected would lead to downgrading of forecast. Share price will be susceptible to strengthening of sterling.
County Natwest	03/18/88	125	• Good results. Disposal of snack business an excellent move.
Kleinwart Grievson	03/18/88	129	• Hold—Fully valued.

Source: Stock brokerage reports.

Exhibit 19:   **The City Code and the U.K. Takeover Climate**

Takeover bids for public companies in the U.K. were conducted according to a complex set of formal rules contained in the City Code on Takeovers and Mergers. The City Code was designed to ensure fair and similar treatment for all shareholders of the same class, mainly through responsible, detailed disclosure and the absence of stock price manipulation. The City Code was administered by the Takeover Panel, a self-regulatory body whose members included Bank of England appointees and representatives of participants in the U.K. securities markets. The Panel was authorized to make rulings and interpretations on novel points arising during the course of a takeover attempt.

The City Code identified consequences associated with the acquisition of certain benchmark percentages of the equity of a takeover target. For example, within 5 days of acquiring 5 per cent or more of the capital of a company, the purchaser was required to inform the target company of its interest; the target company was then required to make an immediate announcement of this fact to the London Stock Exchange.

A purchaser could not acquire 10 per cent or more of the capital of the target within any period of 7 days if these purchases would bring its total interest above 15 per cent of the voting rights in the target company. Between 15 per cent and 30 per cent interest, the purchaser could accumulate shares by tender offer or by a series of share purchases; however, each series of share purchases could not result in the acquisition of more than 10 per cent of the total equity of the target during any 7-day period. Once acquiring an interest totalling 30 per cent, the bidder was obliged to make a general offer for the remaining 70 per cent of the voting capital (at the highest price previously paid by the bidder). After a bidder had obtained 90 per cent ownership of a class of shares, it could compulsorily acquire the outstanding shares from the minority shareholders; similarly, any remaining minority shareholders could require the bidder to purchase their shares at the highest price previously paid by the bidder.

Proposed acquisitions could also be reviewed by the Office of Fair Trading (OFT), a subsection of the Department of Trade and Industry. The OFT had responsibility for deciding whether the competitive implications of the merger warranted investigation. The OFT could refer merger cases to the Mergers and Monopolies Commission (MMC), an independent tribunal which ruled on whether the merger should be blocked in the interests of national competition policy. Referral to the MMC was often prized by managements of takeover targets. Aside from allowing the possibility of a referral decision favouring the target, the referral process gave the takeover target additional time (3–7 months) to mount a more effective takeover defence.

Takeovers of U.K. public companies were either recommended by the Board of the target company or contested. Action by the Board of a target to frustrate an offer for the target company was prohibited without the approval, in a General Meeting, of the shareholders. Recommended offers in the U.K. were generally restricted to smaller companies; they were relatively rare for companies with market capitalization in excess of £200 million.

Between 1985 and 1987, takeover bids were initiated for 14 large U.K. companies, each with individual market capitalizations in excess of £1 billion. Only one of these bids was recommended; the rest were contested. Ultimately, four of these bids were successful while ten failed. For the three successful cash bids, the average share price premium paid was 60 per cent; the individual premiums paid ranged from 40 per cent to 80 per cent.*

More recent acquisition activity in France and the U.K. provided reference points for the value of brand names. During 1987 and 1988, Seagrams (a Canadian drinks group) and Grand Metropolitan (a U.K. drinks and hotel group) waged a fierce takeover battle to acquire Martell (the second largest French cognac house). In February 1988, Seagrams emerged the victor, but only after bidding an estimated 40x the 1987 earnings of Martell. In March 1988, United Biscuits paid a price-earnings multiple of 25x to purchase the frozen and chilled foods division of Hanson Trust. At that time, the average price-earnings ratio for five comparable U.K. food companies was 11.9x.

---

* Share price premiums were calculated by comparing final bid offer prices against the share prices of the target companies two months prior to the date of the final offer.

Exhibit 20: **Selected Financial Market Rates, 1984–87**

	1984	1985	1986	1987	1988 (1ˢᵗ quarter Annualized)
Inflation*(%)					
Switzerland	3.0	1.0	0.8	1.4	3.5
United Kingdom	5.0	6.0	3.4	4.3	1.8
United States	4.3	3.5	2.0	3.6	2.6
Long-Term Government Bond Yield (%)					
Switzerland	4.7	4.8	4.3	4.1	4.1
United Kingdom	10.7	10.6	9.9	9.5	9.4
United States	12.5	10.6	7.7	8.4	8.4

* Based on the Consumer Price Index.

Source: International Monetary Fund.